POLITICAL PHILOSOPHY

THE SEARCH FOR HUMANITY
AND ORDER

JOHN H. HALLOWELL

JENE M. PORTER

Prentice Hall Canada Inc., Scarborough, Ontario

Canadian Cataloguing in Publication Data

Hallowell, John H. (John Hamilton), 1913–
    Political philosophy: the search for humanity and order

ISBN 0-13-063991-5

1. Political science – Philosophy. I. Porter, J.M.
(Jene M.), 1937–   . II. Title.

HA71.H35 1997 320'.01 C96-930714-4

 © 1997 Prentice-Hall Canada Inc., Scarborough, Ontario
A Viacom Company

Prentice-Hall, Inc., Englewood Cliffs, New Jersey
Prentice-Hall International (UK) Limited, London
Prentice-Hall of Australia, Pty. Limited, Sydney
Prentice-Hall Hispanoamericana, S.A., Mexico City
Prentice-Hall of India Private Limited, New Delhi
Prentice-Hall of Japan, Inc., Tokyo
Simon & Schuster Asia Private Limited, Singapore
Editora Prentice-Hall do Brasil, Ltda., Rio de Janeiro

ISBN 0-13-063991-5

Acquisitions Editor: Allan Gray
Developmental Editor: Maurice Esses
Production Editor: Kelly Dickson
Copy Editor: Marie Graham
Production Coordinator: Jane Schell
Permissions: Marijke Leupen
Cover Design: Margot Boland
Interior Design: Petra Phillips
Cover Image: The Granger Collection
Page Layout: Arlene Edgar Graphic Design and Formatting

1 2 3 4 5   RRD   99 98 97 96

Printed and bound in the United States

We welcome readers' comments, which can be sent by e-mail to
    collegeinfo_pubcanada@prenhall.com

TABLE OF CONTENTS

PREFACE   ix

INTRODUCTION   xi

CHAPTER 1   PLATO   1

THE PRE-SOCRATIC PHILOSOPHERS   1

THE SOPHISTS   3

SOCRATES   5

PLATO: His Life and Works   7

THE GORGIAS   10

THE REPUBLIC   16

THE REPUBLIC: Selection of the Guardians   20

THE REPUBLIC: The Definition of Justice   22

THE REPUBLIC: Education of the Guardians   26

THE REPUBLIC: The Four Stages of Cognition   28

THE REPUBLIC: The Allegory of the Cave   31

THE REPUBLIC: The Decline of the Best State   34

THE REPUBLIC: Concluding Observations   40

THE LAWS   41

CONCLUSIONS   49

SUGGESTIONS FOR FURTHER READING   51

CHAPTER 2   ARISTOTLE   55

ARISTOTLE: His Life and Works   55

ARISTOTLE'S METAPHYSICS   57

NICOMACHEAN ETHICS   62

THEORETICAL AND PRACTICAL REASON   67

THE POLITICS: The Nature of the Polis   72

HOUSEHOLD MANAGEMENT   75

HIS CRITICISM OF PLATO'S REPUBLIC   77

TYPES OF POLITICAL ORDER   79

CONCLUSIONS   90

SUGGESTIONS FOR FURTHER READING   93

CHAPTER 3   THE HELLENISTIC AGE   96
AND THE ROMAN
LAWYERS

THE EARLY CYNICS   97

EPICUREANISM   99

STOICISM   102

THE REVISION OF STOICISM   107

POLYBIUS   108

CICERO   110

THE ROMAN LAW   117

CONCLUSIONS   120

SUGGESTIONS FOR FURTHER READING   122

CHAPTER 4   ST. AUGUSTINE AND THE EARLY MIDDLE AGES   126

THE HEBRAIC TRADITION   127

EARLY CHRISTIANITY   133

THE CHRISTIAN CREEDS   136

AUGUSTINE: His Life and Works   140

AUGUSTINE'S CONCEPTION OF HUMAN NATURE   142

THE CITY OF GOD AND THE CITY OF BABYLON   146

AUGUSTINE'S CONCEPTION OF THE STATE   148

AUGUSTINE ON SLAVERY AND PROPERTY   152

GREEK AND CHRISTIAN THOUGHT COMPARED   155

CHURCH AND STATE IN THE EARLY MIDDLE AGES   160

LAW IN THE EARLY MIDDLE AGES   166

FEUDALISM   169

CONCLUSIONS   171

SUGGESTIONS FOR FURTHER READING   172

CHAPTER 5   ST. THOMAS ACQUINAS   175
             AND THE HIGH
             MIDDLE AGES

RECOVERY OF GREEK PHILOSOPHY   175

ACQUINAS: His Life and Works   183

REASON AND REVELATION   186

POLITICAL PHILOSOPHY   194

CONCLUSIONS   216

SUGGESTIONS FOR FURTHER READING   220

CHAPTER 6   MACHIAVELLI   225

THE RENAISSANCE   225

MACHIAVELLI: His Life and Works   229

THE PRINCE   233

THE DISCOURSES   247

CONCLUSIONS   268

SUGGESTIONS FOR FURTHER READING   273

CHAPTER 7   THOMAS HOBBES AND   277
             THE PHILOSOPHICAL
             REVOLUTION OF THE
             SEVENTEENTH CENTURY

THE RISE OF MODERN SCIENCE   278

RENÉ DESCARTES (1596–1650)   287

HOBBES: His Life and Works   295

LEVIATHAN   298

CONCLUSIONS   333

SUGGESTIONS FOR FURTHER READING   335

CHAPTER 8   JOHN LOCKE   341

LOCKE: His Life and Works   341

AN ESSAY CONCERNING HUMAN UNDERSTANDING   348

THE TWO TREATISES   366

CONCLUSIONS   402

SUGGESTIONS FOR FURTHER READING   411

CHAPTER 9   JEAN-JACQUES ROUSSEAU   417

ROUSSEAU: His Life and Works: 419

DISCOURSE ON THE SCIENCES AND ARTS   425
(The First Discourse)

THE DISCOURSE ON INEQUALITY   427
(The Second Discourse)

ON THE SOCIAL CONTRACT   436

CONCLUSIONS   458

SUGGESTIONS FOR FURTHER READING   481

CHAPTER 10   UTILITARIANISM: 487
JEREMY BENTHAM AND
JOHN STUART MILL

BENTHAM: His Life and Works   488

MILL: His Life and Works   502

CONCLUSIONS   543

SUGGESTIONS FOR FURTHER READING   546

CHAPTER 11   KARL MARX   551

MARX: His Life and Works   551

PHILOSOPHIC BACKGROUND   557

HISTORICAL MATERIALISM   570

ECONOMICS   592

CONCLUSIONS   597

SUGGESTIONS FOR FURTHER READING   601

CHAPTER 12   THE END OF HISTORY   605
               AND FRIEDRICH
               NIETZSCHE

MEANING IN HISTORY   605

NIETZSCHE: His Life and Works   608

SUGGESTIONS FOR FURTHER READING   629

CREDIT LIST   635

GLOSSARY   638

SUBJECT INDEX   645

INDEX OF PERSONS   652

PREFACE

John Hallowell (1913–1991) suggested that this book should be dedicated to our students. I am happy to do so. But as his student, I would also like to pay homage to John Hallowell as a teacher. We students were taken by him on a thorough tour of the major works in political philosophy, and those struggling with dissertations in the field of political philosophy were taught two inestimable guides for writing clearly: when to cut and where to omit. These are debts that happily can be willed to the next generation.

One sabbatical ago, John Hallowell asked me to expand five chapters he had written and to add more chapters to complete a book on political philosophy. We decided to write such a book with three major goals. Our first goal was to present a guide to the classic works in political philosophy so that students could better read and understand them. It is a delusion to think that an unaided person can simply pick up the works of Plato or Hobbes or Marx and easily comprehend what is being discussed. Accordingly, we carefully take the reader through each classic work, step by step. We also rely upon an extensive use of quotations so that the reader may become aware of the eloquence and rhetoric that are a necessary part of a thinker's intellectual arsenal. For instance, without directly experiencing Rousseau's writing style and dramatic eloquence, much of Rousseau's extraordinary persuasive power and influence would be incomprehensible.

The second goal was to provide the necessary background for reading each philosopher. Although the meaning of a work cannot be confined to an historical context, the discussion of that meaning is enhanced by knowledge of its intellectual, cultural, and social background. Such knowledge can also aid in evaluating a thinker's influence. We have not written a work in intellectual history, but we have provided critical information for understanding major shifts in thought. For example, it makes little sense to discuss Augustine and Aquinas if one does not understand the great shift that took place with the introduction of the Judaic and Christian traditions into Western civilization. Similarly, one has difficulty understanding Machiavelli without an awareness of the impact of the Renaissance, nor are Hobbes and modernity in general (1600 to the present) understandable without an awareness of Descartes's influence and the Scientific Revolution. Our main focus, nevertheless, remains the philosophic arguments themselves.

Finally, for our third goal, we have provided brief commentaries on the major interpretations and controversies associated with each thinker. The text itself, the notes for each chapter, and the "Suggestions for Further Readings" will provide guidance on where to pursue a variety of issues, including questions of the continuing influence of a particular political philosophy and its possible application.

This project began when I was on sabbatical in California. The hospitality of the Department of Government of Pomona College was immensely helpful. Lee McDonald, whose own work is a model for any history of political philosophy, was always available and encouraging. My former colleague, and permanent friend, Fred Barnard, was my constant companion in thought as well as letter. My colleague at the University of Saskatchewan, Don Story, cheerfully read early chapters and made excellent suggestions. Peter McCormick, University of Lethbridge, arranged for me to have peace and quiet to finish the work, for which I am most grateful. Various papers and lectures, which have been given over the years, have found their way into this book. I am deeply endebted to many friends and colleagues for their responses and for many discussions. In the hope that neither career nor reputation will be damaged, I would like to thank them: Don Carmichael, Barry Cooper, Leon Craig, Tom Flanagan, Bob Grogin, T. Y. Henderson, Bill Marty, Allan MacLeod, Wally Mead, Tony Parel, Denny Pilant, Tom Pocklington, Ken Reschaur, and Ellis Sandoz. The patience, forbearance, and encouragement of Maurice Esses, editor at Prentice-Hall, were beyond reasonable expectations and deeply appreciated. Also, the work would not have been completed without the gracious support of Sally Hallowell Schumaker.

Finally, one person has read every page more than once and has made innumerable corrections and suggestions regarding both style and content, and all of this was done while completing a Ph.D., raising five children, teaching, and writing. To Susan Porter I owe a debt that words and deeds cannot repay, but there is a joy in trying.

JENE M. PORTER

INTRODUCTION

The political slogans that drive public discourse are often superficial remnants of philosophical systems of the past. In other words, yesterday's philosophy becomes today's clichés. This seems particularly true of political thought where we seem prone to accept peer group leads and to rely upon the clichés of the day. There are, of course, the brave and pragmatic lot who, after a smile, remark that they have no abstract political philosophy but rely upon their own common sense. In spite of such claims, the human condition compels us to have a political philosophy of some sort. Consider these indisputable features of our political-social existence. As humans, we live in groups; decisions are forced upon us by our own interests, by conflicts with others, and, sometimes, by sheer chance and fate. These decisions will then have to be implemented, obeyed, and enforced; and, the decisions will also have to be explained and justified. These features are common to all human societies, from our earliest, primitive tribal origins to contemporary, industrialized democracies. It follows that humans are constantly evaluating, assessing, and judging their political conditions. Sometimes, this general weighing activity leads to a formal political act, as in voting; at other times, the activity of evaluating is simply an addition to the political discourse and culture of one's nation. Whatever the case, the activity of evaluating inescapably requires the use of the principles, categories, and metaphors of political philosophy.

Thus, it is not the case that one has a choice between having a political philosophy and not having a political philosophy. The choice is between, on the one hand, holding a political philosophy that is derived from habit or from an intellectual fad shared by a peer group and, on the other hand, holding a political philosophy that is created through encounters with fundamental principles. By knowing the arguments of such thinkers as Plato, Hobbes, Rousseau, and Marx we have a far better chance of understanding our own clichés and confusions. Clarity helps to free us from our limits and by so doing provides an essential condition that is necessary for responsible political discussions. The possibility for becoming better citizens is thus enhanced.

It may be misleading to speak of "holding" a political philosophy as if one could possess a device for solving political problems analogous to the way a calculator solves mathematical problems or a dictionary solves the puzzle of a word's etymology. The subject of political philosophy is much more complex than either mathematics or etymology. A better analogy for political philosophy would be with love or friendship. Neither of these subjects can be solved. It would be non-sensical to argue that Shakespeare's love sonnets have solved the question of love or that Aristotle's discussion of friendship is the final and complete word on that subject. These would be silly claims.

Love and friendships are continual human activities. However eloquent and in-sightful a description of either may be, each has to be thought through and lived or else the description ceases to illuminate and evoke. It ossifies and becomes the source for mere slogans. One should not conclude that love and friendship are therefore hopelessly subjective. Reason is not impotent. Thanks in part to what Shakespeare and Aristotle have taught us, we are quite capable, however difficult it may be, of perceiving when love turns into jealousy or friendship turns into sycophancy. These are also not distinctions relative to an age, gender, or culture but are derived from the constitution of human nature.

Political philosophy, too, is a continual human activity that requires constant reflection. Political societies live within an historical continuum of new and pass-ing generations, of constant and changing challenges, and of an undetermined future. As a consequence, there are two tasks all societies have to face. First, they have to address the unending task of how to organize themselves and how to dis-tribute the "goods" of society (i.e., wealth, positions, status, and honours). What is fair and what is just in these distributions are, thus, inescapable questions found in all societies. Second, societies have the task of articulating and defending their purposes and goals. A society that can no longer justify its existence will experience a loss of meaning and authority. Societies that can integrate these two tasks will maintain a successful political order; societies that cannot will experience disorder. This truth was dramatically demonstrated at the end of the twentieth century. The Soviet Union did not collapse because of a loss of power. There was no sud-den shortage of tanks, warships, or nuclear weapons. There was, however, a loss of authority: the official goals and purposes of the Soviet Union had become hollow and were unpersuasive to its citizens. In short, the Soviet Union was no longer successful in integrating the two great tasks facing all political societies.

There is no formula for love that can be blindly and mechanically applied to a human relationship, and there are similarly none for creating and maintaining a successful political order. Still, reflection and reason are most valuable for un-derstanding both love and politics, and one should obviously listen to those who have reflected with the greatest perspicuity. To understand the nature and practice of love, one can hardly do better than to study Shakespeare or Jane Austen; to understand the nature and practice of politics, one can hardly do better than to study the great political philosophers.

How one should study political philosophy is a matter of some controversy. We have chosen a middle course between two approaches. There is an historical approach, sometimes called the Cambridge School, which stresses that a particular political philosophy can be understood only with reference to the institutions and ideas of that particular time period.[1] The precise degree to which the historical context inscribes a political philosophy varies among the members of this School, but the general approach is to associate a philosopher's thought and, indeed, its pertinence to a particular historical context. To illustrate, a Lockean scholar within the historical approach has written: "I simply cannot conceive of constructing an analysis of any issue in contemporary political theory around the affirmation or negation of anything which Locke says about political matters."[2]

A second approach, for lack of a better name, might be called textual. Here the key works are examined for the arguments they contain about perennial questions in political philosophy. In some philosophy textbooks the impression is left that the history of political philosophy is a kind of handbook of arguments into which one can dip as need requires. An historical sense is virtually non-existent. A variant is provided by Leo Strauss and his followers. With these scholars the great political philosophers are taken very seriously indeed. The contemporary world is viewed

---

[1] Some of the well-known scholars who follow this approach, with some variation, are: Quentin Skinner, J. G. A. Pocock, John Dunn, Richard Ashcraft, and Richard Tuck. The following are a few of the works in which this methodological approach is discussed. Richard Rorty, J. B. Schneewind, and Quentin Skinner, eds., *Philosophy in History* (Cambridge: Cambridge University Press, 1984); "Political Thought and Political Action: A Symposium on Quentin Skinner," *Political Theory* 2 (1974), pp. 251–303; James Tully, ed., *Meaning and Context: Quentin Skinner and His Critics* (Princeton: Princeton University Press, 1988). Quentin Skinner has written three seminal articles on his approach: "Meaning and Understanding in the History of Ideas," *History and Theory* 8, No. 1 (1969), pp. 3–53; "'Social Meaning' and the Explanation of Social Action," in *Philosophy, Politics and Society*, 4th ser., eds. Peter Laslett and W. G. Runciman (Oxford: Basil Blackwell, 1972), pp. 136–57; "Some Problems in the Analysis of Political Thought and Action," *Political Theory* 2, No. 3 (August, 1974), pp. 277–303. See also, Richard Ashcraft, "On the Problem of Methodology and the Nature of Political Theory," *Political Theory* 3, No. 1 (February, 1975).

[2] John Dunn, *The Political Thought of John Locke* (Cambridge: Cambridge University Press, 1969), p. x. He has since modified his claim: *Interpreting Political Responsibility* (Princeton: Princeton University Press, 1990), pp. 9–25.

with considerable anxiety and disdain, and the classic works alone are viewed as providing the necessary guidance for clarifying fundamental political questions. The great works are consequently much more than handbooks of arguments. To study political philosophy, to quote Leo Strauss "consists … in listening to conversations between the great philosophers … the greatest minds, and therefore in studying the great books."[3] History does not inscribe the meaning of these texts; in fact, there is little historical sense at all in this approach. There is history only in the trivial sense that the eldest speaks first. With the text approach the pertinence of political philosophy is very great since the ideas found in these texts are alive within the permanent conversation among philosophers, and the ideas continue to be indispensable for understanding political life. To illustrate, a follower of Leo Strauss has written:

> What was acted out in the American and French Revolution had been thought out beforehand in the writings of Locke and Rousseau, the scenarists for the drama of modern politics …. Locke was the great practical success; the new English and American regimes founded themselves according to his instructions.[4]

The two approaches—historical and textual—are polar opposites. For John Dunn, Locke's thought is of little pertinence for understanding the present, and for Allan Bloom, John Locke is a scriptwriter for the drama of modern politics. Even allowing for literary licence, both positions seem to us exaggerated, and we propose to weave our way between these two poles.[5]

---

[3] *Liberalism: Ancient and Modern* (New York: Basic Books, 1968), p. 7. An explanation and defence of the Straussian approach is provided by Nathan Tarcov and Thomas L. Pangle, "Epilogue," in *History of Political Philosophy,* 3rd ed., eds. Leo Strauss and Joseph Cropsey (Chicago: University of Chicago Press, 1987), pp. 907–938.

[4] Allan Bloom, *The Closing of the American Mind* (New York: Simon and Schuster, 1987), p. 162.

[5] For an antidote to the historical approach, see the critics Tully, *Meaning and Context.*. Of great value, too, is the judicious and perceptive article by the historian Francis Oakley: "Against the Stream: In Praise of Lovejoy," *Omnipotence, Covenant, and Order: An Excursion in the History of Ideas from Abelard to Leibniz* (Ithaca: Cornell University Press, 1984). For a critique of the textual approach, see Conal Condren, *The Status and Appraisal of Classic Texts: An Essay on Political Theory, Its Inheritance and the History of Ideas* (Princeton: Princeton University Press, 1985); John G. Gunnell, "Political Theory: The Evolution of the Sub-field," in *Political Science: The State of the Discipline,* ed. Ada Finifter (Washington, D.C.: American Political Science Association, 1983) and "American Political Science, Liberalism, and the Invention of Political Theory," *American Political Science Review* 82, pp. 71–87. Arlene W. Saxonhouse surveys the different approaches in "Texts and Canons: The Status of the 'Great Books' in Political Theory," in *Political Science: The State of the Discipline,* Vol. II, ed. Ada Finifter (Washington, D.C.: American Political Science Association, 1993).

Political disorder of some kind is usually the catalyst that activates philosophical thought. Certainly, political and social philosophers of the stature of Plato, Hobbes, Rousseau and Marx begin their inquiries into the nature of politics and of humanity with some perception of disorder. What is the nature of this disorder and how did it come about? How can it be overcome, if it can? Their diagnoses of social disorder vary greatly and are often at odds with one another, but each claims to have discovered a true understanding of what is wrong and proposes an appropriate remedy. Both their perceptions of disorder and their remedies stem from presuppositions and convictions about the nature of reality, and the nature and destiny of humanity. We propose to present these perceptions and remedies, as found in each thinker's central writings, and to uncover the basic presuppositions from which they derive.

Our interest in the history of political philosophy is not antiquarian. We, too, live in times of social disorder. We, too, experience anxiety and uncertainty. The way in which we perceive social disorder will greatly influence our choice of the appropriate remedy. By examining the diagnoses of some of the most brilliant minds in Western culture we may come to a better understanding of our own predicaments. We should be led, in this encounter, to discover our own inarticulate premises and to test the adequacies of these against those of great minds in other times and in other societies.

While we do not subscribe to the notion that history follows some predetermined course, that it has some immanent meaning of its own, we do recognize that the course of history has determined, to some extent, the nature of the problems encountered and the sequence of proposed "solutions." There is a sense in which the "solution" of one age becomes the problem of the next. Plato cannot be understood without Socrates, nor Aristotle without Plato. The same holds for modern philosophers. G. W. F. Hegel would not have written as he did had he not first encountered Immanuel Kant, and Kant would not have been led to find his "solution" to the problem of knowledge had he not encountered David Hume and John Locke. There is continuity in this sense in history, but the course of that history is not predetermined. What Alfred N. Whitehead has called the intellectual "climate of opinion" is important to an understanding of every political philosophy, and we shall seek to describe briefly the climate of opinion in which each theory emerged. Although all great philosophies have roots in particular times and societies, they also transcend the concerns of time and place to speak to the human predicament in every age. In this sense all political philosophies have contemporary significance, and all great political philosophers are our contemporaries. At least it is in that philosophic spirit that we shall approach their writings and insights.

The philosophic approach requires us to work through the arguments found in the primary source itself. One justification for this type of approach, which needs to be emphasized these days, is that it puts muscles in the cerebrum. Working through the arguments is as pertinent to a student's learning how to think as skipping rope is to the boxer, although the boxer does not skip rope when in the ring. It is as fundamental to the ability to address political issues as calculus is to the future engineer. As an illustration of the pertinence of the arguments found in great philosophers, we doubt that a person could sensibly discuss the problem of justice (What is it? Is it more or less desirable than equality?) without having read Plato or Aristotle. Another advantage to learning from the classic texts is that the arguments and even styles are removed from the emotions and colouring metaphors of our time. We are not personally involved with their political causes and parties. We are more able dispassionately to examine their arguments than if these arguments were couched in the contexts of our own time. The possibility of gaining the perspective that distance provides is enhanced. Lastly, the texts are not newspaper items of the day. They do not address the ephemera of journalism; rather, they are the fruit of serious thought by brilliant thinkers on questions not confined to one time but addressed to humanity's political existence. Fundamental questions are always relevant.

PLATO

Philosophy and science, as we have known them in the Western world, owe their existence to the early philosophical speculation of Greek thinkers between the sixth and fourth centuries B.C. To think philosophically still means in large part to think like a Greek, for it was the Greeks who provided us with the words and concepts that we associate with rational thinking. Plato and Aristotle were the most pre-eminent and influential among these Greek philosophers, but they were not the first; they represented the culmination of a long development.

THE PRE-SOCRATIC PHILOSOPHERS

The earliest Greek philosophers were Ionians who lived in the coast cities of Asia Minor, in cities such as Ephesus, Samos and Miletus. We know very little about most of them since only fragments of their written work have survived, and about some of them we have knowledge only through anecdotes. Rejecting the popular mythology found in the poetry of Homer that explained reality in terms of the activities of a multiplicity of gods and goddesses, the Ionian thinkers sought to replace this mythological explanation with a more rational one. Conscious of change and movement, these early philosophers asked themselves if anything persists unchanged. What is the "stuff" out of which the universe is made? The earliest Greek philosopher, Thales of Miletus, said it was water; Anaximenes said it was air; and a third, Heraclitus, suggested it was fire. If we think of water as energy in a fluid state, then Thales's answer may not be as naive as it first appears, but of course the answers of these early Ionian philosophers were simplistic. Their importance lies less in the answers they provided than in the questions they raised. They were the first to ask what the nature of ultimate reality might be, and they were the first to try to answer that question rationally. By such questioning, they gave the initial impetus to thinking philosophically and scientifically. The early Greek thinkers, it should be noted, made no distinction between science and philosophy.

If philosophy is conceived of as the exploration of the meaning of reality (Being), then Parmenides of Elea (born towards the end of the sixth century B.C.) might well be called the father of philosophy since it was he who first used the symbol, Being. For a time he was a Pythagorean. The Pythagoreans were a religious community founded by disciples of the Ionian, Pythagoras. They were ascetic in ideas and practices and devoted themselves to the study of mathematics as the key to the understanding of all things. They also had a keen interest in music. Aristotle tells us that "they saw that the modifications and the ratios of the musical scales were expressible in numbers;—since, then, all other things seemed in their whole nature to be modelled on numbers, and numbers seemed to be the first things in the whole of nature, they supposed the elements of numbers to be the elements of all things and the whole heaven to be a musical scale and a number."[1] Change or movement, Parmenides taught, is illusory even though it is attested to by the senses. He is saying that there is a reality behind the appearance of things that is more real than that which appears to our senses to be real. He thus draws a distinction between Truth and Appearance and between Reason and Sense. Being is uncreated, imperishable, and immovable; it is without past and future; it is altogether Now. Reality is one, homogeneous, and indivisible.

Parmenides wrote in verse, and an important poem of his, *The Way of Belief*, has survived in part. Composed around 485 B.C., it consists of a prologue and two parts, one concerning Truth and the other Delusion, but only fragments survive of the last part. In the Prologue he describes his journey into the realm of philosophy as a journey towards an unnamed goddess of Light, guided by the maidens of the sun. He is impelled by his "heart's desire" to leave the realm of darkness and mortality and to enter the realm of light and immortality. Parmenides was the first to conceive of human beings having souls consisting of both mortal and immortal elements, and through the immortal element participating in the immortal

---

[1] *Metaphysics*, 985, b32–986, a3. Richard McKeon, ed., *Introduction to Aristotle*, trans. W.D. Ross, *Metaphysics* (New York: Modern Library, 1947), p. 255. For a general introduction to the pre-Socratic philosophers and Ionian science, see: Francis MacDonald Cornford, *Before and After Socrates* (Cambridge: Cambridge University Press, 1932); W.K.C. Guthrie, *The Greek Philosophers: From Thales to Aristotle* (New York: Harper & Brothers, 1960); J.B. Bury and Russell Meiggs, *A History of Greece*, 4th ed. (New York: St. Martin's Press, 1978).

life of the gods. We possess a special faculty of the soul that enables us to experience Being. This faculty Parmenides calls the *Nous*, the rational organ of cognition. The suggestion is that Thinking and Being are one and the same, but Parmenides does not mean to say that anything that can be thought is real; rather, thinking about that which is immortal is the way in which we experience Being. An additional faculty is required to articulate the content of this experience; this faculty is called ***logos***, or the capacity to argue logically. What is grasped by the *Nous* and the aid of *logos*, however, is a personal experience rather than a set of verbal propositions. The conflict between Truth and Error is not a conflict between true and false propositions but a conflict between two ways of living. If, by Truth, we mean only an "adequate and consistent articulation of an experience," then Delusion may be as "true" as the Truth. The conflict, rather, is between types of experience. The question is, Which kind of experience is more real, more authentic? According to Parmenides, Truth is the philosophy of the reality we experience "if we follow the way of immortalization of the soul; Delusion is the philosophy of the reality that we experience as men who live and die in a world that itself is distended in time with a beginning and an end. The characterization of this philosophy of reality as a Delusion derives its justification from the experience of a superior reality, of an immortal ground of the natural world. The conflict goes ultimately back to the experience of the mortal and immortal component parts of the soul."[2] Parmenides is saying that we can approach the Truth only by living in a way that makes the Truth accessible to us. This is a theme that is to be pursued by Plato and one that, several centuries later, is given an unique and concrete meaning by the Christian thinkers, St. Augustine and St. Thomas.

THE SOPHISTS

The Sophists were itinerant, foreign teachers who were prominent in Athens during the fifth century B.C. Among the most well known were Protagoras, Prodicus, Hippias, and Gorgias. Athens had become a political and cultural centre of considerable prominence following her victory in the Persian wars. The Sophists taught those subjects that would be useful to a young man in a cultivated, competitive, and democratic society. One of the chief subjects they taught was rhetoric, or the art of

---

[2] Eric Voegelin, *Order and History,* Vol. II:, *The World of the Polis* (Baton Rouge: Louisiana State University Press, 1957), p. 216.

public speaking, and the Sophists were often accused by their critics of being more concerned with the skill with which an argument was presented than with the substance of the argument. In addition to grammar and rhetoric, the Sophists taught arithmetic, geometry, music, and astronomy. They laid the foundations for the liberal arts curriculum that was to influence education for many centuries.[3]

The Sophists were uninterested in speculation about the nature of ultimate reality, and many of them professed a profound **skepticism** about the possibility of answering questions of that kind. In a fragment of a work, *On the Gods*, Protagoras declares: "About the gods I am not able to know either that they are, or that they are not, or what they are like in shape, the things preventing knowledge being many, such as the obscurity of the subject and that the life of man is short."[4] With the Sophists, concern with **transcendent** (spiritual) reality is subordinated to concern with life in the world. It is the social environment that engages their attention, and it is man, rather than God, who becomes the measure of all things. As Protagoras says: "Of all things the measure is man, of the being that they are, of the not being that they are not."[5] This can mean either that the human species is the judge of what is true or that each person is the judge of what is true for him or her. Considerable controversy has arisen over the exact meaning of Protagoras's pronouncement, but he is generally thought to have been a relativist who taught that it is possible to argue for and against any proposition equally well. An anonymous fragment entitled *Dissoi Logi* illustrates this with respect to ethical questions:

> Satisfaction of wants with regard to food, drink and sex is good for the healthy, but bad for the ill man. Immoderate consumption of food and drink is bad for the immoderate consumer, but good for the tradesman. Victory at the games is good for the victor, but bad for the defeated....
>
> To put on finery and cosmetics is indecent for a man, but decent for a woman. In Macedonia it is decent for a girl to have premarital relations, in Hellas it is not.

---

[3] For surveys of the writings by Sophists, see: H.D. Rankin, *Sophists, Socratics and Cynics* (London: Croom Helm, 1983); Mario Untersteiner, *The Sophists*, trans. Kathleen Freeman (Oxford: Basil Blackwell, 1954); G.K. Kerferd, *The Sophistic Movement* (Cambridge: Cambridge University Press, 1981).

[4] Quoted by Voegelin, *Order and History*, Vol. II, *The World of the Polis*, p. 295.

[5] *Ibid.*, p. 294.

To deceive an enemy is just, to deceive a friend is unjust.... Temple robbery is unjust, but to take the treasure of Delphi when Hellas is threatened by the barbarians is just.[6]

Some Sophists used this kind of argument to suggest that there is no one or universal moral truth about anything but that all moral judgments are relative to the person or community pronouncing them. Long before Plato taught, controversy had arisen whether justice was natural or conventional. The Sophists generally taught that human beings are naturally predisposed to seek power and to satisfy their desires, and that justice is simply that which a community agrees to call justice. Much of Plato's teaching was intended to provide an answer to such arguments. And his interest in politics was awakened, in part, by the theory of politics taught by the Sophists.[7]

SOCRATES

Very little is known for certain about the life of Socrates. All we know about him we have learned from the writings of Xenophon, Plato, Aristotle, and Aristophanes. Socrates was born around 470 B.C. and was brought to trial and condemned to death in the Spring of 399 B.C. Apparently he wrote nothing but won his great fame as an influential teacher. Socrates is ridiculed in Aristophanes's play *Clouds* as an "intellectual" who does not have his feet on the ground and whose brain consists of empty space filled with air. This is one of the first of many attempts to disparage the utility of intellectual speculation. Despite this popular impression of his activity, Socrates had a profound influence upon the thought of Plato and Aristotle.

Aristotle says that Socrates's greatest contribution was his use of inductive argument and his careful use of words. He taught by the method of questioning and, through questioning, sought to elicit more accurate definitions of words; he insisted that one start with particular examples before proceeding to enunciate universal principles. He would ask his pupil, for example, to give a definition of justice, piety, or courage and then, by questioning, demonstrate the inconsistency or inadequacy of the answers given. This method led some people to the conclusion that Socrates was a skeptic who believed that we can know nothing for

---

[6] *Ibid.*, pp. 296–97.

[7] Christian Meier, *The Greek Discovery of Politics*, trans. David McLintock (Cambridge: Harvard University Press, 1990).

certain. He did believe, however, that we can know nothing until we first ac-knowledge our ignorance, but it was not his intention to leave men in ignorance.

Humans, he thought, are woefully ignorant of the one question that they should address above everything else, namely, how to nurture their souls, how to live as good a life as possible. Socrates believed that his divine mission was to discover the principles of a good life and to impart this knowledge to all who would listen. By posing the question of how one should live, he became the founder of what we have since come to call moral philosophy.[8] He was convinced that virtue could be taught and learned since he tended to equate virtue with knowledge. No one, in his view, would knowingly choose evil as such. Socrates de-scribed his method of teaching as a form of "midwifery" since he believed that knowledge is a form of recollection and that teaching is a stimulus to this recol-lection. The teacher of moral philosophy does not impose new ideas upon us; he simply elicits the knowledge that we already have but have not yet articulated.

In 399 B.C. Socrates was brought to trial on the charge of corrupting the young, introducing new gods, and undermining the popular religion. Socrates had questioned the foundation of all authority, and he encouraged his pupils to question everything. He taught that there is a life that is better than political life and a standard of right that is not derived from society or the will of the people, but he was not an atheist, though some accused him of atheism. He said in his de-fence: "But that is far from so; I do acknowledge them, Gentlemen of Athens, as none of my accusers does, and to you and to the God I now commit my case, to judge in whatever way will be best for me and also for you." He refused to weep, wail, and lament at his trial, "I did not then think it necessary to do anything unworthy of a free man because of danger; I do not now regret so having conducted my defense; and I would far rather die with that defense than live with the other.... It is not difficult to escape death, Gentlemen; it is more difficult to escape wicked-ness, for wickedness runs faster than death.... I desire next to prophesy to you who condemned me. For I have now reached that point where men are especially prophetic—when they are about to die. I say to you who have decreed my death

---

[8] "The aims of moral philosophy, and any hopes it may have of being worth serious atten-tion, are bound up with the fate of Socrates' question...." Bernard Williams, *Ethics and the Limits of Philosophy* (Cambridge: Harvard University Press, 1985), p. 1. For a modern analysis of Socrates's and Plato's positions, see: Terence Irwin, *Plato's Moral Theory: The Early and Middle Dialogues* (Oxford: Clarendon Press, 1977).

that to you there will come hard on my dying a punishment far more difficult to bear than the death you have visited upon me. You have done this thing in the belief that you would be released from submitting to examination of your lives.... If you think by killing to hold back the reproach due you for not living rightly, you are profoundly mistaken."[9]

It was Plato's encounter with Socrates that determined the course of his own life—a life dedicated to the vindication of Socrates's manner of living and dying.

PLATO: His Life and Works

Plato was born to an aristocratic family in Athens in 428 B.C. He lived in times not unlike our own. It was a time of political unrest, of war, and of spiritual malaise; Greek civilization was beginning to decline and pass away. Twenty years before Plato's birth a war had broken out between the two principal Greek cities, Athens and Sparta. His youth was spent in the shadow of what was called the Peloponnesian War. The war came to an end in 404 B.C. when Athens lost her empire to Sparta. An oligarchic revolution took place in Athens that same year when a group of citizens known as the Thirty Tyrants (some of whom were relatives of Plato) seized political power. After about a year in power they were displaced by a democratic government.

Plato, at first, was attracted to a career in politics, but he became disillusioned with the original promise shown by the democratic revolution when the democratic regime charged his teacher, Socrates, with impiety and found him guilty. They put to death a man who taught and lived by the principle that it is more evil to cause suffering and injustice than it is to suffer injustice. Plato saw in Socrates a man in love with truth, a good man, a man not at war with himself or other men—a man, indeed, who encouraged his students to ask questions about the meaning of justice, which might lead them to question the legitimacy of prevailing social authority, but not a man of violence. The only weapon he employed against his opponents was that of speech; his authority was that of reasoned argument. It seemed to the young Plato that there was something radically wrong

---

[9] Plato, *Apology*, 35d, 38e, 39c–d. R.E. Allen, trans., *The Dialogues of Plato*, Vol. I (New Haven: Yale University Press, 1984). For a detailed study of Socrates's defence at the trial, see Richard Kraut, *Socrates and the State* (Princeton: Princeton University Press, 1984).

and disoriented about a society that could put a man of such integrity and wisdom to death. Unlike the politicians, who had caused Socrates to be sentenced to death, it seemed to Plato that Socrates had a much better claim to the true art of statesmanship than did the leaders of the age and that the educational enterprise in which Socrates was engaged was a more likely way out of social disorder than that promised by existing politics. Following the example of his teacher, Plato decided to pursue the life of philosophy.[10]

When Plato was approximately 40 years of age, he left Athens to visit Italy and Sicily. In Sicily he became a friend of Dion, at whose invitation he visited Sicily a second time in 367 B.C. He visited Sicily still a third time in 361 B.C., as a political adviser to Dionysius II. Plato had hoped to draft a constitution that would make possible a confederation of Greek cities, but opposition led him to abandon his plan.

After his first visit to Sicily, Plato founded his Academy in Athens around 388 B.C. His Academy was the parent of all modern colleges and universities. It attracted students not only from Athens but also from abroad and included in its curriculum not only the study of philosophy but also mathematics and the physical sciences. Plato was not uninterested in educating future statesmen, but he disagreed with the methods of the Sophists, who relied chiefly upon the teaching of rhetoric as the foundation of statesmanship. Plato thought of his curriculum as providing a more appropriate preparation for a life of politics.

Plato wrote numerous dialogues on a variety of subjects, and all of them have been preserved. Two of the earliest dialogues, the *Apology* and the *Crito*, are concerned with the trial and death of Socrates. For our purpose of eliciting Plato's political philosophy, the most important dialogues are the *Gorgias*, the *Republic*, and the *Laws*. The *Symposium* is concerned with the meaning of friendship and love, the *Phaedo* with immortality, the *Theaetetus* with knowledge, and the *Statesman* with the general art of the dialectic. Perhaps the most profound of

---

[10] Some scholars have decried this picture of Athenian democracy and have asserted that Plato and Aristotle have created a distorted and elitist perspective on Athens. See, J. Peter Euben, *The Tragedy of Political Theory: The Road Not Taken* (Princeton: Princeton University Press, 1990); Mogens H. Hansen, *The Athenian Democracy in the Age of Demosthenes: Structure, Principles and Ideology* (Oxford: Blackwell, 1991); Josiah Ober, *Mass and Elite in Democratic Athens: Rhetoric, Ideology, and the Power of the People* (Princeton: Princeton University Press, 1989); Jennifer Tolbert Roberts, *Athens on Trial: The Antidemocrataic Tradition in Western Thought* (Princeton: Princeton University Press, 1994).

all the dialogues is the *Timaeus* which is concerned, among other things, with the nature of the cosmos. In addition to the dialogues, we have some of Plato's purported letters. We have no record of his lectures at the Academy since, apparently, he lectured without a manuscript.[11]

Plato did not think that the truth about anything could be expressed in the form of a doctrine. That is, he did not think that the truth could be captured and passed on in verbal propositions. Furthermore, he was as much concerned that we ask the right questions as that we arrive at the right answers, and the answers that really matter are the answers we give to ourselves. Nevertheless, the attainment of knowledge does involve a quest and an encounter with other minds. Plato chose to dramatize this quest in dialogue form because the dramatic dialogue most nearly preserves both the form of living speech and the dialectical give and take of personal encounter.

For Plato, answers to philosophical questions, when we find them, present themselves more in the form of self-authenticating experience than in the form of verbal statements to which we give verbal assent. But there is always the danger that when something is written down the words may be taken as having some kind of reality apart from the experience that they symbolize and seek imperfectly to communicate. Men then argue endlessly about the words, and forget the experience that engendered their use. Of written words, Plato said: "And once a thing is put in writing, the composition, whatever it may be, drifts all over the place, getting into the hands not only of those who understand it, but equally of those who have no business with it; it doesn't know how to address the right people, and not address the wrong. And when it is ill-treated and unfairly abused it always needs its parent to come to its help, being unable to defend or help itself."[12] The dialogues are not intended to be read as containing philosophical doctrine but are intended to engage the reader in the quest for truth, which they represent. To attain knowledge of what is true, good, and beautiful by engaging in such a quest requires an act of will on our part since to know is to decide between various plausible possibilities.

---

[11] For historical evidence about Plato, see John Herman Randall, Jr., *Plato: Dramatist of the Life of Reason* (New York: Columbia University Press, 1970); W.K.C. Guthrie, *A History of Greek Philosophy*, Vol. IV (Cambridge: Cambridge University Press, 1975), pp. 8–38.

[12] *Phaedrus*, 275e, R. Hackforth, trans., *The Collected Dialogues of Plato*, eds. Edith Hamilton and Huntington Cairns (Princeton: Princeton University Press, 1961), p. 521.

In creating the literary form of the dialogue, Plato wanted to avoid presenting systematized doctrines, and, at the same time, he wanted to engage his audience without directly appealing to their emotions and feelings—as was done by the tragic poets of his time. The dialogues were written on papyrus rolls and were not used for reading as we read books but, rather, were used for recitations or dramatic readings. The dialogues, thus, are both literature and philosophy. But even where Plato resorts to powerful **myths** (stories or fables with philosophic points) or other literary devices, they are aimed at illuminating the power of the rational faculty. The dialogue, with its new style of writing, invites the listener to think along with Socrates and his interlocutors.[13]

Throughout the dialogues Plato uses Socrates as the spokesman for his ideas, and this has given rise to the question whether the Platonic Socrates is the historic Socrates. Scholars disagree, but it seems likely that in the early dialogues Plato was reproducing arguments that he had heard Socrates expounding and in the later dialogues he was using the name of Socrates to expound arguments of his own. The dialogues do contain some arguments that were advanced by actual persons with whom Plato was familiar; the characters in the dialogues are, thus, not entirely fictional.

THE GORGIAS

Although ostensibly a conversation about the meaning of rhetoric, the *Gorgias* actually is concerned with contrasting two competing views of the meaning of existence. The dialogue consists of three conversations involving Socrates and Gorgias, Socrates and Polus, and Socrates and Callicles.

Gorgias, a Sophist who teaches rhetoric, is asked by Socrates to describe the art that he teaches. Gorgias replies that it is the art of speaking. Speaking about what? Socrates asks. Gorgias replies that it is speech about the greatest and best of human concerns. But what is the greatest of all human concerns? Some would say that it

---

[13] The interrelationship of Plato's philosophy and the dialogue form are fully discussed in the following works: Charles L. Griswold, Jr., ed., *Platonic Writings: Platonic Readings* (New York: Routledge, 1988); Martha C. Nussbaum, *The Fragility of Goodness: Luck and Ethics in Greek Tragedy and Philosophy* (Cambridge: Cambridge University Press, 1986); John Sallis, *Being and Logos: The Way of Platonic Dialogue*, 2nd ed. (Atlantic Highlands: Humanities Press International, 1986); Michael C. Stokes, *Plato's Socratic Conversations: Drama and Dialectic in Three Dialogues* (Baltimore: Johns Hopkins University Press, 1986).

is good health; others would say that it is wealth; still others would say that it is the enjoyment of beauty. Gorgias replies that the chief concern is freedom. Freedom, as Gorgias understands it, is the ability to have one's own way to do what one wants. This involves imposing one's will on others, and it is rhetoric, the art of persuasion, which makes this possible. But there are other arts that use persuasion; we must ask, says Socrates, what kind of persuasion rhetoric employs and about what matters. Gorgias answers that rhetoric is the kind of persuasion needed in courts of law and other large assemblies; it is most effective when employed before large groups of people, and it seeks to persuade them about matters of right and wrong.

Socrates points out that there is a difference between a conviction produced by instruction and one produced without instruction. The first is based upon knowledge, the second simply upon belief. The art of rhetoric, Socrates declares, is frequently employed to produce convictions without knowledge. An orator does not teach juries and other large bodies of people about right and wrong; an orator merely persuades them to accept certain beliefs. It is the manner in which the orator speaks that is persuasive, not his knowledge of the subject matter. Gorgias agrees and observes that an orator is often more effective in persuading people to a point of view than the specialist who knows much more about the subject but who is deficient in oratorical ability. Indeed, Gorgias declares, there is no subject on which the orator could not speak before a popular audience more persuasively than any professional of whatever kind. That is the nature and power of the art of oratory. The orator who knows nothing about medicine may be more persuasive, even on medical matters, than the physician who has no oratorical ability.

Since the orator need have no knowledge of the truth about things, it is enough for him to have discovered the knack of convincing the ignorant that he knows more than the experts. Is it not likely, Socrates asks, that this will be employed by bad men for the worst of purposes? That is possible, Gorgias concedes, but you should not blame the teacher of rhetoric from whom the orator learned the art. Gorgias does admit that the orator should be a moral man, but it is not clear how, in Gorgias's view, he comes to this knowledge of right and wrong.

Polus now enters the conversation, and he challenges Socrates to submit his own definition of rhetoric for examination. Socrates replies that it is not an art but a "knack" gained by experience and, more precisely, it is the knack of producing gratification and pleasure. The orator typically tells his audience what it wants to hear; he panders to their desires and gives them pleasure.

Socrates says that one must distinguish genuine arts from their spurious counterfeits. There is a double art of nurturing the body and a double art of nurturing the soul.

Gymnastics is an art genuinely concerned with promoting the good of the body. It preserves bodily well-being. Its spurious counterfeit seeks to create the appearance of bodily well-being by the application of cosmetics. When the body becomes disordered or diseased, medicine prescribes an appropriate remedy or regimen to help the body to recover its normal state of well-being. Cookery puts on the mask of medicine and pretends to know what foods are best for the body. Cookery prescribes what the body finds pleasant; medicine prescribes what the body needs in order to correct a defect. It is characteristic of all the genuine arts that they are guided by rational principles to promote the genuine good of the person. In contrast, their spurious counterfeits only pretend to knowledge and are not concerned with what is good for the person but with what is pleasant. The word "cookery", which Socrates uses, might be better understood today if we substituted the word "drugs," the substances used by many persons today to simulate the feeling of physical well-being by producing momentary pleasure. It is the illusion of physical well-being that is created by the use of drugs, however, rather than genuine well-being.

Polus, however, is not persuaded by Socrates's distinctions between genuine and spurious arts. He counters that the man skilled in oratory is able to get his own way, to do as he pleases. It is an exercise of power that anyone would like to be able to practise if he could, he argues. Since it is clearly better to be in a position to do

	GENUINE ARTS	SPURIOUS ARTS
TENDING THE BODY		
Preservative:	Gymnastics	Cosmetics
Corrective:	Medicine	Cookery
TENDING THE SOUL		
Preservative:	Legislation	Sophistry
Corrective:	Administration of Justice	Oratory

a wrong than to suffer a wrong, the tyrant, as the most powerful of men, is enviable. Socrates disagrees. I would rather avoid both, he says, but if I had to choose I would rather suffer a wrong than do a wrong. Men and women are happy when they are upright and honourable, and miserable when they are vicious and wicked. Socrates goes further and says that the wicked are even more miserable when they escape punishment for their crimes than when they pay the appropriate penalty. The man who commits the greatest crimes and yet never undergoes re-proof or punishment is like the man suffering from a serious physical ailment who avoids seeking medical advice and help because, like a child, he fears the pain of the treatment that might be prescribed to cure him.

Callicles breaks into the discussion with the indignant remark that if what Socrates is saying is true then all human life as we ordinarily experience it is turned completely upside down. We are doing precisely the opposite of what we ought to do. Socrates tells Callicles that the difference between them is that he (Socrates) takes his bearings from philosophy, and Callicles takes his from de-mocratic society. According to Socrates right is not determined by what the ma-jority of men declare it to be or by what they practise. Right is what is right by nature not what is regarded as right by conventional agreement.

Callicles accuses Socrates of using a dishonest argument, of pretending to pursue the truth while actually only appealing to conventional opinion, for it is conventional opinion that it is better to suffer a wrong than to do a wrong. Socrates was able to silence Gorgias and Polus only because he shamed them into agreement by appealing to conventional opinion. Callicles says that he will not be so easily defeated because he alone is indifferent to conventional opinion. The truth is that anyone who calls himself a man will never tolerate suffering a wrong. It is natural for the better man to prevail over the worse and the stronger over the weaker. Just as in the animal kingdom the stronger prevails over the weaker, so in human society right consists in the superior man ruling the inferior. It is the weaklings, those who make up the majority of mankind, who invent the con-ventional opinion that it is better to suffer a wrong than to do a wrong.

It is no disgrace for a young man to ask philosophical questions, to pursue the study of philosophy, says Callicles, but a mature man ought to know when to give up asking childish questions and talking like a child. Such a man deserves a whip-ping for his unmanly behaviour. Those persons who are successful in the world—businessmen, politicians, leaders generally—have no time for philosophy; they are too busy pursuing those activities that really matter. No one cuts a more ridiculous figure than the philosopher who seeks to enter the world of business or politics; he appears to be a stumbling idiot, which in fact he is.

Despite the unmannerly way in which Callicles attacks Socrates, Socrates patiently asks Callicles to explain more specifically what he means by the "better" man. Socrates asks Callicles if the better man is not, in fact, the man who has learned to master his own appetites and passions, who has learned self-control. How can a man who has not yet learned how to rule himself possibly benefit and rule others? The good, Callicles replies, is the gratification of desire, the pursuit of pleasure, and "anyone who is to live aright should suffer his appetites to grow to the greatest extent and not check them, and through courage and intelligence should be competent to minister to them at their greatest and to satisfy every appetite with what it craves." It is because the many cannot attain to this life and because they are ashamed of their weakness that "they are led by their own cowardice to praise temperance and justice."[14] The truly great and noble man is the one who lives by the biological law of nature, which decrees that the weakest should go to the wall. Might makes right is the first law of nature and no man or society can stand up against it. In reality, the ugly thing is not to commit a wrong or an injustice but to suffer one. The right of the strong to impose their will on the weak, although contrary to conventional morality, is the first principle of natural morality. The real world—the world of politics and business—is not in need of moral principles but of aggressive men who know that justice is nothing else than the will of the stronger.

Socrates replies to the argument of Callicles by pointing out that the pursuit of pleasure itself is an endless pursuit and that the sensual desires of men are insatiable. The more our desires are satisfied, the more they crave, and our soul becomes like leaking casks that can never be filled. The impossibility of satisfying our desires shows the absurdity of the attempt. It is not the satisfaction of all kinds of desire without limit that men really want but happiness; and how is happiness possible without some rational principle by which we can differentiate good pleasures from bad? A man who does exactly as he pleases in response to the desires of the moment is neither a free man nor a happy one, but a slave to his passions, miserable in his bondage. He cannot be said to do as he pleases, for what he pleases

---

[14] *Gorgias*, p. 492. W.D. Woodhead trans., *The Collected Dialogues of Plato*, eds. Hamilton and Cairns, p. 274.

is not within his rational control. If he would pursue that which is truly good for him as a human being, he must have some rational understanding of that good and exercise rational restraint over his desires. Freedom consists not in the pursuit of pleasure but in a disciplined, ordered life, directed to the perfection of that which is distinctively human.

There is a good of the soul, just as there is a good of the body, and there is a science appropriate to each. The good of the body we call health, and the science of health is medicine. It is this standard of health that the physician tries to reproduce in his patients. Corresponding to the science of medicine, there is a moral science, which is concerned with the health of the soul. Just as the physician aims to produce order and regulation in the human body, so the statesman should aim at producing temperance and justice in the souls of the citizens. Politics is a practical art demanding a knowledge of human nature and that which is its distinctive good. Citizens are not things but persons embodying ends in themselves—to minister to those ends is the distinctive art of statesmanship.

Callicles may be right in thinking, says Socrates, that the rule of life, which Socrates prescribes, is liable to leave an individual at the mercy of an aggressor, but he is wrong in thinking that life is ugly. The "leviathan", says Callicles, will kill you if you do not humour it. Socrates replies that the important thing is not to live long but to live well. The dreadful thing is not to die but to enter the unseen world with a soul laden with guilt. No one, says Socrates, can escape Divine judgment, and before that judgment it is not the life prescribed by Socrates that will appear ugly but, rather, the way of life prescribed by Callicles.

Callicles is not convinced. Socrates suggests that Callicles will be plagued to the end of his life with a contradiction in his soul and this self-contradiction in the long run will make him miserable. As judged by philosophy, a man, like Callicles, who lives lustfully for the moment is already a dead soul, for he refuses to acknowledge that anyone can judge him or show him that he stands in need of judgment. The successful politicians whom Callicles admires have no real knowledge of justice or any genuine concern for the well-being of the souls of the citizens. They practise the spurious arts of sophistry and rhetoric, not the genuine art of politics. Plato argues that Socrates was the only genuine statesman of his time, for he was the only Athenian who used speech not to give pleasure to his audience but to help them to discover the nature of the good. Plato suggests that education, as exemplified by the manner and substance of Socrates's teaching, is a truer form of statesmanship than the counterfeit form practised by politicians.

Earlier in the dialogue Callicles had contended that Socrates must be joking when he asserted that injustice in the soul is the worst evil that a man can experience. For if this is true, then most men are doing precisely the opposite of what they ought to be doing; they are living an inverted existence. Socrates is not joking. He contends that the life of most men is an inverted life, and the problem is how to turn it right side up.[15] This is a task more appropriately performed by education than by politics in the usual sense of the word. And that theme is pursued in the *Republic.*

THE REPUBLIC

The setting for the dialogue is the descent by Socrates to the commercial port city of Piraeus, some six miles from Athens. The characters in the dialogue are Cephalus, a wealthy non-Athenian, his son Polemarchus, Thrasymachus (a sophist), and Plato's older brothers, Glaucon and Adeimantus, plus assorted friends. Socrates and his party have come to see a festival, and as they start back to Athens, some young men stop them and playfully refuse to let them go until Socrates agrees to talk with them. In particular, they want to know about justice and, ultimately, about the best way to live. The dialogue concludes with the myth of Er. Er, who died in war, inexplicably is able to ascend from Hades after death and can now see which life is actually best. By answering the question about justice and the best way to live, Socrates and his party, it appears, are enabled to leave the unhealthy port city of commerce and ascend to the just city of the Republic, which they have founded in their discourse.[16]

The *Republic* opens as an old man (Cephalus) is approaching death. The prospect of dying awakens in him some misgivings about his past life. He wonders how his life will be judged, and he is led to examine his conscience. Cephalus is a man of wealth, and he derives some satisfaction from the fact that he has paid his debts, owes no one anything, and has never deceived or cheated anyone. Socrates asks whether paying one's debts and telling the truth can be the

---

[15] James L. Kastely provides a survey of the significant secondary literature on the *Gorgias* and a sympathetic interpretation of its meaning. "In Defense of Plato's *Gorgias,*" *PMLA,* Vol. 106, No. 1 (January, 1991), pp. 96–109.

[16] For fuller interpretations of the setting of the dialogue, see: W.K.C. Guthrie, *A History of Greek Philosophy,* Vol. IV, *Plato The Man and His Dialogues: Earlier Period* (Cambridge: Cambridge University Press, 1975), pp. 434–49; Nussbaum, *The Fragility of Goodness,* pp. 136–39; Sallis, *Being and Logos,* pp. 312–20.

whole of virtue. He asks others to tell him what righteousness or justice (*dike*) really is. **Justice** has a broader connotation for Plato than it has for us today and is best understood as synonymous with right.

Polemarchus offers the argument that justice or right consists in helping one's friends and harming one's enemies, which was the conventional Greek view in that day. How, Socrates asks, does one distinguish friends from enemies? What if one is mistaken for the other? Can it ever be right to do injury to anyone? Repeating the position taken in the Gorgias, Socrates contends that the person inflicting injury, not the person suffering it, becomes the worse person.

Thrasymachus enters the discussion and repeats the kind of arguments encountered in Socrates's conversation with Callicles. Justice, Thrasymachus contends, is nothing else than that which is to the advantage or interests of the stronger party. The common element found in all just acts, he asserts, is that all just acts can be used by the strong and intelligent to their own advantage or interest. A true ruler or statesman, Socrates replies, is not one who serves his own interests but one who seeks to benefit those over whom he rules. Just as the art of medicine does not consist of the physician's knowledge of how best to promote his own interests but rather of how to benefit his patients, the art of statesmanship is concerned with what is good and proper for those for whom the art is practised rather than the interests of those who practise it.

Thrasymachus replies that the shepherd tends and fattens his flock to make a profit for himself, and that the physician charges a fee for his services. But Socrates answers that Thrasymachus is confusing a by-product of the practice of an art with the art itself. There is an art of shepherding that has nothing to do with making money, and the physician's art consists not of making money but of curing patients. The practice of any genuine art involves the consideration of what is best for those for whom the art is practised.

Undeterred, Thrasymachus contends that happiness consists in getting as much as you can of pleasure, wealth, and power. The man who is capable of getting more than his fair share proves himself more intelligent and stronger. Socrates points out that any group of persons united for a common purpose, whether it be a political community, a family, an army, or a band of robbers, is not likely to achieve its purpose if each member is trying to get the better of everyone else. There is such a thing as "honour among thieves." Just as injustice produces hatred and feuding among individuals, so injustice will divide an individual so that he is incapable of acting with any singleness of purpose. Also, there is no natural limit to self-assertion, and it is unintelligent to pursue a goal that is unachievable.

Anything is good or excellent (**arete**), according to Socrates, when it performs well that function for which it is designed. The function of the eye is to see, that of the ear to hear. Indeed, we speak of someone having "good" eyesight or "bad" in regard to the ability of the eye to do what it is designed to do. The virtue of anything is what it is good for, and just as the organs of the body have certain specific functions to perform, so the soul of man has its own peculiar function, something it alone can do. The proper work of the soul is to deliberate rationally over alternative courses of action and, after deliberation, to take charge and to exercise control. When it does its work well we say that it is acting justly or virtuously. Therefore, the proper life that human beings should strive for is the life of reason.

Glaucon and Adeimantus are dissatisfied with the easy victory of Socrates over Thrasymachus. They restate with more powerful arguments Thrasymachus's position that the best life for the strong (if not the many) is to lead the life of injustice. They do not necessarily agree with Thrasymachus, but they do want better arguments from Socrates. Glaucon notes that the origin of justice seems to be merely convention. People, he says, often do think that it is desirable to do wrong if they can remain undetected. To illustrate, he tells the story of the shepherd Gyges who found a powerful ring that enabled him to become invisible. Using the ring, Gyges was able to seduce the Queen, kill the King, and attain power. Who would not use such a ring?[17] It would be natural to do so. On the other hand, it is not at all desirable to suffer wrong. When the many have had a taste of both and lack the power to do wrong with impunity, they decide that it would be better for all concerned if they made a compact or agreement neither to do wrong nor to suffer it. They agree to make laws, which all will obey, and the laws will prescribe what is right. That, says Glaucon, is how justice originated. Justice or right stands midway between the best thing of all (to be able to do wrong with impunity) and the worst (to suffer wrong without the power of retaliation). Justice, in short, is a compromise made by the many weak. It is not good in itself or natural to do what is just, but we do what is just (as defined by convention and **law**) in order to make life in society tolerable.

---

[17] The Ring of Gyges can be equated with the rhetoric of the Sophists, which also enables a person to attain power through keeping his true intentions and nature invisible.

Glaucon's brother, Adeimantus, goes on to say that when children are told to be good, honest, and just the clinching argument frequently is that such conduct will lead to respectability. It is important to have a good name, a good reputation, and it also pleases the gods who will reward good conduct in an afterlife. In reality, he continues, we all know that dishonesty generally pays better than honesty and that the practice of self-control and virtue is difficult and unpleasant. A man who is rich and powerful, even if dishonest, is usually loaded with honours and high esteem. The important thing is to conceal wrong-doing under a veneer of decent behaviour. No man of any power, social status, wealth, or intelligence will set any value on justice itself, and he is more likely to laugh when he hears it praised. It is only a lack of courage or the infirmity of age or some other weakness that leads men to condemn the evil they have not the strength to practice.

Both Glaucon and Adeimantus challenge Socrates to demonstrate that the life of justice and virtue, which he recommends, is really good and worthwhile in itself, that such a life really makes a person a better person. Socrates accepts, and the rest of the *Republic* is devoted to meeting that challenge. Socrates suggests that they examine together the origin, nature, and function of the political community or state, for in the state we see the individual writ large. If we can first determine what constitutes justice in the state, we shall then be in a better position to say what constitutes justice in the life of the individual.[18]

The state comes into being originally, Socrates says, because individuals are not economically self-sufficient; they have different talents and skills and are fitted for different occupations. If each one performs that task for which he is naturally fitted, then more things will be produced efficiently and the needs of all will be better satisfied. The division of labour according to natural aptitudes is the first principle of justice. It enables each individual to fulfill his potential and to contribute to the common good of the whole. However, no state exists for long simply to supply elementary physical needs. Humans desire luxuries as well as necessities, and often this desire inflames the natural appetites. The desire for luxuries, in fact, is one of the principal causes of warfare between states.

---

[18] One scholar reads the *Republic* as primarily a discourse between Socrates and Glaucon. Plato's focus is less about political rule than it is about self-rule, which can be attempted only by a natural warrior such as Glaucon. Leon Harold Craig, *The War Lover: A Study of Plato's Republic* (Toronto: University of Toronto Press, 1994).

But human needs are not just physical; they are also cultural and spiritual. It is not life alone that men desire but the good life, and the state exists above all to promote that good life. Therefore, in addition to the farmers, artisans, and traders who supply the economic needs of the political community, the state requires leaders, who Plato calls "guardians." The guardians consist of two groups: the auxiliaries and the philosophic rulers. The auxiliaries perform military and administrative duties; the philosophic rulers perform legislative and deliberative functions.

THE REPUBLIC: Selection of the Guardians and Their Manner of Living

The guardians are selected after a long process of education (to be described later). All will have the same education up to the age of 20. At that time, after taking examinations, a few will be selected to pursue their education further and to serve ultimately as philosophic rulers. The rest will move into the ranks of the auxiliairies. Neither wealth nor birth will determine who is eligible to serve as a guardian—only natural aptitude, character, and educational achievement. Women, as Plato makes clear later in the dialogue, will have the same opportunity as men to serve as guardians and the same education.[19] The children of farmers, artisans, and traders will have the same opportunity to rise to the rank of guardian as the children of the guardians. He is clear on the point that the children of guardians do not automatically become guardians but must earn that rank through merit and demonstrated educational achievement.

Despite the claims of some of Plato's critics, it was clearly not his intention to establish a class or caste system of rulership.[20] It was an **aristocracy** of merit that

---

[19] *The Republic,* III, 451c. Some have argued that the equality of women is designed to introduce gentleness into the guardian class. Allan Bloom, "Interpretative Essay," *The Republic of Plato* (New York: Basic Books, 1968), p. 384. Others have claimed that the equality of women actually is a "defeminization" or "de-sexing" of the female. For a full treatment of sexual equality in Plato, see Arlene W. Saxonhouse, *Women in the History of Political Thought: Ancient Greece to Machiavelli* (New York: Praeger, 1985), pp. 37–62; Susan Moller Okin, *Women in Western Political Thought* (Princeton: Princeton University Press, 1979), pp. 15–70, 305–8; Julia Annas, *An Introduction to Plato's Republic* (Oxford: Oxford University Press, 1981), pp. 181–85; Gregory Vlastos, "Was Plato a Feminist?" *Time Literary Supplement,* March 17–23 (1989), pp. 276, 288–89.

[20] Karl R. Popper contends in his *The Open Society and Its Enemies,* 2 Vols. (Princeton: Princeton University Press, 1950) that Plato did intend to create a caste system. This accusation is effectively answered by Ronald B. Levinson, *In Defense of Plato* (Cambridge: Harvard University Press, 1953)

Plato advocated with equality of opportunity for all. It is a significant fact that although slavery was an accepted institution in the Greek world of Plato's time, there is only one passing mention of slavery[21] and a clear injunction prohibiting slavery of fellow Greeks[22] in the *Republic*. Plato uses the "Myth of the Metals" from the Phoenician story to illustrate the proper relations among the citizens. All would be told the "noble fiction" that they were born from the mother earth. Socrates tells the story:

> All of you in the city are brothers we shall tell them as we tell our story, but the god who fashioned you mixed some gold in the nature of those capable of ruling because they are to be honoured most. In those who are auxiliaries he has put silver, and iron and bronze in those who are farmers and other workers.... If [the guardians'] own offspring should be found to have iron or bronze in his nature, they must not pity him in any way, but give him the esteem appropriate to his nature; they must drive him out to join the workers and farmers. Then again, if an offspring of these is found to have gold or silver in his nature they will honour him and bring him up to join the rulers or guardians, for there is an oracle that the city will be ruined if ever it has an iron or bronze guardian.[23]

This myth is not intended to deceive anyone but simply to express in allegorical language a few basic truths, namely: (1) that all humans share a common humanity by virtue of their common origin; (2) humans differ in their natural endowments, some being born with greater capacities and potentialities than others; (3) there should be equality of opportunity with merit alone determining

---

and by John Wild, *Plato's Modern Enemies and the Theory of Natural Law* (Chicago: University of Chicago Press, 1953). A useful series of articles can be found in Renford Bambrough, ed., *Plato, Popper and Politics: Some Contributions to a Modern Controversy* (Cambridge: Heffer, 1967). The controversy continues over whether there is a Greco-totalitarian dimension in Plato, with the charge by Stephen T. Holmes, "Aristippus In and Out of Athens," *American Political Science Review* 73 (March 1979), pp. 113–29, and with a defense by James H. Nichols, "On the Proper Use of Ancient Political Philosophy," *American Political Science Review* 73 (March 1979), pp. 129–33.

[21] *The Republic*, IV, 433d.

[22] *Ibid*, V, 469c.

[23] *Ibid*, III, 415a–d. G.M.A. Grube, trans., *Plato's Republic* (Indianapolis: Hackett Publishing, 1974). All translations are from this edition.

one's place in society. There is no doubt that Plato believed that one can inherit greater or less intelligence, but it does not necessarily follow, as some of his critics have alleged, that he believed that hereditary characteristics are racial. Plato nowhere speaks of a "master race."

The guardians are not to possess any private property beyond the barest necessities. They may not possess gold or silver and are forbidden even to handle it. They are to live in communal dwellings and share all things in common. Superficially, it sounds as though Plato is advocating a kind of communism, but he is not. He is suggesting that the guardians live a monastic-like existence under ascetic discipline. It is his intention that the rulers should be freed as much as possible from the cares and anxieties produced by the possession of things. It is detachment from material things and their temptations that he seeks to achieve rather than the more abundant enjoyment of material things. The community of goods, moreover, is prescribed only for the guardians; it would not apply to the farmers, artisans, and traders.

Socrates is asked whether the guardians will be happy living in this way.[24] He replies that they probably will not be perfectly happy. The aim in founding a community along these lines, however, is not to make any one group of people happy but to secure the greatest possible happiness for the community as a whole. Whatever the practicality of Plato's plan, it is clear that he has no intention of setting up a community designed to secure the well-being or happiness of a select few.

THE REPUBLIC: The Definition of Justice

Virtue consists for Plato in wisdom, courage, moderation, and justice. Having described **Kallipolis,** the best kind of political community, he now asks where one finds these elements of virtue in the community. Wisdom consists in the knowledge that the philosophic rulers possess and that enables them to lead and to govern. Courage is defined as knowing what ought to be feared and what ought not to be feared, in knowing what is truly good and evil. Only the philosophic rulers possess this kind of knowledge completely, but the auxiliaries peculiarly exemplify it in the state. They have learned through education what should and should not be feared and hold fast to this knowledge through conviction. Moderation does not reside in any particular part of the community but extends throughout the state. It is the harmonious agreement as to who should govern and who should perform

---

[24] *The Republic*, IV, 419a.

the other functions necessary for the state. Justice consists in each part of the community—tradesman, auxiliary, and guardian—doing that work which it can do best. A just state is one in which each person has the opportunity to perform that social function for which that person is best fitted by character and ability.

Corresponding to the three parts of the state are three parts of the individual soul. One part of the soul is appetitive, the desire for the pleasures of food and sex. Such desires are nothing more than blind cravings for the object towards which they are impelled. A second part of the soul is that which has the capacity to feel anger and indignation. Plato calls this the **spirit** element. The third part of the soul is the ability to reason. Justice or virtue in the individual consists in each part performing its proper function, with no one part seeking to usurp the role of another. Plato explains in the following passage:

> Therefore it is fitting that the reasonable part should rule, it being wise and exercising foresight on behalf of the whole soul, and for the spirited part to obey it and be its ally. —Quite so....
>
> These two parts, then, thus nurtured and having truly learned their own role and being educated in it, will exercise authority over the appetitive part which is the largest part in any man's soul and is insatiable for possessions. They will watch over it to see that it is not filled with the so-called pleasures of the body, and by becoming enlarged and strong thereby no longer does its own job but attempted to enslave and to rule over those over whom it is not fitted to rule, and so upsets everybody's whole life. —Quite so, he said....
>
> It is this part which causes us to call an individual brave, when his spirit preserves in the midst of pain and pleasure his belief in the declarations of reason as to what he should fear and what he should not. —Right.
>
> And we shall call him wise because of that small part of himself which ruled in him and made those declarations, which possesses the knowledge of what is beneficial to each part, and of which is to the common advantage of all three. —Quite so.
>
> Further, shall we not call him moderate because of the friendly and harmonious relations between these same parts, when the rulers and the ruled hold a common belief that reason should rule, and they do not rebel against it?— Moderation, he said, is surely just that, both in the individual and the city.[25]

---

[25] *Ibid.*, 442a–d.

Plato likens injustice to a kind of civil strife among the three elements of the soul when one part rises up in rebellion against the whole. Just as health consists of each bodily organ performing that function for which it was designed and acting in harmony with all other organs, so justice in the soul is produced by each part performing its own proper function under rational control and subordination. No one seriously asks whether health is desirable or not. No sane person would wish to be unhealthy or diseased. Similarly, no sane person would wish not to be virtuous. A person is a better person and more truly human when just. This is Socrates's answer to the challenge presented to him earlier in the *Republic* by Glaucon and Adeimantus when they insisted that he demonstrate that the life of virtue is worthwhile in itself: justice, like health, is desirable in itself.

The harmony of the parts, which constitutes justice, is brought about by education, which immediately introduces the question whether justice is, in principle, attainable by all humans. On the one hand, the analysis of human nature apparently was meant to apply to all humans as humans. Each person has a rational, spirited, and appetitive faculty. On the other hand, the rational faculty, which is critical in guiding the other faculties to a state of harmony and justice, appears to vary in degrees among people to the same extent other faculties vary. There are degrees of intelligence as there are degrees of courage. Is it possible for all humans to be sufficiently "educated" to attain justice in their souls, or can only philosophers be truly just?[26] The nature of education is, accordingly, a central topic. Socrates proceeds to describe a formal curriculum for educating, and he also indirectly educates through his dialogue, myths, and stories. Both types of education are designed to persuade his listeners to choose the life of justice or virtue.

Before Socrates can develop his scheme of education, he is interrupted by Polemarchus who asks Socrates to explain in more detail the offhand remark made earlier in the dialogue about a community of women and children.[27] There are actually three "waves" of arguments, Socrates complains, which may

---

[26] See the exchange between Dale Hall and Allan Bloom: Dale Hall, "The Republic and the 'Limits of Politics,'" *Political Theory* 5 (August 1977), pp. 293–313; Allan Bloom, "Response to Hall," *Political Theory* 5 (August 1977), pp. 315–20. Thomas Landon Thorson, *Plato: Totalitarian or Democrat?* (Englewood Cliffs: Prentice-Hall, 1963); Terence Irwin, *Plato's Moral Theory: The Early and Middle Dialogues* (Oxford: Clarendon Press, 1977), pp. 283–84; R.W. Hall, *Plato* (London: Allen & Unwin, 1981), pp. 54–80, and *Plato and the Individual* (The Hague: Martinus Nijhoff, 1963), pp. 9–33.

[27] *The Republic*, V, 423e.

well engulf him. First is the assertion that women should be educated equally with men. Women, too, can be part of the guardian class and can perform all of the required tasks. Men and women have the same nature.[28] The second wave is equally radical. The guardians, during the time they serve as guardians, will not be allowed to marry and have children, and they are forbidden to have private property. The guardians will constitute, so Plato hoped, a single family in which there will be a community of wives and children. Sexual promiscuity is not tolerated, and sexual intercourse is strictly controlled in the interest of breeding children by eugenic methods. Parents, presumably, will not know their children, nor the children their parents. The children will be raised communally, and all adults will be parents to all. Plato's intention in suggesting this arrangement is to free the guardians from the temptation to show preference to the members of one's own family and, thus, to help create unity in the political community.[29] The third wave is that philosophers must become kings, or kings philosophers, before political regimes can be happy. Power and wisdom need to be tied.[30] Both marriage and private property have a far greater significance in modern society than in ancient Greece. Consequently, Plato's proposals will appear to us more politically radical than they would to Plato's contemporaries.

One commentator on Plato says that "no sane and sober human being can regard the ideas put forward in Book V as a serious political proposal."[31] Most interpreters have argued that Plato is serious and at least wants to indicate how difficult it is to create a just regime.[32]

---

[28] *Ibid.*, 451c.

[29] *Ibid.*, 457d.

[30] *Ibid.*, 473d.

[31] Leon Harold Craig, *The War Lover: A Study of Plato's Republic* (Toronto: University of Toronto Press, 1994), p. 204.

[32] Should Plato's proposals be taken seriously? One group argues that Plato clearly conceived of the proposals as actual possibilities which could be implemented. The following are examples: Ernest Barker, *Greek Political Theory: Plato and His Predecessors* (London: Methuen & Co., 1964); Francis MacDonald Cornford, trans. with introduction, *The Republic of Plato* (New York: Oxford University Press, 1945); George Klosko, "Implementing the Ideal State," *The Journal of Politics* 43 (May, 1981), pp. 365-89; R.L. Nettleship, *Lectures on the Republic of Plato* (London: Macmillan, 1963). The opposite is argued by Leo Strauss, *The City and Man* (Chicago: University of Chicago Press, 1977); Bloom, *The Republic of Plato*; I.M. Crombie, *An Examination of Plato's Doctrines*, 2 Vols. (London: Methuen, 1962-3); Guthrie, *The Greek Philosophers: From Thales to Aristotle*; Adi Ophir, *Plato's Invisible Cities: Discourse and Power in the Republic* (London: Routledge, 1991).

THE REPUBLIC: Education of the Guardians

Plato first describes the kind of elementary education that children should have. That education would consist of gymnastics to train the body and music to nurture the soul. The purpose of musical training is to help to discipline the passions. Young children are notoriously wild and loud in their play. Musical training seeks to discipline these impulses by introducing children to rhythm and harmony in order to bring these wild impulses under control.

The education of young children begins with the telling of stories about the gods and heroes. The purpose of such stories is to inspire the children with love of the good at a very early age. Plato has been accused of wanting to censor what children should be permitted to read and to hear. He did think that some rational criteria should be used to determine what kind of literature would be appropriate to use in the education of children. Parents and teachers today have to decide on some basis what kinds of stories to tell children and what kind of literature to make available to them. The only difference is that Plato was conscious of the principles he wanted to instill in the light of what reason discovered to be true, and he was more consistent in the application of this knowledge than we frequently are today. To call the process of selecting appropriate literature for children "censorship" only confuses the issue and avoids the problem. By what criteria, if any, does a parent or teacher decide what stories to tell children and what literature to make available to them? There can be no education of children without employing some criteria of selection.

Plato seems to have an animus against using poetry in the education of children; he would forbid them to read Homer or Hesiod. This seems curious since Plato himself often writes like a poet. It is less an animus against poetry, however, than it is a desire to prevent children from being exposed to false teaching about heroes and gods. The gods were often depicted in the poetry of Homer and Hesiod as being deceitful, engaging in intrigues and warfare with other gods, committing the foulest of crimes, and appearing in various shapes disguised as strangers. Plato wants to replace this false teaching with the truth. "Surely the god, and all that is his, are in every way best?" Plato argues. Accordingly, one cannot hold that the god is deficient in beauty or virtue or that gods change shapes and delude us. "Nor must our mothers, believing [the poets], terrify their children by telling bad stories, saying that some gods wander at night in the shape of strangers from many lands."[33] God is not the source of evil but only of good. We must look for the cause of evil in men. God is not a magician, and cannot be bribed. A poet, Plato concludes, should represent the divine nature as it really is.

For the proper development of the child, physical training is as necessary as literature and music. The purpose is not only to develop the muscular strength of the body but also to bring the two elements of the soul, the spirited and the philosophic, into harmony with one another. "Do you not realize," Socrates asks, "the state of mind of those who practise physical culture throughout their life but do not touch the arts, and of those in the opposite case?"

> I get the point, he said. You mean that those who devote themselves exclusively to physical culture turn out to be harsher than they should be, while those who devote themselves to the arts become softer than is good for them.
>
> And further, said I, it is the spirited part of one's nature which provides the harshness; rightly nurtured it becomes courageous, but if strained too far it would be likely to become rigid and harsh....
>
> And is it not the wisdom-loving nature which provides the gentleness, and, if relaxed too far, becomes softer than it should, though if properly nurtured it is gentle and orderly? —That is so.
>
> We said that our guardians must have both these natures.[34]

Elementary education, with emphasis upon literature and music, would continue until the age of 17 or 18. This would be followed by two years of compulsory gymnastics and military service. Then a select few would be chosen on the basis of academic promise to pursue a higher education where the emphasis would be placed upon the study of mathematics. Those not chosen would be absorbed into the ranks of the auxiliaries. After a 10-year course of study in higher mathematics, a final selection would be made of those worthy to pursue the study of philosophy and the principles of morality. This study

---

[33] *The Republic*, II, 381. For a discussion of Plato's assessment of poetry, see Iris Murdock, *The Fire and the Sun: Why Plato Banished the Artist* (Oxford: Oxford Unversity Press, 1977); and Julius A. Elias, *Plato's Defense of Poetry* (Albany, N.Y.: SUNY Press, 1984).

[34] *The Republic*, III, 410c–e.

would require approximately 5 years. Then, between the ages of 35 and 50, those completing this course of study would serve the government in positions of public service. At the age of 50, the better ones would divide their time between studying and serving as members of the supreme governing council.

The purpose of this higher education is to lead the student to an understanding of the reality that lies behind the appearances of things and, ultimately, to a vision of the Good.

THE REPUBLIC: The Four Stages of Cognition

The lowest stage of cognition (knowledge) Plato calls *eikasia* or, as it is frequently translated, imagining. At this stage we take as "real" shadows, reflections in water, and close-grained polished surfaces. In the second stage of cognition we are able to distinguish the reflections of objects from the objects themselves. We are conscious of trees, animals, all the works of nature, and of human hands, and we know the difference between them and the shadows they cast. We have correct opinions (*Doxa*) but no knowledge; this stage is called the stage of belief (*pistis*). In both these stages seeing is believing, real is what we see to be real. We are still inhabiting, however, what Plato regards as the World of Appearances.

The purpose of higher education is to help us to escape from the World of Appearances to the Intelligible World, which is known by rational insight. Rational insight is divided into two stages. We begin to enter the Intelligible World when we begin to think, that is, when we learn how to think mathematically. This stage of thinking is called *dianoia*. The teacher of mathematics typically uses diagrams and models as imperfect representations of the objects of thought. For example, in the study of geometry we use imperfect models of circles, squares, and triangles to discover the distinguishing properties of circles, squares, and triangles. These models serve as a bridge from the visible object to the abstract reality.

What Plato wants to say, in part, is that there is a world of **forms** or ideas (*eidos*) more real than the visible world of things of which these things are imperfect representations. What is a chair? You might say that it is a wooden seat with four legs and a back, but a chair can be made of materials other than wood, and some chairs have fewer than four legs, some have none. In short, a chair cannnot be adequately defined in terms of its physical characteristics. What makes a chair a chair is the function that it alone can perform, namely, to support a human body in a comfortable upright position. The idea or form of the chair is, in short, more real than any particular chair. Particular chairs are perishable, but the form or idea of the chair is not. Just as chairness is more real than any actual chair, no actual circle or square that we can draw perfectly represents the idea of circularity or squareness that we seek to represent in our drawings of circles and squares.

This first stage of rational insight is comparable to the stage of understanding that we achieve when we pursue the study of science. The physicist begins his research with visible, tangible objects but proceeds to discover less visible, and even invisible, realities that explain the structure and function of these objects. The world, as the physicist understands it, is not the world of appearance as we ordinarily experience it. There is a reality behind the world of physical appearance that is more real than the world of physical appearance. At this stage of thinking certain assumptions are made, and we do not inquire about their validity.

The second stage of rational insight (the fourth stage of cognition) employs intelligence (*noesis*) and **dialectic** inquiry. In this stage the assumptions, which were accepted without question in the preceding stage, are now themselves subjected to inquiry. The assumptions are treated as hypotheses. The effort is made to find something that is not hypothetical, something that is the first principle of everything in existence. In this stage of cognition we encounter the eternal and unchanging Forms themselves and, ultimately, the Good (***agathon***), which is the highest object of knowledge.

Plato likens the Good to the Sun. It is by virtue of the existence of the Sun that we are able to see. The Sun is not vision but the cause of vision. When daylight fades vision dims, and we become almost blind.

> Which of the gods in the heavens can you [name] whose light causes our sight to see as beautifully as possible, and the objects of sight to be seen?— The same as you would, he said, and as others would; obviously the answer to your question is the sun…. Sight is not the sun, neither itself nor that in which it occurs which we call the eye. —No indeed…. And it receives from the sun the capacity to see as a kind of outflow. —Quite so. The sun is not sight, but is it not the cause of it, and is also seen by it? —Yes.
>
> Say then, I said, that it is the sun which I called the offspring of the Good, which the Good begot as analogous to itself. What the Good itself is in the world of thought in relation to the intelligence and things known, the sun is in the visible world, in relation to sight and things seen….

Say that what gives truth to the objects of knowledge, and to the knowing mind the power to know, is the Form of Good. As it is the cause of knowledge and truth, think of it also as being the object of knowledge. Both knowledge and truth are beautiful, but you will be right to think of the Good as other and more beautiful than they. As in the visible world light and sight are rightly considered sun-like, but it is wrong to think of them as the sun, so here it is right to think of knowledge and truth as Good-like, but wrong to think of either as the Good, for the Good must be honoured even more than they….

And say that as for the objects of knowledge, not only is their being known due to the Good, but also their reality being, though the Good is not being but superior to and beyond being in dignity and power.[35]

Philosophy, for Plato, is not a disinterested, dispassionate search for truth; it is not simply a theoretical exercise of reason. Reason can be trusted to lead us to the truth only when it is motivated by the love of the Good.

… For Plato philosophy is a way and a life, a way to a moment of existence in which there is direct confrontation with reality. Correspondingly, Plato's conception of wisdom is governed by his conviction that trust relating to ultimate reality resists propositional status and cannot be corraled and contained. Truth *about* reality is subordinated to truth *as* reality. Where man's relation to ultimate Being is involved, truth and reality are inseparable, for reality is embraced in immediate apprehension. Manifestly, then, trust *as* reality is not something admissible of transference by some men to others. Accordingly, the function of philosophy is that of rightly disposing men toward truth.[36]

---

[35] *The Republic*, VI, 508c–509c.

[36] Robert E. Cushman, *Therapeia: Plato's Conception of Philosophy* (Chapel Hill: University of North Carolina Press, 1958), p. xviii. A controversy exists over the nature of the knowledge claim made by Plato for philosophy. Some interpreters hold that Plato does claim that one can have true knowledge of reality through the forms. Others hold that such a claim both depreciates Plato's use of dialogue and dialectic and treats Plato as if he were a modern philosopher concerned primarily with epistemology. The former position has predominated, as the perusal of an introductory textbook in philosophy will show. The second view has more recently gained adherents. See, for example, Voegelin, *Order and History*, Vol. III, *Plato and Aristotle* (Baton Rouge: Louisiana State University Press, 1957), pp. 273–92 and Hans-Georg Gadamer, *Dialogue and Dialectic*, trans. P.C. Smith (New Haven: Yale University Press, 1980). A sample of the controversy can be seen in the essay by Nicholas P. White and the reply by Gadamer: Griswold, Jr., *Platonic Writings: Platonic Readings*, pp. 247–66.

Philosophy seeks to bring men to a decision about reality. It involves the whole man, his affections as well as his reason, his capacity to choose no less than his mind. It seeks his acknowledgment of the Good, of what, in a sense, he already knows but only dimly perceives; thus, cognition is a form of recognition. The truth about reality can never be captured in propositional form or described in a treatise. The purpose of philosophy, as Plato conceives it, is not to lead a person to accept certain propositions about the Good but to *experience* the Good. The Good is indefinable in propositional form, but this is not to say that it is unreal. The most profound of human experiences (e.g., love and suffering) defy attempts to comprehend them in propositional form, but they are no less real for that, as anyone who has been in love or who has suffered will testify. In the final analysis, Plato wants to say, as one commentator has pointed out, "that the primary assumptions on which argument necessarily proceeds are irreducible choices of personality."[37] Plato would have found the modern attempt to distinguish between subjective and objective judgments incomprehensible.[38]

THE REPUBLIC: The Allegory of the Cave

Plato's most famous allegory is probably the "Allegory of the Cave," which he recounts in Book VII. It is intended to further illustrate the four stages of cognition and the analogy of the Good with the Sun. Imagine, Plato suggests, the condition of men living in a large, underground cave with an entrance open to the light and a long passage from the entrance all the way down into the cave. These men have been chained from childhood. They can neither turn their heads nor move from their position and they can see only what is in front of them. Behind them there is a fire burning, and in front of the fire there is a parapet built like a stage for a puppet show. Imagine persons carrying objects that project above the parapet, artificial objects shaped

---

[37] Paul Shorey, *Plato: The Republic*, Vol. II (Cambridge: Harvard University Press, 1935), p. 174, fn. c. In her excellent work, *The Fragility of Goodness*, Martha Nussbaum characterizes Plato's dialogues as follows: "By writing philosophy as drama, Plato calls on every reader to engage actively in the search for trust.... Each of us has the choice, in fact; but it will be an appropriate choice only if it is made by the highest element in us, viz. intellect" (p. 134).

[38] It is in part the dominance of the scientific method in the modern world that has fostered the notion that we can clearly distinguish objective judgments from subjective ones. Yet there are indications that the procedures of even the physical sciences cannot be completely impersonal. See Michael Polanyi, *Personal Knowledge: Towards a Post-Critical Philosophy* (New York: Harper & Row, 1964); Imre Lakatos and Alan Musgrave, eds., *Criticism and the Growth of Knowledge* (New York: Cambridge University Press, 1975); Paul Feyerabend, *Against Method* (London: NLB, 1975).

like animals, human beings, and other forms in wood or stone or other materials. These objects cast their shadows on the wall that the prisoners are facing. (A modern Plato would likely have used the analogy of an underground movie theatre.)

The prisoners in the cave, unable to see one another and seeing only the shadows on the wall, would undoubtedly insist that the shadows of the artificial objects are real. But consider what would happen Socrates suggests:

> Whenever one of them was freed, had to stand up suddenly, turn his head, walk, and look up toward the light, doing all that would give him pain, the flash of the fire would make it impossible for him to see the objects of which he had earlier seen the shadows. What do you think he would say if he was told that what he saw then was foolishness, that he was now somewhat closer to reality and turned to things that existed more fully, that he saw more correctly? If one then pointed to each of the objects passing by, asked him what each was, and forced him to answer, do you not think he would be at a loss and believe that the things which he saw earlier were truer than the things now pointed out to him? —Much truer.
>
> If one then compelled him to look at the fire itself, his eyes would hurt, he would turn round and flee toward those things which he could see, and think that they were in fact clearer than those now shown to him. —Quite so.[39]

Suppose, further, that he were forcibly dragged up the steep incline into the sunlight outside of the cave. Would he not be even more perplexed and in greater pain? In time, however, he would become accustomed to the world outside the cave and would be able to distinguish real objects from their shadows. Eventually he would be able to look up into the sky, but at first he would look up only at night and see the Moon. Last of all he would be able to look at the Sun itself and learn that it is the Sun that governs the seasons and controls everything in the visible world.

Having achieved this knowledge, he would feel sorry for the prisoners in the cave, but only with the greatest reluctance would he go back into the cave to inform the prisoners of the truth that he has discovered. With considerable reluctance he re-enters the cave in the hope of freeing the prisoners from their illusions. Coming out of the sunlight and into the cave, he stumbles and gropes

---

[39] *The Republic*, VII, 515d–c.

his way in the darkness and is ridiculed by the prisoners, who are perfectly content with their condition. "As for the man who tried to free them and lead them upward, if they could somehow lay their hands on him and kill him, they would do so."[40]

The prisoners in the cave correspond to most people living in the world. Most live in that condition where "seeing is believing." Chained by their appetites and their reliance upon sensory experience, they are complacent in their ignorance and resentful of anyone who suggests that there is a reality that lies behind the appearance of things. The painful ascent from the cave, the long and arduous pursuit of truth, which the freed prisoner must endure, is the process of education.

It is interesting that Plato speaks of the prisoner who has been freed from his chains as having "to stand up suddenly, turn his head, walk, and look up toward the light." There is the suggestion that some force outside of the person is needed to effect this change, and there is the further suggestion that unless one is turned around completely (***periagoge***) and faced toward the light, one will be unable on one's own to begin the ascent towards reality. The acquisition of true knowledge involves a turning around of the self and the breaking of the bonds of appetite and sense. Eric Voegelin warns us to avoid the "extravagant interpretations" that link the turning around with "conversion in the religious sense."[41] Nevertheless, later Christian theologians did refer to the whole process found in the allegory of the cave as conversion and grace, and they did use Platonic concepts (such as *periagoge*) to develop Christian theology.[42]

---

[40] *Ibid.*, 517. The allusion, of course, is to the fate of Socrates.

[41] Voegelin, *Order and History*, Vol. III, *Plato and Aristotle*, p. 115; Robert Cushman does find strong links: *Therapeia: Plato's Conception of Philosophy* (Chapel Hill: University of North Carolina Press, 1958).

[42] Although Friedrich Nietzsche was characteristically excessive in dismissing Christianity as Platonism for the people, the influence of Plato and Neo-Platonists on Christian theology is indisputable. As one contemporary philosopher has noted: "The thought of the great Christian theologians up to and including Aquinas is to an incredible extent Platonic." J.N. Findlay, *Plato and Platonism: An Introduction* (New York: Times Books, 1978), p. 207. See also, H.J. Blumenthal and R.A. Markus, eds., *Neo-Platonism and Early Christian Thought* (London: Variorum Publications, 1981); C.J. De Vogel, *Rethinking Plato and Platonism* (Leiden: E.J. Brill, 1986); J.H. Burns, ed., *The Cambridge History of Medieval Political Thought* (Cambridge: Cambridge University Press, 1988); Frederick Copleston, *A History of Philosophy*, Vol. II, *Medieval Philosophy: Augustine to Scotus* (London: Burns Oates & Washbourne, 1959).

THE REPUBLIC: The Decline of the Best State

The concluding chapters of the *Republic* are concerned with a description of the ways in which degenerate forms of political community come into existence. It is unlikely, in Plato's view, that the best state will come into existence and more unlikely that it would continue in existence. Thus, Plato develops for contrast a taxonomy of degenerate forms of political community: timocracy, oligarchy, democracy, and tyranny. However, he is not arguing that this sequence is historically inevitable.

The first degenerate form of political community comes into being when dissension breaks out among the members of the ruling group. The ruling group is forced to accept a compromise between the men of gold and silver and those of bronze and iron. Private ownership of land and property is introduced, and the state is converted into a kind of military establishment. This form of government is called a **timocracy**. War will be its constant occupation, and the military virtues will be prized above those of the intellect. It is as though the spirited element in a man's soul subdued the philosophic and subordinated it. At first the ruling group disguises and subordinates its greed and governs itself by a sense of honour. Gradually, however, the spirit of ambition, motivated by a desire for honour, gives way to the passion for gain, and the oligarchic state (**oligarchy**)comes into being.

> First they find ways of spending [money] on themselves, they twist the laws for this purpose, and they themselves disobey it along with their wives. —Likely enough.
>
> Then as one man sees another doing this and envies him, they make the masses like themselves in this. —That is probable.
>
> Then as they proceed further into money making, the more they honour this the less they honour virtue....
>
> When wealth and the wealthy are honoured in a city, virtue and the virtuous are prized less. —Clearly.
>
> What is honoured is always practised, and what is slighted is neglected. —That is so.
>
> In the end the lovers of victory and honours become money-lovers and money-makers; they praise and admire the wealthy man and appoint him to office while they disregard the poor man. —Quite so.[43]

---

[43] *The Republic*, VIII, 550d–551a.

Wealth becomes the criterion for selecting rulers, and the populace is divided into the few rich and the many poor. A class of drones is created, which consists of persons who are neither tradesmen, artisans, nor soldiers. Some of these become criminals; others are simply paupers. This is caused by "the lack of education and a poor upbringing, as well as the condition of the city."[44] The oligarchic man is held in some restraint by his desire to hoard what he has acquired. Because he values money above everything, the oligarchic man is not disposed to spend it in licentious living, and his appetites, though uncontrolled by reason, are still restrained by greed. He is confined to calculating how money may breed more money. The aim of life in an oligarchy is to become as rich as possible.

The son of the oligarchic man resents the stinginess he sees in his parent. His father appears to him to be a miser; moderation and frugality seem to him nothing but churlish meanness. The young man vows to spend the money that his father has accumulated once he gets in possession of it, in order to satisfy the appetites his father has suppressed. In this way the democratic man emerges from the oligarchic family.

> The democratic man sets all of his pleasures on an equal footing, and so spends his life, always surrendering the government of himself to one, as if chosen by lot, until he is satisfied and then to another, not disdaining any but fulfilling them all equally.... He does not welcome true reasoning or allow it into the guardhouse; if someone tells him that some pleasures belong to good and beautiful desires, but others belong to evil ones, that one should prize and pursue the former while the latter must be restrained and mastered, he denies all this and declares that all pleasures are equal and must be equally prized.... And he lives on, yielding day by day to the desire at hand. At one time he drinks heavily to the accompaniment of the flute, at another he drinks only water and is wasting away; at one time he goes in for physical exercise, then again he does nothing and cares for nothing; at times he pretends to spend his time on philosophy; often he takes part in public affairs; he then leaps up from his seat and says and does whatever comes into his mind; if he happens to admire military men, he is carried in that direction, if moneyed men, he turns to making money; there is no plan or discipline in his life but he calls it pleasant, free, and blessed, and he follows it throughout his time....[45]

---

[44] *Ibid.*, 552e.

[45] *Ibid.*, 561b–d.

The democratic state (**democracy**) values what it calls freedom above everything else. It understands freedom as the opportunity to pursue, without limit, whatever it is that one desires. Each man will have the freedom to arrange his own manner of life to suit his own pleasure. This is the condition that we would describe today as anarchy. It is not intended by Plato as a description of modern constitutional, representative democracy, a form of government with which he was unfamiliar; nevertheless, it is evident that there are anarchic elements and pressures in modern democratic government.

As the passion for liberty grows, the infection of anarchy spreads and, paradoxically, the way is prepared for the introduction of despotism or tyranny.

> [A] father will accustom himself to behave like a child and to fear his sons, while the son behaves like a father, and feels neither shame nor fear before his parents, in order to be free. A resident alien is the equal of a citizen and a citizen the equal of a resident alien, and so too a foreign visitor…. A teacher in such a community is afraid of his pupils and flatters them, while the pupils think little of their teachers or their tutors. Altogether the young are thought to be the equals of the old and compete with them in word and deed, while the old accommodate themselves to the young, and are full of playfulness and pleasantries, thus aping the young for fear of appearing disagreeable and authoritarian….
>
> All these things together, you notice, make the soul of the citizens so sensitive that if anyone brings up a word about slavery, they become angry and cannot endure it. And you know that in the end they take no notice of the laws, written or unwritten, in order that there should in no sense be a master over them.[46]

The democratic state consists of three parts: the few rich who are intent upon making money and are industrious, an increasingly large number of drones, and the largest group of all, the farmers and workers. Because the last group is the largest when assembled, but also the group least interested in politics, the politicians are able to take increasing amounts of money from the rich, ostensibly on behalf of the people's welfare, but they keep the lion's share for themselves. The plundered rich seek to defend themselves and are accused of being

---

[46] *Ibid.*, 563a–e.

reactionary and hostile to democracy. Then, a leader arises as a self-announced champion of the people's interests and leads a revolt against the rich.

> Will he not, during the first days, and indeed for some time, smile in wel-come at anyone he meets. He says he is no dictator and makes many promises both in private and in public. He has freed people from debt and redistributed the land to the people and to his own entourage, and he pretends to be gracious and gentle to all…. But I think that when he has dealt with his outside enemies by making peace with some and destroying others, and all is quiet on the external fronts, the first thing he always does is to stir up a war, so that the people shall feel the need of a leader…. Also in order that by paying war taxes they become poor and are com-pelled to concern themselves with their daily needs and thus are less likely to plot against him….[47]

The man who, at first, was championed by the people as their saviour be-comes hated, and he rules by instilling fear in his subjects. When bolder men, who hold positions of power, begin to criticize him and his policies, the despot has them exiled or killed. This form of rule is **tyranny**. At the end, the tyrant finds him-self with no friends at all, living in an atmosphere of hate, fearful every moment for his own life. The citizens have become slaves of the tyrant.

And what is the despotic man like? The democratic man was the man who sought to satisfy all of his appetites equally, but lurking behind the natural ap-petites are the unnecessary and unlimited appetites that are revealed to most men only in their dreams. The tyrant emerges when these appetites obtain com-plete control of his soul. He will commit any crime, however sordid or foul, to satisfy them.

> Then, with madness as his bodyguard, this champion of the soul becomes fren-zied; if he finds in the man some beliefs or desires which are thought to be good and still have some feeling of shame, he destroys them and throws them out, until he has cleansed him of moderation and filled him with imported mad-ness…. Is this not the reason why Love has of old been said to be a tyrant?…. And so, my friend, I said, a drunken man has something of a dictatorial or

---

[47] *Ibid.*, 566e–567a.

tyrannical mind…. Moreover, a man who is mad expects to be able to rule not only over men but over the gods, and attempts to do so…. This, my dear friend, I said, is precisely how a man becomes dictatorial, when his nature or his pursuits or both make him intoxicated, lustful, and mad.[48]

Of all the degenerate forms of political community, despotism is the worst and the condition of its people the most wretched, and the despot himself is the most miserable, unhappy, and wretched of men. He is a slave and a coward. What sane person would wish to exchange places with him? To wish to be like the despot would be like wishing to be diseased and unhealthy. This is Plato's answer to Callicles and Thrasymachus, and he sums up his answer to them in the image of a fabulous monster.

Fashion me then one kind of multiform beast with many heads, a ring of heads of both tame and wild animals, who is able to change these and grow them all out of himself…. Then one other form, that of a lion, and another of a man, but the first form of all is much the largest, and the second second…. Gather the three into one, so that they somehow grow together…. Model around them on the outside the appearance of being one, a man, so that anyone who cannot see what is inside but only the outside cover will think it is one creature, a man….

Let us now tell the one who maintains that injustice benefits this man, and that justice brings him no advantage, that his words simply mean that it benefits the man to feed the multiform beast well and make it strong, as well as the lion and all that pertains to him, but to starve and weaken the man within so that he is dragged along withersoever one of the other two leads. He does not accustom one part to the other or make them friendly, but he leaves them alone to bite and fight and kill each other. —This is most certainly what one who praises injustice means.

On the other hand, one who maintains that justice is to our advantage would say that all our words and deeds would tend to make the man within the man the strongest. He would look after the many-headed beast as a farmer looks after his animals, fostering and domesticating the gentle heads

---

[48] *The Republic*, IX, 573b–d.

and preventing the wild ones from growing. With the lion's nature as his ally, he will care for all of them and rear them by making them all friendly with each other and with himself. —This is most definitely the meaning of him who praises justice.[49]

Although Plato does not claim that the successive forms of degenerate states are found in exactly this sequence in actual political history, he does want to say that the historical process will reflect a process of psychic decomposition. In describing the stages of timocracy, oligarchy, democracy, and tyranny, he shows that there is a close relationship between types of human character and political regimes. Political regimes do not "grow out of trees and stones" but out of the characters of the persons who inhabit them.

The *Republic* concludes with Socrates relating the story of Er, a Pamphylian, who after dying, arises from his funeral pyre to recount his journey through the afterlife. Er describes the cosmos, the orbits of the planets and stars, held by Necessity to an axis and spun by the Fates, the three daughters of Necessity. He sees souls who, after a thousand years, descend from Heaven and ascend from Hades. They meet on a meadow and, as in a lottery, are given random numbers to determine their place in a line for choosing their future lives. There are many types of lives from which to choose, combining all the features of human existence, but the first in line have the greater choice. The charge is made by Lachesis, a daughter of Necessity, to the assembled souls that they are responsible for their choice: "The responsibility is his who makes the choice, the god has none."[50] Although chance and circumstances—one's parents, genetic endowment, country—are beyond individual control, choice is still inescapable. After choosing, the souls drink from the river of Unforgetfulness and are shot like stars into their new existence. The choice is thus made in the interval between the past, which is no more, and the future; in other words, the choice is always now. 'How to choose correctly' is the crucial question. And Socrates interrupts his story of Er by repeating the theme: "He will call the worse that which leads the soul to being more unjust, the better that which leads it to

---

[49] *Ibid.*, 588d–589b.

[50] *The Republic*, X, 617e.

being more just; for we have seen that this is the best choice for a man, both in life and after."[51] From the perspective of the lasting and significant, i.e., immortality, justice benefits the persons who choose it.[52]

THE REPUBLIC: Concluding Observations

Plato is described by some commentators as presenting an "ideal state" in the *Republic*, and he is frequently characterized as a Utopian. If one means by a Utopian one who dreams of creating the perfect society by organizing the lives of humans in accordance with a blueprint, then Plato was no Utopian. He did not think that human beings could, or should, be manipulated as though they were inanimate things, though he did think that their characters could be formed, in part, through an educational process. Plato does not expect salvation from evil to come through politics or social engineering. The best one can achieve must be achieved through education, and one must always recall that, unlike a Utopia, even the best state, the Republic, will fall. It is Socrates, the teacher, who best exemplifies the true art of statesmanship. And he is less concerned in the *Republic* with the right kind of political constitution than he is with the right order of the soul. He is not concerned with delineating the features of an "ideal state" (a mistranslation of *ariste politeia*) but with constructing a paradigm of right social order in the image of the well-ordered soul.[53]

Plato makes the remarkable observation, which many today find incomprehensible, namely, that "the ills of the human race would never end until either those who are sincerely and truly lovers of wisdom come into political power, or the rulers of our cities, by the grace of God, learn true philosophy."[54] Plato thought that the actualization of a political commonwealth in which philosophers would reign was most unlikely, that such a commonwealth would come about only as a result of miraculous chance. "I understand," said Glaucon, "you mean in the city which we were founding and described, our city of words, for I do not

---

[51] *Ibid.* 618e.

[52] For an analysis of the Myth, see Richard Lewis Nettleship, *Lectures on the Republic of Plato* (London: Macmillan, 1963), pp. 353–64; Voegelin, *Order and History*, Vol. III, *Plato and Aristotle*, pp. 54–62.

[53] Voegelin, *Order and History*, Vol. III, *Plato and Aristotle,* pp. 62–70.

[54] *Epistle* VII, 326b, in Glenn R. Morrow, trans., *Plato's Epistles* (Indianapolis: Bobbs-Merrill, 1962), p. 217.

believe it exists anywhere on earth." "Perhaps" Socrates replies, "it is a model laid up in heaven, for him who wishes to look upon, and as he looks, set up the government of his soul."[55]

THE LAWS

Three elderly gentlemen—the Cretan, Cleinias, the Spartan, Megillus, and an Athenian stranger—start on a journey from Cnossos, on the island of Crete, to a famous cave sanctuary of Zeus. Crete, Sparta, and Athens represent admired political orders, and the discussion turns to the founding of a colony. The topics discussed include the institutions and laws required as well as a wide range of other practical considerations: drinking, sexual practices, population, education, punishment, and religion. This is the longest of Plato's works and also the one with the least dialogue among the characters. A considerable portion of the text consists of monologues by the Athenian stranger, whose voice is, in effect, that of Plato.[56]

The commonwealth described in the *Laws* is characterized by Plato himself as "second-best," but this is sometimes misunderstood. It is sometimes understood as meaning that the commonwealth described in the *Republic* is "ideal" and that described in the *Laws* represents a retreat from this Utopian vision to a more practicable possibility. As pointed out earlier, however, Plato is neither a Utopian nor an idealist. The commonwealth described in the *Republic* is the Idea (not ideal) of the state or *polis*, but the extent to which that Idea can be realized in actuality depends upon the quality of the human beings who inhabit any state.

When Plato wrote the *Republic*, he was not sanguine about the possibility of philosophers becoming rulers or of rulers becoming philosophers; that would occur only by "some miraculous chance." When Plato wrote the *Laws*, he was

---

[55] *The Republic*, IX, 592b. Some have argued that the institutions and practices espoused in the *Republic*, plus the wedding of philosophic wisdom with political power are impossible to realize. Thus, it was Plato's intention in the *Republic* to show the limits on politics, the impossibility of trying to realize Utopian goals. Strauss, *The City and Man* and Bloom, *The Republic of Plato* have made this argument. The continuing debate can be found in: Hall, "The Republic and the 'Limits of Politics,'" *Political Theory* 5 (August 1977), pp. 293–313; Bloom, "Response to Hall," *Political Theory* 5, pp. 315–20; and M.F. Burnyeat, "Spinx Without a Secret," *New York Review of Books* 32 (30 May 1985), pp. 30–36.

[56] For discussions of the setting for the dialogue, see: Guthrie, *A History of Greek Philosophy*, Vol. V, pp. 321–25; Glenn R. Morrow, *Plato's Cretan City: A Historical Interpretation of the Laws* (Princeton: Princeton University Press, 1960), pp. 3–92.

even less confident that one could find any philosopher-kings to rule even if, by miraculous chance, the opportunity should present itself. Accordingly, the guardian class disappears in the *Laws*, and the commonwealth is devised for a community consisting of a free citizenry, slaves, and alien residents. Plato had abolished slavery among fellow Greeks in the *Republic*; in the *Laws* it is reintroduced. Some men are unable to be educated, and they become slaves. Given a situation where a large number of the inhabitants of a commonwealth are unable to be educated and none can be found who are able to pursue the kind of education that was devised for the guardians in the *Republic*, what kind of a commonwealth can be hoped for? That is the subject matter of the *Laws*, and it is in that sense that the commonwealth described therein is "second-best." It is "second-best" because of the inferior quality of the inhabitants with whom one has to deal, not "second-best" as an "ideal." The Idea of the best still provides the principles underlying the commonwealth in the *Laws* and there is no departure from those principles.

In the first book of the *Laws* Cleinias and Megillus suggest that the supreme good for the city is victory over its enemies. A citizen should know how to be a good soldier, and the virtue most highly to be prized is courage. The Athenian stranger (Plato) disagrees. It is not victory over the enemy without that is the most important thing but victory over the enemy within—the conquest of the better parts of the soul (and the community) over the worse. A wise statesman will have peace, not war, as his objective; and while he will respect courage as a virtue, he will subordinate it to wisdom and justice. The better part of courage, the true test of manliness, is not ferocity in the face of danger but the ability to resist the seductions of pleasure. For this reason the wise statesman will give considerable attention to the right kind of education. He will be concerned that children are taught how to feel pleasure and pain rightly, first by habit and then by reason: "Pleasure and liking, pain and hatred, become correctly arranged in the souls of those who are not yet able to reason, and then, when the souls do become capable of reasoning, these passions can in consonance with reason affirm that they have been correctly habituated…. This consonance in its entirety is virtue."[57] Book II elaborates upon the elementary education of children in much the same way as was done in the *Republic*.

---

[57] *The Laws*, II, 653b. Thomas Pangle, trans., *The Laws of Plato* (New York: Basic Books, 1980).

In Book III Plato asks the fundamental question, What is a "city" and how does it arise? Plato brings an historical perspective to bear upon our understanding of how political civilizations grow, mature, and decline. He is one of the first both to appreciate the importance of history in the shaping of institutions and to suggest a cyclical theory of their rise and decline: periodically the arts of civilization are lost and have to be recovered.

Plato traces the growth of political communities over a long period of time. From a nomadic existence men turn to agriculture and settle down in the uplands. The head of each household is its ruler, but as families tend to unite for the purpose of defence, an aristocracy of household leaders emerges. Eventually some leave the uplands and venture into the plains, where they build cities. This is the age of powerful monarchs and of warfare.

In building new political communities men should learn from the mistakes of the past, but they frequently do not. One lesson that should have been learned is that the most stable government will combine features of monarchy and democracy in a "mixed" form. In Persia, the autocratic rulers were more concerned with their own material welfare than they were with the welfare of the people, so the people came to hate them. The rulers had been brought up by eunuches and women, who ruined them by seeking to satisfy their every wish. They did not know how to govern themselves properly and could not govern others. In Athens, the trouble started when the uneducated masses began to think that their own judgments about music and drama were superior to those of the educated, and subsequently, democracy degenerated into mob rule. It was ignorance of the true principles of education that was at fault in both Persia and Athens. In Persia, no one was taught how to command; in Athens, no one learned how to obey.

A wise statesman will avoid setting up a democracy, an oligarchy, an aristocracy, or a monarchy since each of these tends to create a sovereignty of some one class or group of persons. Each promotes factionalism. In a true constitution the sovereign is, in a certain sense, God, and God makes his commands known through the law. Impersonal law, not a person or group of persons, should be sovereign. Neither birth nor wealth shall determine who shall occupy positions of political authority but only whole-hearted devotion to the law. "Friends," the Athenian stranger would say to a people intent upon founding a city,

> the god, just as the ancient saying has it, holding the beginning and the end
> and the middle of all the beings, completes his straight course by revolving,

according to nature. Following him always is Justice, avenger of those who forsake the divine law. He who is going to become happy follows Her, in humility and orderliness. But anyone who is puffed up with boastfulness, or who feels exalted because of riches or honours or good bodily form accompanied by youth and mindlessness, anyone whose soul burns with insolence and hence regards himself as needing neither ruler nor any leader but rather considers himself capable of leading others, is left behind, abandoned by the god.[58]

This is known as the "great preamble" to all legislation. God is the measure of all things, not man, and to be like God is to follow the life of right measure. We shall honour the gods and heroes, our ancestors and our parents, and we shall show reverence for the law, fulfilling all the obligations it lays upon us. We shall teach our children reverence for the law not by admonitions but by example. We must learn reverence ourselves, preferring the goods of the soul to those of the body and those of the body to mere possessions.

Wise physicians seek to enlist the co-operation of their patients in their own cure by explaining to them the reasons for the regimen or course of treatment that they are prescribing. Similarly, the legislator should prefix the whole body of legislation and sections of it with "preambles" that explain the purpose of the regulations. It will be pointed out that the source of most evils is love of self—the partiality we tend to show to our own interests. The preamble will tell us that we should always be truthful and trustworthy and should never take advantage of the weak and defenseless. It will tell us that the good life is the happiest and most pleasant.

A considerable portion of the *Laws* describes in detail the size of the community and the kind of territory that is most favourable to stability. The community will aim at achieving economic self-sufficiency, avoiding commercialism and imperialism. It will be primarily an agricultural economy. No citizen shall engage in trade or possess gold or silver; only alien residents may engage in trade. There will be no lending of money at interest and no credit. Property may be held unequally, but regulations will prevent any excessive accumulation of property in order to avoid the emergence of a few rich and many poor. The normal family will have one or two children, and if moral suasion does not limit the population, colonies will be sent away to avoid overpopulation.

---

[58] *The Laws*, IV, 716a.

Book VI is devoted to a description of the various offices and administrative boards. There will be a "great council" consisting of 360 members, elected by a complicated scheme, which is intended to result in the selection of the more moderate members of each economic class. The aim is not the accurate representation of economic interests but the selection from different groups of the persons most likely to be fair-minded and public-spirited. A chief board of magistrates, "guardians of the law," will consist of 37 persons between the ages of 50 and 70. They will be selected by a complicated process out of a group of 300 names by a threefold election. The chief board of magistrates will elect a Minister of Education who will serve as a kind of prime minister. He will serve for a period of five years. Presumably, this minister will be the most respected and most honourable member of the community.

Marriage and family life will be closely supervised and regulated. Men must marry between the ages of 30 and 35, and women between 16 and 20. The equality of women expressed in the *Republic* is considerably reduced in the *Laws*, where the requirements of childbearing and of the family limit women's public role. After childbearing, however, women can again enter the public sphere. The women would bear arms, have the same moral education as men, and have common meals, separate from the men.[59]

Book VII of the *Laws* describes the features of universal education. The principles are the same as those described earlier in the *Republic*, but the treatment is more detailed. It starts with the care of the baby, and Plato's description of how one should care for a baby is most modern. Everything should be done to keep the baby from being frightened. It should be held when it cries, danced about, and sung to. Education should become formal at the age of six. Plato is one of the first to advocate compulsory, universal education with salaried teachers. The purpose of early education is to inculcate standards of good taste and of morality.

Probably the most important book in the *Laws* is Book X. It is also one of the most controversial. A large portion of this book is devoted to a refutation of atheism. Atheism had been nurtured by the early Ionian scientists, who taught that everything has a natural, materialistic cause and that the cosmos embodies no

---

[59] For a discussion of the role of women in the *Laws*, see: R.F. Stalley, *An Introduction to Plato's Laws* (Indianapolis: Hackett, 1983), pp. 104–6; Morrow, *Plato's Cretan City*, pp. 127, 397; Okin, *Women in Western Political Thought*, pp. 28–50; Saxonhouse, *Women in the History of Political Thought*, pp. 37–62.

conscious design or plan, and by the Sophists, who taught that all moral judgments are relative and conventional. Atheism is the combination of these two doctrines. This is a dogmatic assumption on the part of its adherents, which they do not try to support with proof. In refutation of this belief, Plato endeavours to show that mind (*logos*) is antecedent to body and that the motions of the body are caused by movements in the "soul," which would, in turn, suggest that there is some design and purpose in the universe.

Plato argues that if all things are in motion, there must be some first principle of motion, some "first cause" that generates motion. If self-moving motion is the starting point of all motions, it must be something other than earth, air, fire, or water, which is the subject of motion. It must be something "alive," not lifeless like earth, air, fire, and water. The proper name for this is the soul, or *logos*, and the soul exists as much by nature as do the material elements. The regularity we observe in nature (the movement of the planets, the sun, and the orderly succession of seasons) suggests some motion originally moved by mind or reason. There must be at least two souls: one to account for the irregularity, which is also observable. Disorderly motion is due to an inferior soul, but the best soul, or God, is the source of all that is good and orderly. The universe, in Plato's view, is a reflection of divine activity and purpose. Plato is not a pantheist but a theist, and he is the first to create what has since come to be called "natural theology."

Plato next seeks to refute the belief that the gods are unconcerned with human affairs. They have both the power to know and to order all things. Like true physicians who do not neglect the smallest detail in the care of a patient, nothing is too trivial or insignificant to escape the gods' attention and care. Just as "like gravitates to like" in the natural world, so the souls of men, when properly nurtured, gravitate towards God. The man who lives an orderly, disciplined life is a man beloved of God and most like Him; the man who is self-willed and proud, who proclaims that he needs no guide, is abandoned by God. Such a man brings misery to himself, his family, and his country.

Plato also disposes of the idea that God can be bribed by sacrifices or flattering words. Evil manifests itself in the body in the form of disease; in the natural environment in the form of drought, blight, and pestilence; and in the cities and politics of men in the form of injustice. There are men who say that we can tolerate these evils and escape their penalties. Are the gods to be likened to a pilot who, persuaded by gifts and wine, runs his ship aground? If the gods ignored the transgressions of men they would be like a shepherd who allows a wolf to slaughter his flock on the condition that he share in the kill. Such thoughts are too blasphemous to contemplate.

The propagation of these heretical teachings cannot be tolerated, and Plato prescribes punishment for those who persist in error and decline to listen to the voice of reason. Anyone who, in word or deed, commits impiety shall be brought before a magistrate. The penalty on conviction will be imprisonment in a House of Correction for a period of at least five years. The prisoner will be visited from time to time by members of the Nocturnal Council, who will reason with him and endeavour to persuade him of his error. A second conviction will result in death.

The Nocturnal Council is described in Book XII. It is in perpetual session and meets daily between dawn and sunrise. It consists of the 10 oldest of the 37 guardians of the law, the minister and ex-ministers of education, and 10 younger men. It is charged primarily with preserving and perpetuating the creed that underlies the foundation of the community. The Nocturnal Council takes the place of the philosopher-king in the *Republic*.

The institution of the Nocturnal Council and the punishment for the propagation of heresy is repulsive to modern minds. As one commentator, however, has pointed out:

> As long as one could believe in good faith that the alternative to spiritual control and enforcement of a creed should be the freedom of the spirit, the Nocturnal Council looked sinister indeed. Plato, however, could not consider this alternative, for the horizon of his experience was filled with the tyranny of the rabble and the murder of Socrates. Today our horizon is filled with similar experiences. We have good reasons to doubt that a project of the Platonic type would solve the problems of the age on the pragmatic level of history; but we have lost our illusion that "freedom" will lead without fail to a state of society that would deserve the name of order.[60]

Plato, moreover, was unable to envisage the separation of the spiritual and temporal realms in a way that was made possible after the advent of Christianity.

---

[60] Voegelin, *Order and History*, Vol. III, *Plato and Aristotle*, p. 265.

Just as the philosopher-king has been replaced in the *Laws* by the Nocturnal Council, the vision of the Good (*agathon*) has been replaced by adherence to a creed. Ultimately, law itself, which embodies both persuasion (in the form of the preambles) and coercion (sanctions for disobedience), in effect performs the function of the philosopher-king, constituting the next best form of polity in a society in which one can find no persons capable of becoming philosopher-kings. A government of laws and law-abiding rulers, if not the best polity, is at least preferable to tyranny, oligarchy, or the rule of the mob.

The parable of the cave, which we encountered in the *Republic*, is replaced in the *Laws* by the symbol of the player and the puppets.

> … let's consider each of us living beings to be a divine puppet, put together either for their play or for some serious purpose—which, we don't know. What we do know is that these passions work within us like tendons or cords, drawing us and pulling against one another in opposite directions toward opposing deeds, struggling in the regions where virtue and vice lie separated from one another. Now the argument asserts that each person should always follow one of the cords, never letting go of it and pulling with it against the others; this cord is the golden and sacred pull of calculation, and is called the common law of the city; the other cords are hard and iron, while this one is soft, inasmuch as it is golden; the others resemble a multitude of different forms. It is necessary always to assist this most noble pull of law because calculation, while noble, is gentle rather than violent, and its pull is in need of helpers if the race of gold is to be victorious for us over the other races.[61]

The "golden cord of the law" is what holds the community together in the polity described in the *Laws*, and the law is a kind of crystallization of the wisdom embodied in the life of the philosopher-king. Such a community presumably would require a founding-father of the stature of a Plato to inspire the creed that will lie at the heart of the laws. Consistent adherence to the creed would be required to perpetuate this community, and that adherence would entail not only the use of persuasion but the use of coercion to restrain the recalcitrant. Moderation or a law-abiding spirit becomes one of the principal virtues in such a state.

---

[61] *The Laws*, I, 644d–645a.

CONCLUSIONS

Part of the difficulty in understanding Plato's works arises because his thought cannot be adequately described in modern political terminology. It is quite apparent, and his critics are quick to point out, that Plato was no liberal democrat. The poverty of our modern political vocabulary is such that if one is not a liberal democrat, he or she is branded a fascist or a reactionary. Plato's thought fits into none of these categories. He does not believe that freedom is the ultimate good nor that the principle of freedom itself is an adequate normative standard for choosing among alternative courses of action. He does not believe that the state comes into existence primarily for the purpose of promoting and preserving individual freedom. He does not believe in the unrestrained rule of the majority in its own interest, nor, for that matter, in the self-sufficiency of the democratic process as the best means of determining the requirements of justice. To those who believe that liberalism embodies the ultimate political wisdom, the acknowledgment that Plato is no liberal democrat justifies dismissing anything that he may have to say as irrelevant.

If Plato is no liberal democrat, neither is he an individualist nor a collectivist. Despite the claims of some of his critics, Plato does not conceive of society as an entity having a life or thoughts apart from the individuals who compose it. There is no reference in Plato's writings to a group mind or a group will. Plato does believe that there is a common good that is something more than the sum of the interests of the individuals who compose society. This common good, however, is not the good of some super-entity with a life and purpose distinct from that of its members. For Plato, the common good is a harmonious relationship among all those parts of which a society is composed. The unity of society is a moral unity, and that unity exists only in the minds of the individuals who compose the society and in their co-operative attempts to realize it in practice. It is a kind of unity, moreover, that can be perpetuated only by education. The critics who charge that Plato intends to sacrifice the individual to the state would be right if Plato believed that the state embodied an interest or a good apart from that of its members. Some subsequent political theorists have taught that doctrine, but it is not Plato's. Plato does not expect salvation from evil to come through politics but only through the kind of education that leads to a vision and experience of the Good.

For Plato, philosophy calls humans to a personal commitment to a Good which transcends, but which might inform, the good of the city. While civil society comes into being in order to promote the good of its citizens, society is not qualified to define that good. It is that teaching that distinguishes a free society from a totalitarian one. In a free or open society a person's loyalty to the state is necessarily a conditional and qualified one, for each person acknowledges a loyalty to a truth and justice that transcends the demands of citizenship. Each person is a citizen, if you like, of two kingdoms. It is this duality of citizenship that gives substance and meaning to constitutional government, for it is one of the express purposes of constitutional government to preserve the integrity of the individual in the exercise of responsible freedom. The totalitarian regime denies that the individual can claim such a sphere of freedom since it denies the existence of any standard or authority beyond the state or party that could be capable of determining what is good and just.

It is the loss of conviction in the existence of a transcendent order of truth and justice (such as Plato believed in) that gravely endangers the perpetuation of free societies. Walter Lippmann has pointed out that

> The freedom which modern men are turned away from, not seldom with relief and often with enthusiasm, is the hollow shell of freedom. The current theory of freedom holds that what men believe may be important to them but it has almost no public significance. The outer defenses of the free way of life stand upon legal guarantees against the coercion of belief. But the citadel is vacant because the public philosophy is gone, and all that the defenders of freedom have to defend in common is a public neutrality and a public agnosticism....
>
> In the prevailing popular culture all philosophies are the instruments of some man's purpose, all truths are self-centered and self-regarding, and all principles are the rationalization of some special interest. There is no public criterion of the true and the false, of the right and the wrong, beyond that which the preponderant mass of voters, consumers, readers and listeners happen at the moment to be supposed to want.
>
> There is no reason to think that this condition of mind can be changed until it can be proved to the modern sceptic that there are certain principles which, when they have been demonstrated, only the willfully irrational can deny....[62]

---

[62] Walter Lippmann, *Essays in the Public Philosophy* (New York: New American Library, 1955), pp. 113–14.

The skepticism against which we must contend in the modern world is not essentially different from the skepticism against which Plato had to contend in the ancient world, for the Sophists, by whatever name they are called, are forever with us.

SUGGESTIONS FOR FURTHER READING

This bibliography contains four kinds of works. First, there are general, descriptive introductions to Plato's thought and works. Annas, Grube, Nettleship, and White are page-by-page guides to the *Republic* and those by Morrow and Stalley assist the reader through the *Laws*. Second, there are works presenting original and provocative interpretations. Strauss, Bloom, Craig, and Klosko provide singular, controversial interpretations of Plato. Popper and Ryle are highly critical. Hall, Melling, Levinson, Voegelin, and Cushman are Plato's defenders. Third, there are general works explaining the philosophic background. Sallis, Nussbaum, Griswold, and Stokes illustrate how to approach the dialogue as a philosophic writing. Guthrie, Barker, Friedlander, and Voegelin provide excellent summaries of Greek philosophy and of Plato, and Kraut and Vlastos are collections of articles discussing many of the central controversies about Plato's philosophy. Fourth, there are works on the social and political context. Cornford, Vlastos, and Snell describe the extraordinary influence of Greek thought on Western Civilization.

Translations

Bloom, Allan. Translated with notes and an Interpretative Essay. *The Republic of Plato*. New York: Basic Books, 1968.

Grube, G.M.A., trans. *Plato's Republic*. Indianapolis: Hackett, 1974.

———. *Trial and Death of Socrates: Euthyphro, Apology, Crito, and death scene from Phaedo*. Indianapolis: Hackett, 1980.

Hamilton, Edith, and Huntington Cairns, eds. *The Collected Dialogues of Plato*. New York: Pantheon, 1961.

Kirk, G.S., J.E. Raven and M. Schofield, eds. *The Presocratic Philosophers*. 2nd ed. Cambridge: Cambridge University Press, 1983.

Pangle, Thomas. Translated with notes and an Interpretative Essay. *The Laws of Plato*. New York: Basic Books, 1980.

Commentaries

Annas, Julia. *An Introduction to Plato's Republic.* Oxford: Oxford University Press, 1981.

Barker, Ernest. *Greek Political Theory: Plato and His Predecessors.* London: Methuen & Co., 1918.

Craig, Leon Harold. *The War Lover: A Study of Plato's Republic.* Toronto: University of Toronto Press, 1994.

Crombie, I.M. *An Examination of Plato's Doctrines.* 2 Vols. London: Methuen, 1962-3.

Cushman, Robert E. *Therapiea: Plato's Conception of Philosophy.* Chapel Hill: University of North Carolina Press, 1958.

Euben, J. Peter. *The Tragedy of Political Theory: The Road Not Taken.* Princeton: Princeton University Press, 1990.

Friedlander, Paul. *Plato.* 3 Vols. Translated by Hans Meyerhoff. Princeton: Princeton University Press, 1969.

Griswold, Jr., Charles L., ed. *Platonic Writings: Platonic Readings.* New York: Routledge, 1988.

Grube, G.M.A. *Plato's Thought.* 2nd ed. Indianapolis: Hackett, 1980.

Guthrie, W.K.C. *A History of Greek Philosophy.* Vols. IV, V. Cambridge: Cambridge University Press, 1975.

———. *Socrates.* Cambridge: Cambridge University Press, 1971.

Hall, Robert W. *Plato.* London: George Allen & Unwin, 1981.

———. *Plato and the Individual.* The Hague: Martinus Nijhoff, 1963.

Hansen, Mogens H. *The Athenian Democracy in the Age of Demosthenes: Structure, Principles and Ideology.* Oxford: Blackwell, 1991.

Hare, R.M. *Plato.* New York: Oxford University Press, 1982.

Havelock, Eric A. *Preface to Plato.* Cambridge: Harvard University Press, 1963.

Irwin, Terence. *Plato's Moral Theory: The Early and Middle Dialogues.* Oxford: Clarendon Press, 1977.

Jaspers, Karl. *Plato and Augustine.* Taken from *The Great Philosophers.* Vol. I. New York: Harcourt, Brace, 1966.

Kelly, Eugene, ed. *New Essays on Socrates.* Lanham: University Press of America, 1984.

Klosko, George. *The Development of Plato's Political Theory.* New York: Methuen, 1986.

Kraut, Richard, ed. *The Cambridge Companion to Plato.* Cambridge: Cambridge University Press, 1992.

Levinson, Ronald B. *In Defense of Plato.* Cambridge: Harvard University Press, 1953.

Melling, David J. *Understanding Plato.* Oxford: Oxford University Press, 1987.

Morrow, Glenn R. *Plato's Cretan City: A Historical Interpretation of the Laws.* Princeton: Princeton University Press, 1960.

Murdoch, Iris. *The Fire and the Sun: Why Plato Banished the Artist.* Oxford: Oxford University Press, 1977.

Nettleship, Richard Lewis. *Lectures on the Republic of Plato.* London: Macmillan, 1963.

Nussbaum, Martha C. *The Fragility of Goodness: Luck and Ethics in Greek Tragedy and Philosophy.* Cambridge: Cambridge University Press, 1986.

Ober, Josiah. *Mass and Elite in Democrataic Athens: Rhetoric, Ideology and the Power of the People.* Princeton: Princeton University Press, 1989.

Ophir, Adi. *Plato's Invisible Cities: Discourse and Power in the Republic.* London: Routledge, 1991.

Popper, Karl. *The Open Society and Its Enemies.* 2 Vols. Princeton: Princeton University Press, 1950.

Roberts, Jennifer Tolbert. *Athens on Trial: The Antidemocrataic Tradition in Western Thought.* Princeton: Princeton University Press, 1994.

Ryle, Gilbert. *Plato's Progress.* Cambridge: Cambridge University Press, 1966.

Sallis, John. *Being and Logos: The Way of Platonic Dialogue.* 2nd ed. Atlantic Highlands: Humanities Press International, 1986.

Stalley, R.F. *An Introduction to Plato's Laws.* Indianapolis: Hackett, 1983.

Stokes, Michael C. *Plato's Socratic Conversations: Drama and Dialectic in Three Dialogues.* Baltimore: Johns Hopkins University Press, 1986.

Strauss, Leo. *The Argument and Action of Plato's Laws.* Chicago: University of Chicago Press, 1975.

———. *The City and Man.* Chicago: Rand McNally, 1964.

Taylor, A.E. *Plato: The Man and His Works.* 7th ed. London: Methuen, 1960.

Thorson, Thomas L., ed. *Plato: Totalitarian or Democrat?* Englewood Cliffs: Prentice-Hall, 1963.

Vlastos, Gregory, ed. *Plato: A Collection of Critical Essays.* 2 Vols. Notre Dame: University of Notre Dame Press, 1978.

Voegelin, Eric. *Order and History.* Vol. III. *Plato and Aristotle.* Baton Rouge: Louisiana State University Press, 1957.

White, Nicholas P. *A Companion to Plato's Republic.* Indianapolis: Hackett, 1979.

Social and Political Background

Cornford, Francis M. *Before and After Socrates.* Cambridge: Cambridge University Press, 1932.

Finley, M.I. *Democracy: Ancient and Modern.* Rev. ed. New Brunswick, N.J.: Rutgers University Press, 1985.

————. *Politics in the Ancient World.* Cambridge: Cambridge University Press, 1983.

Grene, David. *Greek Political Theory: The Image of Man in Thucydides and Plato.* Chicago: University of Chicago Press, 1965.

Guthrie, W.K.C. *Socrates.* New York: Cambridge University Press, 1971.

Harrison, A.R.W. *The Law of Athens.* Vol. 1. *The Family and Property.* Oxford: Clarendon Press, 1968.

Jaeger, Werner. *Paideia: The Ideals of Greek Culture.* 3 Vols. Translated by Gilbert Highet. New York: Oxford University Press, 1939–44.

Kagan, Donald. *Pericles of Athens and the Birth of Democracy.* London: Secken and Warburg, 1990.

Kitto, H.D.F. *The Greeks.* London: Penguin Books, 1951.

Meier, Christian. *The Greek Discovery of Politics.* Translated by David McLintock. Cambridge: Harvard University Press, 1990.

Sinclair, R.K. *Democracy and Participation in Athens.* Cambridge: Cambridge University Press, 1988.

Snell, Bruno. *The Discovery of the Mind: The Greek Origins of European Thought.* Translated by T.G. Rosenmeyer. Oxford: Basil Blackwell, 1953.

Vlastos, Gregory. *Plato's Universe.* Seattle: University of Washington Press, 1975.

Voegelin, Eric. *Order and History.* Vol. II. *The World of the Polis.* Baton Rouge: Louisiana State University Press, 1957.

ARISTOTLE

In the history of political philosophy no other philosopher can claim to have been more influential through as many centuries as Aristotle. In the Middle Ages, he was simply called The Philosopher. Although a student of Plato's for 20 years, Aristotle developed his own political philosophy, and he also pioneered in the empirical study of political systems. He justly deserves to be called the father of modern political science.

ARISTOTLE: His Life and Works

Aristotle was born in 385 B.C. at Stagira, a small town on the Aegean coast on the Chalcidic peninsula. His father, Nichomachus, was a physician to King Amyntas II of Macedonia. His father's profession may have stimulated Aristotle's keen interest in biology, which is apparent throughout Aristotle's writings. When he was approximately 17 years of age, he entered Plato's academy where he remained until Plato's death 20 years later. When Plato died, Aristotle, apparently dissatisfied with the choice of Speusippus as Plato's successor, left with his fellow student Xenocrates to join two other Platonists in the little town of Assus. There he became friendly with Hermias, an ex-slave who had become wealthy and politically powerful. Plato married Hermias's niece, Pythias, and, after three years, he moved to Mytilene on the island of Lesbos. Two years later he was invited by Philip of Macedon to come to Pella, the capital of Macedonia, to serve as tutor to Philip's 13-year-old son, who was destined to become Alexander the Great. A year after Alexander succeeded his father as king, Aristotle returned to Athens (around 335 B.C.) to found his own school, known as the Lyceum. He taught there until a wave of anti-Macedonian feeling swept Athens following Alexander's death in 323 B.C. Aristotle fled from Athens and sought refuge in Chalcis on the island of Euboea. While in exile, he was indicted in Athens for impiety. He died and was buried in Chalcis in 322 B.C.

Aristotle argues that humans need a political society to best actualize their potential, however, he, himself, was not a citizen of Athens and could not participate in its political life. There is speculation that he may have been involved in some political activity in Macedonia, but he does not speak of the possibility of an empire as a desirable form of political rule. He did state that the character of the Hellenes was such that they could rule all if they were united in a single regime. He makes clear, though, that mastery over others is not a just political goal. As one commentator has noted, Aristotle's political theory "shows a quite remarkable degree of detachment from his own particular circumstances."[1]

Only fragments of Aristotle's earliest writings exist today, but they indicate that, as a young man, Aristotle closely followed the literary style and thought of his teacher, Plato. His dialogue *Eudemus* or *On the Soul* argues for the immortality of the soul along the lines of Plato's *Phaedo* and embraces Plato's theory of knowledge by recollection. The *Gryllus* or *On Rhetoric* is comparable to Plato's *Gorgias*. A prose work, the *Protrepticus*, belongs to the same period and is a discourse on the philosophical life as the movement of the soul toward the Good. Aristotle soon abandoned the dialogue form of writing, however, and he is best known today for his numerous treatises. His collected works include treatises on metaphysics, physics, logic, meteorology, comparative anatomy and physiology, psychology, rhetoric, aesthetics, ethics, and politics. The collection of 158 Constitutions, which he initiated and supervised, demonstrates the strong bent for empirical detail that distinguishes him, in part, from his teacher, Plato.[2] The finished works that Aristotle wrote are lost, and the treatises through which his thought has come down to us today are collections of lectures and notes for lectures prepared over long periods of time. Many of them have been edited and put together under one title by others. For instance, his *Metaphysics* is a

---

[1] Steven Everson, ed., *Aristotle: The Politics* (Cambridge: Cambridge University Press, 1988), p. xi. A full discussion of Aristotle's life can be found in W.K.C. Guthrie, *A History of Greek Philosophy,* Vol. VI, *Aristotle: An Encounter* (Cambridge: Cambridge University Press, 1981) and Carnes Lord, trans. and with an Introduction, *Aristotle: The Politics* (Chicago: University of Chicago Press, 1984).

[2] All of these constitutions have been lost except for the Constitution of Athens, which was discovered in 1890. Kurt von Fritz and Ernst Kapp, eds., *Aristotle's Constitution of Athens and Related Texts* (New York: Hafner Publishing, 1950).

collection of lectures composed at different times and put together by someone else. The *Nicomachean Ethics* was edited by Aristotle's son after his death.

Although classifications and collections are typical features of Aristotle's writings, it is not clear how he achieved the reputation for being a systematic thinker, for the works by which he is known today are frequently unsystematic, incomplete and sometimes contradictory. The work on *Politics* is particularly exasperating: the topics are sometimes not organized in any systematic fashion, and even prior announcements of topics to be discussed often are ignored or left incomplete. Some scholars, like Professor Werner Jaeger, have endeavoured to clear up the confusion and contradictions by attributing some of the writings to Aristotle's youthful period and others to his more mature years.[3] From this perspective Aristotle's thought is said to move from an early attachment to the otherworldly thought of Plato to a more independent, scientific and empirical point of view in his later life. But there is no universal agreement among scholars on this point. Eric Voegelin, for example, suggests that "Aristotle ... was not interested in systematic unification of his written thought; he was interested in the completeness of his problems. When his various inquiries led to conflicting results, he simply let the results clash; and the conflicting views were peaceably recorded side by side."[4] Although Aristotle clearly had a stronger interest in empirical details than his teacher, Plato, and a passion for classification, he has little kinship with modern behavioural social science. For instance, he did not think that it was possible to distinguish "facts" from "values" (the words were unknown to him) nor to describe something without making normative judgments, and his thought culminated, as it did for Plato, in metaphysics.

ARISTOTLE'S METAPHYSICS

Aristotle's collection of lectures on *Metaphysics* begins by saying: "All men by nature desire to know." But not all men desire to know in the same way; most are content with knowledge that has practical consequences. **Metaphysics** is a search

---

[3] Werner Jaeger, *Aristotle: Fundamentals of the History of His Development*, trans. Richard Robinson (New York: Oxford University Press, 1962); Guthrie, *A History of Greek Philosophy*, Vol. V, *The Later Plato and the Academy*, pp. 18–45; W.D. Ross, "The Development of Aristotle's Thought," in *Articles on Aristotle*, Vol. I, eds. Jonathan Barnes, Malcolm Schofield, Richard Sorabji (London, Duckworth, 1975), pp. 1–13.

[4] Eric Voegelin, *Order and History*, Vol. III, *Plato and Aristotle* (Baton Rouge: Louisiana State University Press, 1957), p. 280.

for the ultimate cause and nature of Reality; it is a science that "considers What Is simply in its character of Being and the properties which it has as such." It is knowledge for the sake of knowledge alone, a search for the ultimate Ground of Being, the unity that underlies all of existence and all specific sciences. That Aristotle believes that such a science is possible distinguishes his position sharply from a modern, empirical conception of science.

Metaphysics seeks to understand what is, simply as such, but the word *is* has more meanings than one. Things or substances have their own mode of being, and attached to things are qualities, like green and sweet, that represent another mode of being. These are the attributes of things. In addition, there are actions that are neither things nor qualities but processes that are capable of modifying things. Metaphysics is concerned with all these modes of being but, primarily, with unchangeable and self-existent substance, with being *qua* being.

Aristotle rejects Plato's theory of Forms on a number of grounds. It is not clear to him how the Forms can have a separate existence apart from the things that they inform. He argues that Plato's theory of Forms is a purposeless doubling of visible things. The theory does not adequately account for the visible world: the Forms "help in no wise towards the knowledge of the other things (for they are not even the substance of these, else they would have been in them)."[5] Plato's concern with the visible world is only that it may serve as a bridge to the invisible world, but, for Aristotle, the visible world is just as real. Moreover, Plato's theory is an impossible one: "it would seem impossible that the substance and that of which it is the substance, should exist apart; how, therefore, can the Ideas, being the substance of things, exist apart?"[6] To say that sensible things "are patterns and the other things share in them, is to use empty words and poetical metaphors."[7] Furthermore, Aristotle finds that the Platonic Forms are useless when it comes to explaining motion. Since the Forms themselves are motionless, things that are copies of them should be motionless, too, but things do, in fact, move. How are we to account for this movement? Aristotle also criticizes Plato's theory that the Forms are Numbers. Some scholars think that Aristotle's arguments against Plato's

---

[5] *Metaphysics*, 991a, 12–13. As found in Richard McKeon, ed., *Introduction to Aristotle, Metaphysics*, trans. W.D. Ross (New York: Modern Library, 1947).

[6] *Ibid.*, 991b, 1–3.

[7] *Ibid.*, 1079b, 24–26.

theory are telling, while others suggest that he has not fully understood Plato's theory, or at least has not taken cognizance of Plato's complete position. It is significant, for example, that Aristotle does not discuss the Demiurge, which Plato introduced precisely to account for movement in the world.[8] Although Aristotle is critical of Plato's theory of Forms, he recognizes that the universal is necessary if we are to have scientific knowledge, and he is in agreement with Plato that the universal is neither a mental construct nor a subjective concept.

For Aristotle every sensible thing is composed of both Matter (*hyle*) and Form (*eidos*). By Matter he means the literal stuff out of which something is made, such as wood or copper, but he means something more as well. He posits what he calls "prime matter," which never exists independently of an actual object but is simply that which possesses the potentiality for receiving some form. The simplest material things, such as earth, fire, air, and water, are not identical with prime matter. Water is capable of being changed into air and air can be changed into water. It is logically necessary, therefore, to posit the existence of something behind air and water that is subject to change—this is nothing but sheer potentiality or prime matter.

By Form Aristotle means not only the literal shape, which everything has, but also the determinate structure, which makes a thing this particular thing. We distinguish trees, horses, dogs and men by virtue of that determinate structure characterizing trees, horses, dogs and men. Everything belonging to the same class of things has its own **nature**; it serves some purpose or has some use, and this is its form. Matter and form never exist apart from one another but are always conjoined in some actual object.

Plants and animals both exhibit the phenomenon of growth, and Aristotle introduces the concepts of actuality and potentiality to explain this. The seeds of plants look very much alike, but when planted one will grow into an oak tree and another into a flower. Sperm cells and ova resemble one another but some develop into chimpanzees and others into men. This suggests to Aristotle that each may be said to have latent possibilities that proper care will develop. By knowing what something is potentially capable of becoming (its **essence**), we know what it *is*. We know what an acorn is because we have seen the oak tree into which the acorn has grown.

---

[8] Plato had argued in the *Republic* and the *Timaeus* that the cosmos was constituted by four factors: the Demiurge (sometimes called Maker, Father, Craftsman or God), the eternal model or structural plan, unformed matter, and necessity. Guthrie, *A History of Greek Philosophy*, Vol. V, pp. 253–74.

Although the acorn is temporarily prior to the oak tree, the oak tree is logically prior. We know what a human embryo is because we have seen such embryos born as infants and raised through childhood into adulthood. When potentiality becomes actuality in the process of development, development ceases. The Form is the actuality and Matter the potentiality. It is as though Form "wants" to be actualized, and this inherent drive towards its proper **end**, when completed, Aristotle calls *entelechy*. Thus, there is a **teleology** in nature, a purposeful development towards a given end. This idea becomes an important element in Aristotle's ethics, as we shall see.

Aristotle says that of things that come to be, some come to be by nature (as in the generation and growth of plants and animals) and some by art (as in the manufacture or production of objects). Aristotle explains how things come into being by a four-fold scheme of "causes" (*aitia*). He uses the word "**cause**" in a somewhat different sense than it would be used today, and it is helpful to conceive of his "causes" as simply levels of explanation. The acorn is the *material* cause of the oak; the tendency of the young plant to grow in the particular way in which oak trees grow is the *formal* cause. Since the acorn did not come from nowhere but grew on a mature oak tree, the parent oak and its capacity to produce acorns is the *efficient* cause. The "efficient" cause is the normal use of cause today, i.e., the immediate instigating factor for something to occur. The mature oak tree bearing acorns of its own completes the process of growth and is termed the *final* cause. Man-made objects are also to be understood in terms of this four-fold scheme of causes. Houses, unlike horses, do not beget other houses. Here the efficient cause is some agent outside the objects—the builder. Houses are made of wood, bricks and stone and these constitute the material cause. The conception of the kind of house the builder wants to build constitutes the formal cause. The purpose for which the house is built—the end it is designed to serve—constitutes the final cause. In a full explanation of something, then, Aristotle will discuss the constituents (the *material* level), the idea or plan (the *formal* level), the agent or action that brings it into existence (the *efficient* level), and the completely realized purpose of a thing (the *final* level).

Everything comes into being through a movement from potentiality to actuality. Motion (*kinesis*) has, for Aristotle, a much broader meaning than it has today since it includes the entire process by which things come into being and pass away. Aristotle does not have the modern mechanistic conception of motion; his conception of nature is more organic and vital than mechanical. Nor does he have any modern idea of evolution. Biological species remain separate and distinct, and the perpetuation of the species goes on eternally. The process has no beginning and no end. The cosmos itself is eternally in motion.

This suggests to Aristotle that there must be some ultimate source of motion that is itself motionless; there must be some First Cause or Prime Mover that sets everything in motion and exists eternally. This ultimate efficient cause or source of motion is what Aristotle calls God. God does not create the world. He forms it by being the object of desire, but God is not conscious of being an object of desire as he is immaterial and not a person. The desire that God inspires is like "the desire of the moth for the star." No Divine plan is fulfilled in this world, and there is no idea of a Providential God presiding over the affairs of men. God wholly transcends the world and is indifferent to the desire that he inspires. He is not an object of worship nor one to whom one could, or should, pray. God, for Aristotle, is more of a metaphysical necessity than a Creator-God. But what kind of activity can be ascribed to God?

> We assume the gods to be above all other beings blessed and happy; but what sort of actions must we assign to them? Acts of justice? Will not the gods seem absurd if they make contracts and return deposits, and so on? Acts of a brave man, then, confronting dangers and running risks because it is noble so to do? Or liberal acts? To whom will they give? It will be strange if they are really to have money or anything of the kind. And what would their temperate acts be? Is not such praise tasteless, since they have no bad appetites? If we were to run through them all, the circumstances of action would be found trivial and unworthy of gods. Still, everyone supposes that they *live* and therefore that they are active; we cannot suppose them to sleep like Endymion. Now if you take away from a living being action, and still more production, what is left but contemplation? Therefore, the activity of God, which surpasses all others in blessedness, must be contemplative; and of human activities, therefore, that which is most akin to this must be most of the nature of happiness.[9]

God's activity, then, consists of thinking—thinking about thinking. Aristotle's God knows only himself, and the object of his thought is himself. When men

---

[9] *Nicomachean Ethics*, Bk. X, 8, 1178b. David Ross, trans., revised by J.L. Ackrill and J.O. Urmson, *Aristotle: The Nicomachean Ethics* (Oxford: Oxford University Press, 1980). Aristotle uses the words "God" and "the Gods" interchangeably. In the *Metaphysics* he speaks of the Prime Mover as one but also develops the conception of 47 divine prime movers. This kind of contradiction is never resolved in the texts.

engage in contemplation upon the noblest objects in existence, when they use their reason to meditate upon the ultimate mysteries of existence, they share, for that moment, in the life of the gods and in their happiness.

Early in his *Metaphysics* Aristotle criticized Plato's doctrine of the transcendent Forms, but he concludes the *Metaphysics* by telling us that the ultimate source of the process by which potentiality becomes actuality is an immaterial activity. While Aristotle's God lives above the world, indifferent towards it, Plato emphasizes the presence of God in the world. Plato's God inspires humanity, through love of him and of his goodness, to combat the evil in the world that constantly threatens to reduce the cosmos to chaos. It is not through cognitive activity alone that order is realized, but through love. This dimension of God's activity tends to disappear in Aristotle.[10]

NICOMACHEAN ETHICS

Aristotle's *Ethics* and *Politics* are published as separate works but, in fact, they were meant to be read as one. The *Ethics* should be read first as it is the proper introduction to the study of politics. The *Ethics* is concerned with describing the moral and intellectual virtues that human beings are potentially capable of realizing and that they should recognize if they want to complete their humanity or true nature. But Aristotle is aware that this will be possible only within a social and political environment that encourages and sustains a life of virtue (*arete*).[11] The *Politics* is concerned, accordingly, with the institutional means that are likely to promote virtue in the citizens.

---

[10] Although Aristotle rejects Plato's theory of Forms as separate existences, he did not, as Eric Voegelin notes, "repudiate the experiences in which the notion of a realm of ideas originated nor did he abandon the order of being that had become visible through the experiences of the philosophers ever since Heraclitus, Parmenides, and Xenophanes. The consequence is a curious transformation of the experience of transcendence which can perhaps be described as an intellectual thinning-out. The fullness of experience which Plato expressed in the richness of his myth is in Aristotle reduced to the conception of God as the prime mover.... The Eros toward the Agathon correspondingly is reduced to...the delight in cognitive action for its own sake. Moreover, no longer is the soul as a whole immortal but only that part of it which Aristotle calls active intellect.... And, finally, the mystical *via negativa* by which the soul ascends to the vision of the Idea in the Symposium is thinned out to the rise toward the dianoetic virtues and the *bios theoretikos*." Voegelin, *Order and History*, Vol. III, *Plato and Aristotle*, p. 276.

[11] The word *arete* refers to the proper function or operation of something and can be translated as excellence, goodness, or virtue. For example, the full and proper development of a human's faculties is the life of virtue.

The kind of knowledge yielded by a study of ethics and politics is not theoretical knowledge but practical knowledge, not knowledge of what is abstractly good but knowledge that will be useful in actually producing goodness of character. Aristotle cautions us at the outset not to expect the kind of precision and exactitude that we find in mathematics: "It is the mark of an educated man to look for precision in each class of things just so far as the nature of the subject admits."[12] In thinking about what is good for humans we do not start from general principles and argue to conclusions; we start with the ordinary moral judgments of people, which are often obscure and confused, and by comparing them we come to more general principles. This method of inquiry typifies all of Aristotle's works and gives his philosophic treatises, particularly those on politics and ethics, their practical and realistic tone.

The virtue of anything is what it is good for. The virtue of the eye, for example, is to see, and when the eyes perform their function well we say that a person has good eyesight. What, Aristotle asks, is the virtue or function of humans as such? It cannot be the mere act of living since we share this with both plants and animals. Like them, we are subject to nurture and growth. What distinguishes humans from animals and plants is our ability to communicate with others through language and our capacity to reason. A person is able to deliberate rationally over alternative ways of acting. Hence, the good person is the one who pursues activity in accordance with reason. This includes both moral and intellectual virtues, which shall be discussed below.

All humans seem to agree that what they desire above everything is happiness. But different people have different ideas about what constitutes happiness, for example, some identify it with health, others with wealth, and still others with honour. When any activity is done properly it is accompanied by pleasure, and so it follows that the life of reason can be a happy life. Happiness is not happiness for the moment; it cannot be achieved in less than a complete lifetime. Happiness, Aristotle recognizes, does require some modicum of external prosperity, and fortune plays a role in providing some of the means to happiness.

Now, how do humans acquire goodness of character? They acquire it by the repeated performance of good acts that eventually become habitual. We do not learn to become good by reading books on ethics or by memorizing moral principles; we acquire moral virtues in the same way in which we learn to play the piano

---

[12] *Ethics*, Bk. I, 3, 1094b.

or a game of tennis. We learn to be brave by acting bravely in situations that call for that kind of behaviour; we acquire the virtue of temperance by repeated acts of self-control. At first children act under compulsion, under the authority of their parents. With the guidance of their parents children are urged to act in certain ways and to refrain from acting in other ways. Good habits are inculcated by parental discipline, but as children mature and learn to reason, they come to understand what impelled their parents to recommend good conduct and they become self-disciplined. Moral virtues are produced neither by Nature nor against Nature. Nature does provide the ground for their reception but their formation is the product of habit.

It is not enough that right actions be taken; the person who acts must be in a certain frame of mind: "in the first place he must have knowledge, secondly he must choose the acts, and choose them for their own sakes, and thirdly his action must proceed from a firm and unchangeable character.... Actions, then, are called just and temperate when they are such as the just or the temperate man would do; but it is not the man who does these that is just and temperate, but the man who also does them *as* just and temperate men do them."[13] The moral virtues are neither feelings nor capacities but dispositions. We do not blame a person for feeling angry or for having the capacity to feel anger, but we blame them for being angry in a particular way, on the wrong occasion, towards the wrong person, or in excess of the provocation.

The moral virtues are associated with certain kinds of action and certain kinds of feeling. From Aristotle's perspective, virtue is a mean between two extremes, between two vices, a mean between excess and deficiency. The mean is not an arithmetic mean; it is not the midpoint between two extremes but a mean that varies with the person and the circumstances. An athlete with a big frame requires more food to nourish his body than does a smaller man engaged in a sedentary occupation. There is no right amount of food that it would be appropriate for both to consume, but there is a right amount for each, and this will differ from person to person. The analogy holds for the virtues: "fear and confidence and appetite and anger and pity and in general pleasure and pain may be felt both too much and too little, and in both cases not well; but to feel them at the right times, with reference to the right objects, towards the right people, with the right motive, and in the right way, is what is both intermediate and best, and this is characteristic

---

[13] *Ibid.*, Bk. II, 4, 1105a–b.

of virtue. Similarly with regard to actions also there is excess, defect, and the intermediate." Aristotle defines moral virtue as "a state of character concerned with choice, lying in a mean, i.e., the mean relative to us, this being determined by a rational principle, and by that principle by which the man of practical wisdom would determine it."[14]

---

[14] *Ibid.*, Bk. II, 6, 1106b–1107a. For a detailed explanation see, Nancy Sherman, *The Fabric of Character: Aristotle's Theory of Virtue* (Oxford: Clarendon Press, 1989); Sir W.D. Ross in his *Aristotle,* 5th ed. (London: Methuen, 1949), gives the following tabulation of the moral virtues (p. 203):

Feeling	Action	Excess	Mean	Defect
Fear Confidence		Cowardice Rashness	Courage Courage	Unnamed Cowardice
Certain pleasures of touch (Pain arising from desire for such pleasures)		Profligacy	Temperance	Insensibility
	Giving of money Taking of money	Prodigality Illiberality	Liberality Liberality	Illiberality Prodigality
	Giving of money on large scale	Vulgarity	Magnificence	Meanness
	Claiming of honour on large scale	Vanity	Self-respect	Humility
	Pursuit of honour on small scale	Ambitiousness	Unnamed	Unambitiousness
Anger		Irascibility	Gentleness	Unirascibility
Social intercourse	Telling the truth about oneself	Boastfulness	Truthfulness	Self-depreciation
	Giving of pleasure— By way of amusement	Buffoonery	Wittiness	Boorishness
	In life generally	Obsequiousness	Friendliness	Sulkiness
	Mean states of feeling			
Shame		Bashfulness	Modesty	Shamelessness
Pain at good or bad fortune of others		Envy	Righteous indignation	Malevolence

Aristotle gives us some guidance when aiming at the mean. We should particularly note the errors into which we, personally, are most liable to fall and be on guard against our own peculiar weakness. We should keep away from that extreme which is most opposed to the mean, for one of the extremes is always a more dangerous error than the other. And we should avoid following the lure of pleasure, "for we do not judge it impartially." *Ethics*, Bk. II, pp. 9, 1109b. Aristotle notes that the doctrine of the mean does not adequately describe all moral actions or feelings. There are some acts such as adultery, theft and murder or feelings such as spite, shamelessness and envy, which are evil in themselves and circumstances do not make any difference in the rightness or wrongness of them. *Ibid.*, Bk. II, 6, 1107a.

In Book V of the *Ethics* Aristotle discusses the meaning of justice. He acknowledges that justice (**dike**) in the broadest sense of the word is synonymous with the whole of virtue, but here he is concerned about dealing with more particular manifestations of justice. For his purpose he distinguishes four kinds of justice: distributive justice, corrective or remedial justice, commercial justice, and equity. Since justice signifies what is fair and equal, distributive justice is concerned with the fair allocation of the material necessities of life, honours, leisure, and responsibilities. These things, he thinks, should be distributed in accordance with merit, i.e., unequally but fairly. Justice is not a mean between two vices, like the moral virtues, but a mean between having too much and having too little, and it is not a mean within the individual but a mean between the acts of two or more individuals. The principle of distributive justice raises such questions as, What are the legitimate needs of individuals in society, and are they being barely satisfied? Do I want my fair share of the good things or more than I deserve? What kind of person merits our respect? Whom should we honour? Do I accept my fair share of social responsibility or less than I should? It would not be fair for all citizens in a given family to be allotted precisely the same allowances or the same responsibilities because these vary with age, need and capacity. Therefore, a fair distribution of goods and responsibilities requires not arithmetic equality but proportional equality.

If proportional equality is appropriately achieved, then the principle of arithmetic equality should be followed; any further exchange should be on the basis of strict equality. In all private transactions the principle of arithmetic equality should be followed. Aristotle calls this remedial or corrective justice. It operates in civil law when a plaintiff seeks damages from a defendant who has inflicted some damage upon him. The judge seeks to restore the "balance," or equality, that has been disturbed by the injury. Aristotle endeavours to apply the same principle to criminal law. In this instance, the penalty imposed on the criminal by the court is an effort to "balance" the crime committed against society. It is, in a sense, a way of equalizing the injustice that has been done.

Commercial justice is concerned with the exchange of goods. "Money ... acting as a measure, makes goods commensurate and equates them."[15] Goods are rarely of equal value but money makes it possible to exchange them fairly. Equity is a special kind of justice that operates when the law is defective due to

---

[15] *Ibid.*, Bk. V, 5, 1133b.

its universality. It allows us to make exceptions to the law when the lawgiver, owing to the generality of language, left a loophole for error to creep in.

THEORETICAL AND PRACTICAL REASON

It is in Book VI of the *Ethics* that Aristotle discusses the intellectual virtues and distinguishes between theoretical and practical **sciences** (*Episteme*), a distinction that is not found in Plato's thought. According to Aristotle, there are two rational faculties, one that aims at knowledge for the sake of knowledge and the other that aims at knowledge for the sake of action.

Theoretical or scientific knowledge is knowledge that does not admit of any variation, which is not subject to change by human volition, and which exists by an unalterable necessity. Metaphysics (what Aristotle sometimes calls First Philosophy), physics and mathematics are sciences of this kind. Practical reason, or the calculative faculty, is concerned with that which is contingent and subject to change by human volition and which admits of exceptions. It aims not at knowledge for the sake of knowledge but at knowledge for the purpose of action. Ethics, political science, and economics are practical sciences. Not only do the two kinds of sciences differ in the objects investigated but also they differ in the kinds of conclusions they reach. The theoretical sciences yield truths that are universal and necessary, truths that are deducible with logical necessity from self-evident principles. The practical sciences, however, yield truths that hold true only in the majority of cases, and their conclusions are always subject to exception.

Associated with the use of theoretical reason are the intellectual (*dianoetic*) virtues, or ways of knowing. The most fundamental of these is insight (*nous*), or what might be called rational intuition, the capacity to grasp the truth of first principles. It includes the capacity to define our terms with precision. When it becomes a fixed habit, we say that a person has intelligence. Another intellectual virtue is the ability to think syllogistically, i.e., to arrive at a correct conclusion from a given premise through a middle term. The highest intellectual virtue is wisdom (*sophia*), which Aristotle defines as "intuitive reason combined with scientific knowledge—scientific knowledge of the highest objects which has received as it were its proper completion."[16] The ability to engage in contemplation about ultimate reality is what Aristotle means by wisdom.

---

[16] *Ibid.*, Bk. VI, 7, 1141a.

Among the things that can be changed by human volition (and, thus, are the proper subjects of the practical sciences) are (a) the manufacture or production of articles, and (b) human actions. Making and doing are different kinds of activities; consequently, the rational faculty exercised in doing something is different from that exercised in making something. The task of every art is to bring something into existence that did not exist before. When the rational faculty is employed in making something, we describe the activity as an art. It involves the calculation of the best means to achieve the purpose we have in mind in producing an object. Art or skill (*techne*) is one of the intellectual (*dianoetic*) virtues but it differs from those just mentioned. It is a virtue acquired through experience.

For example, when we require an operation to correct a defect in our body, we do not go to a professor of anatomy or physiology, we go to a surgeon. A surgeon has to have knowledge of human anatomy and human physiology but that knowledge alone is not adequate to perform a successful operation. The calculative knowledge of the skilled surgeon is different from the theoretical knowledge of human anatomy. Surgical practice is, indeed, dependent upon theoretical knowledge, but it is wider in scope. The surgeon has to apply theoretical knowledge to patients who are suffering from particular diseases or defects and must be able to recognize anatomical abnormalities. The surgeon is engaged not in the theoretical study of the human body but in practice. The knowledge possessed by the surgeon is real knowledge, but it is a knowledge learned less from textbooks than from experience. The surgeon learns by watching more experienced surgeons perform operations and then, in fact, by operating.

Whereas art is concerned with non-human objects, another kind of calculation is required when we are concerned with actions. When a person uses rational faculty to deliberate over the best means to achieve that which is humanly good, that person is said to possess **prudence (*phronesis*)** or **practical wisdom.** Prudence is not science since it is concerned with that which is contingent and subject to change by human volition, and it is not art since it is not concerned with making but with doing. It involves more than a knowledge of general principles since it is concerned with particular actions in particular situations. The kind of knowledge possessed by a person of practical wisdom is acquired through experience much like the kind of knowledge acquired by the surgeon through the practice of surgery.

The exercise of prudence or practical wisdom always involves an element of cleverness, but it is not the same thing as cleverness. Cleverness is the faculty or talent for choosing the best means to achieve any given end, and cleverness itself is indifferent to the end chosen. A burglar may be clever. Prudence is similar to cleverness but not identical with it since prudence always aims at the good of man. The exercise of prudence is only possible in men who possess the moral virtues. Without having first acquired the virtues of courage, self-control, liberality, friendliness, and so forth, we are not likely to be able to choose intelligently the best means to promote our human potentiality.[17] True virtue cannot exist without prudence any more than prudence can exist without virtue. This is Aristotle's answer to Socrates's dictum that "knowledge is virtue." Socrates, he says, is partly right and partly wrong.

Both economics and political science are sciences requiring the exercise of prudence or practical wisdom. Political science is somewhat like engineering in that both are interested in knowledge that can be put to practical use, but there is a significant difference between them: the one is concerned with *doing* and the other with *making*. The objects with which engineering deals are inanimate, material things, and the engineer is concerned with shaping or making those things into useful objects, such as buildings, bridges, highways, and so forth. The materials are transformed by the engineer in conformity with a useful purpose—a purpose which does not inhere in the things themselves but in the mind of the engineer. The products of a science of making, i.e., of a technology such as engineering, may be used for good purposes or bad, and, once made, the technician's task is completed.

Although the objects with which engineering deals are inanimate and material things, the objects with which political science is concerned are human beings—not things, but personalities. Human beings cannot be manipulated like material objects, and any attempt to do so will tend to destroy their very essence. They are not like so many bricks or pieces of steel that have only to be laid in the right place according to a blueprint. They can co-operate or rebel, and to enlist their co-operation in right action is one of the tasks of statesmanship.

---

[17] "Again, the work of man is achieved only in accordance with practical wisdom as well as with moral virtue; for virtue makes us aim at the right mark, and practical wisdom makes us take the right means." *Ibid.*, Bk. VI, 12, 1141.

Political science, Aristotle reasons, comes into being in order to assist humans in doing what they are naturally predisposed to do from the beginning, for Man does not create society but is born into it. Steel is not born to be made into bridges. Because it has no inherent predisposition to *be* anything, it can be manipulated and used in any fashion the engineer decides is appropriate. Human beings, however, are predisposed to live in society and embody ends in themselves. They are, by nature, social beings and require the fellowship and services of other humans. Furthermore, humans are not content simply to exist. It is not life alone they want but a good life. Political science, then, has developed in order to help humans live a good life in society. It ministers to an end that is not of its own devising but is inherent in life itself, and it is a source of the practical wisdom that the statesman needs, rather than productive or technical knowledge. Aristotle, thus, would not agree that politics is, or could be, a form of social engineering.

In Book VII of the *Ethics* Aristotle discusses the relationship between the good and the pleasurable. He rejects the theory of ***hedonism***, which forms the basis for utilitarianism in the nineteenth century and which suggests that the good is simply that which gives us pleasure, but he tells us that we should not succumb to the opposite error of saying that all pleasure is bad. Pleasure is not simply the absence of pain; it is something positive accompanying different kinds of activity. Therefore, we cannot pursue pleasure for pleasure's sake; we have to perform some kind of activity that yields pleasure as an accompaniment to it. For instance, some persons find pleasure in playing a good game of tennis or golf, others in reading a good book, still others in playing a musical instrument. Although we speak loosely of pleasure in all these instances, in fact, the pleasures vary in kind and are not commensurate, and they generally increase in proportion to the skill with which we use the faculty that gives us pleasure. Pleasure is that which accompanies the use of our faculties and helps to perfect their exercise. There is no pleasure without some activity, and every activity is crowned with pleasure. Aristotle returns to this topic in Book X. Here, he recognizes that pleasures differ in quality and that some kinds of pleasurable activities are more desirable than others, i.e., more befitting human nature. Just as there are some depraved human beings, so there are some depraved pleasures, and to pursue these pleasures is disgraceful. The most pleasurable existence—the happiest life—is a life that is devoted to the employment of that faculty which distinguishes humans from animals. Since the intellect is the highest thing in us and the objects that come within its range are the highest that can be known, contemplation is the highest form of human activity.[18] It is the most self-sufficient activity, the least dependent upon other persons or circumstances for its existence, the one that can be carried on longest, and the activity that is most like that of the Gods.

Books VIII and IX of the *Ethics* are devoted to a detailed discussion of the meaning of friendship. Aristotle defines friendship as mutual affection mutually known. He distinguishes among friendships of pleasure, those based upon utility and those based on true friendship. Friendship based upon utility, i.e., upon the advantages one can derive from it, is the lowest form of friendship since it is based not on love but on mutual advantage. Business friendships are of this kind. Friendships of pleasure are found mostly among young people when they engage in activities that each finds pleasurable. These friendships tend to be unstable and short-lived since, as one's tastes and interests change, one acquires new friends. True friendship, which is the rarest but most perfect kind of friendship, is based upon mutual love of the good. True friends desire what is good for the other person, they desire the existence and preservation of a friend for the friend's sake, and they share the joys and sorrows of the friend. True friends, who are also good persons, desire the same things for a friend as for themselves. No one is naturally a recluse, and friendship is a prerequisite for happiness.[19] Friendship is the source of order in human relationships, and the perfect community is one based upon true friendship. Justice, ultimately, is rooted in friendship or love and in the capacity of reason (*nous*) that enables humans to discover

---

[18] "That which is proper to each thing is by nature best and most pleasant for each thing; for man, therefore, the life according to reason is best and pleasantest, since reason more than anything else *is* man. This life therefore is also the happiest." *Ibid.*, Bk. X, 7, 1178b.

[19] "Surely it is strange, too, to make the supremely happy man a solitary; for no one would choose the whole world on condition of being alone, since man is a political creature and one whose nature is to live with others. Therefore, even the happy man lives with others; for he has the things that are by nature good. And plainly it is better to spend his days with friends and good men than with strangers or any chance persons. Therefore the happy man needs friends." *Ibid.*, Bk. IX, 9, 1169b.

the good. A community of good men living in harmony with themselves and with others Aristotle calls *homonoia*, and this is the basis for political stability.[20]

THE POLITICS: The Nature of the Polis

"State" is a relatively modern word and one not known to the Greeks. When Plato and Aristotle spoke of the political community they used the word **polis**. This has sometimes been translated as "city-state," but, in fact, there is no exact equivalent to the Greek polis, and we shall use that word rather than an inaccurate substitute. At the time Plato and Aristotle lived political communities were small in area and in population. When Plato suggests that a good polis should have approximately 5,000 citizens, he is thinking in terms of actual communities he knows. Athens in the fifth century B.C. was part of a larger territory known as Attica. Attica comprised about 1,060 square miles, and the total population of the area was approximately 350,000, about half of them Athenians. Only two other poleis had a comparable population (Syracuse and Acragas in Sicily). Sparta was larger in area but had a much smaller citizen population. In short, Attica was like a large county in the United States rather than a modern nation-state of several million inhabitants, and Athens was like a small city.[21]

Aristotle begins the *Politics* by observing that every polis is a kind of community (*koinonia*) and that every community is instituted for the purpose of attaining some good. The polis is the highest form of community since it aims at the highest good and embraces all of the lesser forms of community. The most fundamental community is the household, which comes into existence naturally because of men's

---

[20] Perhaps the best contemporary analysis of human nature can be found in the stark and candid testaments given by survivors of twentieth-century concentration camps. Terrence des Pres describes the seemingly natural human need for friendship and community found even in these indescribable conditions, and he thus supports an Aristotelian conception of human nature over an egocentric or self-interest conception. *The Survivor: An Anatomy of Life in the Death Camps* (New York: Oxford University Press, 1976). Viktor E. Frankl, a survivor, argues a similar thesis in *Man's Search for Meaning* (New York: Washington Square Press, 1984). See also: Langdon Gilkey, *Shantung Compound* (New York: Harper & Row, 1966); Irina Ratushinskaya, *Grey is the Color of Hope*, trans. Alyona Kojevnikov (New York: Knopf, 1988); Alexander Wat, *My Century: The Odyssey of a Polish Intellectual*, trans. Richard Lourie (Berkeley: University of California Press, 1988). There is also an immense literature by modern sociobiologists: Edward O. Wilson, *On Human Nature* (Cambridge: Harvard University Press, 1978).

[21] The exact composition—citizens, slaves, aliens—of Athens is difficult to ascertain. M.I. Finley, *Democracy in the Ancient World*, rev. ed. (New Brunswick, N.J.: Rutgers University Press, 1985); R.K. Sinclair, *Democracy and Participation in Athens* (Cambridge: Cambridge University Press, 1988).

and women's desire to have children and in order to supply everyday needs. Because families are not economically self-sufficient, associations of households lead to the formation of villages. The association of several villages, serving the interests of all and striving for self-sufficiency, leads to the creation of the polis. It is not economic interests alone that account for the emergence of the polis. Humans desire not life alone but the good life and the polis comes into being in order to promote the good life for humans within a community. Although the family is temporarily prior to the polis, the polis is prior to the family and the individual in the order of nature.

Life in a political community is natural, Aristotle argues, not conventional as the Sophists had maintained. Man is, by nature, an animal intended to live in a polis; he requires the fellowship and services of others in order to realize his potentialities as a human being. Only a beast or a god can live apart from community. It is as natural for humans to live in a polis as it is for a bee to live in a beehive, but a beehive differs from the polis just as a human differs from a bee. Bees build their hives by following animal instinct; they do not deliberate over alternative ways of acting, and, unlike all other animals, humans alone have a sense of good and evil, of just and unjust. It is not a gregarious instinct that produces a political association; the polis does not emerge from the biological nature of humans. There is nothing automatic about the process, though Aristotle maintains that the impulse to live in political community is present by nature.

> A social instinct is implanted in all men by nature, and yet he who first founded the state was the greatest of benefactors. For man, when perfected, is the best of animals, but, when separated from law and justice, he is the worst of all; since armed injustice is the more dangerous.... That is why, if he has not excellence [*arete*, virtue], he is the most unholy and the most savage of animals, and the most full of lust and gluttony. But justice is the bond of men in states; for the administration of justice, which is the determination of what is just, is the principle of order in political society.[22]

In his description of the polis and the way in which it comes into being, Aristotle employs some of the concepts encountered in his metaphysics, namely, nature, potentiality and actuality. The polis comes into being in order to help humans actualize their human potentiality. Indeed, the human community can come into existence only through sharing speech (*logos*), i.e., rational thought.

---

[22] *Politics*, Bk. I, 1253a30–40. Stephen Everson, ed., *Aristotle: The Politics*, trans. Benjamin Jowett and revised by Jonathan Barnes (Cambridge: Cambridge University Press, 1988).

It is this natural capacity that enables a mere aggregate of individuals to form themselves into a community.

> Nature, as we often say, makes nothing in vain, and man is the only animal who has the gift of speech. And whereas mere voice is but an indication of pleasure or pain, and is therefore found in other animals ... the power of speech is intended to set forth the expedient and inexpedient, and therefore likewise the just and the unjust. And it is a characteristic of man that he alone has any sense of good and evil, of just and unjust, and the like, and the association of living beings who have this sense makes a family and a state.[23]

Thus, rather than stifling human development, as some of the Sophists had contended, political institutions and laws are necessary to human development. The polis exists not for the sake of life alone but for the sake of a good life:

> It is clear ... that a state is not a mere society, having a common place, established for the prevention of mutual crime and for the sake of exchange. These are conditions without which a state cannot exist; but all of them together do not constitute a state, which is a community of families and aggregations of families in well-being, for the sake of a perfect and self-sufficing life.[24]

In Aristotle's thought there is no sharp distinction between state and society, such as we frequently find in modern political thought. The state of polis, from Aristotle's point of view, comes into being not simply to facilitate the exchange of products and to prevent crime but to educate men to virtue. Modern liberal theory would insist that you "cannot legislate morality" and would assume that if any moral training takes place it appropriately takes place in the family, church, or some private association. Morality from the modern liberal point of view is a private, not a public, concern. And it is freedom rather than virtue that the liberal state comes into being to promote. By contrast, Aristotle insists that education, in the broadest sense of the word, is the proper function of the state, and that function is to help humans to become good. Although you cannot literally make a person good by law, you can discourage immoral conduct and encourage good conduct through proper laws, and you can create, through proper institutions and through rewards and punishments, an environment that will encourage the development of good character. The unity of the

---

[23] *Ibid.*, Bk. I, 1253a7–18.

[24] *Ibid.*, Bk. III, 1280b30–35.

polis consists not only in the fact that a certain people inhabit a given territory under one government but also in the fact that they share a common moral purpose. It is a kind of unity that depends upon education for its perpetuation.

HOUSEHOLD MANAGEMENT

The household, as Aristotle describes it in Book I of the *Politics*, consists of husband and wife, parents and children, master and slave. The legitimacy of each of these natural relationships (marriage, paternal, master) is determined by the purpose of the relationship and the nature of the participants. The rule of husband or parent or master accordingly differs. Children do not have fully developed reason and are not equals of parents. The relationship of husband and wife is also not of equals: "the male is by nature superior, and the female inferior; and the one rules, and the other is ruled." Yet, the female is to be distinguished from the slave. The master-slave relationship has a clear superior since slaves, by nature, lack the full capacity of reason. Husband-wife thus differs from parent-child or master-slave. The household, which includes children, women, and slaves, has monarchical rule rather than constitutional or political rule. The latter requires equals who can fully participate in reason.[25]

---

[25] *Ibid.*, Bk. I, 1254b14–15, 1252a1–5, 1255b15–21. Susan Okin argues that the inequality of women found in Aristotle flows in large measure from his prejudice for the family. *Women in Western Political Thought* (Princeton: Princeton University Press, 1979), pp. 73–96. Jean Bethke Elshtain also argues that Aristotle "absorbs woman completely within the *oikos* or household." *Public Man, Private Woman* (Princeton: Princeton University Press, 1981), pp. 4–54. For a counter to Okin and Elshtain, read Judith A. Swanson, *The Public and the Private in Aristotle's Political Philosophy* (Ithaca: Cornell University Press, 1992), pp. 44-68; Mary P. Nichols contends that Aristotle's position is not a matter of prejudice, but rather results from his effort to "preserve a distinct role for women" because "women could make a unique and necessary contribution to human life." "Women in Western Political Thought," *Political Science Reviewer* (Fall, 1983), pp. 242, 241–60 and *Citizens and Statesmen: A Study of Aristotle's Politics* (Lanham, My.: Rowman and Littlefield, 1992), pp. 37-38. A similar argument is made by Arlene W. Saxonhouse, *Women in the History of Political Thought* (New York: Praeger, 1985), pp. 63–92. Mary G. Dietz argues, in agreement with Aristotle, that politics is about citizenship and justice rather than the family virtues of love and compassion. "Citizenship with a Feminist Face: The Problem with Maternal Thinking," *Political Theory* 13 (February 1985), pp. 19–37. See also, Leah Bradshaw, "Political Rule, Prudence and the 'Woman Question' in Aristotle," *Canadian Journal of Political Science*, XXIV:3 (September, 1991), pp. 557–73; Harold L. Levy, "Does Aristotle Exclude Women from Politics?" *The Review of Politics* 52 (Summer, 1990), pp. 397–416; Stephen G. Salkever, "Women, Soldiers, Citizens: Plato and Aristotle on the Politics of Virility," *Essays on the Foundations of Aristotelian Political Science*, eds. Carnes Lord and David K. O'Connor (Berkeley: University of California Press, 1991), pp. 165–190; Darrell Dobbs, "Family Matters: Aristotle's Appreciation of Women and the Plural Structure of Society," *American Political Science Review* 90 (March, 1996), pp. 74–89.

Aristotle's justification of slavery shocks the modern reader, but however shocking, it is necessary to try to understand the principle he is endeavouring to defend. Aristotle starts from the assumption, which is frequently challenged today, that humans are essentially unequal. They differ in physical and intellectual capacities, in virtue and in wisdom. They are fitted, as a consequence, for performing different functions in society. There is one kind of slavery that exists by convention and another that exists by nature. Those who have been enslaved by virtue of military conquest may be said to be slaves by convention, but this is not the kind of slavery Aristotle seeks to justify. Anybody who by his nature is not his own, but another's, is by nature a slave. Some are born with a slavish disposition fit only to be ruled by others of superior virtue and intelligence. In Aristotle's view such people are less than human, nothing more than "living instruments."[26] Not all who are legally slaves are naturally slaves, and not all free men merit their freedom.[27] To draw this distinction between slaves by nature and by convention is an advance over the practice of the time, since slaves by convention would simply be a matter of might rather than right. Still, there does appear to be a fundamental incoherence in Aristotle's argument. He sometimes notes that a slave can have the virtues of courage and moderation, that slaves do have some reasoning powers, and that slaves and masters can be friends. All of these traits entail that slaves could not by nature be subhuman. Nevertheless, Aristotle does not draw the seemingly logical conclusion that slavery is unjustifiable.[28] His observation that humans differ in abilities and character and that some merit positions of leadership over others could have been made without justifying slavery. Aristotle's arguments about slavery and the natural inferiority of women are instances in which he was unable to free himself wholly from the customs of his own day.

---

[26] *Ibid.*, Bk. I, 1253b30.

[27] "The abuse of this authority is injurious to both: for the interests of part and whole, of body and soul, are the same, and the slave is a part of the master, a living but separated part of his bodily frame. Hence, where the relation of master and slave between them is natural they are friends and have a common interest, but where it rests merely on convention and force the reverse is true." *Ibid.*, Bk. I, 1255b9–15.

[28] *Ibid.*, Bk. I, 1259b21–29, 1260a33–36. An excellent treatment of this issue can be found in R.G. Mulgan, *Aristotle's Political Theory* (New York: Oxford University Press, 1977), pp. 40–44. Stephen Everson provides a limited defence of Aristotle. He argues that Aristotle should be read as justifying paternalism when the subjects are, say, children or the mentally disabled. "Aristotle on the Foundations of the State," *Political Studies* 36 (March, 1988), pp. 89–101.

The art of household management is not identical with the art of acquiring wealth. There are, according to Artistotle, natural and unnatural modes of acquiring wealth. The natural mode consists in such activities as farming, hunting, and fishing. It is natural to acquire those material things that are necessary to life and that can be stored for later use by the family and community. These are the objects that may be regarded as constituting true wealth. True wealth has a limit of size determined by the purpose of the association it serves. When goods are bartered for other goods, Aristotle regards this as a natural mode of acquiring wealth, but when money is used as a means of exchanging goods, he calls it unnatural. He not only condemns retail trade but also the practice of usury. The pursuit of money for its own sake, for the sake of accumulating more money, is the wrong goal: "The origin of this disposition in men is that they are intent upon living only, and not upon living well; and, as their desires are unlimited, they also desire that the means of gratifying them should be without limit."[29] There is no limit to trying to satisfy one's desires, and those whose desire for enjoyment is excessive seek an art of acquisition that acknowledges no limit. Some turn every art into a means of getting wealth since they conceive of this as the end of life. The art of acquiring wealth is proper, in Aristotle's view, when it aims not at producing the largest amount of wealth possible but the right amount, i.e., the amount appropriate for a good life. Insatiable desires lead to a pursuit of wealth without limit. He concludes by saying that the art of "household management attends more to men than to the acquisition of inanimate things, and to human excellence more than to the excellence of property which we call wealth, and to the excellence of freemen more than to the excellence of slaves."[30]

ARISTOTLE'S CRITICISM OF PLATO'S REPUBLIC

Aristotle begins Book II of his *Politics* with a detailed criticism of Plato's *Republic* and, particularly, of Plato's advocacy of a community of wives, children, and property. His criticisms are curious in that they sound as if Aristotle knew of the *Republic* only by rumour. For example, he claims that Plato advocates the community of property, wives, and children for the whole population rather than

---

[29] *Ibid.*, Bk. I, 1257b41–1258a3.

[30] *Ibid.*, Bk. I, 1259b18–21.

only for the guardians and only while they are in power.[31] Nevertheless, the principles used in criticizing the *Republic* do illustrate key features of Aristotle's political science. He accuses Plato of seeking to achieve an undesirable and unnatural degree of unity in his community. A true polis consists of a plurality: the harmonious living together of different kinds of persons, possessing different capacities and sharing different kinds of services. Not only would a community of women and children produce an undesirable kind of unity but also it would be impracticable. It would dilute parental feeling and responsibility to the point where no one would feel genuinely responsible as a parent: "Each citizen will have a thousand sons who will not be his sons individually, but anybody will be equally the son of anybody, and will therefore be neglected by all alike."[32] Moreover, it will not achieve the purpose that Plato intended. Plato advocated a community of wives and children in part to avoid nepotism, to prevent parents who were guardians from showing favouritism towards their own offspring. But, Aristotle points out that children do tend to resemble their parents: "for children are born like their parents, and they will necessarily be finding indications of their relationship to one another."[33] It may also lead to offences against natural piety, e.g., incest, matricide, patricide. The deterrent that kinship provides against the commission of such crimes will have disappeared.

What is the proper system of property for citizens who are to live in the best polis? Is it a system of communism or one of private property? It is commonly observed, says Aristotle, that people generally take better care of property that is their own than they do of property that is held in common. Individuals do not take the same responsibility for public property that they do for their own because

---

[31] Of Aristotle's criticisms Bertrand Russell quipped: "I do not agree with Plato, but if anything could make me do so, it would be Aristotle's arguments against him." *A History of Western Philosophy* (New York: Simon and Schuster, 1945), p. 189. Eric Voegelin suggests that there may be some "subdued animosity" in Aristotle toward Plato. Voegelin, *Order and History*, Vol. III, *Plato and Aristotle*, p. 294. Martha Nussbaum defends Aristotle's criticisms of Plato, however, in "Shame, Separateness, and Political Unity," in *Essays on Aristotle's Ethics*, ed. Amelie Oksenberg Rorty (Berkeley: University of California Press, 1980), pp. 395–435.

[32] *Politics*, Bk. II, 1261b37–40. "But which is better—for each to say 'mine' in this way, making a man the same relation to two thousand or ten thousand citizens, or to use the word 'mine' as it is now used in states? … how much better is it to be the real cousin of somebody than to be a son after Plato's fashion!" *Ibid.*, Bk. II, 1262a7–14.

[33] *Ibid.*, Bk. II, 1262a16–19.

they assume that someone else will look after the public property. Whether it is admirable or not that people take more responsibility for what they call "mine" than what they call "ours," it is a fact of human nature that they do. Plato's community of property was supposed to do away with the covetousness and discord occasioned by holding property privately, but it is doubtful, Aristotle reasons, if the equalization of property can cure a defect of human nature.

> [The] avarice of mankind is insatiable … men always want more and more without end; for it is of the nature of desire to be unlimited, and most men live only for the gratification of it. The beginning of reform is not so much to equalize property as to train the nobler sort of natures not to desire more, and to prevent the lower form getting more; that is to say, they must be kept down, but not ill-treated.[34]

Aristotle criticizes Plato for neglecting one of his own principles: that one should rely upon education rather than upon institutional arrangements for dealing with evil.

These criticisms, however questionable, illustrate Aristotle's fundamental belief that in politics one must work with natural tendencies within humans: affection for one's family and pride in one's own property. The potential defects within both (nepotism and favouritism with family, and greed and covetousness with property) cannot be addressed by futile schemes and regulations. Human nature cannot be changed by institutional measures nor wickedness cured by regulations. We have to deal with people as we find them, not as we would like them to be.

TYPES OF POLITICAL ORDER

In Book I of the *Politics* Aristotle was concerned with describing the nature of the polis and concluded that the polis comes into being in order to assist people in realizing their potentialities as human beings. It is neither artificial nor conventional, but natural. Humans are, by nature, inclined to live in a political community. In Book III of the *Politics* Aristotle shifts his attention from the idea of the polis to a description and analysis of actual polities. In Book I he is looking at the polis from the perspective of the philosopher, and in Book III

---

[34] *Ibid.*, Bk. II, 1267b1–8.

he is looking at actual political regimes from the perspective of the lawgiver. The lawgiver is less concerned with the nature of the polis as such than with the possibility of actualizing a regime.

Aristotle now gives us a new definition of the polis as consisting of a multitude of citizens. But, who may properly be called citizens? They are those persons who participate in deliberative and judicial functions. He would exclude from citizenship the larger number of the residents of any state: women, children, slaves, resident aliens, mechanics, farmers, and tradesmen. He would exclude the mechanics, farmers, and tradesmen since they do not have the leisure necessary for the development of virtue nor for the performance of political duties. Aristotle shared the rather common Greek view that manual work and trade were somehow ignoble and an obstacle to the development of human excellence. The aristocratic gentleman of leisure was his idea of a citizen.[35] In effect, he would limit citizenship to two classes (guardians and auxiliaries), which comprised Plato's rulers. Plato would have made the craftsmen and farmers an organic part of the polity; Aristotle was content to leave them simply as producers.

In the best polis the good citizen would be identical with the good man, and all the citizens alike would take their turn governing and being governed. Aristotle is not advocating equalitarian democracy of the modern kind but is simply saying that among equally virtuous persons there should be equal opportunities to govern. It is precisely because he conceives of citizens being equal and free in the best polis that he excludes those persons from citizenship whom he does not believe are capable of acquiring, by virtue of their occupation, this kind of equality and freedom. Aristotle's ideal form of polity is aristocratic not democratic. The best polis consists of citizens who are mature men of practical wisdom (**Spoudaioi**). It is in the lives of such men that the full nature of humans has been actualized and in the polis composed of such men as citizens that the full unfolding of human nature is possible.

All actual polities, however, fall short of the best polis. For actual polities are simply the reflection of the way of life of the ruling class, and the ruling class, in actuality, is not composed of mature men of virtue. Although all humans desire the good life and happiness, only some have the capacity to attain it. Others are stopped

---

[35] When Aristotle speaks of leisure he uses the word in quite a different sense from our modern usage. The Greek word is *schole* and it does not mean the absence of activity nor is it synonymous with recreation or amusement. By leisure, Aristotle means time spent in the cultivation of the mind.

from attaining it: "from some accident or defect of nature, the attainments of them is not granted.... Others again, who possess the conditions of happiness, go utterly wrong from the first in the pursuit of it."[36] He describes the best polis as,

> a community of equals, aiming at the best life possible. Now, whereas happiness is the highest good, being a realization and perfect practice of excellence, which some can attain, while others have little or none of it, the various qualities of men are clearly the reason why there are various kinds of states and many forms of government; for different men seek after happiness in different ways and by different means, and so make for themselves different modes of life and forms of government.[37]

In actuality there is more than one form of constitutional order (*politeia*). In Book III Aristotle defines the constitution or polity as "the arrangement of magistracies in a state, especially of the highest of all. The government [*politeuma*, civic ruling body] is everywhere sovereign in the state, and the constitution is in fact the government."[38] The word we are translating as constitution (*politeia*) has a much broader meaning than the English word and, perhaps, would be better understood if we thought of it as the "way of life" which characterizes any particular society.[39] That "way of life" or constitution is determined by those who constitute the ruling part of society (*politeuma*), those who have the power to make all of the important decisions affecting the life of the political community. Every form of political **regime** will reflect the ideas and desires of those who command the ruling power, and in that sense the civic body or ruling power *is* the regime.

Political regimes may be created to serve the interest of all or only the interest of the rulers. Those forms that serve the interest of all Aristotle regards as legitimate or good forms of polity; those that serve only the interests of the rulers he regards as perverted forms. Another characteristic of the good forms is that all are restrained by law; in the perverted forms the ruling power is unrestrained

---

[36] *Politics*, Bk. VII, 1331b39–1332a3.

[37] *Ibid.*, Bk. VII, 1328a35–1328b2.

[38] *Ibid.*, Bk. III, 1278b8–11.

[39] The word *politeia* can be translated as a life, constitution, polity, political system, or regime. Aristotle gives a definition: "A constitution is the organization of offices in a state, and determines what is to be the governing body, and what is the end of each community." *Ibid.*, Bk. I, 1289a15–17.

by law. Following the classification of political regimes given by Plato in the *Statesman*, Aristotle lists the following types of political order:

Rule in the interest of all and restrained by law:

- Monarchy (the rule of one)
- Aristocracy (the rule of the few)
- Polity (the rule of the many)

Rule in the interest of the rulers who are unrestrained by law:

- Tyranny (the rule of one)
- Oligarchy (the rule of the few)
- Democracy (the rule of the many)

Polity in this classification is used in a special sense to designate one particular form of good government. In other contexts the word polity is used to refer to all forms. Aristotle goes on to say that in classifying forms of government we must also look at the social composition of the ruling group. It is not enough to distinguish forms of government simply by the number (one, a few, or many) who constitute the ruling group since the few, in actuality, may be the rich, or in some unusual cases, the poor. He now defines oligarchy as rule by the few rich in their own interest and democracy as rule by the many poor in their own interest. Empirically, we observe that many political struggles involve a conflict between the interests of the rich and those of the poor.[40]

In actual polities, different claims to rule are advanced by different groups of people. The wealthy claim that they should rule since they have the largest stake in the community and the most to lose by the pursuit of bad policies. The poor advance their claim to rule in the name of freedom. Each claim is advanced in the name of justice, but each claim is partial to its own interest and falls short of true justice. The oligarchs think that being superior in one respect, namely, the possession of wealth, entitles them to be superior in all respects. The democrats think that equality in one respect, namely, free birth, entitles them to equality in all respects. Aristotle replies to these claims by saying:

---

[40] When Aristotle uses the word "democracy" he does not mean precisely what we mean today when we talk about representative, constitutional democracy. The Framers of the United States Constitution also spoke of democracy in a pejorative sense, and both they and Aristotle meant by it something which, today, we would likely characterize as mob rule. It is Aristotle's "polity" that most nearly resembles modern constitutional democracy, but Aristotle had no conception of representative government.

... both the parties to the argument are speaking of a limited and partial justice, but imagine themselves to be speaking of absolute justice. For the one party, if they are unequal in one respect, for example wealth, consider themselves to be unequal in all; and the other party, if they are equal in one respect, for example free birth, consider themselves to be equal in all. But they leave out the capital point ... a state exists for the sake of a good life, and not for the sake of life only....

Our conclusion, then is that political society exists for the sake of noble actions, and not of living together. Hence they who contribute most to such a society have a greater share in it than those who have the same or a greater freedom or nobility of birth but are inferior to them in political excellence; or than those who exceed them in wealth but are surpassed by them in excellence.

From what has been said it will be clearly seen that all the partisans of different forms of government speak of a part of justice only.[41]

A polis is something more than a group of persons living in a given territory, more than an alliance for mutual defence, and more than an organization for the prevention of crime or for the purpose of facilitating exchange. Since the true polis exists to actualize human excellence, those who contribute the most through virtue to promote this purpose have the most just claim to govern, though there may be others who exceed them in wealth or who are their equals by free birth. Although this may be a sound argument philosophically, in actual polities the problem is how best to approximate true justice. The virtuous are too few in number to constitute a polis. They are also reluctant, as Plato pointed out in the *Republic*, to seek political office. And although the few rich and the many poor have no absolute right to govern, they do have a legitimate claim to participate in political decisions since they contribute to the necessities without which there could be no political association. In actual politics the political problem, then, is not how to achieve perfect justice but how best to approximate justice. The problem is how to combine the partially legitimate claims of the wealthy, the free, and the virtuous in such a way that no one claim may disallow the claims of others and all may be combined to serve the common good. In actuality we have to be content with a political virtue that resembles, but is not

---

[41] *Politics*, Bk. III, 1280a21–33, 1281a2–10.

identical with, true virtue. In actual states you find the good, the wealthy and well-born, and the many poor all living together in a single community. When no one group is sovereign, who then is to govern when the claims of different groups are simultaneously present?

> Suppose the good to be very few in number: may we consider their numbers in relation to their duties, and ask whether they are enough to administer the state, or so many as will make up a state? Objections may be urged against all the aspirants to political power. For those who found their claims on wealth or family might be thought to have no basis of justice; on this principle, if any one person were richer than all the rest, it is clear that he ought to be ruler of them. In like manner he who is very distinguished by his birth ought to have the superiority over all those who claim on the ground that they are free-born. In an aristocracy a like difficulty occurs about excellence; for if one citizen is better than the other members of the government, however good they may be, he too, upon the same principle of justice, should rule over them. And if the people are to be supreme because they are stronger than the few, then if one man, or more than one, but not a majority is stronger than the many, they ought to rule, and not the many.
>
> All these considerations appear to show that none of the principles on which men claim to rule and to hold all other men in subjection to them are right.[42]

If the question of who is to govern when the claims of different groups are simultaneously present cannot be answered on principle, then the next best thing is to try to combine the principles in a practical way so that each is restrained from serving his own interest exclusively, and all are harmoniously united in the promotion of the common good of all citizens.

In Book IV of the *Politics* Aristotle turns his attention to a more detailed discussion of actual polities and their varieties. The study of politics, he tells us, is a practical science not a theoretical one. Although it is important to know which is the best constitution and what qualities a polity ought to have in order to approximate this standard, it is also important to realize that the attainment of the best regime is likely to be impossible for most states: "the true legislator and statesman ought to be acquainted, not only with that which is best in the abstract,

---

[42] *Ibid.*, Bk. III, 1283b9–30.

but also with that which is best relatively to circumstances."[43] The student of politics must know how actual polities are governed, how they have arisen, and how they may be made to enjoy the longest possible life. "We ought, moreover, to know the form of government which is best suited to states in general.... We should consider, not only what form of government is best, but also what is possible and what is easily attainable by all."[44] It is important for the student of politics and the statesman to know how to improve existing polities and how to enact laws or statutes appropriate to each constitution or way of life.[45]

In Book III, as we saw earlier, Aristotle listed six forms of government—three good and three perverted. But, in Books IV through VI, he points out that this is too simplified a classification. In actuality there are many varieties of each form, and with his penchant for classification and taxonomy he analyzes each of these in some detail. There are at least five varieties of democracy and four varieties of oligarchy. Earlier he had suggested that states were composed of the rich, the poor and the virtuous. Now he says that it is a little more complicated. Actual poleis consist of at least eight necessary elements:

1. farmers and agricultural labourers
2. artisans
3. those engaged in commerce and trade
4. workers
5. soldiers
6. those engaged in the administration of justice and in political deliberation
7. the wealthy
8. public servants and administrators.[46]

These are not distinct and separate groups of people, however, since some persons may perform two or more functions, for example, a person may serve as a farmer, a soldier and a craftsman. "And all claim to possess political ability, and think that they are quite competent to fill most offices. But the same persons cannot be rich and poor at the same time. For this reason the rich and the poor

---

[43] *Ibid.*, Bk. IV, 128826–28.

[44] *Ibid.*, Bk. IV, 1288b34–39.

[45] *Ibid.*, Bk. IV, 1289a.

[46] *Ibid.*, Bk. IV, 1291a1–35.

are especially regarded as parts of a state."[47] It is the relative domination of one part of the state over others that leads, in some measure, to the emergence of different varieties of the same form of government. When, for example, you have a farming class of moderate wealth in a position to make the important political decisions, you have, in Aristotle's view, one of the better forms of democracy. When the mass of the poor are sovereign, you have one of the worst varieties of democracy. When the majority of citizens have property in moderate amounts and all who acquire this moderate amount participate in political decisions, you have the best form of oligarchy. When the wealthy are few in number and their wealth is excessive and they make all of the political decisions, you have one of the worst forms of oligarchy. Most actual states do have one form or another of democracy or oligarchy. The reason is that there are many fewer men of excellence or virtue than there are men in general, and in almost every state you will find a large number of wealthy men. Although an aristocracy is the best constitution, it is beyond the reach of most states. The practical problem, then, is what is the best way of life or constitution for the *majority* of states, what kind of constitution is it *possible* for most states to enjoy?

Referring back to the *Ethics*, Aristotle says that if goodness consists in a mean, then probably the best *practicable* political regime would be a **polity**. Here he uses the word polity in a special sense. It will have to be a blend of democracy and oligarchy (since these are the most common types in existence). Such a blend will be possible only if you have a middle class, which can serve as a kind of buffer between the very rich and the very poor. Persons who enjoy too many advantages, e.g., wealth, good connections, or superior strength, tend to be arrogant. Nurtured in luxury, they have never acquired the habit of discipline. Always ready to rule, they have never learned how to obey. The very poor, on the other hand, are often mean and poor-spirited. They are inclined to be consumed by envy and, frequently, are slavish in disposition. One group, in short, knows how to rule but not how to obey, and the other knows only how to obey. In such a situation the spirit of friendship is lacking, and there is no basis for genuine community or mutual respect. A state composed of a large middle class is a better state than one in which the vital political decisions are made by the rich or the poor.

---

[47] *Ibid.*, Bk. IV, 1291b5–9.

In Aristotle's view, the middle class is economically secure so they are not apt to be envious of the rich and they suffer less from excessive ambition, also they are not apt to be contemptuous of the poor. Since they are secure both economically and psychologically, they are less given to factionalism and divisiveness. They have a capacity for mutual respect and friendship. They are also, in Aristotle's view, more amenable to reason. The most secure polity will exist when the middle class is larger in numbers than both of the other classes. The moderation that characterizes the polity is a political virtue, which resembles, but is not identical with, true virtue. It is the best, however, that we can expect in most actual situations. At least it encourages virtue in its citizens and makes it possible for men of true virtue to live in peace. Such a polity is a mean between two degenerate forms of government. One of the tests of whether you have achieved this mean is how the regime is described. "In a well tempered polity there should appear to be both elements and yet neither" since it will, in fact, contain both democratic and oligarchical elements.[48]

In Book V Aristotle turns his attention to a detailed analysis of the causes of revolution and to the means of preserving constitutions. He examines both the "formal" cause of **revolution**, i.e., the general or guiding principle, and the "efficient" causes, i.e., the actual immediate "triggers" for change, that are peculiar to each type of regime. It is impossible to do justice in a brief summary to the detail with which he examines the problem. It is a remarkably perceptive analysis that, in many particulars, is still helpful in understanding revolutions today. The formal or general cause of revolution, he says, is always a quarrel about justice and equality. The partial justice based on different conceptions of equality, which gives rise to different kinds of political regimes, is precisely what arouses resentment among those who do not share the conception of justice held by those in power. Revolutions, thus always involve a quarrel over the meaning of justice. The motives and actions (efficient causes) that lead to revolution are fear, insolence, and contempt on the part of the rulers towards those being governed, the use of public office for personal and monetary advantage, the unfair distribution of honours, the disproportionate increase of one class at the expense of another, election frauds, and too great a heterogeneity among the members of the state. In democracies, revolutions

---

[48] *Ibid.*, Bk. IV, 1294b35.

generally occur when demagogues attack the rich and egg the people on against them; in aristocracies, revolutions occur when the ruling group seeks to limit the offices and honours to an increasingly smaller number of persons.

The causes of revolution suggest some of the means that should be taken to preserve constitutional stability. No confidence, says Aristotle, should ever be placed in political devices "invented only to deceive the people."[49] The people eventually will see through them and resent them. Petty lawlessness should never be tolerated either since petty infractions of the law lead, ultimately, to a disrespect for the law itself. Aristotle gives many other common sense axioms for preserving a regime: no matter what the form of government, there should be some frequent rotation in the holding of public office; honours should be given out sparingly and only because they are merited; every precaution should be taken so that the "magistrates cannot possibly make money from their offices."[50] Good education for the citizens is also an important safeguard against revolution. It should not, however, be a partisan education (in the sense of instilling democratic or oligarchic principles) but should be the kind of education that will enable citizens to govern with prudence.

Aristotle's discussion of tyranny is sometimes misunderstood. He talks about the traditional method in which tyrants seek to perpetuate themselves in power, and much of this has contemporary relevance. He is not, however, recommending tyranny as a form of government; he is simply observing what tyrants frequently do to maintain themselves in power. Tyrants (we would say dictators today) breed mutual distrust among their subjects; they try in every way to break their subjects' spirit and make them incapable of action. A tyrant will forbid the creation of private clubs or independent associations for cultural purposes in order to keep people from forming friendships. Only mass meetings and public gatherings will be allowed, and the tyrant will encourage his subjects to spy upon their neighbours and report to secret police. The tyrant will keep his subjects so impoverished and hard at work that they have no time for plotting. Of tyrants who practise these traditional techniques, Aristotle says, "there is no wickedness too great" for them.[51]

---

[49] *Ibid.*, Bk. V, 1308a1.

[50] *Ibid.*, Bk. V, 1308b34.

[51] *Ibid.*, Bk. V, 1314a14.

There is another method for preserving a tyranny and that is to use various techniques that will provide far greater stability and security. Here, Aristotle suggests that the tyrant use taxes and revenues for public services and give a public account of their use. He should, as Aristotle says, "appear" to be a guardian and a "steward of the public." In his personal behaviour the tyrant should become moderate and religious. He should "honour men of merit" and let the courts and the law administer punishment. These expedient rules for preserving a tyranny would seem to lead quickly to a kingship, as may well have been Aristotle's intention.[52]

Books VII and VIII of the *Politics* seek to delineate the features of the best constitutions or regime (*ariste politeia*). This is sometimes referred to as Aristotle's "ideal state," but it should be noted that neither Plato nor Aristotle use the word "ideal" or any equivalent. Unfortunately, we have only an incomplete portion of Aristotle's discussion on this topic. Book VIII breaks off in the middle of a discussion of musical education and, obviously, something of importance has been lost.[53] Some of the discussion contains arguments encountered earlier in the *Politics*. Aristotle repeats that to know what is the best regime we first have to know what is the best life for man. The best political order will be that which makes it possible for persons to realize their potentialities as human beings. The best regime will be an aristocracy of good men under the law. We have encountered much of this discussion before. He now describes the external factors, which would have to be be present to actualize such a regime, such as the size of the population, the extent and nature of the territory, and the character of the population. He devotes considerable space to the discussion of the principles of education that should be followed, but the manuscript ends abruptly during this discussion. It is his contention that "the excellence of the citizen and ruler is the same as that of the good man, and that the same person must first be a subject and then a ruler, the legislator has to see that they become good men, and by what means this may be accomplished, and what is the end of the perfect life."[54] He does not tell us here how this Good is to be instilled in the citizens, but he has already instructed us on this point in some detail in the *Ethics*.

---

[52] *Ibid.*, Bk. V, 1314b1–25.

[53] The final two books are examined with care by Carnes Lord, *Education and Culture in the Political Thought of Aristotle* (Ithaca: Cornell University Press, 1982).

[54] *Politics,* Bk. VII, 1333aa11–15.

CONCLUSIONS

It is fashionable among some scholars to contrast Aristotle's thought with that of Plato and to say that whereas Plato's thought is otherworldly and mystical, Aristotle's is empirical, practical, and scientific. We are told that we have to choose between them and that their thought is not really compatible. This judgment has some obvious basis in fact, but it appears to us exaggerated. Aristotle is certainly more of what we would call today a political sociologist than Plato, and he paid considerably more attention to the empirical observation of political reality. His sights, too, are considerably lower as he constantly asks what is practicable, what is possible. He does not abandon normative judgments, however, even in his description of actuality, and he would insist that such judgments are absolutely essential to a genuine knowledge of this actuality. If "science" is conceived as being "value-free," Aristotle was no scientist. If, by empirical, we simply mean what we, in fact, experience in life, then both Plato and Aristotle were empirical, but that, of course, is not the meaning usually attached to the word today. Today, the word "empirical" is usually associated with the use of quantitative language and the possibility of verifying one's hypotheses by experimentation under laboratory conditions or conditions approximating those of the laboratory. If history, however, is thought of as a laboratory of human experiences, then Aristotle could be said to be willing to learn from history, though he would reject the notion that history has some meaning of its own that it "intends" to impart to those who study it. Meaning is something we bring to the historical experience of humans, and for that we need philosophy. Aristotle, like Plato, is first and foremost a philosopher, not essentially a political sociologist or scientist in the sense in which those words are frequently used today.

Aristotle was, after all, Plato's most famous pupil. If he is critical of his teacher, and he frequently is, it is not the kind of criticism that involves a total rejection of everything that he has learned at his master's feet. Much of Plato's teaching he takes for granted as he seeks to improve upon it or extend it to practical matters, and in this endeavour he is clearly indebted to suggestions found in Plato's *Statesman* and *Laws*. Aristotle shares Plato's conception of the Good, he is concerned with the souls of men and knows that the order of the polis will reflect the order, or disorder, in the souls of the men who comprise and govern it. The criteria of judgment that he brings to bear upon actual polities he derives from Plato.

Aristotle differs from Plato in the kinds of problems that engage his attention, and most importantly, in the distinction that he draws between theoretical and practical reason. Although he never wholly forsakes the perspective of the philosopher, he is most concerned, especially in the *Politics*, with looking at problems from the perspective of the lawgiver or statesman who has to concern himself with actual situations. He is, indeed, more practically oriented than Plato in this regard, and it is practical knowledge, he constantly tells us, that the statesman needs, not simply theoretical knowledge. In place of the ambitious with their hunger for power, Plato presents the philosopher-king. Philosophers, however, are rare and prefer a life free of political care. Aristotle suggests a third option for political life: the mature man or gentleman of common sense (the *Spoudaios*) who, rare though he may be in actual societies, is to be found in greater numbers than Plato's philosopher. It is to such men that we must look for political leadership, for the devising of institutions and the formulate of laws that can approximate the good polis. Even so, Aristotle is not sanguine about the probability of achieving this approximation of the best, and much of his analysis is concerned with what might appropriately be called the pathology of politics. Only a very few men can speak with authority about what is good; some can recognize their authority and follow it, but the mass of men neither possess authority nor recognize it. In the *Nichomachean Ethics* Aristotle quotes the poet Hesiod on this point:

> He who understands everything himself is best of all; he is noble also who listens to one who has spoken well; but he who neither understands it himself nor takes to heart what he hears from another is a useless man.[55]

For all his concern with politics, Aristotle has, in fact, given up Plato's hope of uniting wisdom and power and, ultimately, he looks for the fulfillment of his life in the life of contemplation. As Eric Voegelin puts it:

> In Plato's work we feel the somber tension that stems from his theocratic will to achieve the impossible and to restore the bond between spirit and power. In Aristotle we feel a coolness and serenity which stems from the fact, if we may express it drastically, that he has "given up." He can accept the polis as the adequate form of Hellenic civilizational existence; he can dispassionately survey the varieties of his vast collection of 158 studies of constitutions; he can formulate standards and give therapeutic advice for treating unhealthy cases; he has no dreams of a spirituality reformed, national Hellenic empire…. His life is no longer centered in politics, but in his stellar religion,

---

[55] *Ethics*, Bk. I., 1095b10. Terence Irwin, trans., *Aristotle: Nicomachean Ethics* (Indianapolis: Hackett, 1985).

and in the bios theoretikos; his soul is fascinated by the grandeur of the new life of the spirit and intellect; and his work, ranging over the realms of being, brings them into the grip of his imperatorial mind. For such a man the accents of the crisis will no longer lie on the misery of Athens; they will lie on the new life that begins with Plato.[56]

Neither Plato nor Aristotle could prevent the decline of Greek civilization that was taking place during their lifetimes, though they understood very well the reasons for that decline. If both seemed to desert the world of politics in order to find fulfilment in a life of contemplation, ultimately, it was not indifference to the fate of political societies that motivated them in this direction but a recognition of the fact that societies will always be in trouble so long as men seek to live with unresolved contradictions in their souls. For Plato and Aristotle, it is only in the acknowledgment and loyalty to a Good, which transcends the good as pursued by particular societies, that we can live a life that is better than the political life and more fulfilling and befitting our true nature. This Good will always be relevant to life in actual societies but never defined by them. Perhaps the best we can hope for, in Aristotle's view, is a regime good enough to permit the pursuit of a life of contemplation in peace and security by those who are so inclined. Both Plato's and Aristotle's diagnoses of the human predicament remain as relevant to the twentieth century as they were to their own times since the nature of human beings and the rational faculty (*nous*), despite the vicissitudes of history, remains essentially the same.[57] History alters neither the nature of ultimate reality nor the nature of human beings.

---

[56] Voegelin, *Order and History*, Vol. III, *Plato and Aristotle*, p. 289. Wendy Brown contends that Plato has the more radical view of philosophy in that he tries to break the male mode of thinking in contrast to Aristotle. See, "'Supposing Truth Were a Woman …': Plato's Subversion of Masculine Discourse," *Political Theory* 16 (November, 1988), pp. 594–616; *Manhood and Politics: A Feminist Reading in Political Theory* (Totowa, N.J.: Rowman & Littlefield, 1988), pp. 32–52.

[57] For examples of some contemporary uses of Aristotle for analyzing modern philosophical and political issues, see: Bernard Crick, *In Defense of Politics*, 2nd ed. (Chicago: University of Chicago Press, 1972); Ronald Beiner, *Political Judgment* (Chicago: University of Chicago Press, 1983); Richard J. Bernstein, *Beyond Objectivism and Relativism: Science, Hermeneutics, and Praxis* (Philadelphia: University of Pennsylvania Press, 1988); Alasdair MacIntyre, *After Virtue: A Study in Moral Theory* (Notre Dame: University of Notre Dame Press, 1981) and *Whose Justice? Which Rationality?* (Notre Dame: University of Notre Dame Press, 1988); Roger D. Masters, *The Nature of Politics* (New Haven: Yale University Press, 1989); Stephen G. Salkever, *Finding the Mean: Theory and Practice in Aristotelian Political Philosophy* (Princeton: Princeton University Press, 1990); Bernard Yack, *The Problems of a Political Animal* (Berkeley: University of California Press, 1993).

Platonic philosophy, as we shall see, had an important impact on early Christian thought, but Aristotle's writings were lost for several centuries. It was not until they were rediscovered in the early part of the thirteenth century, through Arabic and Jewish translations and commentaries, that they began to exercise an influence upon Western thought that has continued to this day.

SUGGESTIONS FOR FURTHER READING

With respect to Aristotle's life, Carnes Lord, in the "introduction" to his translation of *The Politics*, provides an excellent short summary. Guthrie, Randall, and particularly, Chroust, are more detailed. Ackrill, Barnes, Ferguson, and Veatch give brief and introductory surveys of Aristotle's whole philosophy. Grene, Guthrie, Lloyd, and Ross are larger works with good general surveys. Sherman, Veatch, MacIntyre, Yack, and Irwin's "introduction" to his translation of the *Nichomachean Ethics* are sympathetic treatments of Aristotle's ethical theory. Clark, Cooper, and Hardie give analytical assessments, and Nussbaum provides an original and provocative interpretation of both Plato's and Aristotle's ethical theories. Morrall, Mulgan, and Nichols are excellent short treatments of Aristotle's political philosophy. Keyt and Miller, and Lord and O'Connor are collections of essays on central themes in Aristotle's political philosophy. Voegelin and Barker are larger works with more analysis and interpretation. The bibliography for Plato (in Chapter 1) also contains works useful to understanding Aristotle and ancient Greece.

Translations

Barker, Ernest, trans. *The Politics of Aristotle*. Oxford: Oxford University Press, 1946.

Everson, Stephen, ed. *Aristotle: The Politics*. Translated by Benjamin Jowett and revised by Jonathan Barnes. Cambridge: Cambridge University Press, 1988.

Irwin, Terence, trans. Aristotle: *Nicomachean Ethics*. Indianapolis: Hackett, 1985.

Lord, Carnes, trans. *Aristotle: The Politics*. Chicago: University of Chicago Press, 1984.

Ross, David, trans., and revised by J.L. Ackrill and J.O. Urmson. *Aristotle: The Nicomachean Ethics*. Oxford: Oxford University Press, 1980.

Thomson, J.A.K., trans. *The Ethics of Aristotle*. London: Penguin Books, 1955.

Commentaries

Ackrill, J.L. *Aristotle the Philosopher*. Oxford: Oxford University Press, 1981.

Arnhart, Larry. *Aristotle on Political Reasoning*. DeKalb: Northern Illinois University Press, 1981.

Bambrough, Renford, ed. *New Essays on Plato and Aristotle*. London: Routledge & Kegan Paul, 1965.

Barker, Ernest. *The Political Thought of Plato and Aristotle*. New York: Dover Publications, 1959.

Barnes, Jonathan. *Aristotle*. New York: Oxford University Press, 1982.

Barnes, Jonathan, Malcolm Schofield and Richard Sorabji, eds. *Articles on Aristotle*. 4 Vols. London: Duckworth, 1975–79.

Chroust, Anton-Hermann. *Aristotle*. Vol. I. Notre Dame: University of Notre Dame Press, 1973.

Clark, Stephen R.L. *Aristotle's Man*. Oxford: Clarendon Press, 1975.

Cooper, John M. *Reason and Human Good in Aristotle*. Cambridge: Harvard University Press, 1975.

Ferguson, John. *Aristotle*. New York: Twayne Publishers, 1972.

Grene, Marjorie. *A Portrait of Aristotle*. Chicago: University of Chicago Press, 1963.

Guthrie, W.K.C. *A History of Greek Philosophy*. Vol. VI. *Aristotle: An Encounter*. Cambridge: Cambridge University Press, 1981.

Hardie, W.F.R. *Aristotle's Ethical Theory*. New York: Oxford University Press, 1968.

Jaeger, Werner. *Aristotle: Fundamentals of the History of His Development*. Translated by Richard Robinson. New York: Oxford University Press, 1962.

Keyt, David, and Fred D. Miller, Jr., eds. *A Companion to Aristotle's Politics*. Oxford: Blackwell, 1991.

Lloyd, G.E.R. *Aristotle: The Growth and Structure of His Thought*. Cambridge: Cambridge University Press, 1968.

Lord, Carnes. *Education and Culture in the Political Thought of Aristotle*. Ithaca: Cornell University Press, 1982.

Lord, Carnes, and David K. O'Connor, eds. *Essays on the Foundations of Aristotelian Political Science*. Berkeley: University of California Press, 1991.

MacIntyre, Alasdair. *After Virtue: A Study in Moral Theory*. Notre Dame: University of Notre Dame Press, 1981.

Morrall, John B. *Aristotle.* London: George Allen & Unwin, 1977.

Mulgan, R.G. *Aristotle's Political Theory.* New York: Oxford University Press, 1977.

Nichols, Mary P. *Citizens and Statesmen: A Study of Aristotle's Politics.* Lanham, My.: Rowman and Littlefield, 1992.

Nussbaum, Martha. *The Fragility of Goodness: Luck and Ethics in Greek Tragedy and Philosophy.* Cambridge: Cambridge University Press, 1986.

Randall, John Herman. *Aristotle.* New York: Columbia University Press, 1960.

Rorty, Amelie Oksenberg, ed. *Essays on Aristotle's Ethics.* Berkeley: University of California Press, 1980.

Ross, W.D. *Aristotle.* 5th ed. London: Methuen, 1949.

Sherman, Nancy. *The Fabric of Character: Aristotle's Theory of Virtue.* Oxford: Clarendon Press, 1989.

Strauss, Leo. *The City and Man.* Chicago: University of Chicago Press, 1977.

Veatch, Henry B. *Aristotle: A Contemporary Appreciation.* Bloomington: Indiana University Press, 1974.

Voegelin, Eric. *Order and History.* Vol. III. *Plato and Aristotle.* Baton Rouge: Louisiana State University Press, 1957.

Yack, Bernard. *The Problems of a Political Animal.* Berkeley: University of California Press, 1993.

Social and Political Background

Bowra, C.M. *The Greek Experience.* New York: Mentor, 1957.

Finley, M.I. *Democracy in the Ancient World.* Rev. ed. New Brunswick, N.J.: Rutgers University Press, 1985.

Hamilton, Edith. *The Greek Way.* New York: Norton, 1958.

Marrou, H.I. *A History of Education in Antiquity.* Translated by George Lamb. New York: Sheed and Ward, 1956.

Sinclair, R.K. *Democracy and Participation in Athens.* Cambridge: Cambridge University Press, 1988.

Snell, Bruno. *The Discovery of the Mind: The Greek Origins of European Thought.* Translated by L.G. Rosenmeyer. New York: Harper & Row, 1960.

Vernant, Jean-Pierre. *The Origins of Greek Thought.* Ithaca: Cornell University Press, 1982.

Chapter 3

THE HELLENISTIC AGE
AND THE
ROMAN LAWYERS

The rise of the Macedonian Empire under the leadership of Alexander the Great marked the decline of the independent Greek polis. Cities like Athens, Sparta, and Corinth, once proud of their independence and cultural superiority, were submerged into a larger unit that included both Greeks and barbarians. When Alexander died at a relatively young age in 323 B.C., his generals fought among themselves for the remnants of his empire, but the Greek city-state never was able to reassert its independence. Some unsuccessful and short-lived attempts were made to unite the Greek cities into leagues. The cities were no longer the centres of religion and law, and the immigrants, who increasingly settled in the old Greek cities, felt no ties of loyalty to the cities they inhabited. It would not be long before Greece would become simply another province in the Roman Empire. The period from the death of Alexander to the Roman conquest of Egypt (30 B.C.) is referred to as the Hellenistic Age.

Philosophy, in the sense in which it had been pursued by Plato and Aristotle, was no longer pursued by men of comparable intellectual stature. Cults of oriental dieties, astrology, and mystery-religions abounded.[1] Cut adrift from their moorings in Greek traditions and ways of life, individuals floundered in their efforts to find some meaning in existence, and reason was often overwhelmed by superstition. The Hellenistic age was an age of anxiety, the kind of anxiety that

---

[1] Two excellent works surveying the mystery religions are: Hans Jonas, *The Gnostic Religion*, 2nd ed. (Boston: Beacon Press, 1963); Marvin W. Meyer, ed. *The Ancient Mysteries: A Sourcebook* (New York: Harper & Row, 1987).

occurs at different periods of history when traditional sources of authority disappear or are severely challenged, an age of anxiety that bears some close resemblance to our own.

Intellectual attention shifted away from metaphysics, as individuals seeking for some kind of guidance in this age of uncertainty turned toward ethical speculation in an effort to redefine "the good life." With the demise of the polis, it was understandable that philosophers would think less of the link between the good man and the good citizen or would seldom discuss the relationship between virtue and types of regimes. People turned inward in order to find the self-sufficiency necessary to withstand the age, and the quest for the best social and political institutions seemed of less importance, or even futile, in the midst of large empires. As a consequence, there was a clear decline in political philosophy from the heights of Plato and Aristotle.

If the Hellenistic Age is not notable for political philosophy, it is notable for the extraordinary flowering of new schools of philosophy. With Plato's Academy and Aristotle's Lyceum in existence, it was natural for Athens to become a flourishing centre. The two most prominent schools of thought that emerged were Stoicism and Epicureanism. Both, in a sense, were outgrowths of pre-Socratic metaphysics and owed something to the teaching of the early Cynics, as shall be seen. Although science and mathematics tended to predominate rather than ethics and political philosophy, philosophy, including some political philosophy, had become popular. In a time when the city-states ceased to be the all-encompassing centres, when a multitude of peoples and traditions were mixed, when chance and luck appeared to rule, philosophers could claim the authority to guide. Here is a key distinctive feature of the philosophies of these schools. It would be misleading to claim that Plato and Aristotle created philosophical systems but the Cynics, Stoics, and Epicureans wanted precisely to provide systematic guides for individual life. Philosophy had become denominational.

THE EARLY CYNICS

Although there is no agreement among scholars on this point, the founder of the Cynic school is frequently acknowledged to be Antisthenes (c. 445–365 B.C.). He first studied rhetoric under Gorgias and later became an admirer of Socrates. He founded a school at Cynosarges, which may account for the origin of the name "cynic." Neither Plato nor Aristotle had a high opinion of his intellectual ability. Antisthenes admired the independence of Socrates but wrongly interpreted his teaching as embodying a contempt for learning. He copied what he regarded as Socrates's flouting of conventional opinion but ignored the positive convictions that Socrates opposed to that opinion. Antisthenes taught his students that virtue alone was all that was required for happiness, and virtue implied, for him, not only indifference to the opinions of others but freedom from all earthly pleasures and property. Virtue consists in recognizing that what most people prize—good reputation, property, family life, marriage, learning, citizenship—is really not important for individual happiness. Self-sufficiency is happiness.

This way of looking at life was revived in the Hellenistic Age by Diogenes of Sinope. He lived most of his life in Athens but died in Corinth (c. 324 B.C.). Diogenes was nicknamed "the Dog," and the Corinthians, after his death, erected a monument in his honour on which there rested a marble dog. Since the Greek word for dog is *cynos*, this may also account for the name of the school. He acquired the nickname in part because he held up the way in which animals live as a proper model for human beings. Dogs behave more "naturally" than most human beings who are hypocritically tied to social conventions. For human beings to behave in public as dogs do is to act with sincerity. And a life of poverty is a positive advantage since it frees the individual from all dependence upon external things. Nor, he claimed, should one feel tied to a homeland or city: a virtuous man is a citizen of the world. Indeed, he coined the word "cosmopolitan." Another of his teachings was that a community of wives is preferable and more "natural" than family life. Some of the disciples of this way of thinking affected rude manners and, by their crude utterances and unconventional dress, deliberately sought to shock their neighbours and to call them back to a life "according to nature." Lucian, a Greek writer of the second century, has a character in his dialogue *Cynicus* give the Cynic's catechism:

> I have no desire to be like the men of modern fashion…. I boast that my feet are just like the hoofs of horses. I need an artificial bed no more than the lion does. I need expensive food no more than a dog does. Be it mine to have the whole earth for my bed, the whole world for my house, and the food which comes readiest to hand for my fare. Is my appearance not that most seemly for a good man—to be unwashed, to be hairy, to wear a poor man's cloak, to walk bare-foot? …. This cloak of mine, which you mock at, this long hair, this appearance of mine, has such power that it enables me to live in peace of mind, to do what I will, go

consort with whom I will. For my appearance frightens off all who are fools and uninstructed; soft-livers give me a wide enough berth; but the men of finest temper, the men most truly reasonable, those who hunger after virtue, seek my companionship.[2]

One of Diogenes's disciples was Crates of Thebes, who lived during the latter half of the fourth century B.C., and it was he who taught Zeno, the founder of the Stoic school. There was a strong revival of Cynicism in the first and second centuries A.D. when the writings of Diogenes and Crates were widely circulated and read in Rome. In general, the Cynics sought self-sufficiency against the dominion of luck, chance, or fortune, and they thought that it could be attained by repudiating the insatiable, but unnecessary, desires. Their intellectual significance is primarily as precursors of Stoicism. But the attitudes towards traditional ways of thinking and acting, which characterize the Cynics, arise frequently in history at those times when there is a crisis of authority.[3]

EPICUREANISM

The founder of the Epicurean school was Epicurus (341–270 B.C.) who was born at the Athenian colony on Samos. After teaching at Mitylene and Lampsacus, he came to Athens around 307 B.C. and founded a school. The school was located in a house and garden where he lived in seclusion with his pupils, women, and slaves. He was greatly admired by his followers, and a kind of cult developed which treated him as a divinity. He is reputed to have written over 300 works, but only fragments of these exist today. Upon his death, he left his house and garden to his followers who sought to perpetuate his teaching. Epicurus's teachings were designed so that a person could learn to constrict his focus and, thus, withstand the vagaries of fortune. One should concentrate on pleasure or, more precisely, the absence of pain. Probably his best-known disciple was the Roman poet Lucretius (91–51 B.C.) whose poem *De Rerum Naturae* preserves much of his teaching.

---

[2] Quoted by Edwyn Bevan, "Hellenistic Popular Philosophy," in *The Hellenistic Age*, eds. J.B. Bury et al. (Cambridge: Cambridge University Press, 1925), p. 88.

[3] M.I. Finley, "Diogenes the Cynic," in *Aspects of Antiquity: Discoveries and Controversies*, 2nd ed. (London: Penguin Books, 1977), pp. 88–98; A.A. Long and D.N. Sedley, translations with commentary, *The Hellenistic Philosophers: Translation of the Principal Sources with Philosophical Commentary*, Vol. I (Cambridge: Cambridge University Press, 1987), pp. 434–37.

Epicurus taught that pleasure is the beginning and end of living happily, but pleasure is not to be sought in satisfying lust, in eating rich foods, drinking and revelling, rather in avoiding and suppressing those physical desires that inflame the appetite. Intellectual pleasures are to be preferred to bodily pleasures. Happiness consists not in the pleasures of the moment but in a life of serenity free from pain, worry, and anxiety. Epicurus distinguished between natural and unnatural desires. The desires for food and sleep are natural, but most other desires are unnatural. Sex is natural but not absolutely necessary. It is relatively easy to satisfy our natural desires since they have a limit, and we should seek to confine our desires to these.

The natural desire for sleep is a desire for repose, for freedom from worry, for peace of mind. The two things that make it difficult for most men to achieve this state of serenity are fear of death and fear of the gods. Epicurus did not deny the existence of the gods, but he said that we need not fear the gods since they have no interest in human affairs and do not intervene in them. It is not necessary, as a consequence, to seek to propitiate them by sacrifices or by other means. Fear of death stems from ignorance concerning our true nature. Human beings are nothing but a bundle of physical sensations: there is nothing in us but that which is material. All good and evil consists of sensations. Since death is the deprivation of sensation, then death is nothing, certainly nothing to be feared. In Epicurus' words:

> Accustom yourself to the belief that death is nothing to us. For all good and evil lie in sensation, whereas death is the absence of sensation. Hence a correct understanding that death is nothing to us makes the mortality of life enjoyable, not by adding infinite time, but by ridding us of the desire for immortality. For there is nothing fearful in living for one who genuinely grasps that there is nothing fearful in not living.[4]

Epicurus derived his notion of what constituted human nature and what was the proper way to live from a rather simplistic view of ultimate reality that was based upon the teaching of the pre-Socratic writings of Democritus. Democritus taught that the universe consists of atoms and empty space, everything else is merely thought to exist. An accidental collision of atoms brought the world into existence. It serves no purpose and has no meaning. What we call thought is nothing but a jostling of our mind-atoms by other atoms flung off by physical objects. What we call reasoning

---

[4] Epicurus, *Letter to Menoeceus*, pp. 124–27; Long and Sedley, *The Hellenistic Philosophers*, Vol. I, p. 149.

is only the mechanical movement of one thing literally striking another. Truth is that which we correctly perceive, and perception takes place when the images of things impinge upon our sense-organs. It is from this materialistic and non-teleological metaphysics that Epicureans derive their views.[5]

Since the most pleasant life is that which is free from worry, it is advantageous to have friends rather than enemies, to extend kindnesses to our neighbours, and to live in a society where there is a rule of law. None of these pleasures, however, can be at the expense of self-sufficiency. We need not trouble ourselves over the question whether the law is just since justice is what is conventionally thought to be just. If the law provides a secure life and a peaceful one, it is all we can expect. In any case, the wise man will avoid participating in politics since such participation can only disturb his peace of mind. Epicurus intentionally created an alternative community with himself as the god-like master and apparently had strict rules limiting contacts with the outside world.[6] Similar to Glaucon in Plato's *Republic*, Epicurus taught that the state comes into existence as the result of a contractual agreement for the purpose of making life in society tolerable. He is generally indifferent to the forms of government but appears to have favoured monarchy as the one form most likely to enforce peace.[7]

---

[5] "The Epicurean must first set out his view of the world—that it, and everything on it, is a chance creation of atoms and space, fortuitously formed and destined at some time to break up, neither process depending in any way on divine intervention, for although gods exist they are not concerned with terrestrial affairs—and then he must deduce from this what man, a creature of a day, must do to achieve peace of mind while he lives." C.W. Chilton, *Diogenes of Oenoanda: The Fragments* (London: Oxford University Press, 1971), p. xxviii.

[6] Women fully participated in the community, and intermarriages and families were allowed. Bernard Frischer, *The Sculpted Word: Epicureanism and Philosophical Recruitment in Ancient Greece* (Berkeley: University of California Press, 1982), pp. 52–66.

[7] The best general discussion of Epicurus is by J.M. Rist, *Epicurus: An Introduction* (Cambridge: Cambridge University Press, 1972). James H. Nichols, Jr., admits that Epicureanism is not a political philosophy in the Platonic-Aristotelian mode: "The Epicurean views the whole of nature as fundamentally matter in motion, moving without purpose, unformed by anything like Platonic ideas, unguided by natural ends. Within this mechanistic, unteleological universe, man is a naturally individual being. He is not by nature a political animal: nature does not directly lead him into political society, nor give him direct guidance in political life. Man does not have natural inclinations that can find fulfillment only in political life as such; rather, political society rests on a compact, a convention, that aims at essentially individual or private goods." But Nichols concludes that, while strikingly modern and scientific in its metaphysical premises, Epicureanism does not advocate social schemes for human happiness but teaches the individual how to achieve happiness. It "enables us to see the limits of what politics can achieve for men." *Epicurean Political Philosophy: The 'De rerum natura' of Lucretius* (Ithaca: Cornell University Press, 1976), pp. 20–21, 210.

In an age of anxiety and despair, Epicurus sought to provide a "philosophy" of conduct that would console the individual, justify his withdrawal from politics, and encourage him to live a life of self-sufficiency. By the middle of the fourth century A.D., Epicureanism was effectively dead. Still, throughout its life it remained little changed and, for its followers, was a storehouse of solid, reliable axioms and philosophical amulets for warding off the cares of existence. An amateur follower, Diogenes of Oenoanda, illustrates this use of Epicureanism. In the second century A.D. he had constructed an enormous platform with colonnades (120 or more columns in a row) and inscribed them with the sayings of his Master and with his own comments. As he said: "I wished by making use of this colonnade to set forth in public the remedies which bring salvation, remedies of which I would say in a word that all kinds have been revealed. The fears that gripped us without reason I have abolished, as to pains some I have utterly eradicated, those that are natural I have reduced to quite small measure, making their severity infinitesimal...."[8] Philosophy as Socratic dialogue has been hardened into a closed system.

STOICISM

From the third century B.C. until the third century A.D., Stoicism was the dominant philosophy in the West. The founder of the Stoic school was Zeno, who was born in Cyprus around 336 B.C. and died in 262 B.C. Zeno went to Athens when he was about 21 years of age, arriving there just after Aristotle's death. At first he was a disciple of Crates the Cynic, but he founded a school of his own around 300 B.C. The school took its name from the porch (*stoa*) or open colonnade where he taught. He had a number of influential students who perpetuated his teaching. Cleanthes (330–232 B.C.) and Chrysippus (280–208 B.C.) were the most important. In general, the Atomists, Democritus and Epicurus, were opposed by the successive schools of Plato, Aristotle, and the Stoics. The first three Stoics and their immediate disciples are called, collectively, the Old Stoa. In the first century B.C. there was some revision by Panaetius and Posidonius. This is called the Middle Stoa. After the Roman Empire was firmly established throughout the Mediterranean, the final revision occurred, Roman Stoicism. Among the Late Stoics, Marcus Aurelius and

---

[8] Chilton, *Diogenes of Oenoanda*, p. 4.

Epictetus are important examples. Stoicism by then had become less a philosophy than a wise guide for living a good life. The Stoics reasserted a stress on man's rational faculty and his attunement with a rational reality, and particularly in later revisions, the Stoics continually stressed man's moral and political duty to serve and help others. Following Plato, they divided philosophy into logic, physics (nature), and ethics, but they always insisted on the linkage of these three topics. As Émile Bréhier comments: "they are for the Stoics inseparably linked since one and the same reason connects consequent proposition to antecedent propositions in the dialectic, links together all causes in nature, and establishes perfect agreement between acts in the realm of conduct. It is impossible for the physicist and dialectician not to be a good man."[9] It is this rational coherence that gave Stoicism its distinctive character and eventually established its influence.[10]

Zeno rejected both Plato's transcendental theory of forms and Aristotle's doctrine of immanent form. All knowledge, he taught, derives from sense-perception (**empiricism**). At birth, the mind of man is like a blank slate and through perception it acquires impressions, just as a piece of wax acquires the impression of a seal. These impressions remain in the mind as memories which can be compared and give rise to thoughts. But Zeno's theory of knowledge included the conviction that reason develops along with the accumulation of perceptions and is formed around the fourteenth year of life. There was an element of **rationalism** in the Stoic theory of knowledge that was inconsistent with its sensualist presuppositions. For, in addition to sense-perception, the mind of man is predisposed to form **innate ideas**, and it is ultimately through reason that we penetrate the nature of reality.

The cosmos came into existence, according to Stoic teaching, from primeval fire (an idea derived from Heraclitus) and will end in a universal conflagration.

---

[9] Émile Bréhier, *The History of Philosophy*, Vol. II, *The Hellenistic and Roman Age*, trans. Wade Baskin (Chicago: University of Chicago Press, 1965), p. 36.

[10] Regrettably only fragments are left of Old and Middle Stoa, which were the most original phases. F.H. Sandbach, *The Stoics* (London: Chatto & Windus, 1975), pp. 11–27, 109–22; A.A. Long, *Hellenistic Philosophy: Stoics, Epicureans, Sceptics* (New York: Scribner's Sons, 1974), pp. 107–21; R.D. Hicks, *Stoic and Epicurean* (New York: Russell & Russell, 1962), pp. 3–53, 113–52; Marcia L. Colish, *The Stoic Tradition from Classical Antiquity to the Early Middle Ages*, Vol. I (Leiden: Brill, 1985), pp. 7–60.

But a new world will be born again which is likewise destined to die. The construction and destruction of worlds will continue without end. Each world is an exact replica of the world preceding it, and every individual is born again to live the same life he lived in his previous existence. This primal or creative or designing fire, which lies at the heart of the cosmos, is referred to variously as Zeus, nature, providence, reason, and logos. As conceived by the Stoics, God and the world are composed of essentially the same material, and their cosmology is a form of monistic materialism. Although everything—universe, nature, and God—is composed of one material substance, this substance has two aspects, God (active) and matter (passive). The Stoics argued that there was a total mixture and interpenetration of matter by God or spirit: "God is mixed with matter, pervading all of it and so shaping it, structuring it, and making it into the world."[11] Material reality was thus animated by spirit, and it worked, as one modern commentator has noted, as,

> a sort of force-field between all parts of the universe, so that one part of it moved in unison with the movement of another (as, for example, is the case with the moon and the tides); the mutual interaction of parts was called "sympathy," and the force with which all parts were held together by spirit was described metaphorically as a "bond." And as there was spatial interconnection between parts of the universe as a result of the cosmic tension, so necessarily was there temporal interconnection between events; whence the Stoic theory of fate as a "chain" or "interweaving" of causes. Every creature and every event was a link in the interconnected chain of fate: in other words, the fate of every creature is predetermined and ineluctable. Indeed the fate of the universe itself is predetermined, so that the universe periodically dissolves in fire … and then water, and from these two agents a new universe is created.[12]

---

[11] Long and Sedley, *The Hellenistic Philosophers*, Vol. I, p. 273.

[12] Michael Lapidge, "The Stoic Inheritance," in *A History of Twelfth-Century Western Philosophy*, ed. Peter Dronke (Cambridge: Cambridge University Press, 1988), p. 101. The texts for the Stoics theory of the universe can be found in Long and Sedley, *The Hellenistic Philosophers*, Vol. I, pp. 266–343. H.A.K. Hunt, *A Physical Interpretation of the Universe: The Doctrines of Zeno the Stoic* (Carlton: Melbourne University Press, 1976).

Thus, the Stoics always maintained that the universe is governed by unalterable laws which reflect both the reason of God and his providential concern for the soul. Everything is determined including man's actions. The only freedom man has is the freedom to control his emotions.[13]

The Stoics taught men not to moderate their emotions but to suppress them. Because everything in the universe is determined, the only choice a man has is whether he will resign himself to his fate or fight unsuccessfully against it. The wise man co-operates with rational necessity and strives to achieve a state of apathy or indifference, or literally in Greek, "without passion." This means that a wise man must be "indifferent" to such conventional goals as long life, food, wealth, and power. Virtue consists in living in harmony with Nature. Human emotions, such as fear and sorrow, are unnatural and unnecessary. The wise man practises self-control and suppresses all desire and all emotion. Virtue does not consist in the right performance of external acts; it consists solely and wholly of the right attitude towards life. What men conventionally call good and evil is all the same ultimately since there are no actions which, in themselves, can be called evil absolutely.[14] Motive alone defines virtue, and only when we are motivated to accept the universe as it is, and our place in it, are we truly virtuous.

The wise man is truly free because he is without passion for those things that enslave other men. We are able to control our passions because of the capacity of the mind to give or to withhold assent to our impulses or passions. By assenting or choosing correctly, one acts appropriately as a human with a certain nature and within a universe constituted in a certain manner. Acting appropriately is fulfiling one's "duty," a word continually used by Stoics. Then a person will be able to live harmoniously with nature. As one can imagine, the virtue of the Stoics is attained only over a long period of time and by arduous effort. Although there was

---

[13] Stoics were continually criticized for holding both to determinism and to personal freedom and responsibility. A.A. Long defends Stoicism by arguing that the capacity for a rational decision is internal to the person: "At the very least he can have the consciousness of determining his own attitude to events and a feeling of freedom about the actions he performs." "Freedom and Determinism in the Stoic Theory of Human Action," in *Problems in Stoicism*, ed. A.A. Long (London: The Athlone Press, 1971), p. 175.

[14] The all-encompassing rational nature of reality made the existence of evil very difficult to explain. A.A. Long comments: "But even at its noblest ... there is something chilling and insensitive about the Stoic's faith that all will turn out well in the end." Long, *Hellenistic Philosophy*, 2nd ed. (Berkeley: University of California Press, 1986), p. 170.

no universal agreement among the Stoics on this point, some of them suggested, particularly the later Roman Stoics, that man could assert his freedom ultimately by an act of suicide.[15]

There are some similarities to Cynicism and Epicureanism since all three of these schools of thought sought to teach the individual how to live a life of self-sufficiency. The Stoics added a universal dimension that was missing in Cynicism and in Epicureanism—a dimension that was to have considerable influence in the development of Western thought.[16] Stoicism emphasized the idea that all men live in one universe under one law and one sovereign. This view finds expression in a hymn to Zeus composed by Cleanthes (331 – 232 B.C.):

> Supreme of gods, by titles manifold
> Invoked, O thou who over all dost hold
> Eternal dominance, Nature's author, Zeus,
> Guiding a universe by Law controlled....
>
> Whereby thou guid'st the universal force,
> Reason, through all things interfused, whose course
> Commingles with the great and lesser light—
> Thyself of all the sovereign and the source.[17]

All men are citizens of one world, brothers who are equal in their dependence upon a common sovereign which is Reason. The gods and men alike owe allegiance to the universal law of nature which defines what is right and what is wrong. Chrysippus (280 – 207 B.C.) in his work *On Law* declares:

> Law is king of all things human and divine. Law must preside over what is honourable and base, as ruler and as guide, and thus be the standard of right and wrong, prescribing to animals whose nature is political what they should do, and prohibiting them from what they should not do.[18]

---

[15] Hicks, *Stoic and Epicurean*, pp. 98–102; J.M. Rist, *Stoic Philosophy* (Cambridge: Cambridge University Press, 1969), pp. 233–55; Sandbach, *The Stoics*, pp. 48–52.

[16] Rist examines the connections and differences between Cynicism and Stoicism. *Stoic Philosophy*, pp. 54–80.

[17] E. Vernon Arnold, *Roman Stoicism* (London: Routledge & Kegan Paul, 1911), pp. 85–86; Long and Sedley, *The Hellenistic Philosophers*, Vol. I, pp. 326–27.

[18] Long and Sedley, *The Hellenistic Philosophers*, Vol. I, p. 432.

This law applies equally to slaves and to freemen, to Greek and to barbarian, to the rich and to the poor. For the Romans, who were creating an empire that aspired to include all the known world and to include under its jurisdiction all of mankind, this Stoic teaching had great appeal.[19]

THE REVISION OF STOICISM

Roman thinkers who sought to adapt the teaching of Stoicism to the needs of their time had to revise some of the Stoic teaching and include other teachings that gave the revised Stoicism an eclectic quality. The early Stoic virtue of apathy or indifference was submerged, and the Stoic teaching that all men are players in a drama that requires them to play their roles well was emphasized.

Panaetius of Rhodes (c. 185–110 B.C.), who lived for some time in Rome, rejected the ideal of indifference and emphasized the virtues of benevolence, liberality, and magnanimity. He dismissed the early Stoic teaching that one should strive for the suppression of all feeling and, in place of self-sufficiency, spoke of the desirability of performing public duties. He developed a more practical "second-best" ethical system which became immensely influential among the Romans. He spoke of the unity of the human race, the equal worth of men and women, charity towards one's fellowman, and equality under the law.[20] He had a strong influence both upon his friend and contemporary the Greek historian Polybius and upon Cicero. Both Panaetius and Polybius were friends of Scipio Aemilianus (c. 185–129 B.C.) a general who, in addition to destroying Carthage, was an important personality in Roman politics for nearly 20 years. The friends are now referred to as the Scipionic Circle, and this circle is often credited with exercising considerable influence upon Roman literature and thought.[21]

---

[19] The Stoic fragments on ethics are collated by Long and Sedley, *The Hellenistic Philosophers*, Vol. I, pp. 344–429. See also, N.P. White, "The Basis of Stoic Ethics," in *Harvard Studies in Classical Philology* LXXXIII (1979), pp. 143–209; Long, *Hellenistic Philosophy*, pp. 179–209; Sandbach, *The Stoics*, pp. 28–68.

[20] For the impact of Rome on the development of Stoic thought from the austere non-political Old Stoa to the Middle and Roman Stoa, see H.C. Baldry, *The Unity of Mankind in Greek Thought* (Cambridge: Cambridge University Press, 1965).

[21] Sandbach, "Panaetius and Posidonius," in *The Stoics*, pp. 123–39; Long, *Hellenistic Philosophy*, pp. 210–16; Rist, *Stoic Philosophy*, pp. 173–200; Margaret E. Reesor, *The Political Theory of the Old and Middle Stoa* (New York: Augustin, 1951), pp. 26–58.

POLYBIUS

Polybius was born around 200 B.C. at Megalopolis, a leading city of the Greek Achaean League. He lived during the time when the Romans, having defeated Hannibal, proceeded to extend their sovereignty over Greece, Macedonia, and Asia Minor. He was brought to Rome in 168 B.C. as one of a thousand hostages taken after a Roman victory over Macedon, and in time became a friend of Scipio Aemilianus, a young boy. Polybius followed Scipio's career and through him became acquainted with many leading Roman politicians. Polybius was a politician himself but was also a historian, and it is to him that we owe much of our knowledge of early Roman political institutions. He was motivated to undertake the study of history, particularly the history of Rome, during his lifetime, in order to try to understand by "what means, and under what kind of polity, almost the whole inhabited world was conquered and brought under the dominion of the single city of Rome, and that, too, within a period of not quite fifty-three years (219–167 B.C.)."[22] The Roman political system appeared to him to have admirable qualities that gave it strength and stability. Of his histories containing 40 books, unfortunately, only a few are available today.

Polybius describes in detail the Roman polity as it existed at the time of the Second Punic War. He examines not only the political system but also its military organization and the ways in which the Roman politicians made use of religion for political purposes. He describes the Roman political constitution of that time as a mixed one, embracing features of monarchy, aristocracy, and democracy. Unlike Aristotle, he does not mention the balancing of social classes but stresses the institutional system of checks and balances. He concludes that this peculiar political system explains the ascendancy of Rome: "in every practical undertaking by a state we must regard as the most powerful agent for success or failure the form of its constitution; for from this as from a fountainhead all conceptions and plans of actions not only proceed, but attain their consummation."[23] There is some question whether his description of the actual working of the Roman polity at the time is accurate, but his idea of the nature of the mixed form of government influenced Montesquieu and the framers of the United States Constitution.

---

[22] *Polybius on Roman Imperialism: The Histories of Polybius*, trans. Evelyn S. Shuckburgh (South Bend: Regnery/Gateway, 1980), Bk. I, p. 1.

[23] *Polybius*, Bk. VI, pp. 179–80.

Using a classification of the forms of government that he derived from Plato and Aristotle, Polybius propounded a cyclical theory of the rise and fall of political regimes which he thought had some relevance to Roman history. It is more interesting as speculation than as actual history. Governments, he argued, arise initially in periods of chaos, brought about by famine, floods or some other calamity, when the strongest impose their will on the many in an effort to create a tolerable social existence. In this context, monarchy arises as the most "natural" form of government. At first this monarchy is a kind of despotism, but with the development of reason and civilization the monarchy is gradually transformed into a true kingship. After a time, however, the king repudiates the demands of justice and morality and turns into a tyrant. The best people in the society rise up against him and create an aristocracy. At the beginning they rule with wisdom, but eventually they, too, are corrupted by power, and the aristocracy degenerates into an oligarchy. At this point the people prize the freedom and equality that they have wrested from the oligarchs, but eventually the wealthier among them seek greater privileges than the others. They seek to bribe the mass of the people. Their activity arouses deep resentment and many of the wealthy are killed and their lands taken away from them. A champion of the people encourages all of this, and the end result is mob rule (ochlocracy), which is marked by violence and rioting. Polybius thus predicted the coming of a time when the Roman people would no longer be willing to obey their betters, or even wish to attain equality with them, but would want everything for themselves, and as a result freedom and democracy would turn into anarchy and mob rule. Society would be reduced to chaos and the cycle would begin again.

> This is the regular cycle of constitutional revolutions, and the natural order in which constitutions change, are transformed, and return again to their original stage. If a man has a clear grasp of these principles, he may perhaps make a mistake as to the dates at which this or that will happen to a particular constitution; but he will rarely be entirely mistaken as to the stage of growth or decay at which it has arrived, or as to the point at which it will undergo some revolutionary change. However, it is in the case of the Roman constitution that this method of inquiry will most fully teach us its formation, its growth, and zenith, as well as the changes awaiting it in the future; for this, if any constitution ever did, owed, as I said just now, its original foundation and growth to natural causes, and to natural causes will owe its decay.[24]

---

[24] *Ibid.*, Bk. VI, 9, p. 185.

Polybius appears to have converted Plato's description of the decline of the best polis (in Books VIII and IX of the *Republic*) into an inevitable law of history.

Although Polybius could not be called a Stoic philosopher, his thought is shaped by Stoic themes. The polis, for him, is not the moulder of character, the centre of human life, a necessary medium for human development. On the contrary, he asks little of a political system: stability, protection from enemies, and prosperity. The Roman hegemony could provide these, and the poleis, by the second century, could not. The duty to play one's part was expected in return—a duty Polybius nobly performed as an agent of Rome. The natural and providential cycle of regimes was not to be escaped. This lesson applied to Carthage in its defeat and Rome in its victory. Polybius records with approval Scipio's reflections while watching Carthage burn:

> At the sight of the city utterly perishing amidst the flames, Scipio burst into tears and stood long reflecting on the inevitable change which awaits cities, nations, and dynasties, one and all, as it does every one of us men. This, he thought, had befallen Ilium, once a powerful city, and the once mighty empires of the Assyrians, Medes, Persians, and that of Macedonia lately so splendid…. "O Polybius, it is a grand thing, but, I know not how, I feel a terror and dread, lest someone should one day give the same order about my own native city…." Any observation more practical or sensible it is not easy to make. For in the midst of supreme success for one's self and of disaster for the enemy, to take thought of one's own position and of the possible reverse which may come, and in a word to keep well in mind in the midst of prosperity the mutability of Fortune, is the characteristic of a great man, a man free from weaknesses and worthy to be remembered…."[25]

Such knowledge provides the Stoic courage to counter the purchase of Fortune.

CICERO

Marcus Tullius Cicero lived during the last years of the Roman Republic. He was born in 106 B.C. to well-to-do parents in Arpinum. He received an excellent education, first in Rome and later in Greece, where he studied both in Athens and in Rhodes. He was a brilliant lawyer, a noted orator, and an active but not always

---

[25] *Ibid.*, Bk. XXXIX, 5, pp. 510–11.

successful politician. The height of his political career came in 63 B.C. when he was appointed to the consulship. Subsequently, he opposed Caesar's rise to power, and during Caesar's reign he retired from politics. It was during this period of retirement that he was active as a writer. After the murder of Caesar, he returned briefly to the political arena and denounced Marc Anthony (one of the contenders for Caesar's power) in speech after speech. He was unsuccessful in persuading the Senate to join him in this denunciation and only succeeded in provoking Marc Antony. It was on the command of Marc Anthony that Cicero was killed by soldiers in 43 B.C.

Cicero was a prolific writer whose works include not only orations and letters but also essays on rhetoric, ethics, theology, **epistemology** (the science of knowing), and some poetry. His two most important political writings were dialogues, entitled the *Republic* and the *Laws*. Although he was greatly influenced by Stoicism, his own mode of thought included ideas derived from a number of schools, and his thought is usually characterized as eclectic. Although he is not noted for his originality nor for his ability as a philosopher, he is known for his attempt to explain the Roman political system and to show, with some inaccuracy, that it derived from Greek philosophy. He was familiar with the thought of Plato and Aristotle and made some use of their ideas.[26]

He was attracted to the Stoic doctrine that the good life is one lived in accordance with nature, but he was critical of the idea held by some of the early Stoics that virtue is wholly unitary and indifferent to what many men call duty. He held that there are duties of life, such as the care of one's health, the management of one's estate, participation in politics, and the conduct of public affairs that a man of virtue must perform. At the same time, he opposed the Epicurean notion that the only good is that which gives us pleasure. It is often desirable to do that which is morally worthy whether it yields pleasure or not, or whether the action is profitable or not.

> Good men do a great many things from which they anticipate no advantage, solely from the motive of propriety, morality and right. For among the many points of difference between man and the lower animals, the greatest difference is that Nature has bestowed on man the gift of Reason....

---

[26] Elizabeth Rawson, *Cicero: A Portrait* (Ithaca: Cornell University Press, 1983); D.R. Shackleton Bailey, *Cicero* (New York: Scribner's Sons, 1971); T.N. Mitchell, *Cicero: The Ascending Years* (New Haven: Yale University Press, 1979); David Stockton, *Cicero: A Political Biography* (London: Oxford University Press, 1971); Neal Wood, *Cicero's Social and Political Thought* (Berkeley: University of California Press, 1988).

It is Reason, moreover, that has inspired man with a relish for his kind
... she has prompted the individual, starting from friendship and from
family affection, to expand his interests, forming social ties first with his
fellow-citizens and later with all mankind.... Nature has also engendered
in mankind the desire of contemplating truth.... This primary instinct
leads us ... to hate things insincere, false and deceptive, such as cheating,
perjury, malice and injustice. Further, Reason possesses an intrinsic element of dignity ... suited rather to require obedience than to render it....
These three kinds of moral goodness being noted, there follows a fourth
kind ... combining in itself the other three. This is the principle of order
and of restraint.[27]

We are confronted with moral duties in every aspect of our lives, whether private or public, whether at business or at home, whether one is working on what
concerns oneself alone or is dealing with another. To neglect these duties is always
morally wrong.

Cicero defines justice as rendering to every man his due, with the faithful dis-
charge of all obligations occasioned by that principle.

The first office of justice is to keep one man from doing harm to another,
unless provoked by wrong; and the next is to lead men to use common
possessions for the common interests, private property for their own.

There is, however, no such thing as private ownership established by
nature, but property becomes private either through long occupancy ...
or through conquest or by due process of law, bargain, or purchase, or by
allotment....

Again, there are certain duties that we owe even to those who have
wronged us. For there is a limit to retribution and to punishment; or rather,
I am inclined to think, it is sufficient that the aggressor should be brought
to repent of his wrong-doing, in order that he may not repeat the offence
and that others may be deterred from doing wrong.

---

[27] *De Finibus Bonorum et Malorum [About the Ends of Goods and Evils]*, trans. by H. Rackham,
The Loeb Classical Library (Cambridge: Harvard University Press, 1914), II, xiv, 45–47, pp.
133–35. Cicero's four kinds of moral goodness are simply a restatement of the Platonic four virtues:
wisdom ("contemplating truth"), justice ("to hate things, etc."), courage ("element of dignity"), and
temperance ("principle of order and restraint").

Then, too, in the case of a state in its external relations, the rights of war must be strictly observed. For since there are two ways of settling a dispute: first, by discussion; second, by physical force; and since the former is characteristic of man, the latter of the brute, we must resort to force only in case we may not avail ourselves of discussion. The only excuse, therefore, for going to war is that we may live in peace unharmed; and when the victory is won, we should spare those who have not been blood-thirsty and barbarous in their warfare....

But let us remember that we must have regard for justice even towards the humblest. Now the humblest station and the poorest fortune are those of slaves; and they give us no bad rule who bid us treat our slaves as we should our employees; they must be required to work; they must be given their dues.[28]

It is Cicero's conviction that there is a natural law that governs the entire universe. Inanimate objects are compelled to obey it by natural necessity; animals conform to it by instinct; humans are obliged to obey it by virtue of their capacity to reason. Humans are not compelled to obey the law, they are obliged to do so. Cicero identifies this law with the primal and ultimate mind of God, the right reason of supreme Jupiter. He explains his conception in a passage of the *Republic*, which has become a classic description:

True law is right reason in agreement with nature; it is of universal application, unchanging and everlasting; it summons to duty by its commands and averts from wrongdoing by its prohibitions. And it does not lay its command or prohibitions upon good men in vain, though neither have any effect on the wicked. It is a sin to try to alter this law, nor is it allowed to attempt to repeal any part of it, and it is impossible to abolish it entirely. We cannot be freed from its obligations by senate or people, and we need not look outside ourselves for an expounder or interpreter of it. And there will not be different laws at Rome and at Athens, or different laws now and in the future, but one eternal and unchangeable law will be valid for all nations and all times, and there will be one master and ruler, that is, God, over us

---

[28] *De Officis [On Moral Duty]*, trans. W. Miller, The Loeb Classical Library, Vol. XXI (Cambridge: Harvard University Press, 1975), I, vii, 20–21; xi, 33–35; xiii, 41, pp. 23, 35–37, 45.

all, for he is the author of this law, its promulgator, and its enforcing judge. Whoever is disobedient is fleeing from himself and denying his human nature, and by reason of this very fact he will suffer the worst penalties, even if he escapes what is commonly considered punishment....[29]

This idea of a natural law is taken over by many Christian thinkers and persists for several centuries. It is not seriously challenged until relatively modern times, and it still has its defenders in the twentieth century.[30] It is one of the great legacies of Roman thought. The conviction that there is such a law carries with it the notion that the allegiance that the citizen owes to the laws of his own state is conditional, not absolute, and that laws that do not conform in principle to the natural law no more deserve to be called laws than the rules of a band of robbers.

Plato taught us in the *Statesman* that laws that do not conform to reason are not true laws, but he thought only a philosopher like himself was qualified to make this kind of political judgment. Cicero, by way of contrast, appears more sanguine about the possibility of most persons using their reason to make a similar judgment:

> This is a sufficient proof that there is no difference in kind between man and man; for ... reason which alone raises us above the level of the beasts and enables us to draw inferences, to prove and disprove, to discuss and solve problems, and to come to conclusions, is certainly common to us all, though varying in what it learns, at least in the capacity to learn it is invariable.... In fact, there is no human being of any race who, if he finds a guide, cannot attain to virtue.[31]

It is this professed emphasis upon the essential equality of human beings that distinguishes Cicero's thought from that of Aristotle and, some would argue, even from that of Plato. The equality comes from the common potential capacity (reason)

---

[29] *De Re Publica [The Republic]*, trans. C.W. Keyes, The Loeb Classical Library, Vol. XVI (Cambridge: Harvard University Press, 1977), III, xxii, 33–34, p. 211.

[30] A superb case for the philosophical viability of natural law, unmediated by later Catholic thought, is made by John Finnis, *Natural Law and Natural Rights* (Oxford: Oxford University Press, 1980). The liveliness of the tradition is demonstrated by the contemporary articles in Robert P. George, ed., *Natural Law Theory* (New York: Oxford University Press, 1992).

[31] *De Legibus [Laws]*, trans. by C.W. Keyes, The Loeb Classical Library, Vol. XVI (Cambridge: Harvard University Press, 1977), I, x, 30–31, pp. 329–31.

to participate in the *logos* of Nature. This ability provides the consoling perspective of philosophy for all of the Stoics. It is not equality among unique persons but rather the "equality" that comes from the loss of the individual's particular but ephemeral attributes, woes, and delights into the universal *logos*. Cicero is quite explicit: "We must realize also that we are invested by nature with two characters as it were: one of these is universal, arising from the fact of our being all alike endowed with reason and with superiority which lifts us above the brute. From this all morality and propriety are derived, and upon it depends the rational method of ascertaining our duty. The other character is to be assigned to individuals in particular."[32]

Although the Stoic's concept of natural law—even the explicit and eloquent egalitarian version of Cicero—was held implicitly to be compatible with sexual inequality, class differences, and slavery, the clear enunciation of the idea of a mankind or a human race with its universal common nature was an enormous achievement.[33] Nevertheless, the concern for equality expressed by Cicero was not meant to weaken the need for aristocratic rule or, at least, for the rule by those knowledgeable in the art of government. More so than the Greeks, the Romans, a generally unphilosophical people, accentuated the duty to take part in governing and political life. This political participation, however, was primarily limited to men. The family was in the private realm and ruled by the husband. For Cicero particularly, there is no equality of sexes, and women are politically invisible. Aristotle, some would argue, sees a political contribution of sorts made by women; Plato has equality and full participation; and Cicero has no role for women.[34]

All humans (and gods) are members of a universal commonwealth of reason, and it is this commonwealth that is "natural" to man, not the particular political society in which the individual holds his citizenship. This idea of a

---

[32] *De Officis*, I, xxx, 107, p. 109.

[33] A philosophical analysis of the idea of mankind and of an ecumenic age is given by Dante Germino, *Political Philosophy and the Open Society* (Baton Rouge: Louisiana State University Press, 1982), pp. 83–108, and Eric Voegelin, *Order and History*, Vol. IV, *The Ecumenic Age* (Baton Rouge: Louisiana State University Press, 1974).

[34] Some of the early Stoics and later Stoics, such as Seneca, did explicitly recognize women as equal: "But who has asserted that Nature has dealt grudgingly with women's natures and has narrowly restricted their virtues? Believe me, they have just as much force, just as much capacity, if they like, for virtuous action…." Seneca, "To Marcia: On Consolation," *Seneca: Moral Essays*, Vol. II, trans. John W. Basore, The Loeb Classical Library (Cambridge: Harvard University Press, 1935), I, xvi, p. 49. Arlene W. Saxonhouse has a full discussion of women in ancient Rome. *Women in the History of Political Thought: Ancient Greece to Machiavelli* (New York: Praeger, 1985), pp. 93–124.

"dual citizenship" is a representation of the "dual loyalty" theme found in the thought of Plato and Aristotle, and it is an idea that is taken over by Christian thinkers and perpetuated by them.[35]

Membership in the universal commonwealth of reason does not exclude membership in a particular state. Indeed, it requires the individual to perform the duties of citizenship in particular states so long as those duties conform to the natural law. It is precisely because humans are social by nature and have a capacity to understand the demands of justice that states come into existence. Says Cicero:

> ... a commonwealth is the property of a people. But a people is not any collection of human beings brought together in any sort of way, but an assemblage of people in large numbers associated in an agreement with respect to justice and a partnership for the common good. The first cause of such an association is not so much the weakness of the individual as a certain social spirit which nature has implanted in man. For man is not a solitary or unsocial creature, but born with such a nature that not even under conditions of great prosperity of every sort (is he willing to be isolated from his fellow men)....[36]

The state, for Cicero, is a "partnership in law" (*juris societas*) and comes about by virtue of an "agreement" among the people with respect to the law. Some scholars have interpreted Cicero's theory as implying that the state comes into being as the result of a contract. Although his theory obviously implies that the people "consent" to government, it is not clear that he thought in terms of an actual contract. But here is certainly found the germ of the idea that government should rest upon the consent of the governed. Legitimate political power derives from the people.

---

[35] In the *Republic*, Plato described a commonwealth better than any actual commonwealth, a "city in speech," and said that whether such a city ever will exist in fact is of no matter, for the philosopher will "live after the manner of that city and of no other." But his invitation to join him in the life of such a city is extended, some think, only to the very few who have the capacity to be philosophers. Only the philosopher would then participate in that "dual citizenship" which Cicero would extend to all reasonable men. Others argue that, for Plato, all humans as humans are capable of attaining justice in their souls. See the discussion in Chapter 1.

[36] *De Re Publica*, I, xxv, 39–40, p. 65.

In his emphasis upon the *law* as the source of the state itself, there is a marked departure from the thought of Plato and Aristotle. Cicero's theory differs from theirs not only in this respect but also by virtue of his insistence that all men have equal rights under the law. The idea of individual rights protected by the law is peculiarly Roman in origin. The law, moreover, is binding alike upon the governor and the governed: "… the function of the magistrate is to govern and to give commands which are just and beneficial and in conformity with the law. For as the laws govern the magistrate, so the magistrate governs the people, and it may be truly be said that the magistrate is a speaking law, and the law a silent magistrate."[37] This is one of the first expressions of the thought that a government of men is legitimate only when it is also a government of laws.

Although not a philosopher, Cicero was more successful than he knew at introducing philosophy, particularly Stoic ethics, to the practical Romans. His eloquent writings were immensely influential and remained so even after the entrance of Christianity into the Western world.[38]

THE ROMAN LAW

Around 450 B.C. the customary law peculiar to the Romans was written down in a code known as the Twelve Tables. This came to be known as the *jus civile* (civil law). It was one of the functions of the consul to interpret this law. Around 367 B.C. this function was entrusted to a new elective magistrate known as the *praetor*. As the alien population of Rome increased, and as her contact with foreigners broadened, it was necessary to provide some way of adjudicating disputes among foreigners and between Romans and foreigners. Consequently, in 247 B.C. a new praetorship was created to serve this function. The *praetor peregrinus*, as he came to be known, based his judicial judgments on the principles of Roman civil law, on the customs of the persons whose cases he was adjudicating, and on

---

[37] *De Legibus*, III, i, 2–3, pp. 459–61.

[38] The following contain brief but useful surveys: Robert N. Wilkin, "Cicero and the Law of Nature," in *Origins of the Natural Law Tradition*, ed. Arthur L. Harding (Port Washington: Kennikat Press, 1971), pp. 1–25; Paul E. Sigmund, *Natural Law in Political Thought* (Cambridge: Winthrop Publishers, 1971), pp. 20–35; Passerin A. d'Entrèves, *Natural Law: An Introduction to Legal Philosophy* (London: Hutchinson University Library, 1951), pp. 17–32; Lloyd L. Weinreb, *Natural Law and Justice* (Cambridge: Harvard University Press, 1987), pp. 1–46; Wood, *Cicero's Social and Political Thought*, pp. 1–14.

his own common sense of justice. At the beginning of his term of office, each praetor issued an edit summing up the law he intended to administer and giving him an opportunity to modify it when he thought that was desirable. Gradually, there developed a new body of law known as the ***jus gentium*** (or the law of the tribes). This was essentially judge-made law based upon custom and common sense. It was not law that had been legislated. The task of blending the two systems of law, the *jus civile* and the *jus gentium*, fell to the great Roman jurists writing during the second and third centuries A.D. Roman law was susceptible to change and development, and it came to be regarded as a law for persons as persons, not simply as a law for men as citizens. During the Republic the law was studied and expounded by educated persons who came to be known as *jurisprudentes*, and their opinions were often sought by judges and influenced the judges' decisions. Even under the Empire, when emperors became the supreme lawgivers, the emperors frequently consulted these "licensed consultants" for authoritative answers to legal questions. And it was through the commentaries of the *jurisprudentes* that Greek philosophical ideas, as filtered through the Hellenistic schools, came to be perpetuated through the Roman law.

Two of the most famous jurists who wrote commentaries during the period of the Empire were Gaius (A.D.110–180) and Ulpian (A.D. 170–228). Following the lead of Cicero, Gaius declared that "Whatever any people itself has established as law for it, this is confined to it alone and is called the *jus civile*, as a kind of law peculiar to the state; whatever, on the other hand, natural reason has established among men, this is observed uniformly among all peoples and is called the *jus gentium*, as a kind of law which all races employ. And so the Roman people employ a law partly peculiar to themselves and partly common to all men."[39] In short, Gaius identified the *jus gentium* with the natural law. He distinguishes between the *lex* established by the people and the *jus gentium*.[40] There is a clear implication in the commentaries of Gaius that the validity of all enactments stems from the authorization of the people. Even the Emperor himself, Gaius argued, receives his authority from a *lex*. This idea is repeated in Justinian's *Institutes* where it says that "what

---

[39] Quoted by C.H. McIlwain, *The Growth of Political Thought in the West* (New York: Macmillan & Co., 1932), p. 122.

[40] It is interesting to note that in most every language except English there are two words that can be translated as law. In Latin, the two words are *lex* and *jus*, in German *Gesetz* and *Recht*, in French *loi* and *droit*. The words *jus*, *Recht*, and *droit* mean not only law but also right.

the prince has pleased to ordain has the force of law since by a regal law (*lex regia*) enacted concerning his *imperium* (authority), the people has conceded to him and conferred upon him the whole of its *imperium* and *potestas* (power)."[41] By whomever a law may be enacted, whether a popular assembly, a vote of some part of the people, a Senate, an edict of a magistrate, or a decree by an emperor, it is ultimately law because the people have authorized it. The Roman jurists did not discuss, however, the question whether a law could be revoked by the people nor suggest, apart from the idea of a *lex regia*, how popular responsibility might be enforced.

A generation after Gaius, Ulpian distinguished the *jus gentium* from the natural law. He taught that the natural law was a law common to all animals and not peculiar to humans. From it, however, he derived the sanction for marriage, the duty to care for one's offspring, and the right to repel violence. He described the *jus gentium* as being common only to humans in relation to each other. Slavery was a creation not of the natural law but of the *jus gentium*, for by the natural law all born were born free.[42] By the *jus gentium* another jurist, Hermogenian, said:

> wars were introduced, nations marked off, realms established, rights of ownership distinguished, bounds set to fields, houses built, traffic, purchase and sale, letting and hiring and all sorts of obligations instituted except a few introduced under the *jus civile*.
>
> The *jus gentium* is common to the whole human race. For, urged on by custom and human needs, tribes of men established certain rules for themselves....[43]

The distinction Ulpian drew between the natural law and the *jus gentium* was followed by the jurists who came after him. By the middle of the third century A.D. there is no longer any important writing by jurists. An effort was

---

[41] Quoted by McIlwain, *The Growth of Political Thought in the West*, p. 128. McIlwain relates that a part of such law "conferring the *imperium* and *potestas* upon Vespasian in 69–70 A.D. was found on a bronze tablet unearthed in Rome in the fourteenth century," p. 129.

[42] "Natural law is that which all animals have been taught by nature; this law is not peculiar to the human species, it is common to all animals.... *Jus gentium* is the law used by the various tribes of mankind, and there is no difficulty in seeing that it falls short of natural law, as the latter is common to all animated beings, whereas the former is only common to human beings in respect of their mutual relations...." Ulpian, "On Justice and Law," in Sigmund, *Natural Law in Political Thought*, pp. 32–33.

[43] Quoted by McIlwain, *The Growth of Political Thought in the West*, p. 127.

made to codify the Roman law in the fourth century under the Emperor Diocletian, but the great work of codification took place in the sixth century A.D. under the Emperor Justinian.[44]

Roman law declined in importance with the collapse of the Roman Empire, but it survived, in part, through its influence upon Roman Catholic canon law and its rediscovery by scholars at the University of Bologna in the twelfth century A.D. When the modern nation-state began to emerge, Roman law was used by national monarchs in constructing their own legal systems. With the notable exception of England, the Roman law provided the foundation for almost all modern European and Latin American legal systems. The law was Rome's greatest legacy to the modern world.[45]

CONCLUSIONS

Of the many schools and philosophies that appeared during the Hellenistic Age, Stoicism was the most important. After its introduction to the Romans, it became dominant within the Western world. It cannot be said that Stoicism had a political program or, perhaps, even a political philosophy, but, at its best, Stoicism enabled its practitioners to conduct themselves ethically and honourably and to meet courageously the vicissitudes of human existence.

---

[44] P.G. Stein, "Roman Law," in *The Cambridge History of Medieval Political Thought: c. 350 – c. 1450* (Cambridge: Cambridge University Press, 1988), pp. 37–47; Barry Nicholas, *An Introduction to Roman Law* (Oxford: Clarendon Press, 1962), pp. 1–59; Michael Bertram Crowe, *The Changing Profile of the Natural Law* (The Hague: Martinus Nijhoff, 1977), pp. 28–135; Charles Howard McIlwain, *Constitutionalism: Ancient and Modern* (Ithaca: Cornell University Press, 1940).

[45] Two other contributions should be mentioned, though they are not strictly philosophical. Hannah Arendt, a modern political philosopher, has argued that Rome integrated the inherently "utopian" Greek political philosophy with authority and tradition. She believes that the Roman understanding of authority and tradition was original and has made an essential contribution to the West. Authority and religion for the Romans, unlike the Greeks, were tied to the tradition flowing from the original act of founding Rome. The sacredness of the foundation, she contends, gave Rome its political authority. Patriotism and obligation were derived from this particular tradition rather than from a philosophical realm. "The Roman trinity of religion, authority, and tradition," she states, was "taken over by the Christian era." The Church as an institution thus is, in part, a reflection of the Roman legacy. *Between Past and Future* (New York: Viking Press, 1968), pp. 120, 126–27. In another work she suggests that the theme of a foundation "might well have been the most important single notion which the men of the [American] Revolution adopted, not by conscious reflection, but by virtue of being nourished by the classics and of having gone to school in Roman antiquity." *On Revolution* (New York: Viking Press, 1965), pp. 202–03.

The Stoics taught, as we have seen, that the human capacity for thinking and speaking, the *logos*, was also immanent in reality. The rational structure of reality was a reflection of the same *logos*. Nature in the cosmos was fundamentally one with nature within mankind. Thus, cosmic events and human events are intertwined. To act with Nature is to be true to oneself and to Providence, and to act harmoniously with Nature, they repeatedly claimed, is to be good and wise. As Zeno originally argued, following Socrates, knowledge and goodness are thus tied. With knowledge, one can engage in right action and avoid evil. This Stoic philosophy is more clearly within the political philosophy tradition of Plato and Aristotle than those of the competing schools.[46] A wise man would, when possible, take part in political life.[47]

Stoicism, for a time, seemed to fit the needs of a ruling class with an empire. Providence did rule the world they inhabited and ran, and Stoicism was also a source of consolation when something went wrong within it. But with the collapse of Rome—civil war, barbarism, and plagues—other philosophies, particularly neo-Platonism, and religions emerged, promising their adherents more. Christianity was one of these. To a greater extent than Stoicism, Christianity appealed to more than a courageous and wise elite, and it promised personal and eternal happiness rather than the consolation of enduring within an impersonal, providential Nature. Nevertheless, Stoicism did leave its mark on Christian ethics and, above all, on the evolution of law.[48]

---

[46] Long, *Hellenistic Philosophy*, pp. 150–52.

[47] Sandbach, "Stoicism and Politics," in *The Stoics*, pp. 140–48. Sandbach concludes that Stoicism "must have had some undefinable general influence that favoured conscientious administration for the benefit of the ordinary man and a humanitarianism that resulted in a little legislation and some charitable foundations. The Greco-Roman world would have been a worse place without its philosophers." (p. 148)

[48] Long, *Hellenistic Philosophy*, pp. 232–48; Edwyn Bevan, "Hellenistic Popular Philosophy," in Bury, *The Hellenistic Age*, pp. 97–107; E.R. Dodds, *Pagan and Christian in an Age of Anxiety* (Cambridge: Cambridge University Press, 1965), pp. 102–38; Marcia L. Colish, *The Stoic Tradition from Classical Antiquity to the Early Middle Ages*, examines the precise influence of Stoicism on Roman Law, Vol. II, pp. 341–89. For later influence, see: Gerhard Oestreich, *Neo-Stoicism and the Early Modern State* (Cambridge: Cambridge University Press, 1983); Marc Raeff, *The Well-Ordered Police State* (New Haven: Yale University Press, 1983).

SUGGESTIONS FOR FURTHER READING

For beginning a study of the Hellenistic Age Ehrenberg, "The Hellenistic Age," in *Man, State and Deity* and Bevan, "Hellenistic Popular Philosophy," in Bury et al., *The Hellenistic Age* are excellent essays. Bréhier and Copleston provide short introductions to major figures. Zeller, Rist (*Stoic Philosophy*), Hicks, and Colish are all full studies of the period. Long (*Hellenistic Philosophy*), and Sandbach are particularly valuable, and Colish is encyclopedic in tracing the influence of Stoicism on later thinkers.

For Epicurus, Rist (*Epicurus: An Introduction*) provides a complete treatment. Nichols and Frischer examine special themes. Furley is a careful treatment of Epicurean philosophy, and comparisons are made with Aristotle and modern thought.

For Cicero, Rawson is a large standard biography. Mitchell and Stockton study Cicero's political career. Bailey is a highly readable introduction to Cicero's thought and life, and Wood gives an excellent description of Cicero's political philosophy.

Schofied and Striker, Long (*Problems in Stoicism*), Burnyeat, and Rist (*The Stoics*) contain specialized essays on philosophical problems of the different schools.

Hunt explains the materialist conception of nature held by Zeno. Sambursky relates the Stoic position to modern science.

Baldry and Voegelin (*The Ecumenic Age*) deal with the emergence of the idea of mankind, one common humanity.

D'Entrèves, Harding, Weinreb, and Sigmund provide introductory essays on the evolution of the idea of natural law. Finnis reargues the case for natural law and analyzes the original Stoic arguments.

Translations

Chilton, C.W. *Diogenes of Oenoanda: The Fragments.* London: Oxford University Press, 1971.

Inwood, Brad, and L.P. Gerson, trans. *Hellenistic Philosophy: Introductory Readings.* Indianapolis: Hackett, 1988.

The Loeb Classical Library (Cambridge: Harvard University Press) has translated the main surviving works of the Stoics and other Hellenistic philosophers.

Long, A.A., and D.N. Sedley, trans. *The Hellenistic Philosophers: Translation of the Principal Sources with Philosophical Commentary.* 2 Vols. Cambridge: Cambridge University Press, 1987.

Commentaries

Bailey, D.R. Shackleton. *Cicero.* New York: Scribner's Sons, 1971.

Baldry, H.C. *The Unity of Mankind in Greek Thought.* Cambridge: Cambridge University Press, 1965.

Barnes, J., M. Burnyeat, and M. Schofield, eds. *Doubt and Dogmatism: Studies in Hellenistic Epistemology.* New York: Oxford University Press, 1979.

Bréhier, Émile. *The History of Philosophy.* Vol. II. *The Hellenistic and Roman Age.* Translated by Wade Baskin. Chicago: University of Chicago Press, 1965.

Burnyeat, M., ed. *The Skeptical Tradition.* Berkeley: University of California Press, 1983.

Bury, J.B., et al. *The Hellenistic Age.* Cambridge: Cambridge University Press, 1925.

Carlyle, A.J., and R.W. Carlyle. *History of Mediaeval Political Thought in the West.* 6 Vols. Edinburgh: Blackwood and Sons, 1903–1936.

Colish, Marcia L. *The Stoic Tradition from Classical Antiquity to the Early Middle Ages.* 2 Vols. Leiden: Brill, 1985.

Copleston, Frederick. *A History of Philosophy.* Vol. I, Part II. Garden City, N.Y.: Image Books, 1962.

D'Entrèves, Passerin Alexandra. *Natural Law: An Introduction to Legal Philosophy.* London: Hutchinson University Library, 1951.

Finnis, John. *Natural Law and Natural Rights.* Oxford: Clarendon Press, 1980.

Frischer, Bernard. *The Sculpted Word: Epicureanism and Philosophical Recruitment in Ancient Greece.* Berkeley: University of California Press, 1982.

Furley, David J. *Two Studies in the Greek Atomists.* Princeton: Princeton University Press, 1967.

Harding, Arthur L., ed. *Origins of the Natural Law Tradition.* Port Washington, N.Y.: Kennikat Press, 1971.

Hicks, R.D. *Stoic and Epicurean.* New York: Russell & Russell, 1962.

Hunt, H.A.K. *A Physical Interpretation of the Universe: The Doctrines of Zeno the Stoic.* Carlton, Aust.: Melbourne University Press, 1976.

Inwood, Brad. *Ethics and Human Action in Early Stoicism.* Oxford: Clarendon Press, 1985.

Long, A.A. *Hellenistic Philosophy.* 2nd ed. Berkeley: University of California Press, 1986.

_____, ed. *Problems in Stoicism.* London: The Athlone Press, 1971.

McIlwain, C.H. *The Growth of Political Thought in the West.* New York: Macmillan & Co., 1932.

Mitchell, T.N. *Cicero: The Ascending Years.* New Haven: Yale University Press, 1979.

Nichols, Jr., James H. *Epicurean Political Philosophy: The "De rerum natura" of Lucretius.* Ithaca: Cornell University Press, 1976.

Nicolas, Barry. *An Introduction to Roman Law.* Oxford: Clarendon Press, 1962.

Rawson, Elizabeth. *Cicero: A Portrait.* Ithaca: Cornell University Press, 1983.

Reesor, Margaret E. *The Political Theory of the Old and Middle Stoa.* New York: Augustin, 1951.

Rist, J.M. *Epicurus: An Introduction.* Cambridge: Cambridge University Press, 1972.

_____. *Stoic Philosophy.* Cambridge: Cambridge University Press, 1969.

_____, ed. *The Stoics.* Berkeley: University of California Press, 1978.

Sambursky, S. *Physics of the Stoics.* London: Routledge & Kegan Paul, 1959.

Sandbach, F.H. *The Stoics.* London: Chatto & Windus, 1975.

Schofied, M., and G. Striker, eds. *The Norms of Nature.* Cambridge: Cambridge University Press, 1986.

Sigmund, Paul E. *Natural Law in Political Thought.* Cambridge: Winthrop Publishers, 1971.

Stockton, David. *Cicero: A Political Biography.* London: Oxford University Press, 1971.

Voegelin, Eric. *Order and History.* Vol. IV. *The Ecumenic Age.* Baton Rouge: Louisiana State University Press, 1974.

Weinreb, Lloyd L. *Natural Law and Justice.* Cambridge: Harvard University Press, 1987.

Wenley, *Stoicism and Its Influence.* New York: Cooper Square, 1963.

Wood, Neal. *Cicero's Social and Political Thought.* Berkeley: University of California Press, 1988.

Zeller, E. *The Stoics, Epicureans and Sceptics.* Translated by Oswald J. Reichel. New York: Russell & Russell, 1962.

Social and Political Background

Adcock, F.E. *Roman Political Ideas.* Ann Arbor: University of Michigan Press, 1959.

Boardman, Jasper Griffin, and Oswyn Murray, eds. *The Oxford History of the Classical World.* Oxford: Oxford University Press, 1986.

Cantarella, Eva. *Pandora's Daughter: The Role and Status of Women in Greek and Roman Antiquity.* Baltimore: Johns Hopkins University Press, 1987.

de Ste. Croix, G.E.M. *The Class Struggle in the Ancient World.* Ithaca: Cornell University Press, 1981.

Dodds, E.R. *Pagan and Christian in an Age of Anxiety.* Cambridge: Cambridge University Press, 1965.

Earl, Donald. *The Moral and Political Tradition of Rome.* Ithaca: Cornell University Press, 1967.

Ehrenberg, Victor. *Man, State and Deity: Essays in Ancient History.* London: Methuen, 1974.

Finley, M.I., *Aspects of Antiquity: Discoveries and Controversies.* 2nd ed. London: Penguin Books, 1977.

Grant, Michael. *History of Rome.* New York: Scribner's Sons, 1978.

Jonas, Hans. *The Gnostic Religion.* 2nd ed. Boston: Beacon Press, 1963.

Lefkowitz, Mary R., and Maureen B. Fant, trans. *Women's Life in Greece and Rome: A Source Book in Translation.* Baltimore: Johns Hopkins University Press, 1982.

Meyer, Marvin W., ed. *The Ancient Mysteries: A Sourcebook.* New York: Harper & Row, 1987.

Rawson, Elizabeth. *Intellectual Life in the Late Roman Republic.* Baltimore: Johns Hopkins University Press, 1985.

Starr, Chester G. *The Roman Empire, 27 B.C.–A.D. 476: A Study in Survival.* New York: Oxford University Press, 1982.

ST. AUGUSTINE AND THE EARLY MIDDLE AGES

Western civilization is a cultural fabric woven of many strands. Its understanding of ultimate reality and the nature and destiny of humanity, its aspirations, and its peculiar institutional forms derive not only from Greek philosophy, Stoicism, and Roman law but also from a religious tradition, which we frequently refer to as Hebraic-Christian. The Christian tradition is indeed an important element in the formation of the Western consciousness of the meaning of existence, and it has a close affinity, as we shall see, with the Greek philosophical tradition and with Judaism.[1]

Christianity emerged not as a philosophical system of thought but as a religion centred upon the life and teaching of a particular person, in a particular historical setting. The New Testament is not a philosophical work but is an account of the life and teaching of the man Jesus whom his followers, then and now, believed to be the Son of God. Jesus was a Jew, as were his original disciples and the great majority of his early followers, and throughout his lifetime he preached in the Jewish synagogues. The Old Testament is an integral part of the Christian Bible and without it there would have been no New Testament. It is essential to

---

[1] The historians, J.H. Hexter and Hugh Trevor-Roper, have each written an excellent brief introduction to the Hebraic-Christian tradition: J.H. Hexter, *The Judaeo-Christian Tradition* (New York: Harper & Row, 1966); Hugh Trevor-Roper, *The Rise of Christian Europe* (New York: Harcourt, 1965). See also, Emil Fackenheim, *What Is Judaism? An Interpretation for the Present Age* (New York: Summit, 1987).

an understanding of Christianity to understand the Hebraic tradition from which it has sprung, but that tradition has an importance of its own wholly apart from its influence upon Christianity.[2]

THE HEBRAIC TRADITION

In the Greco-Roman world the Jews were a tiny minority, bound together as a community by a common faith and a common history. They regarded Palestine as their homeland and Jerusalem as their capital city, but for a period of five centuries they had no political power and no political homeland. They had been driven out of Palestine and had lived dispersed throughout the Greco-Roman world. They had been enslaved by the Babylonians, who had destroyed the Temple in Jerusalem in 586 B.C. In 538 B.C. the Babylonians gave their Jewish captives permission to return to their homeland, and by 516 B.C. the Temple in Jerusalem had been rebuilt. Although Jerusalem again became the centre of Jewish religious life, the Jews remained politically subject to Persia. When Alexander the Great conquered the Persians the Jews were temporarily liberated, but following the death of Alexander they were ruled first by the Ptolemies and then by the Seleucids.

In spite of being a subject people, until the reign of the Seleucid king, Antiochus IV Epiphanes (175 – 164 B.C.), they enjoyed religious freedom. In 168 B.C. he forbade all Jews to celebrate their religious festivals or even to observe the Sabbath, and he ordered all copies of the Law to be destroyed. He also commanded the Jews to worship at pagan altars. King Antiochus's attempt to Hellenize the Jews, however, met with resistance. Although virtually without weapons and military experience, the Jews, under the leadership of Judas Maccabaeus, managed to defeat their oppressors. They secured a peace treaty from Antiochus, and reoccupied the Temple at Jerusalem; for a short time they again enjoyed a measure of political independence. This victory is celebrated by Jews today in the festival of Hannukah.

---

[2] For the Old Testament and political theory, see Ernest Barker, *From Alexander to Constantine: Passages and Documents Illustrating the History of Social and Political Ideas* (Oxford: Clarendon Press, 1956), pp. 129–66; William A. Irwin, "The Hebrews," in H. and H.A. Frankfort, *The Intellectual Adventure of Ancient Man* (Chicago: University of Chicago Press, 1946), pp. 223–359; Eric Voegelin, *Order and History*, Vol. I, *Israel and Revelation* (Baton Rouge: Louisiana State University Press, 1956); Nicholas De Lange, *Judaism* (Oxford: Oxford University Press, 1986).

As Roman political power increased, however, the Jews sought the protection of the Roman authorities, and in 63 B.C. the territory in which they lived came under Roman rule. Rome first sent Pompey, and later Herod, as ruler of Judaea and Samaria. Herod, who was installed as a puppet king in 37 B.C. and ruled until 4 B.C., again sought to Hellenize the life of Palestine and, again, met with resistance. From A.D. 6 until A.D. 66 Palestine was governed by Roman procurators. One of these procurators was Pontius Pilate (A.D. 26 – 36). In A.D. 66, when Roman procurators attempted to interfere with their religious practices, the Jews staged an armed rebellion. Once again Jerusalem was under attack, and the Temple was destroyed in A.D. 70. Following the conquest of Jerusalem by the Romans, the Jews were ordered to leave Palestine and not until the twentieth century was a portion of Palestine restored to them as their homeland.

The peculiarly Hebraic understanding of the way in which God reveals himself is through history, and much of the Old Testament (the first 17 books) records the trials and sufferings experienced by the Jews throughout many centuries. The prophetic books of the Old Testament record the responses of particular Hebrew prophets to actual historical situations. History is experienced as a dialogue between Yahweh (Jehovah) and his creature, man.

Many images are invoked throughout the Old Testament to try to capture the nature of Yahweh (judge, king, father, mother, husband, potter), and the language is often anthropomorphic, yet no image or symbol can wholly capture his nature. God is the Creator and Sustainer of the universe, the Source of all that is, and the Sovereign Ruler whose concern for his creatures is Providential. He is good and is the source of all righteousness. God is both near and remote, both the Eternally Present and the Wholly Other, and this tension can never be resolved. God remains an awful Presence and yet a mysterious Absence, for no one can see him and live. The commandment that "Thou shalt have no other gods before me" is an injunction not to attempt to define God or to conceptualize him, for in that endeavour lies man's temptation to try to manage him for his own purposes.

In the Old Testament, God is shown to reveal himself not in words but in historical experiences. Thus, it was through God's revelation (disclosure) of himself when the Jews were brought out of slavery in Egypt that they became a nation (Israel). It is recorded in Exod. 19:1–6:

> On the third new moon after the people of Israel had gone forth out of the land of Egypt, on that day they came into the wilderness of Sinai....

And Moses went up to God, and the Lord called to him out of the mountain, saying, "Thus you shall say to the house of Jacob, and tell the people of Israel:

You have seen what I did to the Egyptians, and how I bore you on eagles' wings, and brought you to myself.

Now therefore, if you will obey my voice and keep my covenant, you shall be my own possession among all peoples; for all the earth is mine,

And you shall be to me a kingdom of priests, and an holy nation."

Through Moses, God extends an invitation to the Jews to enter into a covenant with him. The Ten Commandments, revealed through Moses, disclose the nature of God's order in this world, and by accepting the obligation to receive and follow them, Israel testifies to God's righteousness and mercy to all the nations of the world. Israel is chosen by God to represent him as the fount of justice, and in choosing to enter into this covenant with God, Israel becomes a community anointed not only as a holy people but also one that may be called upon to endure suffering for the sake of righteousness. The story of the Exodus relates the escape from Egyptian oppression, the struggles in the wilderness, and the goal of the promised land in Canaan. It is a story of both a spiritual and a historical progression from political oppression and suffering to spiritual redemption. Later works reiterate and expand these themes. Isaiah 49:3 and 6 declares: "You are my servant, Israel, in whom I will be glorified.... I will give you as a light to the nations, that my salvation may reach to the end of the earth." There is also the suggestion that in witnessing to God's concern that justice should triumph upon this earth Israel would have to suffer vicariously for all the nations who rebelled against him. Isaiah 53:4–6, speaking of Israel through the personal pronoun, says:

Surely he has borne our griefs and carried our sorrows; yet we esteemed him stricken, smitten by God, and afflicted.

But he was wounded for our transgressions, he was bruised for our iniquities; upon him was the chastisement that made us whole, and with his stripes we are healed.

And we like sheep have gone astray;

We have turned everyone to his own way; and the Lord has laid on him the iniquity of us all.

The Book of Psalms weaves together all the strands of the Jewish faith as it speaks of the majesty of the law, the love and mercy of God, his providential concern for all of his creatures, his concern for social justice, and the fulfilment of his judgment in history. The devotional poetry of the Psalms not only lies at the heart of Jewish piety but also is an integral part of the Christian liturgy. It has a universal appeal; it speaks to every human emotion and describes the plight and hopes not only of Jews but also of humankind.

The prophetic literature with which the Old Testament closes speaks frequently of the great gulf that separates God's intentions for the world from the rebellious activities of human beings in defiance of his will. Israel is frequently accused of being unfaithful to the Covenant, and the judgment of God is called down upon the iniquity of humanity. There are no more passionate expressions of righteous indignation in the face of social injustice than in this prophetic literature. "For the first time," Eric Voegelin suggests, "men experienced the clash between divinely willed and humanly realized order of history in its stark brutality, and the souls of the prophets were the battlefield in this war of the spirit."[3] The prophets were speaking of that struggle for order or meaning in history that takes place in the existence of every human being whose soul is open to the Word of God. What, they were asking, is the proper source of order or meaning in human existence? Is it to be found in human creations, great empires and civilizations, or, as the prophets proclaimed, in following Yahweh and the Covenant? Professor Voegelin summarizes the universal significance of Hebraic prophecy by saying:

> "Israel" is not the empirical human beings who may or may not keep the Covenant, but the expansion of divine creation into the order of man and society. No amount of empirical defections can touch the constitution of being as it unfolds in the light of revelation. Man can close the eye of his soul to its light; and he can engage in the futility of rebellion; but he cannot abolish the order by which his conduct will be judged. Modern symbolic expressions of the crisis, as Hegel's dictum, "God is dead" or Nietzsche's even stronger "He has been murdered," which betray the degree to which their authors were impressed by massive events of their times, would have been inconceivable to the prophets—to say nothing of the rebellious fantasy of having the order of history originate in the will of

---

[3] Voegelin, *Order and History*, Vol. I, *Israel and Revelation*, p. 461.

ideological planners left and right.... The prophets could suffer with God under the defection of Israel, but they could not doubt the order of history under the revealed will of God.... They knew that history meant existence in the order of being as it had become visible through revelation.... One could not pretend to live in another order of being than the one illuminated by revelation. And least of all could one think of going beyond revelation replacing the constitution of being with a man-made substitute. Man exists *within* the order of being; and there is no history *outside* the historical form under revelation. In the surrounding darkness of Israel's defection and impending political destruction—darker perhaps than the contemporary earthwide revolt against God—the prophets were burdened with the mystery of how the promises of the Message could prevail in the turmoil. They were burdened with this mystery by their faith; and history continued indeed by the word of God spoken through the prophets. There are times when the divinely willed order is humanly realized nowhere but in the faith of solitary sufferers.[4]

How did a covenant lead to such extraordinary views? Certainly, the idea of a covenant or contract between the gods and a people is not unique to the Hebrews. Other societies held that their laws and moral commands came from gods, and treaties or contracts between nations in Near Eastern cultures were often witnessed by gods to give them due sanction.[5] But the covenant of the Hebrews had several unique features providing a rich source of religious insight and a sustaining identification. It was with one God and with a whole people who collectively took the oath; it contained, or evolved over time, a personal and social ethic; in history it promises a just and merciful response by God. In contrast with the other Near Eastern cultures, here was a peculiar God, a peculiar people, and a peculiar history.[6]

---

[4] *Ibid.*, pp. 464–65. The Nazi holocaust presents in the twentieth century the challenge again of relating a God of mercy and love, acting in history, with the existence of devastating evil. See the discussion and survey of literature in De Lange, *Judaism*, pp. 122–24; Elie Wiesel, *The Trial of God*, trans. Marion Wiesel (New York: Summit Books, 1981).

[5] Eric Voegelin, *The New Science of Politics* (Chicago: University of Chicago Press, 1952), pp. 52–63, and "Mesopotamia," in *Order and History*, Vol. I, *Israel and Revelation*, pp. 16–45; Chester G. Starr, *A History of the Ancient World* (New York: Oxford University Press, 1983), pp. 123–42.

[6] Alan F. Segal, *Rebecca's Children: Judaism and Christianity in the Roman World* (Cambridge: Harvard University Press, 1986), pp. 1–12; Fackenheim, *What Is Judaism?* pp. 107–27.

There was just the one God, separate from, and creator of, the material universe. The physical world, accordingly, was not divine, as with the Stoics, nor was reality polytheistic. It is indicative that the very name "Yahweh" is etymologically derived from "to be" and can be translated as "I am who I am" or "I am the one who causes things to happen." God and the world are thus separate. As Hans Jonas notes, in the classical Greek and Roman position, "a pervading homogeneity of being unites Man, Nature and God." The *logos* is inherent in all. But, the Hebrew doctrine of creation denies this homogeneity, and, of equal importance for Western civilization, the Hebrew doctrine of the will by which the creation of the world is explained takes precedence over intellect or reason. "And this emphasis on the divine will," Jonas argues, "was soon reflected in the emphasis on man's will—first as the respondent of God's will, which in his commandments addresses itself to will more than to anything else in man; then increasingly as the dominant attribute of man himself."[7]

Further, through the covenant this God has become personal in that he underwrites both Israel and the individual members of the community: the people are chosen collectively and individually. The chilling silence of the physical universe and the cycle of history, so powerfully enunciated by Polybius and others in ancient Greece and Rome, is replaced by a God who responds. Lastly, through the advent of Christianity, the Exodus story with its linear progression through oppression and suffering to the promised culmination in the land of Canaan replaces the cycle as the dominant paradigm in the West for understanding history. History thus becomes teleological and a locus of unique and divinely significant acts.[8]

---

[7] Hans Jonas, "Jewish and Christian Elements in Philosophy: Their Share in the Emergence of the Modern Mind," in *Philosophical Essays: From Ancient Greece to Technological Man* (Englewood Cliffs: Prentice-Hall, 1974), pp. 28, 39.

[8] The influence of the Exodus myth, particularly as it was adapted by the Christian millenarians, would be difficult to exaggerate. Michael Walzer, *Exodus and Revolution* (New York: Basic Books, 1985); Frank E. Manuel, *Shapes of Philosophical History* (Stanford: Stanford University Press, 1965); Voegelin, *The New Science of Politics*, pp. 107–32; Norman Cohn, *The Pursuit of the Millennium: Revolutionary Messianism in Medieval and Reformation Europe and Its Bearing on Modern Totalitarian Movements* (New York: Harper Torchbooks, 1961); J.L. Talmon, *Political Messianism: The Romantic Phase* (New York: Praeger, 1960); Karl Löwith, *Meaning in History* (Chicago: University of Chicago Press, 1949).

EARLY CHRISTIANITY

Christianity began as an extremely small community of Jews who were attracted to the person of Jesus of Nazareth. Jesus was born about 4 B.C. in a small village in Galilee. At an early age he was baptized by a prophet, John the Baptist, who, like previous prophets, had been calling the Jews to repentance. Jesus went about the countryside teaching and healing the sick. This career was short-lived, for in A.D. 29 he was executed by the Roman authorities. His teaching did not depart radically from that of the Hebraic tradition. He preached the Jewish vision of one God who was concerned with man's salvation, a God of love and mercy. There was little, if anything, that was unique in his ethical message. He did chide the more pedantic Jewish teachers who insisted that salvation lay in conforming to ritualistic practices and in strict observance of every aspect of Jewish Law. Salvation lay not in properly understanding and following the Law to the letter but in following the two great commandments—to love God with all thy heart and soul and to love thy neighbour as thyself. But, here, he was simply repeating the words of Lev. 19:18 and Deut. 6:5. And he was not alone among Jewish teachers in emphasizing that the true fulfilment of the Law lay in the spirit in which it was followed rather than in the letter. A famous rabbi of the same period, Hillel, was saying much the same thing. Jesus did repeatedly proclaim that the Kingdom of God was at hand, that the world would soon come to an end, and that no one could escape the judgment of God. At the last Passover meal, which he shared with his 12 disciples, Jesus predicted that one of them would betray him to the authorities and that he, Jesus, would soon be put to death. He was, in fact, arrested the next day on the charge of blasphemy and immediately put to death on a cross. As the Roman soldiers mocked him as "King of the Jews" his small band of disciples dispersed and fled from the scene. He died alone.

His life and death might never have been noticed by history were it not for the tradition that soon sprang up concerning his true mission. Jesus himself wrote nothing, and what we now know as the New Testament is an anthology of writings by his early disciples, written over a period of time (A.D. 48 –95), and based upon an oral teaching that preceded these writings. The event that is often regarded as the cornerstone of the Christian faith was his appearance to various disciples after his death. He appeared first to his disciple Peter, then to other disciples, including Paul, who is first to record the Resurrection in written form. The centrality of the Resurrection in the Christian faith is attested to, in part, by Paul's statement in I Cor. 15:14, that "if Christ has not been raised, then our preaching is in vain and your faith is in vain."

The Resurrection rekindled the faith of those disciples who had been plunged into despair at the time of Jesus' execution. His small band of disciples was reunited in a community of faith that very gradually attracted more and more adherents. An oral tradition began teaching that Jesus was, in fact, the Messiah (Christ), whose coming the Jewish prophets had predicted, and the extraordinary claim was made that the same God who had been revealed in the events described in the Old Testament was now revealed in the person of Jesus himself. A doctrine, which came to be known as the Incarnation, claimed that Jesus, though wholly a human being with the same capacity as all human beings to experience thirst and hunger, joy and sorrow, was at the same time wholly God. In the most philosophical book of the New Testament, the Gospel of John, Jesus is described as the incarnation of the *logos*. The word *logos* has two meanings in this context. It refers to the word that God spoke, in Gen. 1:3, when he created the world—the Hebraic meaning of the word—but it also implies the Stoic meaning of the word—the reason that governs the universe.

The early Christians believed, as do Christians today, that by becoming man, God disclosed himself in human terms so that he could more easily be understood; that by enduring suffering and death, God shared all men's experiences; and that somehow, by virtue of the fact that Jesus was also God, Jesus vicariously atoned through the sacrifice of himself for the sins of the whole world. The vicarious suffering of the nation Israel, which we earlier noted in the words of Isaiah, is now seen as the suffering of Jesus the Christ. The Christian community thinks of itself as having entered into a New Covenant with God and of itself as a new Israel.

The Resurrection is understood by Christians to demonstrate God's power over all the evil in the world including death itself. "For as in Adam all die, so also in Christ shall all be made alive" (I Cor. 15:22). Christ is understood to be the Saviour of all mankind, not of Jews alone nor of Gentiles but of freemen and slaves, of men and women belonging to all races in all parts of the world. Jesus inaugurates the Kingdom of God on earth. One is not born into this Kingdom by nature but becomes a member of it by faith, and by faithful obedience to Christ, one achieves salvation not only from the evil in this world but also from death itself. The Kingdom of God is conceived of as a spiritual kingdom, not as a temporal kingdom. As Jesus said: the Kingdom of God is within you.

The early Christians were zealous missionaries who preached the "good news" to all whom they encountered, and their missionary efforts gradually led to the establishment of other Christian communities throughout the Mediterranean world. Probably the most zealous missionary was Paul. Paul was born in Tarsus, one of the principal centres of intellectual life in the first century A.D. He was brought up in the Judaic tradition, but it is of some interest that the language employed in the synagogue of Tarsus was Greek rather than Hebrew and that the Bible of the Jewish community there was the Septuagint (the Old Testament translated into Greek). The common speech of the Roman Empire was a rather simplified version of classical Greek. At first Paul was repelled by the Christians and was one of those who joined in seeking to repress them and their teaching. Sometime around A.D. 33 he had an experience that converted him from a hostile opponent of Christianity to one of its most influential missionaries. He began his preaching in Jerusalem but soon left to travel throughout Asia Minor. It was he who was largely responsible for winning many Gentile converts. Paul extended his missionary activities beyond Asia Minor to the Italian peninsula and to the city of Rome, which he first visited in A.D. 60. He was imprisoned there but given considerable freedom to engage in preaching the gospel. While he was in Rome he wrote letters to Christian communities in other parts of the world. These letters became an integral part of the New Testament.

As the Christian communities multiplied and more and more Gentiles converted, Christians encountered increasing hostility. There was not only hostility from those who remained faithful to the Judaic tradition—a hostility that engendered a counter-hostility on the part of many Christians—but also there was a conflict between the Christians and adherents of the various mystery religions that were common at the time. These mystery religions of Eastern origin were popular among the uneducated masses of people. They contained elements of belief comparable to those of the Christians, but they generally sought to stimulate emotional ecstasy and were frequently erotic in their appeals. Among the highly educated people of the time, Stoicism remained the dominant philosophy of life. All of these religions were competing with one another with different messages of personal salvation. In that sense the time was ripe for the Christian message, which ultimately, and despite repeated persecutions, conquered the mind of the Roman Empire. Perhaps the most severe persecutions took place in Rome when Christians refused to acknowledge the divinity of the state as symbolized in the person of the Emperor. The first persecution of the Christians took place under the Emperor Nero in A.D. 64 and the last in A.D. 311. For over 250 years Christians lived under the constant fear of discovery, arrest, and the sentence of death. Their persecution seemed only to kindle their zeal for missionary activity. It was in the year A.D. 312 that the Emperor Constantine became converted to Christianity. He issued an edict the following year giving the Church the special protection of the state, but it was not until the year A.D. 380, during the reign of Theodosius the Great, that Christianity became the official religion of the empire.[9]

The establishment of the Christian community as a church is a matter of controversy among Christians today.[10] But, however explained, it is agreed that the Church in Rome eventually assumed a position of leadership. Rome was the political capital of the ancient world, and it was in the Roman Christian community that Peter and Paul suffered their final martyrdom. Roman Catholics claim that Jesus himself conferred supreme authority upon Peter and that the Bishops of Rome are his legitimate successors. Protestants dispute the claim but do acknowledge the fact that the Church of Rome acquired a supremacy that lasted for several centuries.

THE CHRISTIAN CREEDS

The earliest Christians lived as though they expected the world to come to an end in their lifetime, and most of them were not persons who had high social status or who occupied prominent positions in society. They were not much concerned, as

---

[9] We can only briefly outline the features of this crucial period in which there was a gradual expansion of Christianity, many doctrinal controversies, attempts by some Christians at accommodation with the Empire, and persecutions. See, Elaine Pagel, "Christians Against the Roman Order," in *Adam, Eve, and the Serpent* (New York: Random House, 1988), pp. 32–56; R.M. Grant, *Early Christianity and Society* (New York: Harper & Row, 1977); Ramsay MacMullen, *Christianizing the Roman Empire* (New Haven: Yale University Press, 1984); R.L. Wilken, *The Christians as the Romans Saw Them* (New Haven: Yale University Press, 1984); Peter Brown, *The Rise of Western Christendom: Triumph and Adversity, A.D. 200–1000* (Cambridge: Cambridge University Press, 1996).

[10] The archeological discovery of ancient Gnostic texts in 1945 and their public release in the 1960s have fueled the controversy. Elaine Pagel has written one account relating the doctrinal controversies with the establishing of the church as an organization. She argues, as one instance, that the doctrine of physical resurrection was used by one group of Christians to show their direct lineage to Jesus and, thus, superiority over the groups who advocated a doctrine of mystical or spiritual resurrection (the Gnostics). The first groups claimed to have physically seen Jesus after the crucifixion and were authorized to speak and rule for him. An organizational hierarchy of bishop, priests, and deacons was thereby authorized and instituted. *The Gnostic Gospels* (New York: Random House, 1979).

a consequence, about political arrangements or practices and developed no distinctly Christian political philosophy. The only explicit reference Jesus made to politics was the advice to render unto Caesar the things that are Caesar's and unto God the things that are God's. Gradually, the expectation that the world would soon come to an end faded and successive generations of Christians were forced to come to terms with life in this world. As more and more educated persons converted to Christianity, a need arose to try to explain the Christian faith in language that such persons would find acceptable.

As Christians became more numerous it was inevitable that controversies should arise among them as to what precisely Christians did believe. It was necessary to decide very early which writings of Christians should be incorporated into the New Testament. In an effort to distinguish between genuine and spurious accounts of the life and teaching of Jesus, the Church adopted a canon at the end of the second century A.D. that defined the New Testament in essentially the form in which we know it today.

Not only did spurious accounts of Jesus' life have to be eliminated, but heretical teaching about him also had to be countered if the faith was to be preserved and perpetuated in its authentic form. A number of heresies arose among Christians when they sought to explain what it was that they believed. Some contended that Christ was not really a man but God in human disguise. Others contended that he was wholly human and divine only by adoption. The creeds came into being in order to settle controversies of this kind. There were a number of creeds adopted by the Church at different times. The earliest was the Apostles' Creed, but probably the most important was the Nicene Creed, which was reaffirmed at a meeting of Church fathers in Constantinople in A.D. 381. For many centuries the Nicene Creed was regarded as the definitive statement of Christian belief. It still remains an authoritative creedal formulation of Christian belief for large numbers of Christians today, though there are differences in the ways in which its language is interpreted.

When Christians began to reflect upon the experiences that engendered their faith and sought to explain and to convert the meaning of those experiences, they began to develop, especially during the second century A.D., a body of thought known as theology. Theology developed both as an attempt to answer the charge of their critics that their faith was nothing but irrational superstition and as a response to what some of the Church fathers thought to be heretical Christian teaching. Living in the Hellenistic Age when Greek was the common language, it was inevitable that these Christian theologians should use Greek words and concepts to communicate the meaning of their faith. To reflect upon experience meant, in fact, to think like a Greek, for it was the ancient Greeks who first introduced the world to rational reflection, or philosophy.

Some of the early Church fathers resisted what they regarded as an intrusion of Greek thought into the Christian faith, but the majority of Church fathers welcomed Greek philosophy as an ally. Typical of those who condemned the attempt to relate the Christian faith to Greek philosophy was Tertullian (c. A.D. 155 – c. 222). "What has Jerusalem to do with Athens, the Church with the Academy, the Christian with the heretic?" he asked.

> Our principles come from the Porch of Solomon, who had himself taught that the Lord is to be sought in simplicity of heart. I have no use for a Stoic or a Platonic or a dialectic Christianity. After Jesus Christ we have no need of speculation, after the Gospel no need of research. When we come to believe, we have no desire to believe anything else; for we begin by believing that there is nothing else which we have to believe.[11]

But many of the Church fathers regarded Greek philosophy, especially the thought of Plato, as a preparation for the reception of the Christian faith. St. Justin Martyr (c. A.D. 110 – c. 164), for example, saw Socrates's mission as one of leading men away from error towards the truth and as a preparation for the completion of this task by Christ.

> I am proud to say that I strove with all my might to be known as a Christian, not because the teachings of Plato are different from those of Christ, but because they are not in every way similar…. The truths which men in all lands have rightly spoken belong to us Christians. For we worship and love, after God the Father, the Word who is from the Unbegotten and Ineffable God, since He even became Man for us, so that by sharing in our sufferings He also might heal us. Indeed, all writers, by means of the engrafted seed of the Word which was implanted in them, had a dim glimpse of the truth.[12]

---

[11] S.L. Greenslade, ed. and trans., "On Prescription Against Heretics," ch. VII, in The Library of Christian Classics, Vol. V., *Early Latin Theology: Selections from Tertullian, Cyprian, Ambrose and Jerome* (London: SCM Press, 1956), p. 36.

[12] Ludwig Schopp, ed., *The Second Apology*, xiii, in *The Fathers of the Church*, Vol. VI, *Writings of Saint Justin Martyr*, trans. Thomas B. Falls (Washington, D.C.: The Catholic University of America Press, 1965), pp. 133–34.

We have been taught that Christ was First-begotten of God [the Father] and we have indicated above that He is the Word of whom all mankind partakes. Those who lived by reason are Christians, even though they have been considered atheists: such as, among the Greeks, Socrates, Heraclitus, and others like them....[13]

Following the same line of thought, Clement of Alexandria (c. A.D. 150– c. 219) declared:

Thus philosophy was necessary to the Greeks for righteousness, until the coming of the Lord. And now it assists towards true religion as a kind of preparatory training for those who arrive at faith by way of demonstration. For "thy foot shall not stumble" if thou attribute to Providence all good, whether it belong to the Greeks or to us. For God is the source of all good things; of some primarily, as of the old and new Testaments; of others by consequence, as of philosophy. But it may be, indeed, that philosophy was given to the Greeks immediately and primarily, until the Lord should call the Greeks. For philosophy was a "schoolmaster" to bring the Greek mind to Christ, as the Law brought the Hebrews. Thus philosophy was a preparation, paving the way towards perfection in Christ.[14]

Clement warns his readers not to try to penetrate the ultimate nature of God, which must always remain an ineffable mystery. No name that we apply to God can possibly exhaust his meaning. He cannot be captured in words or in propositions about him. To say what God is not is always easier than to say what he is.[15]

The most influential of the early Christian thinkers was undoubtedly St. Augustine, and both Roman Catholics and Protestants acknowledge him as a primary source of their thought, even today. From the fifth until the thirteenth century it was his thought that dominated the Western mind.

---

[13] *The First Apology*, xlvi, in *The Fathers of the Church*, Vol. VI, p. 83.

[14] *Stromateis*, I, v. 28. Quoted by Henry Bettenson, ed., *Documents of the Christian Church* (London: Oxford University Press, 1947), pp. 8–9.

[15] Henry Chadwick, "Christian Doctrine," in J.H. Burns, ed., *The Cambridge History of Medieval Political Thought: c. 350 – c. 1450* (Cambridge: Cambridge University Press, 1988), pp. 11–20; John Herman Randall, Jr., *Hellenistic Ways of Deliverance and the Making of the Christian Synthesis* (New York: Columbia University Press, 1970), pp. 135–88; Jean Danielou, *A History of Early Christian Doctrine Before the Council of Nicaea*, 2 Vols., trans. John Austin Baker (London: Darton, Longman & Todd, 1973).

AUGUSTINE: His Life and Works

Augustine was born in North Africa in the small town of Tagaste, not far from Carthage, in A.D. 354. It was an area that still remained close to the Roman world. His father was a local Roman official and a pagan. His mother, Monica, was a Christian. As a child, he was taught both Latin and Greek but showed a predisposition for Latin. When he was about 11 years of age he was sent to a school in the town of Madaura, a centre of pagan learning, where he studied the Latin classics. When his father died in A.D. 370, Augustine went to study rhetoric at Carthage. Here, he was attracted to the erotic rites of Eastern cults and in his *Confessions*, the source of our knowledge of his early life, he said of this period that he "walked the streets of Babylon! I rolled in its mire and lolled about on it, as if on a bed of spices and precious ointments."[16] He describes how he seemed to be passionately attracted to evil itself. When he was 17 years of age he took a mistress with whom he lived for 13 years and who bore him a son.

While in Carthage he attached himself to the Manichaean sect, a cult that originated in Persia. Its founder, Mani, was regarded as a prophet sent by God to deliver men from evil. He taught that although God was good, he was not all-powerful and that his power was limited by that of Satan. It was Satan who created the material world and the human body. The torments of the body are humanity's punishment for evil deeds committed in a previous existence. The cure is the recognition of the evil inherent in all material things and the living of an ascetic life. Many of the Manichaeans regarded themselves as Christians, and the sect was, for a time, very popular. Orthodox Christians, however, condemned it as a heresy, since it was obviously incompatible with the doctrines of creation and of the omnipotence of God. Augustine was later to renounce Manichaeism, but for nine years it seemed to him to provide the best answer he had yet encountered to the problem of evil.

In A.D. 373 Augustine became a teacher and, in 374, he opened a school at Carthage. Ten years later he was offered, and accepted, a position as a professor of rhetoric in Milan, Italy. Here, he heard sermons delivered by St. Ambrose, the Bishop of Milan, but he was not yet ready to convert to Christianity. It was at this

---

[16] Albert C. Outler, trans., "The Confessions of St. Augustine", in The Library of Christian Classics, Vol. VII, *Augustine: Confessions and Enchiridion* (Philadelphia: Westminster Press, 1955), Bk. II, p. 3, para. 8, pp. 53–54.

time that he left his first mistress and took a second. Intellectually, he was at first attracted to neo-Platonism as it found expression in the writings of Plotinus, but by A.D. 387 Augustine asked the Bishop of Milan to baptize him in the Christian faith. He subsequently remained in Rome for two years and then returned to his home village of Tagaste where he founded a monastery. He was ordained a priest in 391 and was consecrated auxiliary Bishop of Hippo in 395. In 429 the Vandals invaded North Africa and lay siege to Hippo. Augustine died during the siege in 430.

Throughout his lifetime Augustine wrote voluminous works including commentaries on the Scriptures, sermons, letters, treatises attacking heresies and defending the faith. His most important work was *City of God* (*Civitas Dei*), which he began in 413 following the sacking of Rome by Alaric. Augustine had two guiding purposes for writing this vast work: first, to defend Christianity against the charge that the Christian faith had so weakened the Roman virtues and the will to fight that it was responsible for Rome's downfall, and second, to comfort those Christians who had mistakenly held Rome to be eternal and had suffered a loss of faith by its fall. It was written over a period of 13 years and was published in parts as it was written.

It is impossible, for several reasons, to give a systematic treatment of Augustine's thought. Above all, he wrote in response to particular events and to defend the faith against specific heresies that he encountered, and, for this reason, one frequently finds contradictions in his writings that are never resolved. Toward the end of his prolific life, he, too, felt the need to establish more coherence in his writings, and he wrote a retrospective on his works, *Retractationes*. Also, Augustine truly inhabited two worlds, the Greco-Roman world and the newly arising Christendom. The intellectual tools available to him were from Greek philosophy, particularly Plato and the neo-Platonist Plotinus and Porphyry, and Roman Stoicism and skepticism, particularly Cicero. Tensions, if not contradictions, were inescapable. Lastly, his philosophy, at its core, was less an expository and rational demonstration than a passionate exploration of the hopes and fears of human existence. Étienne Gilson, a sympathetic defender, writes:

> Perhaps the lack of order we find in Augustinism is due merely to the fact that it has an order different from what we expect. Instead of the synthetic, linear order displayed by doctrines which follow the process of the intellect, we find a method of exposition necessarily different because it is suited to a doctrine whose center is grace and charity. If we are dealing not so much

with knowledge but with love, then the philosopher's task is not so much to cause knowledge as to cause love. Now in order to arouse love we do not prove, we show. Augustine never tires of doing this.[17]

All of his writings reflect the conversion experience, which is described in detail in his *Confessions*. Unlike the confessions that Rousseau is to write in the eighteenth century, Augustine's *Confessions* are addressed less to the reader than to God. They are not a plea to his readers for sympathy or understanding but a genuine confession to God—a confession that is usually made in private rather than in public.

His writings reflect an extensive knowledge of the Scriptures and of Greek philosophy, and he does not distinguish theology from philosophy. Although he was apparently aware of the thought of Aristotle, it has little or no influence upon him. The philosopher whom he admires is Plato, but it is Plato's thought mediated through the neo-Platonists rather than the Platonic dialogues themselves with which he is acquainted. In addition to being familiar with Stoic thought and an admirer of Cicero, he is thoroughly acquainted with Latin literature and frequently quotes from Horace, Virgil, and Varro.[18] However impressive Augustine's considerable learning is, his extraordinary influence could not have occurred without his own original contributions. As Socrates turned from the concerns of the Ionian scientists to a study of human nature, so, too, does Augustine turn from inanimate nature to human nature: "Men go forth to marvel at the heights of mountains and the huge waves of the sea, the broad flow of the rivers, the vastness of the ocean, the orbits of the stars, and yet they neglect to marvel at themselves."[19]

AUGUSTINE'S CONCEPTION OF HUMAN NATURE

Prior to Augustine no thinker had developed a clear understanding of the will, but, for Augustine, the will was as central to his thought as the rational faculty was for the Greeks. He explained the Christian descriptions of human experiences and actions found in the New Testament in terms of the will, and, thus, he was able

---

[17] Étienne Gilson, *The Christian Philosophy of Saint Augustine*, trans. L.E.M. Lynch (New York: Random House, 1960), p. 236.

[18] Marcia L. Colish, "St. Augustine," in *The Stoic Tradition from Classical Antiquity to the Early Middle Ages*, Vol. II (Leiden: Brill, 1985), pp. 142–238.

[19] "The Confessions of St. Augustine," Bk. X, p. 8.

to show the fundamental differences between the Greco-Roman view of human nature and the Christian view. In place of the Greek's tripartite conception—reason, appetites, and spirit—Augustine has a monist conception. The will, he argues, predominates within the soul, not the rational faculty. It is a confusion to think of the faculty of reason ruling another part, as if there were three separate parts. Rather, the person acts and thinks according to the nature of the end sought by the will-desire. If the end sought requires possession and control, one becomes grasping and fearful. If the end sought recognizes the autonomy and distinctness of the other, then one can relate by being open and trusting. In the operation of the will, the end sought and the mode of relating are inseparable. Love and friendship, as examples, occur when the autonomy of the other is recognized, and one can then be open and trusting. When the will-desire is directed to possessing and controlling the other, a fearful, grasping, jealousy results. A will that is properly directed toward God can experience a full and happy life. Rather than develop your reason for living fully, Augustine declares: "Love, and do what you will."[20] Thus, love through the will, not justice through the rational faculty, is the highest virtue. It is in the *Confessions* that Augustine can best be seen probing the nature of the will.[21]

Throughout his *Confessions* Augustine seems to be preoccupied with the problem of evil. At first he was unwilling to exercise self-scrutiny; but when he was confronted by God, he saw, "how ugly I was, and how crooked and sordid, bespotted and ulcerous. And I looked and I loathed myself; but whither to fly from myself I could not discover."[22] Some persons reading Augustine's *Confessions* describe

---

[20] John Burnaby, trans., "Ten Homilies of the First Epistle of St. John," in The Library of Christian Classics, *Augustine: Later Works*, Vol. VII, p. 8; Augustine, *The City of God*, trans. Marcus Dods (New York: Random House, 1950), Bk. V, ch. 12; Bk. XIV, ch. 7; Bk. XV, ch. 22; Bk. XIX, ch. 25. For a fuller treatment of the will in Augustine, see: R.A. Markus, *"Saeculum": History and Society in the Theology of Saint Augustine* (Cambridge: Cambridge University Press, 1970), pp. 91–102, 202–206; Hannah Arendt, *The Life of the Mind: Willing* (New York: Harcourt, Brace, Jovanovich, 1978), pp. 84–110; Albrecht Dihle, *The Theory of Will in Antiquity* (Berkeley: University of California Press, 1982), pp. 123–44. "Love through the will" (caritas).

[21] The Augustinian view of the operation of the will is often portrayed in great literature: Shakespeare's *Othello* or Dostoyevsky's *Crime and Punishment*. A superb modern example is Margaret Laurence's, *The Stone Angel* (Toronto: McClelland and Stewart, 1968). Oliver O'Donovan provides an excellent analysis of Augustine's views on love: *The Problem of Self-Love in St. Augustine* (New Haven: Yale University Press, 1980). James Wetzel does the same for Augustine's conception of the will and also discusses some of the key modern interpretations: *Augustine and the Limits of Virtue* (Cambridge: Cambridge University Press, 1992).

[22] *Confessions*, Bk. VIII, p. 7.

his self-analysis as morbid, and they are repelled by his description of the miserable predicament in which humans find themselves. But it is essential to understand Augustine's conception of that predicament, for it lies at the heart of the Christian tradition.

We are told in Genesis that God, being omnipotent, all-wise, and good, created the universe and everything in it out of nothing. He created humans in his own image and gave them dominion over the entire earth. "And God saw everything that he had made, and behold, it was very good" (Gen. 1:31). In creating humans, Augustine reasons, God made them creatures with a free will, for without free will they would have been puppets or automatons not persons. God did want us to love him, but love cannot be forced and still be love. Love must be given freely and willed.

Augustine argues that the story of Adam and Eve expresses symbolically how the first humans, exercising their freedom of will, disobeyed God's commandment not to eat the fruit of the tree of the knowledge of good and evil, and, thus, introduced wickedness into the world. This is what Augustine and Christians call "original sin." It is the cause of all particular sins. By "original sin" Augustine means the rebellion of humans against their creaturely status in the universe. "Sin" consists of their declaration of independence from God. They become arrogant, self-centred, and intent upon usurping God's role in the universe: it is not God's will that shall prevail but mine. Augustine recounts in his *Confessions* how he was constantly asserting his own will and, as a consequence, bringing misery upon himself. Instead of making him happy, this self-assertion made him miserable. He tells how, as a boy, he stole some pears, not because he really wanted them but that "I might produce a sort of counterfeit liberty, by doing with impunity deeds that were forbidden, in a deluded sense of omnipotence."[23] Apparently, he could find pleasure only by doing something that was unlawful. Wickedness stems from pride, from the desire to be the centre of the universe and to bend everything to one's own will. As a consequence of Adam and Eve's defiance of God, the whole human race is infected with this spirit of rebellion, and it is passed on from generation to generation. It leads to the predicament, as expressed by Paul, that humans find it much easier to do the evil that they would prefer not to do than the good that they

---

[23] *Ibid.*, Bk. II, p. 6.

want but are unable to do.[24] The human race finds itself in bondage to sin, and what it conceives frequently as the expression of freedom is, in reality, slavery to one's own desires.

There is no way, in Augustine's view, that human beings can rescue themselves from this predicament, and no one is exempt from the just punishment that God metes out to those who are disobedient. Although no one can be said to merit salvation from this predicament, God in his mercy does save some from themselves. By his grace, some are spared the punishment that all deserve. The proper response to that grace is gratitude to God for his loving mercy, not self-congratulation on one's virtues. Augustine's doctrine of predestination, that some are chosen to be saved while others are eternally damned, appears from the human perspective to be unjust and arbitrary. Augustine answers that it is not unjust, for if justice were the criterion for salvation no one could be said to merit it. Ultimately, it is a mystery that cannot be fathomed by the human mind. Augustine developed this doctrine of predestination, in part, to answer the Pelagian heresy, which taught that humans can merit salvation through the performance of good works. The worst kind of pride, Augustine says, is the pride of the self-righteous person who *knows* that he is better than others and more deserving of God's favour. Augustine wanted to emphasize humanity's total dependence upon God. Although infected by original sin, human beings, in Augustine's view, do presumably retain the freedom to choose to commit this or that particular act. But when they act to do the good it is because they are inspired by the love of God within, so that only those who are receptive to God's grace are liberated from the bondage to sin. Augustine repeatedly declares that no person acts rightly save by the assistance of divine aid.

Augustine wrestled with four different conceptions of the nature of evil. First, neo-Platonism held that God, the divine, is immanent in reality. Everything that exists is good; therefore, evil is only an illusion. Augustine recognizes that he, himself, did evil and that it is no illusion. Second, there is the Manichean view that evil is an independent force in a struggle with God and the good. Augustine rejects **dualism** because it contradicts the omnipotence of God. Third, some have argued that evil is only the lower realm of the hierarchy of God's good actions. God, by definition, cannot do wrong and what appears to be evil actually,

---

[24] Romans 7:19.

and ultimately, works into the whole or the good. This view ignores the reality of evil and is also rejected by Augustine. Fourth, evil results from the misdirection of the individual will. Evil is not itself real or an inherent faculty. Just as reason can be directed toward good or evil ends, or just as the arm can be used to commit good or evil deeds, so can the will. Evil actions and deeds do occur and are real, but reason, the arm, and the will are not in themselves evil. Rather, evil is a falling away from God, from the good, a privation of right order. And humans alone are responsible for it.[25]

THE CITY OF GOD AND THE CITY OF BABYLON

Mankind can be divided into two great camps, those who love God and subordinate their desires to his and those who exalt their own desires above God's. Just as there are two kinds of love—love of God and love of self—so there are two kinds of cities—the city of Babylon and the city of Jerusalem—and these two cities shall remain commingled until the end of time.

> Accordingly, two cities have been formed by two loves: the earthly by the love of self, even to the contempt of God; the heavenly by the love of God; even to the contempt of self. The former, in a word, glories in itself; the latter in the Lord…. And therefore the wise men of the one city, living according to man, have sought for profit to their own bodies or souls, or both …. But in the other city there is no human wisdom, but only godliness….[26]

We gave the name of the city of God, says Augustine, to that society to which Scripture bears witness. We find frequent references in the Psalms to the city of God and know that it was God's original intention that all should be citizens of this city. But, Augustine argues, since Adam's rebellion against God, no one can become a member of this city except by God's grace. If many are excluded, it is not by virtue of their sex, their race, their earthly citizenship or class, but by

---

[25] G.R. Evans, *Augustine on Evil* (Cambridge: Cambridge University Press, 1983); Margaret R. Miles, *Fullness of Life: Historical Foundations for a New Asceticism* (Philadelphia: Westminster Press, 1981), pp. 62–76; Linwood Urban, *A Short History of Christian Thought* (Oxford: Oxford University Press, 1986), pp. 125–55.

[26] Augustine, *The City of God*, trans. Marcus Dods, Bk. XIV, ch. 28.

virtue of their sin. The one thing that all the members of the city have in common is their love of God. The city consists of all those who enjoy community with God and with one another in God.

The city of God, Augustine believes, is the true Jerusalem; it is the Kingdom of God mentioned by Christ, which he explicitly said is not of this world. It is what is frequently referred to by Christians as heaven. Heaven is understood not as something that can be located on some celestial map but as a state of being in which humans live in harmony with God and with one another. It is a kingdom of eternal love. It includes all of those persons in the past, present, and future who have loved or do or will love God.

As a consequence, it cannot be identified with any earthly institution. The Church is the closest approximation of this city on the earth, but it is not identical with it. A person may be a member of the Church, and yet may be guided by self-love rather than love of God. Augustine says:

> We see now the citizen of Jerusalem, citizen of the kingdom of heaven, have some office upon earth: to wit, one weareth purple, is a Magistrate … but he hath his heart above, if he is a Christian, if he is a believer … if he is despising those things wherein he is, and trusteth in that wherein he is not yet.… Despair we not then of the citizens of the kingdom of heaven, when we see them engaged in any of Babylon's matters, doing something earthly in republic earthly: nor again let us forthwith congratulate all men that we see doing matters heavenly; because even about sons of pestilence sit sometimes in the seat of Moses.… But there will come time of winnowing, when both are to be severed with greatest diligence, in order that no grain may pass over unto the heap of chaff that is to be burned.…[27]

In addition to faithful Christians the city of God includes those lovers of God who preceded Christ, from Abel onwards. Augustine describes the members of the city of God as pilgrims or sojourners who are "passing on through the world, endeavoring to reach Him who created it. Let not the lovers of the world, who wish to remain in the world … let them not disturb you, let them not deceive nor seduce you."[28]

---

[27] *A Select Library of the Nicene and Post-Nicene Fathers of the Christian Church*, Vol. VIII, *Saint Augustine: Expositions on the Book of Psalms* (Grand Rapids: Eerdmans, 1956), Psalm LII, 2.

[28] *A Select Library of the Nicene and Post-Nicene Fathers of the Christian Church*, Vol. VI, *Saint Augustine: Sermons on New Testament Lessons*, Sermon XXXI, para. 7.

Like the city of God, the earthly city, Babylon, cannot be identified with any particular human institution. Members of the earthly city consist of all the fallen angels and all the men, from the time of Cain, who lust after the things of this world and whose love is self-centred. Yet, Augustine does frequently suggest that the kingdoms and states of this world are but divisions of the city of Babylon. Nevertheless, they are not identical since members of the city of God are also citizens of earthly cities. The two cities are commingled and not until the Day of Last Judgment shall the two cities and their members be separated. God alone knows to which city the citizens belong.[29]

AUGUSTINE'S CONCEPTION OF THE STATE

Augustine shows that he is familiar with Cicero's definition of the state as "an assemblage of people in large numbers associated in agreement with respect to justice and a partnership for the common good," but, despite the opinion of some scholars, it appears that he notes it only to reject it.[30] If we discard Cicero's definition and assume, says Augustine,

---

[29] Although generally appreciative of the insights of Augustine, a modern Protestant theologian, Reinhold Niebuhr, declares that "When Augustine distinguished between the 'two loves' which characterize the 'two cities,' the love of God and the love of self, and when he pictured the world as a commingling of the two cities, he does not recognize that the commingling is due, not to the fact that two types of people dwell together but because the conflict between love and self-love is in every soul. It is particularly important to recognize this fact in political analyses for nothing is more obvious than that personal dedication is no guarantee against the involvement of the dedicated individual in some form of collective egoism." *Christian Realism and Political Problems* (New York: Scribner, 1953), p. 138. Augustine does speak, especially in *The City of God*, as though there are two sharply delineated groups of people, those who love God and those who love self. But in his *Confessions* he clearly recognizes that the conflict between love of God and love of self is one that occurs in every soul. "Thus did my two wills—one old and the other new, one carnal, the other spiritual—contend within me; and by their discord they unstrung my soul" (Bk. VIII, ch. 5). Again Augustine says: "While I was deliberating whether I would serve the Lord my God now, as I have long purposed to do, it was I who willed and it was also I who was unwilling. In either case, it was I. I neither willed with my whole will nor was I wholly unwilling. And so I was at war with myself and torn apart by myself" (Bk. VIII, ch. 10).

[30] C.H. McIlwain defends the proposition that Augustine is in basic agreement with Cicero in *The Growth of Political Thought in the West* (New York: Macmillan & Co., 1932), pp. 154ff. John N. Figgis denies this in *The Political Aspects of St. Augustine's 'City of God'* (London: Longmans, Green and Co., 1921), as does Herbert A. Deane in *The Political and Social Ideas of St. Augustine* (New York: Columbia University Press, 1963), pp. 120–38. We are in agreement with Figgis and Deane. The extensive literature on this controversy is surveyed by J.D. Adams, *The Populus of Augustine and Jerome* (New Haven: Yale University Press, 1971).

… that a people is an assemblage of reasonable beings bound together by a common agreement as to the objects of their love, then, in order to discover the character of any people, we have only to observe what they love. Yet whatever it loves, if only it is an assemblage of reasonable beings and not of beasts, and is bound together by an agreement as to the objects of love, it is reasonably called a people; and it will be a superior people in proportion as it is bound together by higher interests, inferior in proportion as it is bound together by lower. According to this definition of ours, the Roman people is a people, and its weal without doubt a commonwealth or republic. But what its tastes were in its early and subsequent days, and how it declined into sanguinary seditions and then to social and civil wars and so burst asunder or rotted off the bond of concord in which the health of a people consists, history shows and in the preceding books I have related at large…. But what I say of this people and of this republic I must be understood to think and say of the Athenians or any Greek state, of the Egyptians, of the early Assyrian Babylon, and of every other nation, great or small, which had a public government. For, in general, the city of the ungodly, which did not obey the command of God that it should offer no sacrifice save to Him alone, and which, therefore, could not give the soul its proper command over the body, nor to the reason its just authority over the vices, is void of true justice.[31]

If justice, according to the traditional definition, is giving everyone his due, then a people who do not acknowledge the commandments of God cannot be just since they are not giving God that which is due him. The only kingdom in which God is given his due, Augustine reasons, is in the city of God, and only in that kingdom can true justice be found.

In Book IV of *The City of God*, Augustine likens kingdoms to robber bands.

Justice being taken away, then, what are kingdoms but great robberies? For what are robberies themselves, but little kingdoms? The band itself is made up of men; it is ruled by the authority of a prince; it is knit together by the pact of the confederacy; the booty is divided by the law agreed on. If, by the admittance of abandoned men, this evil increases to such a degree that

---

[31] Augustine, *The City of God*, Bk. XIX, ch. 24.

it holds places, fixes abodes, takes possession of cities, and subdues people, it assumes the more plainly the name of a kingdom, because the reality is now manifestly conferred on it, not by the removal of covetousness, but by the addition of impunity. Indeed, that was an apt and true reply which was given to Alexander the Great by a pirate who had been seized. For when the king had asked the man what he meant by keeping hostile possession of the sea, he answered with bold pride, "What thou meanest by seizing the whole earth; but because I do it with a petty ship, I am called a robber, whilst thou who dost it with a great fleet are styled emperor."[32]

Augustine is not saying that all kings are necessarily wicked men but that kingdoms more often resemble bands of robbers than they do the community of those who love God. He recognizes, as we have said earlier, that the two kingdoms are commingled, and that sometimes one finds Christians in positions of political leadership, but even in these cases we cannot expect the kingdom itself to embody true justice. Despite the participation of Christians in government, there will never be any such thing on earth as a truly Christian state or a perfectly just one. He does have some advice to give to Christians who find themselves in a position of political leadership; it is intended not necessarily as a description of how Christians do, in fact, behave in such situations but rather how they ought to behave. From the following passage a genre of literature developed in the middle ages providing a "Mirror to Princes" for their edification:

> For neither do we say that certain Christian emperors were therefore happy because they ruled a long time ... or subdued the enemies of the republic.... But we say that they are happy if they rule justly; if they are not lifted up amid the praises of those who pay them sublime honors, and the obsequiousness of those who salute them with an excessive humility, but remember that they are men; if they make their power the handmaid of His majesty by using it for the greatest possible extension of His worship; if they fear, love, worship God; if more than their own they love that kingdom in which they are not afraid to have partners; if they are slow to punish, ready to pardon ... if they compensate with the leniency of mercy and the liberality of benevolence for whatever severity they may be compelled

---

[32] *Ibid.*, Bk. IV, ch. 4.

to decree; if their luxury is as much restrained as it might have been un-restrained; if they prefer to govern depraved desires rather than any na-tion whatever; and if they do all these things, not through ardent desire of empty glory, but through love of eternal felicity, not neglecting to offer to the true God, who is their God, for their sins the sacrifices of humility, contrition, and prayer.[33]

Augustine is not describing the function of the state in this passage but the conduct that ought to characterize a Christian who is in a position of political leadership.

Since the overwhelming majority of the citizens of any state are unredeemed sinners, the state comes into existence both as a consequence of sin and as a par-tial remedy for it. A fallen man is self-centred, covetous, lustful, and desirous of exercising power over others, and the state becomes necessary to keep people from destroying one another. Without it we would have anarchy. The power of the state to coerce and punish wrongdoers is a direct result of man's sinfulness, and it is a remedy for that sin to the extent that it is able to impose order and to main-tain a measure of domestic peace. Order and peace are necessary to the earthly ex-istence of all sinners and pilgrims alike.

The order and peace that the state provides is always an imperfect peace when compared with the peace of the city of God. In seeking peace, however, the state, even when it acts unjustly, testifies to the natural, i.e., before the Fall, desire of man for fellowship and peace with all men.

> … even wicked men wage war to maintain the peace of their own circle, and wish that, if possible, all men belonged to them, that all men and things might serve but one head, and might, either through love or fear, yield themselves to peace with him! It is thus that pride in its perversity apes God. It abhors equality with other men under Him; but, instead of His rule, it seeks to impose a rule of its own upon its equals. It abhors, that is to say, the just peace of God, and loves its own unjust peace; but it cannot help loving peace of one kind or other. For there is no vice so clearly con-trary to nature that it obliterates even the faintest traces of nature.[34]

---

[33] *Ibid.*, Bk. V, ch. 24.

[34] *Ibid.*, Bk. XIX, ch. 12.

The peace that the state provides is, indeed, a genuine kind of peace, though it falls short of the peace of the city of God. Because it is a genuine kind of peace, Christians will have no scruples about obeying the laws of the state, and so long as the state does not interfere with the freedom of Christians to worship God, they will support its laws and institutions.

> The earthly city, which does not live by faith, seeks an earthly peace and the end it proposes, in the well-ordered concord of civic obedience and rule, is the combination of men's wills to attain the things which are helpful in this life. The heavenly city, or rather that part of it which sojourns on earth and lives by faith, makes use of this peace only because it must, until this mortal condition which necessitates it shall pass away. Consequently, so long as it lives like a captive and a stranger in the earthly city, though it has already received the promise of redemption … it makes no scruple to obey the laws of the earthly city, whereby the things necessary for the maintenance of this mortal life are administered; and thus, as this life is common to both cities, so there is harmony between them in regard to what belongs to it.[35]

The peace provided by the state is a good, but not the highest good. And the same consideration that obliges the Christian to obey the laws of the state also defines the limits of the state's authority. There is "harmony between them," i.e., the two cities, only so long as the state confines itself to what properly "belongs to it." The Christian is obliged to renounce his allegiance to the state whenever the state seeks to limit or to destroy the worship of the true God.

AUGUSTINE ON SLAVERY AND PROPERTY

Like the state, slavery and property are products of the sinful rebellion of humans against God. Originally, God intended that all should be free and equal and share all things in common. Slavery, Augustine says, "was introduced by sin and not by nature."[36] It is both a punishment for man's sinfulness and also a partial remedy. He does not mean that slaves are personally being punished for being sinful, and he recognizes that the slave may, in fact, be better, spiritually, than

---

[35] *Ibid.*, Bk. XIX, ch. 17.

[36] *Ibid.*, Bk. XIX, ch. 15.

the master. It is the institution of slavery that he seeks to justify, as a consequence and remedy for sin, not the position of any particular person. He thinks of the slave more as a servant than as a piece of property. Augustine's attempt to justify the institution of slavery is no more admirable than Aristotle's, but at least it represents some advancement over Aristotle's view that the slave is nothing but an animated tool. The master can claim no inherent superiority over the slave and, if wicked, may be in graver danger than the faithful servant.

> … there are many wicked masters who have religious men as their slaves, and who are yet themselves in bondage…. And beyond question it is a happier thing to be the slave of a man than of a lust; for even this very lust of ruling, to mention no others, lays waste men's hearts with the most ruthless dominion. Moreover, when men are subjected to one another in a peaceful order, the lowly position does as much good to the servant as the proud position does harm to the master. But by nature, as God first created us, no one is a slave either of man or of sin.[37]

Aristotle had argued that some are slaves "by nature"; Augustine, at least, denies this.

Private property, like the state and like the institution of slavery, is also a consequence of man's rebellion against God and a partial remedy for it. It comes into existence because of the covetousness of fallen man, and it canalizes that covetousness and makes it more socially tolerable than it would be if there were no institution of private property. The civil law of kings and emperors originally brought private property into existence and continues to sustain it. It is not wealth *per se* that Augustine condemns but covetousness, and clearly, the poor may be as much infected by the spirit of covetousness as the rich.

Augustine follows the teaching of the Church fathers in this matter. When Christ declares that the rich shall have greater difficulty entering the Kingdom of God than the poor, it is a warning against the *temptations* involved in the possession of wealth rather than a condemnation of wealth itself. It will be impossible, Christ declared, for those who *trust* in riches to enter the Kingdom of God. That applies equally to the poor who think that their salvation lies in the attainment of riches and to the rich who think that, being rich, they have everything they need for their own salvation.

---

[37] *Ibid.*

> Fear not, little flock, for it is your Father's good pleasure to give you the king-
> dom. Sell your possession, and give your alms; provide yourselves with
> purses that do not grow old, with a treasure in the havens that does not
> fail, where no thief approaches and no moth destroys....

is Augustine's version of Christ's injunction, "for where your treasure is, there will
your heart be also."[38] His message is that only the love of God endures forever.

Wealth itself is a neutral thing, which can be used in the service of God or of
Self. Christ teaches that wealth is given to us that we may satisfy human needs; if
we do not use it as it was intended to be used, but for our exclusive benefit and enjoyment, then it is a curse. Christ warns against the temptations involved in the possession of wealth and against the lack of charity that frequently accompanies its
possession, but it is the lack of charity he condemns rather than the possession of
wealth itself: "But if any one has the world's goods and sees his brother in need, yet
closes his heart against him, how does God's love abide in him?"[39]

The parable of the rich young man seeking Christ's counsel illustrates the traditional Christian teaching on this point. When the young man asks what he
should do to inherit eternal life, Christ tells him to follow the Ten Commandments.
When the young man replies that he has done so and asks what *more* he should do,
Christ tells him: "If you would be perfect, go, sell what you possess and give to the
poor ...."[40] This is not an injunction to redistribute the wealth more equitably
but to detach one's self completely from the things of this world. Read in context, this is a counsel of perfection rather than a commandment meant to be binding upon all individuals in all circumstances. It is a counsel of perfection that is as
difficult for the poor to follow as for the rich. St. Clement of Alexandria, one of the
early Church fathers, points out in his interpretation of the parable that there is no
special merit in poverty. The real meaning of the story, he says, is that we should
"banish from the soul its opinions about riches, its attachment to them, its excessive desire, its morbid excitement over them, its anxious cares, the thorns of our
earthly existence which choke the seed of the true life."[41] Unless the renunciation

---

[38] Luke 12:32–34.

[39] I John 3:17.

[40] Matthew 19:21.

[41] T.E. Page, ed., "The Rich Man's Salvation," in *Clement of Alexandria*, trans. G.W. Butterworth,
The Loeb Classical Library (Cambridge: Harvard University Press, 1953), pp. 291–93.

of wealth leads us closer to the love of God there is no special merit in poverty—no more, of course, than there is in the possession of wealth. Wealth is an instrument that can be used for good purposes or bad, and it is the way in which it is used that is the important consideration. Evil lies not in the possession of things but in the passions of men. Pride, avarice, and anxiety are the real evils, and pride, covetousness, and anxiety infect the poor as well as the rich. They are human infirmities, not peculiar to any one class of people. The counsel of perfection, nevertheless, does remain for those Christians who are especially called to the service of God. In Augustine's view, which is that of the Roman Catholic Church, it is appropriate for priests, monks and nuns to renounce the ownership of all earthly goods; it is also appropriate that they live a life of complete chastity. Christians who do not have a special calling to the service of God are enjoined to act as trustees and to use their property for good purposes.

GREEK AND CHRISTIAN THOUGHT COMPARED

One of the marked differences between the Greek tradition, as exemplified in the thought of Plato and Aristotle, and that of the Christian tradition, as exemplified by Augustine, is the emphasis that the Christian tradition places upon sin. The contrast, however, is more apparent when one compares the thought of Augustine with that of Aristotle than when one compares Augustine's thought with that of Plato.[42] Both Plato and Aristotle were well aware of the fact that the majority of mankind is deficient in virtue, though neither used the word sin to describe that deficiency.

Plato repeatedly tells us that most humans live an inverted existence, that the life they follow is "turned upside-down." He frequently contrasts the sleeping or dreaming state of existence of most people with the waking state of the person who loves the Good. Plato tells us in the famous myth of the cave in the *Republic* that a redirection (*perigogia*) is required to turn souls around. Chained by their senses

---

[42] The complex relationship between Greek and Christian thought is well explored by the following: A.H. Armstrong and R.A. Markus, *Christian Faith and Greek Philosophy* (New York: Sheed and Ward, 1960); Charles Norris Cochrane, *Christianity and Classical Culture* (Oxford: Oxford University Press, 1957); Werner Jaeger, *Early Christianity and Greek Paideia* (Cambridge: Harvard University Press, 1961); John Herman Randall, Jr., *Hellenistic Ways of Deliverance and the Making of the Christian Synthesis* (New York: Columbia University Press, 1970); James Shiel, *Greek Thought and the Rise of Christianity* (London: Longmans, 1968).

and their sensual desires, most people live in darkness and in bondage to themselves. It is ignorance (*amathia*) that is the source of evil. This ignorance comes not simply from an inability to reason correctly but from a turning away from the Good which solicits reason. Ignorance exists when someone "hates, what in his opinion is noble or good, and likes and welcomes what in his opinion is wicked and unjust. This dissonance between pleasure and pain on the one hand, and the opinion that is according to reason on the other, I assert to be the ultimate and greatest ignorance, because it belongs to the major part of the soul."[43]

Plato tells us that what humans take to be Real will depend, ultimately, upon what they conceive to be Good. And if they mistake a lesser good for the true Good they will necessarily fall into error. Most live a life of self-contradiction in perpetual disagreement with themselves. A coherent, full life, or what Christians call salvation, begins with honest self-inquiry when we are made aware, by dialectical inquiry, of our inability to hold contradictory points of view. Self-knowledge is the beginning of wisdom. According to Plato, however, wisdom, or true knowledge of reality, requires redirection, from concern with ourselves, our desires, and the perspectives of the world of the senses to the contemplation of the Good. Although education cannot compel assent to the truth of reality, it can turn the soul around if, in fact, the person wants to see. The attainment of wisdom requires a personal decision, and the quest for truth can only be undertaken successfully by one who has a desire to be good. Although Aristotle differs from Plato in some important matters, he, too, maintains that there can be no true virtue without prudence and no prudence without virtue.

Augustine shares Plato's conviction that there is no such thing as "disinterested" or dispassionate reason and that reason can be trusted to lead us to an understanding of reality only when it is motivated by love of the Good. "Socrates," says Augustine,

> is said to be the first who directed the entire effort of philosophy to the correction and regulation of morals, all who went before him having expended their greatest efforts in the investigation of physical, that is, natural phenomena ... he did it because he was unwilling that minds defiled by earthly desires should essay to raise themselves upward toward divine things. For he saw that the causes of things were sought for by them—which causes

---

[43] Thomas Pangle, trans., *The Laws of Plato* (New York: Basic Books, 1980), p. 689a.

he believed to be ultimately reducible to nothing else than the will of the one true and supreme God—and on this account he thought they could only be comprehended by a purified mind; and therefore that all diligence ought to be given to the purification of the life by good morals, in order that the mind, delivered from the depressing weight of lusts, might raise itself upward by its native vigor to eternal things, and might, with purified understanding, contemplate that nature which is incorporeal and unchangeable light, where live the causes of all created natures.[44]

This passage reminds us of Plato's analogy of the Good with the Sun. Although it is frequently asserted that Plato had no idea of God as a creator, there is evidence in the *Timaeus* that he did, in fact, have such a conception.[45] "If, then, Plato defined the wise man as one who imitates, knows, loves this God, and who is rendered blessed through fellowship with Him in His own blessedness, why discuss with other philosophers? It is evident that none come nearer us than the Platonists."[46]

Augustine does not mention Aristotle in the same way. And, indeed, in Aristotle there is a significant departure from the thought of Plato. The God of love, whom we encountered in Plato's dialogues, is absent from Aristotle's thought and is replaced by a god who is nothing more than a metaphysical necessity.

---

[44] *The City of God*, Bk. VIII, ch. 3. Augustine agreed with the neo-Platonic stress on man's rational nature. Says Augustine: "For I do not travel very far for examples, when I mean to give thee some similitude to thy God from thy own mind; because surely not in the body, but in that same mind, was man made after the image of God." *A Select Library of the Nicene and Post-Nicene Fathers of the Christian Church*, Vol. II, *St. Augustine: Ioannis Evangelicum*, XXIII, 10. In another passage Augustine states: "we must find in the soul of man, i.e., the rational or intellectual soul, that image of the Creator which is immortally implanted in its immortality ... so although reason or intellect is one time torpid in it, at another appears small, and at another great, yet the human soul is never anything save rational or intellectual; and, hence, if it is made after the image of God in respect to this, that it is able to use reason and intellect in order to understand and behold God, then from the moment when that nature so marvellous and so great began to be, whether this image be so worn out as to be almost none at all, or whether it be obscure and defaced, or bright and beautiful, certainly it always is." *A Select Library of the Nicene and Post-Nicene Fathers of the Christian Church*, Vol. VIII, *St. Augustine: On the Trinity*, XIV, pp. 4, 6.

[45] "When the father and creator saw the creature which he had made moving and living, the created image of the eternal gods, he rejoiced, and in his joy determined to make the copy still more like the original; and as this was eternal, he sought to make the universe eternal, so far as might be." *Timaeus*, p. 37d, Edith Hamilton and Huntington Cairns, eds., *The Collected Dialogues of Plato* (New York: Pantheon, 1961). This and other passages from the *Timaeus* are strikingly similar to the account of the creation in Genesis.

[46] *The City of God*, Bk. VII, ch. 5.

Plato's dialectical mode of inquiry, moreover, is replaced by an inductive logic that is intended by Aristotle to yield more certain knowledge of ultimate reality and a knowledge that is not dependent upon the character of the inquirer for its discovery. In this sense Aristotle moves much closer to the modern view of dispassionate reason that is supposed to characterize what we call today thinking "scientifically." Because Aristotle's God is indifferent to men and their affairs, there is no sense, moreover, in which evil can be conceived as a form of rebellion against God.

Neither Plato nor Aristotle has a conception of a Redeemer or Saviour (in the Christian sense) nor a conception of grace mediated for humans through the self-sacrifice of such a Redeemer. Yet, in Plato's thought, there is a parallel to the conception of grace, though it does not go by that name. We recall how, in the allegory of the cave, one of the prisoners is "set free and forced suddenly to stand up, turn his head, and walk, with eyes lifted to the light." This experience at least resembles the Christian experience of conversion, and it is motivated, like the Christian experience, by the love of God, what Plato calls the "divine mania" (*theia mania*).[47] There is a great deal in Plato's thought that appears compatible with Christianity, and it is for this reason that Augustine, along with other Church fathers, thought of him as an invaluable, intellectual ally.

Augustine's conception of the Kingdom of God is thought by many to have been prefigured by Plato's construction of the "city in speech" and by the Stoic conception of a universal community of humanity ruled by reason. In the Stoic view, however, all were members of this community by nature; whereas, in Augustine's view, humans, though originally intended by their nature to be members of the city of God, now, in their fallen state, can become members only by the grace of God. Both Plato and Aristotle recognized that there is a life "better than the political" and that the criteria of that better life were useful as

---

[47] In one of the best commentaries upon the thought of Plato in relation to Christianity, Robert Cushman declares that "... in the *Phaedrus* Plato unveiled his discovery of something that might be called the 'expulsive power of a new affection.' It is none other than philosophic love or *theia mania*—the love of abiding and eternal Good. He asserted that it worked, as a by-product to eliminate enmity among men (253b) and to introduce amity and friendship (255b). The divine eros did not eliminate self-interest, but it had the capacity to transform expressions of self-regard. More exactly, the higher madness pointed out the direction in which true 'self-advantage' was to be found. It transmuted the old reprobate eros, accepted with complacency by the many, into an uncalculating, free, and 'generous love.'" *Therapeia: Plato's Conception of Philosophy* (Chapel Hill: University of North Carolina Press, 1958), p. 204.

standards with which to measure the quality of life in actual states. Although it is sometimes said that Christianity introduced into Western political thought the idea of a dual citizenship, this is not true. The same idea can be found in Plato and Aristotle. What Christianity did was to institutionalize the two cities, and the tension between the two cities came to be seen as a tension between church and state.

Although the early Church fathers saw many areas of compatibility between Christianity and the Greek philosophers, in retrospect there were critical differences. Politics, as one striking example, is viewed by Augustine as more about coercion and order than about virtue. It is mainly a palliative for the inescapable conflict born from flawed human nature. The human condition, as Augustine describes it in *The City of God*, is inherently unstable, and human laws and institutions cannot promise to deliver us from its harshness. It is only after we have left the boundaries of politics that we can find true virtue, justice, community, peace, and happiness within the city of God. In short, there is a hardheaded realism in Augustine about the inevitable tensions and conflicts in political life and about man's inability to achieve a lasting convergence of human law and virtue or human institutions and justice. There is a striking lowering of importance of the political realm.[48]

The most significant differences can be traced to the Hebraic conceptions of will and of history. Augustine's development of these two ideas permanently altered Western culture. For Augustine, the Christian God was not a God for a chosen people or empire but was a God for all people and equally for male and female. Accordingly, Augustine introduces a picture of human nature or personhood that is different from that of the Greeks: one that accents equality and virtues such as love, forgiveness, mercy, and gratitude. These virtues are not listed by Aristotle, for example, in the *Nichomachean Ethics*. The equality of male and female, espoused first by Plato, is given far greater stress by Augustine. Although the exact influence of this spiritual equality on the political, social, and family realms is still disputed, few would disagree with the statement that "Christianity

---

[48] The most influential modern exponent of Augustinian political realism has been Reinhold Niebuhr: *Christian Realism and Political Problems* (New York: Charles Scribner's Sons, 1953) and *Faith and History* (New York: Charles Scribner's Sons, 1949). More recent examples are: Richard John Newhaus, *The Naked Public Square* (Grand Rapids, Mich.: Eerdmans, 1984) and Graham Walker, *Moral Foundations of Constitutional Thought: Current Problems, Augustinian Prospects* (Princeton: Princeton University Press, 1990).

ushered a moral revolution into the world which diametrically, and for the better, transformed the prevailing images of male and female, public and private."[49]

Augustine develops the Hebraic idea of a providential history in order to dismiss the predominant cyclical view of history and to remind some Christians and Romans that Rome could not be eternal. Only the heavenly city is eternal. History, through God's providence, does have a beginning, middle, and end, but its meaning is not found in the rise and fall of secular empires. Augustine sees a pattern of five stages in the old Testament: Adam to Noah, Noah to Abraham, Abraham to David, David to the Babylonian captivity, the captivity to the birth of Christ. The world entered the last stage with the advent of Christ. In this last dying stage, however, humans cannot see any clear pattern but must rely upon their faith to provide meaning. Although secular history, politics, and empires, cease to be essential for developing and displaying one's faculties and virtues, there is still a goal and meaning to human history. The new institution of the Church becomes the focus of a person's most important responsibilities. Although we are citizens of both cities, the goal of salvation in the city of God diminishes, in contrast, the importance of the political realm. Here again, Augustine broke with the ancient world and introduced new ideas. Whether there is a meaning or pattern in history has become a perennial question in Western philosophy.[50]

CHURCH AND STATE IN THE EARLY MIDDLE AGES

Although for the sake of brevity we refer to the tension that existed throughout the Middle Ages as a tension between church and state, actually the tension is between the spiritual and the temporal spheres of jurisdiction. Neither the concept of the state nor the word "state" existed during the Middle Ages, nor was

---

[49] Jean Bethke Elshtain, *Public Man, Private Woman: Women in Social and Political Thought* (New York: Princeton University Press, 1981), pp. 56, 64–74; Peter Brown, *The Body and Society: Men, Women, and Sexual Renunciation in Early Christianity* (New York: Columbia University Press, 1988), pp. 5–32; Diana H. Coole, *Women in Political Theory: Ancient Misogyny to Contemporary Feminism* (Boulder, Col.: Lynne Rienner, 1988), pp. 49–64; Miles, *Fullness of Life: Historical Foundations for a New Asceticism*, pp. 62–78; Arlene W. Saxonhouse, *Women in the History of Political Thought: Ancient Greece to Machiavelli* (New York: Praeger, 1985), pp. 125–40.

[50] R.A. Markus, "*Saeculum*": *History and Society in the Theology of Saint Augustine*; Jaroslav Pelikan, *The Mystery of Continuity: Time and History, Memory and Eternity in the Thought of Saint Augustine* (Charlottesville: University of Virginia, 1986).

the word "political" used before the thirteenth century. In modern times we are inclined to distinguish among religious, moral, political, and economic standards and activities, but no such distinctions were made during the Middle Ages. In the early days of Christianity there were "two powers"—the Christian Church and the pagan empire of Rome—and they were frequently in conflict with one another. But after Christianity became the official religion of the Roman Empire, during the fifth century A.D., the distinction between the two powers became a distinction between two orders within the Church—the laity and the clergy.[51]

In the fifth century Pope Gelasius laid down a doctrine that is called "the doctrine of the two swords." It is a doctrine that subsequent writers refer to again and again throughout the Middle Ages. Pope Gelasius notes that in the classical political regimes of Greece and Rome no distinction was drawn between duties to the polity and duties to the gods. Pagan emperors also bore the title of Chief Priests.

> Admittedly, before the advent of Christ there actually existed—though in a prefigurative sense—men who were concurrently kings and priests; sacred history records that such a one was Saint Melchizedek [Gen. 14]. This the Devil, who tyrannically arrogates to himself what is proper to divine worship, has imitated, so that pagan emperors caused themselves to be called supreme pontiffs. But when the One came who was truly King and Pontiff, then no emperor accepted the name of pontiff and no pontiff claimed the supreme dignity of king. Indeed, parts of Him—of the true King and Pontiff—splendidly obtained of either, in participation of his nature, so that there continue both a kingly and a priestly class. Christ, however, mindful of human frailty, has, by a marvelous dispensation, regulated what would serve the salvation of His own and has separated the offices of the two powers [*officia utriumque potestatis*] by means of distinctive functions and

---

[51] "Whilst the early and high Middle Ages did not distinguish between religious, political, moral (etc.) norms, but considered only the faithful, there was nevertheless a crucial distinction between the members of the Church, that is, the clergy and the laity. It would be quite erroneous to think and speak of the Church in the sense of the clergy only. Since both constituted the Church, the problem of the relations between the two formed an essential topic in the Middle Ages. Clergy and laity were epitomized in priests and kings and focalized as priesthood (*sacerdotium*) and kingship (*regnum*).... However often it is repeated that there was a conflict between Church and State in the Middle Ages, the assertion still does not make historical sense. What there was, was a conflict between the *sacerdotium* and the *regnum*, but this conflict was fought *within* one and the same body, and not between two autonomous and independent bodies, a Church and a State." Walter Ullmann, *Medieval Political Thought* (New York: Penguin Books, 1975), pp. 17–18.

dignity, intending that His own should be saved by salutary humility and not be carried away by human pride. Hence, Christian emperors are in need of pontiffs for their eternal life, and pontiffs must make use of imperial regulations for temporal necessities.[52]

In a letter, which Pope Gelasius wrote to the Roman Emperor, he declared:

There are mainly two things, August Emperor, by which this world is governed: the sacred authority [*auctoritas*] of the pontiffs and the royal power [*potestas*]. Of these, priests carry a weight all the greater, as they must render an account to the Lord even for kings before the divine judgement. You know, most merciful son, that though you surpass the human race in divinity, yet you must bend a submissive head to the ministers of divine things, and that it is from them that you must receive the conditions of your salvation…. In things concerning the public weal, religious leaders realize that imperial power has been conferred on you from above, and they themselves will obey your laws, for fear that in worldly matters they should seem to thwart your will.[53]

Pope Gelasius enunciated a doctrine that might be called a doctrine of "dual sovereignty." Each sphere of jurisdiction is supreme within the range of activity that is properly its own. The priests are supreme in all spiritual matters, the king in all temporal matters. How one distinguishes between matters spiritual and temporal is not spelled out, and it was precisely because of this ambiguity that serious conflicts arose. The very concept of dual sovereignty is a contradiction since there cannot be two supreme authorities. Pope Gelasius does say that the spiritual power of the priests is superior to that of the king, since their burden is "the heavier," but he does not provide criteria by which to clearly delineate spiritual from temporal matters.

To appreciate the power of the Church in the Middle Ages it is essential to understand that the Church and society were one and that the Church regarded the sacraments administered by priests as the principal means by which the grace of God was made available to the faithful. The Church, through its priests, administered

---

[52] Quoted in Francis Dvornik, *Early Christian and Byzantine Political Philosophy: Origins and Background* (Washington, D.C.: The Dumbarton Oaks Center for Byzantine Studies, 1966), II, p. 807.

[53] *Ibid.*, pp. 804–5.

(and still does) seven sacraments: baptism, confirmation, Holy Eucharist, Holy Orders, penance, matrimony, and extreme unction. From birth to death, the Church is ever present. The greatest spiritual power possessed by the Church is the power of excommunication, which is the denial of the sacraments to someone whom the Church regards as wholly unworthy of receiving them. During the Middle Ages, this power of excommunication was sometimes invoked against kings whose actions the Church regarded as encouraging heresy or corrupting the integrity of the Church. The practical effect of the excommunication of a king was to relieve his Christian subjects of any obligation to obey him—in effect, therefore, to depose him as king. Kings often regarded the use of this power as an illegitimate interference in temporal matters and often claimed that its use was motivated by political, rather than spiritual, concerns.

It was not until the eleventh and twelfth centuries that serious conflicts arose between secular rulers and the Church. By that time the papacy had grown in stature and power within the Church. During the earliest days of Christianity, the word *papa* (pope) was simply an affectionate way of addressing a bishop, but after the fourth century it was used to refer to the Bishop of Rome. To understand the rise of the papacy in Rome, it is essential to recall briefly the historical context of the Church in the early Middle Ages.

The Roman Empire was gradually eroded by the pressure of various barbarian invasions. In August 410, the sacking of Rome by the Visigoths was the most dramatic blow. As would be expected, even the distinction between Romans and non-Romans became blurred as the Germanic tribes gained dominance and the Empire fragmented. Furthermore, around the year 700 many of the lands that had been Christian were taken over by Islam, including North Africa, Syria, Palestine, and Spain.[54] The ancient Christian churches in Jerusalem, Antioch, and Alexandria lost contact with the Latin Church. The first great division within Christendom took place when the Latin Church claimed primacy over all Christian churches and, as a result, in time, came into conflict with the Eastern Orthodox Church (Greek), whose leader was the patriarch of Constantinople. At first the relationship between the two Churches was cordial and close, but, gradually, the Eastern Orthodox Church developed some differences in ritual and in belief. The Eastern Church became independent of the Latin Church and refused to acknowledge the

---

[54] Judith Herrin, *The Formation of Christendom* (Princeton: Princeton University Press, 1987).

Bishop of Rome as the head of the Church. In the year 1054 the relationship between the two Churches became severely strained when, using some rather scurrilous language, the Pope in Rome denounced the Eastern Church as a "confabulation of heretics, a conventicle of schismatics, a synagogue of Satan."[55]

The political dissolution of the Roman Empire under the successive waves of barbarian invaders left the Church in Rome as one of the few remaining sources of ancient authority. The Church survived the barbarian invaders, as other Roman institutions did not, and even converted most of them to Christianity. The conversion of the Franks proved to be especially fortuitous or providential since it was the Frankish monarchy that strongly supported the Roman Church. The papacy fell heir to the Empire's former political position and traditions.

It was in the eleventh century that one of the first great conflicts between Pope and Emperor took place. When Hildebrand became Pope Gregory VII in 1073, he immediately sought to bring the new Emperor, Henry IV of Germany, into line. One of the causes of the conflict was a common practice known as simony. Some of the secular rulers were playing a prominent part in offering important ecclesiastical posts (bishoprics) to the highest bidder. Kings frequently were governed in their selection of bishops less by the spiritual qualifications of the candidates than by their political loyalty to the secular ruler. Henry IV had just appointed a Bishop of Milan (which city was under his control) whom Gregory considered unfit for the office. Pope Gregory's displeasure was answered by Henry's calling of a council of nobles and bishops. This council rejected the Pope's authority and sought to depose Gregory as Pope. Gregory replied to this action by excommunicating Henry, and Henry sought unsuccessfully to replace Gregory with another pope. This was only the first of several such clashes that were to take place during the next three hundred years. During this period a considerable volume of literature was produced justifying either the imperial or the papal claims. Although the Gelasian doctrine of the two swords was generally acknowledged by both sides to be valid, as time went on increasingly extreme positions were taken that repudiated that doctrine, and those who sided with the imperial power often challenged the authority of the Pope as the supreme head of the Church.

---

[55] Quoted by R.W. Southern, *Western Society and the Church in the Middle Ages* (Harmondsworth: Penguin Books, 1970), p. 71.

In the twelfth-century controversy over investiture between Anselm and Henry I of England, strong anti-papal arguments were advanced in the so-called York Tracts. The unknown author of the York Tracts not only repudiated the doctrine that bishops have a superiority over kings but also further repudiated the doctrine that the Pope is superior to all bishops. Both kings and priests, the author declares, owe their authority to God as mediated through Christ. "Each of them is in the spirit both Christ and God, and in his office is the figure and image of Christ and of God, the priest the image of Him as priest, the king the image of Him as king, the priest the image of an inferior office and nature, that is His humanity, the king the image of a superior, that is His divinity."[56] The author declares that, in spiritual matters, Christians are obliged to obey not a man but the Church, and the Church, he suggests, consists of the body of the faithful not a hierarchy. Some scholars see the seeds of Protestantism in this early statement rejecting papal claims of authority. The thought contained in the York Tracts is not typical of thought in the twelfth century, but it anticipates the increasingly extreme claims for complete political independence from the Church that are to be made in successive centuries.

The most extreme statement on behalf of the papal claim is made in the papal bull *Unam Sanctam* (1302). The bull was issued during the conflict between Philip the Fair of France and Pope Boniface VIII. The bull declares:

> The true faith compels us to believe that there is one holy Catholic Apostolic Church and this we firmly believe and plainly confess. And outside of her there is no salvation or remission of sins.... Therefore there is one body of the one and only Church, and one head, not two heads, as if the Church were a monster. And the head is Christ, and his vicar, Peter and his successor.... Whoever denies that the temporal sword is in the power of Peter does not properly understand the word of the Lord.... Both swords ... the spiritual and the temporal, are in the power of the Church; the one by the hand of the priest, the other by the hand of kings and knights, but at the command and permission of the priest. Moreover, it is necessary for one sword to be under the other, and the

---

[56] Quoted by McIlwain, *The Growth of Political Thought in the West*, p. 212.

temporal authority to be subjected to the spiritual; for the apostle says, "For there is no power but of God; and the powers that be are ordained by God" (Rom. xiii, 1).... Therefore, whosoever resisteth the power thus ordained of God resisteth the ordinance of God.... We therefore declare, say, and affirm that submission on the part of every man to the bishop of Rome is altogether necessary for his salvation.[57]

The original conception of the two swords, that is, that each is sovereign within its own sphere of jurisdiction, is overturned by this bull. Pope Boniface effectively claims both swords for the Church and asserts the supreme authority of the papacy in all matters temporal and spiritual. The Roman Catholic Church was forced by the pressure of historical events to retreat from this position in subsequent centuries, though it still clings to the affirmation that there is but one holy Catholic Apostolic Church and that all priests, bishops, and laity within the Church are subject to the authority of the Pope on matters of faith and morals.

LAW IN THE EARLY MIDDLE AGES

We cannot conclude an examination of significant developments during the early Middle Ages without mentioning the prevailing conceptions of the nature of law. As Professor Ullmann declares:

> From the fifth to the eleventh century very few individual writers can be detected who had made it their business to expound political theses.... For it was the governments themselves, the popes, kings and emperors who by their governmental measures created, shaped, and applied political ideas. Whatever there was in political doctrine was contained in actions which the governments themselves took and these actions were as often as not responses to actual and concrete situations and challenges.... The vehicle which served the governments to express their political views was, for ostensible reasons, the law. For the business of any government is to govern, and government can be executed—within civilized societies—only by means of the law.[58]

---

[57] Frederic Austin Ogg, ed., *A Source Book of Mediaeval History* (New York: Cooper Square, 1972), pp. 385–88.

[58] Ullmann, *Medieval Political Thought*, pp. 14–15.

The Church fathers took over from the Stoics and the Roman jurists the idea that there is a natural law, which is the rule of right reason. The classic description of this law we encountered earlier in the writings of Cicero. St. Augustine follows St. Paul in recognizing that there is a law written in the hearts of all that enables them, if they will but consult their reason, to distinguish right from wrong. The basic precept of this law is the Golden Rule, "do not unto others what you would not have others do unto you." Following that precept it is wrong to lie, to defraud, to murder, to steal, or to use violence to get one's way. It is a law implanted in the conscience of all. Athough this law is not recognized by children, it is a law that children perceive when they mature and learn to use reason. It is a law that is in conformity with the will of God, an expression of his own nature. The natural law is not the product of will but of the discovery of reason.

In addition to the natural law, the Church fathers also spoke of a divine law. The divine law includes the moral law of the Old Testament, especially the Ten Commandments. The only portion of the Ten Commandments that St. Augustine would exclude is "the carnal observance of the Sabbath," i.e., the literal prohibition against performing any form of labour. The divine law includes the two great commandments that "thou shalt love the Lord thy God with all thy heart, with all thy soul and with all thy mind and thou shalt love thy neighbour as thyself." Some portions of the divine law simply make explicit what is implicit in the natural law.[59] The early Middle Ages did not sharply differentiate the divine law from natural law. It was St. Thomas Aquinas, in the thirteenth century, who provided more precise distinctions.

There is also human law or what is called statute or positive law. This is the law that political authorities make. Such legislation varies in content from time to time and from place to place. In the early Middle Ages it was frequently associated with custom. One of the purposes of human law is the application of the principles contained in divine and natural law to particular situations, but the content of this law will vary with circumstances and needs. St. Augustine was well aware of this:

---

[59] One of the documents used to study canon (Church) law was the *Decretum* of Gratian (c. 1139). It is said there that "... since nothing is commanded by the law of nature but what God wishes, and nothing forbidden but what God forbids, and since there is nothing in the canonical scriptures other than what is found in divine law and divine law is consistent with nature, it is clear that whatever is demonstrably contrary to the divine will or canonical scripture is also opposed to natural law." Quoted by Paul E. Sigmund, *Natural Law in Political Thought* (Cambridge: Cambridge University Press, 1971), p. 51.

Therefore, it is not true to say that a thing rightly done once should not be changed. Obviously right reason demands a change in what was right to do at some earlier time, if the time circumstances is changed, so, when objectors say it is not right to make a change, truth answers with a shout that it is not right not to make a change, because then it will be right both ways, if the change accords with the variation in time.[60]

The principles of justice remain always and everywhere the same but their application may require variations with changed circumstances.

An important ingredient of law in the early Middle Ages was the conception of law brought into Western Europe by the successive waves of barbarian invaders. When the Franks, the Visigoths, Ostrogoths, Vandals, Lombards, and Burgundians crossed the frontiers of the Roman Empire and settled within it, they brought with them their own peculiar ideas of law. They had no written law but they did have laws that had been handed down from generation to generation by an oral tradition. It was not law that had been enacted by any assembly or decreed by any king but that was simply the immemorial custom of the tribe. At first, and when they were nomadic, the law was conceived as being peculiar not to any particular place but to particular peoples. Visigoths, for example, would be subject to Visigothic law (custom) throughout their lives and wherever they might live. This conception of the law enabled the Roman law to persist throughout the early Middle Ages as the law peculiar to Romans. From the perspective of the Germanic tribes, law was not something made but something discovered and even when it was written down, as it came to be later, it was conceived, as Professor Jenks points out, "not as legislation but record."[61]

By the ninth century, the Germanic tribes had generally ceased to be nomadic and had settled down in particular areas. The idea of law as being peculiar to particular peoples was transformed into the idea of law as being peculiar to particular territories. Law was still thought of as an immemorial custom, but it was now conceived as the custom of the territory or of the community, i.e., the law of the land.

---

[60] *Epistula*, CXXXVIII, I, 4. Quoted by Deane, *The Political and Social Ideas of St. Augustine*, p. 91.

[61] Edward Jenks, *Law and Politics in the Middle Ages* (London: Murray, 1913), p. 7.

FEUDALISM

As the Germanic tribes settled down in various parts of Western Europe, there gradually developed a system of relationships, which we now characterize as feudalism. Under this system no clear-cut distinctions were made between political, social, and economic activities or functions. The system prevailed in varying forms from approximately the ninth to the eleventh centuries. The word feudalism comes from the word "fief" (*feodum*) and the English word that most nearly approximates its meaning is "tenure." Everything of value, whether it was a piece of land, an office, or a licence to perform some activity, was a "fief," something held by a person as a consequence of some grant by another person. Feudalism was a system of reciprocal rights and duties based upon personal relationships organized hierarchically. The distinction between political authority and personal rights was blurred. During this period it was difficult to distinguish public law from private law. The feudal system consists of a vast and complicated network of contractual relationships between lords and vassals.

The system arose, in part, precisely because there was no centralized authority capable of imposing order in an age that was marked by violence and private wars. The kinds of public duties that the modern citizen is conceived as owing to the state were conceived then as personal duties that a citizen owed to a person who was in a position to protect the citizen from others. The private services, which a vassal owed to a lord, were conceived of as a kind of "rent," which one was obliged to pay for the granting of the fief. Whereas the citizen of the modern state looks to the government for protection of life, liberty and property, the individual in the early Middle Ages looked to another individual who was able to provide this protection. All land was held in tenure by someone from someone else. A vassal who held land as a fief from a lord was obligated to come to the lord's defence if he was attacked by enemies and to help pay the lord's ransom if he was captured. Disputes among vassals in a given territory were settled by the vassals coming together and forming a court, the verdict being rendered by one's peers. There was no "public" authority to perform this function.

Kings themselves were a part of this feudal system and their relationship to their vassals was conceived as a kind of contract. As yet, there were no institutions available to interpret or enforce this contractual relationship, but kings did feel some restraints as a result of it. And, through the idea of law as immemorial custom, the vassals had certain specific expectations as to what was just. Typical of such expectations was a feudal law declaring that "No freeman shall be captured and imprisoned or disseized or outlawed or exiled or in any case harmed, except by a legitimate court of his peers and by the law of the land."[62] Justice was not an abstract idea; it consisted of the recognition of certain specific rights and duties, which were to be found in immemorial custom. The king, moreover, was conceived as being as much bound by immemorial custom as the vassals, and any legislation that was enacted was supposed to be a product of the joint consultation of the king and his nobles.

The Church itself was involved in the feudal system, particularly as it acquired land and property. The Church wanted to invest the powers of bishop on men whom it regarded as spiritually worthy of that position; the kings wanted bishops who would be loyal vassals, since bishops held land in tenure from kings. The ambiguity of the bishop's role—priest and vassal at one and the same time—was one of the principal reasons for the investiture controversy. The king was conceived both as a feudal overlord and as a protector, entrusted by the sanction of God to preserve the true religion. This led to difficulties, as Professor Ullmann points out:

> The feudal function of the king was diametrically opposed to his theocratic function, and in this respect the mediaeval king was an ambiguous being, for according to the latter function it was his will that created law and in its exercise he was unimpeded and independent, whilst according to the former it was the implied or explicit consent of the feudal tenants-in-chief to the law of the king which was the constitutive element. This entailed that the king had to proceed by consultation and agreement with the other parties in the feudal contract.... In this function the king did not stand outside and above the community, but was in every respect a member of it; hence within this structure there was no margin for the sovereign display of the prince's will.[63]

The contradiction between the roles was never resolved.

---

[62] Quoted by Ullmann, *Medieval Political Thought*, p. 150. The words quoted are from the thirty-ninth chapter of the *Magna Carta*. It is interesting to note that the phrase "law of the land," which is still in use, derives from the Germanic idea of law.

[63] *Ibid.*, pp. 146–47.

One thing is clear. The mediaeval king, at least in theory, was never conceived to have absolute power. The king was supposed to be under the law, and a distinction was made between true princes and tyrants. The only remedy for tyranny that mediaeval writers could conceive of was tyrannicide and some of them justified it in extreme cases. This had the obvious disadvantage of giving the decision as to when a king had become a tyrant to the person who would commit the murder. But the idea of institutional restraints had not yet emerged. Professor McIlwain summarizes the situation well when he says:

> … with medieval monarchy, as with feudal relations, the prevailing theory was one thing, the actual facts were often quite another. A nobler conception of kingship—a higher conception of government even —has seldom been expressed than that of the middle ages. Yet injustice was rife and private war almost constant, and lords and kings alike often ruled arbitrarily and oppressively. The main political defect of the time was not a lack of principles, but an almost total absence of any effective sanction for them, and this is undoubtedly one of the chief reasons for the later acquiescence in royal absolutism. One tyrant was preferable to a thousand.
>
> Though the king was under the law in theory, there was little effective machinery in existence to make this theory a practical reality.[64]

CONCLUSIONS

In the fourth and fifth centuries A.D., the Roman Empire slowly collapsed. With its demise, the nomadic and barbarian tribes came to fill the temporary void, and Christianity expanded to replace the thought and institutions of the Greco-Roman culture. Philosophically and theologically, Augustine's understanding of human nature, will, and history became major seminal ideas affecting the course of Western civilization to the present. The meaning ascribed to the individual and to the political community by Greek and Roman thinkers was permanently altered. The purpose of human existence was no longer found in the link provided by the *logos* between human nature and the eternal cosmos. Rather, meaning in existence was purported to be found in the relation of the human race to history and God.

---

[64] McIlwain, *The Growth of Political Thought in the West*, p. 197. A reliable general survey of feudalism is provided by John Critchley, *Feudalism* (London: George Allen & Unwin, 1978).

Politically, Augustine's de-divinization of the political realm and his insistence on the priority of a separate sacred realm were persistent themes throughout the Middle Ages. The inevitable tensions between Church and state increasingly led to the development of separate institutions. Nevertheless, the politico-religious goal remained—a united Christendom where the two realms, *Sacerdotium* and *Regnum*, the sacred and the political authorities, would be connected in an hierarchy in which the political realm was justified primarily by its contribution to the sacred.

SUGGESTIONS FOR FURTHER READING

Hexter, Trevor-Roper, and Fackenheim provide brief but excellent introductions to the Judaic and Christian traditions. Voegelin, De Lange, Danielou and Urban are more extensive works on the philosophic and religious background, and Burns and Armstrong are invaluable guides.

Brown provides an authoritative biography of Augustine. Smith and Chadwick are concise surveys of Augustine's life and thought. Gilson gives a general and sympathetic introduction to Augustine's theology and Kirwan provides an examination from the perspective of a contemporary analytic philosopher.

Translations

Bettenson, Henry, trans. *City of God.* Harmondsworth: Penguin, 1972.

Bourke, Vernon J., ed. *The Essential Augustine.* Indianapolis: Hackett, 1974.

Danielou, Jean. *A History of Early Christian Doctrine Before the Council of Nicaea.* Translated by John Austin Baker. 2 Vols. London: Darton, Longman & Todd, 1973.

Oates, Whitney J., ed. *Basic Writings of Saint Augustine.* 2 Vols. New York: Random House, 1948.

Paolucci, Henry, trans. *The Political Writings of St. Augustine.* Chicago: Gateway, 1962.

Commentaries

Battenhouse, Roy, ed. *A Companion to St. Augustine.* New York: Oxford University Press, 1955.

Borresen, Karl Elisabeth. *Subordination and Equivalence: The Nature and Role of Women in Augustine and Thomas Aquinas.* Washington, D.C.: University Press of America, 1981.

Brooks, Edgar H. *The City of God and the Politics of Crisis*. New York: Oxford University Press, 1955.

Brown, Peter. *Augustine of Hippo*. New York: Dorset Press, 1987.

———. *The Body and Society: Men, Women, and Sexual Renunciation in Early Christianity*. New York: Columbia University Press, 1988.

Chadwick, Henry. *Augustine*. Oxford: Oxford University Press, 1986.

Deane, Herbert A. *The Political and Social Ideas of St. Augustine*. New York: Columbia University Press, 1963.

Evans, G.R. *Augustine on Evil*. Cambridge: Cambridge University Press, 1983.

Figgis, John N. *The Political Aspects of St. Augustine's 'City of God'*. London: Longmans, Green and Co., 1921.

Gilson, Étienne. *The Christian Philosophy of St. Augustine*. New York: Random House, 1960.

Kirwan, Christopher. *Augustine*. London: Routledge, 1989.

Markus, R.A. *Augustine: A Collection of Critical Essays*. New York: Doubleday, 1972.

———. *"Saeculum": History and Society in the Theology of Saint Augustine*. Cambridge: Cambridge University Press, 1970.

Meagher, Robert. *Augustine: An Introduction*. New York: Harper & Row, 1979.

Miles, Margaret R. *Fullness of Life: Historical Foundations for a New Asceticism*. Philadelphia: Westminster Press, 1981.

O'Donovan, Oliver. *The Problem of Self-Love in St. Augustine*. New Haven: Yale University Press, 1980.

Pelikan, Jaroslav. *The Mystery of Continuity: Time and History, Memory and Eternity in the Thought of Saint Augustine*. Charlottesville: University of Virginia, 1986.

Smith, Warren Thomas. *Augustine: His Life and Thought*. Atlanta: John Knox Press, 1980.

Wetzel, James. *Augustine and the Limits of Virtue*. Cambridge: Cambridge University Press, 1992.

Social and Political Background

Armstrong, A.H. *The Cambridge History of Later Greek and Early Medieval Philosophy*. Cambridge: Cambridge University Press, 1967.

Brown, Peter. *The Rise of Western Christendom: Triumph and Adversity, A.D. 200–1000*. Cambridge: Cambridge University Press, 1996.

Burns, J.H., ed. *The Cambridge History of Medieval Political Thought: c. 350–c. 1450.* Cambridge: Cambridge University Press, 1988.

Cochrane, Charles Norris. *Christianity and Classical Culture.* Oxford: Oxford University Press, 1957.

De Lange, Nicholas. *Judaism.* Oxford: Oxford University Press, 1986.

Dodds, E.R. *Pagan and Christian in an Age of Necessity.* New York: Norton, 1970.

Fackenheim, Emil. *What Is Judaism? An Interpretation for the Present Age.* New York: Summit, 1987.

Grant, R.M. *Early Christianity and Society.* New York: Harper & Row, 1977.

Hexter, J.H. *The Judaeo-Christian Tradition.* New York: Harper & Row, 1966.

Jaeger, Werner. *Early Christianity and Greek Paideia.* Cambridge: Harvard University Press, 1961.

MacMullen, Ramsay. *Christianizing the Roman Empire.* New Haven: Yale University Press, 1984.

Markus, R.A. *From Augustine to Gregory the Great.* London: Varkiorum Reprints, 1983.

McIlwain, Charles H. *The Growth of Political Thought in the West.* New York: Macmillan, 1932.

Randall, Jr., John Herman. *Hellenistic Ways of Deliverance and the Making of the Christian Synthesis.* New York: Columbia University Press, 1970.

Segal, Alan F. *Rebecca's Children: Judaism and Christianity in the Roman World.* Cambridge: Harvard University Press, 1986.

Smalley, Beryl, ed. *Trends in Medieval Political Thought.* Oxford: Basil Blackwell, 1965.

Southern, R.W. *Western Society and the Church in the Middle Ages.* Harmondsworth: Penguin Books, 1970.

Trevor-Roper, Hugh. *The Rise of Christian Europe.* New York: Harcourt, 1965.

Ullmann, Walter. *Medieval Political Thought.* New York: Peregrine Books, 1975.

Urban, Linwood. *A Short History of Christian Thought.* Oxford: Oxford University Press, 1986.

Voegelin, Eric. *Order and History.* Vol. I. *Israel and Revelation.* Baton Rouge: Louisiana State University Press, 1956.

———. *Order and History.* Vol. IV. *The Ecumenic Age.* Baton Rouge: Louisiana State University Press, 1974.

ST. THOMAS AQUINAS AND THE HIGH MIDDLE AGES

In A.D. 529, within a century of Augustine's death (A.D. 430), the Emperor had closed a unique institution of the ancient world, the schools of Plato, Aristotle, and the other Greek philosophers. Fittingly, that same year a different kind of institution, the great Benedictine Abbey, Monte Cassino, was founded, inaugurating the "Middle Ages," as that time period between the ancient and the modern worlds has come to be called. Similarly, philosophy was being replaced by Augustinian theology, which dominated until the thirteenth century when the Greek philosophers began to be rediscovered. These eight hundred years from the death of Augustine, sometimes referred to as the Dark Ages, were critical to the development of Western civilization.

It was during these eight hundred years, especially the High Middle Ages from the eleventh century to the thirteenth century when relative stability finally occurred, that cathedrals, universities, and cities painfully, but successfully, transformed a continent devastated by nomadic tribes and wars. It is a common prejudice to describe the history of political philosophy as one that begins with the originality of Socrates, Plato, and Aristotle, becomes diverted if not suppressed by Augustinian orthodoxy in the fifth century, and then revives in the sixteenth century with Machiavelli and the Renaissance.

RECOVERY OF GREEK PHILOSOPHY

Two developments took place that were of crucial importance to political philosophy. First, there was a revival of the study of Roman law, particularly after the production, in 1140, of Gratian's *Concord of Discordant Canons* (sometimes called the *Decretum*). This revival produced a great mass of literature on representation, authority, and consent. Even though this literature was primarily directed at the government of the Church, these discussions of church customs and law were immensely influential on secular political theory as well.[1] Second, during the thirteenth century the rediscovery of Aristotle's philosophy precipitated a crisis in theological and political thought in the West. Whether this crisis was successfully met is still debated, but the synthesis of Greek philosophy and Christianity created by St. Thomas Aquinas during this century is still viewed as an original achievement that had profound political, philosophic, and religious consequences for the West. As J. G. Canning writes:

> The thirteenth century marked the great turning-point in medieval political thought: an idea of the state was clearly acquired and located within an overtly political and this-worldly dimension. This development had its roots in the twelfth century and was the product of the assimilation of ideas derived from the study of Aristotle and Roman law in universities.[2]

The greatness of Aquinas's work can best be seen against the backdrop of the tensions and problems of the twelfth and thirteenth centuries, which sorely tested the unity of Christendom. It had become obvious that the Holy Roman Empire was neither Holy, Roman, nor an empire. Although emperors would still claim to be the 'lords of the whole world', as the Justinian code described the ancient Roman emperors, they, in fact, were not Romans but Germans and instead of being 'lords of the whole world' were in constant tension and conflict with the French, Spanish, and English. Moreover, Italy itself was divided into little kingdoms and city-states. Many of the latter were republican, and both kingdoms and city-states were *de facto* independent of the Empire, as were the great kingdoms of France, Spain, and England. In time, the papacy itself became a kingdom with an army in the field fighting the Emperor. In reality, there clearly was no empire. Even the emperors' claims

---

[1] Brian Tierney, *Religion, Law, and the Growth of Constitutional Thought (1150–1650)* (Cambridge: Cambridge University Press, 1982), pp. 8–28; K. Pennington, "Law, Legislative Authority and Theories of Government, 1150–1300," in *The Cambridge History of Medieval Political Thought, c. 350–c.1450,* ed. J. H. Burns (Cambridge: Cambridge University Press, 1988), pp. 424–53.

[2] B. Canning, "Introduction: Politics, Institutions and Ideas," in *The Cambridge History of Medieval Political Thought, c. 350–c.1450,* p. 341.

of suzerainty, however nominal, were disputed by some who reinterpreted the Roman law to mean that sovereignty resided ultimately in the people.

There was a ferment of new ideas along with a slow evolution of religious and political institutions. Throughout the Middle Ages there had been two competing theories of authority. The ascending theory of authority, associated at the beginning with the Germanic tribes, is that authority is located in the political community, and then, through consultation and election, the community chooses a leader whom it would then also have the authority to depose. The descending theory was that authority is from God but is delegated to rulers through various means. The latter theory was the orthodox position of both the Emperor and the Church. With the revival of interest in the Roman law, some jurists again took up the ascending theory. As Azo, a famous teacher of jurisprudence at the University of Bologna, argued, the people had the authority to make and break a government.[3] With the ascending theory of authority came supporting ideas about popular sovereignty, consent, and accountability of rulers. New institutions were also growing throughout the eleventh and twelfth centuries. The papacy led the way by establishing supremacy over the entire Western church and by declaring its independence from secular powers. Governments with their separate institutions and processes followed and also began to have their own trained and loyal staff rather than relying upon the clergy, as had been the custom. These governments were embryonic, but they did have a central administration, a rational jurisprudence, and legislation derived from deliberation and promulgated by a recognized public authority; and they were supported by claims of representation and consent. There was also the quick development of professional courts, a legal profession and literature, and a bewildering variety of legal systems: canon law, urban law, royal law, feudal and manorial law. The stage had been set for the development of the modern state.[4]

---

[3] Quentin Skinner, "Political Philosophy," in *The Cambridge History of Renaissance Philosophy*, eds. Quentin Skinner, Eckhard Kessler, Jill Kraze (Cambridge: Cambridge University Press, 1988), pp. 391–95; Tierney, *Religion, Law and the Growth of Constitutional Thought*, pp. 54–60.

[4] Harold J. Berman, *Law and Revolution: The Formation of the Western Legal Tradition* (Cambridge: Harvard University Press, 1983), pp. 49–51; Joseph R. Strayer, *On the Medieval Origins of the Modern State* (Princeton: Princeton University Press, 1970), pp. 16–36; Heinrich Mitteis, *The State in the Middle Ages: A Comparative Constitutional History of Feudal Europe*, trans. H. F. Orton ((Amsterdam: North-Holland, 1975).

While secular authority was stabilizing and new political and legal institutions were evolving, creating new tensions and problems for the unity of Christendom, there was a renewal of religious practices and beliefs from the eleventh to the thirteenth centuries. As early as 910 a monastery at Cluny, in French Burgundy, was founded, which led to religious reforms and a cleansing of the papacy. A second impetus for reform began in 1198 at a Benedictine monastery in Citeaux, France. The Cistercians, as they were called, attempted again to lead the Church to religious purity. They established many monasteries far away from the temptations and corruptions of the world. They were, paradoxically, eminently successful throughout the twelfth century in spreading settlements and contributing to the rise of prosperity, from which followed the inevitable corruptions of the world. A third movement began in the thirteenth century, the mendicant Friars of the Franciscan and Dominican orders. The Friars, who attracted the young Aquinas, conceived of their task as one of working in the world rather than one of retreating to a monastery. They took vows of poverty and dedicated their lives to preaching. These two orders came to provide the major thinkers of the High Middle Ages (1100-1300) and to dominate the universities.

All of these movements for reform took place within the general institutional framework of the Church. For many, these reforms were not radical enough. By this time the Church was indeed a privileged institution, demanding independence from secular authorities but still insisting on playing a leading role in governing. It seemed to be far removed from the simple, poor mass of people. As Gordon Leff comments, the Church appeared to many as just another layer of government:

> ...it collected its dues in the form of tithes, enforced tariffs for marriage, baptism, and burial; it often occupied the finest lands with which it had been endowed; in the cities of Northern Europe especially, the bishops were usually the most obdurate opponents of communal liberties. Thus there were very real signs that the Church as an institution was losing contact with its flock and had forgotten its first principles.[5]

Since, for many, religious belief could not be adequately expressed within the established Church, there were continual millenarian movements and various heretical groups trying to purify and even to replace the established Church.[6]

---

[5] Gordon Leff, *Medieval Thought: St. Augustine to Ockham* (Baltimore: Penguin, 1958), p. 83.

[6] Bernard McGinn, *Visions of the End: Apocalyptic Traditions in the Middle Ages* (New York: Columbia University Press, 1979).

Even though secular authorities and the Church would eventually suppress them, their influence persisted. **Millenarian** movements had occurred throughout the Middle Ages. They promised the attainment of salvation and happiness in this world, and soon. Moreover, some viewed the Pope as the anti-Christ who should be destroyed by force. Such movements were given a new, more powerful and influential formulation by Joachim of Fiore (1145-1202). Whereas Augustine had seen no pattern to the rise and fall of civilization in the time between the birth of Christ and the end of history, and whereas he also viewed his time as, at best, one of waiting for the end, Joachim of Fiore developed an ideology to explain and forecast the progress of civilization. His views became quite influential, in part because the Augustinian picture of a dying, senile world, as Eric Voegelin writes, simply did not fit the twelfth-century European's experience:

> ...for his world was quite obviously not in its decline, but, on the contrary, on the upsurge. Population was increasing, areas of settlement were expanding, wealth was growing, cities were being founded, and intellectual life was intensifying, especially through the emergence of the great religious orders since Cluny. The idea of senility must haved seemed preposterous to this vital, expanding age, relishing the exercise of its civilizing powers.[7]

Joachim argued that world history moved in three stages, representing the Trinity. There was the age of the Father, lasting from Creation to the birth of Christ; the second age began with Christ but would be followed, after 1260, by the third age, that of the Holy Ghost. This would be the final stage of perfect Christianity. The first age was one of law as described in the Old Testament, the second of the Church, and in the third all would freely will the good in harmony with one another. For Joachim and his followers, the triadic view of history made sense of the development of civilization and, moreover, was theologically sound. In a rough sense there did seem to be a progression from the Old Testament to Christianity, and now a new prophet and leader would inaugurate a third age befitting the final stage of civilization and progress. Some thought that the new leader would be St. Francis of Assisi and that the prophet who

---

[7] Eric Voegelin, *Science, Politics, and Gnosticism* (Chicago: Regnery, 1968), pp. 93–94.

knew the course of history was Joachim. In any case, the new age would be one of perfect community and of the common man, without institutions, laws, or an oppressing hierarchy.[8]

The religious world had not fragmented to the extent that the Holy Roman Empire had; yet, it was clear that Augustinian theology did not appear to be able to explain the new growth of civilization, and the speculations of Joachim of Fiore indicated the need for a new and, perhaps, better understanding than that found in Augustinianism. But the main threat to the unity of the religious realm came from the rediscovery of Aristotle. A foretaste of the difficulty that faced Aquinas can be perceived in the earlier effect Aristotle had on Judaism and Islam. Between 700 and 1200 the Arab world was clearly the more advanced civilization. It had universities, great libraries, science, and a revival of Greek learning. Consequently, the Islamic scholars, and also the Judaic ones within the Arab world, had to address the challenges to revelation and the Divine Law implicit in Greek philosophy: theology or philosophy, the religious life or the life of reason, the ethics of Aristotle or the ethical commands of the Koran or the Old Testament. How could these alternatives be made compatible? The solution proposed by the greatest Arabic commentator on Aristotle, Ibn Roschd (latinized as Averröes), 1126-1198, was to draw sharp lines separating those capable of rational demonstration (the philosophers) from the dialectician or apologists (the theologians) and both from those who learn by rhetoric (the average person). Truth could be expressed in various ways, in short, depending upon the capacities of the listener. But, in the main, Averröes establishes the compatibility of philosophy and the Koran by arguing that revelation enjoins philosophic speculation, and since only the philosopher can truly know by rational demonstration, it does appear that philosophy ranks higher than theology.[9]

---

[8] Echoes of Joachim's key themes can still be heard today in secular form: a triadic view of history, a leader or prophet who knows the future course of history and inaugurates the new stage, and the final age of perfection, harmony, and the common man free of stifling institutions and regulations. For a full discussion of the transformation of these themes see the studies by Norman Cohn and Eric Voegelin. Voegelin, "Ersatz Religion," in *Science, Politics and Gnosticism*, pp. 83-114; Norman Cohn, *The Pursuit of the Millennium* (London: Temple Smith, 1970); Morton Wilfred Bloomfield, "Joachim of Fiore: A Critical Survey of his Canon, Teachings, Sources, Biography and Influence," *Tradition* 13 (1957), pp. 249–311.

[9] Averröes, "The Decisive Treatise, Determining What the Connection is Between Religion and Philosophy," in *Medieval Political Philosophy: A Sourcebook,* eds. Ralph Lerner and Muhsin Mahdi, (New York: MacMillan, 1963), pp. 168–69, 181–85.

The Jewish philosopher Maimonides (1135-1204) took the opposite tack from Averröes by subordinating philosophy to revealed religion. As one example of his position, he reasoned that since theology teaches the creation of the world in time out of nothing, God must be the author of matter as well as of form and the world cannot be eternal, contrary to the theories of the Greek philosophers. If the eternity of the world could be demonstrated by philosophy (i.e., reason) in such a way that the opposite was clearly seen to be an impossibility, then we should have to modify Scriptural teaching, but the Scriptural teaching is clear on this point and the philosophic arguments adduced to prove the eternity of the world are inconclusive. Moreover, the miracles further attest to the truth of the Biblical view of creation. So, Maimonides concludes, we must reject Aristotle on this point.[10]

That philosophy was recognized as a potential threat to the unity of a religious world, whether Islamic or Judaic, is attested to by the fact that both Averröes and Maimonides spent some time in exile as a consequence of their writings.[11] Whether the relation between philosophy and theology was one that clearly separated philosophy from theology and the philosopher from the society, as advocated by Averröes, or a relation in which Scripture is given the benefit of the doubt in any conflict with philosophy, the potential danger to the unity of Christendom inherent in the conflict was well understood.

It is not surprising then that Aristotle was banned at various times by several Church authorities throughout Europe. The Council of Paris forbid the study of Aristotle's natural philosophy in 1210, and papal bulls were issued in 1231 and 1263 further restricting the study of Aristotle.[12] The rediscovery of Aristotle indeed raised two fundamental challenges. The first challenge had been addressed by Averröes and Maimonides: Are theology and philosophy, reason and revelation, compatible? The second challenge was to medieval political theory: Are the political teachings of theology compatible with the political philosophy of Aristotle?

---

[10] Maimonides, "Guide to the Perplexed," Part I, ch. 71, in Lerner and Mahdi, *Medieval Political Philosophy: A Sourcebook*, pp. 195–98.

[11] Both Averröes and Maimonides were born in Cordova, Spain, lived within the Arabic world, and wrote in Arabic. For a general treatment of Arabic and Jewish philosophy, see David Knowles, *The Evolution of Medieval Thought*, 2nd ed. (London: Longmans, 1988), pp. 175–86.

[12] Fernand Van Steenberghen documents the increasing influence of Aristotle. *Aristotle in the West* (Louvain: Nauwelaerts, 1955).

Christianity, as does Islam and Judaism, requires its believers to assent to divine revelation in order to understand the meaning and destiny of human life. Such a stance appears to be diametrically opposite to Aristotle. Did he not embrace the natural material world, a human's natural power of reason, and a unified knowledge of reality? Christian theology, on the other hand, focusses on the supernatural and immaterial world, faith and revelation, salvation and redemption, and God's design for human life. Yet, Aristotle also covered remarkably similar topics of human nature, ethics, and purposes through recourse to philosophy, and reason, not revelation. To compound the challenge to theology, Aristotelian philosophy, as explained by the chief commentator, Averröes, was clearly viewed as superior to theology. In contrast to philosophy, the occupation of the learned, theology and belief were meant for the average and unlearned person, or so Averröes and his followers claimed.

It seems appropriate to ask why theology is needed if one has the capacity to read and to understand Aristotle. Certainly, the fundamental concepts of Augustinian theology did not appear to lend themselves to reconciliation or a synthesis with philosophy, as David Knowles writes:

> For Aristotle, the philosopher of common sense and this world, knowledge comes from the mind working on experience, the visible universe is the only field of operation, the immortality of the soul is not personal, and God is needed only as a logical postulate, an ultimate linch-pin to hold the universe together. For Augustine, God and the soul alone are of interest; knowledge is an illumination of the mind in contact with the divine idea of things; and the whole life of a Christian is a growing absorption into God.[13]

Such seeming lack of compatibility would inevitably lead to questioning the very need for theology. Was not the political realm in Aristotle natural and sufficient for the full development of human potential? Theology and theocracy appeared to some as no match for Aristotelian philosophy and political order. As one theologian has written, the intellectual life of the Christian world was in peril: there was potentially "the danger of a complete de-Christianization."[14]

---

[13] David Knowles, "The Historical Context of the Philosophical Work of St. Thomas Aquinas," in *Aquinas: A Collection of Critical Essays*, ed. Anthony Kenny (Notre Dame: University of Notre Dame Press, 1976), p. 17.

[14] Josef Pieper, *Guide to Thomas Aquinas* (New York: Pantheon, 1962), p. 120.

The political challenge of Aristotle was as critical as the challenge to theology. The whole foundation of Christendom had to be rethought. The legal and predominantly religious categories that characterized most political thought after Augustine were clearly inadequate when placed alongside the new, vital ideas of Aristotle and were also clearly inadequate in expressing and evaluating the new civilizational developments seen in the universities, cities, and the political realm. The Augustinian legacy, as we have seen, stressed the tale of two cities, and the earthly, political city belonged to fallen man and was of little worth. By the time of Aquinas, Western Europe had clearly passed into another stage. As Eric Voegelin has noted, a "Western civilization that began to feel its muscles would not easily bear the Augustinian defeatism with regards to the mundane sphere of existence."[15] The stark contrast of the two Augustinian cities, the city of God and the city of man, could not express or explain the extraordinary development of civilization. In the seemingly hopeless task before Aquinas—of providing a synthesis of Aristotelianism with theology—he had to develop for Christianity a new theory of the state and of political authority, relate law to theology, and weave together the obligations of the spiritual with the temporal, the person with the community, and prudence and political realism with theological principles and premises.

ACQUINAS: His Life and Works

Within 50 years of his death Aquinas was canonized as a saint, the first teacher to be so recognized, and within a century his works had rapidly become the major source of theological training for the Catholic Church. This was recognized in 1879 when the Pope proclaimed Aquinas's writings as the official works to be used by all seminaries.

Most of Aquinas's 49 years (1225-1274) were spent in teaching and writing. At the age of five, his family had placed him in the Benedictine monastery Monte Cassino. It was a common practice for noble families to show prudence by sending some sons into the service of the king or emperor and some into service of the Church. All of Thomas's older brothers had joined the service of Emperor Frederick II, and this may explain why Thomas was sent to the monastery to prepare for the more peaceful life of religious service. Monte Cassino also served as a fortress

---

[15] Eric Voegelin, *The New Science of Politics* (Chicago: University of Chicago Press, 1952), p. 119. See also, A. P. D'Entrèves, ed., *Thomas Aquinas: Selected Political Writings* (Oxford: Blackwell, 1965), pp. ix–xi.

during this time, and after one of many quarrels with the Pope, Frederick sent his army, in 1238, to besiege the monastery. Aquinas's education was interrupted and he was sent to Naples. This was an opportune move, which fundamentally altered Aquinas's life in two ways. First, he now had the good fortune of receiving his early university education (from 14 to 20 years of age) at the University of Naples. This university had been established by the Emperor in 1224 and, in effect, was a state university free of the Church's ban against Aristotle. Naples was also a centre for translations of the Arabic commentator on Aristotle, Averröes. Aquinas also had the good fortune to be taught by Peter of Ireland, who knew Arabic. Thus, at a formative age, he was introduced to Aristotle, particularly the scientific works, and Averröes's commentaries. Unlike most educated youth of the time, Aquinas became acquainted with Greek and Arabic, as well as Latin, culture. The second fundamental change that occurred was that Aquinas was converted to the new Order of Preachers, the Dominicans. This was a mendicant order similar to the Franciscans except there was considerably more stress on teaching and on the study of Aristotle. His decision to join the Dominicans, taken in 1244, caused enormous stress with his family. Instead of having a future as a potential abbot of the prestigious Monte Cassino, Aquinas was joining an order of beggars. His brothers actually kidnapped him for a year, but neither their persuasion nor their procurement of a courtesan as a temptation would change Aquinas's decision. Upon his release he was sent by the Dominican order to the greatest university of the age, Paris.

In spite of the official ban Aquinas studied Aristotle in Paris under Albert the Great, who held the Dominican chair of theology. From 1245 to 1248 Aquinas was Albert's student and continued his studies with him at the University of Cologne from 1248 to 1252. Aquinas then returned to Paris and began his study to be a professor of theology. He received his licentiate and professorship in 1256. Neither the Dominican order nor Aristotle was in great favour in Paris. In fact, the university barred Aquinas's appointment to the faculty and ordered students not to attend his inaugural lecture at the Dominican academy. The Pope personally intervened in 1257 to secure the appointment for Aquinas.

The remaining 25 years were spent at Paris, Rome, a return to Paris, and Naples. His last tour of duty at the University of Paris, 1269-1272, was particularly onerous. It was a time of intense controversy between advocates of Aristotelianism, led by Siger of Brabant, and the traditional theological orthodoxy. Aquinas had to separate his views from both sides and also convince both that a synthesis was possible. He wrote over a million words on theology in this three-year period as well as commentaries on most of Aristotle's works. He would dictate to three or four secretaries in sequence. At the same time he had a full slate of classes and was bound to the regular duties of a friar. A few months after returning to Naples (1273) he suffered from exhaustion. On December 6, 1273, he collapsed after Mass and upon reviving, it is reported, told his secretary: "All that I have written seems to me nothing but straw." He continued his other duties, and a couple of months later Pope Gregory X called for a Council of the Church to meet at Lyons to discuss the reconciliation of the Greek and Latin Churches. As an expert on the theology of the Greek Church, Aquinas was asked to go. He was in poor health, and during the journey he sustained a minor head injury and died on March 7, 1274.[16]

The writings that contain most of his political ideas are the *Summa Theologiae* (1266-72), *On Kingship* (1260-66) and his commentaries on Aristotle's *Ethics* (1271) and *Politics* (1269-72). Except for Aquinas's commentary on Aristotle's *Politics*, which was never finished, there is no one work that purports to deal with political philosophy, and most of this commentary is meant to be an explanation of Aristotle rather than a development of Aquinas's own political philosophy. Even *On Kingship*, which he also never finished, is narrowly directed toward the art of governing. His political philosophy, in short, is embedded within his theology. Topics in political philosophy are discussed only as a consequence of pursuing more general theological issues. It is, as one example, the relationship between reason and revelation, discussed in both the *Summa contra Gentiles* (1258-1264) and the *Summa Theologiae*, that leads Aquinas to an explanation of the different kinds of law: eternal, natural, divine, and human. Accordingly, Aquinas's general theological framework and its relation to political philosophy have to be examined first in order to achieve a full understanding of his political philosophy.

---

[16] For brief surveys of Aquinas's life see: Anthony Kenny, *Aquinas* (New York: Hill and Wang, 1980); Ralph McInerny, *St. Thomas Aquinas* (Boston: Twayne, 1977); Kenelm Foster, trans. and ed., *The Life of St. Thomas Aquinas: Biographical Documents* (London: Longmans and Green, 1959). The standard full length biography is by James Weisheipl, *Friar Thomas d'Aquino* (London: Blackwell, 1974).

REASON AND REVELATION

The *Summa contra Gentiles* (*Summary against the Gentiles* or, in English translation, *On the Truth of the Catholic Faith*) is not actually against non-Christians but was written to aid the missionary work of the Dominican order by building on the common philosophical ground shared by Christians, Jews, and Moslems. The importance of the work derives from its attempt to speak about theological questions, but without relying upon the authority of faith, to those Jews and Moslems who were knowledgeable about Aristotelian philosophy.

The work is divided into four books. The first book discusses the existence and nature of God; the second book is on God as creator and on human nature; the third book considers God as the good, the proper end of human action, and God's providential rule. These first three books use only philosophical reasoning to demonstrate theological positions. It is only the last book that relies upon scripture and revelation. Here the topics are the Christian teachings on the trinity, the incarnation, the sacraments, and the resurrection of the dead. Aquinas keeps these topics distinct because they can be known only through revelation, not through natural reason.

The line between reason and revelation is drawn between what can be shown by reason and what requires revelation. Aquinas also notes that many truths, which can be reached by philosophy, can be known to the vast majority only through the authority of revelation. Most people have neither the time nor the ability to use philosophy. To illustrate, for those capable of reasoning Aquinas uses Aristotle's *Physics* to present two proofs of the existence of God, and he also reasons that God must be immaterial, eternal, and unchanging. But, other features of God's nature, he argues, cannot be philosophically demonstrated; they are known by the authority of revelation. For example, when speaking of God's love, wisdom, or knowledge, we can only use words analogically, i.e., as we would use these words about humans. Even when speaking in book three of God's grace and of predestination, Aquinas purports to use only the language and arguments of natural reason. However unwarranted it may appear to modern thinkers, Aquinas clearly held that the use of Aristotelian philosophy was not antithetical to either faith or theology.

It is in the later *Summa Theologiae*, written for theology students, that Aquinas addresses most clearly the relationship between philosophy and theology. The *Summa* is one of the greatest works in the history of philosophy and theology, not only because it examines such fundamental questions as the relation between philosophy and theology but because it is designed to elicit a full and disciplined discourse on each side of an issue. It is written in the form of a disputation: an article or position is stated, objections are given, and Aquinas replies. Great care is given to present as strong objections as possible and to present them as fairly and clearly as possible, i.e., in such a way that the opponents would agree with the formulation. In reply, Aquinas states his position and then follows by detailed replies to each objection. Throughout the *Summa* he vigilantly maintains the line between the arguments derived from natural reason and from the authority of revelation.

The *Summa* has three major parts which are designated as: 'First Part'; 'First Part of the Second Part' and 'Second Part of the Second Part'; and 'Third Part'.[17] The First Part begins with a general discussion of the nature of theology, God, and creation, and it also presents Aquinas's theory of human nature and of reason. The whole of the Second Part is an extensive treatment of ethics and is modelled on the *Nichomachean Ethics*. The First Part of the Second Part considers the moral life of humans in general, and the Second Part of the Second Part discusses specific virtues and vices. The Third Part was never finished but outlines some central theological topics, such as the incarnation and the sacraments.

The first article of the *Summa Theologiae* states the key question: "Whether, besides the philosophical disciplines, any further doctrine is required?" Aquinas replies that theology, the "sacred science," is necessary:

> Even as regards those truths about God which human reason can investigate, it was necessary that man be taught by a divine revelation. For the truth about God, such as reason can know it, would only be known by a few, and that after a long time, and with the admixture of many errors; whereas man's whole salvation, which is in God, depends upon the knowledge of this truth. Therefore, in order that the salvation of men might be brought about more fitly and more surely, it was necessary that they be taught divine truths by divine revelation. It was therefore necessary that, besides the philosophical sciences investigated by reason, there should be a sacred science by way of revelation.[18]

---

[17] Abbreviations are normally used for this voluminous work, such as S. T. I, 1, 8. This means *Summa Theologiae*, Part One, Question 1, article 8. The article contains both the objections and Aquinas's replies. The translation used is that of the Fathers of the English Dominican Province, 3 Vols. (New York: Benzinger Bros., 1948).

[18] S.T.I, 1, 1.

The sacred science is distinctive in several ways. Perhaps most important is that philosophy cannot argue from authority, but in theology one can because the authority is divine revelation, not mere human reason. One could not prove articles of faith by reason, he notes, but one could use rational arguments that start from articles of faith. Even so, such rational arguments are persuasive only to those who have accepted, as premises, Christian revelation.

Beside arguments from authority, theology is distinguished from philosophy in that it cannot, by reason alone, fully grasp its subject matter, God.

> Although we cannot know in what consists the essence of God, neverthe- less in this doctrine we make use of His effects, either of nature or of grace, in the place of a definition, in regard to whatever is treated in this doc- trine concerning God; even as in some philosophical sciences we demon- strate something about a cause from its effect, by taking the effect in the place of a definition of the cause.[19]

The theological method begins with an article of faith or revelation and then ap- plies reason. The proofs of theology thus depend upon their ultimate ground- ing in revelation.

Aquinas further argues that, in addition to being distinctive from philoso- phy, the sacred science "has no science above itself." He gives two reasons. First, theology alone can tell humans about salvation and redemption, the trinity, in- carnation, and other necessary truths found in revelation. Second, even the ar- gument from authority used by theology shows the superiority of the sacred science: "although the argument from authority based on human reason is the weakest, yet the argument from authority based on divine revelation is the strongest."[20] Such an infallible truth about man's highest goal—salvation—ob- viously cannot be claimed by philosophy.

The claim of certitude provided by revelation is not to be confused with that provided by reason. As Aquinas explains, the non-sacred sciences "derive their certitude from the natural light of human reason, which can err, whereas [the sacred science] derives its certitude from the light of the divine knowledge, which cannot err."[21] He does admit that humans, of course, can have doubts about

---

[19] S.T.I, 1, 7, obj. 1.

[20] S.T.I, 1, 8.

[21] S.T.I, 1, 5.

matters of faith, but this reflects upon the "weakness of the human intellect" and not upon the particular article of faith. Echoing Artistotle's remark that one should seek as much certainty as the subject matter allows, Aquinas adds: "yet the slenderest knowledge that may be obtained of the highest things is more desirable than the most certain knowledge of the lowest things."[22]

Although reason and revelation are distinct, and different types of proofs are appropriate to each, Aquinas emphatically maintains that they are not antithetical and can be compatible. To make the case, Aquinas begins by drawing clear differences in starting points and subjects. Even where there are truths common to theology and philosophy, Aquinas shows that they are reached differently. For example, the existence of God is known by the philosopher through rational arguments for a First Cause; the theologian accepts God's existence by the evidence of revelation. Theology, in short, begins with revelation and has such subjects as the mystery of the trinity. Philosophy begins with nature and apprehends through demonstration and the senses.

Aquinas argues that these distinctions between theology and philosophy, revelation and reason, are not antithetical because of the relationship that exists between grace and nature, the supernatural and the natural. As Aquinas repeats through his prolific writings, grace perfects nature.

> The gifts of grace are added to nature in such a way that they do not destroy but rather perfect nature. Thus the light of faith which is infused in us by grace does not destroy the natural light of reason divinely given us. And although the natural light of the human mind is insufficient to manifest what is manifested through faith, nonetheless it is impossible that what has been divinely given us by faith should be contrary to what is given us by nature.[23]

It is by virtue of this hierarchy that the compatibility of theology and philosophy, revelation and reason, is consistently maintained, and Aquinas is able to construct his synthesis. The theologian, as would be expected, is concerned with the supernatural end of man and the philosopher with the natural end.

---

[22] S.T.I, 1, 5.

[23] "Exposition of Boethius's On the Trinity," S.T.I, 2, 3. Ralph McInerny, *A First Glance at St. Thomas Aquinas: A Handbook for Peeping Thomists* (Notre Dame: University of Notre Dame Press, 1990), p. 18.

It should be remembered that the pervasive model of reality throughout the Middle Ages, one that had its origins in neo-Platonism, was of a hierarchy with levels of being and goodness leading through the natural to the supernatural. This motif was also used to portray the ecclesiastical hierarchy and even a celestial hierarchy. Perhaps the most famous and influential work devoted to this model of reality was Dante Alighieri's *The Divine Comedy*. The original contribution of Aquinas was that the relationship between the natural and the supernatural was not simply one of levels; rather, the natural cannot be fulfilled, completed, or perfected without the supernatural. Because of this feature, Aquinas claimed to provide a true synthesis with grace completing nature.[24]

The synthesis enabled Aquinas to answer affirmatively the question: Are divine law and revelation compatible with Aristotle? More specifically, it enabled him to distinguish in the eyes of his contemporaries his thought from Averröes and Christian Aristotelians, such as Siger of Brabant. The theological followers of Averröes were often charged with having a theory of the double truth, one for faith and one for philosophy. In contrast with Aquinas's synthesis, one was not forced to conclude that a proposition was true by philosophy but false by faith. There was a continuity that led from nature to the truth of faith and revelation.

At the same time, to those who wanted to dismiss Aristotle as a threat to Christianity, Aquinas could show how one could build upon Aristotle. Perhaps the single best illustration of this can be found in the Second Part of the *Summa Theologiae*. Here, Aquinas develops a Christian theory of ethics constructed initially on Aristotle. In form, the positions of Aristotle and Aquinas are similar: virtues are psychic dispositions, and happiness is consistent with them and directed toward the highest object of contemplation. The meaning changes, however, and a synthesis emerges when Aquinas fits the revealed supernatural end and the theological virtues onto the general Aristotelian frame. The compatibility of divine law and revelation with Aristotle is thus claimed.

According to Aristotle, as we saw earlier, true happiness results from living according to the virtues, both intellectual and moral. Aristotle's moral virtues, which are psychic dispositions, are means between excessive or deficient emotions

---

[24] Jaroslav Pelikan, *The Christian Tradition*, Vol. 3, *The Growth of Medieval Theology (600–1300)* (Chicago: University of Chicago Press, 1978), pp. 284–95; Etienne Gilson, *Dante and Philosophy*, trans. David Moore (New York: Harper and Row, 1963); Arthur O. Lovejoy, *The Great Chain of Being* (Cambridge: Harvard University Press, 1936).

and actions. In order to discover the golden mean, i.e., the appropriate emotion or action, one needs the intellectual virtues of prudence (*phronesis*) and of wisdom (*sophia*). Prudence, as defined by Aristotle, comes from experience, and wisdom from theoretical speculation. Aquinas agrees with this main outline: happiness is the goal of human life and, thus, happiness must be consistent with human virtues and not with power, wealth, or the appetites. Further, natural reason could disclose the cardinal virtues of prudence, temperance, courage, and wisdom, and the other virtues disclosed in the *Nichomachean Ethics*. Aquinas, in general, extends virtues to all rather than limiting their realization to the statesman, or potential statesman, and this includes the political virtue of prudence.[25] All of these virtues, Aquinas reasons, "arise from certain natural principles pre-existing in us."[26]

At this point, Aquinas relies upon his position of a continuity leading from reason to revelation. The "naturally instilled principles," he argues, do not "extend beyond the capability of nature. Consequently, man in addition needs to be perfected by other principles in relation to [his] supernatural end."[27] Thus, Aquinas cites, as necessary, the theological virtues of faith, hope, and charity. These are clearly different for they are known by revelation, directed at God, and infused within us by God.[28] There is also the moral virtue of religion, a subspecies of the general virtue of justice. As Aquinas reasoned, the just debt owed to God is worship and reverence. Aristotle did not perceive this virtue because he conceived of the unmoved Mover as a fit subject only for philosophic contemplation. There could be no sense of a just debt being owed, and reason could not establish the moral virtue of religion. Again, we can see how the theological dimension is not merely an addition to Aristotle; rather, it is a synthesis that has changed the perception of human nature.[29]

---

[25] S.T.II-II, 50, 2.

[26] S.T.I-II, 63, 1.

[27] *Ibid.*

[28] S.T.I-II, 62, 1.

[29] An excellent modern defence and explanation of the traditional four cardinal virtues and the three theological virtues is given by Peter Geach, *The Virtues* (Cambridge: Cambridge University Press, 1977). Alasdair MacIntyre argues for the continuing superiority of Aquinas's moral theory: *Three Rival Versions of Moral Enquiry* (Notre Dame: University of Notre Dame Press, 1990).

Aristotle's understanding of the goal of happiness is also altered by Aquinas. Happiness is broadened to include a happiness consistent with theological virtues rather than simply the natural virtues. The happiness of this life is always imperfect given the imperfect conditions and powers of human life. Perfect happiness requires the supernatural end of eternal life and the contemplation of God: "man is directed to God as to an end that surpasses the grasp of his reason."[30] The theological virtues, Aquinas claims, point to this goal and provide a happiness richer than any foreseen by Aristotle. Again, by utilizing the theme that grace completes and perfects nature, Aquinas can build upon Aristotle while retaining his own Christian theory of ethics.

There were, nevertheless, two particular doctrines of Aristotle that seemed clearly incompatible with Christianity and threatened Aquinas's synthesis. First was the heterodox view that the world was eternal. From Aristotle's *Physics*, and other sources in Greek philosophy, this view appeared to be rationally unassailable. To hold that the universe was not eternal, according to Aristotle, one would have to defend the ridiculous and irrational proposition that something—the universe—somehow came from nothing. Later neo-Platonists, such as Plotinus, added that reality was a continual emanation from an eternal and unchanging cause, the One. However expressed, it was agreed by Greek and Islamic philosophers alike that the world was eternal. In contrast, the Judaic and Christian traditions were united in the position that the universe was created out of nothing by God.

The controversy was sufficiently serious at the universities that Aquinas addressed a separate essay to the question, *On the Eternity of the World*, and several articles in the *Summa Theologiae*. In addressing this issue, Aquinas first goes back and carefully examines Aristotle's own arguments. He finds that Aristotle does not claim to have conclusively demonstrated the eternity of the world: "wherever he speaks of the subject, he quotes the testimony of the ancients, which is not the way of a demonstrator, but of one persuading what is probable." Also, Aristotle "expressly says that there are dialectical problems which we cannot solve demonstratively, as, whether the world is eternal."[31] Aristotle's position, in short, is not as the Averröists and others have claimed. Aquinas is now able to reconcile the two sides in the controversy by returning to his great theme of the synthesis of the natural and

---

[30] S.T.I, 1, 1.

[31] S.T.I, 46, 1.

the supernatural, philosophy and revelation. Reason and philosophy can go no further than to demonstrate that there must have been a First Cause and an Unmoved Mover to instigate change and motion in the world. Revelation does not dispute nor contradict this conclusion of natural reason; revelation completes the story by showing that the First Cause is God who created the world *ex nihilo*: "that the world began to exist is an object of faith, but not of demonstration or science."[32]

A second position held by the radical Aristotelians, and apparently incompatible with Christianity, was that of monopsychism, i.e., there is one immaterial soul for all of mankind in which individuals merely participate. This, too, was a serious controversy in the universities, and Aquinas devoted a separate work to it, *The Unity of the Intellect*, and several articles in the *Summa Theologiae*. Roughly, the idea behind such a seemingly strange doctrine was that individuals come in and out of existence but immaterial, uncorruptible, eternal thought does not. The authority for this view was, purportedly, Aristotle since he had described intellectual contemplation as the goal for human perfection. For Aquinas, such a doctrine was contrary to the sanctity and immortality of the individual personality and contrary to individual moral responsibility. But, Aquinas did not rely only on an appeal to tenets of faith. He cited new and more reliable translations of Aristotle to show that Aristotle himself argued for a plurality of individual souls. He accused Averröes and his Latin followers of being corrupters of Aristotle's philosophy.[33] Again, Aquinas concludes that Aristotle's teachings do not contradict Christian belief.

Through his great synthesis of Aristotelian philosophy and Christian theology, Aquinas was able to distinguish his theological position from that of the radical Aristotelians, the Averröists, and the followers of Siger of Brabant. He also could respond to the recovery of Greek philosophy by incorporating much of Aristotelian philosophy. He absolutized neither Aristotle nor the Bible and Augustine. In the eyes of his followers, he did achieve a true synthesis, escaping, on the one hand, the spiritual unworldliness of traditional orthodoxy and, on the other, the self-sufficient philosophy of the natural, material world associated with Aristotle.

Two provisos should be added about this synthesis. First, theology, for Aquinas, is higher than philosophy in importance simply because it interprets revelation. But, theology must rely, in part, upon the intellectual tools of science and philosophy

---

[32] S.T.I, 46, 2.

[33] S.T.I, 76, 2.

for its task. It would be misleading to say that theology is all encompassing and submerges philosophy or even that philosophy serves theology. Thus, the independence of philosophy and science is not questioned. Second, there is, in Aquinas, explicit warnings against a systematic and total claim for knowledge about God and reality. Near the beginning of the *Summa Theologiae*, for example, he states: "we cannot know what God is but rather only what he is not."[34] And, of reality he states: "The essence of things is unknown to us."[35] Systematic certainty or absolute knowledge of the whole is impossible, but the quest is continual for what can be known. For the human mind, reality is inexhaustible. The synthesis, thus, was not designed to chose either theology or philosophy.

POLITICAL PHILOSOPHY

Prior to Aquinas the Christian teachings on secular authority were a mass of conflicting elements. There were sayings strongly supporting the political order: "The powers that be are ordained of God, and he that resisteth the power, resisteth the ordinance of God";[36] "render therefore to Caesar, the things that are Caesar's and to God the things that are God's."[37] There were other passages clearly 'non' if not 'anti' political: "My kingdom is not of this world";[38] "we must obey God rather than men."[39] One passage was particularly cited by the various millenarian movements in condemning political authority: "And all who believed were together and had all things in common; and they sold their possessions and goods and distributed them to all, as any had need."[40] Augustine also had left an ambivalent heritage of maintaining that a loving and benevolent God created and maintained the world but that political order was the consequence of sin. Augustine's assessment of the political realm tended to stress its

---

[34] S.T.I, 3, 3, prologue.

[35] *On Truth*, 10, 1.

[36] Romans 13:1-2.

[37] Matthew 22:21.

[38] John 18:36.

[39] Acts 5:29.

[40] Acts 2:44-45.

negative function as a bulwark against sin. Moreover, there was a live tradition within the Church that supported those who withdrew entirely from the social realm and chose the life of a hermit or joined a monastery.

Aquinas provided the first systematic attempt to combine Christian themes, Stoic and Roman legal thought, and Aristotelian philosophy into a Christian political philosophy. Using the classical Aristotelian method, Aquinas begins with what is natural in humans and upon that inherent potentiality constructs a political philosophy in which the state is more than a palliative for sin. Laws and institutions can contribute to the realization of virtue in humans and society; justice can be more than simply the order one finds among thieves; and the happiness possible in the natural order can lead to the happiness found in the supernatural order.

The shape of Aquinas's political philosophy is determined by his reliance on Aristotle. Aquinas accepts Aristotle's fundamental approach to understanding political reality. We begin reasoning through knowing sensible objects from which the intellect forms concepts. Humans can then attempt to understand the nature and causes of sensible objects. Following Aristotle, Aquinas holds that the nature or the structure of things is determined by their end or final causes. All things develop according to an inherent nature or structure that has a potential realized in a specific end. Potentiality and actuality are, thus, central principles to knowing. An acorn, through the activity of developing, achieves the perfection, or end, of a mature oak tree; a baby, through its activities, achieves the end of adulthood. Potentiality becomes actuality.

Useful as this framework is for understanding, it is limited to the natural world, and Aquinas, as we have seen, insists upon relating the natural to the supernatural. For the political realm, Aquinas must relate human potentialities to both the political or human community and to the supernatural order. In brief, Aquinas argues that the goal of human life is happiness, and this is achieved by a way of life in which both the Aristotelian and theological virtues, or excellences, are practised. Reason, theoretical and practical, can aid us in creating the requisite habit, or way of life, that nature has implanted as a potential in us. But, political society, government, and law can also aid in cultivating the life of virtue, which leads to happiness. The Augustinian view of the secular authority as providing mainly order has clearly been dropped; secular authority can have a positive and constructive part to play in realizing human potentialities and happiness.

Virtue

With Aristotle, Aquinas places the cultivation of virtue as the foremost political end. He also uses the Christian ideas of the will and conscience in explaining virtue and human nature. Conscience is defined as an act or judgment of practical reason in Aristotle's sense. It is an application of knowledge or reason to what we do, and, in Aquinas's words, "is said to witness, to bind or incite, and also to accuse, torment, or rebuke."[41] Conscience works as a psychological register entailing these responses: to witness, to incite, to rebuke.

Unlike our modern usage, conscience, for Aquinas, can be laid aside. Since conscience does depend upon knowledge and reason, since we can be mistaken and in error, and since our consciousness that we are doing wrong can be extinguished, we are provided in human nature with a natural disposition to grasp a universal precept of human action. This capacity, or in Aquinas's terms "natural habit," is called **synderesis**. It is infallible and can never be completely obliterated: it is "said to incite to good and to murmur at evil, inasmuch as we proceed from first principles to discover and judge of what we have discovered."[42] Humans, thus, can judge not only by reason using conscience but also by this natural habit, *synderesis*. Although, as Aquinas notes, *synderesis* may not be destroyed, in practice it, too, may be rendered ineffective through errors in reason or sinful practice. Conscience and, particularly, *synderesis* do show that human nature is constituted for a certain form of human life and directed toward a certain end.

The chief difficulty is to make conscience and *synderesis* operative in humans and society so that the goal of a life of virtue can be obtained. Nature inclines us toward good habits, but education, personal endeavour, laws, and institutions are necessary to acquire the virtues for a good life.

Law

Central to Aquinas's political philosophy is the concept of law by which he weaves together themes from Aristotle, Stoicism and Roman jurisprudence, and Christian moral teachings. He begins by defining law in the manner of Aristotle:

---

[41] S.T.I, 79, 13.

[42] S.T.I, 79, 12.

Law is a certain rule and measure of acts whereby man is induced to act
or is restrained from acting.... Now the rule and measure of human acts
is reason, which is the first principle of human acts...since it belongs
to reason to direct to the end, which is the first principle in all matters
of action, according to the Philosopher.[43]

He gives as the definition of law that "it is nothing else than a certain ordinance
of reason for the common good, made by him who has care of the community, and
promulgated."[44]

Each of these four features can be found in four kinds of law: eternal, divine, natural, and human. Eternal law is the first feature explained because it
supports all the others. The eternal law is promulgated by God, who created
and rules the world by divine reason and directs all things to their ordained end.
"Hence the eternal law is nothing else than the plan of the divine wisdom considered as directing all the acts and motions of creatures."[45] The essential idea is
that what is in reality (Being) embodies a direction, inclination, or ordering toward fulfilment or realization (Good). As Aquinas explains, "God imprints on the
whole of nature the principles of its proper actions." There is an "inward active
principle" in all natural things, including the physical universe and irrational
creatures. All are commanded by God through the eternal law. As a result, being
and goodness are tied in the sense that the good is the realization of a thing's
potential. The move from potentiality to actuality shows that the good is an inherent tendency striving to be fulfilled.[46]

This movement from potentiality to actuality, i.e., to the appropriate end or
good, is a fundamental feature of reality. According to Aquinas, natural inclinations
are found in all three levels of nature: inanimate and plants, animals, and humans.
In the first natural level of plants and inanimate bodies, the inclinations are simply physical or biological necessities; at the animal level, the inclination is seen in
the appetites or instincts for the useful or pleasing; at the human level, the incli-

---

[43] S.T.I-II, 90, 1.

[44] S.T.I-II, 90, 4.

[45] S.T.I-II, 93, 1.

[46] S.T.I, 5, 1-4.

nation is called will and is guided by reason and knowledge. Here the 'good' is not simply instincts or necessity; rather, humans, through reason, can know the nature of the good. The natural inclination for humans, then, is not toward a particular good driven by necessity but is "toward good in general."[47] Humans must habituate the will and use reason to choose the good. Humans are not bound by necessity, but they are bound or obligated in the sense that if they do not act according to their natural inclinations they will hinder their ability to be full persons.

It is because humans can perceive the purposive order of nature intended by God, which he calls the eternal law, that **natural law** is possible. Aquinas has a two-fold task: to delineate the inherent potentialities or inclinations in humans, which are in general good and are the subjects for natural law; to demonstrate how natural law can direct and guide human society and the political order.

First, he argues that practical reason shows that all actions are aimed at an end or good:

> ...the first principle in the practical reason is one founded on the notion of good, viz., that good is that which all things seek after. Hence this is the first precept of law, that good is to be done and pursued, and evil is to be avoided. All other precepts of the natural law are based upon this, so that whatever the practical reason naturally apprehends as man's good (or evil) belongs to the precepts of the natural law as something to be done or avoided.[48]

Second, he argues that there are three natural inclinations toward the good found in human nature: our biological nature inclines us toward self-preservation; our social and animal nature inclines us to propagate and raise children; our rational nature inclines us to seek God and to live in society with other rational creatures. From these three natural inclinations and the first precept of 'do good and avoid evil' other primary precepts of natural law are often formulated: "Act according to reason" or "you ought to act in such a manner that the good is realized."[49]

More precise topics can be derived from the three natural inclinations: humans should seek in rational ways to preserve their lives, to procreate and raise children, and to seek truth and live co-operatively with others. Such primary precepts are

---

[47] S.T.I, 59, 1.

[48] S.T.I, 94, 2.

[49] S.T.I-II, 94, 4.

general, non-specific, and, according to Aquinas, self-evident. All humans have the natural capacity to grasp the truth of these precepts, and, thus, natural law can direct and guide human society and the political order.

It is because humans have *synderesis*, i.e., the habitual capacity to grasp immediately general, moral principles, that Aquinas calls these first precepts of natural law "self-evident." Once we have used the minimal reasoning required to know the meaning of terms, the truth of the first precepts of natural law are immediately seen by all people. He illustrates his point by showing how key propositions are formed, as Aristotle taught, by speculative reason:

> "Man is a rational being," is in its very nature self-evident, since who says "man" says "a rational being," and yet to one who knows not what a man is, this proposition is not self-evident. Hence it is that…certain axioms or propositions are universally self-evident to all, and such are those propositions whose terms are known to all, as, "Every whole is greater than its part," and, "Things equal to one and the same are equal to one another."[50]

Just as the intellect allows us to grasp self-evident propositions in speculative reason, so too *synderesis* allows us to grasp self-evident propositions or primary precepts of natural law.

There are also secondary precepts of the natural law. These are conclusions drawn by reason and experience from the primary precepts. They can tell us what specific human acts are moral. But, these secondary precepts are analogous to practical reason rather than to speculative reason in that some are valid in most cases but not all. He gives as an example the secondary precept of returning goods held in trust. This is morally required in most cases but not when the goods "are claimed for the purpose of fighting against one's country."[51] Secondary precepts are also not self-evident: reason can be "perverted by passion or evil habit or an evil disposition of nature; thus, formerly, theft, although it is expressly contrary to the natural law, was not considered wrong among the Germans, as Julius Caesar relates."[52]

---

[50] S.T.I-II, 94, 2.

[51] S.T.I-II, 94, 4.

[52] *Ibid.*

Aquinas further distinguishes between proximate and remote secondary precepts. The proximate precepts require only a minimum use of reason but the remote precepts are perceived only by the wise. He gives as examples of the proximate secondary precepts what "the natural reason of every man of its own accord and at once judges to be done or not to be done: e.g., 'Honour thy father and thy mother', and 'Thou shalt not kill'." On the other hand, a remote secondary precept cannot be known "without much consideration of the various circumstances, which all are not competent to do carefully but only those who are wise." The example he gives is "honour the person of the aged man."[53]

As with the primary precepts, Aquinas does not give many examples of secondary precepts. For illustrations, he normally cites the Ten Commandments or other commandments from the Old Testament.[54] He does state of both the Old and New Testaments that "whatever belongs to the natural law is fully contained in them."[55] All secondary precepts of natural law are formed by using the primary precepts as directives for determining the proper conduct for a particular situation. As an illustration, the prohibition against lying is a secondary precept and can be derived in the following way. Speech was created by God for the social purpose of communicating with others. When one lies, this purpose is clearly violated. Thus, by reason one can conclude that lying violates what we are, by nature, inclined and designed to do with speech. Here, the general self-evident, primary precept of "act according to reason" and the natural inclination to "live co-operatively with others" lead us to the prohibition against lying. There are, of course, contingencies in which the obligation to tell the truth does not hold, e.g., when one must lie to protect the innocent.

Recognition of the precepts of natural law and their application in a particular situation varies among individuals, societies, and historical periods. This puts into question whether natural law can, in practice, direct and guide human society and political order. The primary or general precepts that constitute "natural law in the abstract", he states, "can nowise be blotted out from men's hearts." He immediately acknowledges that they can be "blotted out in the case of particular action insofar as reason is hindered from applying the general principles to a particular point

---

[53] S.T.I-II, 100, 1.

[54] S.T.I-II, 100, 1-3.

[55] S.T.I-II, 90, 4.

of practice on account of concupiscence or some other passion...." The secondary precepts of natural law also "can be blotted out from the human heart either by evil persuasion, just as in speculative matters error occurs in respect of necessary conclusions, or by vicious customs and corrupt habits...."[56]

Aquinas is well aware that the closer one gets to a particular case the more difficult it is to apply the natural law. Nevertheless, he holds that humans are provided direction and guidance by general primary precepts that are immediately and self-evidently true, such as 'do good and avoid evil' and 'act rationally'. Further, we can, through reason and experience, form precepts from the three natural inclinations of our nature. Also, the secondary precepts, proximate and remote, are perceivable through our natural capacity to reason. Lastly, humans do have conscience and, above all, *synderesis*. Thus, Aquinas and his followers maintain that natural law can provide norms for guiding human actions, laws, and regimes.[57]

Because passions, errors of reason, and distorting social prejudices interfere with the application of natural law, human law and divine law are required to help provide the necessary specifics to guide human life. Aquinas gives four reasons for having the divine law. The first and most important reason is that humans are "ordained to an end of eternal happiness which is inproportionate to man's natural faculty." The divine law, revealed primarily in the Old and New Testaments, directs humans to their supernatural end and also shows humans the means, such as the sacraments, necessary for achieving the end. Reason is not capable of discovering either. Second, human judgment on matters that can be known can still be uncertain, "different people form different judgments on human acts, whence also different and contrary laws result." Even in those areas where the natural law could be applicable, divine law eliminates confusion and uncertainty. There is, accordingly, a very useful overlap between natural and divine laws: the latter includes part of the natural law as well as the commandments in the Bible. Third, divine law, particularly as found in the New Testament, covers human will and intention. Humans, Aquinas writes, are "not competent to judge of interior movements that are hidden." For the "perfection of virtue," the interior movements of the will or,

---

[56] S.T.I-II, 94, 6.

[57] R.A. Armstrong, *Primary and Secondary Precepts in Thomistic Natural Law Teaching* (The Hague: Martinus Nijhoff, 1966); Richard J. Regan, *The Moral Dimension of Politics* (Oxford: Oxford University Press, 1986), pp. 12–33; Alasdair MacIntyre, *Whose Justice? Which Rationality?* (Notre Dame: University of Notre Dame Press, 1988), pp. 183–208.

as we would say today, motives and intentions, are as necessary for the virtuous life as exterior actions. Last, if human law tried to punish all evil deeds, it would sometimes cause more harm than good. But through the divine law, all evil deeds can be forbidden by God.[58]

Human law, sometimes called "man-made" law, has the essential four ingredients found in all law: "a certain ordinance of reason for the common good, made by him who has care of the community, and promulgated."[59] Aquinas claims that "all laws proceed from the eternal law."[60] But he also notes that "the natural law is a participation in us of the eternal law, while human law falls short of the eternal law."[61] His explanation is that human errors and ill intentions interfere in the realization of eternal and natural law. Nevertheless, human law should clearly try to apply the natural law to particular cases and provide for enforcement.

It is, accordingly, critical to determine precisely how human law can be derived from natural law. Aquinas presents two methods. One he calls a conclusion: "that 'one must not kill' may be derived as a conclusion from the principle that 'one should do harm to no man'." The other is a determination, e.g., one determines precisely the penalty for crime: "the law of nature has it that the evildoer should be punished; but that he be punished in this or that way is not directly by natural law but is a determination of it."[62] These two methods coincide with the traditional distinction in Roman law between the *jus civile*, which is the law peculiar to a particular people and political system, and *jus gentium*, which is a compilation of the rules common to all legal systems. The latter was held to be a "conclusion" and, by its universality, more directly linked to the natural law.[63]

Aquinas is aware that not all provisions of the natural law can be easily applied—in some cases more harm than good would come in trying—but in all cases positive law is to be judged by natural law and must be consistent with it:

---

[58] S.T.I-II, 91, 4.

[59] S.T.I-II, 90, 4.

[60] S.T.I-II, 93, 3.

[61] S.T.I-II, 96, 2.

[62] S.T.I-II, 95, 2.

[63] P. G. Stein, " Roman Law," in Burns, *The Cambridge History of Medieval Political Thought, c. 350–c.1450*, pp. 37–47.

"Every human law has the nature of law in so far as it is derived from the law of nature. If in any case it is incompatible with the natural law, it will not be law, but a perversion of law."[64]

Aquinas does stipulate at some length when the citizen's obligation to human law ceases. Just laws are binding upon conscience and obligatory only when three conditions are met. The laws must be "ordained to the common good," and must not "exceed the power of the lawgivers," and the burden of the law must be shared among the subjects "according to an equality of proportion."[65] By definition, an unjust law violates one of these three conditions. Obligation would then cease unless, as he explains, prudence shows that a scandal or public disturbance would occur. For example, it is possible that disobedience could lead to general violence, which could cause greater disturbance to the public good than an unjust law. He gives the same prudential advice when a ruler has usurped his power. Second, laws are unjust when they are contrary to the divine law. In this case, there is no obligation because such a law is "beyond the scope of human power."[66]

The chief purpose of human law is to aid in developing our "natural aptitude for virtue, but the perfection of virtue must be acquired by man by means of some kind of training." Education and custom often suffice for the young, but this, regrettably, is not ever sufficient: "since some are found to be depraved and prone to vice and not easily amenable to words, it was necessary for such to be restrained from evil by force and fear." A special training is clearly needed, and "this kind of training which compels through fear of punishment is the discipline of laws."[67]

The principle followed by Aquinas is that a law is morally good to the extent that it encourages the development of human potentialities or needs, and a law is morally bad if it keeps humans from being fully human. The end for Aquinas, as it was for Aristotle, is a fully actualized human being. Political society and the law, thus, have a primarily moral purpose:

---

[64] S.T.I-II, 95, 2.

[65] S.T.I-II, 96, 4.

[66] *Ibid.*

[67] S.T.I-II, 95, 1.

It is evident that the proper effect of law is to lead its subjects to their proper virtue: and since virtue is that which makes its subjects good, it follows that the proper effect of law is to make those to whom it is given, good, either simply or in some particular respect.[68]

Besides the overall goal of virtue, Aquinas also mentions other purposes of law. Peace and order are often cited. He particularly stresses that the "end of law is the common good."[69] He also cites with approval a seventh-century Bishop of Seville, Isidore, who lists three conditions for a proper law: "foster religion," "be helpful to discipline," and "further the commonweal."[70] All of these formulations about the purposes of law are linked by Aquinas's position that human law should directly contribute to the development of good character through providing the regulations and coercion that lead to those habits that shape interior wills (motives and intentions) as well as exterior acts.

Although human law appears to have an all-encompassing jurisdiction, Aquinas actually places sharp limitations on its scope. First and most important, Aquinas argues that the law leads "man to virtue by habituating him to good works." That is, human law can affect only the "outward acts" of humans and cannot judge "the inward movements of will," which is the domain of the divine law. Aquinas gives an example: "For human law does not punish the man who wishes to slay but slays not, whereas the divine law does."[71] Second, the fact that the law has a moral purpose does not entail a detailed regulation of all of life. Aquinas agrees with Aristotle that politics is the realm of the practical. Law must fit the majority of cases and aim at vices that it can affect:

Now, human law is framed for a number of human beings, the majority of whom are not perfect in virtue. Wherefore, human laws do not forbid all vices from which the virtuous abstain but only the more grievous vices from which it is possible for the majority to abstain and chiefly those

---

[68] S.T.I-II, 92, 1.

[69] S.T.I-II, 96, 1.

[70] S.T.I-II, 95, 3.

[71] S.T.II, 100, 9.

that are to the hurt of others, without the prohibition of which human society could not be maintained; thus human law prohibits murder, theft, and suchlike.[72]

Moral perfection cannot be achieved by human law. Aquinas agrees with Augustine that true moral perfection is not of this earth but is found in the city of God. Here, one must have laws that are practical and realistic: "The purpose of human law is to lead men to virtue, not suddenly but gradually."[73]

A third limitation on the scope of law is found in Aquinas's insistence that law must limit itself to what actually is appropriate to a particular people and their customs: "Wherefore laws imposed on men should also be in keeping with their condition, for, as Isidore says, laws should be 'possible both according to nature and according to the customs of the country'."[74] In fact, Aquinas views customs as a legitimate source of law: custom "seems to proceed from a deliberate judgment of reason"; custom can be a training for virtue as "by repeated external actions, the inward movement of the will and concepts of reason are most effectually declared"; a law from custom is properly promulgated and "counts far more in favour of a particular observance than does the authority of the ruler." Custom cannot change the natural and divine laws, he argues, but in practice it does set some limits to human law: "For it is not easy to set aside the custom of a whole people."[75]

Even given these limitations to law, it would be difficult to overemphasize the importance of law for Aquinas. It is so essential to the political community that Aquinas finds that something of the nature of law survives even in tyrannical law, which is "not a law, absolutely speaking." But even here peace and order are possible, and in a sense some good is sought "with respect to that particular government."[76] In his work *On Kingship* he also cautions against overthrowing a tyrant too quickly: "this should be tolerated so that greater evils

---

[72] S.T.I-II, 96, 2.

[73] S.T.I-II, 96, 1.

[74] S.T.I-II, 96, 2.

[75] S.T.I-II, 97, 3.

[76] S.T.I-II, 92, 1.

can be avoided."[77] Law, in principle, aims at training humans for the life of virtue and, in practice, provides the necessary conditions of peace and order.

Political Structure

The short essay *On Kingship, to the King of Cyprus* (approximately 80 pages) is as close as Aquinas came to writing a treatise directly on politics. It was never finished, and the King of Cyprus never received it. The essay was written in the tradition of the "Mirror for Princes" literature and contains the usual exhortations to virtuous rule. By using Aristotle, Aquinas does provide more substance than found in the standard "Mirror for Princes" essay, but it still must be augmented by passages from other works in order to see clearly his views on the origin and nature of a political system. The first section or "book" of *On Kingship* outlines a theory of monarchy and follows Aristotle by arguing that political systems evolve from the political and, as Aquinas adds, "social" nature of man. The second book expounds upon the duties of monarchs and, again following Aristotle, discusses some practical considerations in founding a state.

As we have seen from the original precepts of natural law, humans are initially described by Aquinas according to our biological nature: "it is natural for man, more than for any other animal to be a social and political animal, to live in a group." Since we humans are not sufficiently endowed by nature with "teeth, horns, and claws" for procuring our needs, we have to use reason, speech and the help of others to survive.[78] A government is required not only for bodily necessities but, in agreement with Aristotle, one is needed so that humans can develop and express their rational and non-animal dimension. Contrary to Augustine, Aquinas holds that even in "the state of innocence" there would have been social life and political institutions in order to have full human development.[79]

By adding "social" to Aristotle's famous dictum that "man is by nature a political animal," Aquinas meant to accent the natural sociality of human beings separate from the dimensions of law, decision making, power, and governmental institutions. Family, work, worship, and play are all necessary for

---

[77] Gerald B. Phelan and I. Th. Eschmann, trans., *On Kingship, to the King of Cyprus*, (Toronto: The Pontifical Institute of Mediaeval Studies, 1949), I, ch. 6.

[78] *On Kingship*, I, ch. 1.

[79] S.T.I, 96, 4.

human development and become proper concerns for the community as a whole. Accordingly, Aquinas viewed society as an organism with the individual subordinate to, or developing within, the community. Society was also naturally hierarchical because of the differences in knowledge, virtue, and abilities among humans.[80] Because humans have free will and reason, they still have the capacity and responsibility to mould their societies into just communities, grounded on natural law and directed to the common good. The chief instruments to be used for moulding societies are laws and institutions. To the topic of laws, Aquinas devoted considerable attention, as we have seen, but to the question of the best form of government, Aquinas is curiously ambiguous.

In *On Kingship* Aquinas uses Aristotle's definition of a just regime: one directed toward the common good and ruled by laws. He also repeats Aristotle's classification of three just and three parallel unjust regimes: monarchy-tyranny, aristocracy-oligarchy, and polity-democracy. Because the essay was prepared for a king, perhaps it is not too surprising that he finds rule by one the preferable just form. Aquinas gives several practical reasons for this non-Aristotelian conclusion. He argues that it is "in accord with nature" to have "governance by one"; "a unified force is more efficiacious in producing its effects than a force which is scattered or divided"; "the government is better in proportion as the ruling power is one–thus monarchy is better than aristocracy, and aristocracy better than polity"; "lesser evil follows from the corruption of a monarchy (which is tyranny) than from the corruption of an aristocracy."[81] In addition to these practical considerations, monarchy is supported by Divine Providence because everything is so ordered that "good ensues from one perfect cause."[82]

Aquinas describes the office and duties of the king in grandiose terms. As reason rules within the human and as God rules the universe, "the multitude of one is governed by the reason of one man. This is what first of all constitutes the office of a king." Or, the king "is to be in the kingdom what the soul is in the body, and what God is in the world."[83] The duties of the king are also conceived as analogous to God's creation and governing of the world. However flattering the comparison,

---

[80] S.T.I, 96, 3; I, 108, 4.

[81] *On Kingship*, I, chs. 2, 3, 5.

[82] *Ibid.*, ch. 3.

[83] *Ibid.*, ch. 1.

Aquinas reminds the king that he is in charge of intermediate and practical ends and, as such, "should be subject to him to whom pertains the care of the ultimate end, and be directed by his rule.... Kings should be subject to priests."[84] The practical duties listed by Aquinas are "to establish a virtuous life in the multitude," peace, and "a sufficient supply of the things required for proper living."[85]

The king that follows these homilies is promised "stability of power, wealth, honour and fame."[86] Such a king will also have friendship, virtue, and happiness as rewards. Indeed, because the king has greater responsibility within the political hierarchy, he is greater in virtue and will receive proportionately greater happiness.[87] These rewards are contrasted with the fate awaiting a tyrant, in the next life if not in this.

Although these exhortations and homilies seem little protection against tyranny, they do evidence a true concern by Aquinas. He accepts Aristotle's definition of tyranny—rule for oneself and by decree—and believes that education, such as provided by the Church and by reading *On Kingship*, would provide some protection. He does give the advice that the "government of the kingdom must be so arranged that opportunity to tyrannize is removed."[88] What precisely is meant by this lone sentence is not discussed. He is very cautious about removing a tyrant from power, since one should prefer suffering, lest an even worst tyranny should result, but in an extreme case he does allow that a "public authority" could justifiably kill a tyrant. If there is no higher secular authority, such as an emperor over a subordinate prince, however, "recourse must be had to God."[89] This is obviously a very limited doctrine of tyrannicide (the just killing of a tyrant).

The unequivocal defence of monarchy found in *On Kingship* is not maintained in other writings. In the *Summa Theologiae* consent and representation are mentioned as requisite elements for a just political structure. When Aquinas defines law as an ordinance for the common good, he adds that "the making of

---

[84] *Ibid.*, ch. 3.

[85] *Ibid.*, ch. 4.

[86] *Ibid.*, ch. 11.

[87] *Ibid.*, ch. 9.

[88] *Ibid.*, ch. 6.

[89] *Ibid.*

the law belongs either to the whole people or to a public personage who has care of the whole people."[90] This is a formulation of the ascending theory of secular authority, which is that the political source of law must be based on the populace or its representatives. While defending customs as source of law, Aquinas repeats this ascending theory: "For if they are free and able to make their own laws, the consent of the whole people expressed by a custom counts far more in favour of a particular observance than does the authority of the ruler, who has not the power to frame laws except as representing the people."[91]

Yet another difference between *On Kingship* and the *Summa Theologiae* is his advocacy in the *Summa* of the mixed regime rather than monarchy:

> …all should take some share in the government, for this form of constitution ensures peace among the people, and all love and defend it…. Accordingly, the best form of government is in a political community or kingdom wherein one is given the power to preside over all according to his virtue, while under him are others having governing powers according to their virtue, and yet a government of this kind is shared by all, both because all are eligible to govern, and because the rulers are chosen by all. For this is the best form of polity, being partly kingdom since there is one at the head of all, partly aristocracy insofar as a number of persons are set in authority, partly democracy, i.e., government by the people, insofar as the rulers can be chosen from the people, and the people have the right to choose their rulers.[92]

Just as the teachings on the best form of government is ambivalent, so are Aquinas's assessments of the central issues and policies of his day. In some cases his views can be clearly ascribed to an hierarchical paternalistic, and organic political framework. In other cases his views may appear consistent with a limited conception of governmental power, but even in such cases it is the Aristotelian common good, transformed and expanded by the theological virtues, that guides his political thought.

The limited conception of government is expressed in his argument that unjust laws are not binding on conscience. A law is unjust when it is not directed to the common good, exceeds the power of the lawgiver—such as laws contrary to divine

---

[90] S.T.I-II, 90, 3.

[91] S.T.I-II, 97, 3.

[92] S.T.I-II, 105, 3.

law–or lays a disproportionate burden on the subjects. He does note that there may be prudential grounds for the individual to obey; yet, the principle is clear that governments are limited.[93] Another example of this limited conception of the state can be found in his theory of the just war. The state cannot go to war unless certain conditions are met: the proper constitutional authority must decide, not an individual; the war must be for a just cause; the intention should not be wicked, i.e., the motives should not be revenge or cruelty.[94] In both of these cases, Aquinas's concern for the person and the common good provides some limits on government.

With respect to property, Aquinas follows Aristotle and allows individual ownership but with some general direction for the common good by the state. He gives three reasons for preferring private ownership to communal ownership: a person would be more motivated to "procure what is for himself alone," but with communal ownership he would be apt to "shirk the labour and leave to another" a communal task; since a person is more concerned with his own, the general management of the economy would be done better and in a "more orderly fashion"; each person will be more contented and there will be less chance for quarrels.[95] Aquinas also agrees with Aristotle that usury (the charging of interest) is morally wrong: one should not try to profit from someone else's need or to make profit for profit's sake. But, with his usual sense of political realism, Aquinas does not wholly prohibit it since he admits that it can have certain advantages to the economy. He accepts Aristotle's distinction between natural and unnatural modes of exchange for evaluating economic activity. Little that is new is added to the original Aristotelian framework.

The critical point is that the economy is to be subordinate to the common good of the community. Private property fundamentally is a human convention and can be trumped by human need. As Aquinas warns:

> ...whatever goods some have in superabundance are due, by natural law, to the sustenance of the poor.... [It] is lawful for a man to succor his own self by means of another's property...nor is this properly speaking theft or robbery.[96]

---

[93] S.T.I-II, 96, 4.

[94] S.T.II-II, 40, 1.

[95] S.T.II-II, 66, 2.

[96] S.T.II-II, 66, 7.

The common good may also require that unbelievers forfeit their property, as the public authority decides.[97] The view that property rights are inalienable and prior to the community would be inconceivable to Aquinas. A contemporary Thomist, Richard J. Regan, rightly concludes that for Aquinas, "the good of the community goes beyond maximizing the freedom of individuals to do whatever they wish to do; the good of the community includes the whole material and spiritual environment in which individual citizens exercise their freedom."[98]

The concern for the social and communal life of humans can serve to place human welfare at the top of a political agenda, but it may also lead, as critics have contended, to supporting the prevalent social patterns and even prejudices of the day. Aquinas's own reliance on the dominant hierarchical, paternalistic, and organic motifs of feudalism can be seen in his treatment of church-state relations, religious toleration, and the position of women.

As the term was used by Aquinas, slavery refers to medieval serfdom rather than to the absolute slavery of the ancient world or to that practised in the antebellum South. In principle at least, feudalism did provide some reciprocal duties and obligations between serf and master. Aquinas thus views slavery as referring only to external actions where obedience can be rightly demanded. But, "in matters touching the internal movement of the will, man is not bound to obey his fellowman, but God alone." Moreover, "since by nature all men are equal, he is not bound to obey another man in matters touching the nature of the body, for instance, in those relating to the sustenance of his body and the begetting of children."[99] Nevertheless, Aquinas also holds that "a slave is a kind of possession" and anyone who induces a slave to leave his master has committed theft.[100] He also draws an anology between a son and a slave: "each is something belonging to another, the perfect idea of right or just is wanting to them."[101] The themes of hierarchy and paternalism clearly permeate his views.

---

[97] S.T.II-II, 66, 8.

[98] Regan, *The Moral Dimension of Politics*, p. 79; Anthony Black, "The Individual and Society," in Burns, *The Cambridge History of Medieval Political Thought, c. 350–c. 1450*, pp. 588–606.

[99] S.T.II-II, 104, 5.

[100] S.T.II-II, 61, 3.

[101] S.T.II-II, 57, 4.

As to church-state relations, Aquinas advocates neither a clear separation of the two nor a complete dominance of one over the other. In principle, the temporal authority of the state is derived from nature and is independent of the Church. The former's purpose is civic welfare; the latter's purpose is salvation of souls. The obedience of the subjects is divided accordingly by the difference in purposes: "secular power is subject to spiritual power insofar as God so disposes, i.e., in those things pertaining to the salvation of souls. In such matters, one should obey the spiritual rather than the secular power."[102] He further protects the autonomy of the secular realm by arguing that the "distinction between faithful and unbelievers, considered in itself, does not do away with the dominion and authority of unbelievers over the faithful." The next sentence, however, shows that this autonomy is only prudential: "this right of dominion or authority can be justly done away with by the sentence or ordination of the church…since unbelievers in virtue of their unbelief deserve to forfeit their power over the faithful.…"[103] In short, there is clear supremacy of the Church over the state. Temporal authority does come from the natural law as ordained by God and not from the Church; yet, in practice, what is Caesar's and what is God's is decided by the Church since it has the higher calling.[104] The supernatural goal comes within the purview of the Church, and it also provides the perspective for guiding the civic activities of the state. Frederick Copleston rightly concludes that the Church has "indirect power" over the state and that the state "is very much a handmaid of the church."[105] The hierarchy is not altered.

As one would expect, a policy of religious plurality or toleration does not follow from this conception of church-state relations. Although Aquinas argues that heathens and Jews, "who have never received the faith," should not be compelled to believe since that is a matter of the will, they can be subjected to considerable pressure "in order that they may not hinder the faith by their blasphemies or by their evil

---

[102] *Commentary on the Sentences*, II, dist. 44, ad. 4, as found in *Saint Thomas Aquinas: On Law, Morality, and Politics*, eds. William B. Baumgarth and Richard J. Regan (Indianapolis: Hackett, 1988), pp. 259–60.

[103] S.T.II-II, 10, 10.

[104] S.T.III, 8, 1.

[105] *A History of Philosophy: Mediaeval Philosophy*, Vol. II, Part II (Garden City: Doubleday, 1962), pp. 136–37.

persuasions or even by their open persecutions."[106] Aquinas, with approval, quotes Augustine who came to believe that fear and pain were useful to break the willful adherence to heretical arguments. In the same vein, he holds that the Church has the authority to grant freedom to any slave belonging to a Jew, "without paying any price," if the slave becomes a Christian: "nor does the Church inflict harm in this, because Jews themselves are slaves of the Church, and so she can dispose of their possessions...."[107] Given these positions, Aquinas predictably argues that the rites of unbelievers were to be tolerated only "lest certain goods be lost or certain greater evils be incurred." It could cause a great disturbance to forbid them, and besides, he reasons, if they are "unmolested, might gradually be converted to the faith."[108] The severest restrictions are for the heretics or the unbelievers who once did believe. They are rightly subject to "bodily compulsion, that they may fulfil what they have promised and hold what they, at one time, undertook."[109] If the heretics persevere after two admonitions, they are to be delivered to the "secular tribunal to be exterminated thereby from the world by death."[110]

In discussing the role of women, Aquinas sees an equivalence between males and females in some features found in their common human nature, but in general his hierarchical framework and the teachings of Aristotle lead to the subordinate position for women commonly found in the Middle Ages.[111] Relying upon Aristotelian biology, he traces this subordination to nature and to procreation:

> ...the active power in the seed of the male tends to produce something like itself, perfect in masculinity; but the procreation of a female is the result either of debility of the active power, of some unsuitability of the material or of some change affected by external influences, like the south wind, for example, which is damp, as we are told by Aristotle.[112]

---

[106] S.T.II-II, 10, 8.

[107] S.T.II-II, 10, 10.

[108] S.T.II-II, 10, 11.

[109] S.T.II-II, 10, 8.

[110] S.T.II-II, 11, 3.

[111] Eileen Power, *Medieval Women* (Cambridge: Cambridge University Press, 1975); Angela M. Lucas, *Women in the Middle Ages: Religion, Marriage and Letters* (New York: St. Martin's Press, 1983).

[112] S.T.I, 92, 1.

He does add a note of equivalence between male and female by arguing that from the standpoint of the species as a whole, the female is not misbegotten in some way but is natural and derived from God too.

Because of this biological origin, one can understand that at the social level, indeed in the Garden of Eden before sin, there would be natural and necessary subjection of woman to man: "For the human group would have lacked the benefit of order had some of its members not been governed by others who were wiser. Such is the subjection in which woman is by nature subordinate to man because the power of rational discernment is by nature stronger in man."[113] Indeed, the origin of woman from the rib of man in Genesis is fitting: "So the woman was rightly formed from the man, as her origin and chief."[114] In another passage, the same position is repeated: the female has an "intelligent nature" and, thus, is in the image of God, which again provides some equivalence with the male, but "God's image is found in man in a way in which it is not found in woman; for man is the beginning and end of woman, just as God is the beginning and end of all creation."[115]

Such subjection of women, grounded in the order of creation, clearly bars women from partaking in the spiritual powers of the Church, according to Aquinas. Also, there would be little reason for women to take part in political life. He does, accordingly, place women, outside of female religious orders, in the family. Again, he follows Aristotle in finding an intermediate position for women. They are not at the level of two equal men but between children and slaves, and they are capable in marriage of achieving a "domestic" justice rather than a political or civic justice.[116]

Most commentators would agree that Aquinas's view of women "represents a retrogressive dimension" of the return to Aristotle.[117] Some argue that Aquinas has actually further removed women from political life; others find that the stress on the social and family levels, where women are active, has "enhanced [the] dignity of woman":

---

[113] *Ibid.*

[114] S.T.I, 92, 2.

[115] S.T.I, 93, 4.

[116] S.T.II-II, 57, 4.

[117] Jean Bethke Elshtain, *Public Men, Private Women: Women in Social and Political Thought* (Princeton: Princeton University Press, 1981), p. 76.

Aquinas, unlike Aristotle, must grant activities *within* the private sphere a sanctity as well, not simply because they carry over into the public realm but because they express certain Christian virtues and values. Christian morality has a profound effect on the nature and dignity of the public sphere as well.[118]

Whatever judgment is made, the views of Aquinas are far removed from the equality found in Plato.

Understandably, there is a continual debate whether hierarchy or constitutionalism is the dominant motif in Aquinas's political philosophy. It is clear that law and morality are mutually supportive, but this did not lead him to advocate a theocracy or to support the divine right of kings to rule. The state's legitimacy is not provided by the Church nor should law be used in an attempt to "transform" human nature, as Jean-Jacques Rousseau would argue in the eighteenth century. Private morals belonged to the Church and to Providence. Law, however, was directed at the general population and at preventing those grievous acts, as Aquinas says, that "are to the hurt of others, without the prohibition of which human society could not be maintained."[119] There are clear limits, therefore, on the scope and purpose of the state's institutions and laws. Yet, there are also clear hierarchical and organic positions in his thought: witness his views on heresy, women, Jews, slavery, and church-state relations. Both constitutional and heirarchical elements are present with little attempt made to make a synthesis, as he had done in theology. Some modern neo-Thomists have argued that democratic government follows from Aquinas's natural-law theory, but the overwhelming evidence of his writings is for a limited or constitutional monarchy at best.[120]

---

[118] *Ibid.*, p. 79. See also, Margaret R. Miles, *Fullness of Life: Historical Foundations for a New Asceticism* (Philadelphia: The Westminster Press, 1981), pp. 113–34; Arlene W. Saxonhouse, *Women in the History of Political Thought: Ancient Greece to Machiavelli* (New York: Praeger, 1985), pp. 144–50; Kari Elisabeth Børresen, *Subordination and Equivalence: The Nature and Role of Woman in Augustine and Thomas Aquinas* (Washington, D. C.: University Press of America, 1981), pp. 141–306; Diana H. Coole, *Women in Political Theory: From Ancient Misogyny to Contemporary Feminism* (Boulder: Lynne Rienner, 1988), pp. 64–70.

[119] S.T.I-II, 96, 2.

[120] For the view that Aquinas is an unredeemable monarchist, see: Charles Howard McIlwain, *The Growth of Political Thought in the West* (London: Macmillan, 1932), pp. 329–33; Samuel H. Beer, "The Rule of the Wise and Holy: Hierarchy in the Thomistic System," *Political Theory* 14 (August, 1986), pp. 391–422. For those who stress the "democratic" themes in Aquinas, see: Mortimer Adler, *A Dialectic of Morals* (Notre Dame: University of Notre Dame Press, 1941); Yves Simon, *Philosophy of Democratic Government* (Chicago: University of Chicago Press, 1951); Jacques Maritain, *The Rights of Man and Natural Law* (New York: Charles Scribner's Sons, 1943); Regan, *The Moral Dimension of Politics*, pp. 37–46.

CONCLUSIONS

Aquinas's great synthesis was designed primarily to address the question: Are theology and philosophy, reason and revelation, compatible? An evaluation of his synthesis turns to a considerable extent upon the success attributed to his answer. The Augustinian tradition through the Reformation to the present has always criticized the very idea of a synthesis. The major criticism has been that the synthesis blurs the line between the sacred and the secular. H. Richard Niebuhr explains:

> The effort to bring Christ and culture, God's work and man's, the temporal and the eternal, law and grace, into one system of thought and practice tends, perhaps inevitably, to the absolutizing of what is relative.... It is one thing to assert that there is a law of God inscribed in the very structure of the creature, who must seek to know this law by the use of his reason and govern himself accordingly; it is another thing to formulate the law in the language and concepts of a reason that is always culturally conditioned.[121]

The terms we use to understand can never be completely free of our own historical context, and yet the synthesis by definition claims to be able to identify clearly the sacred, eternal, and absolute within the secular, mortal, and historical context. Thus, there is the inescapable consequence with the synthesist approach, as we can see in retrospect, of treating some culturally conditioned practices as if they were divinely sanctioned.

An excellent illustration of this fundamental flaw in the synthesist approach, according to critics, can be found in the natural-law theory. Whereas Plato and Aristotle would argue for a source of right inherent to human nature and reality, Aquinas transforms this idea, using Stoic and Roman views on law, into a theory of natural law. The extent of this transformation or derailment can be seen in two contrasts: the knowledge claimed by Aquinas; and the conception of politics entailed by his theory of natural law.

First, a lawlike ethical code, inscribed in nature and rationally uncovered, is always suspect: it presumes that historical, or fallen and sinful humans as Protestant critics argue, could by untainted reason attain objective moral knowledge. Reinhold Niebuhr has written that it is an illusion to look for "alleged fixities" when the answer is in "the law of love itself":

---

[121] *Christ and Culture* (New York: Harper & Brothers, 1951), p. 145.

The whole concept of natural law rests upon a…rationalism which assumes fixed historical structures and norms which do not in fact exist. Furthermore, it assumes a human participation in a universal reason in which there is no ideological taint. The moral certainties of natural law…are all dubious….[122]

Neither Plato's inner state of being, Aristotle's ethics with the Golden Mean, nor Christian ethics, at least as understood by non-Roman Catholics, can be adequately expressed within the rational, objective framework of the natural law. The source of ethics has been distorted, the critics charge, and the historical human context must temper the claims of moral certainties. What is right to do cannot be logically captured through universally valid rules with secondary precepts and rational deductions. An attempt to do so leads to sanctifying the dominant cultural and social attitudes and practices of the day in the name of natural law and its secondary precepts—just as Aquinas did with his views on Jews, heretics, and women.

Second, the conception of politics implicit in Aquinas's natural law distorts our views of political life. As critics charge, the conflicts, tension, complexity, and plurality of politics, emphasized by Plato and Aristotle, cannot be adequately expressed through a rational theory of natural law. At best, law should provide a framework and general guidance, but even here it must be institutionally possible to amend and develop it. Law's logical, systematic, inflexible, and impartial nature is incompatible with the sensitivity to circumstances and the exercise of judgment required of political decisions. Such decisions are not simply deductions from legal rules but are analogous to judgments in art: there are standards and criteria, but their application to an individual work of art is never simple and deductive.[123] In trying to use natural law for political decisions and judgments, two consequences thus appear inevitable. Culturally-conditioned opinions and decisions are made but covered by the sanctification of natural law, as occurred in the case of Aquinas. Or, the political judgments entailed by natural law are trivial, axiomatic, or abstract: do good, avoid evil;

---

[122] *Christian Realism and Political Problems* (New York: Charles Scribner's Sons, 1953), pp. 172–73.

[123] Ronald Beiner, *Political Judgment* (London: Methuen, 1983), chs. 6–7; Leo Strauss, *Natural Right and History* (Chicago: University of Chicago Press, 1953), pp. 156–64.

act rationally. The political value appears minimal. In either case, according to the critics, the discussion and persuasion necessary for political judgments is not enhanced by the claims of natural law.[124]

Even assuming that these criticisms of the great synthesis are sound, it is still impossible not to accredit the enormous achievements of Aquinas. Prior to his writings, the legal tradition and theology provided the framework in which politics was studied. Aquinas added Aristotelian philosophy and successfully restored the political order. He re-established the classical position that law and institutions actively contribute to the moral development of humanity. Because this is the case, citizens had civic as well as spiritual responsibilities, and the political community as well as the spiritual community was perceived to be a necessary and compatible home for human development. Secular authority, thus, was provided a relative independence from religious dogma, and politics became again an activity intellectually and morally valuable.

Although it would be rash to cite Aquinas as the source of a modern theory of the state or of constitutional monarchy, it would be wrong to deny Aquinas's contribution to the development of both. It is doubtful if the ascending theory of authority could have been revitalized without Aquinas's introduction of Aristotle into the debate. However successful the synthesis may now appear to modern philosophers, it historically freed political philosophy from the stultifying charge of endangering theology and the Church. Perhaps of equal importance in the development of the modern state, Aquinas stressed that prudence was a moral virtue in politics. In spite of his theory of natural law, it seems Aquinas again and again refers to what is practical, prudential, or realistic.

---

[124] The literature defending and criticizing the theory of natural law is immense. A survey of contemporary positions can be found in the collection of articles by Robert George, *Natural Law Theory* (New York: Oxford University Press, 1992). For criticism, in addition to the works of H. Richard Niebuhr and Reinhold Niebuhr, see: Michael Bertram Crowe, *The Changing Profile of the Natural Law* (The Hague: Martinus Nijhoff, 1977); Emil L. Fackenheim, *Metaphysics and Historicity* (Milwaukee: Marquette University Press, 1961). For a defence of Aquinas and with some modifications, see: Armand Maurer, *St. Thomas and Historicity* (Milwaukee: Marquette University Press, 1979); Alan Donagan, "The Scholastic Theory of Moral Law in the Modern World," in *Aquinas: A Collection of Critical Essays*, ed. Anthony Kenny (Notre Dame: University of Notre Dame Press, 1976), pp. 325–39; Daniel J. O'Connor, *Aquinas and Natural Law* (New York: Crowell-Collier-Macmillan, 1968); Anthony Parel, "History and Thomistic Natural Law," in *Vital Nexus* 1:2 (November 1991), pp. 75–90.

He did not let theological abstractions determine his political advice on types of political institutions or practices. The justifying of political activity and institutions was not subsumed by theology or natural law.

There are two other contributions that flowed from Aquinas's synthesis. The two defining institutions of Western civilization were immeasurably improved. The Church was able to survive the recovery of Greek philosophy and, indeed, strengthen itself. The synthesis convinced the Church that the teaching of philosophy was, in principle, non-threatening and could be useful to theology itself. The university also was strengthened through the integration of philosophy with Western civilization. The relative autonomy of philosophy in the West contrasts sharply with its fate in Islam and helps to explain the slow evolution of modern autonomous universities.[125]

It would be quite misleading to leave the impression that Aquinas's political philosophy characterized the Middle Ages. Duns Scotus (1300) forcefully argued that political authority came from the consent and choice of the community. Marsilius of Padua (1325) also argued that government should be derived from the consent and election of the people. William of Ockham (1340) repeated these themes of consent and election. There were unambiguously egalitarian and consent theories associated with Christian theology throughout the Middle Ages, and they helped form the foundations for modern political institutions.

The direct, long-term effect of Aquinas's grand synthesis has been confined mainly to the Roman Catholic Church and its followers. Modern thinkers seldom even attempt to relate the *sacrum et imperium*, reason and revelation, the temporal and eternal. Indeed, modern liberal thinkers, such as Hobbes, Locke, and Mill view such an attempt as fundamentally harmful to the well-being of the individual and to the community. It was certainly clear by the sixteenth century that the persuasive power of the synthesis would be limited: theologically, Luther led the Reformation, in part, to break the Aristotelian influence on Christianity; politically, Machiavelli broke with both medieval and classical political philosophy.

---

[125] David Knowles, *The Evolution of Medieval Thought*, 2nd ed., ed. D. E. Luscombe and C. N. L. Brooke (London: Longman, 1988), pp. 139–98; A. B. Cobban, *The Medieval Universities: Their Development and Organization* (London: Methuen, 1975); Gordon Leff, *Paris and Oxford Universities in the Thirteenth and Fourteenth Centuries: An Institutional and Intellectual History* (New York: Wiley, 1968); Stephen C. Ferruolo, *The Origins of the University* (Stanford: Stanford University Press, 1985).

SUGGESTIONS FOR FURTHER READING

Most works on Aquinas begin with a brief biography, but Weisheipl provides the definitive work. Kenny and McInerny have particularly good chapters, and Foster contains the primary sources of Aquinas's life.

For a general background, J. H. Burns is the indispensable work. Knowles and Murray are short but excellent surveys, particularly for the introductory student. Ullmann's works are also useful short surveys and Berman, Black, Haren, Tierney, Strayer, and Mitteis are valuable for political and legal developments.

There are several good general treatments of Aquinas's whole thought. McInerny's books are highly readable. Copleston is one of the single best works; it is reliable and thorough. Chenu's larger work is also thorough and reliable. Kenny presents Aquinas from the perspective of a modern philosopher and, for the beginning student, Regan applies Aquinas to contemporary issues. MacIntyre's works justify and apply Aquinas to contemporary moral and political topics.

Pelikan is one of the best theological studies and also provides the theological context, as do Copleston's two volumes, *A History of Philosophy*. Gilson and Pieper are in the Thomist tradition. Lonergan gives an astute modern interpretation of Aquinas both as a theologian and philosopher. Geach, Miles, and Jordan are excellent specialized studies.

The readers edited by Sigmund, Parel, and Kenny provide many articles on Aquinas's political philosophy. Gilby's works expound and defend Aquinas. O'Connor, D'Entrèves, Simon, and Armstrong explicate Aquinas's theory of natural law, and Crowe, Finnis, and MacIntyre discuss and criticize Aquinas within the tradition of natural law.

Translations

Baumgarth, William B., and Richard J. Reagan, eds. *Saint Thomas Aquinas: On Law, Morality and Politics*. Indianapolis: Hackett, 1988.

D'Entrèves, A. P., ed. *Thomas Aquinas: Selected Political Writings*. New York: Barnes & Noble, 1981.

Lerner, Ralph, and Mushin Mahdi, eds. *Medieval Political Philosophy: A Sourcebook*. New York: Macmillan, 1963.

Lewis, Ewart, ed. *Medieval Political Ideas*. 2 Vols. New York: Knopf, 1954.

Pegis, Anton, ed. *Basic Writings of Thomas Aquinas*. 2 Vols. New York: Random House, 1945.

————. *Introduction to St. Thomas Aquinas: The Summa Theologica and The Summa contra Gentiles*. New York: Modern Library, 1948.

Phelan, Gerald B., and I. Th. Eschmann, trans. *On Kingship, to the King of Cyprus*. Toronto: Pontifical Institute of Mediaevel Studies, 1949.

The Summa Theologica of St. Thomas Aquinas. 2nd ed. Rev. 3 Vols. New York: Benziger, 1947.

Commentaries

Armstrong, R. A. *Primary and Secondary Precepts in Thomistic Natural Law Teaching*. The Hague: Martinus Nijhoff, 1966.

Chenu, Marie Dominique. *Toward Understanding Saint Thomas*. Chicago: Regnery, 1964.

Copleston, Frederick. *Aquinas*. Baltimore: Penguin, 1955.

Foster, Kenelm, trans. and ed. *The Life of St. Thomas Aquinas: Biographical Documents*. London: Longmans and Green, 1959.

Gilby, Thomas. *The Political Thought of Thomas Aquinas*. Chicago: University of Chicago Press, 1958.

————. *Principality and Polity: Aquinas and the Rise of State Theory in the West*. London: Longmans, 1958.

Gilson, Etienne. *The Christian Philosophy of St. Thomas Aquinas*. New York: Hippocrene Books, 1983.

————. *The Elements of Christian Philosophy*. New York: Mentor, 1960.

Jaffa, Harry V. *Thomism and Aristotelianism*. Chicago: University of Chicago Press, 1952.

Jordan, Mark D. *Ordering Wisdom: The Hierarchy of Philosophical Discourses in Aquinas*. Notre Dame: University of Notre Dame Press, 1986.

Kenny, Anthony. *Aquinas*. New York: Hill and Wang, 1980.

————, ed. *Aquinas: A Collection of Critical Essays*. Notre Dame: University of Nortre Dame Press, 1976.

Lonergan, Bernard. *Verbum: Word and Idea in Aquinas*. Edited by David B. Burrell. Notre Dame: University of Notre Dame Press, 1967.

Maritain, Jacques. *St. Thomas Aquinas*. New York: Sheed and Ward, 1946.

Maurer, Armand. *St. Thomas and Historicity*. Milwaukee: Marquette University Press, 1979.

McInerny, Ralph. *Ethica Thomistica: The Moral Philosophy of Thomas Aquinas*. Washington: The Catholic University of America Press, 1982.

————. *A First Glance at St. Thomas Aquinas: A Handbook for Peeping Thomists*. Notre Dame: University of Notre Dame Press, 1990.

————. *St. Thomas Aquinas*. Boston: Twayne, 1977.

Miles, Margaret R. *Fullness of Life: Historical Foundations for a New Asceticism*. Philadelphia: Westminster Press, 1981.

O'Connor, Daniel J. *Aquinas and Natural Law*. New York: Crowell-Collier-Macmillan, 1968.

Parel, Anthony, ed. *Calgary Aquinas Studies*. Toronto: Pontifical Institute of Medieval Studies, 1978.

Pieper, Josef. *Guide to Thomas Aquinas*. New York: Pantheon, 1962.

Regan, Richard J. *The Moral Dimension of Politics*. Oxford: Oxford University Press, 1986.

Sigmund, Paul E., ed. *St. Thomas Aquinas on Politics and Ethics*. New York: Norton, 1988.

Weisheipl, James. *Friar Thomas d'Aquino*. London: Blackwell, 1974.

Social and Political Background

Berman, Harold J. *Law and Revolution: The Formation of the Western Legal Tradition*. Cambridge: Harvard University Press, 1983.

Black, Antony. *Political Thought in Europe, 1250–1450*. Cambridge: Cambridge University Press, 1992.

Burns, J. H., ed. *The Cambridge History of Medieval Political Thought, c. 350–c. 1450*. Cambridge: Cambridge University Press, 1988.

Copleston, Frederick. *A History of Philosophy: Mediaeval Philosophy*. Vol. II, Part II. *Late Mediaeval and Renaissance Philosophy*. Vol. III, Part I. Garden City: Doubleday, 1962.

Crowe, Michael Bertram. *The Changing Profile of the Natural Law*. The Hague: Martinus Nijhoff, 1977.

D'Entrèves, A. P. *The Medieval Contribution to Political Thought*. New York: Oxford University Press, 1937.

———. *Natural Law.* London: Hutchinson's University Library, 1950.

Finnis, John. *Natural Law and Natural Rights.* Oxford: Clarendon Press, 1982.

Geach, Peter. *The Virtues.* Cambridge: Cambridge University Press, 1977.

Gilson, Etienne. *Dante and Philosophy.* Translated by David Moore. New York: Harper and Row, 1963.

———. *Reason and Revelation in the Middle Ages.* New York: Scribner's Sons, 1938.

Haren, Michael. *Medieval Thought: The Western Intellectual Tradition from Antiquity to the Thirteenth Century.* New York: St. Martin's, 1985.

Hearnshaw, F. J. C., ed. *The Social and Political Ideas of Some Great Medieval Thinkers.* New York: Barnes & Noble, 1967.

Huizinga, J. *The Waning of the Middle Ages.* New York: Anchor Books, 1954.

Knowles, David. *The Evolution of Medieval Thought.* 2nd ed. Edited by D. E. Luscombe and C. N. L. Brooke. London: Longman, 1988.

Leff, Gordon. *Medieval Thought: St. Augustine to Ockham.* Baltimore: Penguin, 1958.

Lovejoy, Arthur O. *The Great Chain of Being.* Cambridge: Harvard University Press, 1936.

MacIntyre, Alasdair. *Three Rival Versions of Moral Enquiry.* Notre Dame: University of Notre Dame Press, 1990.

———. *Whose Justice? Which Rationality?* Notre Dame: University of Notre Dame Press, 1988.

Mitteis, H. *The State in the Middle Ages: A Comparative Constitutional History of Feudal Europe.* Amsterdam: North-Holland, 1975.

Morrall, John B. *Political Thought in Medieval Times.* New York: Harper, 1958.

Murray, Alexander. *Reason and Society in the Middle Ages.* Oxford: Clarendon Press, 1985.

Pelikan, Jaroslav. *The Christian Tradition.* Vol. 3. *The Growth of Medieval Theology* (600–1300). Chicago: University of Chicago Press, 1978.

Pieper, Josef. *Scholasticism: Personalities and Problems of Medieval Philosophy.* New York: Pantheon, 1960.

Sigmund, Paul E., ed. *Natural Law in Political Thought.* Cambridge: Winthrop Press, 1971.

Simon, Yves. *The Tradition of Natural Law: A Philosopher's Reflections.* New York: Fordham University Press, 1965.

Skinner, Quentin, Eckhard Kessler and Jill Kraze, eds. *The Cambridge History of Renaissance Philosophy.* Cambridge: Cambridge University Press, 1988.

Strayer, Joseph R. *On the Medieval Origins of the Modern State.* Princeton: Princeton University Press, 1970.

Tierney, Brian. *Religion, Law, and the Growth of Constitutional Thought (1150–1650).* Cambridge: Cambridge University Press, 1982.

Ullmann, Walter. *A History of Political Thought: The Middle Ages.* Baltimore: Penguin, 1965.

———. *The Individual and Society in the Middle Ages.* Baltimore: The Johns Hopkins Press, 1966.

Van Steenberghen, Fernand. *Aristotle in the West.* Louvain: Nauwelaerts, 1955.

Vignaux, Paul. *Philosophy in the Middle Ages.* Translated by E. C. Hall. New York: Meridian, 1959.

MACHIAVELLI

The period from the fall of Constantinople (A.D. 1453) to the end of the sixteenth century has frequently been spoken of as the Renaissance. Most historians today, however, would extend the initial period and some would contend that the category itself is misleading. We now know that the so-called Dark Ages of the medieval period were not as "dark" as we had been led to suppose and we know that the transition from medieval thought and institutions to those of modernity was gradual, not abrupt. It is difficult to precisely date the so-called Renaissance since, on the one hand, there were indications as early as the eleventh and twelfth centuries that the climate of opinion was changing, but, on the other hand, there were many elements of medieval thought still lingering in the seventeenth century. The important thing, however, is not the precise length of its duration but the gradual change in the climate of opinion that took place between the time of St. Thomas Aquinas and that of John Locke.

THE RENAISSANCE

The Renaissance was an age of exploration, adventure, and discovery. Marco Polo had already explored China, India, and Persia as early as the thirteenth century but in the fifteenth century many explorers sought new routes to the Far East. It was the age of Diaz, Vasco da Gama, Columbus, and Magellan. New scientific instruments such as the quadrant, the sextant and chronometer, ways of distilling sea water, maps and improvements in shipbuilding—all contributed to making journeys by sea safer, and longer journeys became possible. These overseas explorations had a stimulating effect on commerce. Trade increased both in volume and in geographical scope. A money economy gradually replaced the medieval barter system, and a new social class of merchants and bankers challenged the dominance of the feudal landowners. New cities arose whose prosperity rested upon trade. It was the new mercantilists and investors who financed many of the voyages of exploration and discovery in the expectation of making profits.

Politically, the period witnessed the rise of large centralized territorial states. The commercial class and the great princes collaborated in breaking the declining power of feudal ties and restrictions, which were an obstacle to the establishment of territorial hegemony. In this last development, however, Italy lagged significantly behind. While the medieval kings of England, Spain, and France were consolidating their kingdoms and creating the institution of absolute monarchy, Italy remained a congeries of independent cities and principalities. The major principalities were Florence, Milan, Naples, Venice, and the papal states (a collection of small principalities under some control by the Pope). There were shifting alliances and continual conflicts among them. At various times during Machiavelli's life Swiss, German, French, and Spanish armies fought on Italian soil, often at the invitation of one or more of the feuding and weak Italian principalities. Italy was disunited and impotent, with its fate apparently decided by others.

Intellectually, the period was characterized by an increasing interest in things secular and temporal. The Italian writer Petrarch (1304-1374) began the now traditional distinction between classical, dark, and modern ages. In the latter age humanity would experience a rebirth—a renaissance as it came to be called by later historians. One striking feature of this periodization of history was that Christianity became relegated to the dark age, and the classical age of Greek and Roman cultures was viewed as a period of great achievement for humanity. There was, consequently, a great revival of interest in the Greek and Roman classics and in ancient institutions. The thought of Plato and Aristotle had never completely disappeared in the Middle Ages, but often that thought was appropriated second-hand from commentators and corrupt texts. In this period there was a revival of interest not only in Plato and Aristotle but also in the works of pagan historians, essayists, dramatists, and poets. Vergil, Livy, and Thucydides were read with keen delight and enthusiasm. The works of Cicero were held up as a model of Latin prose. The revival of learning stimulated a demand for books in place of the old parchment manuscripts, and the invention of printing in the fifteenth century increased the supply. The pursuit of learning that had formerly been restricted to the clergy was gradually broadened. There was even a small but significant number of women humanists, which is amazing given that women's opportunities for a career were virtually non-existent. The options were the convent, marriage, or solitude, and none of these provided much of a stage for developing and showing one's learning. Yet, against immense odds, a few women did have a public presence in which their ideas were heard and debated.[1] Libraries and universities, as one would expect, began to multiply throughout Europe. Men like the Florentine banker Lorenzo the Magnificent vied with one another to serve as patrons for this outpouring of the arts and letters. A new cultural movement emerged that we have since come to call **humanism**.

In large part **humanism** was a revival of the thought of the pre-Socratic Protagoras who had taught that "Man is the measure of all things." Petrarch had already anticipated this point of view in the fourteenth century, but it remained for contemporaries of Machiavelli—men like Marsilio Ficino and Pico della Mirandola in the fifteenth century—to express it more explicitly. Ficino calls humanity the "terrestrial God" who can shape its own destiny. In his *Oration on the Dignity of Man* Pico tells us that humans stand at the centre of the world and that to humans it has been granted to have whatever they choose and to be whatever they will. By their own free will, and with the aid of their intellect, humans can define their nature for themselves. Poetry, music, art, and literature flourished under the spell of the belief that humans are their own masters and appropriate objects of adulation. Words were hardly adequate to describe, nor the skill of the artist great enough to do homage to the magnificence of the human body, the nobility of its features, and the "agony" of human love. The skill that had previously been directed to building cathedrals proclaiming the glory of God was now directed to singing the praises of humanity.

Many humanists came to the conclusion that ancient learning before the Dark Age provided a deeper and truer knowledge of reality, humanity, and society than that found in contemporary theology. They pursued interests in the ancient traditions of the occult, alchemy, magic, gnosticism, Kabbalah, and Hermetism.

---

[1] Margaret L. King, "Book-lined Cells: Women and Humanism in the Early Italian Renaissance," in Albert Rabil, Jr., *Renaissance Humanism: Foundations, Forms, and Legacy*, Vol. I, *Humanism in Italy* (Philadelphia: University of Pennsylvania Press, 1988), pp. 434–53; Constance Jordan, "Feminism and the Humanists: The Case of Sir Thomas Elyat's Defence of Good Women," *Renaissance Quarterly* 36 (1983), pp. 181-201 and *Renaissance Feminism: Literary Texts and Political Models* (Ithaca: Cornell University Press, 1990); Ian Maclean, *The Renaissance Notion of Woman* (Cambridge: Cambridge University Press, 1980).

The latter purportedly refers to the writings of one Hermes Trismegistus, an alleged teacher of both Moses and Plato. As fantastical as it now seems, many argued that through Hermetism, for example, Christianity and philosophy would be united, and humanity would be seen to be a co-creator with God of reality. All of these ancient learnings claimed to provide esoteric knowledge through which reality could be understood and even controlled.

The revival of science was interwoven with this confidence in human power and the search for esoteric knowledge about reality. Particularly important for Machiavelli was the development of astrology. It was generally held in the fifteenth century that astrology contained universal natural laws: the motion of the heavenly bodies affected not only all individuals but states and religions as well. What we would now call pseudo-sciences were clearly part and parcel of the development of science itself, and they continued to be influential well into the modern age. Even the great Isaac Newton (1642-1727) spent more time writing on his alchemy studies than he did on physics. There was great confidence among the early humanists that we could control our own destiny by discovering such God-like knowledge and power over nature.[2]

The spirit of humanism was also vividly reflected in the sculpture and painting of the period and especially in Florence in the fifteenth century. Throughout the Middle Ages the human body had remained concealed in paintings and treated as an object of shame. The rediscovery of the ancient pagan worlds of Athens and Rome led to the celebration of the human body as a thing of beauty. Donatello's *David* is a magnificent example of this appreciation. Realistic portraiture was introduced as painters increasingly chose as their subject matter

---

[2] The relation of humanism to the development of modern science is a complicated and controversial topic. For an excellent survey of the literature, see: Pamel O. Long, "Humanism and Science," in *Renaissance Humanism: Foundations, Forms, and Legacy*, ed. Albert Rabil, Jr., Vol. III pp. 486–512; Anthony Grafton, "Humanism, Magic and Science," in *The Impact of Humanism on Western Europe* eds. Anthony Goodman and Angus MacKay (London: Longman, 1990), pp. 99–117; Ingrid Merkel and Allen G. Debus, eds. *Hermetism and the Renaissance: Intellectual History and the Occult in Early Modern Europe* (Washington: Folger Books, 1988); D. P. Walker, *Spiritual and Demonic Magic: From Ficino to Campanella* (London: Warburg Institute, 1958); Frances A. Yates, *Giordano Bruno and the Hermetic Tradition* (London: Routledge and Kegan Paul, 1964); Wayne Shumaker, *The Occult Science in the Renaissance: A Study in Intellectual Patterns* (Los Angeles: University of California Press, 1972); Stephen A. McKnight, *Sacralizing the Secular: The Renaissance Origins of Modernity* (Baton Rouge: Louisiana State University Press, 1989); Betty Jo Teeter Dobbs, *The Foundations of Newton's Alchemy or "The Hunting of the Greene Lyon"* (Cambridge: Cambridge University Press, 1975).

scholars, doctors, princes, and businessmen. Self-portraits became more common. Nature, as we encounter it in landscape, was increasingly used to frame the individual figures. The painters rediscovered perspective and used it to place humans in harmony with their natural environment. The supernatural was gradually receding from view. This world and all that is within it seemed more than enough to satisfy human desires. Humanness was becoming more prominent and more individualistic. In some paintings there was a curious commingling of pagan and Christian themes. Botticelli's *Birth of Venus* appears to celebrate the pagan goddess, but it is also suggestive of the Virgin Mary. The new humanism still sought a reconciliation of pagan and Christian deities, and not all fifteenth-century intellectuals or artists were prepared to repudiate their Christian heritage and convictions. But the seeds of modernity had been sown.[3] And some, like Machiavelli, were ready to embark upon a wholly new journey.

MACHIAVELLI: His Life and Works

Machiavelli was born in Florence, in 1469, to a family that lived in modest comfort but was not rich. His father, a lawyer, came from impoverished landed gentry. Florence, in the fifteenth century, was an independent city, owing political allegiance to no one. It was a city of prosperous woolmerchants, bankers, and tradesmen with a population exceeding 100,000. It was also a centre of learning and of considerable artistic creativity. In the fifteenth century the city was ruled by members of the Medici family—a family that was destined to play a prominent role in the history of Florence well into the eighteenth century.

The Medici were temporarily expelled from Florence in 1494. A Dominican friar, Savonarola, carried on an intensive campaign against both ecclesiastical and municipal corruption. He enlisted popular support for his reforms and established

---

[3] The legacy of humanism can be seen in all aspects of civilization. The classic introduction is still by Jacob Burckhardt, *The Civilization of the Renaissance in Italy,* trans. S.G.C. Middlemore (London: Oxford University Press, 1960). See also: Ernst Cassirer, *The Individual and the Cosmos in Renaissance Philosophy,* trans. Mario Domandi (New York: Harper and Row, 1963); Wallace Ferguson, *The Renaissance in Historical Thought* (Cambridge: Harvard University Press, 1948); Hans Baron, *The Crisis of the Early Italian Renaissance,* rev. ed. (Princeton: Princeton University Press, 1966); Paul Oskar Kristeller, "Humanism," in *The Cambridge History of Renaissance Philosophy,* eds. Quentin Skinner, Eckhard Kessler, and Jill Krage (Cambridge: Cambridge University Press, 1988), pp. 111–37 and "The Cultural Heritage of Humanism: An Overview" in Rabil, *Renaissance Humanism: Foundations, Forms, and Legacy,* Vol. III, pp. 515–28; William Kerrigan and Gordon Braden, *The Idea of the Renaissance* (Baltimore: The Johns Hopkins Press, 1989).

a republic. To some, Savonarola appeared as a moral reformer, to others as a self-righteous moral fanatic. The Franciscans supported the political party in opposition to Savonarola, and Pope Alexander VI excommunicated him in 1497. He was brought to trial on charges of treason and heresy by Florentine authorities and was condemned to death in 1498. He was succeeded in power by Piero Soderini, a public-spirited man who had no party ties.

A month after the execution of Savonarola, Machiavelli, now a young man of 29, was appointed secretary to the Second Chancery. This was not an elective office but was the second-highest-paid position in the bureaucracy of the Florentine government. Machiavelli's duties involved more than merely the keeping of records. He was called upon to handle municipal problems and was frequently asked to participate in diplomatic negotiations with foreign powers. It was a position he was to hold for 15 years. A large part of this time was spent in travels as Piero Soderini entrusted him with important diplomatic missions. He was sent to France on four occasions and to the papal court twice. He represented Florence in Cesare Borgia's court at Imola and conferred with the Emperor Maximilian I. Soderini clearly valued his judgment in both domestic and foreign affairs. It was at Machiavelli's suggestion that Soderini created a national militia. Machiavelli became acquainted with military strategy and actually directed a military operation against the neighbouring city of Pisa.

In 1510 Pope Julius II began a military campaign to expel the French from Italy. The French resisted and called a council meeting in Florentine territory. In 1512 the Pope made an alliance with King Ferdinand of Spain, placed Florence, as an ally of France, under an interdict, and sent a Spanish mercenary army to invade Tuscany. After a short and bloody siege of Florence, the city capitulated. Soderini left the city, and the Medici family returned to Florence and to the seats of power. In 1513, on the death of Julius II, Giovanni de Medici was elected Pope Leo X. Another member of the family would be elected Pope in 1523. The ascendancy of the Medici effectively finished the republican government of Florence for the remainder of Machiavelli's life.

With the return of the Medici family to political power, Machiavelli lost his post in the Florentine government. He was forbidden to leave Tuscany for a year and even to enter the City Hall. In February 1513, he was accused of being a member of a conspiracy to overthrow the rule of the Medici. He was put in prison and tortured. He was eventually found innocent and was released from prison on the occasion of Giovanni de Medici's election as Pope Leo X. Shortly thereafter Machiavelli left the city and went to live on a family farm in the hills outside of Florence. During the next 14 years, until his death in 1527, he was effectively barred from the life of action he loved and, instead, devoted himself to studying—particularly the history of Rome—and to writing. There is a very obvious personal element to this writing. Machiavelli wants to understand and to explain the reasons for the failure of the republic in Florence and for his own bitter misfortune.[4] During this whole period he also wrote numerous letters to the Medici and to the Pope pleading for reinstatement, but to no avail. He finally did receive a minor post in 1526. When the Medici were overthrown shortly afterwards, however, he was dismissed, this time for being pro-Medici. The work by which he is best known, *The Prince,* although completed in 1513 and circulated privately during his lifetime, was published posthumously in 1532. Less well known, but equally important to an understanding of his political theory were his *Discourses on the First Ten Books of Titus Livius* (1513-1519), *The Art of War* (1520), *The Life of Castruccio Castracani* (1520), and a *History of Florence* (1525), which had been commissioned by Guilio de Medici. Machiavelli is also credited with the authorship of a number of literary works, of which the play *Mandragola* (1518) is the best known. A large number of Machiavelli's letters are also available. In a letter that he wrote near the end of his life, he said: "I love my native city more than my own soul."[5] Some commentators might think this a fitting epitaph to the life and works of a man who devoted himself both to the practice and observation of what we have since come to call power politics.

---

[4] Three excellent works probing the relation between Machiavelli's personal life and his political philosophy are: Sebastian de Grazia, *Machiavelli in Hell* (Princeton: Princeton University Press, 1989); Wayne A. Rebhorn, *Foxes and Lions: Machiavelli's Confidence Men* (Ithaca: Cornell University Press, 1988); Charles D. Tarlton, *Fortune's Circle: A Biographical Interpretation of Niccolò Machiavelli* (Chicago: Quadrangle Books, 1970).

[5] Letter to Francesco Vettori, 16 April 1527, no. 225. Allan Gilbert, ed. and trans., *The Letters of Machiavelli: A Selection of His Letters* (New York: Capricorn, 1961). There is no doubt that Machiavelli deeply felt the impotence of Florence in facing the great powers and the general humiliation of Italy. For the political background, see: H. C. Butters, *Governors and Government in Early Sixteenth-Century Florence 1502–1519* (Oxford: Clarendon Press, 1985); J. M. Stephens, *The Fall of the Florentine Republic 1512–1530* (Oxford: Clarendon Press, 1983); Eric Voegelin, "Machiavelli's Prince: Background and Formation," *The Review of Politics* XIII (1951), pp. 142–68.

Machiavelli wrote at a time when the personal loyalties of the feudal age were disappearing, when the moral restraints of the Middle Ages were felt less keenly, and when Italy was ruled by a number of petty tyrants. The popes of Machiavelli's day were often corrupt and immoral. Some fathered bastard sons who were put in positions of political power. The papal state itself had gained in political power and stability but stood as an obstacle to the political unification of Italy. Civic loyalty was frequently non-existent, and the tyrants had to rely upon foreign troops and ruthless tactics in order to sustain their power. It was an age in which compassion was scorned as weakness, when justice was no more than the will of the stronger, when treachery, and even murder, were regarded as "normal" expressions of diplomacy. The age confirmed Aristotle's observation that when man is separated from law and justice, he is the worst of all animals.[6]

Some commentators regard Machiavelli's work as nothing more than a record of the political practices of his day, but whether this is an adequate account we shall, for the moment, pass over. Historically, Machiavelli (1483-1546) was the first of a remarkable group of political thinkers who, independent of each other, became precursors of modern political thought: Luther (1483-1546), Bodin (1530-1596), and Hobbes (1588-1679). Each wrote in his own vernacular, rather than only in Latin, and in the context of his own emerging nation: Italy, Germany, France, and England. Each wrote using the intellectual tools from his own background: Machiavelli used history; Luther was a theologian; Bodin relied on law and history; and Hobbes turned to the new sciences of physics and geometry. Yet, their perceptions of politics were strikingly similar. Where the classical and medieval writers were concerned with the source of authority, of right, and of justice, these thinkers studied the reality of power. It could be explained and utilized, for it had a rationally detectable pattern and development. Power certainly could not be understood or constrained simply by discussing religious and philosophic sources of authority. Politics, for them, was the realm of force, selfishness, conflict

---

[6] The standard biography is by Roberto Ridolfi, *The Life of Niccolò Machiavelli,* trans. Cecil Grayson (Chicago: University of Chicago Press, 1963). For a useful description of Machiavelli's diplomatic and political career see J. R. Hale, *Machiavelli and Renaissance Italy* (London: The English Universities Press, 1961). For biographies that relate Machiavelli to the intellectual context, see Federico Chabod, *Machiavelli and the Renaissance,* trans. David Moore (New York: Harper Torchbooks, 1965); Felix Gilbert, *Machiavelli and Guicciardini: Politics and History in Sixteenth-Century Florence* (Princeton: Princeton University Press, 1965).

and domination, and political institutions and statecraft should be formed accordingly. The state or temporal authority must concern itself primarily with peace and order, and so, too, should the political philosopher. Questions of right and justice are of little import. Machiavelli was the first, but Hobbes, as we shall see, was the greatest of these founders of modern political thought.

THE PRINCE

The Prince is a small work, actually more of a pamphlet than a book. Machiavelli dedicated it to Lorenzo the Magnificent, a Medici, but actually a grandson of the original Lorenzo the Magnificent, in the hope that he might secure his favour and employment. Perhaps because Machiavelli's friends did not respond very enthusiastically to its content, the book was never sent to the Medici. Still, Machiavelli's original intention was not just a vain hope. He did have practical knowledge of statecraft. After all, he had observed first-hand two great powers outside of Italy: the king of France, Louis XII, and the Holy Roman Emperor, Maximilian I. He also had direct contact with two major powers within the tense world of Italian principalities: Cesare Borgia, the Duke of Romagna, who attempted to unite northern Italy, and Julius II, the warrior-pope. His assessments of the strengths and weaknesses of these leaders were a significant part of his diplomatic dispatches to Florence, and he clearly relied upon them in composing *The Prince*. He also studied assiduously the classical literature, which was, for him, a storehouse of knowledge about politics. In a letter to his friend Francesco Vettori, he describes his daily life in exile on his farm:

> On the coming of evening, I return to my house and enter my study; and at the door I take off the day's clothing, covered with mud and dust, and put on garments regal and courtly; and reclothed appropriately, I enter the ancient courts of ancient men, where, received by them with affection, I feed on that food which only is mine and which I was born for, where I am not ashamed to speak with them and to ask them the reason for their actions; and they in their kindness answer me; and for four hours of time I do not feel boredom, I forget every trouble, I do not dread poverty, I am not frightened by death; entirely I give myself over to them.[7]

---

[7] Letter to Francesco Vettori, 10 December 1513, no. 137.

It was with some justification, then, that he could claim in his dedication to the book that he had "knowledge of the conduct of great men, learned through long experience of modern affairs and continual study of ancient history."

After reading the laudatory dedication, one might expect the usual exhortation to virtues found in the "Mirror for Princes" genre. It is quickly clear to a reader that scandalously different advice is being offered to the ruler. The contrast with Aquinas's *On Kingship* (1260) or with the standard humanist "Mirror for Princes" of his own day could not be sharper. There is none of the usual moral guidance, or discussion of natural law, or lists of ethical precepts. Indeed, Machiavelli radically criticizes the fundamental premise of such books: that rational political action, moral principles, and even expediency can be bound together. An unjust act that seemed expedient and successful, these books warned, would exact a penalty on the health of the ruler's soul in this life and punishment in the next. Since this view had come to permeate the culture, Machiavelli's statecraft was revolutionary and shocking. J. R. Hale, a noted Renaissance historian, has written that "Machiavelli's *Prince* was like a bomb in a prayerbook."[8] It was not published until five years after his death, and, in 1557, Pope Paul IV placed the book on the *Index Expurgatorious.*

The Prince has four main sections in which Machiavelli organizes and collates his historical data. After describing this structure of the work we will examine the key terms through which he constructs his whole political philosophy: particularly important are his understandings of *virtù*, fortune, necessity, and human nature.

The first part of *The Prince,* chapters I-XI, is organized around the theme of how different forms of states can be governed and maintained. Machiavelli begins by making several key distinctions. States are classified as either republics or principalities, i.e., rule by a prince. He eliminates republics as a subject, since that will be discussed in the *Discourses,* and turns to principalities. As he says, they can be gained through the arms of others (mercenary troops) or one's own arms (a citizen army) or through fortune (good luck) or by "cleverness" (*virtù*). He concludes that there are three classes of principalities, and he explains how power can be consolidated in each. The first class is acquired through inheritance. These are easier to govern and maintain since "ancient custom" or tradition preserves stability. The second class is called "mixed": a new prince acquires an old state. These

---

[8] Hale, *Machiavelli and Renaissance Italy,* p. 23.

states are very difficult to maintain since the very act of acquisition will have offended the new subjects. If the principality has the same language as the prince, it can be maintained, as history demonstrates, by following two rules: "the family line of the old prince must be extinguished," and neither the laws nor the taxes should be changed.[9] If the language and culture of the new subjects are quite different from the new prince, Machiavelli's advice is to establish colonies, as did the ancient Romans. If the acquired state has a history of being free, it will be particularly difficult to maintain. Citing historical examples, Machiavelli finds three methods that could work: destroy it, go and live in it, or create a puppet state to pay tribute but keep the old laws. It becomes clear by chapter VI that the primary focus of the book is with the third class of principalities, the wholly new state. Here, the prince is a founder and innovator.

With the second part of the book, chapters XII to XIV, Machiavelli turns from discussing forms of states to the general methods to be used for founding and preserving them, and this requires a knowledge of military and foreign affairs. He reasons that "since there cannot exist good laws where there are not good armies, and where there are good armies there must be good laws, I shall leave aside the treatment of laws and discuss the armed forces."[10] Chapters XV to XXIII constitute the third major section of the book. Here, Machiavelli presents the actual "methods and procedures of a prince in dealing with his subjects and friends." The result, as we shall see, is a purportedly new knowledge with new rules of conduct toward "subjects and friends" quite unlike those of conventional morality.[11]

The last three chapters of the book provide the fourth and concluding part of the work. Chapter XXIV takes the analysis of the preceding chapters and applies it to Italy: "Why Italian Princes Have Lost Their States." Machiavelli believes that there are two general reasons. First, they used unreliable mercenary troops, and, second, they did not know how to secure support among either subjects or nobles. Chapter XXV is titled: "On Fortune's Role in Human Affairs and How She Can Be Dealt With." Machiavelli argues that his new, realistic, political knowledge

---

[9] Peter Bondanella and Mark Musa, eds. and trans., *The Prince*, in *The Portable Machiavelli* (New York: Penguin, 1979), ch. III, p. 82. All quotations in the text are from this translation unless otherwise noted.

[10] *The Prince,* ch. XII, p. 116.

[11] *Ibid.*, ch. XV, p. 126.

can lead to effective political action, provided that the prince has the correct character and cleverness (*virtù*). In fact, the final chapter, XXVI, is a call for political action, the liberation of Italy. The chapter can be read as the final test for his realistic statecraft and as the promise contained in his political advice. It would appear to be directed at the Medici. There was a Medici pope and the new ruler of Florence, to whom *The Prince* was dedicated, was also a Medici. In principle, there could be other potential princes for the great task of liberation, but whoever leads, Machiavelli predicts, will receive the ardent support of all Italians.

The political philosophy found in *The Prince* could be best described as a statecraft. However shocking, the components he used were innovative and instrumental in recasting political thought. The key components to the statecraft are: human nature and history; necessity and prudence; *virtù* and fortune; form and matter; the state and power. In linking these components the Renaissance tone of the work becomes obvious: Machiavelli and his Machiavellian prince look at the political world afresh; they are free of the old traditions of politics and philosophy; they want to create a new world by human power, one that will reflect and glorify their achievements. Machiavelli may sound like an Aristotelian when he explains how a prince must form through his knowledge and ability (*virtù*) the material, i.e., the subjects and regime, into a stable, successful, and free country. But, as will become clear, the Renaissance confidence in human power and knowledge, which permeates *The Prince*, is decidedly not Aristotelian.[12]

Machiavelli clearly states his purpose in chapter I of *The Prince*: "I shall discuss how these principalities can be governed and maintained." The knowledge of statecraft needed for this task, which he gained from his own experience and from studying the ancients, is derived from a particular view of human nature and history. First, Machiavelli holds that history is a storehouse of the actions of great men. His constant advice is to imitate these great men: "a prudent man

---

[12] Over the centuries the interpretations of Machiavelli have fluctuated from a teacher of evil to a literary figure and rhetorician to a patriot and precursor of modern political science. These, plus other interpretations, are still being voiced. Leo Strauss argues that Machiavelli is an immoralist: *Thoughts on Machiavelli* (Glencoe, Ill.: Free Press, 1958). Eugene Garver stresses the rhetoric of Machiavelli, *Machiavelli and the History of Prudence* (Madison: University of Wisconsin Press, 1987), and Wayne A. Rebhorn interprets him through the literary genres of Medieval and Renaissance writings, *Foxes and Lions: Machiavelli's Confidence Men.* Herbert Butterfield outlines the science of statecraft of Machiavelli in *The Statecraft of Machiavelli* (New York: Collier Books, 1962).

should always enter those paths taken by great men and imitate those who have been most excellent."[13] The great men are invariably founders and rulers of a people or are military leaders: Moses, Cyrus, Romulus, Alexander the Great, Hannibal, and, in his own time, Cesare Borgia. Of the latter, infamous for his poisoning, betrayals, and cruelty, Machiavelli writes, "I would not know of any better precepts to give to a new prince than the examples of his deeds."[14] Second, Machiavelli can use the deeds of the great men to advise present or future princes because the problems of governing and maintaining are universal and repeatable. History is not simply a cycle of recurring events, but, there is sufficient similarity between ancient problems and situations and those of the present. For example, the political problem of maintaining rule over a conquered people is common to all times. A lesson learned from the past would, thus, be applicable to the present. Moreover, the character, ability, and cleverness (*virtù)* of the great men of the past can also be noted and imitated. Third, knowledge for the present can be gained from past events and deeds because human nature is predictable. Self-interest predominates: "For one can generally say this about men: that they are ungrateful, fickle, simulators and deceivers, avoiders of danger, greedy for gain; and while you work for their good they are completely yours, offering you their blood, their property, their lives, and their sons...when danger is far away; but when it comes nearer to you they turn away."[15] Consequently, he advises a prince to "keep his hands off the property and the women of his citizens and subjects." He concludes that "men forget more quickly the death of their father than the loss of their patrimony."[16]

With the repetition through history of political problems and solutions coupled with the predictability of egocentric humans, Machiavelli claims to have brought a new solidity to the knowledge of statecraft. For example, Machiavelli continually stresses that his knowledge is real: "it seemed more suitable to me to search after the effectual truth of the matter rather than its imagined one. And many writers have imagined for themselves republics and principalities that have

---

[13] *The Prince,* ch. VI, p. 92.

[14] *Ibid.,* ch. VII, p. 97.

[15] *Ibid.,* ch. XVII, p. 131.

[16] *Ibid.,* ch. XVII, p. 132.

never been seen nor known to exist in reality."[17] The imaginary republics of Plato, Cicero, and their imitators thus are scorned and of no value to this realistic statecraft. Law, justice, and the good were the topics of these republics of the imagination. But governing and maintaining a real state requires, above all, a knowledge of military affairs: "A prince, therefore, must not have any other object nor any other thought, nor must he take anything as his profession but war, its institutions, and its discipline; because that is the only profession which befits one who commands; and it is of such importance that not only does it maintain those who were born princes, but many times it enables men of private station to rise to that position...." Conflict, not conversation, epitomizes politics. It follows that the education of a prince clearly should not follow the schemes of Plato, Aristotle, the Stoics, and the humanists: "For the exercise of the mind, the prince must read histories and in them study the deeds of great men; he must see how they conducted themselves in wars; he must examine the reasons for their victories and for their defeats in order to avoid the latter and to imitate the former."[18]

Military knowledge alone is too limited for a prince to be successful and, thus, is only a part of statecraft. One also must have knowledge of what actually works in politics. An effective prince does not confuse "what is done for what ought to be done." One must be guided, Machiavelli repeatedly states, by necessity: "it is necessary for a prince who wishes to maintain his position to learn how not to be good, and to use this knowledge or not to use it according to necessity."[19] Necessity can refer to the inescapable tendencies of human nature, heredity, even local customs—in short, any factor that has a causal effect on human action. Necessity may also refer to what is required as a means to accomplish a purpose, for example, law is necessary to correct bad customs. Necessity is not insurmountable, but it must be recognized so that realistic choices and actions are possible. Through necessity, choice can be limited and character, or what Machiavelli calls *virtù*, can be strengthened. A ruler can create and use necessity in maintaining a state. A commander, for example, strengthens the resolve of his troops by burning bridges and boats, which could be used for retreat. Similarly, the law and physical pain or punishment can raise the level of courage and dedication within a citizenry. It is

---

[17] *Ibid.*, ch. XV, pp. 126–27.

[18] *Ibid.*, ch. XIV, pp. 124, 126.

[19] *Ibid.*, ch. XV, p. 127.

advice born from necessity that has helped earn Machiavelli his reputation as an immoralist. What is necessary for founding and maintaining a state and, as we shall see, for attaining honour and glory is not a simple list of virtues.

Circumstances may dictate that appearances deceive as to what is a virtue and what is a vice. In chapter XV Machiavelli makes it clear that he is departing from the principles laid down by previous writers and is offering advice that, he hopes, will be recognized for its originality.

> I say that all men…and particularly princes…are judged by some of these qualities which bring them either blame or praise. And this is why one is considered generous, another miserly…; one is considered a giver, the other rapacious; one cruel, another merciful; one treacherous, another faithful; one effeminate and cowardly, another bold and courageous; one humane, another haughty; one lascivious, another chaste; one trustworthy, another cunning; one harsh, another lenient; one serious, another frivolous; one religious, another unbelieving; and the like. And I know that everyone will admit that it would be a very praiseworthy thing to find in a prince, of the qualities mentioned above, those that are held to be good; but since it is neither possible to have them nor to observe them all completely, because human nature does not permit it, a prince must be prudent enough to know how to escape the bad reputation of those vices that would lose the state for him, and must protect himself from those that will not lose it for him, if this is possible; but if he cannot, he need not concern himself unduly if he ignores these less serious vices. And, moreover, he need not worry about incurring the bad reputation of those vices without which it would be difficult to hold his state; since, carefully taking everything into account, one will discover that something which appears to be a virtue, if pursued, will end in his destruction; while some other thing which seems to be a vice, if pursued, will result in his safety and his well-being.[20]

When Machiavelli speaks of "prudence," as in the quotation above, he does not use that word in the Aristotelian sense but in the more modern sense of being cautious or shrewd—calculating how to appear virtuous without actually being virtuous, knowing how to adapt one's actions to the occasion in such a way as to ensure one's own security.

---

[20] *Ibid.*, ch. XV, pp. 127–28.

Both in *The Prince* and in the *Discourses* Machiavelli frequently uses the word "*virtù*." The Latin derivation for **virtù** is *virtus*, which was similar in meaning to the Greek word *areté*, or excellence. This idea of excellence was transformed by the Romans into the active, noble, and manly life of heroic deeds—the life of *virtus*. By Machiavelli's time, *virtù* was also carrying connotations of Christian virtue. Machiavelli himself implicitly redefines the term by coupling it with necessity and (to be discussed later) fortune. Understandably, translators have always had difficulties capturing the layers of meanings in Machiavelli's use of the term. Some have translated it as "prowess," "valour," or "audacity." *Virtù* has been described by Jacob Burckhardt, a noted historian of the Renaissance, as a compound of strength and intellect. As Machiavelli uses the word, it means those "manly" qualities by which an individual is able to attain power and fame. (Machiavelli, often quite deliberately, uses gendered evaluative terms.) *The Prince*, as we have noted, consists largely of rules and advice, and it is directed to those either in positions of political power or aspiring to such power. The *virtù* that Machiavelli admires and recommends for this task reminds one of the kind of "virtue" that Callicles defended as "natural."[21] It is clearly not Christian, and it has specifically masculine tones.

Machiavelli's advice, found in chapter XVIII of *The Prince* where he discusses "How a Prince Should Keep his Word," is typical:

> How praiseworthy it is for a prince to keep his word and to live by integrity and not by deceit everyone knows; nevertheless, one sees from the experience of our times that the princes who have accomplished great deeds are those who have cared little for keeping their promises and who have known how to manipulate the minds of men by shrewdness; and in the end they have surpassed those who laid their foundations upon honesty.
>
> You must, therefore, know that there are two means of fighting: one according to the laws, the other with force; the first way is proper to man, the second to beasts; but because the first, in many cases, is not sufficient, it becomes necessary to have recourse to the second....

---

[21] There is an extensive commentary on the meaning of *virtù*: Isaiah Berlin, "The Originality of Machiavelli," in his *Against the Current*, ed. Henry Hardy (London: Hogarth Press, 1979), pp. 25–79; J. H. Hexter, "The Loom of Language and the Fabric of Imperatives: The Case of *Il Principe* and *Utopia*," in his *The Vision of Politics on the Eve of the Reformation* (New York: Basic Books, 1973), pp. 150–72; Neal Wood, "Machiavelli's Concept of *Virtù* Reconsidered," *Political Studies* 15 (1967), pp. 159–72; I. Hannaford, "Machiavelli's Concept of *Virtù* in *The Prince* and *The Discourses* Reconsidered," *Political Studies* 20 (1972), pp. 185–89; Gilbert, *Machiavelli and Guicciardini*, pp. 179–200.

Since, then, a prince must know how to make good use of the nature of the beast, he should choose from among the beasts the fox and the lion: for the lion cannot defend itself from traps and the fox cannot protect itself from wolves. It is therefore necessary to be a fox in order to recognize the traps and a lion in order to frighten the wolves. Those who play only the part of the lion do not understand matters. A wise ruler, therefore, cannot and should not keep his word when such an observance of faith would be to his disadvantage and when the reasons which made him promise are removed. And if men are all good, this rule would not be good; but since men are a sorry lot and will not keep their promises to you, you likewise need not keep yours to them.... But it is necessary to know how to disguise this nature well and to be a great hypocrite and a liar: and men are so simpleminded and so controlled by their present necessities that one who deceives will always find another who will allow himself to be deceived.[22]

Machiavelli goes on to say that the prince should learn how to "seem merciful, faithful, humane, forthright, religious and to be so in reality; but his mind should be disposed in such a way that should it become necessary not to be so, he will be able and know how to change to the contrary."[23] The truth of the matter, according to Machiavelli, is that a prince sometimes may not have the option to "observe all those things by which men are considered good, for in order to maintain the state he is often obliged to act against his promise, against charity, against humanity, and against religion." Because appearing to have the traditional virtues can be useful, the prince must know how to dissemble and deceive when the occasion warrants it. There is not much danger in doing this because people are easily fooled: "Let a prince therefore act to seize and to maintain the state; his methods will always be judged honourable and will be praised by all; for ordinary people are always deceived by appearances and by the outcome of a thing."[24] A prince must learn how to use both force and fraud.

Machiavelli does use *virtù* to include acts that would normally be viewed as immoral and cruel. His praise of Hannibal is a famous illustration:

---

[22] *The Prince,* ch. XVIII, pp. 133–34.

[23] *Ibid.,* ch. XVIII, p. 135.

[24] *Ibid.,* ch. XVIII, pp. 135-36.

Among the praiseworthy deeds of Hannibal is counted this: that, having a very large army, made up of all kinds of men, which he commanded in foreign lands, there never arose the slightest dissention, neither among themselves nor against their prince, both during his good and his bad fortune. This could not have arisen from anything other than his inhuman cruelty, which, along with his many other abilities [*virtù*], made him always respected and terrifying in the eyes of his soldiers; and without that, to attain the same effect, his other abilities [*virtù*] would not have sufficed.[25]

Yet, it would be misleading to think that *virtù*, for Machiavelli, is simply any means necessary to achieve and secure the power of the prince. Machiavelli also links *virtù* with **fortune**. As one illustration, he argues that great men have *virtù* in the sense that they are able to form what circumstances and fortune have given them into a great achievement. In chapter VI, where he begins his discussion of great men and *virtù*, he characterizes great men in these words: "they received nothing but the opportunity from Fortune, which then gave them the material they could mould into whatever form they desired; and without that opportunity the strength [*virtù*] of their spirit would have been extinguished, and without that strength [*virtù*] the opportunity would have come in vain."[26] *Virtù* is particularly required of the new prince at the moment of founding a regime. No set of rules or natural-law precepts will do.

In the main, Machiavelli is following the humanist tradition in the discussion of fortune.[27] Accordingly, he does not treat fortune either as the Christian equivalent of Providence or as the sum of blind, all-powerful fate controlling human actions. In chapter XXV, "On Fortune's Role in Human Affairs and How She Can Be Dealt With," Machiavelli uses two famous metaphors for fortune. The first is that of a river: "I compare her to one of those ruinous rivers that, when they

---

[25] *Ibid.*, ch. XVII, p. 132.

[26] *Ibid.*, ch. VI, p. 93.

[27] For analyses of Machiavelli's use of fortune see: Thomas Flanagan, "The Concept of *Fortuna*," in *The Political Calculus: Essays on Machiavelli's Philosophy* (Toronto: University of Toronto Press, 1972), pp. 127–56; Robert Orr, "The Time Motif in Machiavelli," in *Machiavelli and the Nature of Political Thought*, ed. Martin Fleisher (New York: Atheneum, 1972), pp. 185–208; Hannah Fenichel Pitkin, *Fortune Is a Women: Gender and Politics in the Thought of Nicolò Machiavelli* (Berkeley: University of California Press, 1984); de Grazia, *Machiavelli in Hell*, pp. 202–16; Timothy J. Lukes, "Fortune Comes of Age in Machiavelli's Literary Works," *The Sixteenth-Century Journal* 11 (1980), pp. 33–50.

become enraged, flood the plains, tear down the trees and buildings...; everyone flees from them, everyone yields to their onslaught, unable to oppose them in any way." The critical point, he continues, is to be prepared: "she shows her force where there is no organized strength [*virtù*] to resist her; and she directs her impact there where she knows that dikes and embankments are not constructed to hold her." This is the present sad state of Italy, "without embankments and without a single bastion." He views his own statecraft as contributing to the "organized strength." Here, fortune works as a force or cause that affects, usually unfavourably, human action. Whether fortune is plain dumb luck or bad luck, fate, chance, or contingencies, it cannot be controlled, but it might be channelled if one is prepared.

The second is that of a woman:

> Fortune is a woman, and it is necessary, in order to keep her down, to beat her and to struggle with her. And it is seen that she more often allows herself to be taken over by men who are impetuous than by those who make cold advances; and then, being a woman, she is always the friend of young men, for they are less cautious, more aggressive, and they command her with more audacity.[28]

Machiavelli is less interested in what fortune is than in how she can be mastered or seduced. His play, *Mandragola,* is about the seduction of a young married woman, and it clearly reveals that Machiavelli sees parallels between seduction in private life and statecraft in public life. Traditional moral rules and virtues are inapplicable to either task, and deceit, trickery, and cunning characterize both. Just as a prince must know how not to be good, so too must a seducer. Indeed, Machiavelli sees the contest between *virtù* and fortune to be as intrinsic to seduction as it is to politics. In love and politics the hero can test himself; fortune provides the opportunity, and even the temptation, for those who have the audacity and strength [*virtù*] to dare.

Although fortune is a force or cause in human affairs, Machiavelli insists that humans do have free will: "in order that our free will not be extinguished, I judge it to be true that Fortune is the arbiter of one half of our actions, but that she still leaves the control of the other half, or almost that, to us."[29] He concludes *The Prince* by repeating the point: "God does not wish to do everything, in order not to take

---

[28] *The Prince*, ch. XXV, p. 162.

[29] *Ibid.*, ch. XXV, p. 159.

from us our free will and that part of the glory which is ours."[30] In short, the field is vacated for human action. Secular action can take the place of divine intervention.

When matched against fortune, *virtù* provides the responses necessary in the circumstances, which are derived from the qualities of the manly or *virtus*: bravery, perseverance, courage, and daring. It is by fortune that we can test our mettle and show our inner strength. Sometimes a man should be cautious, but most of the time impetuousness and vigour will win fortune, and glory can be achieved. After his arrest and torture, Machiavelli wrote to his friend Francesco Vettori: "And as to turning my face to resist Fortune, I want you to get this pleasure from my distresses, namely, that I have borne them so bravely that I love myself for it and feel that I am stronger than you believed."[31] This is not Stoic serenity in the face of adversity but a sense of one's own personal strength and power [*virtù*].

There are passages where Machiavelli actually welcomes the tests of fortune, for fortune provides in political life the occasion and matter that our *virtù* can form and, thereby, show our greatness and glory:

> …it was necessary that the people of Israel be slaves in Egypt in order to recognize Moses' ability [*virtù*], and it was necessary that the Persians be oppressed by the Medes to recognize the greatness of spirit in Cyrus, and it was necessary that the Athenians be dispersed to realize the excellence of Theseus, then, likewise, at the present time, in order to recognize the ability [*virtù*] of an Italian spirit, it was necessary that Italy be reduced to her present condition and that she be more enslaved than the Hebrews, more servile than the Persians, more scattered than the Athenians; without a leader, without organization, beaten, despoiled, ripped apart, overrun, and prey to every sort of catastrophe.[32]

It is when the prince faces the greatest of tasks—the founding or renovating of a state or people—that one can see most clearly the interplay that exists between *virtù* and fortune, form and matter.[33]

---

[30] *Ibid.*, ch. XXVI, p. 163.

[31] Letter to Francesco Vettori, 18 March 1513, no. 19.

[32] *The Prince,* ch. XXVI, p. 162.

[33] J. G. A. Pocock provides an excellent analysis of this interplay in *The Machiavellian Moment: Florentine Political Thought and the Atlantic Republican Tradition* (Princeton: Princeton University Press, 1975), pp. 156–82. William Kerrigan and Gordon Braden insightfully examine form and matter as the themes of artistic creation, *The Idea of the Renaissance*, pp. 55–69.

The stage where we can show ourselves best is in the exercise of power. Machiavelli, fittingly, is the first person to use the word "state," *lo stato,* so extensively.[34] The word does not yet have the modern legal meaning encompassing government, land, people, and sovereignty. Nevertheless, he gives a distinctive and, as usual, an innovative meaning: to control the state is to have command over men, i.e, power. Machiavelli does not discuss founding a body politic in the Platonic or Aristotelian sense, i.e., by nurturing, through education and the political structure, the tenuous link between the good, the virtuous person, and citizenship. Machiavelli looks at power as the foundation of the state. Thus, as noted earlier, he puts good arms as prerequisites to good laws for the founding of a prince's rule. The centrality of power in founding a state is voiced in one of Machiavelli's most famous dicta: armed prophets are victorious and unarmed fail. As he explains in chapter VI, Savonarola, the Dominican priest and evangelist, failed as the ruler of Florence because he relied only on the beliefs he had instilled through his evangelical oratory, but Moses, an armed prophet, used force to support his leadership of the Israelites.[35]

Even the power of the state provides a limited stage for the test of *virtù* against fortune. *The Prince* is primarily about one man gaining and maintaining the power of the state and the *virtù* required for the task. The larger stage is reserved for the final chapter: the people, country, or, in modern language, the nation. It is here that *virtù* can fully be disclosed and glory won. Machiavelli's call to the Medici to deliver Italy from foreign domination foretells the spirit of modern nationalism and patriotism.

This opportunity, therefore, must not be permitted to pass by so that Italy, after so long a time, may behold its redeemer. Nor can I express with what love he will be received in all those provinces that have suffered through these foreign floods; with what thirst for revenge, with what obstinate loyalty, with what compassion, with what tears! What doors will be closed to him? What jealousy could oppose him? What Italian would deny him homage? This barbarian dominion stinks to everyone! Therefore, may

---

[34] Hexter, "The Predatory Vision: Niccolò Machiavelli: *Il Principe* and *lo stato,*" in his *The Vision of Politics on the Eve of the Reformation,* pp. 150–72.

[35] In the long exodus from Egypt Moses's leadership was clearly supported by arms. After one episode when the Israelites had fallen away by worshipping an idol, Moses had three thousand men killed. Exodus 32:28.

your illustrious house take up this mission with that spirit and with that hope in which just undertakings are begun; so that under your banner this country may be ennobled....[36]

Machiavelli makes clear in the *Discourses* that because it is the country, or *patria,* where the prince and also the people can show *virtù*, the power and glory of the prince must flow from more than the ruler himself. It is in conjunction with the *patria* that the greatest glory can be achieved. In *A Discourse on Remodeling the Government of Florence* (1520), Machiavelli writes, "I believe that the greatest honour men can have is that which their native city [*patria*] gives willingly to them; I believe that the greatest good to be done, and the most pleasing to God, is that which is done for one's native city [*patria*]."[37] It is also here that fortune provides the greatest opportunities. A prince can maintain or lose a state, i.e., the power to command, but the *patria* will continue and remains the ultimate justification for power and the ultimate test of *virtù* . In the final sentence to the *Art of War* Machiavelli declares that he would have passed such a test for Italy: "If Fortune had, in the past, conceded me as great a state as is sufficient for such an enterprise, I believe that I would have shown the world in a very short time how much ancient institutions are worth; and, without a doubt, I would have added to the glory of my state or lost it with no shame."[38]

Virtù and glory are not limited to successful princes. There would have been "no shame" if Machiavelli had done all that was necessary but had still lost to bad fortune. Glory comes from how you play the game. Hannibal and Cesare Borgia both showed great *virtù* and achieved glory in their failed endeavours. Neither was squeamish about using the means necessary for the task at hand, and each knew how not to be good. In order to be clear about what is *virtù* and what gains glory, Machiavelli draws a contrast with the Sicilian prince, Agathocles. He was no less cruel and deceitful than Hannibal or Borgia and, moreover, was successful in rising from low station to be ruler of Sicily. But Machiavelli says, "it cannot be called skill [*virtù*] to kill one's fellow citizens, to betray friends, to be without faith, without mercy, without religion; by these means one can acquire power

---

[36] *The Prince,* ch. XXVI, pp. 165–66.

[37] Allan H. Gilbert, ed. and trans. *Machiavelli: The Chief Works and others,* Vol. II (Durham: Duke University Press, 1965), pp. 113–14.

[38] *The Art of War,* Bk. VII in *The Portable Machiavelli,* p. 517.

but not glory." It is clearly not simply the means which disqualify Agathocles but also the purpose. He destroyed a principality rather than founding or preserving one; his means did not lead to a secure regime nor was greatness or glory achieved by the *patria*. Such a ruler always has "to keep his knife in his hand; nor can he ever count upon his subjects who…cannot feel secure with him."[39] Agathocles forgot that the point of the "game" of *virtù* and fortune was not power for power's sake. Indeed, a power, i.e., the ability to command and influence others, that relies only upon violence and force does not require much acumen, intelligence, courage, perseverance, ability, ingenuity or, in short, *virtù* from the prince nor does it build *virtù* in the subjects. Power built only on violence cannot maintain a state very well since the prince always must have a "knife in his hand"; there is little of substance to such a regime and it can easily fall. Thus, since nothing of importance has been achieved, there is no glory for prince or people. Machiavelli does not laud Agathocles. Machiavelli was a patriot and a patriot with a vision: he longed to see Italy united in a state of peace and security. In this sense, he was an early precursor of such nineteenth-century Italian nationalists as Mazzini, Garibaldi, Cavour, and Victor Emmanuel.

THE DISCOURSES

The *Discourses on the First Ten Books of Titus Livius* purports to be a commentary upon the first ten books of Titus Livy's *History of Rome*. Livy (57 to 29 B.C.) had written a much larger work, but most of it had been lost except for the first 10 books. The *Discourses* is a much larger work than *The Prince* and was, presumably, being written at the same time. It was first published 4 years after Machiavelli's death, and, unlike his other works, it does not appear to have received its final revision. The commentary is divided into 3 books, each with a separate introduction. Book I, 60 chapters long, concentrates on the constitutional evolution of Rome and on domestic politics. Book II, 33 chapters in length, turns to military and foreign affairs and the development of the Roman Empire. Book III, containing 49 chapters, looks at how the qualities of the great leaders enabled Rome to sustain its power for so long. Machiavelli's commentary is based on approximately 450 years of Roman history (753 to 293 B. C.). He delineates Rome's rise from a small republic to a great empire and the factors that kept the

---

[39] *The Prince,* ch. VIII, pp. 104, 107.

Romans patriotic, resolute, and, as he often says, incorrupt. More generally, he again presents through the commentary a statecraft, as he remarks in his introduction to Book I, for "instituting republics, maintaining states, governing kingdoms, organizing the army and administering a war, dispensing justice to subjects, and increasing an empire."[40]

Some scholars have found it difficult to reconcile *The Prince* and the *Discourses,* and there are some obvious differences between them. The first work boldly expresses admiration for the realistic and ruthless tyrant; the second work extols the ideals of republican government. The first work is formally dedicated to a prince, but the second is dedicated to two friends and citizens who "deserve to be princes." *The Prince* examines principalities, particularly new ones. The *Discourses* examines several forms of government but mainly focuses on republics. Instead of describing the *virtù* required for a prince, the *Discourses* discusses the *virtù* of a citizenry.

Most scholars now agree that these differences are not fundamental. There is little evidence to support the view that one is a work of political realism supporting autocracy and the other political idealism supporting republicanism.[41] Although one work is about principalities and the other addresses republics, the underlying political philosophy remains unaltered. There are many substantive commonalities linking the works: a great innovator is needed to save a regime; historical examples are applicable to the present; the ancients are generally superior to the moderns and the Republic of Rome is the most instructive; there is, in political existence, an unceasing contest between *virtù* and fortune; necessity changes the pertinence and meaning of virtues and vices; audacity is usually preferable to caution; the Christian religion is inimical to successful politics and a patriotic citizenry; violence, when necessary and justified, should be used unhesitatingly and applied in full measure; statecraft requires knowledge about power and, particularly, about military affairs; human nature is predictably egocentric.

In the dedication and introduction to the *Discourses,* Machiavelli reiterates that he is qualified by "long experience and continuous study of worldly affairs," that he will present real, "practical knowledge," and that he has an original message:

---

[40] *Discourses on the First Ten Books of Titus Livius,* Bondanella and Musa, *The Portable Machiavelli,* Book I, p. 170.

[41] For surveys of this old controversy, see Silvia Ruffo-Fiore, *Niccolò Machiavelli* (Boston: Twayne, 1982), pp. 55–60; John H. Whitfield, *Discourses on Machiavelli* (Cambridge: Heffer & Sons, 1969), pp. 181–206 and his *Machiavelli* (Oxford: Blackwell, 1947), pp. 106–21; Hans Baron, *In Search of Florentine Civic Humanism,* Vol. II (Princeton: Princeton University Press, 1988), ch. 15.

…it has always been no less dangerous to discover new methods and institutions than to explore unknown oceans and lands, since men are quicker to criticize than to praise the deeds of others. Nevertheless, driven by that natural desire I have always felt to work on whatever might prove beneficial to everyone, I have determined to enter a path which has not yet been taken by anyone….[42]

Machiavelli's exploration of history in the *Discourses* is guided by the same principles found in *The Prince*. History is viewed as a storehouse for statecraft, precisely as in *The Prince*, for two reasons: human nature is predictably selfish, and historical situations repeat themselves.

As is demonstrated by all those who discuss civic life (and as history is full of such examples), it is necessary for anyone who organizes a republic and institutes laws to take for granted that all men are evil and that they will always express the wickedness of their spirit whenever they have the opportunity; and when such wickedness remains hidden for a time, this is due to a hidden cause that is not recognized by those without experience of its contrary; but then time, which is said to be the father of every truth, will uncover it.

• • •

Anyone who studies present and ancient affairs will easily see how in all cities and all peoples there still exist, and have always existed, the same desires and passions. Thus, it is an easy matter for him who carefully examines past events to foresee future events in a republic and to apply the remedies employed by the ancients, or, if old remedies cannot be found, to devise new ones based upon the similarity of the events.

• • •

Prudent men often say, neither casually nor groundlessly, that anyone wishing to see what is to come should examine what has been, for all the affairs of the world in every age have had their counterparts in ancient times. This is because these affairs are carried on by men who have, and have always had, the same passions and, of necessity, the same results come from them.[43]

---

[42] *Discourses*, Bk. I, p. 169.

[43] *Ibid.*, Bk. I, ch. III, pp. 181–82; Bk. I, ch. XXXIX, p. 252; Bk. III, ch. XLIII, p. 413.

It follows, again as in *The Prince*, that imitation is the heart of a successful statecraft. In the preface to Book II, Machiavelli states the purpose of historical commentary: "I shall boldly declare in plain terms what I understand of those ancient times and of our own times, so that the minds of young men who read these writings of mine may be able to reject the present and prepare themselves to imitate the past whenever Fortune provides them with an occasion." A change from *The Prince* is that we are advised to imitate republics as well as great men. It is "clearer than the sun" that "ancient Roman times" in particular should be imitated.[44]

Machiavelli's recommendation of evil means to achieve a good end is also not confined to *The Prince* alone. Similar advice is given throughout the *Discourses*. Princes, he tells us in the *Discourses*, ought to exterminate the families of rulers whose territory they wish to possess securely. They ought to murder their opponents rather than confiscate their property since those who have been robbed, but not those who are dead, can think of revenge. "Insofar as threats to one's life are concerned, they are more dangerous than their execution—that is, threats are most dangerous, but when they are carried out there is no danger whatsoever, for one who is dead cannot think about a vendetta...."[45] It is not necessary or desirable to tell someone precisely what you intend to do before you have the means at your disposal to carry out your intention. "One should not show one's mind but try to get one's wish just the same, because it is enough to ask a man for his weapons without saying: I wish to kill you with them. For when you have the weapons in your hands you can satisfy your desire."[46] Maxims and precepts such as these occur not only in *The Prince* and in the *Discourses* but also in the *History of Florence* and in Machiavelli's private letters. As one commentator has said:

> The truth is that to Machiavelli there was no profit in being wicked if you did not know how to be downright. The man who was wholly good might be admirable but Machiavelli despised the wicked man who could not be

---

[44] *Ibid.*, Bk. II, preface, p. 290. For Machiavelli's use of history, see: Bruce James Smith, *Politics and Remembrances: Republican Themes in Machiavelli, Burke, and Tocqueville* (Princeton: Princeton University Press, 1983), pp. 26–38; Butterfield, *The Statecraft of Machiavelli*, pp. 23–66; Mark Hulliung, *Citizen Machiavelli* (Princeton: Princeton University Press, 1988), pp. 130–218; Peter Bondanella, *Machiavelli and the Art of Renaissance History* (Detroit: Wayne State University Press, 1974).

[45] *Discourses*, Bk. III, ch. VI, p. 359.

[46] *Ibid.*, Bk. I, ch. XLIV, p. 287. As found in Gilbert, *Machiavelli: The Chief Works and Others*, Vol. I.

wholly wicked—he taunted him with squeamishness and argued that he would never achieve the greatest heights.... It is not his cunning, indeed, but in his demand for greater consistency in cunning.... [He] had something to teach even to the princes of Renaissance times.[47]

Although Machiavelli promises in the first sentence of Book I "to discover new methods and institutions," he follows Plato, Aristotle, and others by first dissecting (as the initial chapter is entitled), "What the beginnings of all cities have been and what, in particular, was the beginning of Rome." But Machiavelli's story of founding a regime is original and does not follow the classical Greek, Roman, or Christian thinkers. Four major ingredients in his political thought are displayed in his account of the origins of political society. First, political institutions came into being because of fear and insecurity:

The first situation occurs when inhabitants, dispersed in many small groups, feel they cannot live securely, since each single group, because of its location or its small number, cannot resist the assault of anyone who may attack it, and if the enemy arrives, they are not in time to unite for their defense; if there is time, they have to abandon many of their strong fortifications, and then they remain at the mercy of their enemies. Hence, to escape these dangers, moved either by their own decision or by someone among them of greater authority, they join together to live as a group in a place chosen by them that is more convenient to live in and easier to defend.[48]

Moreover, from this origin there develops the institution of a single leader and a whole set of political virtues:

...in the beginning of the world, when its inhabitants were few, they lived at one time dispersed and like wild beasts; then, when their numbers multiplied, they gathered together and, in order to defend themselves better, they began to search among themselves for one who was stronger and braver, and they made him their leader and obeyed him. From this sprang the knowledge of what things are good and honorable, as distinct from the pernicious and evil: for if someone were to harm his benefactor, this aroused hatred and compassion among men, since they cursed the ungrateful and

---

[47] Butterfield, *The Statecraft of Machiavelli*, pp. 77–78.

[48] *Discourses*, Bk. I, ch.I, pp. 171–72.

honored those who showed gratitude; and thinking that the same injuries could also be committed against themselves, they made laws to avoid similar evils and instituted punishments for transgressors. Thus, the recognition of justice came about.[49]

The founding stories of Plato and Aristotle led to the conclusion that humans are naturally political-social animals through the requirements of biology and of reason and speech. Society is viewed as an expression of a potentially rational and ordered human nature. For Machiavelli, conflict and force, and fear and necessity explain our political beginnings. Likewise, morality develops from the necessities of political order, not from God's commands or from the structure of human nature.

Second, politics is about the power required to form, shape, and mould, at least to the extent that fortune allows. Consequently, Machiavelli continually demonstrates the need to use human power and *virtù* in forming political institutions.

And since men act either out of necessity or by choice, and since we know that there is more ability [*virtù*] where free choice has less authority, it must be considered whether it might be best to select barren places for the building of cities so that men, forced to become industrious and less idle, will live more united.... And as for that idleness which the site invites, one should organize the laws in such a way that they force upon the city those necessities which the location does not impose; and one should imitate the wise men who have lived in the most beautiful and fertile of lands, lands more apt to produce idle men unfit for any vigorous activity; in order to avoid the harm which the pleasant nature of the land might have caused because of idleness, they constrained their soldiers to undergo such training and exercise that better soldiers are produced there than in lands which are naturally harsh and barren.[50]

Here, Machiavelli introduces a third ingredient: law is not a derivation from reason or nature but a human tool and creation. Since this is the case, laws can be used as a necessity in forming a citizenry so that they can withstand the inevitable insecurity and change in political life. This, he believes, was the great achievement of

---

[49] *Ibid.*, Bk. I, ch. II, p. 177.

[50] *Ibid.*, Bk. I, ch. I, pp. 173–74.

the founders of Rome: "many necessities were imposed upon her by the laws instituted by Romulus, Numa, and others so that the fertility of the location, the convenience of the sea, the frequent victories, and the grandeur of her empire were not able to corrupt her for many centuries; these laws kept her very rich in ability [*virtù*], richer than any other city or republic that was as well adorned."[51]

Fourth, and with his customary frankness, Machiavelli holds that a founder must concentrate power in his hands in order to be effective and that, to this end, it may prove necessary to resort to force. Romulus, the founder of Rome, murdered his brother Remus and his friend Titus Tatius. Other founders have had to commit similar acts to accomplish their purposes. He cites, as examples, Moses, Lycurgus, who founded Sparta, and Solon, a founder of Athens. Each founder has to be alone because he must have sufficient, unshared power in his hands to accomplish his task. In the case of Romulus, Machiavelli argues that he deserves to be "pardoned for the death of his brother and his companion, and that what he did was for the common good and not for private ambition…." The lesson, also drawn in *The Prince*, is generalized to all founders:

> …a prudent founder of a republic, one whose intention it is to govern for the common good and not in his own interest, not for his heirs but for the sake of the fatherland, should try to have the authority all to himself; nor will a wise mind ever reproach anyone for some extraordinary action performed in order to found a kingdom or to institute a republic. It is, indeed, fitting that while the action accuses him, the result excuses him; and when this result is good, as it was with Romulus, it will always excuse him: for one should reproach a man who is violent in order to destroy, not one who is violent in order to mend things.[52]

In sum, whether a kingdom or a republic, a single leader is needed for the founding of a regime; necessity and fear are tools in the process and acts of violence are inevitable; and, as Machiavelli says, if the acts are done for the common good or fatherland, the "result excuses him." Machiavelli does not directly say that such acts of violence are morally justified. He makes a factual evaluation: it will be forgotten or excused by the people. Nevertheless, there is, at least, the germ of the modern idea, *raison d' ètat*, or reason of state. Put simply,

---

[51] *Ibid.*, Bk. I, ch. I, p. 175.

[52] *Ibid.*, Bk. I, ch. IX, pp. 200–01.

this is the doctrine that the "good of the body politic"—however that may be defined—overrides any private ethic, and, thus, the leader's responsibility for the whole justifies what otherwise would be unethical, such as the murder by Romulus of his brother.[53]

Machiavelli believes that Rome was fortunate in its founding, and this contributes to an answer for a central question of Book I of the *Discourses*: How did Rome become great and remain incorrupt for so long? In probing this question Machiavelli was aided by the great Greek historian Polybius, who had studied the years from 221 to 144 B.C. He, too, had marveled at "how it was and by virtue of what peculiar political institutions that in less than fifty-three years nearly the whole world was overcome and fell under the single dominion of Rome."[54] Machiavelli followed Polybius's well-known account of the forms of government, which, in turn, was based upon Aristotle's typology of six regimes, three just (monarchy, aristocracy, polity) and three unjust (tyranny, oligarchy, and democracy). Polybius had added that the just and unjust regimes alternate in a cycle (monarchy, tyranny, aristocracy, oligarchy, polity) with the democracy leading to a monarchy and the cycle continuing. The best constitution was one that combined all three elements within it (one, few, many). Machiavelli, too, believed that this was the key to explaining the constitutional stability and success of Rome. Within the Roman Republic the monarchical powers were given to the consuls, the senate represented the aristocratic element, and the popular assembly held the democratic faction. The division of legislative powers between nobles and the common people, each having control of one assembly, kept any one faction from dominating. The consent of both was required for a law, and this ensured

---

[53] Hexter, "The Predatory Vision," pp. 167-72. The classic work on the topic is still by Friedrich Meinecke, *Machiavellism: The Doctrine of Raison d' Etat and its Place in Modern History*, trans. Douglas Scott (New York: Praeger, 1965). For a review of the history of the doctrine, see: R. B. J. Walker, "*The Prince* and "The Pauper": Tradition, Modernity, and Practice in the Theory of International Relations," in *International/Intertextual Relations: Postmodern Readings of World Politics*, eds., James Der Derian and Michael J. Shapiro (Lexington: Lexington Books, 1989), pp. 25-48; Maurizo Viroli, *From Politics to Reason of State: The Acquisition and Transformation of the Language of Politics, 1250–1600* (Cambridge: Cambridge University Press, 1992).

[54] "The General History of the Wars of the Romans," as found in *The Ancient World, 800 B.C.–A.D. 800*, ed. Richard J. Burke, Jr. (New York: McGraw-Hill, 1967), p. 215.

that laws would be for the common good. In addition to representing the three elements within the society, this system provided a dictator for an emergency.[55]

In addition to relying upon the theory of constitutional development provided by Polybius, Machiavelli places Rome within a general cosmological or astrological framework. As with other thinkers of his day, Machiavelli held that the "heavens, the sun, the elements" through "their nature, their order, and their power" affected history and human action. These cosmic motions were not determinative, but they apparently provided a general framework for the rise and fall of regimes and the inescapable context for human action and rationality. The general cause would be the motion of the heavens and the particular cause would be an individual's capacity and temperament. To be successful, these two levels must mesh. Individual freedom occurs between these two levels when an individual, or state, has mastered its own capacities and then chooses to act. In the *Discourses* Machiavelli lists plagues, famines, and floods as causes that come from heaven, but humans with *virtù* have the freedom, if limited, to respond: "men always have hope."[56] Thus, at the beginning of each of the three books of the *Discourses* Machiavelli pointedly refers to the general effects of astrology-cosmology on humans and regimes.[57]

Because the constitution of Rome mixed elements of kingly, aristocratic, and democratic authority, "Rome was a perfect state." And, this perfection, Machiavelli continues, "was produced through the friction between plebeians and the senate." Here was an original claim of Machiavelli, and much criticized by his contemporaries: factional conflict was beneficial to the state in that it helped to preserve the liberty and vitality of the state.[58] Furthermore, this mixed constitution nourished other factors,

---

[55] *Discourses*, Bk. I, ch. II, p. 179; Bk. I, ch. XXXIV, pp. 243–46. Kurt von Fritz, *The Theory of the Mixed Constitution in Antiquity: A Critical Analysis of Polybius' Political Ideas* (New York: Columbia University Press, 1954); Bruce James Smith, "The Theory of the Mixed Regime and the Problem of Power: A Machiavellian Meditation" in *Contemporary Political Systems: Classifications and Typologies*, eds. Anton Bebler and Jim Seroka (Boulder: Lynne Rienner Publishers, 1990), pp. 45–68.

[56] *Ibid.*, Bk. II, ch. V; Bk. II, ch. XXIX, p. 345.

[57] *Ibid.*, Bk. I, "Introduction," p. 171; Bk. II, "Introduction," p. 288; Bk. III, ch. I, p. 351. The single best work on astrology and Machiavelli is by Anthony J. Parel, *The Machiavellian Cosmos* (New Haven: Yale University Press, 1992).

[58] *Ibid.*, Bk. I, ch. II, pp. 181, 183–84. This original idea of balancing factions and institutions was quoted with approval by John Adams in his *A Defense of the American Constitutions,* Vol. II (1787).

according to Machiavelli, which contributed to the successful evolution of the Roman Republic into an empire: the people were able to attain liberty and an outlet for their ambition and *virtù*; the assured liberty and *virtù* of the people enabled the Republic to expand; with the expansion of the republic a greater glory was achieved.

Machiavelli continually stresses that a republic with a mixed constitution is able to create and sustain a proper citizenry. This is, perhaps, its major advantage over other regimes. One must never forget "that all men are evil and that they will always express the wickedness of their spirit whenever they have the opportunity."[59] But, this fickleness, ambition, egocentricism and other traits of human nature are here enframed by the balancing of factions, mixed institutions, and the necessity of law. The people, thus, are less inclined, and it becomes more difficult for them, to behave irrationally because of the political structure. Although the *virtù* of the great man is necessary for the founding of a regime, it is just as necessary to implant *virtù* in the citizenry in order to sustain a regime. As Machiavelli writes: "though one man alone is fit for founding a government, what he had founded will not last long if it rests upon his shoulders alone; it is lasting when it is left in the care of many and when many desire to maintain it."[60] The constitutional evolution of Rome, the major theme of the first book of the *Discourses*, provides the best source of practical instructions for accomplishing this larger task and for preventing the corruption of *virtù*. A republic thereby is clearly preferable to a prince: "concerning prudence and stability, let me say that the people are more prudent, more reliable, and have better judgement than a prince does." Machiavelli always insists that a multitude will still need leaders.[61] A republic also positively enhances the attachment of the people to the state through providing some access to office, an outlet for ambition, a right of impeachment of officials, and protection for the many or the plebians: "all countries and provinces living in freedom make very great progress; …every man willingly procreates the children he believes he can provide for without fear that this patrimony will be taken away; he is assured that they will be born free, not slaves, and that they may, through their own ability become great men."[62] All of these features increase the unity and strength of the state.

---

[59] *Ibid.*, Bk. I, ch. III, pp. 181–82.

[60] *Ibid.*, Bk. I, ch. IX, p. 201.

[61] *Ibid.*, Bk. I, ch. LVIII, p. 284; Bk. I, ch. XLIV, p. 261.

[62] *Ibid.*, Bk. II, ch. II, p. 300; Bk. I, ch. VII, pp. 193–94.

A second advantage of a mixed republic is that it is best able to preserve liberty and its fruits. By 'liberty' Machiavelli only means that the state is self-governed: "governed themselves by their own judgment."[63] The republic is far from the modern idea of a democracy. He lauds Sparta rather than Athens. Sparta lasted eight centuries precisely because it was well constituted and not simply democratic. The people in a free republic, such as Sparta or Rome, provide stability and endurance; they remember their liberty and are, consequently, very difficult to conquer; a citizens' militia in a free republic is better than a mercenary army; the people choose leaders more wisely than would a prince who would find it hard to accept potential rivals; the people are not fearful of "valiant men" nor are they ungrateful, as a prince would be; lastly, the people are benefited by seeking the common good of the city, whereas, for a prince, his private interest "harms the city" and "the city's benefit harms him."[64] Machiavelli repeats that a leader is necessary and superior to the people in creating new laws or institutions, but "the people are so much more superior in maintaining the things thus established." So, he concludes "that government by the people is better than government by princes."[65]

A third praiseworthy feature of a republic is its capacity for innovation and expansion: "it is evident that cities in which people are the rulers increase their territories in a very short time, much more so than cities which have always been under a prince."[66] Differing again with Cicero and the predominant humanist tradition, Machiavelli does not believe that peace and concord should be the goals of a republic. Expansion and greatness are thrust upon any city that wants to preserve its liberty. A republic must organize itself so that "should necessity impel it to expand, it may do so and conserve its acquisitions."[67] In short, Machiavelli sees no middle way between peaceful idleness for a regime and the preparedness for war, which was the practice of Rome.

As attested by the history of Rome, when read by Machiavelli, the dedication of a citizenry and the meritocracy nurtured by mixed institutions create an abundance

---

[63] *Ibid.*, Bk. I, ch. II, p. 175.

[64] *Ibid.*, Bk. I, chs. XXIX, XXX, XLIII, LVIII; Bk. II, ch. II.

[65] *Ibid.,* Bk. I, ch. LVIII, p. 285. Marcia L. Colish, "The Idea of Liberty in Machiavelli," *The Journal of the History of Ideas* 32 (1970), pp. 325–50.

[66] *Ibid.*, Bk. I, ch. LVIII, p. 284; Bk. II, ch. II.

[67] *Ibid.*, Bk. I, ch. VI, p. 192.

of leaders over time and enable a republic to expand economically and politically. Thus, of all regimes it is the most capable of responding to challenges and sustaining its growth. In contrast, Alexander the Great's empire was of short duration. Athens was too democratic, did not have a noble ruling class, and, consequently, achieved a short if brilliant glory. Florence, Machiavelli judges, has repeated these errors. Sparta had great civic ethos combined with an extraordinary stability and could last eight centuries, but it was too exclusive and was unable to make an empire. Venice, too, achieved stability and was unable to sustain an empire. Neither knew how to assimilate other people and to grow. Rome alone, he says, had all of the elements and attained the greater glory.[68]

The fourth advantage of a proper republic is this very capacity for attaining glory. The fear of meaninglessness, oblivion, or death is countered by the attainment of glory. It is a secular immortality experienced in the present and grounded on the long and real memory of citizens. As theology can direct one on the path toward immortality, history points the careful student to the path toward glory. Machiavelli discusses glory in the *Prince*, but it is a far more significant theme in the *Discourses*. A republic, for Machiavelli, is a far richer soil for nourishing glory than a princedom. In a republic there were many avenues for many men to obtain glory. A free republic also has that long memory of its citizens, which gives glory its peculiar immortality. An expanding republic has even more opportunities for glory. But not only are single men able to attain glory in a republic, so too is the citizenry itself. It is this glory that excuses the means of power politics. The founders of regimes attain great glory in both the *Prince* and the *Discourses*, but Machiavelli holds that the founders of religion are even more to be praised since their task is the more difficult and since it is religion that permeates the people, "brings them to civic obedience," and helps to form them into citizens.[69] In chapter X of Book I he gives four ranks of "praiseworthy men": founders of religion, founders of republics or kingdoms, military leaders, and men of letters. Machiavelli clearly does not think of himself as a mere humanist man of letters. By implication at least, he reserves the greatest glory for a person, such as himself, who restores through teaching, who has entered "a path which has not yet been taken by

---

[68] *Ibid.*, Bk. I, ch. VI.

[69] *Ibid.*, Bk. I, ch. XI, p. 207.

anyone," who can teach founders of the means to glory followed by the ancients, and who can reach "the minds of young men who read these writings of mine."[70]

The advantages of a mixed constitution help to explain how Rome became great and was able to remain incorrupt for so long. Of equal importance is that interplay of *virtù*, fortune, and necessity first expressed in the *Prince*. In the first sentence of the first chapter of the *Discourses* Machiavelli states that no one knowing the origins of Rome and its empire would be surprised that "so much ability [*virtù*] was preserved in that city for so many centuries." *Virtù* has the same meaning in the *Discourses* as in the *Prince*. Necessity and the preservation of the state are the parameters for justifying actions. Just as Romulus's killing of his brother has a good result and is thus justified so too is the harsh destruction of city after city during Rome's expansion.[71] The humanist tradition from Cicero and others, the Christian tradition, or the ancient Greeks are all repudiated as guides for relating ethics and power: "This thought deserves to be noted and put into practice by any citizen who has occasion to advise his country, for when the entire safety of one's country is at stake, there should be no consideration of just or unjust, merciful or cruel, praiseworthy or disgraceful; on the contrary, putting aside every form of respect, that decision which will save her life and preserve her liberty must be followed completely."[72]

In the *Discourses* this same *virtù* is found in citizens as well as leaders. The goal is always the "common good," i.e., the maintenance and glory of the state, not one's own interest; action to be justified and to qualify as *virtù* must be "for the sake of the fatherland."[73] The difficulty is in maintaining the necessary level of *virtù* and patriotism. There is an inevitable tendency in egocentric men to fall away. Individuals when isolated are selfish, weak, and cowardly, but when constrained and united with their fellows they regain their *virtù*. In Machiavelli's words, "men never do good except out of necessity; but when they have the freedom to choose and can do as they please, everthing immediately becomes confused

[70] *Ibid.*, Bk. I, Introduction, p. 169; Bk. II, Introduction, p. 290.

[71] *Ibid.*, Bk. II, ch. XXIII.

[72] *Ibid.*, Bk. III, ch. XLI, p. 411.

[73] *Ibid.*, Bk. I, ch IX, p. 200.

and disorderly."[74] Great men, the mixed constitutions, and fortune all helped at various times in the history of Rome, but he stresses, in particular, the Roman use of religion and of law in creating and preserving *virtù* and patriotism.

Machiavelli was one of the first, if not the first, to recognize the nature of the new secular state that was emerging at the time of the Renaissance, and he sought to provide a theory appropriate to it. This is most evident in his discussion of religion through chapters XI to XV in Book I. For Machiavelli, politics is separated from all metaphysical, moral, and religious foundations and declared to be an autonomous realm. One theme dominates his thought: "Putting all other considerations aside the only question should be, what course will save the life and liberty of the country?"

The title to chapter XII of the first book of the *Discourses* asks "How much importance must be granted to religion, and how Italy, without religion, thanks to the Roman Church, has been ruined." Machiavelli says that both princes and republics should hold religious ceremonies in veneration for there is no more certain indication of the decline of a country than to see religion condemned and neglected. But religion is conceived by him as a means toward a more ultimate end than the worship of God; its value is only instrumental and relative to secular ends. Although religion is assigned an important role to perform within the state, it is not above the state nor even equal with it. Rulers should always behave devoutly and should display the greatest reverence even, or perhaps especially, when they are convinced that the teaching of religion is quite fallacious. Speaking of the foundation of Rome, Machiavelli declares:

> Even though Rome found its first institution builder in Romulus and, like a daughter, owed her birth and her education to him, nevertheless, as the heavens judged that the institutions of Romulus would not suffice for so great an empire, they inspired the Roman senate to elect Numa Pompilius as Romulus's successor so that those matters not attended to by Romulus could be seen to by Numa. Numa found the Roman people most undisciplined, and since he wanted to bring them to civil obedience by means of the arts of peace, he turned to religion as an absolutely necessary institution for the maintenance of a civic government, and he established it in such a way that for many centuries never was there more fear of God than in that republic—a fact which greatly facilitated any undertaking that the senate or

---

[74] *Ibid.*, Bk. I, ch. III, p. 182.

those great Romans thought of doing…. Thus, anyone who examines Roman history closely will discover how much religion helped in commanding armies, encouraging the plebeians, keeping men good, and shaming the wicked. And so, if one were to argue about which prince Rome was more indebted to—whether Romulus or Numa—I believe that Numa would most easily be first choice: for where there is religion it is easy to introduce arms, but where there are arms without religion the latter can be introduced only with difficulty…. Having considered everything, then, I conclude that the religion introduced by Numa was among the most important reasons for the success of that city, for it brought forth good institutions, and good institutions led to good fortune, and from good fortune came the felicitous successes of the city's undertakings.[75]

Machiavelli asks why it is that in ancient times the people were more fond of liberty than they are today. It is due, he says, to the difference between our education and theirs, between "our religion," i.e., Christianity, and theirs. Christianity teaches humility and the disregard of worldly success, material possessions, and honour. Christianity esteems the man of contemplation rather than the man of action. Roman religion was created by the Roman elite for the very purpose of moulding or forming the populace into a strong and virile citizenry. The civic ethos thus created was one that made the republic great. Pagan religion differed from Christianity most strikingly because of its ability to motivate through terror and fear, rather than through the impotent piety of a Savonarola. The pagan religion thus encouraged men to be ferocious in action while Christianity condemns such ferocity. While the pagan religion exalted the courage to do bold things, Christianity recommends the kind of courage of soul that enables men to endure suffering. Army commanders were regarded with the highest respect by the pagan religion in contrast to the saints and martyrs who were the "heroes" for Christianity. Augustine himself had referred to the motivations behind the great deeds of the republic as "noble vices." Machiavelli concludes that the antipolitical and antipatriotic teachings of Christianity have "rendered the world weak and handed it over as prey to wicked men, who can safely manage it when they see that most men think more of going to Heaven by enduring their injuries than by avenging them."[76]

---

[75] *Ibid.,* Bk. I, ch. XI, pp. 207–09.

[76] *Ibid.,* Bk. II, ch. II, p. 298.

At times Machiavelli seems to waver between Christianity and paganism. He never explicitly calls the wicked good, and when he recommends cruel and deceitful means he does not attempt to deny the cruelty or the deceit involved. This wavering is apparent when Machiavelli says that a prince conquering a city or a province should "destroy existing ones, move the inhabitants from one place to another; in short, leave nothing intact in that province, nor permit either rank, institution, form of government, or wealth in your city which is not recognized as coming from you...." He adds: "These methods are most cruel and are inimical to any body politic, not only to a Christian one but to any human one, and every man should avoid them and should prefer to live as a private citizen rather than as a king who does so much damage to mankind; nevertheless, anyone who does not wish to choose this first humane course of action must, if he wishes to maintain himself, enter into this evil one." He does not say that such means are good in themselves but only that they are expedient and justified. Here again the Romans were able to relate political necessity and ethics. We should imitate the practice of these ancients and have religion instil patriotism. The religion of the Romans tied the citizens and the citizen army to the defence of the state. It was a sacred duty to fight for the state, and all were so pledged.[77]

We have already seen the general importance of law in founding a regime and in nourishing *virtù*. Machiavelli also advocates special laws and institutions for preserving *virtù* and regimes, for responding to dangers, and for retarding the inevitable decline to corruption. The Roman institution of the dictator, as one example, is praised by Machiavelli. It enabled the Republic to concentrate power within a fixed time limit and for specific purposes in order to meet "urgent dangers." Once the danger has been clearly seen and one can cure it, Machiavelli advises: "set yourself to doing so without reservation."[78] Quick and decisive action, as we have seen, is often recommended by Machiavelli. The failure of the Republic of Florence is often paraded as an object lesson. Soderini could have saved the republic if he had decisively acted to defeat the enemies of the regime.

---

[77] *Ibid.,* Bk. I, ch. XXVI, p. 232. Machiavelli's view of religion and Christianity is only one of many areas of controversies among scholars: de Grazia, *Machiavelli in Hell,* pp. 88–121, 376–80; Hulliung, *Citizen Machiavelli,* pp. 219–51; Rebhorn, *Foxes and Lions,* pp. 1–40; Anthony Parel, "The Fatherland in Machiavelli," in *Unity, Plurality, and Politics,* eds. J. M. Porter and Richard Vernon (London: Croom Helm, 1986), pp. 38–51.

[78] *Ibid.,* Bk. I, ch. XXXIII, pp. 240–43; ch. XXXIV.

In Roman history, in contrast, when the sons of Brutus conspired to bring back the kings, Brutus himself ordered and watched the execution of his sons.[79]

The successes and failures associated with the rise of the Roman Republic and Empire commend many such actions, laws and institutions. A few can be mentioned. Laws against slander are necessary to stop the destruction of a government. Again, Rome knew how to act, but Florence did not. Military commands should be ordered for short durations otherwise the regime can be threatened by a military leader who obtains too much power and prestige. The public treasury should be kept rich, but the citizens kept poor in order to contain ambitions and to limit the quarrels between the rich and poor. Such special laws and institutions indicate to Machiavelli that a successful statecraft requires continual vigilance, flexibility in government response, and, above all, decisive action.[80]

Book II recounts the organization and methods used for the expansion of the empire. The ancient historians, Plutarch and Livy, are criticized by Machiavelli for attributing Rome's greatness to fortune. Marchiavelli argues the contrary: "there never has been a republic so organized that she could acquire as Rome did. For the ability of her armies caused her to acquire her empire, and the institution of her conduct and her individual way of living...allowed her to keep her conquests...."[81] As we have already seen, the Roman Republic is lauded by Machiavelli not for its justice but for its successful expansion, its power, and its glory. Here there was scope to achieve *virtù* for a people as well as for a leader. It was Augustine who had first insisted that the history of the rise of the Roman Republic was actually a history of power politics and not one of justice and virtue. He also had criticized its apologists and the way of life propounded by the Roman Stoics. Machiavelli's descriptions of Rome's brutal methods are no less candid than Augustine, but Machiavelli lauds the resulting achievements of power and glory. He also lauds the *virtù* of conquest rather than the virtues of Christianity or of Cicero.

The successful Roman expansion, as he explained in Book I, depended on a balanced constitution and a patriotic religion. In Book II Machiavelli mentions many other factors that contributed. One critical factor was Rome's policy of allowing immigration to increase the pool of subjects. She also knew how to

---

[79] *Ibid.*, Bk. I, ch. XVI; Bk. III, ch. III.

[80] *Ibid.*, Bk. I, ch. VIII; Bk. III, ch. XXIV; Bk. I, chs. XXXVII and LV.

[81] *Ibid.*, Bk. II, ch. I, p. 291.

conduct a foreign policy with her neighbours. Initially, they were treated as equals in a confederation, at other times as allies led by a central command, and eventually as subjects. Another contributing factor to Roman success was their military practice of massing a large, highly disciplined army and conducting campaigns for quick victories. Also, they did not make the mistake of having two great wars simultaneously. Once victorious, they then knew how to keep the losers subject: with monarchs, the ruling family was just eliminated; republics were more difficult to subject, but the use of colonies and the technique of divide and rule normally enabled them to absorb the conquered.[82]

Starting in chapter X Machiavelli describes long lists of "evil examples" not to be imitated. He warns against a singular reliance on wealth rather than arms, on slow decision making, and on an inflexible dependence on artillery, or cavalry, or mercenary troops, or fortresses.[83] These "evil examples," and many others, all have the common effect of dissipating the *virtù* required for an army and a citizenry. It was Machiavelli's continual theme that *virtù* gave the citizens the dedication and courage to defend the community, enabling the state and citizens to remain independent and secure. The expanding Roman Republic did not repeat these "evil examples" and methods, but, as he frequently laments, Florence did.

In general, Machiavelli sees the Roman expansion as relying upon the same statecraft or political arts that are defended in the *Prince*. As usual, he is blunt in characterizing these means as a statecraft of force and, above all, fraud:

> I believe it to be very true that rarely or never do men of humble station rise to high ranks without force and without fraud, although others attain such rank either as a gift or by having it left to them as an inheritance. Nor do I believe that force by itself will ever suffice, although fraud alone surely can be enough.... I do not believe that anyone who has been placed in a humble station has ever attained great authority by employing only open and guileless force....
>
> What princes have to do at the beginning of their expansion republics must also do—at least until they have become powerful and force alone is sufficient.[84]

---

[82] *Ibid.*, Book III, chs. I, III, IV, VI.

[83] *Ibid.*, Book II, chs. XIX, X, XV, XVII, XVIII, XX, XXIV.

[84] *Ibid.*, Bk. II, ch. XIII, pp. 314–15.

Deception, fraud, cunning, force, and other political practices were used as required for Roman expansion. Whatever the means, they were vigorously applied: "in governmental decisions the Romans always avoided a middle course of action and took extreme ones."[85] The Romans, in short, knew when to be lions or foxes and when to use force or fraud as the occasion demanded. They were aggressive, not passive, just as fortune demanded. The wars of Rome, as an instance, were normally instigated by attacking rather than defending. The contrast between the statecraft of Machiavelli and that of Plato and Aristotle is striking. The latter had condemned imperialism and a military or heroic ethic precisely because it would destroy a small republic and its sustaining life of virtue.[86]

Book III is devoted to great men and their contribution to Rome. Machiavelli focuses on their ability to reverse decline, to revise, and to renew Roman institutions and *virtù*. There is a constant need in any regime to constrain individual ambitions and to renew the dedication to the common good. Such a task of innovative leadership can be accomplished only by great men. If such men, he says, "had occurred at least every ten years in that city, it would have necessarily followed that the city would have never been corrupted."[87]

Machiavelli cites the now familiar array of methods. Two are noteworthy. First, he stresses the need for creative violence or terror, and he lists many successful instances from Roman history. As in the *Prince*, Hannibal is used as a model: "in most cases a man who makes himself feared is better followed and more readily obeyed than one who makes himself loved."[88] He compares the harshness of Manlius Torquatus, who had his own son killed, with the kindness of Valerius Corvinus. Both were successful generals for Rome, but, he argues, "I believe the procedure of Manlius to be more praiseworthy and less dangerous. This method works entirely for the well-being of the public and in no way invokes private ambition, for a man cannot acquire partisans by such a method since he always shows himself to be stern toward everyone and to love only the common good."[89] Terror and force can mould and renew the dedication of a citizenry and an army.

---

[85] *Ibid.*, Bk. II, ch. XXIII, p. 327.

[86] *The Politics of Aristotle*, Bk. 7, ch. 14.

[87] *Discourses*, Bk. III, ch. I, p. 354.

[88] *Ibid.*, Bk. III, ch. XXI, p. 392.

[89] *Ibid.*, Bk. III, ch. XXII, p. 398.

The second method is simply that of example. The leadership qualities shown by a great man can also renew: "And if a republic were fortunate enough to have…someone who could renew her laws by means of his example, who would not only keep her from running to her ruin but would pull her back from it, such a state would endure forever."[90] Leaders who showed the many facets of *virtù* at critical moments also prevented Rome's decline. Camillus is called "the most prudent of all the Roman generals" and "considered marvelous" because of "his care, his prudence, his great courage, his excellent method in administering and commanding armies."[91] Prudence is also exemplified by the conduct of the Roman commander Fulvius who discovered the deception of an enemy. This is a prudence, Machiavelli notes with some bitterness, not imitated by Florence. As a consequence, Florence was deceived by its neighbouring city of Pisa and many times by France.[92] Camillus is cited again as a model of steadfastness and dignity. Machiavelli quotes Camillus's own words: "As for me, the dictatorship did not exalt my spirits nor exile depress them." "Fortune," Machiavelli comments, "does not have power over" such great men.[93] The leader of a group of pirates, Timasitheus, is commended for instilling religious fear in his people.[94] Courage is shown by Valerius Corvinus who told his troops, "My deeds, not my words, soldiers, I wish you to follow."[95]

A central lesson that a great leader can exemplify is how to overcome envy. Camillus dispelled envy through a reputation earned of selfless service for the state. The example of his conduct assured all that his attainment of power gave no reason for fear or envy. Machiavelli quickly adds that a second way of dispelling error may be required in a corrupt city: "there is no other method than the death of those affected with it." Regrettably, he adds, Florence under both Savonarola and Soderini did not learn the second method and were overcome by envy.[96]

---

[90] *Ibid.*, Bk. III, ch. XXII, p. 396.

[91] *Ibid.*, Gilbert trans., Bk. III, ch. XII, p. 462; ch. XXIII, p. 484; ch. XXX, pp. 497–98.

[92] *Ibid.*, Bk. III, chs. XLIII, XLVIII.

[93] *Ibid.*, Gilbert trans., Bk. III, ch. XXXI, p. 498.

[94] *Ibid.*, Bk. III, ch. XXIX, p. 405.

[95] *Ibid.*, Gilbert trans., Bk. III, ch. XXXVIII, p. 515.

[96] *Ibid.*, Gilbert trans., Bk. III, ch. XXX, p. 496.

The uniting theme in all of these edifying examples is that the behaviour is directed toward the "survival of Rome." Machiavelli recites the advice of Lucius Lentulus to express again the persistent theme of his statecraft: "one's country is well defended by any means which defends it, whether by disgrace or glory."[97]

Nevertheless, great men, their methods, and their leadership qualities could not prevent the eventual fall of Rome. Machiavelli alludes to three general causes and two specific ones. First, he notes that a republic will have longer duration than a principality because its diverse citizenry provides the potential for meeting changing conditions. Yet, over time, republics too will fail to change, just as Fabius always remained cautious and Pope Julius II remained impetuous even when their times had changed. Then, the inability to meet fortune and change will cause the downfall of cities: "For change results from times in which the entire republic is shaken; and for this to occur, it is not sufficient for one man alone to modify his method of procedure."[98]

Second, there is insatiable ambition: "Whenever men cease fighting through necessity, they go to fighting through ambition, which is so powerful in human breasts that whatever high rank men climb to, never does ambition abandon them."[99] The propensity for instability is, thus, incurable. Third, Romans "become secure in their freedom." There are many variations on this theme. Necessity, laws, and religious fear are all commended by Machiavelli as remedies for countering complacency and maintaining *virtù*. Otherwise, the people choose leaders for their ability "to please men" rather than for their *virtù*; honours are not fairly awarded; and the citizens become incapable of wise decisions. The people become corrupt.[100]

Finally, Machiavelli specifies two immediate causes. First, the Agrarian Law of Rome limited the amount of land that could be owned and provided for the distribution of conquered land. It produced constant friction among the nobles and the people. Second, the prolongation of command in the army led to a few generals having great political influence. This culminated in the control by Caesar, after whom the "city was never again free."[101] With the Empire, the glorious rise of the Republic had come to an end.

---

[97] *Ibid.*, Bk. XLI, p. 411.

[98] *Ibid.*, Bk. III, ch. IX, p. 383.

[99] *Ibid.*, Gilbert trans., Bk. I, ch. XXXVII, p. 272.

[100] *Ibid.*, Bk. I, ch. XVIII, pp. 226–27.

[101] *Ibid.*, Bk. I, ch. XXXVII; Bk. III, ch. XXIV.

CONCLUSIONS

There are almost as many interpretations of Machiavelli's significance as there are commentators upon his work. He has been described as a teacher of evil, an objective historian simply recording the political practices of his time, the first political scientist, and an Italian patriot and father of Italian nationalism. Among his contemporaries he was frequently described as a teacher of evil. English authors of the Elizabethan age—men like Marlowe, Ben Jonson, Shakespeare, Beaumont, and Fletcher—all use his name as synonymous with cunning, crime, deceit, and hypocrisy. As one moves away from the sixteenth century, however, his reputation improves. Francis Bacon, writing in the seventeenth century, hails him as a kindred spirit, an empirically minded man, who described what men do, not what they ought to do. In the eighteenth century Voltaire represents himself as continuing the work of Machiavelli in attacking Christianity and the Church, and Rousseau hails Machiavelli as a true patriot and republican. Hegel, in the nineteenth century, describes him as a "political genius" possessing one of the greatest and noblest minds. The Italian nationalists of the nineteenth century claim him as one of their forerunners. Vittorio Alfieri, a scholar-politician of the time, speaks of him as the "divine Machiavelli." In the twentieth century he is sometimes described as the first genuine political scientist.[102]

Although there is no agreement among scholars as to Machiavelli's influence or his general significance, there are influential themes in his thoughts that collectively distinguish him from his contemporaries and from past thinkers. First, and most important, Machiavelli claims to have provided a new knowledge about political regimes in contrast to the speculations about ideal, imaginary, and "paper" republics of past thinkers. Solid knowledge, he tries to demonstrate, can become a source of power for making and sustaining states. Machiavelli wants to bestow a new confidence and a new degree of certainty that can strengthen a leader and a people so that fortune might be mastered. Here is a modern theme not found in Plato, Aristotle, the Stoics, Augustine, and Aquinas. He has dismissed, for example, the practical wisdom of Aristotle with its modest claim to understanding and its modest assessment of human power. Machiavelli has started, perhaps inadvertently, on the modern journey to a science of statecraft and of politics.

---

[102] See James Burnham, *The Machiavellians: Defenders of Freedom* (New York: John Day, 1943). A selection from the scores of interpretations can be found in Robert M. Adams, trans. and ed. *The Prince: A New Translation, Backgrounds, Interpretations* (New York: Norton, 1992).

Second, Machiavelli bases his knowledge claim on a new understanding of the essential elements constituting politics. Human nature is stripped to its basic and simplest level: humans are fundamentally selfish or egocentric. Fear, as a consequence, can be reliably used to provide power over others, and to change behaviour and attitudes. It follows that human society is characterized by conflict and instability; order can be established only by power and, often, by violence. The goals of political life, which actually guide and mould humans, are power and glory. These enable a regime to attain stability, riches, and the patriotic support of a citizenry. It is these purportedly real and natural elements that Machiavelli uses to explain and predict political behaviour.

The third, and the most controversial theme, is Machiavelli's treatment of political expediency or, as some would argue, political immorality. Defenders of Machiavelli have interpreted his teachings as a call for political realism: one must suspend ethics in order to have successful political action. Machiavelli recognizes, they believe, that no one can be innocent in politics. Power must be used either defensively or offensively, and various ethical rules simply will be violated. Inevitably, people will be treated instrumentally and the innocent will suffer. In short, no one can exercise power without dirty hands. Such interpreters argue that Machiavelli illuminates the inescapable moral dilemmas in exercising power. In addition, some claim that he teaches us the complexity of politics, the incompatibility of public duty and personal ethics or of political activism and Christianity, and the courage to see necessity clearly. Isaiah Berlin, to illustrate, has argued that the "wholly unintended" consequence of Machiavelli's thought was to open the modern path to "empiricism, pluralism, toleration, compromise."[103]

Those who are critical of Machiavelli argue that he does not speak about a moral dilemma in political action. One cannot sense in Machiavelli any anguish about the use of power. Rather, he advocates the means consistent with the goals of establishing or maintaining a state and with achieving fame and glory for

---

[103] "The Originality of Machiavelli," in *Against the Current* (London: Hogarth Press, 1979), pp. 78, 79. See also: Michael Walzer, "Political Action: The Problem of Dirty Hands," in *War and Moral Responsibility,* eds. Marshall Cohen, Thomas Magel, Thomas Scanlon (Princeton: Princeton University Press, 1974), pp. 62–82; Neal Wood, "Machiavelli's Humanism of Action," in *The Political Calculus: Essays on Machiavelli's Philosophy*, ed. Anthony Parel (Toronto: University of Toronto Press, 1972), ch. 2; Sheldon S. Wolin, *Politics and Vision* (Boston: Little, Brown and Company, 1960), ch. 7; Maurice Merleau-Ponty, *Humanism and Terror*, trans. John O' Neill (Boston: Beacon Press, 1969).

oneself and one's people. The usual catalogue of virtues, as we have seen throughout the *Prince* and the *Discourses*, are evaluated from the perspective of their effectiveness in creating or restoring a regime. For these ends, it is sometimes necessary for a prince and a people to learn, in Machiavelli's famous phrase, "how not to be good." Within this framework, he has produced a coherent political "ethic" for justifying, not just condoning, immoral actions. A transformation has thus occurred in *virtù*: it becomes being-good-at the political statecraft of getting and keeping power. Accordingly, critics for centuries have concluded that the significance of his thought is that it is designed to provide a justification for political immorality.

Some critics have claimed that Machiavelli's views of human nature and of politics are clearly distorted by his gender-based categories. That, for Machiavelli, "realism" entails a masculine, public role for the virile and a subordinate, private role for women has been argued by several interpreters. Also, the political-military mode of citizenship advocated by Machiavelli seems to permanently place women outside the public realm. Machiavelli constantly relies on masculine metaphors for illustrating political virtues. He then uses feminine analogies to portray the obstacles and problems hindering successful political action: fortune is a women to be conquered by audacity, and a corrupt citizenry or religion is called effeminate. This one-sided, male understanding of the political realm, these commentators reason, permanently distorts and ultimately undermines Machiavelli's support for republican liberty and politics.[104]

Machiavelli's significance or, at least, originality can be clearly seen when contrasted with classical thinkers. Machiavelli's pictures of humans and society are drawn when humanity confronts the abnormal, emergencies, crises, and necessity. Selfishness, fear, and conflict are now obvious, according to Machiavelli. These qualities predominate and are, therefore, the natural, real features constituting humanity. Plato and Aristotle begin at our biological beginnings and show how

---

[104] The best treatment is by Pitkin, *Fortune Is a Woman: Gender and Politics in the Thought of Niccolò Machiavelli*; see also, Arlene W. Saxonhouse, *Women in the History of Political Thought: Ancient Greece to Machiavelli* (New York: Praeger, 1985), ch. 7; Wendy Brown, *Manhood and Politics: A Feminist Reading in Political Theory* (Totowa, N.J.: Rowman and Littlefield, 1988), ch. 5; Jean Bethke Elshtain, *Meditations On Modern Political Thought: Masculine/Feminine Themes from Luther to Arendt* (New York: Praeger, 1986), ch. 8. For a different reading of Machiavelli, see: J. G. A. Pocock, "Machiavelli in the Liberal Cosmos," *Political Theory* 13 (November, 1985), pp. 559–74; de Grazia, *Machiavelli in Hell*, ch. 6.

humans normally evolve, behave, and reason together. Consequently, the Greeks characterize humanity quite differently. Aquinas provides an equally sharp contrast. In *On Kingship* Aquinas commends to a potential prince the usual set of Christian virtues and promises a commensurate set of rewards; Machiavelli substitutes his *virtù*, and the rewards are power, glory, and riches. Indeed, Machiavelli's *virtù* and rewards consist of the very vices and temptations that thinkers from Plato to Aquinas have consistently warned against and have constructed political systems to thwart. Not surprisingly, political ethics in Machiavelli has changed its moorings from a human nature grounded on the capacity for reason or on God's Providential ordering to one grounded on the necessities of power.[105]

Contrasts can also be drawn between Machiavelli and his fellow humanists. Although many scholars argue that Machiavelli can be best understood as a member of the humanist tradition of classical republicanism,[106] there are still striking discontinuities. As with Christianity, the humanist virtues of Seneca and Cicero, much admired by his contemporaries, are altered by Machiavelli. What is cruel or liberal depends, according to Machiavelli, on the political effect rather than the effect on the soul. When Machiavelli does follow a standard humanist piece of advice, it is for a strategic reason. The prince, for example, is told to exercise self-control over his desire for the property and women of his subjects. This advice is not because of a belief in the Stoic virtue of self-control but because it enables the prince to preserve his position. Machiavelli also decidedly differs with his contemporaries' views on Rome. The great Republic was still the source to be imitated, Machiavelli insists; yet, it was not the Rome perceived through the eyes of Stoicism or Cicero. Machiavelli's Rome rose to greatness using Machiavellian *virtù*, with a citizen army led by rulers who knew how not to be good and who could, without remorse, use force, fraud, and deceit as dictated by necessity.[107] A modern scholar states of Machiavelli that

---

[105] The contrast between Machiavellian and classical Christian perspectives is brilliantly drawn in the novel by Graham Greene, *The Power and the Glory* (London: Heinemann, 1960) and, as usual, by William Shakespeare in *Henry V* and through the character Edmund in *King Lear*.

[106] See the many works of Hans Baron, Felix Gilbert, J. G. A. Pocock, and B. F. Skinner.

[107] Marcia L. Colish tries to show a connection between Stoic thought and Machiavelli: "Cicero's *De Officiis* and Machiavelli's *Prince*," *Sixteenth Century Journal* 9 (Winter, 1978) pp. 81–93. For a sharp contrast, see Horst Hutter on Ciceronian virtue and friendship: *Politics as Friendship: The Origins of Classical Notions of Politics in the Theory and Practice of Friendship* (Waterloo: Wilfred Laurier University Press, 1978).

he took the Roman republicans, whom Cicero had portrayed as pre-Stoics, and turned them into self-conscious power politicans, taking by force and by fraud, by the methods of the lion and the fox, what Cicero had ancient peoples freely giving to the Romans because they were the embodiment of justice, dedicated to the fair and humanitarian treatment of mankind. It was Cicero who invented the imagery of the lion and the fox, the better to congratulate Rome on having disdained their use; it was Machiavelli who maintained that the lion and the fox were evident throughout the history of republican Rome, that the bestial in the Romans was what made them great, and that any modern republic wishing to re-create ancient grandeur had better overcome its denial of the animal inside the man.[108]

It must be reiterated that Machiavelli, contrary to his own rhetoric, did not discover a new world of power politics. Prior thinkers were perfectly aware of the obvious conflicts and wars surrounding them. In Book V of *The Politics*, for example, Aristotle was as knowledgeable and candid as Machiavelli in describing how to get and keep power. Augustine's view of Roman history and political activity is no less frank than that of Machiavelli. But it was Machiavelli who formulated the arguments to justify such practices and goals. He aspired to present a new political and "moral" standard.

There are incontestably modern themes in Machiavelli, but it would be misleading to attribute a revolution in political philosophy to him. Ernst Cassirer has claimed, and we think improperly: "What Galileo gave in his *Dialogues*, and what Machiavelli gave in his *Prince* were really new sciences…. Just as Galileo's Dynamics became the foundation of our modern science of nature, so Machiavelli paved a new way to political science."[109] This is too high a praise given Machiavelli's non-modern philosophic views: Machiavelli held that human nature, society, history, and religion were affected by the motions of the heavens; his key concepts of fortune, *virtù*, and necessity are hopelessly vague. In brief, his philosophic framework is incompatible with modern thought. Although Machiavelli cannot be called a political philosopher, a theologian, or a philosopher of jurisprudence, it would still be fair to accredit the achievements of a thinker who lived between

---

[108] Hulliung, *Citizen Machiavelli*, p. xi.

[109] *The Myth of the State* (New Haven: Yale University Press, 1946), p. 130.

the Middle Ages and modernity: he did reassert, however adequately, the autonomy and value of the political realm; and he explored, as few had done before, the anatomy of power and its effects on creating and sustaining a regime.

SUGGESTIONS FOR FURTHER READING

For the standard historical biography of Machiavelli see the work by Ridolfi. Tarlton, Hale, and Ruffo-Fiore are useful short biographies for the beginning student and Hale relates Machiavelli's diplomatic career to his writings. Skinner, Anglo, and Butterfield provide short surveys of Machiavelli's political thought and writings. De Grazia, the best biography, is a literary masterpiece in its own right and along with the works by Baron, Pocock, Skinner, and Smith place Machiavelli within the civic humanism tradition of classical republicanism. Bondanella, Kerrigan and Braden, Rebhorn, Allan Gilbert, and Garver examine Machiavelli from literary perspectives. Hulliung, Butterfield, Chabod, Strauss, Parel, and Mansfield, Jr. are the most critical treatments of Machiavelli. The works edited by Rabil, and by Skinner and Kessler, as well as the writings of Kristeller are essential sources for the cultural and philosophical context. The works edited by Parel, Jensen, Bock, Skinner and Viroli, and Fleisher, and the edition of the *Prince* edited by Adams represent the many interpretations of Machiavelli. Felix Gilbert and Hulliung discuss contemporary interpretations and provide guides to the immense secondary literature.

Translations

Adams, Robert M., ed and trans. *The Prince: A New Translation, Backgrounds, Interpretations.* New York: Norton, 1992.

Atkinson, James B., trans. *The Prince.* Indianapolis: The Library of the Liberal Arts, 1976.

Bondanella, Peter, and Mark Musa, eds. and trans. *The Portable Machiavelli.* New York: Penguin, 1979.

Gilbert, Allan, ed. and trans. *Machiavelli: The Chief Works and Others.* 3 Vols. Durham: Duke University Press, 1965.

Lerner, Max, ed. *The Prince and the Discourses.* Translated by Luigi Ricci. Revised by E. R. P. Vincent. *The Discourses.* Translated by Christian E. Detmold. New York: Modern Library, 1950.

Musa, Mark, trans. *The Prince*. Bilingual ed. New York: St. Martin's Press, 1964.

Skinner, Quentin, and Russell Price, eds. *The Prince*. Cambridge: Cambridge University Press, 1988.

Walker, Leslie J., trans. *The Discourses of Niccolò Machiavelli*. 2 Vols. Introduction by Cecil H. Clough. Rev. ed. New Haven: Yale University Press, 1975.

Commentaries

Anglo, Sydney. *Machiavelli: A Dissection*. London: Victor Gollancz, 1969.

Bock, Gisela, Quentin Skinner and Maurizo Viroli, eds. *Machiavelli and Republicanism*. Cambridge: Cambridge University Press, 1990.

Bondanella, Peter. *Machiavelli and the Art of Renaissance History*. Detroit: Wayne State University Press, 1974.

Butterfield, Herbert. *The Statecraft of Machiavelli*. New York: Collier Books, 1962.

Chabod, Federico. *Machiavelli and the Renaissance*. Translated by David Moore. New York: Harper Torchbooks, 1965.

de Grazia, Sebastian. *Machiavelli in Hell*. Princeton: Princeton University Press, 1989.

Fleisher, Martin, ed. *Machiavelli and the Nature of Political Thought*. New York: Atheneum, 1972.

Garver, Eugene. *Machiavelli and the History of Prudence*. Madison: University of Wisconsin Press, 1987.

Gilbert, Allan H. *Machiavelli's Prince and Its Forerunners*. Durham: Duke University Press, 1938.

Gilbert, Felix. *Machiavelli and Guicciardini: Politics and History in Sixteenth-Century Florence*. Princeton: Princeton University Press, 1965.

Hale, J. R. *Machiavelli and Renaissance Italy*. London: The English Universities Press, 1961.

Hulliung, Mark. *Citizen Machiavelli*. Princeton: Princeton University Press, 1983.

Jensen, De Lamar, ed. *Machiavelli: Cynic, Patriot, or Political Scientist?* Boston: D. C. Heath, 1960.

Mansfield, Harvey C., Jr. *Machiavelli's New Modes and Orders: A Study of the 'Discourses on Livy'*. Ithaca: Cornell University Press, 1979.

Parel, Anthony J. *The Machiavellian Cosmos*. New Haven: Yale University Press, 1992.

————, ed. *The Political Calculus: Essays on Machiavelli's Philosophy.* Toronto: University of Toronto Press, 1972.

Pitkin, Hanna Fenichel. *Fortune Is a Woman: Gender and Politics in the Thought of Niccolò Machiavelli.* Berkeley: University of California Press, 1984.

Pocock, J. G. A. *The Machiavellian Moment: Florentine Political Thought and the Atlantic Republican Tradition.* Princeton: Princeton University Press, 1975.

Rebhorn, Wayne A. *Foxes and Lions: Machiavelli's Confidence Men.* Ithaca: Cornell University Press, 1988.

Ridolfi, Roberto. *The Life of Niccolò Machiavelli.* Translated by Cecil Grayson. Chicago: University of Chicago Press, 1963.

Ruffo-Fiore, Silvia. *Niccolò Machiavelli.* Boston: Twayne, 1982.

Skinner, Quentin. *Machiavelli.* Oxford: Oxford University Press, 1981.

Smith, Bruce James. *Politics and Remembrance: Republican Themes in Machiavelli, Burke, and Tocqueville.* Princeton: Princeton University Press, 1985.

Strauss, Leo. *Thoughts on Machiavelli.* Glencoe, Ill.: Free Press, 1958.

Tarlton, Charles D. *Fortune's Circle: A Biographical Interpretation of Niccolò Machiavelli.* Chicago: Quadrangle Books, 1970.

Whitfield, John H. *Discourses on Machiavelli.* Cambridge: Heffer and Sons, 1969.

Social and Political Background

Baron, Hans. *In Search of Florentine Civic Humanism.* 2 Vols. Princeton: Princeton University Press, 1988.

Burckhardt, Jacob. *The Civilization of the Renaissance in Italy.* Translated by S.G.C. Middlemore. London: Oxford University Press, 1960.

Cassirer, Ernst, Paul Oskar Kristeller and John Herman Randall, Jr. eds. *The Renaissance Philosophy of Man.* Chicago: University of Chicago Press, 1948.

Gilbert, Felix. *History: Choice and Commitment.* Cambridge: Harvard University Press, 1977.

Kerrigan, William, and Gordon Braden. *The Idea of the Renaissance.* Baltimore: The Johns Hopkins University Press, 1989.

Kristeller, Paul Oskar. *Renaissance Thought: The Classic, Scholastic, and Humanist Strains.* New York: Harper, 1955.

McKnight, Stephen A. *Sacralizing the Secular: The Renaissance Origins of Modernity.* Baton Rouge: Louisiana State University Press, 1989.

Meinecke, Friedrich. *Machiavellism: The Doctrine of Raison d'Etat and its Place in Modern History.* Translated by Douglas Scott. New York: Praeger, 1965.

Rabil, Jr., Albert, ed. *Renaissance Humanism: Foundations, Forms, and Legacy.* 3 Vols. Philadelphia: University of Pennsylvania Press, 1988.

Skinner, Quentin. *The Foundations of Modern Political Thought: The Renaissance.* Vol. I. Cambridge: Cambridge University Press, 1978.

Skinner, Quentin, and Eckhard Kessler, eds. *The Cambridge History of Renaissance Philosophy.* Cambridge: Cambridge University Press, 1988.

Viroli, Maurizo. *From Politics to Reason of State: The Acquisition and Transformation of the Language of Politics, 1250-1600.* Cambridge: Cambridge University Press, 1992.

THOMAS HOBBES AND THE PHILOSOPHICAL REVOLUTION OF THE SEVENTEENTH CENTURY

The intellectual climate of opinion that emerged in the seventeenth century is the climate that nurtured the spirit of inquiry that is the very essence of modernity. Building upon the sixteenth-century labours of Copernicus, William Gilbert, and Leonardo da Vinci, men like Harvey, Kepler, Galileo, Huyghens, Boyle, and Newton established the foundations of modern physical science. Francis Bacon sought to explain in philosophical terms what the practising scientists were doing. Descartes provided the agenda for modern philosophy. Hobbes and Locke sought to provide a political theory that would be compatible with the new knowledge and new methods of inquiry. As Alfred North Whitehead has said, it was a "century of genius." This age of intellectual ferment was destined to change the social and political world just as it changed the way in which most persons would henceforth look at the natural world.

There were, of course, dissenters and those who clung stubbornly to the ancient wisdom and traditions, but the majority of intellectuals welcomed the new science of inquiry as a breath of fresh air and a liberation from the bondage of error. Theology was dethroned as the queen of the sciences and physics put in her place. Philosophy announced its declaration of independence from theology. Man and nature, not God and Being, would engage the intellectual curiosity of the philosopher. The search for "useful" knowledge would replace that "useless" knowledge that passed for wisdom in earlier centuries. The mystery of the universe was no longer regarded with awe nor submitted to with humility; rather it presented a challenge to those who had the new keys that would open the door that had previously been locked. Above all, the new knowledge would give man new powers.

THE RISE OF MODERN SCIENCE

Leonardo da Vinci (1452–1519) is well known to us as a painter and sculptor, but he was also an astronomer, a geologist, a botanist, an engineer—a restless observer of nature. All of our knowledge, he says, comes from our perceptions. And since experience never errs, we must first "test by experiment" before proceeding further. "Whosoever appeals to authority applies not his intellect but his memory.... Although nature begins with the cause and ends with the experience, we must follow the opposite course, namely...begin with the experience and by means of it investigate the cause."[1] Thus, da Vinci helped launch the modern world on what came to be called the empirical investigation of reality. And the language used to conduct empirical investigation is mathematics.

It was astronomy that first used the technique of mathematics. According to the second-century (A.D.) astronomer Ptolemy, whose views predominated throughout the Middle Ages, the universe was a large, finite sphere, consisting of several concentric spheres. At the centre of this hollow sphere was the earth, and near the periphery were the fixed stars. Between the earth and the stars, in the heavenly sphere, of which they were a part, revolved the planets. The outermost sphere was Paradise or "the abode of the blessed." Although medieval astronomers were able to predict eclipses by means of this conception, it was, we know now, a very crude picture of physical reality. Copernicus (1473–1543) accepted much of this cosmological theory but put the sun at the centre instead of the earth. Kepler (1517–1630) demonstrated that, contrary to the previously accepted theory that the planets move in perfect circles, actually planets move in ellipses, and move more rapidly the nearer they are to the sun. Another brilliant insight enabled him to suggest a formula whereby the movements of the planets in relation to one another might be mathematically computed with exactitude. These laws, to which Kepler's name has been attached, laid the foundations of modern astronomy. Galileo (1564-1641) not only substantiated, by the use of the telescope, the hypotheses

---

[1] J. P. Richter and I. A. Richter, eds., *The Literary Works of Leonardo da Vinci* (Oxford: Oxford University Press, 1939), Vol. II, p. 239.

put forth by Copernicus and Kepler, but also laid the foundations for modern physics. He made use of such newly invented scientific instruments as the telescope, the barometer, and the thermometer. The compound microscope was to make its first appearance around 1650. Although not completely liberated from Aristotelian notions, Galileo successfully contested conventional scientific propositions—for example, that bodies fall at speeds proportional to their weight—and, in general, helped to create a mathematical and mechanical view of reality. He also introduced a new method: mathematical reasoning combined with observation and experiment. Thus he wrote:

> Philosophy is written in this grand book, the universe, which stands continually open to our gaze. But the book cannot be understood unless one first learns to comprehend the language and to read the letters in which it is composed. It is written in the language of mathematics, and its characters are triangles, circles, and other geometric figures without which it is impossible to understand a single word of it.[2]

Galileo was primarily interested in understanding the movement of bodies in space and time. More traditional explanations of motion, such as that of Aristotle, were useless for the purpose of calculating rates of motion or predicting future movements. Aristotle had taught that motion consisted of potentiality seeking to actualize itself. This might or might not be true, but it is only a verbal statement, which is useless for practical purposes. Galileo is not interested in *why* things move but *how* they move. He wants to *measure* movement not explain it. Describing his own achievements he says:

> My purpose is to set forth a very new science dealing with a very ancient subject. There is, in nature, perhaps nothing older than motion, concerning which the books written by philosophers are neither few nor small; nevertheless I have discovered by experiment some properties which are worth knowing and which have not hitherto been either observed or demonstrated. Some superficial observations have been made as, for instance, that the free motion of a heavy falling body is continuously accelerated; but to

---

[2] Stillman Drake, *Cause, Experiment and Science: A Galilean dialogue incorporating a new English translation of Galileo's 'Bodies that Stay atop Water, or Move in it'* (Chicago: University of Chicago Press, 1981), p. 207. Also see Stillman Drake, *Galileo* (New York: Hill and Wang, 1980).

just what extent this acceleration occurs has not yet been announced; for so far as I know, no one has yet pointed out that the distance traversed during equal intervals of time by a body falling from rest, stand to one another in the same ratio as the odd numbers beginning with unity.

It has been observed that missiles and projectiles describe a curved path of some sort; however no one has pointed out that this path is a parabola. But this and other facts, not few in number or less worth knowing, I have succeeded in proving; and what I consider more important, there have been opened up to this vast and most excellent science, of which my work is merely the beginning, ways and means by which other minds more acute than mine will explore its remote corners.[3]

All knowledge of nature must start with the perceptual observation of particular objects in their quantitative aspects. From this observation we may proceed to derive mathematical hypotheses which, if found by further observations and experimentation to explain physical phenomena not previously observed, we may regard as *laws of nature*. Galileo was careful to point out that no such law, however, ever corresponds exactly to actuality but is, in a sense, an ideal law made possible by *abstraction*. Although we may state as a law that all planets move in the form of an ellipse, no particular planet ever moves in a perfect ellipse, but we can calculate the forces that disturb its regular elliptic motion by knowing in advance the form its movement would take if there were no disturbing forces. In effect, Galileo said that we can measure that which is measurable and describe mathematically that which lends itself to mathematical description, but he did not say, as some people thought and think, that *all* phenomena are measurable. It is only by abstracting out of the totality of phenomena that physical science is made possible.

The early work of men like Kepler and Galileo was carried on by others and brought to a culmination by Isaac Newton (1642–1727). Newton was born a year after the death of Galileo, and although his monumental work, the *Philosophiae Naturalis Principia Mathematica* was not published until 1687, he began to make important contributions to physics when he was only 19 years of age. It was at that time that he discovered the general binomial theorem and began to study the problem of gravitation. He made important contributions to

---

[3] Galileo Galilei, *Dialogues Concerning Two New Sciences,* trans. Henry Crew and Alfonso de Saliro (New York: Dover, 1954), pp. 153–54.

the development of analytic geometry and invented the differential calculus. His *Principia* summarizes the famous laws of motion that interpreted the entire universe as one vast system of mechanical motion. The change in the climate of opinion brought about by the Newtonian revolution is described by Professor Burtt in these words:

> Just as it was thoroughly natural for mediaeval thinkers to view nature as subservient to man's knowledge, purpose and destiny; so now it has become natural to view her as existing and operating in her own self-contained independence, and so far as man's ultimate relation to her is clear at all, to consider his knowledge and purpose somehow produced by her, and his destiny wholly dependent on her.[4]
>
> But it was of the greatest consequence for succeeding thought that now the great Newton's authority was squarely behind that view of the cosmos which saw in man a puny, irrelevant spectator (so far as being wholly imprisoned in a dark room can be called such) of the vast mathematical system whose regular motions according to mechanical principles constituted the world of nature…. The world that people had thought themselves living in—a world rich with colour and sound…speaking everywhere of purposive harmony and creative ideals—was crowded now into minute corners in the brains of scattered organic beings. The really important world outside was a world, hard, cold, colourless, silent and dead; a world of quantity, a world of mathematically computable motions in mechanical regularity. The world of qualities as immediately perceived by man became just a curious and minor effect of that infinite machine, beyond.[5]

The "puny, irrelevant spectator" was transformed by scientific knowledge into a creature of enormous and, what Hobbes called, god-like power. The epitome of scientific knowledge was provided by mathematical physics, which was destined to dominate the scientific world until Darwin and biology challenged that ascendancy in the nineteenth century.

---

[4] E.A. Burtt, *Metaphysical Foundations of Modern Physical Science* (New York: Doubleday Anchor, 1955), p. 24. And see Frank Manuel, *Sir Isaac Newton: A Portrait* (Cambridge: Harvard University Press, 1968).

[5] *Ibid.* pp. 238–39. The evolution of physical science from Copernicus, Kepler, and Galileo to Newton is fully described in I. Bernard Cohn, *Revolution in Science* (Cambridge: Harvard University Press, 1985), pp. 105–94; A. Rupert Hall, *From Galileo to Newton* (New York: Dover, 1981).

Actually, two broad streams in the evolution of science developed. Both can be traced to ancient Greece. From the Ionian scientists there developed a materialist and mechanical tradition, and from Pythagoras and Plato there evolved a theoretical and mathematical tradition. These streams, often intermingled, can be identified in the key figures of the scientific revolution. Copernicus and Kepler followed the mathematical and theoretical stream. Galileo participated in both streams, but Newton was clearly in the material-mechanical stream. For thinkers within the materialist stream mathematical knowledge was not about reality, though it may be used to express certain features. Empirical and mechanical knowledge thus came to be held as wholly different from mathematical knowledge. And it was not until Einstein's theory of relativity emerged in the twentieth century that physicists were forced to re-examine some of their basic Newtonian presuppositions.[6]

The activities of the early scientists led to the formation of numerous societies devoted to the promotion of the new knowledge. Probably the earliest such society was the one founded by della Porta in Naples in 1560, the *Academia Secretorum Naturae*. The *Academia dei Lincei* was founded in Rome in 1603 and included Galileo among its members. The Royal Society of London was chartered in 1662 "for the promoting of Physico-Mathematical Experimental Learning" and included Isaac Newton among its earlier members. A French academy was started in 1666, and a German academy was founded in Berlin in 1700. The establishment of an American Philosophical Society for "promoting useful knowledge" was first proposed by Benjamin Franklin in 1743 and was established in 1769. Many of these societies are still active.[7]

THE REACTION OF THE CHURCH

Many Churchmen reacted to the emergence of the modern scientific age with panic. The Copernican theory that the earth is not the centre of the universe seemed to some highly placed Churchmen to be not only philosophically false

---

[6] Michael Polanyi, *Personal Knowledge: Towards a Post-Critical Philosophy* (New York: Harper, 1962), pp. 3–17.

[7] The origins of modern science has a complicated history. The following are useful guides: Herbert Butterfield, *The Origins of Modern Science, 1300–1800* (Toronto: Clark Irwin & Co., 1968); Robert Mandrow, *From Humanism to Science: 1480–1700* (New York: Penguin Books, 1978); A. Rupert Hall, *The Revolution in Science 1500–1750* (London: Longmans, 1983); Allen Debus, *Man and Nature in the Renaissance* (Cambridge: Cambridge University Press, 1978).

but also contrary to the teaching of Holy Scripture. This was curious in that an heliocentric cosmogony was discussed through the centuries. Copernicus himself was taught by a neo-Platonist monk, Domenico Maria de Novara, who had criticized the Ptolemaic system on the Platonic grounds that it was neither mathematically sound nor heliocentric. Nevertheless, many Churchmen failed to understand the significance of what was happening and, in their ignorance, condemned many of the new hypotheses as heresy. Galileo was condemned by the Roman Inquisition for propagating "grievous and pernicious error" and his writings were put on the index of prohibited books. He was forced to sign a formal recantation, obliged to recite daily a number of Psalms praising God in penance, and was confined to house arrest until his death.[8] Such actions added fuel to the flames of controversy, and they had the unfortunate effect of framing the controversy in terms of religion versus science and of authority versus reason. Thereafter, the claims of natural science were advanced in the name of enlightened reason, and the authority of the Church came to be regarded in the minds of many as synonymous with obscurantism. In time, the Church itself recanted, but it was not soon enough to avoid the suspicion of many that the Church was motivated by an opportunistic acceptance of the inevitable rather than by a sincere acknowledgment of error.

The impact of modern science upon the intellectual climate generally need not have been so controversial had philosophy been prepared to meet it. Metaphysics need not have yielded its legitimate speculation concerning the totality of experience, but, discredited and rendered impotent by the late scholastics, it was unprepared to assert its rightful claim to be heard. There was no Christian philosopher of the intellectual stature of St. Thomas Aquinas who was prepared to address the new science. Furthermore, many claims of a metaphysical nature hostile to Christianity were advanced by individuals in the name of science but had nothing to do with science itself.

Some students of intellectual history have been inclined to describe this period in history as one in which "truth" finally conquered over "error" and "reason" replaced "faith." But other scholars suggest that such generalizations

---

[8] For a detailed account of these proceedings see Giorgio de Santillana, *The Crime of Galileo* (Chicago: University of Chicago Press, 1955). Thomas Kuhn describes the background to the theories of Copernicus and Galileo in *The Copernican Revolution* (New York: Random House, 1959), pp. 100–33.

do not adequately account for what was happening. A distinguished philosopher of the twentieth century, Alfred North Whitehead, points out that what really happened was that one kind of faith was exchanged for another. If the Middle Ages can be characterized as an age of faith based upon reason, then the modern age can be characterized as an age of reason based upon faith. Whitehead, and others, argue that without the long antecedent preparation of the European mind, modern science could never have emerged. "The greatest contribution of medievalism to the formation of the scientific movement," he says, was

> the inexpugnable belief that every detailed occurrence can be correlated with its antecedents in a perfectly definite manner, exemplifying general principles. Without this belief the incredible labours of scientists would be without hope....
>
> When we compare this tone of thought in Europe with the attitude of other civilizations when left to themselves, there seems but one source for its origin. It must come from the medieval insistence on the rationality of God, conceived as with the personal energy of Jehovah and with the rationality of a Greek philosopher. Every detail was supervised and ordered: the search into nature could only result in the vindication of the faith in rationality. Remember that I am not talking of the explicit beliefs of a few individuals. What I mean is the impress on the European mind arising from the unquestioned faith of centuries.[9]

The early scientists made no claim to speak about matters that had traditionally constituted the agenda of philosophy. They were interested in answering the question *how* things move, not *why*. "Galileo admitted that he knew nothing about the ultimate nature of the forces he was measuring, nothing about the cause of gravitation, or the origin of the Universe; he deemed it better, rather than speculate on such high matters, 'to pronounce that wise, ingenious, and modest sentence, I know it not.'"[10] And we know, from the perspective of the

---

[9] Alfred North Whitehead, *Science and the Modern World* (New York: Mentor, 1960), p. 19.

[10] Basil Willey, *The Seventeenth-Century Background* (New York: Doubleday Anchor Books, 1953), p. 29.

twentieth century, that there can be more than one theory about natural phenomena and that each can be partially true. As Whitehead points out:

> Galileo said that the earth moves and that the sun is fixed; the Inquisition said that the earth is fixed and the sun moves; the Newtonian astronomers, adopting an absolute theory of space, said that both the sun and the earth move. But now we say that any one of these three statements is equally true, provided that you have fixed your sense of 'rest' and 'motion' in the way required by the statement adopted. At the date of Galileo's controversy with the Inquisition, Galileo's way of stating the facts was, beyond question, the fruitful procedure for the sake of scientific research. But in itself it was not more true than the formulation of the Inquisition. But at that time the modern concepts of relative motion were in nobody's mind; so that the statements were made in ignorance of the qualifications required for their more perfect truth. Yet this question of the motions of the earth and the sun expresses a real fact in the universe; and all sides had got hold of important truths concerning it. But with the knowledge of those times, the truths appeared to be inconsistent.[11]

Throughout the Middle Ages all the branches of knowledge, metaphysics, logic, ethics, politics, and economics were held together in one coherent whole through the mediation of the "queen of the sciences," theology. As we have already seen in the monumental work of St. Thomas Aquinas in the thirteenth century, the realm of nature and the realm of grace, the knowledge yielded by natural reason and the knowledge yielded by revelation, were conceived as complementary. But between the fifteenth and seventeenth centuries the authority of the Church, the guardian of theology, was challenged in the Reformation by nationalistic and intellectual forces with which it was unable to cope successfully. The massive, coherent structure raised by Aquinas had already been attacked within the Church by men like Duns Scotus and William of Ockham, and the Church itself lacked the moral authority necessary to harmonize the new intellectual forces with the old. With the repudiation of the authority of the Church and the disintegration of Scholasticism, the medieval edifice of thought collapsed—the keystone of its arch, theology, discredited. This revolt against authority, which characterized the

---

[11] Whitehead, *Science and the Modern World,* p. 263

period of the Renaissance, necessitated the search for some substitute method of arriving at knowledge, and the intellectual activity of the fifteenth, sixteenth, and seventeenth centuries was directed toward the search for that new method.

Replacing the reliance upon traditional authorities and institutions, a new stress on the autonomy of the individual arose. William Temple explains the shift in sensibility:

> But if the Church and its system were repudiated, what could take its place? If a man's thought and purposes were no longer to take their start from the only tradition available, where could they begin? And the only possible answer was 'with himself.' If a man was not going to start as a member of a system, accepting that system and his own place in it, then he must start with his isolated self. Of course he would submit to the authority of conscience, but it would be *his* conscience. He would submit to the Voice of God as he heard it, but it would be as *he* heard it. So the modern movement was bound to be a movement of individualism. We owe to it the distinctive blessings of modern life, but also its distinctive ills.[12]

This individualism coalesced with a new understanding of reason and knowledge. The thought of the Renaissance was characterized not only by the rejection of the authority of the Church but also, as Machiavelli demonstrated, by the rejection of Aristotle. Roger Bacon in the thirteenth, Peter Ramus in the sixteenth, and Francis Bacon in the seventeenth century all attacked the Aristotelian logic. According to Francis Bacon: "That method of discovery and proof according to which the most general principles are first established, and then intermediate axioms are tried and proved by them, is the parent of error and the curse of all science."[13] For the demonstration of truth Francis Bacon would substitute a method of discovering truth. The discovery of that new method, or at least the

---

[12] William Temple, *Nature, Man and God* (London: Macmillan, 1935), p. 62. For a discussion of the cultural consequences of the new science: Margaret C. Jacob, *The Cultural Meaning of the Scientific Revolution* (Philadelphia: Temple University Press, 1988); Larry Stewart, *The Rise of Public Science: Rhetoric, Technology, and Natural Philosophy in Newtonian Britain, 1660–1750* (Cambridge: Cambridge University Press, 1992).

[13] *Novum Organum*, Bi. I, Aphorism 69. See for an introduction to his thought and influence: Fulton H. Anderson, *Francis Bacon: His Career and His Thought* (Los Angeles: University of Southern California Press, 1962); Anthony Quinton, *Francis Bacon* (New York: Hill and Wang, 1980). Howard B. White has a full discussion of Bacon's political philosophy in *Peace Among the Willows: The Political Philosophy of Frances Bacon* (The Hague: Martinus Nijhoff, 1968).

philosophical formulation of it, was largely the work of a Frenchman, René Descartes. He is often referred to as the "father" of modern philosophy. The characteristic feature of modern philosophy is the emphasis that is placed upon the individual as the source or medium of authority. Repudiating all traditional authority, modern philosophy thus proclaims the autonomy of human reason. According to one authority on this period:

> Philosophically, the Renaissance marks a change in the manner of conceiving truth and knowledge generally. The epistemological transition to be inferred from the scientific attitude of such minds as da Vinci and Galileo is, briefly, from one of unquestioning conviction that truth ultimately related to a reality transcendent and inaccessible to mind, to an active faith in the essential sufficiency of human powers to discover truth, precisely because knowledge is not ultimately of a transcendent reality. Or, as M. Bréhier puts it: 'truth is not disclosed in the form of a systematic and total vision of the universe (whether the vision be due to revelation or reason or both) but is, so to say, distributed in a multitude of propositions.'[14]

Perhaps the change wrought by the new, modern philosophy and science is best illustrated by contrasting remarks of Thomas Aquinas with those of Descartes. Aquinas had argued that "The slenderest knowledge that may be obtained of the highest things is more desirable than the most certain knowledge obtained of lesser things." Descartes, on the other hand, set the tone for modern thought: "in seeking the right path of truth we ought to concern ourselves only with objects which admit of as much certainty as the demonstrations of arithmetic and geometry."[15]

RENÉ DESCARTES (1596–1650)

Descartes has been called the "father of modern **rationalism**." With Descartes the philosophical tradition of **realism**, which dominated philosophical speculation from Thales to William of Ockham, was first seriously challenged. Until the fifteenth and sixteenth centuries nowhere had it been seriously disputed that

---

[14] S.V. Keeling, *Descartes* (London: Oxford University Press, 1934), p. 32. John Cottingham has an excellent short presentation of Descartes's philosophy, *Descartes* (Oxford: Basil Blackwell, 1986).

[15] St. Thomas Aquinas, *Summa Theologica* I, 1, 5ad, 1; Descartes, *Rules for the Direction of the Mind*, in *The Philosophical Writings of Descartes*, 3 Vols., trans. John Cottingham, Robert Stoothoff, and Dugald Murdoch (Cambridge: Cambridge University Press, 1985), Vol. I, Rule Two, pp. 12–13.

knowledge is a knowledge of real objects. It is not the external world of real objects that is the starting point of modern philosophical speculation but rather the individual mind and experience. Although there are numerous suggestions of a changed perspective before Descartes, it is with Descartes that the proclamation of the autonomy of human reason becomes explicit.

Descartes describes in his *Discourse on Method* (1637) how he determined to reject all traditional principles and doctrines and to rely solely upon his own reason to discover the truth.

> At that time I was in Germany, where I had been called by the wars that are not yet ended there. While I was returning to the army from the coronation of the Emperor, the onset of winter detained me in quarters where, finding no conversation to divert me and fortunately having no cares or passions to trouble me, I stayed all day shut up alone in a stove-heated room, where I was completely free to converse with myself about my own thoughts.
>
> …regarding the opinions too which I had hitherto given credence, I thought that I could not do better than undertake to get rid of them, all at one go, in order to replace them afterwards with better ones, or with the same ones once I had squared them with the standard of reason. I firmly believed that in this way I would succeed in conducting my life much better than if I built only upon old foundations and relied only upon principles that I had accepted in my youth without ever examining whether they were true.
>
> But, like a man who walks alone in the dark, I resolved to proceed so slowly, and to use such circumspection in all things, that even if I made but little progress I should at least be sure not to fall. Nor would I begin rejecting completely any of the opinions which may have slipped into my mind without having been introduced there by reason, until I had first spent enough time in planning the work I was undertaking and in seeking the true method of attaining the knowledge of everything within my mental capabilities.[16]

---

[16] *Discourse on the Method of Rightly Conducting the Reason and Seeking for the Truth in the Sciences*, in *The Philosophical Writings of Descartes*, Vol. I, Part Two, pp. 116, 117, 119.

The "true method" of arriving at knowledge was suggested to him by geometry and algebra and could be reduced, he believed, to four basic principles:

> The first was never to accept anything as true if I did not have evident knowledge of its truth: that is, carefully to avoid precipitate conclusions and preconceptions, and to include nothing more in my judgements than what presented itself to my mind so clearly and so distinctly that I had no occasion to doubt it.
>
> The second, to divide each of the difficulties I examined into as many parts as possible and as may be required in order to resolve them better.
>
> The third, to direct my thoughts in an orderly manner, by beginning with the simplest and most easily known objects in order to ascend little by little, step by step, to knowledge of the most complex, and by supposing some order even among objects that have no natural order of precedence.
>
> And the last, throughout to make enumerations so complete, and reviews so comprehensive, that I could be sure of leaving nothing out.[17]

Here are to be found many of the guiding principles of the modern scientific age. Descartes will accept nothing as true except that which is "clear and distinct," by which he means that which can be expressed with the clarity of mathematics. 'Two plus two equals four' is Descartes's conception of a clear and distinct perception. And he will start with what is simple in order to seek an explanation of that which is complex. We have since come to call this reductionism, i.e., trying to explain higher forms of life in terms of lower, a complex experience in terms of the simple components of that experience. Echoes of this characteristic theme of the modern age will be seen in all of the modern political philosophers: Hobbes, Locke, Bentham, Mill, Rousseau, and Marx.

While Descartes was shut up alone in the stove-heated room, he decided to conduct a simple experiment. He picked up a piece of beeswax. It was hard and cold, had a certain shape and colour, was sweet to the taste and gave off an odor. Then he took it close to the fire. The beeswax became liquid and hot; it lost its shape and became larger in size, changed in colour and lost its smell. What then, he asked himself, was distinct about the beeswax? His senses had obviously deceived him. At one

---

[17] *Ibid.*, p. 120.

moment they told him that it was hard and cold and at another moment that it was liquid and hot. Ignoring, then, what his senses had told him about the wax he concluded nothing remained except something that was "extended, flexible and movable." It was not his senses that told him this but his mind.

Descartes concluded from this experiment that it might prove profitable in the search for knowledge to begin with doubt rather than with certainty. He would reject, at least initially, everything that he had ever been taught (and he had been taught the Scholastic philosophy by the Jesuits) and everything that it was possible to doubt. Both his education and his senses had, he concluded, deceived him.

> For a long time I had observed…that in practical life it is sometimes necessary to act upon opinions which one knows to be quite uncertain just as if they were indubitable. But since I now wished to devote myself solely to the search for truth, I thought it necessary to…reject as if absolutely false everthing in which I could imagine the least doubt, in order to see if I was left believing anything that was entirely indubitable. Thus, because our senses sometimes deceive us, I decided to suppose that nothing was such as they led us to imagine. And since there are men who make mistakes in reasoning, committing logical fallacies concerning the simplest questions in geometry, and because I judged that I was as prone to error as anyone else, I rejected as unsound all the arguments I had previously taken as demonstrative proofs. Lastly, considering that the very thoughts we have while awake may also occur while we sleep without any of them being at the same time true, I resolved to pretend that all the things that had ever entered my mind were no more true than the illusions of my dreams. But immediately I noticed that while I was trying thus to think everything false, it was necessary that I, who was thinking this, was something. And observing that this truth '*I am thinking, therefore I exist*' was so firm and sure that all the most extravagant suppositions of the sceptics were incapable of shaking it, I decided that I could accept it without scruple as the first principle of the philosophy I was seeking.[18]

In the process of doubting everything that could possibly be doubted he said:

> In rejecting—and even imagining to be false—everthing which we can in any way doubt, it is easy for us to suppose that there is no God and no

---

[18] *Ibid.,* Part Four, pp. 126–27.

heaven, and that there are no bodies, and even that we ourselves have no hands or feet, or indeed any body at all. But we cannot for all that suppose that we, who are having such thoughts, are nothing. For it is a contradiction to suppose that what thinks does not, at the very time when it is thinking, exist. Accordingly, this piece of knowledge—*I am thinking, therefore I exist*—is the first and most certain of all to occur to anyone who philosophizes in an orderly way.[19]

It is important to notice that Descartes's experiment in doubting has an element of artificiality about it. Descartes is not in genuine despair. His doubting is more in the form of an intellectual game. Let's pretend, he says in effect, that there is no God, no earth, no bodies, etc. and then ask ourselves what, if anything, remains that we can know for certain. But not for a moment is Descartes emotionally upset by the experiment he is conducting. He seems to know, even in advance of the experiment, how it is all going to come out in the end.

In the earlier experiment with the beeswax Descartes, you remember, concluded that only the mathematical properties of the beeswax were real. Only those properties were "clear and distinct." What our senses told us about it— that it was hard or soft, had a certain taste and odor, etc—are, according to Descartes, secondary qualities that derive from us, the observer, and are not a part of the thing itself. As regards material things, they all occupy some space that is measurable, they all have some geometric shape, and they all have the possibility of changing location relative to other things, and this, too, is measurable. Only these measurable characteristics of matter are *real.* Reality consists of two substances, two distinct things, body and mind. The essential feature of mind is thought or consciousness: the mind is a kind of "thinking substance." The body is an "extended substance" independent of the mind. Within each of us is the "thinking substance" or "I" which is distinct from the body and uncontrolled by mathematical laws. Outside of ourselves there is the real world of mathematically defined relationships which are subject to the laws of nature. With these distinctions Descartes bequeathed to the modern world a problem with which philosophers have been wrestling ever since—what is the relationship between body and mind? How, if my mind is distinct from the world outside of it, can I have contact with that world? There is the humanly experienced world of love,

---

[19] *Principles of Philosophy*, Vol. I, Part I, Principle vii, pp. 194–95.

beauty, justice, hope and despair and the world of mathematical relationships (equations, vectors, factoring), and if the latter is the *real* world, how are we to account for the world of common sense and everyday human experience?

In the intellectual experiment that Descartes conducted and in which he resolved to doubt everything that he could possibly doubt, he arrived at the conclusion that there were only two things he could know with certainty. First, he was doubting—I think, therefore I am. From this one axiom he then proceeded to erect an entire philosophy. He regarded intuition and deduction as the most certain routes to knowledge. Second, he thought that he could know with certainty that God exists. The fact that he experienced himself as limited, fallible, and imperfect suggests that there must exist some being who is omniscient, perfect and omnipotent; otherwise he could not have experienced himself as limited and fallible. This suggests to Descartes that God exists and that he is perfect, omniscient, omnipotent, and immutable. If God exists and has these attributes, he would not be a deceiver. Therefore, the conviction Descartes had that there is a world of objects distinct from himself cannot be a delusion. The two certainties, that "I exist" and that God exists, assure Descartes that the objects of mathematical thought are real. He brings God into his philosophy as a kind of intellectual necessity to reassure himself that what he is thinking is real. If the mind is independent of the body and the body of the mind, how, then, do the two manage to work together? How can what is internal and mental reflect what is external and real? Descartes's only answer is that God so constituted the world that they do. Every action and perception, it appears, requires a continuous and miraculous intervention by God.

Descartes's influence merits his title as the founder of modern philosophy. He altered our views of reason and knowledge. Reason becomes epitomized by mathematics and geometry; knowledge is applied to only what can be gained through a reliable method and held with certainty. Here the rational and autonomous individual stands free of authority and tradition. Liberal rationalism was born, and it clearly nurtured the liberal political philosophers of the next three centuries: Hobbes, Locke, Bentham, and Mill. Thomas Spragens, Jr., has encapsulated liberal rationalism in 11 central tenets:

1. The assumptions and methods of the previously dominant Aristotelian-Scholastic tradition are mistaken and must be fundamentally revised or supplanted before genuine "natural philosophy" can be possible.

2. The human understanding, guided by the "natural light" of reason, can be and should be autonomous. Moreover, it constitutes the norm and the means by reference to which all else is to be measured.

3. It is possible and necessary to begin the search for knowledge with a clean slate.

4. It is possible and necessary to base knowledge claims on a clear and distinct, indubitable, self-evident foundation.

5. This foundation is to be composed of simple, unambiguous ideas or perceptions.

6. The appropriate formal standards for all human knowledge are those of the mathematical modes of inquiry.

7. The key to the progress of human knowledge is the development and pursuit of explicit rules of method.

8. The entire body of valid human knowledge is a unity, both in methods and in substance.

9. Therefore, human knowledge may be made almost wholly accessible to all men, provided only that they not be abnormally defective in their basic faculties.

10. Genuine knowledge is in some sense certain, "verifiable," and capable of being made wholly explicit.

11. Knowledge is power, and the increase of knowledge therefore holds the key to human progress.[20]

Ever since Descartes, philosophers have been preoccupied with the problem of knowledge. He had set the philosophical agenda. Metaphysical questions were either ignored or subordinated to the question: How do we know what we know and what does knowing mean? One of the effects of Descartes's separation of mind and body was to encourage some subsequent philosophers to become either idealists or materialists. It also led to a division between rationalism and empiricism.

---

[20] Thomas A. Spragens, Jr., *The Irony of Liberal Reason* (Chicago: University of Chicago Press, 1981), pp. 22–23. For critical assessments of the Cartesian tradition in philosophy, see: Richard J. Bernstein, *Beyond Objectivism and Relativism: Science, Hermeneutics, and Praxis* (Philadelphia: University of Pennsylvania Press, 1983); Richard Rorty, *Philosophy and the Mirror of Nature* (Princeton: Princeton University Press, 1979); Charles Taylor, *Sources of the Self: The Making of the Modern Identity* (Cambridge: Harvard University Press, 1984), pp. 143–58; Michael Polanyi, *The Tacit Dimension* (New York: Doubleday, 1966).

On the European continent Descartes's rationalism was further elucidated by philosophers like Spinoza (1632–1677) and Leibniz (1646–1716). In England, an empirical tradition developed through Locke (1632–1704) and Hume (1711–1776). It was not until the eighteenth century that the great German philosopher Immanuel Kant (1724–1804) sought to reconcile rationalism and empiricism in what some came to regard as "the answer" to the mind-body problem as posed initially by Descartes.

From the perspective of political philosophy, one striking consequence of the tenets of liberal rationalism was the link made between certain knowledge and effective action. Certainly, part of the original impetus that gave rise to modern science, as we have noted, was the desire to find knowledge that would prove to be "useful" or practical. "The true and lawful goal of the sciences," Francis Bacon declared, "is none other than this: that human life be endowed with new discoveries and powers."[21] Science promised, in time, to penetrate the ultimate mysteries and to provide humans with the tools necessary to assert their independence. There was a latent will to power subtly compounded with genuine intellectual curiosity. Science, it was hoped, would unleash the power that would make us masters and possessors of nature. Descartes himself says that knowledge of some general notions of physics

> ...opened my eyes to the possibility of gaining knowledge which would be very useful in life, and of discovering a practical philosophy which might replace the speculative philosophy taught in the schools. Through this philosophy we could know the power and action of fire, water, air, the stars, the heavens and all the other bodies in our environment, as distinctly as we know the various crafts of our artisans; and we could use this knowledge— as the artisans use theirs—for all the purposes for which it is appropriate, and thus make ourselves, as it were, the lords and masters of nature.[22]

---

[21] *Novum Organum*, Bk. I, Aphorism 81.

[22] *Discourse on Method*, Vol. I, Part 6, pp. 142–43. Some have argued that Descartes's conception of reason—enabling humans to be the "lords and masters of nature"—excludes females. This position has been argued by Susan Bordo, *The Flight to Objectivity: Essays on Cartesianism and Culture* (Albany: State University of New York Press, 1987) and Genieve Lloyd, *The Man of Reason: "Male" and "Female," in Western Philosophy* (Minneapolis: University of Minnesota Press, 1987). For the contrary view: Margaret Atherton, "Cartesian Reason and Gendered Reason" in *A Mind of One's Own: Feminist Essays on Reason and Objectivity*, eds. Louise M. Antony and Charlotte Witt (Boulder: Westview Press, 1993).

Curiously, Descartes never applied the new science or his own philosophy to politics. The first and greatest political philosopher to use these themes of liberal rationalism was Thomas Hobbes.

HOBBES: His Life and Works

Thomas Hobbes was born in Malmesbury on April 5, 1588, the second son of the curate of Malmesbury (Wiltshire). His father was barely educated and was an abusive alcoholic, who eventually abandoned his family when Hobbes was 16. His uncle thereafter supported the family. Hobbes demonstrated unusual intellectual ability as a child and became exceptionally well versed in Latin and Greek. When he was only fourteen years of age he translated Euripides's *Medea* into Latin verse. At that same age he entered Magdalen College at the University of Oxford. Although he remained at Oxford for five years, he later described his education there as a waste of time. After graduation he obtained a position as tutor to the son of William Cavendish who was later to become the Earl of Devonshire. He lived in the Cavendish household for the bulk of his life and became acquainted, through this association, with many of the prominent literary and political men of the day. Among his friends were Francis Bacon, Ben Jonson, and Robert Ayton, a Scottish poet.

Most of Hobbes's early life was spent as a tutor to various young men in the Cavendish family and he accompanied them on several occasions on extensive European tours. It was during his third visit to Europe in 1634–37 that Hobbes made the acquaintance of Galileo (1636) in Florence and joined a circle of philosophers in Paris who were concerned with the implications of the newly emerging sciences. Hobbes was a great admirer of Galileo, but his initial attitude to Descartes was quite critical, and this attitude was reciprocated. By the time they eventually met (1648), however, Hobbes recognized that, in spite of their differences, Descartes, too, was obviously on the side of the new sciences. It was, apparently, during this third sojourn to Europe that Hobbes read Euclid's *Elements of Geometry*. He was so struck by its indisputable certainty and logical elegance that he exclaimed: "By God, this is impossible!" He returned to England in 1637 and began composing a three-part work entitled *Elements of Philosophy*. Hobbes wrote both Latin and English versions of the three sections of this work. A portion of the English version, consisting primarily of sections two and three, was reworked and given the title *The Elements of Law, Natural and Politic*. He was 52 years of age when he completed it in 1640. For 10 years it circulated in manuscript form, but it was not published until 1650. He argued in the *Elements of Law* for the necessity of a sovereign with absolute power. This royalist position was clearly dangerous, given the assertion of power by the parliamentary forces that characterized the current political situation in England. When Parliament met in November 1640, signaling the conflict that would lead to the English Civil War in 1642, Hobbes wisely fled to Paris and remained there for over a decade. For 2 of those years he served as tutor to the Prince of Wales (who was later to become Charles II) while the Prince was living in exile. As King, Charles II awarded Hobbes a pension of £100 a year, though it was not regularly paid. During those years in Paris, Hobbes wrote the third section of the *Elements of Philosophy*, entitled *De Cive* (1642), which was an expanded Latin version of the *Elements of Law*. Then, in 1651, he published his most important political work, *Leviathan*.

Hobbes returned to England in 1652 to rejoin the household of the Earl of Devonshire. Now 64 years of age, Hobbes continued his intellectual labours. He published, in Latin, the first part of his *Elements of Philosophy, De Corpore* (Of Body), in 1655 and the second part, *De Homine* (Of Man), in 1658. For the last 20 years of his life he was engaged in rather acrimonious debates with political, philosophical, theological, and mathematical opponents. When he was 90 years of age, he returned to the literary interests of his youth and translated Homer's *Iliad* and *Odyssey* into English verse. He died in the winter of 1679 at the age of 91.

Hobbes's long life spanned one of the most critical periods in English political history. It was an age not only of intellectual ferment but also of political turmoil. He was born during the year of the Spanish Armada (as he often remarked, "fear and I were born twins") and he died 9 years before the Glorious Revolution. He lived through the Stuart attempt to establish an absolute monarchy, the Puritan revolution and the Civil War ("the first of all that fled," he boasted), the republic and dictatorship of Cromwell, and the restoration of the monarchy under Charles II. His political sympathies during the English Civil War were probably with the royalists, but his writings often displeased them, and it is doubtful if his writings' immediate influence was very great. He was also critical of the Calvinist clergy, though he exempted Cromwell himself. As *Leviathan* became widely read, it was increasingly clear to many Royalists that Hobbes was opposed to an established church exercising power over the citizens and the sovereign, which was precisely what many Anglican Royalists desired. In his later years he, in fact, wrote several tracts against a policy advocated by the Anglican Royalists, the punishment of heresy. The most famous of these later writings was *Behemoth, or the Long Parliament* (1668), purportedly a history of the English Civil War, which was published after his death in 1682. These writings were critical of the establishment of Anglican power as well as the excesses of Puritanism. Not surprisingly, these various works did not pass the censor, and, indeed, from 1666 until his death, several bills were introduced in Parliament that were directed specifically at Hobbes. Several times his works were burned by offended clergy and academics.[23] It was not until his ideas were revived by the Utilitarians, and especially by John Austin in the nineteenth century, that Hobbes came to be viewed in an openly favourable light or that his ideas came to exert a considerable influence in a direct way. His justifiable fame flows from the fact that he was the first political theorist to attempt to apply the perspectives of modern natural science to the problems of ethics and politics. Just as Machiavelli had claimed to be the first to understand politics clearly, Hobbes is well aware of his own originality. He declares that "natural philosophy", i.e. natural science, only began with the scientific revolution and "Civil Philosophy [is] yet much younger, as being no older…than my own book *De Cive*" (1642).[24] The boast is not entirely vain. As we shall see by examining his classic work, *Leviathan* (1651), Hobbes's influence has been both subtle and profound.

---

[23] The fierce criticisms aimed at Hobbes by his contemporaries are recounted by John Bowle, *Hobbes and His Critics: A Study in Seventeenth Century Constitutionalism* (London: Frank Cass, 1969), and Samuel I. Mintz, *The Hunting of the Leviathan* (Cambridge: Cambridge University Press, 1962). Several excellent biographies of Hobbes are: George Cromm Robertson, *Hobbes*, first ed. 1886 (New York: AMS Press, 1971); Charles H. Hinnant, *Thomas Hobbes* (Boston: Twayne, 1977); Arnold A. Rogow, *Thomas Hobbes: Radical in the Service of Reaction* (New York: W. W. Norton, 1986); Oliver Lawson Dick, ed., *Aubrey's Brief Lives* (London: Secker and Warburg, 1949), pp.147–59.

[24] Dedicatory epistle to the (third) Earl of Devonshire, *The English Works of Thomas Hobbes*, ed. Sir William Molesworth, Vol. I, *The Elements of Philosophy: The First Section, Concerning Body* (London: Bohn, 1835), p. ix. (The *English Works* will be hereafter referred to as *E. W.*) In 1620, long before his introduction to the new science, Hobbes had published anonymously three discourses—on Tacitus, Rome, and the law—which do contain typical Hobbesian views. In particular, he argued that there is no inherent natural order, as described by Aristotle, that political order must be imposed by human will on the world, and that power has to be used by the ruler to create political order out of chaos. Noel B. Reynolds and Arlene Saxonhouse, *Three Discourses of Thomas Hobbes* (Chicago: University of Chicago Press, 1995).

LEVIATHAN

One would be hard pressed to think of a work more deserving to be titled the greatest work of political philosophy in the English-speaking world. It is a classic work for several reasons: the book is elegantly and tightly reasoned; it has an eloquent and passionate rhetoric designed to convert Christians and Aristotelians to a new scientific understanding of the methods and goals of political philosophy, or what he called the "moral and civil science"; it has given new meanings to such rudiments of modern political thought as rights, state of nature, and social contract.

The *Leviathan* is divided into four parts: Of Man, Of Commonwealth, Of a Christian Commonwealth, and Of the Kingdom of Darkness. The latter two parts are not much read these days, but they compose almost half of the entire works and, as we shall see, were held by Hobbes to be critical to his whole project. In reading the book it is essential to recognize that it was not written for modern readers but for Christians and Aristotelians, and the arguments and rhetoric are designed for them. Hobbes initially speaks with contempt of rhetoric, but in his conclusion he confesses, after he is confident that he has persuaded his readers: "if there be not powerful eloquence, which procureth attention and consent, the effect of reason will be little."[25] To reiterate, this eloquence and rhetoric of Hobbes will not be properly perceived unless it is remembered that it is not directed at us who are heirs of the scientific revolution but to his Christian and Aristotelian cont

The "Author's Introduction" is a dramatic two-page stateme themes of the work. His intention is made clear in the opening s

> Nature, the art whereby God hath made and governs the world,
> of man, as many other things, so in this also imitated, that it c
> artificial animal. For seeing life is but a motion of limbs, the
> whereof is in some principal part within; why may we not say,
> *tomata* (engines that move themselves by springs and wheels as doth a watch)
> have an artificial life? For what is the *heart*, but a *spring*; and the *nerves*, but
> so many *springs*; and the *joints*, but so many *wheels*, giving motion to the

---

[25] *Leviathan*, ed. by Michael Oakeshott (New York: Collier, 1962), A Review, and Conclusion, p. 563. For an insightful treatment of Hobbes's eloquence, see: Norman Jacobson, *Pride and Solace* (New York: Methuen, 1978), pp. 51–92. More generally, Richard Tuck describes the Renaissance background, *Philosophy and Government 1572-1651* (Cambridge: Cambridge University Press, 1993), pp. 1–30; and David Johnston, *The Rhetoric of the Leviathan: Thomas Hobbes and the Politics of Cultural Transformation* (Princeton: Princeton University Press, 1986), places Hobbes within the rhetorical tradition of his time.

whole body, such as was intended by the artificer? *Art,* goes yet further, imitating that rational and most excellent work of nature, *man.* For by art is created that great LEVIATHAN called a COMMONWEALTH, or STATE, in Latin CIVITAS, which is but an artificial man; though of greater stature and strength than the natural, for whose protection and defense it was intended.... Lastly, the *pacts* and *covenants,* by which the parts of this body politic were at first made, set together, and united, resemble that *fiat,* or the *let us make man,* pronounced by God in the creation.[26]

This passage sets a tone of power and optimism not seen before in political philosophy. Machiavelli himself made clear that fortune could destroy a prince's best efforts, and Plato described in detail (Book X of *The Republic*) how the best state, even assuming it came into existence, would fall. But Hobbes declares that as God through his power can create and govern the world so, too, can humanity create and govern its own world, the state. This was a stunning thought to Hobbes's Christian contemporaries. They were well aware of the Biblical Book of Job, from which came Hobbes's title, *Leviathan,* the name of a sea monster. Job had questioned God about the disasters that had plagued his life even though he was a devout believer. God's answer, in Job 38: 3–4, produced silence and humility: "Where were you when I laid the earth's foundations? Tell me, if you know and understand." Hobbes suggests a different stance: as God creates and runs the world, so can we. Humans, through their "art," have similar power; thus, we can address our world, the state and its problems with optimism.

The "art" of God is seen in the laws and forces of physical nature that power the external world. The "art" of humanity can be seen in perceiving humans and society as mechanical contrivances put into motion by wheels, springs, joints, and the like. A knowledge derived from mechanical materialism would be humanity's "art" and would provide us with God-like power over our own little world, the state. It is "to decipher without a key," Hobbes continues, unless we can explain humanity's thoughts and actions. His plan is to discover the passions that cause human thoughts and actions, and in the light of which they can be explained. Hobbes warns: "I say the similitude of *passions,* which are the same in all men, *desire, fear, hope,* etc; not the similitude of the *objects* of the passions, which are the things *desired, feared, hoped....*"[27] In short, human action is to be understood by

---

[26] *Ibid.,* p. 19.

[27] *Ibid.,* p. 20.

recourse to underlying passions, which cause human behaviour. Humans are not to be understood by examining the ends sought—the hopeless quest of classical and Christian philosophers and theologians—but by discovering the underlying causes. Once we have this knowledge we can, by an act of will, covenant, thereby creating our own world just as God by an act of will created the whole world.

If one source were to be cited as the origin of modern social science, Hobbes's "Introduction" would be a contender. His plan is to follow the reductive method of discovering the causes of human beliefs and actions. The passions, he will argue, provide such a causal explanation. Later generations will accept his reductive method but will substitute or add such other purportedly causal factors as economics, social roles, Freudian drives, race, gender, and so on. The essential feature of Hobbes's plan is to delineate the causes of human behaviour, and it is the knowledge of these causes that constitutes the "art" that will give us the God-like power to create and govern our world.

The First Part: Of Man

The First Part sets the philosophical foundation for the entire work. Hobbes begins by first developing an epistemology, chapters 1–5. He then takes this method of knowing and applies it to describing human nature, chapters 6–9. These last four chapters provide the frame for his psychology of human nature. The final chapters to this Part, 10 to 16, present a social psychology; that is, they describe the human condition and indicate how humans living together would interact. By the end of the First Part Hobbes has provided the reader with a new, powerful, scientific approach for addressing the problems of politics.

The first chapter has an odd title for a work in political philosophy, "Of Sense." Hobbes begins by stating his thesis: The "thoughts of man" are "a *representation* or *appearance*, of some quality, other accident of a body without us, which is commonly called an *object*.... The original of them all, is that which we call SENSE, for there is no conception in a man's mind, which hath not at first, totally, or by parts, been begotten upon the organs of sense." By mechanical pressure on the sense organs sensations are transmitted "by the mediation of the nerves" to our brain and heart. We then experience such qualities as heat, cold, hardness, and softness, but these qualities are not in the objects themselves. They are caused by the "several motions of the matter, by which it presseth our organs diversally."[28] In principle,

---

[28] *Ibid.*, ch. 1, p. 21.

Hobbes is following Descartes's distinction between secondary and primary qualities. The latter would be Hobbes's matter in motion which causes a particular sense to respond and, thus, results the secondary qualities.

After stating his thesis and briefly elaborating it, Hobbes proceeds to show how the reader can personally verify the thesis: "And as pressing, rubbing, or striking the eye, makes us fancy a light; and pressing the ear, produceth a din; so do the bodies also we see, or hear, produce the same by their strong, though unobserved action. For if these colours and sounds were in the bodies, or objects that cause them, they could not be severed from them, as by glasses, and in echoes by reflection, we see they are; where we know the thing we see is in one place, the appearance in another." He then concludes by showing the pertinence: "But the philosophy-schools, through all the universities of Christendom, grounded upon certain texts of Aristotle, teach another doctrine, and say, for the cause of *vision*, that the thing seen, sendeth forth on every side a *visible species*, in English, a *visible show, apparition*, or *aspect*, or *a being seen*; the receiving whereof into the eye, is *seeing*." This Aristotelian explanation is clearly ludicrous he concludes, but such is the "frequency of insignificant speech."[29] The reader will have authenticated a new way of knowing, independent of any traditional authority and, while in the process, will have had a quick laugh of contempt at Aristotle and the universities.

The chapters in Parts I and II normally follow the same tripartite structure found in chapter 1. First, there will be a paragraph or two in which the thesis will be stated in neutral and impartial language. Hobbes takes great pains initially to formulate his thesis so that the reader's response will not be predetermined by schooling or religious beliefs. The reader's mind is left open. Second, Hobbes presents evidence, either logical and definitional or empirical, that the reader can authenticate while reading. At this stage, he will often illustrate his points by using as examples the "backward" gentiles and pagans. Pride in one's own scientific superiority is thus triggered. Also, aiming derisive wit at opponents is a technique often used by Hobbes. Contempt, even when cloaked by wit, serves to break the respect and authority the traditional modes of thinking have over the reader. The reader gradually becomes aware of the superior intellectual power provided by this new civil and moral science. Although the gentiles and pagans are normally the ones subjected to a reductive analysis, the principles learned would also be applicable to Christianity or classical political philosophy. The pagan

---

[29] *Ibid.*, ch. 1, p. 22.

historians, for example, cite the vision of Marcus Brutus who, the night before a battle, saw his coming defeat at the hand of Augustus Caesar. But we know, as Hobbes mockingly tells us, the causes of such purported visions: "lying cold breedeth dreams of fear, and raiseth the thought and image of some fearful object."[30] Visions are often cited in Judaism and Christianity as authoritative signs too. The laughter at the pagans and the sword of the reductive analysis will have also cut the readers' ties with their own tradition, and thereby the readers will have been led deeper into accepting Hobbes's position. Third, Hobbes concludes by showing the pertinence of the arguments used. As the book proceeds and the reader becomes ever more tightly caught in the power of the new civil and moral science—and no doubt takes more and more delight in it—Hobbes becomes blunter.

In order to enable his readers to leave the classical and medieval worlds and enter the modern world, Hobbes delicately leads them. After describing in chapter 1 how we know the external world, he next discusses the faculty of reason (chapter 2, "Of Imagination"), the process of reasoning (chapter 3, "Of the Consequence or Train of Imaginations"), and the tools of reasons (chapter 4, "Of Speech"). The explicit title of each chapter does not betray the subject matter, for to do so would only cause the reader to recall the standard position on these topics and, consequently, hinder or block Hobbes's efforts to convince. Within each chapter he uses the previously mentioned three steps: the reader is presented with a seemingly innocuous and philosophically neutral thesis; there is an elaboration and verification of the thesis; and a conclusion provides the pertinence. Only in chapter 5, "Of Reason and Science," do we get a recognizable title, but by then Hobbes has established the fundamental tenets for his new epistemology or science of knowing. He can now safely name and describe these old topics with their new meanings.

As we saw in chapter 1, for Hobbes, everything we know derives originally from sense perception. Sensation is a motion caused in the organs of sense by a previous motion in some external body. Imagination, he says in chapter 2, is simply "decaying sense," the persistence in a less intense form of the process originally stimulated by the movement of an external body when that original stimulus has been withdrawn. Another name for imagination is memory. And the memory of many things is what we call experience. Hobbes's theory of memory and experience is in striking contrast to traditional theories. The Platonic doctrine of recollection, for example, holds that the inherent rational

---

[30] *Ibid.*, ch. 2, p. 25.

structure of the mind reflects the rational structure of reality itself. For Hobbes, the brain is rather like a calculator, a recording mechanism. Speech serves to mark what has been recorded. It is only through the proper signification of words, Hobbes repeatedly warns, that we can gain knowledge. First, we can have knowledge of fact when a word has a clear empirical referent: "words whereby we conceive nothing but the sound, are those we call *absurd, insignificant,* and *nonsense*; or of a *free subject*; a *free will*; or any *free*, but free from being hindered by opposition, I should not say he were in error, but that his words were without meaning, that is to say, absurd."[31] Second, words can be given precise meaning through definitions since

> truth consisteth in the right ordering of names in our affirmations, a man that seeketh precise truth had need to remember what every name he uses stands for, and to place it accordingly, or else he will find himself entangled in words.... And therefore in geometry, which is the only science that it hath pleased God hitherto to bestow on mankind, men begin at settling the significations of their words; which settling of significations they call *definitions*, and place them in the beginning of their reckoning.[32]

He concludes that "whereas sense and memory are but knowledge of fact, which is a thing past and irrevocable; *Science* is the knowledge of consequences, and dependence of one fact upon another: by which, out of that...we see how any thing comes about, upon what causes, and by what manner; when the like causes come into our power, we see how to make it produce the like effects."[33] Science is made possible by a reasoning which, for Hobbes, is a kind of calculation such as is employed in arithmetic and geometry. Reason is "nothing but *reckoning*, that is adding and subtracting, or the consequences of general names agreed upon for the *marking* and *signifying* of our thought; I say *marking* them when we reckon by ourselves, and *signifying*, when we demonstrate or approve our reckonings to other men."[34]

---

[31] *Ibid.*, ch. 5, p. 43.

[32] *Ibid.*, ch. 4, pp. 36–37. For a full discussion of Hobbes's understanding of language, see: John W. Danford, *Wittgenstein and Political Philosophy: A Reexamination of the Foundation of Social Science* (Chicago: University of Chicago Press, 1978), pp. 16–49.

[33] *Ibid.*, ch. 5, p. 45.

[34] *Ibid.*, ch. 5, p. 41.

Like Bacon, Galileo, and Descartes, Hobbes was interested in such knowledge as was useful and practical. Like them, he rejected Aristotle's teaching as useless for the purpose of understanding how things really "work." To know *how* things are caused is more useful than to know *why*. It is the behaviour of material particles in conformity with mechanical law that should engage our attention. Everything knowable can be explained ultimately in terms of the laws of motion. This knowledge is not for aesthetic contemplation: "The end of knowledge is power and the use of theorems…is for the construction of problems; and lastly, the scope of all speculation is the performance of some action or some thing to be done."[35]

Philosophy, as Hobbes conceives it, is concerned with such knowledge of effects as we can acquire from the knowledge we first have of their causes, or, of such causes as we may discover from knowing their effects. Only bodies should be viewed as real, and only bodies move. Descartes contended that there are two distinct knowable substances: matter and mind. Hobbes contends that only matter is knowable, and, therefore, that for philosophy reality consists of matter in motion obeying mechanical laws. Even thoughts, as we have seen, are only expressions of motions in our brains. The method of knowing, thus, determines what is knowable.

We actually know the external world through the recordings in our brain. In contrast to the realism of Plato and Aristotle, Hobbes takes the position that we cannot know forms, essences, or universals since they do not impact on our nervous system and are not recorded (**nominalism**). The internal operation of the mind, such as adding and subtracting, and the recording of the impacts on our sense organs, are the only sources of knowledge. Two questions immediately arise. How reliable is the connection between the brain and matter? Can one assume that all brains record in a similar manner? Descartes, as we saw earlier, solved such problems by arguing that God guarantees that we can know reality and others. Hobbes does not doubt the similarity of the recordings. Our sense organs just do work the same way as can be reliably observed in human behaviour. Strictly speaking, however, what we know is the recordings and their labels. He does not follow Descartes in having God underwrite the link with reality.

The new method of knowing is now directed, in chapters 6–9, at understanding human nature. The title to chapter 6, as in the early chapters, does not make the topic obvious: "Of the Interior Beginnings of Voluntary Motions, commonly called the Passions; and the Speeches by which they are expressed." Hobbes

---

[35] *E.W.* I: *De Corpore*, Part First, i, 6.

has shown us that we can know matter in motion; his next step is to approach human nature by seeing if equivalent features can be seen by this new science. Indeed, Hobbes does detect in humans two kinds of motion: vital, as seen in the blood and breathing, and voluntary, "as to *go*, to *speak*, to *move* any of our limbs, in such manner as is first fancied in our minds." The voluntary motion, called "endeavour" in humans, is further broken down into two kinds.[36]

Endeavour toward something that causes it is called appetite or desire. It involves movement toward or from some perceived object. When it is movement toward an object, we call it desire; when it is movement away from an object, we call it aversion. Other names, like love and hate, are sometimes used to describe this movement but such words express nothing about the movement itself. Whatever is the object of human aversion is called evil. Whatever is the subject of contempt is called vile. And "these words of good, evil, and contemptible, are ever used with relation to the person that useth them: there being nothing simply and absolutely so; nor any common rule of good and evil, to be taken from the nature of the objects themselves; but from the person of the man, where there is no commonwealth; or, in a commonwealth, from the person that representeth it; or from an arbitrator or judge, whom men disagreeing shall by consent set up, and make his sentence the rule thereof."[37] Hobbes tends to equate good with pleasure and evil with pain. Good and evil are matters of individual judgment, that which we happen to like or dislike. We are not attracted to something because it is good, but "good" is the name we give to that to which we are attracted. Humans are not so constituted that the same things cause the same appetites in everyone, and one person's desire may be another's aversion.

Hobbes's point is that the standard words used to delineate human nature have no clear referents. There is nothing in the "objects themselves" to which such words could refer. "Motion" and the human equivalent "passions," however, are words that label detectible features of humans. In short, the host of words we use to explain and evaluate human behaviour are merely sounds until we can relate them to the motion of our passions. For example, "hope" does not label a bodily part nor is it in some object, anymore than red would be in a brick.

---

[36] *Leviathan*, ch. 6, p. 47. Motion is not only a critical concept for explaining physical reality, it is essential for explaining human nature and politics. See the study by Thomas A. Spragens, Jr., *The Politics of Motion: The World of Thomas Hobbes* (London: Croom Helm, 1973).

[37] *Ibid.*, ch. 6, pp. 48–49.

"Hope" works as a word when defined as an "appetite, with an opinion of attaining."[38] The ethical categories of Aristotle, or of the Bible, can all be treated in this fashion, i.e., given a meaning of sorts by relating them to individual passions. A chief difficulty remains with such words: individual passions not only differ among humans but also they vary within a person's own life. Consequently, the only way out of the confusion is to have, as Hobbes says, an "arbitrator" who simply decides on a settled usage.

This new psychology of human nature is superior to the models of the Greek philosophers and Christian theologians. Here, there are objective, non-personal, and measurable categories for explaining human behaviour. One can treat the so-called virtues and vices as measurable effects of motions—the passions. In the new science words label precisely the external, impersonal, objective, effects of matter in motion, enabling us to have an intelligible grasp on reality and some power over it. Such objective words are meaningful regardless of a person's religious or political views, ethnic background, or personal history. Hobbes has applied the new way of knowing to human nature. The result is a human psychology, also promising great explanatory power because of its objective referent, the passions as motion. It is applicable to all humans, independent of their personal religious or philosophical convictions, as would be any science.

Other models of human nature are quickly dispatched. The Greeks had argued that reason was the essential part from which other human faculties and excellences could develop. Using his scientific model for analysis, Hobbes declares that what we call deliberation is nothing but the succession of alternating impulses towards and from an object. Hobbes explains it this way:

> When in the mind of man, appetites and aversions, hopes and fears, concerning one and the same thing, arise alternately; and divers good and evil consequences of the doing, or omitting the thing propounded, come successively into our thoughts; so that sometimes we have an appetite to it; sometimes an aversion from it; sometimes hope to be able to do it; sometimes despair, or fear to attempt it; the whole sum of desires, aversions, hopes and fears continued till the thing be either done or thought impossible, is that we call DELIBERATION.[39]

---

[38] *Ibid.*, ch. 6, p. 50.

[39] *Ibid.*, ch. 6, p. 53.

Hobbes's conception of the process of deliberation is in marked contrast to that of Aristotle. Deliberation, for Hobbes, is not a rational evaluation of alternative courses of action in terms of a good that transcends our animal desires, but it simply describes the seesawing of conflicting animal impulses. According to Hobbes, beasts also deliberate. Deliberation ceases when a human or a beast decides to will something. There is no such thing as a "rational appetite" as Aristotle and the scholastics had contended—appetite is simply appetite, and reason is incapable of pronouncing one appetite superior to another.

The 'will' model of human nature, as espoused in the Judaic and Christian traditions, is also given short shrift. Within Hobbes's scientific framework, 'will' would refer only to "the last appetite, or aversion, immediately adhering to the action, or to the omission thereof, is that we call the WILL; the act, not the faculty, of *willing*."[40] Happiness, too, is given a new meaning by Hobbes's model. Continual success in obtaining those things that we desire Hobbes calls felicity or happiness: "I mean the felicity of this life. For there is no such thing as perpetual tranquility of mind, while we live here; because life itself is but motion and can never be without desire, nor without fear, no more than without sense. What kind of felicity God hath ordained to them that devoutly honour Him, a man shall no sooner know, than enjoy; being joys, that now are incomprehensible, as the word of Schoolmen *beatifical vision* is unintelligible."[41]

In chapter 9 Hobbes shows how his new epistemology, psychology, and all other disciplines should be related. He presents a chart dethroning philosophy or theology and showing the unity of all knowledge through science. From this new science all subjects now become simply branches, ranging from geometry to ethics and politics.[42]

---

[40] *Ibid.*, ch. 6, p. 54.

[41] *Ibid.*, ch. 6, p. 55.

[42] A controversy persists as to the centrality of science to Hobbes's moral and political philosophy. A few scholars have argued that his political philosophy uses science as a rhetorical cover when, in fact, his moral and political views belong within the natural law tradition. For those who view Hobbes as a moralist and not a scientist see: Leo Strauss, *The Political Philosophy of Hobbes: Its Basis and Its Genesis* (Chicago: University of Chicago Press, 1952); A. E. Taylor, "The Ethical Doctrine of Hobbes," in *Hobbes Studies*, ed. K. C. Brown (Oxford: Blackwell, 1965); Howard Warrender, *The Political Philosophy of Hobbes: His Theory of Obligation* (Oxford: Oxford University Press, 1957). For criticisms of this view see, J. W. N. Watkins, *Hobbes' System of Ideas: A Study in the Political Significance of Philosophical Theories* (London: Hutchinson, 1965); M. M. Goldsmith, *Hobbes' Science of Politics* (New York: Columbia University Press, 1966); Spragens, Jr., *The Politics of Motion*; and Tom Sorell, *Hobbes* (London: Routledge & Kegan Paul, 1986).

In chapters 10–16 Hobbes examines human social psychology, our goals and behaviour. According to his model of the human condition, we need, above all, power as a means for satisfying our appetites. One can conclude that individual power is the good which is actually behind all of the quests of humanity. Hobbes lists dozens of goals that humans seek, but each can be reduced to a type of power-seeking. Wealth is power "because it procureth friends, and servants"; nobility, reputation, affability, dignity, victory and other goals of human behaviour can similarly all be reduced to power-seeking. As a consequence, power becomes the essential means by which we obtain those things that we want. Moreover, since desire persists throughout life and is never satisfied, the quest for power is perpetual. Says Hobbes: "I put for a general inclination of all mankind, a perpetual and restless desire for power after power, that ceaseth only in death. And the cause of this, is not always that a man hopes for a more intensive delight, than he has already attained to...but because he cannot assure the power and means to live well, which he hath present, without the acquisition of more."[43]

Religion has always played a role in explaining human conduct and even in forming a state. This would immediately occur to Hobbes's contemporaries. Chapter 12 is designed to dispel such views. It is actually the fear of the invisible, according to Hobbes, that has lead humanity to form religions, which, in turn, have led some "to nourish, dress, and form it into laws...by which they thought they should be best able to govern others."[44] Hobbes finds four natural seeds of religion. He explains each seed, which he cleverly names through safe examples from the gentiles and pagans, but his arguments are actually designed to undermine the authority and pertinence of Christianity. The first seed is called the "opinion of ghosts" or "of powers invisible." The pagans have "ascribed divinity, and built temples to mere accidents, and qualities; such as time, night, day, peace, concord, love, contention, virtue, honour, wealth, rust, fever, and the like."[45] Some of these "qualities and accidents" have been viewed as defining attributes of human nature. By associating these attributes with ignorant pagans, Hobbes undermines their authority. A second seed, "ignorance of second causes," is the penchant gentiles had of giving names to features of nature, such as the seasons. Not knowing

---

[43] *Leviathan*, ch. 11, p. 80.

[44] *Ibid.*, ch. 11, p. 86.

[45] *Ibid.*, ch. 12, p. 91.

causes, they again give names. The third seed is "devotion toward what men fear." Thus it is that ignorant pagans worship merely the names and representations or idols of what they do not know but fear. With both of these seeds Hobbes is subtly calling into question the pertinence of two formative experiences of the Greek, Judaic, and Christian traditions, i.e., reality has an order and purpose, and the proper stance is one of awe and wonder. The ignorance of second causes, from Hobbes's scientific perspective, is the only real meaning to the classical view that reality has an inherent order and purpose; likewise, worship itself is an expression of what humans fear rather than a behaviour born from awe and wonder. The last seed is prognostics of time to come. Instead of trying to understand future developments through "conjectures upon experience of time past," pagans try to predict through such ignorant devices as astrology, the croaking of ravens, palmistry, and the like. Through such silly means they try to "take hold of their fear, and ignorance." Here, Hobbes has debunked hope as a reliable clue to the meaning of human existence. Hope, as was discussed in the chapter on Aquinas, is a central theological virtue for Christianity.[46]

These four natural seeds of religion are utilized by two kinds of humans. One group uses them for its own purposes, but another group uses them "by God's commandments." Regardless of the group, the function of religion is the same: "a purpose to make those men that relied on them, the more apt to obedience, laws, peace, charity, and civil society." The lesson indirectly taught is that there is nothing substantial in the experiences associated with religion that could serve as clues for understanding humans or God. Such experiences are fundamentally subjective: "the different fancies, judgments, and passions of several men, hath grown up into ceremonies so different, that those which are used by one man, are for the most part ridiculous to another."[47] Religion, thus, can serve neither as a solid foundation of a civil order nor as a standard or judge of a civil order. Hobbes's position is often called Erastian—the view that religion must function as an instrument of the state. Instead of religion, we need real knowledge of humans and their behaviour in order to have a solid, objective foundation for the state. Chapter 12 thus prepares the reader for chapter 13 where the foundation is presented.

---

[46] *Ibid.*, ch. 12, pp. 90–93.

[47] *Ibid.*, ch. 12, p. 90.

What can we know? Humans are naturally selfish because we are attracted to that which we desire. And we are naturally equal. If one excels another in intelligence, the other excels in bodily strength.

> Nature hath made men so equal, in the faculties of the body, and mind as that though there be found one man manifestly stronger in body, or of quicker mind than another; yet when all is reckoned together, the difference between man, and man, is not so considerable that one man can thereupon claim to himself any benefit, to which another may not pretend, as well as he.[48]

Hobbes offers proofs that humans share this fundamental equality of strength and mind: the weakest can, in secrecy or with others, kill the strongest; humans are also equal through pride in their own minds in that they "hardly believe there be many so wise as themselves."[49]

From this equality of ability there arises equality in the hope of attaining our desires. This equality of hope makes us all enemies, especially when two of us desire something that we cannot both enjoy. If one should "plant, sow, build, or possess a convenient seat, others may probably be expected to come prepared with forces united, to dispossess, and deprive him, not only of the fruit of his labour, but also his life or liberty. And the invader again is in the like danger of another."[50] It is also natural that humans want to be valued as highly as possible, and they respond quickly to contempt or undervaluing. In addition to psychological conflicts, there are actually some who take pleasure in conquest. In short, "where there is no power able to overawe them all," humanity's condition is inherently unstable and quarrels become inevitable.

There are, Hobbes says, three principal causes of these inevitable quarrels among humans: competition, **diffidence**, and glory.

> The first maketh men invade for gain; the second, for safety; and the third, for reputation. The first uses violence, to make themselves masters of other men's persons, wives, children, and cattle; the second, to defend them; the third, for trifles, as a word, a smile, a different opinion, and any other sign

---

[48] *Ibid.*, ch. 13, p. 98.

[49] *Ibid.*

[50] *Ibid.*, ch. 13, p. 99.

of undervalue, either direct in their persons, or by reflection in their kindred, their friends, their nation, their profession, or their name.[51]

This is the natural condition of humanity prior to the establishment of civil society; all seek to gratify their own desires, to keep what they have, and to preserve their reputations.

Hobbes concludes by calling the **state of nature** a **state of war**. That is, there is a "state" or an inclination over time for a war "of every man against every man." There may not be actual fighting at any one time, but without a common power to keep them all in awe the instability remains. Hobbes provides a stark description of our condition:

> …during the time men live without a common power to keep them all in awe, they are in that condition which is called war; and such a war, as if of every man, against every man…. In such condition, there is no place for industry, because the fruit thereof is uncertain: and consequently no culture of the earth; no navigation, nor use of the commodities that may be imported by sea; no commodious building; no instruments of moving, and removing, such things as require much force; no knowledge of the face of the earth; no account of time; no arts; no letters; no society; and which is worst of all, continual fear, and danger of violent death; the life of man, solitary, poor, nasty, brutish, and short.[52]

In this war of every person against every person there is nothing just or unjust, right or wrong, but force and fraud everywhere prevail. It is not until humans enter society that such a thing as justice is possible for "where there is no common power, there is no law: where no law, no injustice."[53]

Hobbes provides evidence for this analysis of human behaviour when there is no common power to overawe. Do we not lock our doors and our chests? There is further demonstration provided by "the savage people in many places of America." Finally, one need only look at the behaviour of sovereign states. Empirically, the evidence is clear, he claims, as to how humans behave without an ordering common

---

[51] *Ibid.*, ch. 13, pp. 99–100.

[52] *Ibid.*, ch. 13, p. 100.

[53] *Ibid.*, ch. 13, p. 101.

power.[54] Thus, by placing us in an imaginative state of nature, Hobbes has used reason plus our greatest passion—fear for our self-preservation—to create a "powerful eloquence" which "procureth attention and consent."

Hobbes's conception of the human condition as a war of all against all was, no doubt, inspired, in part, by the civil wars through which he lived. But Hobbes's identification of the lust for power as characteristic of humanity's nature also suggests an affinity with the thought of St. Augustine with this significant difference: that what St. Augustine identifies as "sin," Hobbes simply notes as "fact." What St. Augustine regards as characteristic of "fallen man," Hobbes regards as "natural" to humans. Hobbes conceives of our selfish nature not as a defect of human nature but simply as a scientific description of that nature. Whereas St. Augustine looks to "grace" to heal and deliver humans from their predicament, Hobbes looks at the formation of civil society not to "heal" but to make life with others tolerable. Later thinkers, such as Rousseau and Marx, will go further and will argue that a properly constructed society can, in effect, "heal" or transform humanity.

Inspired by fear of violent death and desirous of peace, humans are impelled to enter society. "The passions that incline men to peace, are fear of death; desire of such things as are necessary to commodious living; and a hope by their industry to obtain them. And reason suggesteth convenient articles of peace upon which men may be drawn to agreement. These articles are they, which otherwise are called the Laws of Nature."[55] Although Hobbes uses the phrase "laws of nature," he means something quite different from what has traditionally been called "natural law." This becomes evident when Hobbes distinguishes between natural right and natural law and defines **natural right** as the right of self-preservation. "The right of nature . . .," Hobbes declares, "is the liberty each man hath, to use his own power, as he will himself, for the preservation of his own nature, that is to say, of his own life; and consequently, of doing any thing, which in his own judgment, and reason, he shall conceive to be the aptest means thereunto."[56] This "natural right" has no moral content for Hobbes; it is not a statement of how humans ought to act but a statement of how, in fact, humans do act, in Hobbes's opinion.

From the fundamental right of self-preservation Hobbes derives three laws of nature or articles of peace: (1) "That every man ought to endeavour peace, so

---

[54] *Ibid.*, ch. 13, pp. 101–02.

[55] *Ibid.*, ch. 13, p. 102.

[56] *Ibid.*, ch. 14, p. 103.

far as he has hope of obtaining it; and when he cannot obtain it, that he may seek, and use, all helps, and advantages of war;" (2) "that a man be willing, when others are so too…to lay down this right to all things; and be contented with so much liberty against other men, as he would allow other men against himself," and (3) "that men perform their covenants made."[57]

The centre of Hobbes's system is not justice but self-preservation. We seek peace, we agree with other humans to give up our liberty of doing as we please, and we keep this agreement once made, not because we ought to but because it is the only way we can escape from the anarchy of the state of nature which constantly threatens our existence. It is not a desire for justice that impels us to follow Hobbes's laws of nature, but a fear of death and a calculated self-interest. There is no moral "problem" for Hobbes because he denies that there is any conflict between what is and what ought to be. Hobbes says, and with considerable optimistic assurance, that humans will, in fact, seek peace because they will realize that it is to their personal advantage to do so. The "laws of nature" are statements of how humans motivated by fear of death will, in fact, act if prudent. Moreover, he refers to these laws of nature, and he has 19 in total, as "dictates of reason" or "theorems" because they are logically deducible from the premise of self-preservation. For instance, the law that 'if others seek peace, you seek peace' is perfectly rational given the premise of self-preservation. If you did not seek peace when all around you did, you would very quickly stand out and put your own preservation in serious jeopardy. All of the 19 laws have this same rational structure. Assuming always that all would seek self-preservation, he claims that these laws of nature have the same certainty of any geometric theorem.[58] In an original use of a famous Biblical injunction, Hobbes says all of these laws of nature can be "contracted into one easy sum, intelligible even to the meanest capacity; and that is, *Do not that to another, which thou wouldest not have done to thyself.*" As Hobbes proceeds to explain, one needs only to put in balance one's own action with another's. The laws of nature will then clearly be seen as reasonable.[59]

---

[57] *Ibid.*, chs. 14 and 15, pp. 103–04, 113.

[58] *Ibid.*, ch. 15, p. 124.

[59] *Ibid.*, ch. 15, p. 122. Hobbes was not the first to have a non-Aristotelian and non-Thomist conception of natural right and natural law. For the historical and philosophical background, see, Richard Tuck, "Grotius and Selden," in *The Cambridge History of Political Thought, 1450–1700*, ed. J. H. Burns (Cambridge: Cambridge University Press, 1991), pp. 499–529.

Nevertheless, Hobbes does realize that unless humans do keep their promises, unless "men perform their covenants made," we will still be in a condition of war. It is this "law of nature" that is the fountain of justice, for "when a covenant is made, then to break it is *unjust*; and the definition of injustice, is no other than the not performance of covenant."[60] It is important to note that Hobbes has not shifted his ground by suggesting that there is some kind of moral obligation to keep one's promise, something more than calculated self-interest, something dictated not by the reasonings of individuals but by reason itself. By referring to the keeping of promises as a "law of nature," he is not invoking the memory and sanctions of the older natural law tradition. Hobbes provides the same ground for obeying this "law of nature" as provided for the others: self-preservation. Humans "perform their covenants made" only when there is some "coercive power, to compel men equally to the performance of their covenants."[61]

Part One concludes with a discussion of representation, "Of Persons, Authors, and Things Personated." Hobbes argues that authority, representation, and acting are bound together through consenting to a proper covenant. In order for an institution ("artificial person") to be authorized to act, a transfer of authority from those who have the right of action is necessary, and then the institution's action will emanate from the authors' own acts of consenting. In Hobbes's language, the "persons artificial [will] have their words and actions *owned* by those whom they represent."[62]

Hobbes has a formal theory of representation. The government ("artificial person") is authorized fully to act in behalf of the constituents, and since the acts are thereby "owned" by the represented, they, in turn, are obligated. This theory of representation contrasts sharply with other theories. The descriptive theory of representation calls for the government to mirror key features of the people, such as age, education, gender, income, ethnicity, and so on. The symbolic theory holds that representation occurs when people feel an emotional identity with the political system. The substantive theory is that constituents authorize and are represented through common issues and interests binding themselves and the government. Hobbes is clear that representation takes place when all formally authorize and are obligated by owning the actions of the "artifical person." A true unity can then

---

[60] *Ibid.*, ch. 15, p. 113.

[61] *Ibid.*

[62] *Ibid.*, ch. 16, p. 125.

be achieved: "A multitude of men, are made *one* person, when they are by one man, or one person, represented; so that it be done with the consent of every one of that multitude in particular."[63] It would inevitably cause contentions to ask such inherently subjective questions as: Does the government represent any particular set of characteristics of the populace? Does the government engender an emotional attachment or commitment? Does the government represent our views on substantive issues? In sharp contrast, the formal and objective question to ask is: Has the government been properly authorized? This question can be answered clearly and precisely; thus, contentions are eliminated. Part Two of the *Leviathan* addresses the question of how to authorize and construct a proper government.

The Second Part: Of Commonwealth

It is critical to note that the laws of nature are only logical truths of the mind, like the laws of geometry. The next step for attaining peace and commodious living is to make these laws operative in guiding political behaviour. A covenant is necessary to implement and enforce them. But, as Hobbes warns at the very beginning of chapter 17, "covenants, without the sword, are but words, and of no strength to secure a man at all."[64] The power must be sufficient to ensure security, yet it must be authorized and representative of all.

A contract meeting these requirements and establishing a state, according to Hobbes's account, is one in which each covenants with each to give the natural right of self-governing to some designated sovereign person or assemblage of persons. In Hobbes's words, it is "as if every man should say to every man, I authorize and give up my right of governing myself, to this man, or to this assembly of men, on this condition, that thou give up thy right to him and authorize all his actions in like manner. This done, the multitude so united in one person, is called a COMMONWEALTH."[65] A commonwealth, then, "is a person, of whose acts a great multitude, by mutual covenants one with another, have made themselves

---

[63] *Ibid.*, ch. 16, p. 127. For a discussion of different theories of representation, see Hanna Fenichel Pitkin, ed., *Representation* (New York: Atherton, 1969); David J. Vogler, *The Politics of Congress* (Boston: Allyn and Bacon, 1974), pp. 35–77. Harvey Mansfield, Jr., argues that Hobbes has changed the question of representativeness from one of when government represents the good (a question of substance) to one of how it represents (a question of process), *The Spirit of Liberalism* (Cambridge: Harvard University Press, 1978), pp. 45*ff.*

[64] *Ibid.*, ch. 17, p. 129.

[65] *Ibid.*, ch. 17, p. 132.

every one the author, to the end he may use the strength and means of them all, as he shall think expedient, for their peace and common defense."[66] This person, or assemblage of persons, is called sovereign, and those over whom the sovereign rules are called subjects.

When a sovereign is authorized by formal consent, Hobbes calls it a commonwealth by institution in contrast to a commonwealth by acquisition. In chapter 18 he describes the "instituting" of a commonwealth as having two steps: everyone covenants and the "major part" determines who will be the government:

> when a *multitude* of men do agree, and *covenant, every one, with every one,* that to whatsoever *man,* or *assembly of men,* shall be given by the major part, the *right* to *present* the person of them all, that is to say, to be their *representative*; every one, as well he that *voted for it,* as he that *voted against it,* shall *authorize* all the actions and judgments, of that man, or assembly of men, in the same manner, as if they were his own, to the end, to live peaceably amongst themselves, and be protected against other men.[67]

A person who did not agree with the "major part" as to who would be the representative is still obligated "for if he voluntarily entered into the congregation of them that were assembled, he sufficiently declared thereby his will, and therefore tacitly covenanted, to stand to what the major part ordain."[68]

It is important to notice that the sovereign is not a party to the contract: "by covenant only of one to another, and not of him to any of them."[69] The sovereign's power is not conditioned by any obligation to the subjects. Once having transferred their right of governing themselves to a sovereign, moreover, the subjects

---

[66] *Ibid.* The general theme of achieving authority through a voluntary act of consenting to a covenant or contract did not originate with Hobbes. The Calvinist churches were established in this manner, and even earlier medieval sources existed. Ralph C. Hancock, *Calvin and the Foundations of Modern Politics* (Ithaca: Cornell University Press, 1989); Francis Oakley, "Legitimation by Consent: The Question of the Medieval Roots," *Viator* 14 (1983), pp. 303–35, and *Omnipotence, Covenant, and Order: An Excursion in the History of Ideas from Abellard to Leibniz* (Ithaca: Cornell University Press, 1984); Quentin Skinner, *The Foundations of Modern Political Thought: The Age of Reformation*, Vol. II (Cambridge: Cambridge University Press, 1978).

[67] *Ibid.*, ch. 18, p. 134.

[68] *Ibid.*, ch. 18, p. 136.

[69] *Ibid.*, ch. 18, p. 135.

(as they now become) "cannot lawfully make a new covenant, amongst themselves, to be obedient to any other, in any thing whatsoever, without his permission."[70] Since the sovereign is not a party to the contract "there can happen no breach of covenant on the part of the sovereign; and consequently none of his subjects, by any pretence of forfeiture, can be freed from his subjection."[71] If any one should seek to withdraw consent from the covenant, that person then becomes in "the condition of war he was in before; wherein he might without injustice be destroyed by any man whatsoever."[72] Nor can any one accuse the sovereign of acting unjustly since justice is, by definition, what the sovereign wills. The sovereign is the sole judge of what is necessary for the peace and defence of his subjects, and this includes the judgment as to which doctrines are permitted to be taught "for the actions of men proceed from their opinions; and in the well-governing of opinions, consisteth the well-governing of men's actions, in order to their peace and concord."[73]

The sovereign who is instituted by the covenant will be the final arbitrator of all matters of contention. Hobbes argues that one should not fear this sovereign power: "the state of man can never be without some incommodity or other." He continues that the greatest incommodity "that any form of government can possibly happen to the people in general, is scarce sensible in respect of the miseries, and horrible calamities, that accompany a civil war, or that dissolute condition of masterless men, without subjection to laws, and a coercive power to tie their hands from rapine and revenge."[74] Moreover, it would not be in the interest of "sovereign governors" to harm their own subjects "in whose vigour, consisteth their own strength and glory." Humans have a confused perspective, Hobbes argues, and, thus, cannot see clearly the institutional solution to the inevitable state of war which follows when there is no common power to overawe. "For all men are by nature provided of notable multiplying glasses, that is their passions and self-love, through which, every little payment appeareth a great grievance; but are destitute of those prospective glasses, namely moral and civil science, to see afar

---

[70] *Ibid.*, ch. 18, p. 134.

[71] *Ibid.*, ch. 18, p. 135.

[72] *Ibid.*, ch. 18, p. 136.

[73] *Ibid.*, ch. 18, p. 137.

[74] *Ibid.*, ch. 18, p. 141.

off the miseries that hang over them, and cannot without such payments be avoided."[75] The rest of Part Two is devoted to teaching us this new civil and moral science through which we can escape the terror of civil war and the "dissolute condition of masterless men."

He begins in chapter 19 with a new scheme for classifying regimes, one in sharp contrast with Aristotle's typology. Aristotle had distinguished between regimes using the criteria of law and the common good, three unjust (tyranny, oligarchy, democracy) and three just (monarchy, aristocracy, polity). For Hobbes, the only criterion is where sovereignty is housed: "When the representative is one man, then is the commonwealth a Monarchy; when an assembly of all that will come together, then it is a Democracy, or popular commonwealth; when an assembly of a part only, then it is called an Aristocracy."[76] Tyranny does not refer to any objective reality but is simply a name which individuals use when they "are discontented under monarchy." Similarly, when they are displeased with aristocracy they "call it oligarchy; so also, they which find themselves grieved under a democracy, call it anarchy."[77] Thus, **sovereignty** may be lodged in one person, in several, or in many, but it is everywhere absolute, and the words used since Aristotle to describe the perverted forms of government are nothing but insignificant sounds.

Hobbes does maintain that the monarchical forms tend to have greater stability than others, but this is not determinative. The central questions are that sovereignty must remain absolute, as he argued in chapter 18, and that the right of succession be clearly stated. We created, as it were, an "artifical man" with our covenant, and we can also create an "artificial eternity of life" for our institutions, whether monarchs or assemblies, by providing clear steps for succession. Otherwise, we would risk a return to the condition of war. Here is a promise of institutional stability that no other political philosopher had thought possible. For Plato, as an instance, even the best state would inevitably fall, and even for Machiavelli *fortuna* would finally bring to ruin all republics and empires.

---

[75] *Ibid.*

[76] *Ibid.*, ch. 19, p. 143.

[77] *Ibid.*, ch. 19, p. 142.

Hobbes sees little difference between a commonwealth by institution and one by conquest. In the former, humans covenant "for fear of one another" and, in the latter, for fear of the conqueror. "In both cases they do it for fear," says Hobbes.[78] The rights of the sovereign are the same for Cromwell as for Charles II. Consent and contract, triggered by fear, authorize both sovereigns and obligate their subjects. The conquered also covenant: "It is not therefore the victory, that giveth the right of dominion over the vanquished, but his own covenant. Nor is he obliged because he is conquered; that is to say, beaten, and taken, or put to flight; but because he cometh in, and submitteth to the victor."[79]

Hobbes insists that authority is based upon consent and contract. This is true in an analytical or definitional sense, as chapters 16 and 17 show. Hobbes also tries to demonstrate that the anatomy of authority is always the same regardless of where it is found: one authorizes by willing consent. The authority found in a family, for example, has identical features. Parents have "dominion" or authority over a child not because of paternity "but from the child's consent, either express, or by other sufficient arguments declared." And, the dominion of a parent over a child is by contract in civil law and often in nature. It is not true that authority belongs to the man "as being of the more excellent sex." If, in nature, there should be no contract between the parents, the dominion belongs to the mother because "the infant is first in the power of the mother." Accordingly, Hobbes sees no difference in principle between a family, a commonwealth by institution or one by conquest.[80] The sovereign rights are the same as outlined in chapter 18 for the commonwealth by institution. He also notes that the absolute obedience required by authority, wherever it may be found, is actually taught by Scripture. Had not both Moses and Samuel demanded absolute obedience? Hobbes admits that humans may fear such an unlimited power and "may fancy many evil consequences, yet the consequences of the want of it, which is perpetual war of every man against his neighbour, are much worse."[81] We are reminded throughout Part Two, chapter by chapter, to keep this perspective in mind. Further, in the past humans have been ignorant

---

[78] *Ibid.*, ch. 20, p. 151.

[79] *Ibid.*, ch. 20, p. 154.

[80] *Ibid.*, ch. 20, p. 152.

[81] *Ibid.*, ch. 20, p. 157.

and have not "with exact reason weighed the causes" of the nature of common-wealths. Hobbes's new civil and moral science will teach us that "maintaining commonwealths consisteth in certain rules, as doth arithmetic and geometry; not, as tennis play, on practice only."[82] With the perspective of the state of war in mind and with geometrical reasoning, we can make and maintain a commonwealth with an artifical eternity.

Hobbes turns, in chapter 21, to a topic that would be foremost on his readers' minds—liberty. He defines liberty as the "absence of opposition…I mean exter-nal impediments of motion."[83] Liberty so understood, he insists, is consistent with fear and necessity. We could refuse to throw our "goods into the sea for fear the ship should sink."[84] Necessity is more difficult to reconcile. It is true, he rea-sons, that all causes have a "continual chain whose first link is in the hands of God…. So that to him that could see the connexion of those causes, the necessity of all men's voluntary actions, would appear manifest."[85] God wills in general our appetites and passions, it appears, but he does not command our particular actions. Rather, God wills our human wills. Logically, God "seeth and disposeth all things," but we are left with a "natural liberty," as he calls it, over our own actions. However inadequate this argument may be, Hobbes wants to maintain that individuals have a true liberty over themselves.

Hobbes's theory of liberty has come to be called the negative or 'freedom from' theory. The absence of physical coercion by itself indicates that liberty ex-ists; there is a 'freedom from' a physical impediment to action. Psychological "coercion," such as fear, and structural "coercion," such as poverty, are not rec-ognized. Hobbes would not accept a positive or 'freedom to' view of liberty. Some philosophers claim that humans do not have true liberty in any real sense when fear or poverty confines human decisions and actions; in these cases, hu-mans are not 'free to' peruse normal activities and goals. Hobbes's conception is also neutral about any needs humans should fulfill, any activities we should pur-sue, or any moral goals we should seek in order to feel free. Such matters are subjective, he thinks, and always contentious. It is essential to Hobbes to have a

---

[82] *Ibid.*, ch. 20, p. 158.

[83] *Ibid.*, ch. 21, p. 159.

[84] *Ibid.*

[85] *Ibid.*, ch. 21, p. 160.

definition of liberty that is clear, objective, and identifiable. Thus, Hobbes's definition of liberty labels an empirical condition: one has a physical impediment and no liberty, or one does not and has liberty.[86]

As Hobbes argues, there is only one liberty consistent with the unlimited power of the sovereign and that is the liberty that individuals retain "to defend their own bodies, even against them that lawfully invade them." Nobody, even on the command of the sovereign, is obliged "to kill, wound, or maim himself" or to abstain from food, water, or medicine. This may appear to be no more than that humans may not be commanded to take their own life. Yet it is critical for Hobbes. The right of self-preservation propels us into the covenant and, thus, into obligation. When self-preservation is not protected by the sovereign, our passion is no longer attached to it and obligation is broken. In such a case self-preservation leads us to look elsewhere for protection and security. Hobbes is unmistakably clear: "The obligation of subjects to the sovereign, is understood to last as long, and no longer, than the power lasteth, by which he is able to protect them."[87] An import of this reasoning in 1651 is that the Royalist living in England must accept the rule of Cromwell. "As for other liberties," Hobbes declares, "they depend on the silence of the law. In cases where the sovereign has prescribed no rule, there the subject has the liberty to do, or forbear, according to his own discretion. And therefore such liberty is in some places more, and in some less; and in some times more, in other times less, according as they that have the sovereignty shall think most convenient."[88]

For the remaining chapters of Part Two, Hobbes examines a large variety of topics that conceivably could be used to restrain and limit the power of the sovereign, such as the roles of private and public organizations and assemblies, the powers of government ministers, property rights, advisors to the sovereign, and criminal and civil law. Hobbes, however, resists any concept or definition that would impede the rights of the sovereign. To illustrate, Hobbes will permit no distinction

---

[86] The controversy between the two theories of liberty is unending: Isaiah Berlin, *Four Essays on Liberty* (Oxford: Clarendon Press, 1969); G. C. MacCallum, "Negative and Positive Freedom," *Philosophical Review* 76 (1967); Charles Taylor, "What's Wrong with Negative Liberty?" in *Philosophy and Human Sciences: Philosophical Papers*, Vol. 2 (Cambridge: Cambridge University Press, 1985).

[87] *Leviathan*, ch. 21, p. 167.

[88] *Ibid.*, ch. 21, pp. 164, 165–66.

to be drawn between the state and society, the state and government, or between law and morality. All authority and all power reside in the sovereign, whom Hobbes appropriately calls a "mortal God." The sovereign is the supreme legislator and is not himself bound by the law since the law is nothing else but what he declares it to be. "It is manifest," Hobbes writes, "that law in general, is not counsel, but command; nor a command of any man to any man; but only of him whose command is addressed to one formally obliged to obey him…. Civil Law, is to every subject, those rules which the commonwealth hath commanded him, by word, writing, or other sufficient sign of the will, to make use of, for the distinction of right and wrong; that is to say, of what is contrary, and what is not contrary to the rule."[89] Because the laws of nature are not properly called laws but are simply "qualities that dispose men to peace and obedience," there can be no conflict between the civil law and the law of nature. They have the same aim: "the law of nature and the civil law, contain each other, and are of equal extent."[90]

Chapter 20 provides a concise summary of Hobbes's central arguments in Part Two: "Of those things that weaken or tend to the Dissolution of a Commonwealth." He repeats his promise that if we would learn his new civil and moral science with its clear geometric reasoning, we could create a political institution that would last "as long as mankind." He cites two causes that would lead to dissolution. First, there are infirmities that rise from an "imperfect institution," i.e., by a want of absolute power. Citing some historical examples, he concludes that the sovereign must have sufficient power to secure public safety. He cites the Magna Carta as an instance where the shift of power to the dukes was "to a degree inconsistent with the sovereign power."[91] Second, there are "seditious doctrines," which can cause dissolution: "that every private man is judge of good and evil actions"; that conscience makes one "subject to no civil law"; that there are absolute property rights; that there should be a division of power; that there is a doctrine of tyrannicide; and that there should be a mixed form of government.[92] Each of these seditious doctrines would cause contention and return us to the state of nature. They are beliefs for which no science can provide clarity; they depend upon subjective commitments, not impersonal, objective, scientific knowledge.

---

[89] *Ibid.*, ch. 26, p. 198.

[90] *Ibid.*, ch. 26, p. 200.

[91] *Ibid.*, ch. 29, p. 238.

[92] *Ibid.*, ch. 29, pp. 238–46.

By the end of Part Two Hobbes has effectively established a political system, scientifically grounded on the central passion of self-preservation and constructed through geometric reasoning. It is "designed to live as long as mankind" itself. Through consenting to a covenant and authorizing the sovereign to be our person, we have created, by an act of will, our own artificial *civitas*, just as Hobbes promised in the Introduction to the *Leviathan*. We are obliged to give our consent to such a political order primarily through the fear of death that we experienced most starkly in the imaginative state of nature. Following Michael Oakeshott, a modern commentator on Hobbes, we can see that there are actually several kinds of obligation woven into the argument. First, we are clearly obliged by simple physical fear. Second, Hobbes again and again reminds us to calculate the consequences of our action. The sovereign has the sword, and we can rationally determine that the punishment outweighs the pleasure of breaking a law. In addition to physical and rational obligation, there is a peculiar moral sense of obligation alluded to by Hobbes. We have authorized the person to act in our behalf and, in this sense, are bound by our own voluntary act. Lastly, there is political obligation in that the end of the covenant is to provide for a civil society where there can be civilization, commodious living, and all those features destroyed in the state of war. We have political reasons for obeying.[93]

The creation of the sovereign power can be viewed as analogous to granting a power of attorney to someone. Hobbes, for example, refers to the sovereign as an "arbitrator" who has been authorized to be our person. The originality, though, is in connecting this extraordinary grant of power to the continuing act of willing by each individual. The relation between subjects and the sovereign resembles a perpetual mobile: the passion of self-preservation of each individual is the gravity running the political system, authorizing and obligating. Hobbes does not call for passions to check one another and, thus, provide for order and liberty. Such a theme is found in many later thinkers who influenced the founding fathers of the

---

[93] Michael Oakeshott, ed., *Leviathan* (Oxford: Blackwell, 1955), Introduction, pp. lix–lxi. C. B. Macpherson has interpreted Hobbes as having a bourgeois morality and as designing the sovereign power to protect the market economy, at least for its early stage, *The Political Theory of Possessive Individualism: Hobbes to Locke* (Oxford: Oxford University Press, 1962). This interpretation has been refuted by Keith Thomas, "The Social Origins of Hobbes's Political Thought," in *Hobbes Studies,* ed. Keith C. Brown (Oxford: Basil Blackwell, 1965), pp. 185–236; D. J. C. Carmichael, "C. B. Macpherson's 'Hobbes': A Critique," *Canadian Journal of Political Science* XVI:1 (March, 1983), pp. 61–80; William Letwin, "The Economic Foundations of Hobbes' Politics," in *Hobbes and Rousseau: A Collection of Critical Essays* (New York: Doubleday, 1972), pp. 143–64.

United States. Nor does Hobbes stress that human passions should be repressed or transformed as, for example, did Augustine. Hobbes builds on the passion for self-preservation. The individual's liberty to determine his or her own self-preservation can never be transferred or eliminated. Moreover, the self-preservation drive, which leads to the state of war when there is no power to overawe, is not transformed by the political system. It is the same natural, raw power and right found in the state of nature. Thus, while authorizing the sovereign for our own self-preservation, we must also be continually directed by the sword of the sovereign and by the new civil and moral science to remain within the civil order.

The actual establishment of a government is not the point of Part Two or, indeed, of the *Leviathan* itself. The oath of covenanting in chapter 17 is said in the subjunctive: "as if every man should say to every man." This is a solution to the hypothetical problem set in chapter 13: what is the natural condition of humanity when there is no "common power to keep them in awe." The final paragraph of Part Two briefly alludes to the possibility of having the "administration of the sovereign power" guided by the "natural reason" of Hobbes's doctrine. "This writing of mine," he closes, "may fall into the hands of a sovereign...and by the exercise of entire sovereignty, in protecting the public teaching of it, convert this truth of speculation, into the utility of practice."[94] He also concludes the book with the hope that the *Leviathan* "may be profitably printed, and more profitably taught in the Universities."[95] In short, the *Leviathan* assumes the prior existence of a government. Hobbes is perfectly aware that in practice a sovereign might act out of personal interest or whim rather than from the right to preserve the commonwealth. In such cases, the self-preservation of citizens is threatened and obligation is broken. As he writes at the end of chapter 31, "negligent government of princes" results in "rebellion, and rebellion with slaughter." The *Leviathan's* chief purpose is to train our imagination and reason so that we can have order within whatever political system we inhabit.

The Third Part: Of a Christian Commonwealth

To the modern reader it seems odd that over half of the *Leviathan* is devoted to religion, theology, and Biblical interpretation. Hobbes, it should be remembered, was writing at a time when England had experienced a civil war. In his judgment

---

[94] *Leviathan*, ch. 31, p. 270.

[95] *Ibid.*, A Review and Conclusion, p. 510.

it had arisen, in part, because political power was divided between the King and the Parliament and, in part, because of the bitter dissension arising from political views that were derived from religious claims.

But it was not the context alone that led Hobbes to discuss questions of theology. Religion was, obviously, a powerful source for human beliefs and actions, often causing conflict. Indeed, he had argued in Chapter 31 that for "the entire knowledge of civil duty" one must know the laws of God. Otherwise, a citizen might obey the civil power and offend God, or out of fear of God offend the civil power. If Hobbes's new civil and moral science could not resolve such contentions in religion as it had in civil matters, peace and order could not be achieved. Hobbes's new theology, thus, had not only to be compatible with modern science, but it had to be capable of sustaining political neutrality and the goal of peace.

There are four central issues in Parts Three and Four. First, Hobbes needs to show that Christian theology can be transformed so that it is compatible with the scientific epistemology of his civil and moral science. Second, he reiterates that the formative experiences of religion are not politically significant and must be confined to the private realm. In earlier chapters this analysis was carefully directed at pagans and gentiles. Now Hobbes specifically discusses Christianity and the Old and New Testaments. Third, he needs to show that the Bible, an indisputable source of authority at the time, was actually consistent with the general position of the *Leviathan*. Fourth, he reaffirms that the proper orientation point for political life is self-preservation or the fear of death. In Part Four he attacks the pretensions, as he views them, of the papacy and of the Puritans to be above the obligation owed to the sovereign. There is also a deeper level to this polemic against churches and clergy. In order to sustain the view that only the fear of death can be reliably known, and thus can serve as a foundation for politics, Hobbes provides reasons designed to disperse the greater fear for his readers—the fear of hell or eternal damnation.

In Parts One and Two Hobbes has already made clear some positions on religion. Generally, he has argued that religion must be subordinate to the state, and theology subordinate to his civil and moral science. While he has argued for the existence of God, as logically demonstrable from the necessity of a first cause, he has also held that God's nature or attributes are strictly unknowable: "by the visible things in this world, and their admirable order, a man may conceive there is a cause of them, which men call God; and yet not have an idea, or image of him

325

in his mind."[96] Thus, instead of worshipping God by responding out of gratitude to God's nature—or God's attributes of love, mercy, forgiveness and so on—humans can only worship God's irresistible power.[97] Hobbes declared that an appeal to conscience cannot trump the command of the sovereign and, moreover, that there is scriptural support for his conception of the laws of nature and for his definition of authority. In the final chapter of Part Two he demonstrated that public worship must be determined by the sovereign.[98] He does not explicitly argue, however, that these points are entailed by, or are compatible with, Christian theology. This is the task of Part Three.

The first chapter in this Part, Chapter 32, "Of the Principles of Christian Politics," begins with the promise to establish the "nature and rights of a Christian Commonwealth." Such a topic, Hobbes notes, must rely upon the "natural word of God, but also the prophetical." He, then, quickly equates the "undoubted word of God [with] our natural reason." It is true, he says, that "there be many things in God's word above reason; that is to say, which cannot by natural reason be either demonstrated, or confused; yet there is nothing contrary to it; but when it seemeth so, the faults either in our unskillful interpretations, or erroneous ratiocination."[99] Hobbes admits that there are mysteries to Christian religion, but these are to be accepted on faith as an act of obedience and, in any case, are not politically significant. He quips: "For it is with the mysteries of our religion, as with wholesome pills for the sick; which swallowed whole, have the virtue of cure; but chewed, are for the most part cast up again without effect."[100]

According to Hobbes, there are two sources for God's words other than natural reason: God speaks "immediately" to a person or God speaks through "mediation," a prophet. The problem with speaking "immediately" is that the message is unknowable to others, in the strict sense of knowing developed in Part One. Even worse, however, such immediate revelation can be false and

---

[96] *Ibid.*, ch. 11, p. 85.

[97] *Ibid.*, ch. 31, p. 262.

[98] *Ibid.*, ch. 31, pp. 268–69.

[99] *Ibid.*, ch. 32, p. 271.

[100] *Ibid.*, ch. 32, pp. 271–72. Hobbes has dramatically altered the meaning of the category "word of God" in this chapter by treating it in the manner he outlined in chapter 4, "Of Speech." The "word" becomes simply a label with a referent. Theologians give a strikingly different meaning: Dallas M. High, *Language, Persons and Belief* (New York: Oxford University Press, 1967).

deceptive: "So that though God Almighty can speak to a man by dreams, visions, voice, and inspiration, yet he obliges no man to believe he hath so done to him that pretends it; who, being a man, may err, and, which is more, may lie." On the other hand, when God's word is mediated, one must confront the contentious question: How can one tell a true from a false prophet? Hobbes cites a passage from Deut. 12: 1–5, purporting to demonstrate the criteria: "that there be two marks, by which together, not asunder, a true prophet is to be known. One is the doing of miracles; the other is the not teaching any other religion than that which is already established."[101] He concludes that "seeing therefore miracles now cease, we have no sign left, whereby to acknowledge the pretended revelations or inspirations of any private man; nor obligation to give ear to any doctrine, farther than it is conformable to the Holy Scripture."[102] The pertinence of this chapter would have been clear to his readers: the claim of the Roman Catholic Church to be the necessary mediator between God and humanity is undercut. The only proper source of God's word is found in Scripture.

Hobbes spends the bulk of Part Three showing how the Bible can be interpreted using natural reason. In this fashion primarily he delineates, as he promised, the "nature and rights of a Christian Commonwealth." Basically, Hobbes provides a materialist interpretation of the Bible. For example, while asserting the Protestant principle of the primacy of Scripture over the Church, Hobbes does not thereby subordinate natural reason. The scriptures, he states in chapter 33, have "no other authority than that of all other moral doctrine consonant to reason; the dictates whereof are laws, not *made*, but *eternal*." Here, the laws of God found in Scripture are equated with those dictates of reason, the laws of nature described in chapters 14 and 15. Further, the sovereign is the judge of what counts as Scripture: "Seeing therefore I have already proved, that sovereigns in their own dominions are the sole legislators; those books only are canonical, that is, law, in every nation, which are established for such by the sovereign authority."[103] The authority of the Bible, a great distinctive theme of the Protestant Reformation, has been as clearly undercut as the authority of the Roman Catholic Church.

---

[101] *Ibid.*, ch. 32, p. 273.

[102] *Ibid.*, ch. 32, p. 275.

[103] *Ibid.*, ch. 33, pp. 284, 276.

Hobbes systematically goes through the Bible demonstrating the power of his new materialist method of interpretation. Chapter 34 shows that a proper signification or meaning to such words as "angel" or "spirit" is possible only by interpreting them as having a corporeal or metaphorical referent. A corporeal use of the word "angel," for example, is when the real person, John the Baptist, is called an angel. At other times, the word refers to God's presence but generally the uses are to show "their materiality." The word thus labels a body; it does not express any spiritual meaning. Precisely the same type of argument is used in chapter 35: "Kingdom of God" simply refers either to the actual earthly kingdom of the Jews up to the election of Saul or to the Kingdom of God that will be established on earth after the second coming of Christ. The phrase has no spiritual meaning. Chapter 36 limits prophecy to those who derive their authority from the sovereign. Prophecy is not some independent means through which God's word is revealed or disclosed. Not only are there no new miracles, but Hobbes shows in chapter 37 that the miracles cited in the Bible itself are easily understood using his epistemology. A miracle refers to what is at first unusual, such as a rainbow, or to something "whereof there is no natural cause known." In either case, there is a danger that miracles can be used to deceive. As with distinguishing between true and false prophets, one must go to the sovereign to determine what is a true or false miracle: "In which question we are not every one, to make our own private reason, or conscience, but the public reason, that is, the reason of god's supreme lieutenant, judge; and indeed we have made him judge already, if we have given him a sovereign power, to do all that is necessary for our peace and defence." A private person may disagree and believe whatever he wants in his heart, but, Hobbes concludes, "the private reason must submit to the public."[104]

Salvation, damnation, and eternal life are critical categories for a Christian. In one of his more remarkable chapters, 38, Hobbes reconciles these ideas with his materialist interpretation. Without explaining how this could happen, Hobbes interprets Scripture to mean that Christ will return to earth, give a new material existence to the dead, damn some to a final death, and bestow eternal material life on the saved. The remaining chapters of Part Three examine many other theological

---

[104] *Ibid.*, ch. 37, pp. 318, 324. For a modern theological explanation of mystery and miracles, see: William Hordern, *Speaking of God: The Nature and Purpose of Theological Language* (New York: Macmillan, 1964), pp. 113–30.

concepts and with the same general results: Biblical words and concepts can all be interpreted using natural reason and Hobbes's epistemology; when there are questions of interpretation or doctrine, the sovereign must be judge.

By far the longest chapter of the *Leviathan*, 42, is entitled "Of Power Ecclesiastical." It is now clear that Hobbes has changed his position on the role of the Church as first enunciated in *De Cive* (1642) and in *The Elements of Law* (1640). In both of these works he had taken the traditional Anglican position that the Church would be the interpreter of Scripture because it had been so consecrated by the apostolic succession from Peter.[105] As we have seen, the Church is now defined as a congregation of citizens, and the sovereign legislator decides contentious theological questions. In 1586, Cardinal Bellarmine had written a famous exposition in defence of papal supremacy, *De summo pontifice*. Hobbes carefully attacks every argument, and consistently defends the supremacy of the civil sovereign. Even in cases where the sovereign is not Christian and has ordered a non-Christian public worship, obedience is required. Hobbes recites, from 2 Kings 5: 17–18, the story of Naaman, the Jewish servant who was forced to attend the pagan rites of his master. "Profession with the tongue is an external thing" and clearly allowed by Scripture when ordered by the sovereign. All that is required of a Christian is to keep the faith "firmly in his heart."[106]

The final chapter of Part Three states the central principles of Hobbes's theology: "All that is NECESSARY *to salvation*, is contained in two virtues, *faith in Christ*, and *obedience to laws*." The laws of God have been so interpreted that they are the laws of nature, which in turn require us "to obey our civil sovereigns, which we constituted over us by mutual pact one with another."[107] So Hobbes concludes that there can be no inconsistency between obedience to God and obedience to the civil sovereign because if the sovereign is a Christian, he will allow his citizens to believe that Jesus is the Christ, and he will require obedience "to all the civil laws; in which also are contained all the laws of nature, that is all the laws of God: for besides the laws of nature and the laws of the Church which are part of the civil law…there be no other laws divine. Whosoever therefore obeyeth his Christian

---

[105] Bernard Gert, ed., *De Cive*, ch. 17 in Thomas Hobbes, *Man and Citizen* (Indianapolis: Hackett, 1991), p. 368; Ferdinand Tönnies, ed., *The Elements of Law, Natural and Politic*, 2nd ed. (London: Cass, 1969), Part I, ch. 11, pt. 10, p. 59.

[106] *Leviathan*, ch. 42, p. 364.

[107] *Ibid.*, ch. 43, pp. 425, 426.

sovereign, is not thereby hindered, neither from believing, nor from obeying God." On the other hand, if the sovereign be not a Christian "every one of his own subjects that resisteth him, sinneth against the laws of God (for such are the laws of nature) and rejecteth the counsel of the apostles that admonisheth all Christians to obey their princes.... But if they do, they ought to expect their reward in heaven, and not complain of their lawful sovereign; much less make war upon him. For he that is not glad of any just occasion of martyrdom, has not the faith he professeth, but pretends it only...."[108]

The Fourth Part: Of the Kingdom of Darkness

Although this is the shortest of the four parts of the *Leviathan*, it still seems fanciful to worry about misinterpretation of such scriptural phrases as the kingdom of Satan, the principality of Beezlebub, and other labels. Nevertheless, Hobbes warns against a "confederacy of deceivers" who try to "obtain dominion over men in this present world, endeavour by dark and erroneous doctrines, to extinguish in them the light, both of nature, and of the gospel."[109] It quickly becomes clear that the "confederacy of deceivers" includes the Roman Catholic Church. The bulk of the arguments in the four chapters of this part are aimed at various beliefs and practices of the Roman Church, but Hobbes explicitly mentions the Presbyterian clergy too.[110]

Hobbes cites two errors that deceive and lead to darkness. The first is the error of thinking that the "Kingdom of God" mentioned in Scripture refers to the "present Church" (an error of the Roman Church), or to the "multitude of Christian men now living" (an error of the Puritan separatists). In both cases these erroneous claims "causeth so great a darkness in men's understanding, that they see not who it is to whom they have engaged their obedience."[111] The second error is to confuse consecration with conjuration or enchantment. The last supper or communion sacrament, as an illustration, in which bread is turned into body and wine into blood, is of the same piece as the ancient Egyptian's rite of worshipping leeks and onions as forms of divinity. Both practices are forms of conjuration and idolatry.

---

108 *Ibid.*, ch. 43, pp. 435, 436.

109 *Ibid.*, ch. 44, p. 437.

110 *Ibid.*, ch. 47, p. 495.

111 *Ibid.*, ch. 44, pp. 438, 439.

All churches, and particularly the Roman Church, are full of similar errors. He scathingly attacks the Roman Church for worshipping images, the canonization of saints, and other forms of idolatry. More importantly, the ideas of hell, purgatory, eternal torments, and everlasting fire are scandalously used by the clergy "to the pretences of exorcism and conjuration of phantasms." Hobbes goes through the scriptural passages for these ideas and gives them a new empirical meaning. Everlasting fire, as one case, can only mean places with fire.[112] There is no spiritual or psychological meaning attached to such phrases. In fact, he holds Aristotle and scholasticism primarily responsible for the longevity of all these errors:

> ...the metaphysics, ethics, and politics of Aristotle, the frivolous distinctions, barbarous terms, and obscure language of the Schoolmen, taught in the universities, which have been all erected and regulated by the Pope's authority, serve them to keep these errors from being detected, and to make men mistake...vain philosophy, for the light of the Gospel.[113]

To demonstrate that these various erroneous doctrines were designed "to obtain dominion over men in this present world" Hobbes asks, Who benefits? Churches were able to get independency, and sometimes even supremacy, over the civil power through the use of these doctrines. People were persuaded by the churches' claims to supernatural authority. The answer then is: "The authors therefore of this darkness in religion, are the Roman, and the presbyterian clergy."[114] Hobbes is especially vehement in his attack on the Roman Church:

> For, from the time that the Bishop of Rome had gotten to be acknowledged for bishop universal, by pretence of succession to St. Peter, their whole hierarachy, or kingdom of darkness, may be compared not unfitly to the *kingdom of fairies*; that is, to the old wives' *fables* in England, concerning *ghosts* and *spirits*, and the feats they play in the night. And if a man consider the original of this great ecclesiastical dominion, he will easily perceive that the Papacy is no other than the *ghost* of the deceased *Roman empire*, sitting crowned upon the grave thereof....

---

[112] *Ibid.*, ch. 44, p. 452.

[113] *Ibid.*, ch. 47, p. 497.

[114] *Ibid.*, ch. 47, p. 495.

The *ecclesiastics* are *spiritual* men, and *ghostly* fathers. The fairies are *spirits*, and *ghosts*. *Fairies* and *ghosts* inhabit darkness, solitudes and graves. The *ecclesiastics* walk in obscurity of doctrine, in monasteries, churches, and churchyards.[115]

The importance of Part Four is not simply the explicit attack on the political pretensions of churches and clergy but the implicit undermining of religious experiences. Hobbes's "powerful eloquence which procureth attention and consent" depended upon the reader accrediting the fear of death as a fundamental and knowable human experience. Fear of eternal damnation, in the minds of the readers of his time, would be a clear alternative, and even a trump, to the fear of death. Thus, Hobbes needs to use natural reason to deprive such ideas as purgatory, eternal damnation, communion, and hell of their traditional meaning. By taking these terms and transforming them, where possible, into labels with purported empirical or material referents he has deprived them of their "powerful eloquence."

It is understandable that the publishing of the *Leviathan* immediately started speculation, which continues to this day, about Hobbes as an atheist. Hobbes's own retort seems clear: "Do you think I can be an atheist and not know it? Or, knowing it, durst have offered my atheism to the press?"[116] Although Hobbes is normally called an Erastian, it would be more precise to say that Hobbes wanted to limit the Church's jurisdiction so that civil power and sovereignty would not be undermined. The sovereign in principle would enter religious disputes only to resolve conflict. He actually preferred the toleration of "the independency of the primitive Christians, to follow Paul, or Cephas, or Apollas, every man as he liketh best: which, if it be without contention… is perhaps the best." Hobbes never assigned the sovereign a religious duty, and he never denigrated religion to

---

[115] *Ibid.*, ch. 47, p. 500.

[116] *E. W.*, Vol. VII, p. 350. The single best study of Hobbes's theology is by A. P. Martinich, *The Two Gods of Leviathan: Thomas Hobbes on Religion and Politics* (New York: Cambridge University Press, 1992). Also of importance: Henning Graf Reventlow, *The Authority of the Bible and the Rise of the Modern World* (Philadelphia: Fortress Press, 1985), pp. 194-222; Mark Goldie, "The Reception of Hobbes," in *The Cambridge History of Political Thought, 1450–1700*, pp. 589–615; Richard Peters, *Hobbes* (Harmondsworth: Penguin Books, 1967), pp. 225–48; Preston King, ed., *Thomas Hobbes: Critical Assessments*, Vol. IV, *Religion* (London: Routledge, 1993). A. E. Taylor and Howard Warrender have argued that God is a necessary part of Hobbes's political philosophy. For this modern controversy see the articles in Brown, *Hobbes Studies.*

an instrumental role for the state. He wanted a properly grounded and coherent theology consonant with his philosophy.[117] The supremacy of the state, however, remained clear, and in this one respect he would agree with Machiavelli, and, a century later, Rousseau would agree with both.

In retrospect Hobbes's philosophy had the unintended consequence of undermining religion, which helps to explain why Hobbes has been continually charged with, or praised for, atheism. His own theological views, learned, no doubt, while in Magdalen Hall at Oxford University, were those of a "high Calvinist." The influence of Calvinism is particularly obvious in three areas: the Calvinist doctrine of the "total depravity of man" is easily seen in Hobbes's egocentric psychology of human motivation and behaviour; Hobbes's discussion of liberty and necessity echoes the Calvinist doctrine of predestination; his insistence that it is God's omnipotence that is to be worshipped fits Calvin, not Augustine, Aquinas, or Luther. His views were those of "high" Calvinism because he also argued for the supremacy of the sovereign. Still, he was unsuccessful in his attempt to synthesize the new science with religion, but his epistemology ultimately did serve to consign the unknowable tenets of faith to the realm of the private. For later generations, these very tenets quickly came to be viewed as irrelevant and meaningless.[118]

CONCLUSIONS

Like Aristotle, Hobbes sought to establish his political theory upon the basis of nature. Hobbes, however, had a very different conception of that nature and self-consciously rejected the teaching of Aristotle. He said: "I believe that scarce anything can be more absurdly said in natural philosophy than what now is called Aristotle's *Metaphysics*; nor more repugnant to government, than much of that he hath said in his *Politics*; nor more ignorantly, than a great part of his

---

[117] *Leviathan*, ch. 43, p. 499.

[118] In addition to Martinich, the following authors argue for the coherence of Hobbes's theological and philosophical views: Eldon J. Eisenach, "Hobbes on Church, State and Religion" *History of Political Thought* 3: 2 (1982), pp. 215–43; R. J. Halliday, Timothy Kenyon and Andrew Reeve, "Hobbes's Belief in God," *Political Studies* XXXI (1983), pp. 418–33; Joshua Mitchell, "Luther and Hobbes on the Question: Who was Moses, Who was Christ?" *Journal of Politics* 53: 3 (1991), pp. 676–700; J. G. A. Pocock, *Politics, Language and Time: Essays on Political Thought and History* (New York: Atheneum, 1971), pp. 148–201; S. A. Lloyd, *Ideals as Interest in Hobbes's Leviathan: The Power of Mind over Matter* (Cambridge: Cambridge University Press, 1992).

Ethics."[119] Aristotle had a teleological conception of nature; he saw in nature the cause of all order and he defined motion as movement from potentiality to actuality. Aristotle saw in humanity's attraction to the **summum bonum** (the highest good) the source of political order.

Hobbes's conception of nature was quite different in three respects. First, motion, for Hobbes, is nothing but change of place. Second, it has no direction and is never completed. The science that Aristotle admired and often drew analogies from was biology; the science that Hobbes admired was geometry. Geometry reveals that motion is nothing but change of place, and place is nothing but a mathematical abstraction. Nature, thus, is characterized by endless motion without direction or completion and by the absence of a teleological order. Third, it was possible to get mastery over nature and to attain certainty through the new science. Since there is no reason (or *logos*) inherent in nature and guiding her, humanity must create through the new science an "artificial man" or Leviathan of greater stature and strength than nature to save itself from destruction. It is not the highest good (or *summum bonum*) that attracts us to society but the *summum malum*; we enter society not to fulfil our nature but to escape from its bad consequences. Hobbes's society is founded not upon reason (or *logos*) but upon will. And the will is simply a reflection of human appetites. In many ways Hobbes's psychology anticipates twentieth-century psychological behaviourism.

Hobbes is a thorough-going individualist. There is nothing wrong with the individual as such; a problem arises only when one individual comes into contact with another. Because he conceives of reason as a handmaid of passion and appetite, individuals are unable to communicate with one another, and there is no common authority to which they are all bound. There is no common good. Since Hobbes denies the authority of reason and of God, the only way out of his predicament is the substitution of an artificial authority created by individual acts of will and embodied in an absolute sovereign. It is authorized to settle all questions and becomes the arbiter of truth and falsehood, right and wrong, justice and injustice. This is not to say that the Leviathan is charged with saving souls, satisfying needs, or nurturing our well-being. It has no moral end other than peace. Nevertheless, some argue that here we have in embryonic

---

[119] *Leviathan*, Part IV, ch. 46, p. 481.

form the beginnings of the modern authoritarian state. Hobbes, in fairness, does not anticipate this phenomenon since he rather optimistically presumes that the sovereign will permit a large area of individual freedom.[120]

SUGGESTIONS FOR FURTHER READING

Many of the works listed in the intellectual background for Machiavelli would also be useful for Hobbes, specifically, the work edited by Burns. Greenleaf, Tuck (*Natural Right Theories*), and Lessnoff are useful for political thought. See Willey, Skinner, Oakley, and pertinent articles in Burns for the Reformation and medieval influence.

Rogow provides the best biography. *Aubrey's Brief Lives*, written by a contemporary, is well worth reading. Hinnant, Robertson, Sommerville, and Tuck (*Hobbes*) are short introductions to Hobbes's whole philosophy. Tuck is particularly good with various influences on Hobbes, but regrettably pays little attention to the *Leviathan*. Hinnant, Tuck, and Raphael provide useful summaries of interpretations and works on Hobbes. Peters and Watkins are larger works with useful treatments of Hobbes's political philosophy.

Hobbes has been interpreted from many perspectives. The quickest way to sample the variety is through a collection of articles. Baumrin, Brown, Cranston and Peters, Dietz, King, Rogers and Ryan, and Sorell are all useful collections. Hinnant's *Thomas Hobbes: A Reference Guide* lists books and articles published from 1679 to 1976 with brief explanatory notes. Boonin-Vail, Flathman, and Tuck (1989) provide excellent reviews of contemporary literature.

The following are a few works interpreting the different sides of Hobbes's philosophy. Oakeshott's essays are brilliant treatments of Hobbes and his enduring contribution to political philosophy and are, in themselves, works of political philosophy and required of any serious student. Warrender, Taylor, Martinich,

---

[120] Richard E. Flathman, *Thomas Hobbes: Skepticism, Individuality, and Chastened Politics* (Newbury, Ca.: Sage, 1993) and *Willful Liberalism: Voluntarism and Individuality in Political Theory and Practice* (Ithaca: Cornell University Press, 1992), pp. 19–49; Deborah Baumgold, *Hobbes's Political Theory* (Cambridge: Cambridge University Press, 1988); R. E. Ewin, *Virtues and Rights: The Moral Philosophy of Thomas Hobbes* (Boulder: Westview Press, 1991); Robert P. Kraynak, *History and Modernity in the Thought of Thomas Hobbes* (Ithaca: Cornell University Press, 1990).

Hood, Ewin, Raphael, and Lloyd focus on the ethical and moral dimension of Hobbes's thought. Spragens, Jr. discusses Aristotelian influence and Sorel and Herbert stress the scientific basis of Hobbes's thought. Brandt, Laird, and Goldsmith are worth reading as works on the purported materialist and scientific unity of Hobbes's philosophy. Hill and Macpherson interpret Hobbes from a Marxist perspective. McNeilly, Kavka, Gauthier, Hampton, and Baumgold are modern philosophers who have explained and argued against Hobbes. Strauss and Kraynak are critical of Hobbes's influence on modernity. Flathman, Connolly, Tuck (1989), and Rapaczynski are more positive.

Works

Gert, Bernard, ed. *Man and Citizen* (*De Homine* and *De Cive*). Indianapolis: Hackett, 1991.

Macpherson, C. B., ed. *Leviathan.* London: Penguin, 1968.

Molesworth, Sir William, ed. *The English Works of Thomas Hobbes.* 11 Vols. London: Bohn, 1839–1845.

Oakeshott, Michael, ed. *Leviathan.* New York: Collier, 1962.

Parasons, Jr., J. E., and Whitney Blair, trans. "The Life of Thomas Hobbes of Malmesbury," *Interpretation* 10: 1 (January, 1982), 1–7.

Reynolds, Noel B., and Arlene Saxonhouse, eds. *Three Discourses of Thomas Hobbes.* Chicago: University of Chicago Press, 1995.

Tönnies, Ferdinand, ed. *Behemoth or The Long Parliament.* Introduction by Stephen Holmes. Chicago: University of Chicago Press, 1990.

———. *The Elements of Law, Natural and Politic.* 2nd ed. Introduction by M. M. Goldsmith. London: Cass, 1969.

Tuck, Richard, ed. *Leviathan.* Cambridge: Cambridge University Press, 1991.

Warrender, Howard, ed. *De Cive, The English Version.* Oxford: Clarendon Press, 1983.

Commentaries

Baumgold, Deborah. *Hobbes's Political Theory.* Cambridge: Cambridge University Press, 1988.

Baumrin, Bernard. *Hobbes's Leviathan: Interpretation and Criticism.* Belmont: Wadsworth, 1969.

Boonin-Vail, David. *Thomas Hobbes and the Science of Moral Virtue.* Cambridge: Cambridge University Press, 1994.

Bowle, J. *Hobbes and His Critics: A Study in Seventeenth Century Constitutionalism.* London: Frank Cass, 1969.

Brandt, Frithiof. *Thomas Hobbes's Mechanical Conception of Nature.* Copenhagen: Levin & Munksgaard, 1928.

Brown, Keith C., ed. *Hobbes Studies.* Oxford: Basil Blackwell, 1965.

Connolly, William E. *Political Theory and Modernity.* New York: Basil Blackwell, 1988.

Cranston, Maurice, and Richard Peters. *Hobbes and Rousseau: A Collection of Critical Essays.* Garden City: Doubleday, 1972.

Dick, Oliver Lawson, ed. *Aubrey's Brief Lives.* London: Secker and Warburg, 1949.

Dietz, Mary G., ed. *Thomas Hobbes and Political Theory.* Lawrence: University of Kansas Press, 1990.

Ewin, R. E. *Virtues and Rights: The Moral Philosophy of Thomas Hobbes.* Boulder: Westview Press, 1991.

Flathman, Richard E. *Thomas Hobbes: Skepticism, Individuality, and Chastened Politics.* Newbury, Ca.: Sage, 1993.

———. *Willful Liberalism: Voluntarism and Individuality in Political Theory and Practice.* Ithaca: Cornell University Press, 1992.

Gauthier, David. *The Logic of Leviathan: The Moral and Political Theory of Thomas Hobbes.* Oxford: Clarendon Press, 1969.

Goldsmith, M. M. *Hobbes' Science of Politics.* New York: Columbia University Press, 1966.

Hampton, Jean. *Hobbes and the Social Contract Tradition.* Cambridge: Cambridge University Press, 1986.

Herbert, Gary B. *Thomas Hobbes: The Unity of Scientific and Moral Wisdom.* Vancouver: University of British Columbia Press, 1989.

Hinnant, Charles H. *Thomas Hobbes.* Boston: Twayne, 1977.

———. *Thomas Hobbes: A Reference Guide.* Boston: G. K. Hall, 1980.

Hood, F. C. *The Divine Politics of Thomas Hobbes.* Oxford: Oxford University Press, 1964.

Johnston, David. *The Rhetoric of the Leviathan: Thomas Hobbes and the Politics of Cultural Transformation*. Princeton: Princeton University Press, 1986.

Kavka, Gregory S. *Hobbesian Moral and Political Theory*. Princeton: Princeton University Press, 1986.

King, Preston, ed. *Thomas Hobbes: Critical Assessments*. 4 Vols. London: Routledge, 1993.

Kraynak, Robert P. *History and Modernity in the Thought of Thomas Hobbes*. Ithaca: Cornell University Press, 1990.

Laird, John. *Hobbes*. London: Ernest Benn, 1934.

Lloyd, S. A. *Ideals as Interests in Hobbes's Leviathan: The Power of Mind over Matter*. Cambridge: Cambridge University Press, 1992.

Macpherson, C. B. *The Political Theory of Possessive Individualism: Hobbes to Locke*. Oxford: Oxford University Press, 1962.

Martinich, A. P. *The Two Gods of Leviathan: Thomas Hobbes on Religion and Politics*. New York: Cambridge University Press, 1992.

McNeilly, F. S. *The Anatomy of Leviathan*. New York: St. Martin's Press, 1968.

Mintz, Samuel I. *The Hunting of the Leviathan*. Cambridge: Cambridge University Press, 1962.

Oakeshott, Michael. *Hobbes on Civil Association*. Oxford: Basil Blackwell, 1975.

Peters, Richard. *Hobbes*. Harmondsworth: Penguin, 1967.

Rapaczynski, Andrzej. *Nature and Politics: Liberalism in the Philosophies of Hobbes, Locke and Rousseau*. Ithaca: Cornell University Press, 1987.

Raphael, D. D. *Hobbes: Morals and Politics*. London: Allen & Unwin, 1977.

Robertson, George Cromm. *Hobbes*. First ed. 1886. New York: AMS Press, 1971.

Rogers, G. A. J., and Alan Ryan, eds. *Perspectives on Thomas Hobbes*. Oxford: Clarendon, 1988.

Rogow, Arnold A. *Thomas Hobbes: Radical in the Service of Reaction*. New York: W. W. Norton, 1986.

Sommerville, Johann P. *Thomas Hobbes: Political Ideas in Historical Context*. New York: St. Martin's Press, 1992.

Sorell, Tom. *Hobbes*. London: Routledge & Kegan Paul, 1986.

———, ed. *The Cambridge Companion to Hobbes*. Cambridge: Cambridge University Press.

Spragens, Jr., Thomas A. *The Politics of Motion: The World of Thomas Hobbes.* London: Croom Helm, 1973.

Strauss, Leo. *The Political Philosophy of Hobbes: Its Basis and Its Genesis.* Chicago: University of Chicago Press, 1952.

Taylor, A. E. *Thomas Hobbes.* Originally published 1908. New York: Kennikat, 1970.

Tuck, Richard. *Hobbes.* Oxford: Oxford University Press, 1989.

Warrender, Howard. *The Political Philosophy of Hobbes: His Theory of Obligation.* Oxford: Oxford University Press, 1957.

Watkins, J. W. N. *Hobbes' System of Ideas: A Study in the Political Significance of Philosophical Theories.* London: Hutchinson, 1965.

Intellectual Background

Allen, J. W. *English Political Thought, 1603–1660.* London: Methuen, 1938.

Burns, J. H., ed. *The Cambridge History of Political Thought: 1450–1700.* Cambridge: Cambridge University Press, 1991.

Burtt, E. A. *The Metaphysical Foundations of Modern Science.* Garden City: Doubleday, 1954.

Butterfield, Herbert. *The Origins of Modern Science, 1300–1800.* Toronto: Clarke, Irwin & Co., 1968.

Greenleaf, W. H. *Order, Empiricism, and Politics: Two Traditions of English Political Thought, 1500–1700.* London: Oxford University Press, 1964.

Hall, A. Rupert. *The Scientific Revolution: 1500–1800.* London: Longmans, 1962.

Hancock, Ralph C. *Calvin and the Foundations of Modern Politics.* Ithaca: Cornell University Press, 1989.

Hill, Christopher. *Puritanism and Revolution: Studies in Interpretation of the English Revolution of the 17th Century.* London: Secker & Warburg, 1958.

Jacob, Margaret C. *The Cultural Meaning of the Scientific Revolution.* Philadelphia: Temple University Press, 1988.

Koyre, Alexandre. *From the Closed World to the Infinite Universe.* Baltimore: Johns Hopkins University Press, 1957.

Lessnoff, Michael. *Social Contract.* Atlantic Highlands: Humanities Press, 1986.

Oakley, Francis. *Omnipotence, Covenant, and Order: An Excursion in the History of Ideas from Abelaard to Leibniz.* Ithaca: Cornell University Press, 1984.

Popkin, Richard. *The History of Scepticism from Erasmus to Descartes.* New York: Humanities Press, 1964.

Reventlow, Henning Graf. *The Authority of the Bible and the Rise of the Modern World.* Philadelphia: Fortress Press, 1985.

Schochet, G. J. *Patriarchalism in Political Thought: The Authoritarian Family and Political Speculation and Attitudes especially in Seventeenth Century England.* Oxford: Basil Blackwell, 1975.

Skinner, Quentin. *The Foundations of Modern Political Thought: The Age of Reformation.* Vol. II. Cambridge: Cambridge University Press, 1978.

Tuck, Richard. *Natural Right Theories: Their Origin and Development.* Cambridge: Cambridge University Press, 1979.

————. *Philosophy and Government 1572–1651.* Cambridge: Cambridge University Press, 1993.

White, Lynn, Jr. *Dynamo and Virgin Reconsidered.* Cambridge: M.I.T. Press, 1968.

Whitehead, Alfred North. *Science and the Modern World.* New York: Mentor, 1960.

Willey, Basil. *The Seventeenth-Century Background.* New York: Doubleday Anchor Books, 1953.

JOHN LOCKE

Although both Hobbes (1588–1679) and Locke (1632–1704) lived during the political upheavals of the seventeenth century, it was Locke who both witnessed the considerable political turmoil and was directly active and influential. As we shall see, Locke's own political activity ebbed and flowed with the influence of his patrons, two of the most powerful men of the age. Most important was Lord Ashley (later the first Earl of Shaftesbury), whom Locke served in various ways from 1667–1675 and 1679–1682. After Shaftesbury's death, Locke's political activity and influence benefited by his ties with Lord Somers, 1674–1700.

LOCKE: His Life and Works

In his youth Locke had the great good fortune to have his career launched by being sent to the prestigious Westminster School in London (1647). His father, an attorney, was a captain in the Parliamentary army against Charles I during the Civil War, 1641–1647. This connection, no doubt, helped Locke attain a position at the Westminster School. In fact, the beheading of Charles I in 1649 took place close to Locke's own school, but he and his classmates were likely not allowed to witness that extraordinary event, the execution of the King by the victorious Parliamentary and Puritan army under Cromwell. In 1652 Locke went from Westminster to Christ Church College at Oxford University. Locke remained connected with Christ Church through various positions for the next 15 years.

Locke did not particularly admire the traditional education of either Westminster or Christ Church as both concentrated on the classical languages, Aristotle, and Scholastic thought. Yet, he earned a Bachelor of Arts in 1656 and a Master of Arts in 1658. He even became a tutor in Greek and medieval

Aristotelianism in 1660, but in order to stay at the university in a permanent teaching position, Locke had to be ordained into the Church. He refused (1663) and, instead, switched to medicine, in which he received a bachelor's degree but not a doctorate.[1] His major interest was now botany. He became acquainted with the new experimental science and joined a circle that included Robert Boyle and others who eventually founded the Royal Society. Locke himself became a member in 1668. He also read Descartes and the host of thinkers constituting the new scientific school. Throughout his education, it should be noted, he did not study philosophy in any formal sense. In fact, he was later to lament that he had lost time "because the only philosophy then known at Oxford was the peripatetic [Aristotle], perplexed with obscure terms and useless questions."[2]

During his time at Oxford Locke wrote two works on political philosophy. In 1662 he completed *Two Tracts on Government*, one in English and one in Latin. Neither was ever published. He was, at the time, clearly on the side of the sovereignty of the ruler, reminiscent of Hobbes and many other supporters of the King. It was indicative of his thought, however, that civil power was not derived from divine right. Locke was primarily worried about human perversity and the potential for civil disorder. His conclusion was that the power of the magistrate must be inclusive and final. He argued, as an instance, that the King must be able to exercise control over both civil and religious ceremonies. These are "indifferent" to Christian liberty, which is only about belief not practices.[3]

He wrote another unpublished work in 1663, and it also foretells the mature Locke. *Essays on the Law of Nature* has several lines of thought that Locke would later develop and bring to print. He states his empirical approach: there is no innate knowledge of rational truths or moral rules built into human nature supposedly linking humanity with a rational universe. Further, tradition or custom can provide no reliable source for such truths and moral rules. It is only through the senses and experience that reason can provide us with knowledge of a law of

---

[1] There is no clear reason for his decision to refuse ordination. His views at the time were not particularly incompatible with ordination. He was actively writing romantic letters at the time, and this could have been a factor since one could not be married and stay in a permanent position at Christ Church.

[2] Cited in Richard I. Aaron, *John Locke*, 3rd ed. (Oxford: Oxford University Press, 1971), p. 5.

[3] John Locke, *Two Tracts on Government*, ed. and introduction by Philip Abrams (Cambridge: Cambridge University Press, 1967).

nature, rational truths, or moral rules. Locke argues that we can observe the regularity and design of the universe, which demonstrates the existence of a Creator, and by our natural faculties we can also see that humans, too, were designed by a Creator. We are subject, accordingly, to the Creator and to the dictates of his will. Natural law flows from the will of this Creator God and is recognizable because of humanity's rational nature. Because there is a "harmony" between the law of nature and human nature, we can draw indubitable and self-evident moral truths:

> In fact it seems to me to follow just as necessarily from the nature of man that, if he is a man, he is bound to love and worship God and also to fulfil other things appropriate to the rational nature, i.e. to observe the law of nature, as it follows from the nature of a triangle that, if it is a triangle, its three angles are equal to two right angles, although perhaps very many men are so lazy and so thoughtless that for want of attention they are ignorant of both these truths, which are so manifest and certain that nothing can be plainer.[4]

Although unpublished, the general themes were made public through an address given in 1664 as Censor of Moral Philosophy for Christ Church. This seemingly paradoxical mixture of theological arguments, empirical premises, and mathematical analogies came to be common throughout Locke's famous published works.

Locke briefly pursued a diplomatic career (1665–1666), with a small assignment as secretary to a special mission to the principality of Brandenburg. After he returned to Oxford, he received another offer to join a diplomatic mission to Spain, but he declined.

In 1666 his life course was set when he met Anthony Ashley Cooper who had come to Oxford for medical treatment. Ashley would soon become Lord Ashley and eventually the Earl of Shaftesbury. He was one of the most powerful figures of the seventeenth century and pursued a career ranging from Lord Chancellor (1672) and other ministerial posts to imprisonment (1678 and 1681) and eventually to exile in Holland where he died (1683). Ashley was clearly impressed by Locke and invited him to stay in London at the Ashley home. In 1668, in this pre-anesthetic age, Locke performed an amazing operation on Ashley's abscessed liver and saved Ashley's life. Becoming more than a medical advisor, Locke advised Ashley (now

---

[4] W. Von Leyden, ed., *Essays on the Law of Nature*, VII (Oxford: Clarendon Press, 1954), pp. 199–200.

the Earl of Shaftesbury) on the political issues of the time; he took charge of the education of the Earl's son and grandson; he was awarded, over the years, several administrative positions in the government; and, most importantly for political philosophy, he was given the time and encouragement by the Earl to write not only on contemporary economic and political issues but also on epistemology, toleration, and political philosophy.

Locke was immediately put to the task of writing what today would be called "position papers": an *Essay Concerning Toleration* (1667) was written to be presented to the King; an essay on interest rates and legislation was composed for Lord Ashley to use; and he helped Ashley write a constitution (never implemented) for the colony of Carolina. He also wrote, in 1671, several drafts of his major work on epistemology, *An Essay Concerning Human Understanding*, which was given to Ashley but not published until 1690.

Locke also became actively involved in Shaftesbury's political career and experienced some perilous adventures as a result. Political and religious toleration was yet to be firmly established, and to say that this was an age of political turmoil understates the brutality and dangers of political life. Charles II, restored to the throne in 1660, was pursuing what appeared to be a contradictory set of policies: he supported the suppression of the Dissenters; he made moves to relieve the fines that were levied on them; he made some moves for toleration of Catholics and Dissenters; and he secretly agreed in the first Treaty of Dover (May, 1670) to accept money from the French King Louis XIV and to work toward the re-establishment of Catholicism and monarchical absolutism. It appears that Charles initially hoped to strengthen the monarchy by gaining support from the Anglican Church with a campaign against the Dissenters. Then, in time, he would get the support of the Dissenters for his toleration, which would include the Catholics. It was, indeed, a time of conspiracy, deceit, paranoia, and terror.

Shaftesbury was politically successful during 1672. He had effectively pushed through the Declaration of Indulgence that suspended the penalties imposed on Puritans and Catholics. When he became suspicious of the King's behaviour as the rumours of the Treaty of Dover spread, he fell out of favour and was removed from office the next year. A considerable opposition to the King quickly formed around Shaftesbury. Locke was clearly involved in this dangerous activity. For example, one of the many anonymous pamphlets of the age, *A Letter from a Person of Quality to His Friend in the Country*, attacked the King's policies and was formally burned. Shaftesbury or Locke probably wrote it. Locke, who was ill at the time, departed for France, where he remained for four years (1675–1679). But even then, he could well have been working on behalf of Shaftesbury. As one commentator remarked, "We cannot be sure whether Locke during these years is best described as a convalescent philosopher, a political exile, or a secret agent."[5]

Shaftesbury returned to a position of power in 1679. Locke was called back from Europe and put to the task of justifying a change in the constitution and civil rule. Shaftesbury, in particular, wanted to legally bar Charles's Catholic brother James from the throne and to have Charles's bastard son the Protestant Duke of Monmouth formally named the heir. The great fear that a Catholic king would impose religious uniformity and erode the power of Parliament helped to produce a major split in politics throughout the 1680s. The coalition supporting the King and his policies would eventually lead to the creation of the Tory party; just as the group coalescing around Shaftesbury would lead to the Whig party. By 1681 the last attempt to get Parliament to pass an exclusion bill barring James failed. Shaftesbury was soon arrested for high treason. Shaftesbury's supporters were also in danger, and some were arrested and executed. Opposition groups then went underground. One such group—the members of the Rye House Plot (1681–1683)—had even planned a coup but were discovered before it could be implemented. Locke's friend, Algernon Sydney, was a member of this group. Sydney and others were executed, an event that could hardly have helped Locke's own peace of mind. Furthermore, while Locke was staying quietly at Oxford, books, which expressed views that he shared, were burned. Locke, who had had enough, fled in haste and by secret passage to Holland. Locke's fear was justified: the King, in 1684, personally forced Christ Church to revoke Locke's "studentship." The precise nature of Locke's involvement in this revolutionary activity is now impossible to know. Nevertheless, it is clear that Locke's relationship with the Whig political faction against the King and Tory party was maintained at a considerable personal risk. He did not return until 1689, a year after the Glorious Revolution and after William and Mary had ascended the throne.

---

[5] David Wootton, ed., *John Locke: Political Writings*, and with an Introduction by David Wootton (London: Penguin, 1993), p. 19. For background on the extraordinary political intrigue prevalent during the Restoration period see: J. R. Jones, *Country and Court: England, 1658–1714* (Cambridge: Harvard University Press, 1978); G. M. Trevelyan, *England under the Stuarts* (London: Methuen, 1965).

Locke continued to face dangers while in exile. Attempts were made by the agents of James II to seize Locke and to return him to England. At one point, Locke was actually expelled from the city of Utrecht through the King's diplomatic efforts. Locke moved several times, used the alias Dr. van der Linden, wrote letters in code, and generally behaved with great care. Again, it is difficult to tell now the precise extent of Locke's involvement with the various efforts to depose James II and to install William and Mary on the throne. Still, it was during this political activity that Locke completed his most famous works, an association that undeniably places Locke and these writings within the larger process of a radical movement organizing for political change.

Some have concluded that Locke's activity throughout the 1680s should remind us to read his writings less as political philosophy and more as political tracts designed to mobilize members of a certain audience and to justify their actions.[6] But, as we have already seen, many of Locke's ideas can be traced to his times at Oxford. It is also true that he examined many of these questions when the idea of insurrection would have been non-existent.

His time in exile, from 1683–1689, was usefully spent in discussions with other philosophers and in completing various works begun earlier. He began to publish in rapid succession the works that would make him a prominent figure. *An Essay Concerning Human Understanding*, begun in 1671, was printed in 1689 under his name. It gave him, in his lifetime, increasing stature as a philosopher. *Some Thoughts Concerning Education* in 1693, and his essays on economics, in 1692 and 1695, were also published under his name. He published anonymously three letters on *Toleration* (1689, 1690, 1692), *The Reasonableness of Christianity* (1695), and *Vindications* (1697). The authorship of these works was quickly suspected, however, and he became the subject of religious controversies for the rest of his life.

What has become his most influential work, *Two Treatises of Government*, was published in 1689 anonymously, and initially only a few attributed it to Locke. He always adamantly denied authorship and was able to hide or destroy any proof of his paternity. Fortunately, his authorship became known upon his death

---

[6] This case is particularly well argued in a fascinating work by Richard Ashcraft, *Revolutionary Politics and Locke's Two Treatises of Government* (Princeton: Princeton University Press, 1986). For the larger historical background see: Christopher Hill, *The World Turned Upside Down: Radical Ideas During the English Revolution* (London: Temple Smith, 1972); J. R. Western, *Monarchy and Revolution: The English State in 1680s* (London: Blandford Press, 1972); J. H. Plumb, *The Growth of Political Stability in England, 1675–1725* (London: Macmillan, 1967).

when the work was mentioned in his will. There is still some dispute about when Locke actually composed the *Two Treatises*. The dates range from the winter of 1679–80 to early 1683. In any case, a few additions were made to the *Second Treatise* (chapters I, IX, XV) after the 1688 Glorious Revolution, and it was these changes that supported the traditional belief that the *Two Treatises* were written intentionally at that time to support the Glorious Revolution. They were clearly written, nevertheless, to support the political activity of resisting an arbitrary government and reinstituting a new one, and it was this activity that culminated in the Glorious Revolution. There were actually many essays written to support the 1688 Revolution, and it is ironic, given the universal acclaim and influence after his death, that the *Two Treatises*, at the time, were not particularly well received by the major actors in that drama.

Locke's political, economic, and administrative career resumed upon his return from the continent. He became the advisor and confidant of Sir John Somers, who exercised considerable political power. Locke served from 1689 to 1700 as a commissioner on the Committee for Trade, which he later helped reorganize into the Board of Trade. He was instrumental in establishing the new coinage policy as well as other economic policies. He was also instrumental, along with the Earl of Halifax, in getting Isaac Newton a position, in 1696, as director of the mint. In addition, he inaugurated a small group of political friends (the "College") who, through correspondence and meetings, tried to establish a coherent set of public policies.

After 1700 Locke retired permanently to the home of Sir Francis and Lady Masham, where he had frequently stayed since returning from Europe. Lady Masham (Damaris Cudworth) had exchanged love letters with Locke during his early Oxford years, and their friendship and letters had continued throughout the years of exile.[7] In October, 1704, Locke quietly died while Lady Masham read the Psalms to him. He left an estate of nearly twenty thousand pounds.

Sir Ernest Barker, a twentieth-century British political philosopher, has noted that English political theorists or philosophers are unique in that they are, in varying degrees, politically active and "immersed" in their times:

---

[7] Lady Masham was a philosopher of some standing. She was knowledgeable about the scientific revolution and the new developments in philosophy. Her philosophic correspondence with Leibniz is still valuable reading. Leibniz was an innatist—i.e., certain truths are embedded in the mind—and was critical of Locke's empirical position. Lady Masham defended Locke. See Margaret Atherton, ed., *Women Philosophers of the Early Modern Period* (Indianapolis: Hackett, 1994), pp. 77–95.

Our English political theorists, like our historians, have often been men immersed and steeped in the general current and sweep of affairs. If they have not been politicians themselves (and some of them have been), they have at any rate been in touch with politicians and the movement of politics.... Indeed, the connection between theory and practice, always notable in England, has worked in a double way. Not only have theorists turned to practical politics: practical politicians, reversing the flow of the stream, have also turned to political theory.[8]

This statement fits John Locke perfectly. He is still the most recognized and influential English political philosopher.[9]

AN ESSAY CONCERNING HUMAN UNDERSTANDING

Locke and five or six friends began a discussion in 1671 to determine the "principles of morality and revealed religion," but they found the task too daunting. As Locke explains,

After we had a while puzzled our selves, without coming any nearer a Resolution of those Doubts which perplexed us, it came into my Thoughts, that we took a wrong course; and that, before we set our selves upon Enquires of that Nature, it was necessary to examine our own Abilities, and see, what Objects our Understandings were, or were not fitted to deal with. This I proposed to the Company, who all readily assented; and thereupon it was agreed, that this should be our first Enquiry.[10]

After writing a draft in 1671, Locke made changes in a sporadic fashion until it was published in 1689. He modestly tells the reader that he is not a "Master Builder" like Robert Boyle or "the incomparable Newton"; rather, he is satisfied to

---

[8] Sir Ernest Barker, "Reflections on English Political Theory," *Political Studies*, Vol. I (1953–54), p. 7.

[9] The standard biography is by Maurice Cranston, *John Locke: A Biography* (London: Longmans, 1966); an earlier biography, but less reliable, is H. R. Fox-Bourne, *The Life of John Locke*, 2 Vols. (London: King, 1876).

[10] "The Epistle to the Reader," in *An Essay Concerning Human Understanding*, ed. Peter H. Nidditch (Oxford: Clarendon Press, 1975), p. 7. For an account of the various influences on Locke, culminating in the writing of the *Essay*, see Wootten, *John Locke: Political Writings*, "Introduction," pp. 26–31; Ashcraft, *Revolutionary Politics*, pp. 108–11.

be "an Under-Labourer in clearing Ground a little, and removing some of the Rubbish, that lies in the way to Knowledge."[11] This was not a feigned modesty. Locke clearly believed that Boyle, the father of modern chemistry, and Newton were the great discoverers and leaders of the new science and he was not. Yet, one would be hard-pressed to find a work so often quoted in the eighteenth century—the Age of the Enlightenment—as the *Essay.* Locke was the first major empiricist, and the *Essay* was central to the development of the experimental or empirical tradition.

The *Essay* is divided into four books: "Of Innate Notions," "Of Ideas," "Of Words," and "Of Knowledge and Opinion." The general purpose of the *Essay* is "to enquire into the Original, Certainty, and Extent of humane knowledge; together, with the Grounds and Degrees of Belief, Opinion, and Assent."[12] Locke wants to establish the limits on human understanding in order to be clear about what can be known and the degree of certainty that can be justifiably claimed. Once epistemological matters are settled, it would then be possible to determine with confidence the principles of morality and political philosophy.

Book I, "Of Innate Notions," disputes two types of claims held in various versions by many people. First, there were speculative principles, as they were called, which were supposedly innate. By speculative principles were meant such logical propositions as "from nothing can come nothing," or "a thing cannot be and not be at the same time," or "a whole is greater than its parts." Many held that unless these logical propositions were innate, rational thought was impossible. Second, there were practical moral principles also supposedly innate such as, "keep promises," "murder is wrong," and "always tell the truth." Many believed that unless these practical principles were innate, there was no solid, incontrovertible base for morality and religion.[13] Whether God imprinted such principles on our minds or whether they are simply part of the structure of the rational faculty, the doctrine of innatism appeared to guarantee the process of reasoning and the permanence of morality and religion.

---

[11] *Ibid.*, pp. 9–10. Peter Winch discusses some of the inherent difficulties of the underlabourer conception of philosophy in *The Idea of a Social Science and Its Relation to Philosophy* (London: Routledge, 1958), pp. 3–24.

[12] Bk. I, i, 2. The citations for the *Essays* are to Book, chapter, and section.

[13] Precisely who held these views is debated. Some scholars have viewed the characterizations as so much empty rhetoric aimed at straw men. See Richard I. Aaron, *John Locke*, 3rd ed. (Oxford: Clarendon, 1970), pp. 83–98. John W. Yolton, however, documents Locke's contemporaries who did profess such views, *John Locke and the Way of Ideas* (Oxford: Oxford University Press, 1956), pp. 26–64.

Locke's purpose is to show that there is no innate knowledge of such principles and that there are also no **innate ideas**—the building blocks or material of knowledge. Locke uses the word 'idea' to refer to "the Object of the Understanding when a Man thinks, I have used it to express whatever is meant by *Phantasies, Notion, Species,* or whatever it is, which the Mind can be employ'd about in thinking."[14]

Locke attacks on several grounds. He begins by arguing that it is a contradiction to hold that there are innate truths imprinted on the soul or mind but that untrained minds—idiots and children—just cannot perceive them. If the untrained must have education and experience to assent to such logical propositions as "a thing cannot be and not be at the same time," then it makes no sense to call such propositions innate.[15] He further notes that the moral, innate principles cannot be seen everywhere, and, clearly, there is no universal assent.[16] There is no consensus within a country either, and even if there were, it could have been learned by common experience. Lastly, it is clear to Locke that reason and experience are required to discover the so-called self-evident and innate truths. Since reasoning is a long and painful process, it is senseless to talk of innate principles as if they were self-evident and easily perceivable.[17]

Locke was only criticizing the idea that there were innate logical rules and moral laws, not that the mind does not have built-in capacities or what Locke calls powers. As Locke remarks,

> Nature, I confess, has put into Man a desire of Happiness, and an aversion to Misery: These indeed are innate practical Principles, which (as practical Principles ought) do continue constantly to operate and influence all our Actions, without ceasing: These may be observ'd in all Persons and all Ages, steady and universal; but these are Inclinations of the Appetite to good, not Impressions of truth on the Understanding.[18]

---

[14] Bk. I, i, 8.

[15] Bk. I, ii, 5.

[16] Bk. I, ii, 2.

[17] The coherence of Locke's arguments against innatism is often questioned by modern philosophers. See John L. Jenkins, *Understanding Locke* (Edinburgh: Edinburgh University Press, 1983). The contemporary linguistic philosopher, Noam Chomsky, has led a revival of interest in innatism and argues that the structure of language appears to be innate to humans. For a full discussion see, Michael Ayers, *Locke*, Vol. 1, *Epistemology* (London: Routledge, 1991), pp. 269–300.

[18] Bk. I, iii, 3.

Locke also denies that there are innate tendencies toward a moral good or evil: "Things then are Good or Evil, only in reference to Pleasure or Pain. That we call *Good*, which *is apt to cause or increase Pleasure, or diminish Pain in us; or else to procure, or preserve us the possession of any other Good, or absence of any Evil.* And on the contrary we name that *Evil*, which *is apt to produce or increase any Pain, or diminish any Pleasure in us; or else to procure us any Evil, or deprive us of any Good.*[19]

Locke concludes Book I by noting two particularly pernicious effects of the doctrine of innate principles. First, by calling the common, accepted, and authoritative opinions of the day innate, we inevitably are hindered from thinking and reasoning for ourselves. Locke admonishes: "we should make greater progress in the discovery of rational and contemplative *knowledge*, if we *sought* it in the Fountain, in the consideration of Things themselves; and make use rather of our own Thoughts, then other Mens to find it." This thought came to be one of the great articles of faith of the Enlightenment: think for oneself; do not rely upon authority. As Locke reminds his readers: "In the Sciences every one has so much, as he really knows and comprehends."[20] A second pernicious effect of innatism is that it re-enforces government and makes us all "more easily governed." Locke explains: "Nor is it a small power it gives one Man over another, to have the Authority to be the Dictator of Principles, and Teacher of unquestionable Truths; and to make a Man swallow that for an innate Principle which may serve to his purpose, who teacheth them."[21] The philosophic stance born of innatism, in sum, is counter to reason and science but also to political liberty.

If the mind does not have ideas imprinted, the obvious question is, What is their source? Locke begins Book II, "Of Ideas," with his answer:

Let us then suppose the Mind to be, as we say, white Paper, void of all Characters, without any *Ideas*; How comes it to be furnished?...Whence has it all the materials of Reason and Knowledge? To this I answer, in one word, From *Experience*. In that, all our Knowledge is founded; and from that it ultimately derives it self. Our Observation employ'd either about *external, sensible Objects; or about the internal Operations of our Minds, perceived and reflected on by our selves, is that, which supplies our Understandings with*

---

[19] Bk. II, xx, 2.

[20] Bk. I, iv, 23.

[21] Bk. I, iv, 24.

all the materials of thinking. These two are the Fountains of Knowledge, from whence all the *Ideas* we have, or can naturally have, do spring.[22]

Experience, thus, provides us with ideas in two ways: directly through the sensations and through the "perception of the operations of our own mind." These actings of our minds include perception, thinking, doubting, believing, reasoning, knowing, and willing. The objects of sensation and the objects of reflection are the two sources of all our ideas.[23]

Locke next divides ideas into two kinds, simple and complex. A simple idea is one that cannot be reduced to any other idea. It gets its meaning solely from a single referent. Whiteness, for example, cannot be further reduced to any other idea. A simple idea has one direct referent or ostensive object. Complex ideas are constructed from two or more simple ideas. Simple ideas from reflection would include thinking, doubting, and willing; and simple ideas from sensation would include white, hard, and bitter. The appeal of this simple-complex scheme is that it appears to provide a solid program for knowing. There should be, in principle, a base of simple ideas for any knowledge claim, and one would then simply reduce a complex knowledge claim to its constituent parts, i.e., the simple ideas. In addition, the validity of simple ideas seems to be guaranteed because the ideas are received into the mind passively, undistorted by personal whims or ideological predilections. In a famous passage Locke uses a mirror analogy to make this point:

> In this Part, the *Understanding* is merely *passive*; and whether or no, it will have these Beginnings, and as it were materials of Knowledge, is not in its own Power. For the Objects of our Senses, do, many of them, obtrude their particular *Ideas* upon our minds, whether we will or no: And the Operations of our minds, will not let us be without, at least some obscure Notions of them. No Man, can be wholly ignorant of what he does, when

---

[22] Bk. II, i, 2.

[23] Bk. II, i, 4. Locke's severe attack on innatism and his insistence on experience as the sole basis of ideas led many to fear that he was undermining natural law, a traditional support for morality, and was echoing Hobbes's nominalism, i.e., there is only knowledge of particular things. Both the German philosopher Leibniz and Locke's friend Newton so read the *Essay.* Mark Goldie, "The Reception of Hobbes," in *The Cambridge History of Political Thought: 1450–1700,* ed. J. H. Burns (Cambridge: Cambridge University Press, 1991), pp. 608–09.

he thinks. These *simple Ideas,* when offered to the mind, *the Understanding can* no more refuse to have, nor alter, when they are imprinted, nor blot them out, and make new ones in it self, than a mirror can refuse, alter, or obliterate the Images or *Ideas,* which, the Objects set before it, do therein produce. As the Bodies that surround us, do diversely affect our Organs, the mind is forced to receive the Impressions; and cannot avoid the Perception of those *Ideas* that are annexed to them.[24]

Locke, at times, does note that the mind has to be active in order to receive even sensations. Unless we are paying attention we may not hear or record a sensation. In this sense at least, the mind needs to be focused and judgment used.[25] Allowing for this qualification, the overwhelming impression still is that the passivity by which simple ideas of sensation and reflection are received provides the requisite objectivity and non-personal base for knowledge.

With these simple ideas the mind is able to be active and to construct complex ideas in three ways: through combining, through comparing and contrasting, and through finding the common element in ideas, which Locke calls abstraction, or the forming of general ideas.[26] It is this active power of the mind that explains the infinite variety of the "Thoughts of Men." Locke further reduces complex ideas into three categories. First, there are complex ideas that refer to substances or things in reality, such as the idea of "lead" or of "man." Locke calls these "Works of Nature" whose constituent simple ideas "have an Union in Nature."[27] Second, there are complex ideas simply made by the mind. These ideas are about "modes," which are expressions or attributes of things. Complex ideas and modes are created by the operation of our minds whereby we combine ideas. They are not about substances or material things.[28] Modes are "considered as Dependences on; or Affections of Substances; such are the *Ideas* signified by the Words *Triangle, Gratitude, Murther, etc.*"[29]

---

[24] Bk. II, i, 25.

[25] Bk. II, ix, 4.

[26] Bk. II, xii, 1.

[27] Bk. III, v, 11–12.

[28] Bk. II, xxii, 1.

[29] Bk. II, xii, 4.

The very idea of a mode is obscure enough, but then Locke proceeds to explain complex ideas by drawing a distinction between simple modes and mixed modes. The simple mode of a complex idea occurs when one adds up a set of experiences or ideas and then gets the simple mode type of a complex idea. As Locke explains, repeating an "*Idea* in our Minds, and adding the Repetitions together, we come by the *complex* Ideas *of the Modes of it.* Thus by adding one to one, we have the complex *Idea* of a Couple; by putting twelve Unites together, we have the complex *Idea* of a dozen, and so a score, or a Million, or any other Number."[30] Or, for another example, by noting repeatedly the passing of time we can extrapulate to the complex idea of eternity.[31] Mixed modes of complex ideas result from the combination of different simple ideas. Locke cites theft and beauty as examples. A combination of such ideas as colour, figure, and delight, when mixed by our minds, produces the attributes or mode of beauty. Theft, too, is a combination of several ideas jointly producing the attribute or mode of theft.[32] It is essential to Locke's later arguments in the *Essay* and in the *Second Treatise* to note that moral and political principles are mixed modes of complex ideas. Consequently, for Locke, moral and political principles and concepts are creations of our minds.

In addition to complex ideas, which refer to things, and complex ideas, which refer to modes, the third category of complex ideas refers to "the consideration and comparing [of] one *Idea* with another."[33] Examples of such complex ideas are "Father, and Son; Bigger, and Less; Cause, and Effect."[34]

Central to Locke's scheme for classifying ideas is the distinction between primary and secondary qualities. This is the same distinction discussed by Hobbes, Descartes, and Locke's friend Robert Boyle. Primary qualities refer to features that are inherent to bodies. These are real attributes of matter: solidity, extension, figure, mobility, and number.[35] Secondary qualities refer to colours, sounds, tastes, and the like. It is the primary qualities that correspond to "real" features in bodies, and they have the power to produce the effects in us of the secondary qualities.

---

[30] Bk. II, xvi, 2.

[31] Bk. II, xiv, 3.

[32] Bk. II, xii, 5.

[33] Bk. II, xii, 7.

[34] Bk. II, xxv, 2.

[35] Bk, II, viii, 9.

… I think it is easie to draw this Observation, That the *Ideas of primary Qualities* of Bodies, *are Resemblances* of them, and their Patterns do really exist in the bodies themselves; but the *Ideas, produced* in us *by* these *Secondary Qualities, have no resemblance* of them at all. There is nothing like our *Ideas,* existing in the Bodies themselves. They are in the Bodies, we denominate from them, only a power to produce those Sensations in us: And what is Sweet, Blue, or Warm in *Idea,* is but the certain Bulk, figure, and Motion of the insensible Parts in the Bodies themselves, which we call so.[36]

Although the primary qualities are the foundations of reality, it is difficult to see how one can know them. Locke followed Robert Boyle in positing an atomistic or corpuscular theory of reality, i.e., all things are composed of insensible, minute particles. As he recognizes, "For our Senses failing us, in the discovery of the Bulk, Texture, and Figure of the minute parts of Bodies, on which their real Constitutions and Differences depend, we are fain to make use of their secondary Qualities, as the characteristical Notes and Marks, whereby to frame *Ideas* of them in our Minds, and distinguish them one from another."[37] Thus, the primary qualities of these material particles have powers to produce ideas in us and to affect other bodies. These physical substances are not all that there is. We also have the idea of an immaterial spirit or soul:

Besides the complex *Ideas* we have of material sensible Substances…by the simple *Ideas* we have taken from those Operations of our own Minds, which we experience daily in our selves, as Thinking, Understanding, Willing, Knowing, and Power of beginning Motion, *etc.* co-existing in some Substance, we are able to frame *the complex* Idea *of an immaterial Spirit.* And thus by putting together the *Ideas* of Thinking, Perceiving, Liberty, and Power of moving themselves and other things, we have as clear a perception, and notion of immaterial Substances, as we have of material.[38]

Given the corpuscular or atomist theory, we obviously cannot have direct knowledge of these particles, which are the real properties of things in nature, and we must rely upon secondary qualities. To complete this picture of reality,

---

[36] Bk. II, viii, 15.

[37] Bk. II, xxiii, 8.

[38] Bk. II, xxiii, 15.

Locke adds the idea of power to explain change and movement in ourselves and in physical objects. According to Locke, there is the simple idea of power, and, as with other simple ideas, it reflects an inherent feature of reality. We see how natural bodies produce differing effects on each other, and we see how we can move several parts of our own body. Thus, by reflection and sensation we get the simple idea of power. Happily, power provides the link for understanding by illuminating the cause and effect relationship in reality.

Power is further divided into active and passive. Active power is clearly seen in thinking and motion. We can see how the active power of a billiard-stick causes a ball to move, and we can see how "a thought of the Mind…can move the parts of our Bodies, which were before at rest."[39] At one point Locke calls active power a "third sort" of quality, after primary and secondary, precisely because it is the source of new qualities not otherwise perceivable.

> To these might be added a third sort which are allowed to be barely Powers though they are as much real Qualities in the subject, as those which I to comply with the common way of speaking call *Qualities*, but for distinction *secondary Qualities*. For the power in Fire to produce a new Colour, or consistency in Wax or Clay by its primary Qualities, is as much a quality in Fire, as the power it has to produce in me a new *Idea* or Sensation of warmth or burning, which I felt not before, by the same primary Qualities, *viz*. The Bulk, Texture, and Motion of its insensible parts.[40]

In sum, the active power of fire produces a new quality—the colour of red—from clay. Fire itself is the source of this new quality or property of red and is the cause of its existence. In this sense, the new quality or property of red belongs to, and is located in, the active power of fire, which caused the change. The passive power in clay—its bulk, texture, and motion—would never produce red without fire.

Here we see a crucial link between Locke's epistemology and his political philosophy: a new quality or property is owned by, belongs to, or is located in, the active power that caused the new quality to come into existence. The great rights mentioned in the *Second Treatise*—such as life, liberty, health, and estates—can be explained through the application of the idea of active power. First, life itself is conceived by Locke as a power: "This at least I think evident, That we find in our selves

---

[39] Bk. II, xxi, 4.

[40] Bk. II, viii, 10.

a *Power* to begin or forbear, continue or end several actions of our minds, and motions of our Bodies, barely by a thought or preference of the mind ordering, or as it were commanding the doing or not doing such or such a particular action."[41] Second, liberty, too, is so conceived by Locke:

> So that *Liberty is not an* Idea *belonging to Volition*, or preferring; but to the Person having the Power of doing, or forbearing to do, according as the Mind shall chuse or direct. Our *idea* of liberty reaches as far as that Power, and no farther. For whereever restraint comes to check that Power, or compulsion takes away that Indifferency of Ability on either side to act, or to forbear acting, there *liberty*, and our Notion of it, presently ceases.[42]
>
> … when any one well considers it, I think he will as plainly perceive, that *Liberty*, which is but a power, belongs only to Agents, and cannot be an attribute or modification of the *Will*, which is also put a *Power*.[43]

Locke connects life and liberty to the pursuit of happiness, both in this life and (for our immortal souls) in the next: "the care for our selves, that we mistake not imaginary for real happiness, is the necessary foundation of our *liberty*. The stronger ties, we have, to an unalterable pursuit of happiness in general, which is our greatest good, and which as such our desires always follow, the more are we free from any necessary determination of our *will* to any particular action…. "[44] Third, estates or private property, which is discussed at great length in the *Second Treatise*, results from the active power of mixing one's labour with nature, whether plowing a field or picking an apple. Locke has thus established that life, liberty, and estates are attributes or modes of the simple idea of power in its active phase. Just as the simple idea of power is an inherent feature of reality, so are the modes of life, liberty, and estates inherent features of human existence.

Locke has laid the epistemological foundations for his political principles. To reiterate, the red colour in clay comes into existence because of the active power of fire; red inheres to, or is a property of, the active power of fire. Reality simply has this built-in structure. Life, liberty, and estates are similarly the consequence

---

[41] Bk. II, xxi, 5.

[42] Bk. II, xxi, 10.

[43] Bk. II, xxi, 14.

[44] Bk. II, xxi, 51.

of, the attributes of, or the property of, human active power. We will see these rather odd formulations repeated in the *Second Treatise*. The epistemological foundation had been prepared in *An Essay Concerning Human Understanding.*[45]

Book III, "Of Words," is concerned with language and, more particularly, the signification and meaning of words. After spending a considerable amount of time explaining the origins and types of ideas, Locke now must explain how ideas in one's mind "might be made known to others, and the Thoughts of Men's Minds be conveyed from one to another."[46] Words are necessary "that Man should find out some external sensible Signs, whereby those invisible *Ideas*, which his thoughts are made of, might be made known to others."[47] For words to have meaning they have to be "*Signs of Internal Conceptions.*"[48] Besides words that name ideas, there are also words that connect ideas in language: prepositions, verbs, and other grammatical terms.[49] The sounds we use for words are simply arbitrary, depending on history and place, but, they serve as public signs for communicating with others.

In the main, Locke views language as a labelling device. Although the ideas do represent objects, language first labels ideas in the mind. Consequently, for Locke, there is an implicit gap between language and reality, which explains the need to achieve the most precise label or definition. Locke's analogy for the way language works seems to be to acquire the proper mirror or focus and then reality becomes perceivable. This way of looking at the relationship between human language with its labelling function and a separate reality introduces several difficulties. First, many contemporary philosophers argue that it makes no sense to think of an intelligible reality independent of language. The very idea of an independent, intelligible reality is embedded in language itself. One cannot conceive of such a reality except through a certain kind of language; if one does not have this kind of language, then one cannot so conceive of reality. As an illustration, when Charles Darwin made his famous voyage to the Galapogas Islands,

---

[45] Max Milam, "The Epistemological Basis of Locke's Idea of Property," *Western Political Quarterly* 20 (March, 1967), pp. 16–30.

[46] Bk. III, i, 2.

[47] Bk. III, ii, 1.

[48] Bk. III, i, 2.

[49] Bk. III, vii, 1.

the natives on the coast marvelled at the rowboats, which seemed like large canoes, but they ignored the big sailing ship. They had no way conceptually or through language, to take in the large ship.[50]

A second difficulty is that Locke's version of how language works does not adequately express how we, in fact, use language. Locke seems to feel that for talk to be meaningful there must be, consciously and simultaneously, a running videotape of ideas in the mind, which are then expressed with the appropriate tag words. Moreover, Locke's position that ideas are mental things in the brain simply does not fit the way that we perceive either the world or ourselves. Seeing a table, for example, is not seeing the idea but is seeing various features in the table, having a prior context for understanding the parts and functions, and being able to relate context and features. Another example where Locke's theory of language appears to fail is in the discussion of a disposition or mood. The mood of a person is not a kind of thing or a mental entity in the mind.[51]

A third difficulty, as Locke himself phrases it, is to ensure that a set of words "excite in the Hearer, exactly the same *Idea*, they stand for in the Mind of the Speaker."[52] Locke's critics would contend that, in effect, Locke has a logically private language: if all one can know is based upon ideas and if ideas are internal constructions, all we can ever know is our own language, ideas, and experience. A full answer to these objections is not developed until Book IV where Locke discusses knowledge, but he does believe that he can address this issue.

Locke argues throughout Book III that there are indeed "unavoidable Imperfections" in words and that the signification of complex ideas, particularly about moral and political ideas, are especially prone to misunderstandings. Still, for Locke, the task is far from hopeless. Perhaps of most importance is the use of words that are "clear and distinct in their signification." In this fashion, it is possible to avoid the "empty Sounds, with little or no signification" so common

---

[50] Michael Polanyi, *Personal Knowledge* (New York: Harper, 1964), p. 291. For a fuller discussion of the role of language, see Winch, *The Idea of a Social Science*; Charles Taylor, *Human Agency and Language: Philosophical Papers*, Vol. I (Cambridge: Cambridge University Press, 1985), ch. 2; John W. Danford, *Wittgenstein and Political Philosophy: A Re-examination of the Foundation of Social Science* (Chicago: University of Chicago Press, 1978), pp. 49–72.

[51] John F. Bennett, *Locke, Berkeley, Hume* (Oxford: Oxford University Press, 1971), ch. 3.

[52] Bk. III, ix, 6.

among the "Schoolmen and Metaphysicians."[53] In short, Locke's advice is to follow the reductive program outlined in Book II. He further warns against figurative speech, eloquence, and rhetoric: "that all the Art of Rhetorick, besides Order and Clearness, all the artificial and figurative application of Words Eloquence hath invented, are for nothing else but to insinuate wrong *Ideas*, move the Passions, and thereby mislead the judgment; and so indeed are perfect cheat."[54]

As a guide to clear and distinct ideas, Locke presents five rules to follow. First, "a Man should take care *to use no word without a signification.*" Second, the words must be based upon clear and distinct ideas, or if the ideas are complex, they must be reducible to simple ideas. He warns that this is especially necessary for moral words such as "justice." Third, words must be attached to ideas "as common use has annexed them to." Fourth, any new signification and meaning of words should be clearly declared. This fourth rule is particularly valuable for moral discourse. Here, the terms are not about natural substance where we can only know nominal essences; rather, moral words are like mathematical notations and capable of precise definition and demonstration: "the precise real Essence of the things moral Words stand for, may be perfectly known." Fifth, words should be used "constantly in the same sense."[55]

It is essential to remember that, for Locke, clear and distinct ideas can come only from an empirical approach. Humans can never know the *real* essence of material things since we cannot perceive the atomistic or corpuscular features of reality. We have to be satisfied with what is empirically detectable. The best approach is to "look on all natural Things to have a real, but unknown constitution of their insensible Parts, from which flow those sensible Qualities, which serve us to distinguish them one from another, according as we have occasion to rank them into sorts, under common Denominations."[56] With respect to the material world, we can only know the *nominal*, and not the real, essence of a thing. There are limits to our understanding because we cannot know the internal constitution of reality, but by labelling clear and distinct ideas we can establish the material for true knowledge.[57]

---

[53] Bk. III, x, 2.

[54] Bk. III, x, 34.

[55] Bk. III, xi, 8–26.

[56] Bk. III, iii, 17.

[57] Locke does hold that there is a *real* essence for concepts: "*Essences* being thus distinguished into *Nominal and Real*, we may farther observe, that *in* the Species of *simple* Ideas *and Modes,*

Locke has now explained the flaws in innatism, the materials of knowledge, and the requisite words and language to communicate that knowledge. He now turns in Book IV, "Of Knowledge in General," to give an account of knowledge itself. He begins with the statement that knowledge can only be about ideas: "Since *the Mind*, in all its Thoughts and Reasonings, hath no other immediate Object but its own *Ideas*, which it alone does or can contemplate, it is evident, that our Knowledge is only conversant about them."[58]

Knowledge, then, can only be about "*the perception of the connexion and agreement, or disagreement and repugnancy of any of our Ideas.*"[59] Locke proceeds to list four possible kinds of knowledge. First, there is knowledge gained by noting the identity or diversity of ideas. One idea is different from another. There is knowledge in recognizing that white is not red. Second, there is knowledge of the relationship between ideas, such as larger or smaller and so forth. Third, there is knowledge gained through perceiving the co-existence of ideas. The complex idea of gold is composed of the co-existence of such ideas as yellow, weight, and malleability. Fourth, there is knowledge of "actual real existence," i.e., of real things.[60]

Knowledge can be further classified according to the degree of certainty. Intuitive knowledge is the most certain. The mind immediately perceives that "white is not black, that a circle is not a triangle, that three are more than two and equal to one and two."[61] There is also intuitive certainty about our own existence. Although Locke's general empirical stance puts him on a different path from the rationalist Descartes, in this instance he follows Descartes:

> As for *our own Existence*, we perceive it so plainly, and so certainly, that it neither needs, nor is capable of any proof. For nothing can be more evident to us, than our own Existence. I *think, I reason, I feel Pleasure and Pain;*

they *are always the same* : But *in Substances, always quite different.* Thus a Figure including a Space between three Lines, is the real, as well as nominal *Essence* of a Triangle; it being not only the abstract *Idea* to which the general Name is annexed, but the very *Essentia*, or Being, of the thing it self, that Foundation from which all its Properties flow, and to which they are all inseparably annexed" (Bk. III, iii, 18).

[58] Bk. IV, i, 1.

[59] Bk. IV, i, 2.

[60] Bk. IV, i, 30–37.

[61] Bk. IV, ii, 1.

Can any of these be more evident to me, than my own Existence? If I doubt of all other Things, that very doubt makes me perceive my own *Existence*, and will not suffer me to doubt of that.[62]

The second type is demonstrative knowledge—the mind has to discover the intervening linkage or entailments between ideas. Each step in establishing linkage can have intuitive certainty, but the process as a whole cannot be grasped intuitively. Although mathematics is an obvious example, Locke also includes the existence of God and the principles of morality as examples. With respect to God, Locke argues that only an intelligent being could have produced us. If matter did create life and intelligence, it could only be because God so designed. Locke also cites the harmony, order, and beauty of the world as signs of God's existence. He concludes that "we have a more certain Knowledge of the Existence of GOD than of any thing our Senses have not immediately discovered to us. Nay, I presume I may say, that we more certainly know that there is a GOD, than that there is anything about us."[63]

He has the same confidence in the demonstrative knowledge of morality. His argument that morality belongs to the science of demonstration is as follows:

The *Idea* of a supreme Being, infinite in Power, Goodness, and Wisdom, whose workmanship we are, and on whom we depend; and the *Idea* of our selves, as understanding, rational Beings, being such as are clear in us, would, I suppose, if duly considered, and pursued, afford such Foundations of our Duty and Rules of Action, as might place *Morality amongst the Sciences capable of Demonstration*: wherein I doubt not, but from self-evident Propositions, by necessary Consequences, as incontestable as those in Mathematicks, the measures of right and wrong might be made out, to any one that will apply himself with the same Indifferency and Attention to the one, as he does to the other of these Sciences.[64]

Locke proceeds to give an example—as certain as "a triangle has three angles equal to two right ones"—of an incontestable, self-evident moral proposition: "*Where there is no Property, there is no Injustice,* is a Proposition as certain as any

---

[62] Bk. IV, ix, 3.

[63] Bk. IV, x, 6.

[64] Bk. IV, iii, 17.

Demonstration in *Euclid*: For the *Idea* of *Property*, being a right to any thing; and the *Idea* to which the Name *Injustice* is given, being the Invasion or Violation of that right."[65] Such moral precepts as do not kill or steal are not innate, as we have already seen, nor are they somehow substantive or built into physical nature. Moral rules, as well as political principles, are mixed modes of complex ideas which we construct by reason in our own minds. Just as the definition of a triangle can allow us to recognize an actual triangle, so moral precepts enable us to recognize virtues and vices in humans.

Nevertheless, by arguing that ethics and mathematics equally belong to the science of demonstration, Locke creates a new problem and subject: the applicability of this logical moral knowledge to actual human situations. Moral theory has to be joined to motivations and reasons for fulfiling theoretical moral obligations. Locke, implicitly and explicitly, does give some reasons for applying the mathematical-like moral precepts. The most important reason, perhaps, is Locke's argument that God has designed humans with certain inclinations, desires, and capacities so that our purposes fit nature.[66]

The infinite wise Contriver of us, and all things about us, hath fitted our Senses, Faculties, and Organs, to the conveniences of Life, and the Business we have to do here. We are able, by our Senses, to know, and distinguish things; and to examine them so far, as to apply them to our Uses, and several ways to accommodate the Exigencies of this Life.… We are furnished with Faculties (dull and weak as they are) to discover enough in the Creatures, to lead us to the Knowledge of the Creator, and the Knowledge of our duty; and we are fitted well enough with Abilities, to provide for the Conveniences of living: These are our Business in this World.[67]

---

[65] Bk. IV, iii, 18.

[66] The centrality of God, for Locke, and the nature of his theology are much debated. Most scholars support the centrality of God to Locke's whole philosophy, though the exact nature of his theology is subject to various interpretations. John Dunn, *The Political Thought of John Locke* (Cambridge: Cambridge University Press, 1969); John Colman, *John Locke's Moral Philosophy* (Edinburgh: Edinburgh University Press, 1983); Joshua Mitchell, *Not by Reason Alone* (Chicago: University of Chicago Press, 1993), pp. 73–97. A contrary view that stresses a Hobbesian and secular treatment of Locke is given by Leo Strauss, *Natural Rights and History* (Chicago: University of Chicago Press, 1953) and Richard H. Cox, *Locke on War and Peace* (Oxford: Clarendon Press, 1960).

[67] Bk. II, xxiii, 12.

The *Second Treatise*, in fact, also spells out some of these features. In general, the pursuit of happiness, our inclinations of pain and pleasure, and our natural capacity to reason can sufficiently move us to apply moral and political principles.[68] Practical judgment, a training in virtue, and education are always necessary since we do have the liberty "to prefer the worse to the better."[69] Although not expressly written to complement the *Essay,* Locke published in 1693 *Some Thoughts Concerning Education.* In it Locke addresses, in practical detail, how to educate children and develop their capacities so that they can fulfil their obligation to be moral and social persons as well as citizens.

After intuitive and demonstrative knowledge, sensitive knowledge is the third and least certain kind of knowledge. Locke is well aware of the difficuties when knowledge is only about "the perception of the agreement or disagreement of our own *Ideas*: but who knows what those *Ideas* may be?"[70] But there can be conformity between our ideas and the reality of things through simple ideas: "Thus the *Idea* of Whiteness, or bitterness, as it is in the Mind, exactly answering that Power which is in any body to produce it there, has all the real conformity it can, or ought to have, with Things without us."[71] As previously established in Book II, the passivity of the mind in recording sensations provides confidence in the validity of the sensations, though we are unable to have direct experience of the primary qualities. There is, accordingly, sufficient solidity to this knowledge that Locke has little patience for a skeptic's contention that ideas may only be a dream or a figment of the imagination. Locke's common sense reply is: "If any one say, a Dream may do the same thing, and all these *Ideas* may be produced in us, without any external Objects, he may please to dream that I make him this Answer.... That I believe he will allow a very manifest difference between dreaming of being in the Fire, and being actually in it."[72] Nevertheless, we cannot have here the same type of certain knowledge found in mathematics or abstract moral

---

[68] Bk. II, xxi, 34–45.

[69] Bk. II, xxi, 56. For an examination of Locke's arguments for applying moral knowledge, see: Ruth W. Grant, *John Locke's Liberalism* (Chicago: University of Chicago Press, 1987), pp. 27–39. Colman, *John Locke's Moral Philosophy*, pp. 206–34; Peter A. Schouls, *Reasoned Freedom: John Locke and Enlightenment* (Ithaca: Cornell University Press, 1992), pp. 204–32.

[70] Bk. IV, iv, 1.

[71] Bk. IV, iv, 4.

[72] Bk. IV, ii, 13.

definitions. For natural philosophy, i.e., the study of physical reality, we must rely upon observation and experiment. Strictly speaking, the knowledge gained is not certain, but probable, since we cannot directly grasp the "atoms." So, Locke warns that "natural philosophy is not capable of being made a science."[73]

In the conclusion to the *Essay* Locke divides human knowledge and science into three divisions: nature, which is natural science in modern terminology; human action, which is the realm of ethics; and signs, which is roughly logic. Here, he relaxes his strict use of the word "science":

> All that can fall within the compass of Humane Understanding, being either, *First,* The Nature of Things, as they are in themselves, their Relations, and their manner of Operation: or, *Secondly,* That which Man himself ought to do, as a rational and voluntary Agent, for the Attainment of any End, especially Happiness: or, *Thirdly,* The ways and means, whereby the Knowledge of both the one and the other of these, are attained and communicated; I think, *Science* may be divided properly into these *Three sorts.*[74]

All three are the proper objects of knowledge or science and are amenable to the methods and framework he has described throughout the *Essay.*

Certainty is, indeed, one feature of knowledge, but this should not mislead us about the general direction of Locke's scientific method. It is not deductive and mechanical, which distinguishes Locke from Hobbes, but it relies upon observation and experiment. Our ideas, as Locke insisted at the very beginning, are ultimately derived from experience. Locke has always had an ambivalent place in the history of philosophy: empiricist or rationalist? He is certainly an empiricist with respect to the origins of ideas and with respect to his stress on observation and experiment, but knowledge, as described in Book IV, is decidedly rational and is a knowledge of propositions and ideas.[75]

---

[73] Bk. IV, xii, 10.

[74] Bk. IV, xxi, 1.

[75] For excellent brief surveys of Locke's *Essay:* Jenkins, *Understanding Locke;* Bennett, *Locke, Berkeley, Hume;* Frederick Copleston, *History of Philosophy,* Vol. 5 (Westminster: Newman Press, 1964), chs. 4–6; F. J. Lowe, *Locke on Human Understanding* (New York: Routledge, 1995). For a large collection of essays on Locke's epistemology, Richard Ashcraft, ed., *John Locke: Critical Assessments,* Vol. 4 (London: Routledge, 1991).

Epistemology has clear consequences for political and moral theories. Locke's original motivation for composing the *Essay* was to find solid grounds, as one has in a true science, for moral principles. He believes that he has done this, and in Book IV, he devotes chapter XIX to applying his framework to a criticism of religious "enthusiasts." These are the people who rely on professed revelation untested by reason. Human knowledge is limited to what can be ascertained by reason and experience, and this realization supports religious toleration. The "enthusiasts" simply cannot speak with such certainty that they are right in their political and religious opinions and that others are wrong. It was not only thought that Locke's epistemology produced toleration, but, in general, the eighteenth century, the Age of the Enlightenment, was also convinced by Locke's arguments that reason and experience were incompatible with authoritarianism and dictators. The epistemology of Locke was understood to support political liberty.[76]

THE TWO TREATISES

First Treatise

Although Locke wrote two treatises, bound together as one work, the *First Treatise* is seldom, or seriously, studied. It is the *Second Treatise*, now often published separately, that receives the most scrutiny. In part, this is because the purpose of the *First Treatise* is to criticize an obscure advocate of the divine right of kings, and there is little doubt that the target of the attack, *Patriarcha* and other writings by Sir Robert Filmer (1588–1653), would be assigned to obscurity except for Locke's attention. At the time, Locke did believe that the contrast between the arguments of Filmer, explained and criticized in the *First Treatise*, and those developed in the *Second Treatise* would enhance the persuasive power of his own position. Although the writings of Filmer seem to have been primarily a foil for Locke, it is also true that many still believed some features of Filmer's argument, and those features needed to be undermined in order to establish Locke's own position. Locke states in the preface that "the Pulpit, of late years, publickly owned

---

[76] Morton White, "The Politics of Epistemology," *Ethics* 100 (October, 1989), pp. 77–92. John W. Yolton gives the most sympathetic and careful treatment of Locke's epistemology and its relation to moral and political philosophy: *Locke and the Compass of Human Understanding* (Cambridge: Cambridge University Press, 1970) and *John Locke: An Introduction* (Oxford: Blackwell, 1985). Ruth W. Grant is also excellent: *John Locke's Liberalism* (Chicago: University of Chicago Press, 1987), pp. 12–51.

his Doctrine, and made it the Currant Divinity of the Times."[77] Thus, while it may appear to modern readers unnecessary to attack Filmer, in Locke's context the critique was a valuable preparation for the readers who would encounter in the *Second Treatise* a realm of new and, for many, disturbing arguments.

That God ordained the institution of the monarchy, derived by analogy from the original parents Adam and Eve before the flood and Noah and his three sons after the flood, was a common enough theme before Filmer wrote *Patriarcha*. It was a standard theological argument with the political purpose of teaching and justifying the duties of the subjects. It was a general, moral argument, prevalent in the medieval world. But, it was not used to allow kings to murder and steal, or to allow taxation to be imposed by simple kingly decree, or to require absolute political obedience of subjects. St. Thomas Aquinas, for example, would hardly have excepted Filmer's position.[78]

Filmer believed that the Bible contained God's will on all matters. From this unimpeachable source, it was clear that human society originated with Adam, who was given the whole world and all that was in it. Because Eve and all others came after Adam, it was also clear that humans were related in a natural sense. Society was intended to be an extended family, subordinate to Adam. Furthermore, there was no natural equality. Eve was created after Adam and, accordingly, was subordinate to Adam, and this subordination of female to male was thereby ordained in all areas of life. Neither Eve nor marriage is given much attention in Filmer's most famous work, *Patriarcha*. The only mention of marriage is in a brief quotation from Aristotle, which Filmer criticizes.[79] In any case, the sovereignty of Adam could not be limited by a marriage contract. The primacy of being first also entailed that the first-born male took precedence over other children. Primogeniture—the right of the oldest male to inherit the father's estate—was ordained by God. Filmer drew the

---

[77] *Patriarcha* was written in the 1620s and privately circulated, but it was not published until 1680. Filmer was well known, but, according to one scholar, his own defence of divine right was curiously not representative of Royalist thought in general, in that Filmer would allow for no limitations on Royalist authority. James Daly, *Sir Robert Filmer and English Political Thought* (Toronto: University of Toronto Press, 1979), pp. 173–93. Gordon J. Schochet draws an opposite conclusion and claims that Filmer's position was almost the "official state ideology." *Patriarchalism in Political Thought* (Oxford: Blackwell, 1975), p. 193; see also W. H. Greenleaf, *Order, Empiricism and Politics: Two Traditions of English Political Thought* (Oxford: Oxford University Press, 1964), pp. 80–94.

[78] Glen Burgess, *The Politics of the Ancient Constitution: An Introduction to English Political Thought, 1603–1642* (University Park: Pennsylvania State University Press, 1992), pp. 134–38.

[79] Peter Laslett, ed., *Patriarcha and other Political Works of Sir Robert Filmer* (Oxford: Blackwell, 1949), p. 76.

conclusion for politics that humans were never naturally free and equal; there was always political order, dependence, and inequality ordained by God at the beginning.

The question of the right to property was answered by Filmer in the same fashion as the political right to rule. Adam was given all possessions, which he could dispose of as he pleased, with the eldest son inheriting the estate at death of the father. There was no state-of-nature stage of communal property or primitive communism. Neither the right to political power nor the right to property depended upon consent. Since society was a natural and extended family, as provided in the Bible, it could not be that society was formed by the consent of autonomous, naturally-free individuals in a state of nature. One does not enter a family by consent, nor does one so enter a society. Neither theology nor history supports the contention that a political society could be based upon consent and a contract.

Just as the Bible explained the origin and nature of political society, so it prescribed the proper political structure. The Bible recounts the direct lineage of sovereign rulers from Adam to Noah and the Flood. After the Flood, Noah divided the earth among his sons, and from this division came rulers to the present time. Filmer is adamant in claiming that neither the Bible nor ancient history has evidence of people properly and rightly authorizing a government. This means that there is no justification for diminishing royal power through some constitutional arrangements. It remains the case that absolute monarchy is the best form of government, and democracy is the worst.

One obvious difficulty that Filmer had to face was that there was no clear line leading from Noah and his sons to the present rulers; moreover, there was irrefutable evidence of individuals deposing kings by force and taking the crown for themselves. Filmer's response, such as it is, is that divine providence is mysteriously at work:

> If it please God, for the correction of the Prince or punishment of the people, to suffer Princes to be removed and others to be placed in their rooms, either by the factions of the nobility or rebellion of the people, in all such cases the judgment of God, who hath power to give and take away kingdoms, is most just. Yet the ministry of men who execute God's judgments without commission is sinful and damnable. God doth but use and turn men's unrighteous acts to the performance of His righteous decrees....
>
> There is, and always shall be continued to the end of the world, a natural right of a supreme Father over every multitude, although, by the secret will of God, many at first do most unjustly obtain the exercise of it.[80]

---

[80] *Ibid., Patriarcha*, p. 62.

Filmer insists that it is irrelevant how a king gets political authority and that in all cases it remains the "natural right of a supreme Father." Yet, one can imagine a situation where one usurper fights another or a situation where an established ruler is defeated but later tries to regain power. Who has divine right, and who must be obeyed? Filmer's reply is that subjects must exercise passive obedience: one must tolerate what an evil ruler inflicts, but one need not actively obey. The individual will have to judge what belongs under the jurisdiction of the king, whoever that may be, and what belongs to God. He quotes the New Testament, Mark 12:17: "Render unto Caesar the things that are Caesar's, and unto God the things that are God's." But, it is never the case that the individual has the right to revolt or to actively resist. It is hard to see how Filmer's arguments are even coherent, let alone how they provide guidance for the citizen during a civil war. God's providence supports continuously, if mysteriously, successful political authority.

The citizen, as a consequence, always has an undiminished obligation to obey the monarchy. There are no other ordained forms of government, and the alternatives of democracy or anarchy would be a disaster for humanity. Filmer himself provides a political catechism as a summation of his political philosophy:

1. That there is no form of government, but monarchy only.
2. That there is no monarchy, but paternal.
3. That there is no paternal monarchy, but absolute, or arbitrary.
4. That there is no such thing as an aristocracy or democracy.
5. That there is no such form of government as a tyranny.
6. That the people are not born free by nature.[81]

Filmer's political tenets had many ramifications. Since God's grant to Adam was unconditional and passed to all sovereign rulers, it followed that subjects and laws were dependent upon the sovereign's will: individual rights were grants from the king; taxation did not require consent; parliament's power derived from the king's grant and not from a contract created by consent; law's authority came from the sovereign king and did not bind the king.

To modern heirs of Locke these political themes seem outrageous. Yet, for many in Locke's time they were quite reasonable. It was often argued, by reputable historians supporting the Royalist cause, that in feudal times kings created parliament only to provide advice. The analogy of a ruler to a father, also, seemed

---

[81] *Ibid.*, "Observations upon Aristotle's Politics Touching Forms of Government," p. 229.

perfectly reasonable: the Lord's prayer, which the vast majority would say daily, begins "Our Father"; the local priest, a person of great authority for many people at the time, is called Father; the first created human was Adam, a father. Authority in religion, family, and state was identified with the father. It seemed to be plain common sense to call a patriarchy "natural" and ordained by God. In order to be persuasive, Locke had to alter or have set aside many deep assumptions, implicitly relied upon by Filmer, which permeated the political culture.

More precisely, Filmer's attack on the notions of consent, contract, and property sets the stage for the *Second Treatise* and the presentation of Locke's own political philosophy. What Locke proposes is what Filmer opposes. Filmer launches the *Patriarcha* with "the dangerous opinion" he will refute, the very same dangerous opinion that Locke will lead his readers to embrace in the *Second Treatise* through a blend of arguments from theology, history, natural reason, and common sense practicality. The dangerous opinion, as formulated by Filmer for refutation, is: "Mankind is naturally endowed and born with freedom from all subjection, and at liberty to choose what form of government it please, and that the power which any one man hath over others was at the first by human right bestowed according to the discretion of the multitude."[82] This view, he notes, has been advocated by both "Jesuits and some zealous favourers of the Geneva discipline [Calvinists]."[83] It was true that from one end of the theological spectrum, the Jesuits Francisco Suarez and Cardinal Bellarmine, and from the other end, certain Calvinist religious leaders had written that citizens authorize rulers. The implication is that Filmer's own position will be in the solid, Anglican, English middle.

Admittedly, Filmer's reliance on the doctrine of Providence and on his peculiar interpretation of the Bible seems muddled and bizarre to modern readers. Yet, in criticizing "the dangerous opinion" Filmer did provide some serious arguments for Locke to address. For instance, there are several difficulties associated with relying upon consent and contract to establish a legitimate government and to derive the obligation of citizens. The principle is that if one has not consented, then obligation does not exist. What then happens to dissenters, women, minorities, and the young? Does each generation have to create a new contract? If consent were to be the criterion for establishing a legitimate government and

---

[82] *Ibid., Patriarcha,* p. 53.

[83] *Ibid.*

370

for instilling a moral obligation among citizens, society, Filmer warns, would inevitably be full of "naturally free" subjects, and society would also be full of strife. In practice, it would be a hopeless situation leading to anarchy. Similarly, it is impossible to see how consent can be used to establish private property once it has been acknowledged, as some thinkers have, that God gave the earth to humanity in common. Filmer continues, if it is held that God initially established a community of all things, it must be a sin to destroy this communism and have private property. If it is argued that God's will did not create private property through Adam, private property becomes simply a human creation: "then the moral law depends upon the will of man. There would be no law against adultery or theft, if women and all things were in common."[84] Filmer's belief is that his approach escapes such difficulties.

In brief, the democratic view—that human are naturally free and that through consent and contract humans construct legitimate government—is, in Filmer's idea, contrary to the Bible, history, and natural reason. The impracticality of using consent and contract as criteria for legitimacy and, if they are used, the inevitable decline to instability and even anarchy are also Filmer's constant themes. Locke first will systematically refute these contentions and then will present in the *Second Treatise*, his own full political philosophy.

Locke begins the *First Treatise* by ridiculing *Patriarcha*: if others had not praised Filmer, Locke says, he would "have taken Sr. Rt. Filmer's *Patriarcha* as any other treatise, which would perswade all Men, that they are Slaves, and ought to be so, for such another exercise of Wit...."[85] By advocating that absolute monarchy is the only legitimate form of government and that "no Man is born Free" Filmer, in effect, is justifying slavery.

It, thus, is clear from the start that Locke's treatise is a polemical piece and, as did other pamphlets of the time, attempts to persuade readers to the author's cause. The 1670s and 1680s were turbulent, and Locke, Shaftesbury, and others needed to convince as many readers as possible that political rule depends upon consent and that resistance and revolution can be justified. These would be disturbingly radical views for many. The arguments used would not be successful if

---

[84] *Ibid.*, p. 65.

[85] IT.1. All citations will be to Laslett ed., *Two Treatises of Government*, rev. ed. (Cambridge: Cambridge University Press, 1963). The citation "IT.1" indicates the *First Treatise*, paragraph 1; "IIT.5" indicates the *Second Treatise*, paragraph 5.

they were easily dismissed as the views of Puritans, "enthusiasts," or radicals.[86] Locke had to tread a careful path between the rhetoric required to undermine Filmer's credibility and the philosophic arguments necessary to lead citizens to a radical view of their power and authority.

Locke argues in chapter two that Filmer's declaration "that men are not naturally free" is built upon the premise that paternal and regal (political) power are the same. Filmer conflates fathers and kings and compounds this confusion by identifying both roles with property ownership.[87] To Locke, it appears Filmer's confusion flows from two sources. Sometimes, Filmer has wrongly interpreted the Bible or some historical source; at other times, it is Filmer's incapacity to have clear and precise definitions that is at fault.

Locke needs to undermine Filmer's appeal to religious authority. That political authority was, directly or indirectly, derived from God was a truism uniting Augustine, Aquinas, Luther, Calvin, and a variety of Protestant theologians. At issue was the precise nature of that derivation. Thus, Locke had to dispute Filmer's position while providing a more plausible interpretation of the Bible. As one instance, Locke heaps scorn on Filmer for citing the commandment "Honour thy Father" as entailing obedience to the ruler. The Biblical commandment actually reads to "Honour thy Father and Mother." The latter is dropped by Filmer. Similarly, Filmer writes that in the first book of the Bible, *Genesis*, God grants dominion to Adam, but Locke points outs that the actual phrase refers to Adam and Eve.[88] Throughout the *First Treatise* Locke ridicules a variety of Filmer's misquotations or even contradictions in the *Patriarcha*.[89]

Locke does not reject the Bible. He, too, relies on Biblical citations for authority, but his method of interpretation is designed to be more plausible and coherent. Locke argues that reason and common sense should be used in interpretations. God uses "ordinary Rules of Language" or else he would "lose his design in speaking," i.e., humans could not understand the message. When God

---

[86] Esmond S. De Beer, "Locke and English Liberalism: the *Second Treatise of Government* in its Contemporary Setting," in *John Locke: Problems and Perspectives*, ed. John W. Yolton (London: Cambridge University Press, 1969), pp. 34–44; Ashcraft, *Revolutionary Politics*, ch. 4.

[87] IT.7–9.

[88] IT.29, 47, 55, 62.

[89] IT.17, 71–72.

speaks to Adam and Eve, he means both Adam and Eve. When God speaks to Noah, he means only Noah and not all subsequent rulers in history. These are the plain meanings available to "any ordinary understanding," though not followed by Filmer.[90] Locke is appealing to his readers to rely on their own understanding and to dismiss the authority of traditional theologians who distort the Bible. This appeal is clearly not a denial of the importance of the Bible, but it does deprive Filmer's position of a major pillar of support.

At other points, Locke cites Filmer's inability to reason with clear and precise definitions. There are many inconsistencies and plain contradictions, which Locke attacks. For example, Filmer has the right to absolute power transferred by inheritance, by grant, by election, and by usurpation, all allegedly derived from the first father, Adam, before he was a father.[91] Toward the end of the treatise, Locke taunts: "And hence not being able to make out any Prince Title to Government, as Heir to *Adam,* which therefore is of no use, and had been better let alone, he is fain to resolve all into present Possession, and makes Civil Obedience as due to an *Usurper's* Title as good."[92]

In addition to polemical and rhetorical attacks, there are substantive criticisms made by Locke. Perhaps the most significant criticism is Locke's contention that Filmer has confused property with political power.

> Property, whose Original is from the Right a Man has to use any of the Inferior Creatures, for the Subsistence and Comfort of his Life, is for the benefit and sole Advantage of the Proprietor, so that he may even destroy the thing, that he has Property in by his use of it, where need requires: but Government being for the Preservation of every Mans Right and Property...is for the good of the Governed.[93]

Filmer conflates the two with his claim that God's grant of dominion over the whole earth to Adam established the divine right of monarchy. To Locke, this shows again Filmer's inability to make clear distinctions. The grant of dominion

---

[90] IT.46, 80.

[91] IT.17, 79–80.

[92] IT.121.

[93] IT.92.

over beasts does not translate into absolute power over humans. The dominion over animals provides for a property to use granted by God, but property ownership is not the same as political rule. In fact, God did not give to one man total control of the goods of the earth.

> But we know God hath not left one Man so to the Mercy of another, that he may starve him if he please: God the Lord and Father of all, has given no one of his Children such a Property, in his peculiar Portion of the things of this World, but that he has given his needy Brother a Right to the surplusage of his Goods; so that it cannot justly be denied him, when his pressing Wants call for it.[94]

If one powerful person did demand obedience for food, this would only demonstrate that political obedience is truly founded upon compact and consent:

> Should any one make so perverse an use of God's Blessings poured on him with a liberal Hand; should any one be Cruel and Uncharitable to that extremity, yet all this would not prove that Propriety in Land, even in this Case, gave any Authority over the Persons of Men, but only that compact might; since the Authority of the Rich Proprietor, and the Subjection of the Needy Beggar began not from the Possession of the Lord, but the Consent of the poor Man, who preferr'd being his Subject to starving. And the Man he thus submits to, can pretend to no more Power over him, than he has consented to, upon Compact.[95]

Ownership of property and political rule are conceptually distinct.

Another of Locke's critisms is Filmer's conflating of parental authority with political rule. Paternal authority no more than property ownership, can be the source of unlimited political authority. Filmer's position, as already noted, rests upon identifying the natural authority of the father (ignoring the mother) over children with the nature of political authority. Locke makes several criticisms. Not only does the mother have an equal entitlement according to Scripture, but there is no passage in the Bible giving unlimited power over children to the father. Indeed, God's will and the law of nature clearly confine and limit parental power: "For Children being by the course of Nature, born weak, and unable to provide for

---

[94] IT.42.

[95] IT.43.

themselves, they have by the appointment of God himself, who hath thus ordered the course of nature, a Right to be nourish'd and maintained by their Parents, nay a right not only to a bare Subsistance but to the conveniences and comfort of Life, as far as the conditions of their Parents can afford it."[96] Moreover, the origin of parental authority does not entail political power. The "Law of Nature gives Fathers Paternal Power over their children, because they did *beget* them." But this can hardly be transferred or inherited: "This is evident, That Paternal Power arising only from *Begetting*, for in that our *A.* [Filmer] places it alone, can neither be *transfer'd*, nor *inherited*: And he that does not beget, can no more save Paternal Power which arises from thence, than he can have a Right to any thing who performs not the Condition, to which only it is annexed."[97] The very origins of paternal power, Locke contends, make it clearly different in kind from political power.

The practical question to be answered is Who has political power and must be obeyed? Filmer's answer fails, Locke argues, since his theory of divine appointment cannot be seen to be transferred, assuming that it was even initially made to Adam. The history since Noah is permanently obscure; moreover, usurpers have clearly been successful over ruling kings. In practice, whoever has power must be obeyed. Consequently, there is "no distinction between Pirate and Lawful Princes, he that has Force is without any more ado to be obey'd, and Crowns and Scepters would become the Inheritance only of Violence and Rapine."[98]

Filmer is not clear, Locke argues, about the origins of the different types of authority, about the different purposes of the types of authority, and about the transferral of authority. When Filmer discusses the origins of political authority, he is hopelessly confused. If political authority originates from being a father, then it could be exercised only by a father and could not be transferred: "For it being a Right that accrews to a Man only by *begetting*, no Man can have this Natural Dominion over any one he does not *beget*.[99] If the origin of political authority is a divine grant, then a divine grant is needed each time.[100]

---

[96] IT.89.

[97] IT.101.

[98] IT.81.

[99] IT.74.

[100] IT.96.

A further confusion occurs because Filmer ignores the purposes or ends of political authority, paternal authority, and ownership. In each case, even if the grant of authority was absolute, it was not arbitrary, i.e., without limits. Political authority has the purpose of the "good of the whole," which cannot be transferred or inherited: "That…was vested in him, for the good and behoof of others, and therefore the Son cannot Claim or Inherit it by a Title, which is founded wholly on his own private good and advantage."[101] Paternal authority is confined by the purpose of providing subsistence and care of children. Children are not property, nor is primogeniture ordained by God or nature: "the First Born has not a sole or peculiar Right by any Law of God and Nature, the younger Children having an equal Title with him founded on that Right they all have to maintenance, support and comfort from their Parents…."[102] Ownership is a major topic of the *Second Treatise*, but here too Locke notes limits to property: it is confined by the true needs of the owner and by the rights of others when "pressing Wants" call for it.[103] In each case, the purpose or end of the type of authority limits power, confuting the claims of Filmer. In the cases of paternal and political authority, since each exists for the good of others, neither can be inherited or transferred unilaterally. These types of authority are relational and constitute the "binding" that makes a family or a political society. As such, they cannot be housed in, or owned by, a single person. An analogy, although one not used by Locke, would be to friendship. Friendship binds people and cannot be owned by one. Again, Filmer is refuted.

The upshot of Locke's critique is that Filmer fails to distinguish who by right should rule:

> For if this remain disputable, all the rest will be to very little purpose; and the skill used in dressing up Power with all the Splendor and Temptation Absoluteness can add to it, without shewing who has a Right to have it, will serve only to give a greater edge to Man's Natural Ambition, which of it self is but to keen. What can this do but set Men on the more eagerly to scramble, and so lay a sure and lasting Foundation of endless Contention and Disorder, instead of that Peace and Tranquility, which is the business of Government, and the end of Humane Society?[104]

---

[101] IT.93.

[102] *Ibid.*

[103] IT.42, 92.

[104] IT.106.

Filmer, the Monarchist, has implicitly recognized usurpation, when successful, as ordained. The irony would not be lost on Royalist supporters. Filmer's position leads to instability, in contrast to a theory of obligation built upon consent and contract.

Locke has carefully prepared the ground for his own position in the *Second Treatise*. While still providing an appeal to the Bible himself, Locke has shown that Filmer's own Biblical interpretations are faulty. He has also shown that history does not support Filmer, nor does natural reason. In contrast to Filmer's charge that democracy, consent, and compact lead to instability, Locke has cleverly shown that Filmer's divine right theory leads to instability.

The critique of Filmer's arguments sets major tasks for Locke to address in the *Second Treatise*. As Filmer noted, all humans are born into a family and into subordination. One task is to explain the claim that humans are still naturally free and can choose their own forms of government. What is the origin and nature of political authority? Can there be a right of resistance to an unjust political authority? Another task is to explain the origin and right of property. Finally, Locke needs to demonstrate that the institutional structure that will arise from his political philosophy will be stable and just.

Second Treatise

In the *Second Treatise* chapters 1 to 3 (paragraphs 1–21) explain the major philosophic premises. Locke describes legitimate political power, the state of nature, natural law, and the state of war. Chapters 4 through 9 (paragraphs 22–131) discuss different kinds of rule, property, and the origins and ends of political society. In chapters 10 through 15 (paragraphs 132–174) Locke develops the institutional framework that flows from his philosophic premises. Chapter 15 summarizes his arguments for distinguishing legitimate and illegitimate governments and chapters 16 through 19 (paragraphs 175–243), provide a guide for analyzing illegitimate governments and conclude with a justification for resisting and replacing an illegitimate government.

Filmer's fundamental difficulty was his inability to distinguish a legitimate from an illegitimate government. Locke begins with a clear, precise definition of "political power," a phrase he uses to indicate legitimate power:

> *Political Power* then I take to be *a Right* of making Laws with Penalties of Death, and consequently all less Penalties, for the Regulating and Preserving of Property, and of employing the force of the Community, in

the Execution of such Laws, and in the defence of the Common-wealth from Foreign Injury, and all this only for the Publick Good.[105]

In this definition of political power the functions of government are plausible enough: preserve property and defend the community for the public good. The issue is the origin of the "Right" to employ such force on behalf of a community.

It is already clear from the *First Treatise* that the origin is not a divine fiat to a particular government. Locke turns, as had Hobbes, to an original state of nature prior to government, in order to discover the origin of Right. The state "all Men are naturally in…is a *State of perfect Freedom* to order their *Actions*, and dispose of their *Possessions*, and *Persons* as they think fit, within the bounds of the Law of Nature…." In addition to freedom, the state of nature is also a state of "*Equality*, wherein all the Power and Jurisdiction is reciprocated, no one having more than another…."[106] Although humans are naturally free and equal, the result is not chaos; or, as Locke phrases it, "though this be a *State of Liberty*, yet it is *not a State of Licence*."[107] There is both law and right in the state of nature.

The state of nature is governed by a law of nature that "obliges everyone: and Reason, which is that Law, teaches all Mankind, who will but consult it, that being all equal and independent, no one ought to harm another in his Life, Health, Liberty, or Possessions" (IIT.6).[108] What is the source of this law, or what makes this right? Locke's answer is that the individual and the community have been so structured by God:

> For Men being all the Workmanship of one Omnipotent, and infinitely wise Maker; All the Servants of one Sovereign Master, sent into the World by his order and about his business, they are his Property, whose Workmanship they are, made to last during his, not one anothers Pleasure. And being furnished with like Faculties, sharing all in one Community of Nature, there cannot be supposed any such *Subordination* among us, that may Authorize us to destroy one another, as if we were made for one anothers uses, as the inferior ranks of Creature are for ours.[109]

---

[105] IIT.3.

[106] IIT.4.

[107] IIT.6.

[108] *Ibid.*

[109] *Ibid.*

Every individual, therefore, is "*bound to preserve himself* and…when his own Preservation comes not in competition, ought he, as much as he can, *to preserve the rest of Mankind*, and may not…impair the life, or what tends to the Preservation of the Life, Liberty, Health, Limb or Goods of another."[110] For Locke, the duty to preserve all mankind—the fundamental law of nature—leads to the four derivative rights belonging equally to each person: life, liberty, health, and possession.

This law of nature in the state of nature would be of no value unless it could be enforced. Since there is no government, each individual executes the law of nature. But this does not lead to chaos because humans can detect through reason the law of nature and guide their actions accordingly. The individual need not act "according to the passionate heats, or extravagancy of his own Will"; the individual can be guided by "calm reason and conscience."[111] Because there is a law found by reason to provide a standard and because the execution of the law is guided by reason and conscience, this is not a state of "Confusion and Disorder."[112]

Critical to this picture is the role of reason. Locke is arguing that humans are capable of reasoning on grounds other than a calculating self-interest. Given the premise that all are equal and independent, reason dictates for those "who will but consult it" that humans should not harm each other or their possessions.[113] Reason is not merely a logical operation, however. It does, in fact, occur in a state of nature. The relation among independent nations is evidence: "all *Princes* and Rulers of *Independent* Governments all though the World, are in a State of Nature,"[114] and agreements and compacts are made among them. Locke also alludes to two shipwrecked sailors on a deserted island and to "a *Swiss* and an *Indian*, in the Woods of *America*." Reason was not impotent in these cases: "For Truth and keeping of Faith belongs to Men, as Men, and not as Members of Society."[115]

The state of nature, as can now be seen, is not automatically a state of war, contrary to Hobbes. In both states there is no "common judge" to adjudicate disputes, but the state of war is distinct because force is used without right, i.e. outside the law

---

[110] *Ibid.*

[111] IIT.8.

[112] IIT.13.

[113] IIT.6.

[114] IIT.14.

[115] *Ibid.*

of nature. There is a right of war when an external aggressor violates the law of nature. But likewise, there is a state of war when one's freedom is taken away by those "appointed to administer Justice."[116] As an illustration, to be put under the absolute power of another, as advocated by Filmer, is to be placed into a state of war in spite of the trappings of law. The state of complete subordination to an absolute power denies the "Right of my Freedom;" therefore, it makes one a slave. The rule of an absolute ruler, strictly speaking, is not even a form of political rule. The fundamental law of nature is the preservation of life, but an absolute dictator deprives one of the very freedom needed for security and life.[117] Through the features discerned in the state of nature, Locke derives a standard of legitimacy for the use of force, a standard independent of the political society.

The state of nature presented in chapters 1 through 3 is a rational demonstration of this moral standard. Assuming that there is no government, individuals would be independent and free to do as they wished (a natural freedom); and individuals would be in an equal condition with no one given a superior position to another (equality). In this state, humans can be seen to have common powers and attributes. They can reason, choose, and act; they are moral agents. These individuals are not isolated from each other but have a communal sense and social relations. Later, Locke will expand these attributes when discussing the role of the family. In these beginning chapters, he refers to preserving mankind, the community of nature, and the public good. Such creatures, independent and equal, should not be harmed; to argue the contrary would be to conceive of humans as animals. Since we are not animals, this would be against reason and common equity.[118] The rational demonstration Locke provides is linked to God's purposes for humanity. Humans have been endowed by God with free will and reason, and it is these attributes, "the Principles of Human Nature," that make moral action and responsibility possible.[119]

---

[116] IIT.20.

[117] IIT.17.

[118] IIT.18.

[119] There is an enormous literature on Locke's state of nature. Particularly valuable are Dunn, *The Political Thought of John Locke*, ch. 6; Richard Ashcraft, "Locke's State of Nature: Historical Fact or Moral Fiction," *American Political Science Review* 62 (1968), pp. 909–15; Grant, *John Locke's Liberalism*, pp. 64–72; A John Simmons, *The Lockean Theory of Rights* (Princeton: Princeton University Press, 1992).

Locke's state of nature is a logical construct, or "demonstrative knowledge" as it is termed in *An Essay Concerning Human Understanding*. In this sense, it is non-historical, but Locke's practical examples indicate that his construct actually does portray actual human nature and action in history. Human reason is more than simply a calculating self-interest; humans do have an awareness of, and duty toward, others that constitute a sense of community; humans are duty-bound by the law of nature created by God. Political power is a right when it evolves from these premises illuminated in the state of nature.

Chapters 4 through 9 show the reader how the state of nature evolves into a political society with a government. This evolution builds upon the premises discerned in the state of nature. In particular, Locke continually reaffirms that all humans are naturally free and independent. The development of any kind of inequality or subordination or rule must be consistent with the original premises. The only way free and independent creatures could justifiably leave a state of nature, form a political society, and establish a government—to peruse the matter hypothetically and logically—would have to be consistent with the use of reason, guided and bound by the law of nature and by free consent. Force and conquest must give way to compact and consent in order to have a legitimate government, or, to use Locke's technical phrase, political power.

In chapter 4, "Of Slavery," political power is contrasted with absolute, arbitrary power. Absolute power is the highest authority and includes the power of life and death. Arbitrary power is the term Locke uses to indicate that the power is used contrary to the law of nature and at the will of the ruler. To be under an absolute, arbitrary power is the condition of slavery. In contrast, a legitimate government is one in which the legislative power to make law is derived from consent and the laws are applicable to all. This would be consistent with our natural liberty in nature. To give an absolute, arbitrary power control over one's life would be inconsistent and a violation of the fundamental law of nature, to preserve life: "No body can give more Power than he has himself; and he that cannot take away his own Life, cannot give another power over it."[120] Although Locke holds that slavery is justified only when there is a continuing state of war, it is difficult to reconcile this position with the moral principles of the state of nature.[121] The chapter

---

[120] IIT.23.

[121] For a discussion of the controversy surrounding Locke's various remarks on slavery, including African slaves and American Indians, see Grant, *John Locke's Liberalism*, p. 68.

on slavery does demonstrate the limits on governmental power and the need for consent and compact to attain legitimacy for governmental power. Also, by applying the moral principles of the state of nature to the extreme case of slavery and despotic government, the reader can see the importance of these principles to the process of forming a legitimate government.

The evolution from the state of nature poses several difficult questions for Locke. The peaceful and generally pleasant description of the state of nature does not include any clear reason why one should leave it. Even transgressions of the law of nature can be punished privately through calm reason and conscience. Why should one leave? The development of property is a major part of Locke's answer. Another question for Locke is the development of inequality in property when originally God "hath given the World to Men in common."[122] Locke needs to provide an explanation and justification for the existence of private property and for inequality. Filmer had argued that material possessions came under the sovereign's control through the original dispensation to Adam. In fact, Charles I had so declared. Neither Filmer's concept of property's originating in the absolute monarchy nor some kind of primitive communism is acceptable to Locke.

Locke begins his discussion by acknowledging that God did give the world to humanity in common but, he adds, for the reason "to make use of it to the best advantage of Life, and convenience."[123] Here is the key to Locke's theory of property. It is through man's use and his labour that Locke discovers how property is created:

> Though the Earth and all inferior Creatures be common to all Men, yet every Man has a *Property* in his own *Person*. This no Body has any Right to but himself. The *Labour* of his Body, and the *Work* of his Hands, we may say, are properly his. Whatsoever then he removes out of the State that Nature hath provided, and left it in, he hath mixed his *Labour* with, and joyned to it something that is his own, and thereby makes it his *Property*. It being by him removed from the common state nature placed it in, hath by this *labour* something annexed to it, that excludes the common right of other Men. For this *Labour* being the unquestionable property of the

---

[122] IIT.26.

[123] *Ibid.*

Labourer, no Man but he can have a right to what that is once joyned to, at least where there is enough, and as good left in common for others.[124]

This is called the **labour theory of value** by which private property is gained and property attains value. In this manner what was originally "in common with others, become my *Property*, without the assignation or consent of any body." Locke proceeds to make clear that the right to private property includes the value instilled through the labour of a paid employee: "the Turfs my Servent has cut...becomes my *Property*."[125]

During the early period of human development there is "little room for Quarrels or Contentions about Property so establish'd" because of the boundaries fixed by the law of nature:

> The same Law of Nature, that does by this means give us Property, does also *bound* that *Property* too.... As much as any one can make use of to any advantage of life before it spoils; so much he may by his labour fix a Property in. Whatever is beyond this, is more than his share, and belongs to others. Nothing was made by God for Man to spoil or destroy.[126]

Furthermore, there was such abundance that "there was still enough, and as good left; and more than the yet unprovided could use."[127] The development of property is natural to humans as humans and is inscribed by the law of nature: "From all which it is evident, that though the things of Nature are given in common, yet Man (by being Master of himself, and *Proprietor of his own Person*, and the actions or *Labour* of it) had still in himself *the great Foundation of Property*."[128]

Locke explains the great discrepancy in wealth through his labour theory of value. By cultivating land one actually increases "the common stock of mankind. For the provisions serving to the support of humane life, produced by one acre of enclosed and cultivate land, are... ten times more, than these, which are

---

[124] IIT.27.

[125] IIT.28.

[126] IIT.31.

[127] IIT.33.

[128] IIT.44.

yielded by an acre of Land, of an equal richnesse, lyeing wast in common."[129]
It is labour that puts the different value on land. Indeed, Locke places the great
chasm between the poverty of the New World, only recently explored, and
Europe on the value fixed by labour:

> There cannot be a clearer demonstration of any thing, than several Nations
> of the *Americans* are of this, who are rich in Land, and poor in all the
> Comforts of Life; whom nature having furnished as liberally as any other
> people, with the materials of Plenty, i.e. a fruitful Soil, apt to produce in
> abundance, what might serve for food, rayment, and delight; yet for want
> of improving it by labour, have not one hundredth part of the Conveniencies
> we enjoy: And a King of a large fruitful Territory there feeds, lodges, and is
> clad worse than a day Labourer in *England*.[130]

The conclusion, for Locke, is that labour determines property: "we see how *labour*
could make Men distinct titles to several parcels of it, for their private uses;
wherein there could be no doubt of Right, no room for quarrel."[131]

A major change occurs when money comes into use. The limit on accumulation provided by spoilage could now be escaped. As a consequence, it became
inevitable that possessions would be increased: "it is plain, that Men have agreed
to disproportionate and unequal Possession of the Earth, they having by a tacit and
voluntary consent found out a way, how a man may fairly possess more land than
he himself can use the produce of, by receiving in exchange for the overplus,
Gold and Silver, which may be hoarded up without injury to any one, these met-
alls not spoileing or decaying in the hand of the possessor."[132] Where once there
was little room for quarrels, there is now a need for government. The need has resulted from a natural evolution without any violation of the law of nature or of
the principles of human nature found in the state of nature.

Commentators have given a variety of interpretations to the relatively few
paragraphs on property. Without straining the text, Locke does seem to have

---

[129] IIT.37.

[130] IIT.41.

[131] IIT.39.

[132] IIT.50.

in mind three stages in the evolution of property. There is the initial stage where the individual "mixes his labour with" nature by plucking an apple or killing a deer in the forest. The next stage is the development of productivity by enclosing and cultivating land. At this point Locke discusses barter and exchange.[133] Finally, there is the development of money by "tacit and voluntary consent." With increased productivity and the advent of money, it became possible to have capital accumulation and a burst of economic activity, which Locke believes explains the differences in wealth between the New and Old Worlds.

In this three-part story the idea of mixing one's labour with nature has been transformed from a simply physical act to the accumulation of capital. His view of actual labourers, accordingly, was not a romantic one of hunters and peasants spending pleasant and leisurely days in a benevolent world. Indeed, to modern ears he sometimes sounds quite harsh. The Constitution of Carolina—partly composed by Locke—was clearly designed to protect the large landholders against the many poor with property. But, in his economic writings of the 1690s he did write against speculators who could cause harm to the poor; he suggested regulations to cut the working days for the poor; he advocated the confiscation of the land of proprietors in Virginia who did not farm at least once every three years. In a recommendation to the Board of Trade in 1697, Locke recommended forced labour at sea for the idle and unemployed, workhouses for orphans with boys working at 3 years of age and girls at 5, for 12 to 14 hours a day, and the serving of a "watery gruel." It is also true that Locke did personally many acts of charity and that he developed philosophically the right or entitlement of the needy to welfare.[134] All in all, it would be best to consider his economic attitude a mix of laissez faire, where individuals have free reign, and mercantilism, where government policy guides.[135]

---

[133] IIT.46.

[134] IT.42. It is possible to argue that Locke's views on the law of nature and on our natural social or community sense would support a governmental welfare policy. James Tully, *A Discourse on Property* (Cambridge: Cambridge University Press, 1980), ch. 6.

[135] Cranston, *John Locke: A Biography*, pp. 424*ff.*, 480*ff.*; John Marshall, *John Locke: Resistance, Religion and Responsibility* (Cambridge: Cambridge University Press, 1994), pp. 324–26; Mitchell, *Not By Reason Alone*, pp. 83*ff.*

Locke took great pride in his theory of property and with good reason.[136] His original natural law argument entails the recognition of the right to private property, a right which exists prior to government. Property, thus, became another way in which Locke could place limits on government. It is also true that no one since Aristotle had provided such a thorough defence of property. Locke believed, first, that he had demonstrated with the labour theory of value how private property became a right, independent of either a government grant or of an act of forceful appropriation. Second, he argued the case that private property enhanced material abundance or the "common stock" of mankind. Property was a positive good. Third, inequality was not automatically an evil but was a natural inevitability and led to more abundance. Fourth, in keeping with his Protestant and Puritan forebears, Locke saw value in the virtue of industriousness: the world was given by God for "the use of the Industrious and Rational...not to the Fancy or Covetousness of the Quarrelsom and Contentious."[137] For centuries the grudging recognition given to property-getting was that it was simply a dike against sin and greater intemperance. At best, it was a necessary vice. Fifth, as will be seen below, Locke held private property to be central to a stable political society, as did Aristotle.

Humanity has developed within the state of nature to the point where a political society and a government are necessary. By using the original premises of natural freedom and independence, of equality, and of the law of nature to preserve all mankind, Locke could logically criticize despotic power for being absolute and arbitrary and could demonstrate the origins of the right of property. He repeats this approach with parental power in chapter 6. Locke apparently wants to foreclose, again, the Filmerian opinion that political power can be modeled on parental power. He also wants to stress the value of the family to political society. The chapter, not surprisingly, is repetitive of much in the *First Treatise*.

By examining the nature of parental authority, Locke shows what is required for political authority. The members of the state of nature are independent and equal; the nature of the family is, as a consequence, radically different from Filmer's. Even though it is temporary, children are not born equal in reality, and parents have

---

[136] In a letter to the Rev. Richard King, Locke's cousin for whom he had great affection, Locke compares the *Two Treatises* to Aristotle and recommends the treatment of property done by the "anonymous" author. *The Works of John Locke*, 10 Vols. (London, 1823), pp. 1801, X, 305. Locke repeated his praise of the "anonymous" work in *Some Thoughts Concerning Reading and Study for a Gentleman* (1803).

[137] IIT.34.

"a sort of Rule and Jurisidiction over them."[138] Parents—or, if necessary, guardians—are obliged by the law of nature "*to preserve, nourish, and educate the Children,* they had begotten, not as their own Workmanship, but the Workmanship of their own Maker, the Almighty, to whom they were to be accountable for them."[139] This rule over children is consistent with the law of nature, Locke insists. The child has merely the potential to reason until the age of maturity has been reached. Once the capacity to reason has been reached—"one and twenty years and in some cases sooner"—then law, whether civil or natural law, can be followed. Freedom is dependent upon reason; law is dependent upon reason; and reason enables humans to follow a rule or a law, civil and natural. Freedom is possible only through law and reason; licence occurs when one follows the will or passion. In the latter case, there is no reason and one is at the level of the brute beast.

> The *Freedom* then of Man and Liberty of acting according to his own Will, is *grounded on* his having *Reason*, which is able to instruct him in that Law he is to govern himself by, and make him know how far he is left to the freedom of his own will. To turn him loose to an unrestrain'd Liberty, before he has Reason to guide him, is not the allowing him the priviledge of his Nature, to be free; but to thrust him out amongst Brutes, and abandon him to a state as wretched, and as much beneath that of a Man, as theirs.[140]

It is the duty of parents, mother and father, so to educate their children. If that purpose is violated, the right of rule over children is then terminated.[141] It is not the "bare *act of begetting*" that gives parental authority, but it is a duty assigned by God, the true Maker, to care for children so that they can attain reason and freedom.[142] When they have attained reason, authority can only be derived from consent and compact, but the family is the necessary condition for the development of reason and eventually the attainment of property. Locke concludes that the "*Society betwixt Parents and Children,* and the distinct Rights and Powers belonging respectively to them…is far different from a Politick Society."[143]

---

[138] IIT.55.

[139] IIT.56, 59.

[140] IIT.63.

[141] IIT.65.

[142] IIT.67.

[143] IIT.84.

More generally, Locke's conceptions of the family, marriage, and the role of women are derived from his oft repeated premises: "Man being born, as has been proved, with a Title to perfect Freedom, and an uncontrouled enjoyment of all the Rights and Privileges of the Law of Nature, equally with any other Man, or Number of Men in the World, hath by Nature a Power, not only to preserve his property, that is, his Life, Liberty, and Estate."[144]

It has already been made clear in the *First Treatise* that the family cannot be a type of society ruled by a father with an absolute and arbitrary power over women and children. The equality of women and children make Filmerian rule a violation of the natural law. It also follows that parental rule itself is terminated when the child reaches the age of reason and has title to perfect freedom. Both parents—or guardians—have a duty to care and educate their children for the purpose of developing their reason so that they may attain their freedom.[145] Finally, Locke's premises lead to equality in parental authority between mothers and fathers.[146]

Marriage, for Locke, is fundamentally a voluntary relationship based upon equality. It is a true contract that could be terminated by mutual consent, i.e., divorce.[147] This contract includes property for the wife, "whether Labour or Compact gave her a Title to it."[148] It could not be taken by the husband. It was common in the seventeenth century to speak of contractual "elements" in a marriage, but Locke has gone much further with an equal and full contractual relationship.[149]

---

[144] IIT.87.

[145] Locke's views of education of the young stressed reasoning rather than the accepted means of physical and psychological pressures to educate. Lawrence Stone, "Children and the Family," in Lawrence Stone, *The Past and the Present Revisted* (London: 1987), p. 315.

[146] For a general treatment of the family as a political model during the seventeenth century, see: Constance Jordan, "The Household and the State: Transformations in the Representation of an Analogy from Aristotle to James I," *Modern Language Quarterly* 54:3 (September, 1993), pp. 307–26; Gordon J. Schochet, "The Family and the Origins of the State in Locke's Political Philosophy," in *John Locke: Problems and Perspectives*, ed. John W. Yolton (London: Cambridge University Press, 1969).

[147] IIT.82.

[148] IIT.183.

[149] Mary Lyndon Shanley, "Marriage Contract and Social Contract in Seventeenth-Century English Political Thought," *Western Political Quarterly* 32 (1979), pp. 79–91; Melissa A. Butler, "Early Liberal Roots of Feminism: John Locke and the Attack on Patriarchy," *American Political Science Review* 72 (1989), pp. 135–50; Simmons, *The Lockean Theory of Rights*, pp. 167–221.

There are many passages in the *Two Treatises* where the equality of women seems to be an indisputable deduction from Locke's premises.[150] These are not sufficient, it appears, to provide for full political equality, even though the philosophical grounds have been prepared by Locke. In speaking of marriage, Locke states: "But the Husband and Wife, though they have but one common Concern, yet having different understandings, will unavoidably sometimes have different wills too; it therefore being necessary, that the last Determination, i.e., the Rule, should be placed somewhere it naturally falls to the Man's share, as the abler and the stronger."[151] Locke immediately proceeds in the same paragraph to reassert the equality and power of the wife. However much an advance on the times, the role of women has not been fully developed by Locke from his own premises.

Chapters 7, 8, and 9 describe the nature of political or civil society, the origins of such a society, and its major purposes. Locke begins with a contrast with what is not a political society. The family or conjugal society, as Locke calls it, is a voluntary compact with the twin ends or purposes (1) of procreation and care of children who have not reached the age of reason, and (2) of a mutual care and affection between the man and the woman. The conjugal bonds are, thus, quite strong. The political society, on the other hand, is also a voluntary compact, but it is constituted of members who are independent and have reached the age of reason. Locke lists the "chief end" of political society as "the preservation of property."[152] "Property," as already noted, includes, for Locke, "life, liberty, and estate."[153] He also often calls these "properties" powers, which is the formulation in the *Essay on Human Understanding*. The "chief end" of political society is not to attain material possessions, but to ensure the protection of these properties or powers or rights.

Another defining feature of a political society is that the power to judge and execute or to enforce the law of nature, which each has in the state of nature, is transferred to public institutions in the civil society: "Where-ever therefore any

---

[150] IT.29, 47, 55, 62.

[151] IIT.82.

[152] IIT.85.

[153] IIT.87.

number of Men are so united into one Society, as to quit every one his Executive Power of the Law of Nature, and to resign it to the publick, there and there only is a *Political, or Civil Society.*"[154] The public institutions Locke mentions are the legislature and the executive. Under the latter, Locke includes the judicial functions. Unless there are such institutions to make, judge, and enforce law, there is no political society, and the individuals are in the state of nature. An absolute monarchy does not have these institutions so that the "Subjects have an Appeal to the Law, and Judges to decide any Controversies, and restrain any Violence."[155] Here, the conditions faced by humans is much worse than in the state of nature because one person has all the power. Humans would be stupid to agree to such a relationship: "This is to think that Men are so foolish that they take care to avoid what Mischiefs may be done them by *Pole-Cats, or Foxes*, but are content, nay think it Safety, to be devoured by Lions."[156] A true political society, then, has the chief end of preserving our property, i.e., the great rights of life, liberty, and estate, and has the public institutions for making, judging, and enforcing law.

Chapter 8 answers two questions: How can a true political society come into existence? and What does history show us about this process? Consent is obviously the catalyst for inaugurating a political society. Locke begins the argument by restating his premises:

> Men being, as had been said, by Nature, all free, equal and independent, no one can be put out of his Estate, and subjected to the Political Power of another, without his own *Consent.* The only way whereby any one devests himself of his Natural Liberty, and *puts on the bonds of Civil Society* is by agreeing with other Men to joyn and unite into a Community, for their comfortable, safe, and peaceable living one amongst another, in a secure Enjoyment of their Properties, and a greater Security against any that are not of it. This any number of Men may do, because it injures not the Freedom of the rest; they are left as they were in the Liberty of the State of Nature. When any number of Men have so *consented to make one Community* or Government, they are thereby presently incorporated, and make *one Body Politick*, wherein the *Majority* have a Right to act and conclude the rest.[157]

---

[154] IIT.89.

[155] IIT.93.

[156] *Ibid.*

[157] IIT.95.

One becomes obliged by the bonds of political or civil society by agreeing with others; moreover, such obligation requires the "consent of every individual."[158] Consent obligates. In contrast with Hobbes, an explicit agreement is made to use the decision-making method of the majority.[159] It is the majority that will actually determine the precise form of government. We have agreed in the original act of consent with each other to abide by the majority decision. We agree to this because it is simply the most practical way for a community to come to a decision. Locke's common-sense explanation is that it is impossible to require unanimity for all decisions and, in any case, the majority by being the "greater force" will eventually determine it anyway.

There are two stages in the full process of establishing a political society and a government. This stage is the establishment of the community or civil society. The first stage requires that each individual consent to the purposes (life, liberty, and estate) and to the majority decision-making device. The second stage occurs when the majority actually establishes a government.

Locke admits that the actual historical record of how governments originate looks rather different: "I will not deny, that if we look back as far as History will direct us, towards the *Originals of Commonwealths*, we shall generally find them under the Government and Administration of one Man."[160] Even here, where there was "Fatherly Authority," there was still consent: "everyone in his turn growing up under it, tacitly submitted to it, and the easiness and equality of it not offending any one...."[161] In any case, no one "dream'd of Monarchy being *Jure Divino* [divine right]."[162]

Locke provides for both express and tacit consent. But, there is considerable ambiguity about what constitutes express consent. The seventeenth century did not have regular elections or universal suffrage. There were, to be sure, formal

---

[158] IIT.96.

[159] Hobbes does hint at the majority method when discussing the third right of the sovereign: "*No man can without injustice protest against the institution of the sovereign declared by the major part.* Thirdly, because the major part hath by consenting voices declared a sovereign; he that dissented must now consent with the rest; that is, be contented to avow all the actions he shall do, or else justly be destroyed by the rest." Michael Oakeshott, ed., *Leviathan* (New York: Collier, 1962), ch. 18, p. 136.

[160] IIT.105.

[161] IIT.110.

[162] IIT.112.

occasions where oaths of allegiance were taken or public prayers of support for a government were given. But, Locke simply does not explain what would count as express consent. He is more precise as to tacit consent:

> And to this I say, that every Man, that hath any Possession, or Enjoyment, of any part of the Dominions of any Government, doth thereby give his *tacit Consent*, and is as far forth obliged to Obedience to the Laws of that Government, during such Enjoyment, as any one under it; whether this his Possession be of Land, to him and his Heirs for ever, or a Lodging only for a Week; or whether it be barely travelling freely on the Highway; and in Effect, it reaches as far as the very being, of any one within the Territories of that Government.[163]

He quickly adds that tacit consent, also recognized by Hobbes, is only the obligation expected of a foreign visitor.[164] As Locke reasons, property ownership or traveling within a country tacitly obliges one to the laws of the country but the enjoyment of such privileges "*make not a Man a Member of that Society....*" Entering a political society requires a "positive Enjoyment, express Promise and Compact. This is that, which I think, concerning the beginning of Political Societies, and that *Consent which makes any one a Member* of any Commonwealth."[165] Express consent is necessary for forming a society, but what would count as express consent is simply not discussed. In general, Locke's intent is to provide an explanation of how governments can have political authority rather than a practical scheme for creating a society and government.

In Chapter 9 Locke now completes his answer to the question of why one should leave the relatively benign state of nature where each individual has full executive power to enforce the law of nature. In the state of nature "all being Kings as much as he, every Man his Equal, and the greater part no strict Observers of Equity and Justice, the enjoyment of the property he has in this state

---

[163] IIT.119.

[164] Hobbes had made a similar argument in the *Leviathan*: "But this promise may be either express, or tacit; express, by promise; tacit, by other signs. As for example, a man that hath not been called to make such an express promise, because he is one whose power perhaps is not considerable; yet if he live under their protection openly, he is understood to submit himself to the government....": Oakeshott, p. 505.

[165] IIT.122.

is very unsafe, very unsecure."[166] The protection of our lives, liberties, and estates, "which I call by the general Name, *Property*," has now become seriously threatened in the last stage of the state of nature.

There are three essential features lacking in the state of nature.

First, There wants an *establish'd*, settled known *Law*, received and allowed by common consent to be the Standard of Right and Wrong, and the common measure to decide all Controversies between them. For though the Law of Nature be plain and intelligible to all rational Creatures; yet Men being biassed by their Interest, as well as ignorant for want of study of it, are not apt to allow of it as a Law binding to them....

Secondly, In the State of Nature there wants a *known and indifferent Judge*, with authority to determine all differences according to the established Law. For every one in that state being both Judge and Executioner of the Law of Nature, Men being partial to themselves, Passion and Revenge is very apt to carry them too far....

Thirdly, In the state of Nature there often wants *Power* to back and support the Sentence when right, and to *give* it due *Execution*....[167]

The need for law, for a judiciary, and for an executive has now become obvious, and this convinces us to leave the state of nature. We are "quickly driven into society."[168] Accordingly, we give up the equality, liberty, and executive power enjoyed in the state of nature, but we do not give a blank check to the government. Locke carefully limits the power to the initial purposes or ends for entering the political society. He, then, turns in the next chapters, 10 through 15, to a description of the precise bounds to governmental powers and the proper institutional structure for exercising power.

Locke classifies forms of government according to who exercises the making of laws. If the community (the majority) makes the laws and appoints others to enforce it, this is designated a democracy. If the power of making laws is given to

---

[166] IIT.123.

[167] IIT.124, 125, 126.

[168] IIT.127. A few scholars have argued that Locke's state of nature and these three reasons for leaving are, in principle, identical to Hobbes's reasoning. Locke has simply made Hobbes more palatable through a gentler language. See Strauss, *Natural Rights and History* and Cox, *Locke on War and Peace*. See the counter arguments and bibliography provided by Grant, *John Locke's Liberalism*, pp. 8–9.

a few, it is called an oligarchy. If it is given to one, either elected or inherited, it is a monarchy. These three types can also be combined in various ways.

The key to Locke's rather prosaic classification is the legislative power. He calls it the "great instrument and means" used by governments for ruling their societies. To keep the use of this great power legitimate, Locke ties it to the law of nature: "the *first and fundamental positive Law* of all Commonwealths, *is the establishing of the Legislative Power*; as the *first and fundamental natural Law*, which is to govern even the Legislative itself, is *the preservation of the Society.*"[169] Apparently, a shift has taken place in Locke's emphasis on the end of the fundamental law of nature: in the state of nature Locke stresses the preservation of all mankind, but here the phrase is amended to refer only to the formal political society and every person in it. Later in the chapter, Locke, without explanation, does revert to his original formulation and say that the legislators' regulations must conform to the "*fundamental law of Nature* being *the preservation of Mankind.*"[170] In either case, Locke says the legislative power is supreme, and it is owed obedience.

The citizens' obligation is tempered by four great limitations. First, the exercise of governmental power cannot be arbitrary. There was no such justified power over individuals in the state of nature; therefore, no such grant could be given to a government in political society. The legislative power, it follows, "in the utmost Bounds of it, is limited *to the publick good* of the Society. It is a power, that hath no other end but preservation, and therefore can never have a right to destroy, enslave, or designedly to impoverish the Subjects."[171]

Second, the legislative power "*is bound to dispense Justice*, and decide the Rights of the Subject *by promulgated standing Laws and known Authoris'd Judges.*"[172] Promulgated standing laws require that the process of making laws should be public and general. These two features will check any attempt to rule by decree or to create laws that apply only to an unfavoured few. The requirement of known and authorized judges implies, but Locke does not expressly state, that the legislative and judicial functions should be separated.

---

[169] IIT.134.

[170] IIT.135.

[171] *Ibid.*

[172] IIT.136.

Third, the legislative or "*Supream Power cannot take* from any man any part of his *Property* without his own consent."[173] In practice, this means that governments cannot tax without "the Consent of the Majority, giving it either by themselves, or their Representatives chosen by them."[174] There is a consent required for forming a political society and forming a government, and there is a second consent required for taxation. The Declaration of Independence, proclaimed by the American Colonies in 1776, made famous the slogan "No Taxation without Representation." Ironically, Locke begins this famous paragraph by also stressing the obligation to pay taxes: "'Tis true, Governments cannot be supported without great Charge, and 'tis fit every one who enjoys his share of the Protection, should pay out of his Estate his proportion for the maintenance of it. But still it must be with his own Consent..."[175] Locke is making an argument in principle. At the time, not even all property holders had a right to vote for a representative.[176]

Fourth, "the *Legislative cannot transfer the Power of Making Laws* to any other hands."[177] The legislators that have been chosen and authorized to make laws for the society are responsible to the majority. The consequent trust and accountability cannot be transferred nor would "laws" made by any other body be properly authorized.[178] Locke does not relate this principle to the governance of the American Colonies.

These constitute the four great "*Bounds* which the trust that is put in them by the Society, and the Law of God and Nature, have *set to the Legislative* Powers of every Commonwealth, in all Forms of Government."[179] Locke has already emphasized that the very ends of government also entail limitations on the

---

[173] IIT.138.

[174] IIT.140.

[175] *Ibid.*

[176] M. Hughes, "Locke on Taxation and Suffrage," *History of Political Thought*, XI, 3 (1990), pp. 423–42.

[177] IIT.141.

[178] During the Depression in the 1930s, the Roosevelt Administration in the United States had a congressional act passed that delegated to a commission of employers and employees the power to regulate the coal industry. The commission regulated prices, wages, and other matters, and penalties were also enacted for any violations of the regulations. The U. S. Supreme Court declared the act unconstitutional and, among other grounds, used the Lockean prohibition of delegating legislative power: *Carter v. Carter Coal Co.*, 298 U.S. 238 (1936).

[179] IIT.142.

reach of government: our properties, i.e., lives, liberties, and estates, are protected. A legitimate government is defined as one that governs within the four limitations and that honours the protection of the great rights or properties of life, liberty, and estate.

What sort of institutions should a properly constituted political society or commonwealth have? Locke's strictures are simple and, given his earlier stress on limiting power, surprisingly broad and flexible. There is a legislative power to make the laws to which the legislators themselves are subject. There is a separate executive power for enforcing the laws. The judiciary function is part of this general power. Lastly, Locke has a separate federative function for the conduct of external or foreign relations.[180] Of the three powers, the legislative is naturally superior. But, Locke makes clear that a legislative body that has fundamentally violated the trust placed in it can be replaced by the people: "thus the *Community* may be said in this respect to be *always the Supream Power....*[181]

The executive power is not supreme, but it is a flexible and broad power. Locke gives the executive the power to call and dissolve the legislative. Moreover, in chapter 14, "Of Prerogative," the executive can act without specific legal authorization: "*Prerogative* can be nothing, but the Peoples permitting their Rulers, to do several things of their own free choice, where the Law was silent, and sometimes too against the direct Letter of the Law for the publick good: and their acquiescing in it when so done."[182] The executive is continuing and permanent whereas legislative sessions are not. Still, given the attempts of monarchs in the seventeenth century to deny the centrality of the legislature, it seems odd that Locke did not insist on regular parliaments.

Equally surprising is Locke's reliance on the executive to create a fairer and more equitable electoral system. Both Charles II and James II manipulated the electoral system and the franchise in order to get favourable majorities. Locke argues that legislators will always act in their own interests and want to keep the electoral system that gave them power; therefore, the executive will have to exercise its prerogative and create a new electoral system.[183] The dilemma is that

---

[180] IIT.143, 148.

[181] IIT.149.

[182] IIT.164.

[183] IIT.158.

the executive is as capable of acting in its own interest as is the legislative, which Locke himself cites in a later chapter.[184] The final arbiter when the legislative or executive violates its trust is the people. If these institutions should exercise their power arbitrarily or deprive the people of their rights, then "the Inconvenience is so great, that the Majority feel it, and are weary of it, and find a necessity to have it amended."[185]

Locke restates in chapter 15 the definitions he has already constructed of parental, political, and despotical power. This prepares the reader for his final section, chapters 16 through 19, where he discusses illegitimate governments and his theory of resistance.

In chapter 16, "Of Conquest," Locke applies his principles to the obedience exacted and due to a conqueror. There was throughout the seventeenth century a debate over the nature of English history. Locke and his Whig compatriots would see history as a series of institutions and evolving principles jointly supporting liberty against despotic rule. From this perspective, the monarchs were viewed as enemies to a libertarian tradition. In contrast, Filmer and many far less extreme thinkers saw the irrefutable evidence of a feudal system, which had grown, in part, from conquest. Since Locke's principles and political activity identify him within the Whig interpretation of history, he is anxious to dispute any claim that conquest can engender legitimate governments.

Locke presents two cases for analysis: Does conquest through an unjust war entail obligation among the conquered? Does conquest through a just war entail obligation? With respect to the first question, Locke is unequivocal: "That the *Aggressor*, who puts himself into the state of War with another, and *unjustly invades* another Man's right, *can*, by such an unjust War, *never* come to *have a right over the Conquered....*"[186] It does not matter if the force is by a robber or a Crown, there is no right to obedience.

The second question is more complicated. The conqueror in a just war gains no control over those that conquered with him. William the Conqueror in the Norman invasion of 1066 did not gain absolute dominion over his fellow Normans, even assuming that the invasion was just. The only dominion can be

---

[184] IIT.222.

[185] IIT.168.

[186] IIT.176.

over those who actually resisted and fought. The dominion does not extend to the rest of the people in the conquered society. It is a clear despotic power over those who fought, but this is justified since they "actually assisted, concurr'd, or consented to that unjust force...."[187] These people placed themselves in a state of war and forfeited their lives to the conquerors. Even in this case of a just war, however, Locke draws two striking limitations. There is no right to the conquered's possessions and no right of rule over the children and wives of those who actively fought. The only just claim that can be made by the conquerors is for reparations, and even this is limited to no more than "the destruction of a Years Product or two."[188] The conclusion is that no government can have a right to obedience unless consent has been freely given. For this to happen, the people must be "put in a full state of Liberty to chuse their Government and Governors, or at least till they have such standing Laws, to which they have by themselves or their Representatives, given their free consent, and also till they are allowed their due property...."[189] Locke apparently thinks that, in some sense, such consent was given after 1066.

Chapter 17 examines the question whether obedience is owed to an usurper, which is a kind of domestic conquest. The answer is obviously the same: there is no right to be obeyed unless the "People are at liberty to consent, and have actually consented to all, and confirm in him the Power he hath then Usurped."[190] One could claim, in principle, that the ascension of William and Mary to the throne in the Glorious Revolution was legitimated through consent, and this may well be what Locke wishes to recognize in this chapter.

The analysis of conquest or usurpation by Locke is, as usual, a logical demonstration rather than an historical examination or a practical scheme for establishing a political solution to a conflict. How far back in history can one return to nurture the wrong of an unjust conquest or usurpation never annulled by free consent? From which century should one begin to remember or forget the unjustified conquest or usurpation? What constitutes a majority freely consenting: Northern Ireland or the whole of Ireland? The concept of sovereignty, as advocated by Hobbes and others, was designed to foreclose such questions and their invitation to unrest.

---

[187] IIT.179.

[188] IIT.184.

[189] IIT.192.

[190] IIT.198.

For Locke, the grounds for self-determination are permanent; the unjustly conquered are never obliged to the conqueror or usurper: "They are free from any subjection to him…they are at liberty to begin and erect another to themselves."[191]

Although consent is a necessary criterion for limiting the claim of legitimacy by usurpers and conquerors, it is not sufficient for determining legitimacy. A tyranny is defined as a case of exercising power "beyond Right."[192] In addition to consent, then, to be legitimate governmental power must be directed by law, not by personal will, and used only for proper ends: "When the Governour, however intituled, makes not the Law, but his Will, the Rule; and his Commands and Actions are not directed to the preservation of the Properties of his People, but the satisfaction of his own Ambition, Revenge, Covetousness, or any other irregular Passion."[193] Locke warns that, tyranny so defined, is not limited to one-man rule: "'Tis a Mistake to think this fault is proper only to Monarchies; other Forms of Government are liable to it, as well as that."[194]

Since all forms of government, "whether those…are one or many," can deteriorate into a tyranny, there needs to be some recourse for the people. The practical problem is that whenever a person is aggrieved the initial response is to claim a right to resist. But, in Locke's words, this "will unhinge and overturn all Politics, and instead of Government and Order leave nothing but Anarchy and Confusion."[195]

To counter this argument, Locke provides several limitations to the citizens' using force as a response to unlawful force. First, the king's person is not to be harmed. Locke then adds a caveat aimed at justifying the execution of Charles II:

---

[191] IIT.185. The contrast with Hobbes is instructive. In the "Review and Conclusion" to the *Leviathan* Hobbes makes it clear that the conqueror should be obeyed—self-preservation so dictated and obliged: "I find by divers English books lately printed, that the civil wars have not yet sufficiently taught men in what point of time it is, that a subject becomes obliged to the conqueror; nor what is conquest; nor how it comes about, that it obliges man to obey his laws…(p. 504).

Thomas Flanagan has perceptively examined the various justifications used for appropriating land in the New World. Locke's theory of property has sometimes been improperly cited as a justification, but Locke's views of conquest would lead to an opposite conclusion: "The Agricultural Argument and Original Appropriation: Indian Lands and Political Philosophy," *Canadian Journal of Political Science* XXII (September, 1989), pp. 589–602.

[192] IIT.199.

[193] *Ibid.*

[194] IIT.201.

[195] IIT.203.

"unless he will be actually putting himself into a State of War with his People, dissolve the Government, and leave them to their defence, which belongs to every one in the State of Nature."[196] Second, force cannot be justifiably used when the remedy of law is available.[197] Third, the right of resistance should not be attempted unless there is a chance of success: "the Right to do so, will not easily ingage them in a Contest, wherein they are sure to perish."[198] There must be a majority of the people, or potentially so, who are threatened by the government's unlawful use of force before resistance is justified. Moreover, there must be a "long Train of Actings" that clearly demonstrate the arbitrary use of power. Then, resistance will be probable and justified.[199]

A theory of active resistance introduces the topic of dissolving and creating a new government. Dissolution of governments occurs in two major ways: when the legislative power is fundamentally altered and "when the Legislative, or the Prince [executive], either of them act contrary to their Trust."[200] The legislative can be altered when the government, in effect, misbehaves. Locke cites examples from the historical experience of England: the "Prince hinders the legislative from assembling in its due time, or from acting freely"; "the Electors, or ways of Election are altered, without the Consent…of the People"; "the delivery…of the People into the subjection of a Foreign Power"; the "Supream Executive Power, neglects and abandons that charge, so that the Laws already made can no longer be put in execution."[201] The last two actions refer to the secret treaty made by Charles II with France and to the flight of James II in 1688. In all of these cases, the people can erect a new legislative: "the *Society* can never, by the fault of another, lose the Native and Original Right it has to preserve it self, which can only be done by a settled Legislative."[202]

---

[196] IIT.205.

[197] IIT.207.

[198] IIT.208.

[199] For the historical background on Locke's theory of resistance, see: Julian H. Franklin, *John Locke and the Theory of Sovereignty: Mixed Monarchy and the Right of Resistance in the Political Thought of the English Revolution* (Cambridge: Cambridge University Press, 1978); Quentin Skinner, "The Origins of the Calvinist Theory of Revolution," in *After the Reformation: Essays in Honour of J. H. Hexter*, ed. Barbara C. Malament (Manchester: University of Manchester Press, 1980).

[200] IIT.221.

[201] IIT.215, 216, 217, 219.

[202] IIT.220.

The second way a government can be dissolved is when its actions are "contrary to their Trust." All actions that are contrary to the proper ends of government constitute a betrayal of trust. When the executive or legislative "endeavour to invade the Property of the Subject, and to make themselves or any parts of the Community, Masters, or Arbitrary Disposers of the Lives, Liberties, or Fortunes of the People."[203] Locke cites the various attempts by the King to alter the electoral system as a case in point.

Locke concludes the *Second Treatise* by defending this theory of resistance. First, he argues that his theory will not lay a "*ferment* for frequent *Rebellion.*" When people are truly miserable, they will revolt regardless of one's theory of government. "Let [the governments] be Sacred and Divine," Locke taunts, people will throw off the burden just as was done in the readers' own time.[204] Second, people do not revolt "upon every little mismanagement in publick affairs. *Great mistakes* in the ruling part, many wrong and inconvenient Laws, and all the *slips* of humane frailty will be *born by the People*, without mutiny or murmur."[205] Third, this theory of resistance will actually impede future rebellions because the government will be aware of the danger of acting unjustly. The people will dispose the government and erect a new one.

Locke is careful to define the unjust government as the rebel. At this time, the connotations to the word "rebellion" were mainly pernicious. Thus, Locke's rhetoric is to label the government the rebel and the people as the restorers of the just government. His final remarks are to reassert that the authority of the government is derived from the people who entrust the government with power and with the responsibility to rule by law and for the proper purposes. It follows that any controversy between the people and the government must be decided by the people: "Here 'tis like, the common Question will be made, *Who shall be Judge* whether the Prince or Legislative act contrary to their Trust?" Locke's famous reply is, "*The People shall be Judge.*"[206] The government is only the "Trustee or Deputy" of the people. The society or community formed by the individuals in the state of nature remains even though a government is dissolved; the people in

---

[203] IIT.221.

[204] IIT.224.

[205] IIT.225.

[206] IIT.240.

the society can judge, dissolve, and re-create a new government to perform in their behalf: "the People have a Right to act as Supream, and continue the Legislative in themselves, or erect a new Form, or under the old form place it in new hands, as they think good."[207]

Locke has developed a theory of revolution, but this word itself is seldom used by Locke. It does not have the commendatory connotations for Locke as it has come to have in later centuries after the American and French revolutions. He is careful to talk about restoring a government that has been dissolved or corrupted, and he calls the unjust government the rebel. In fact, he makes clear that the governmental structure he prefers is that of a "single hereditary Person," "an Assembly of Hereditary Nobility," and an "Assembly of Representatives chosen…by the People."[208] In short, a constitutional monarchy with a strong executive was his preferred option. The goal of a social revolution was far from his mind. Nevertheless, the legacy of trusting the people—"the people shall be judge"—endures.[209]

CONCLUSIONS

Locke's influence has been indisputably enormous. Philosophically, Locke follows Descartes's more original and greater contributions. Still, the impact on the Age of the Enlightenment of Locke's more empirical approach would be difficult to overstate. His epistemology supported religious toleration and political liberty. It strengthened Descartes's famous injunction to make ourselves lords and masters of nature. For Locke, too, humans are potentially autonomous and capable of mastery and self-mastery. In fact, God has created us so that it is our duty to utilize our freedom and reason. Locke's influence is properly called revolutionary.

Politically, Locke's influence increased throughout the next century. Locke and some of his radical contemporaries did not accomplish all that they wished in their own time, but it was their political language of consent, rights, majority, and revolution that came to reconstitute political discourse.

---

[207] IIT.243.

[208] IIT.213.

[209] In a brilliant essay John Dunn discusses the significance and meaning of trust in Locke: "Trust in the Politics of John Locke," in *Rethinking Modern Political Theory* (Cambridge: Cambridge University Press, 1985), ch. 2.

There are four areas where Locke's legacy is particularly clear: limited government, property, political structure, and revolution. First, Locke's theory of a limited government has been central to liberal thought in the West. His arguments are now clichés: a government is a trustee or delegate of the people; governments are justified by their protection of rights for all; governments are accountable, through consent, to the majority, and many more such maxims. Assessments of Locke's theory by contemporary scholars vary according to the degree of individualism assigned to Locke. Some have noted Locke's stress on the public good, equality, the family, the society and community, and the centrality of religion. Even Locke's notion of rights, these scholars argue, depends upon the duties humans have as creatures of God.[210] In this interpretation individualism is balanced with these other features, and the assessment of Locke is fundamentally favourable. The limited government legacy appears well grounded.

There are some who accentuate the individualistic and libertarian theme in Locke and praise Locke precisely for it.[211] In the main, though, it is the purported excessive individualism and its consequences that have lead to critical assessments of Locke. One such scholar has written:

> Rights as properties are to be conceived more as claims *against* others rather than as joint entitlements constituting a moral community. We have rights *against* others as we have duties *towards* one another. Rights as properties are option-rights rather than welfare-rights; they function to secure choice rather than direct us to what is choiceworthy.[212]

When the individual becomes the foundation for political obligations and for a government, so this group of scholars argues, the ties to the community and the sources of civic duties and responsibilities inevitably weaken. Self-interest trumps the common good and the social dimension to human existence. Here, the limited government legacy appears to be based upon philosophically-suspect grounds.

---

[210] Examples would be the works of John Dunn, Nathan Tarcov, and James Tully.

[211] Robert Nozick, *Anarchy, State, and Utopia* (New York: Basic Books, 1974).

[212] Edward Andrew, *Shylock's Rights: A Grammar of Lockian Claims* (Toronto: University of Toronto Press, 1988), pp. 19–20. See the careful analysis by Simmons, *The Lockean Theory of Rights*, pp. 222–306.

Contemporary criticisms of liberalism often refer to Locke or to a vague Lockean influence. It is, no doubt, true that an excessive stress on individual rights, rules, and procedures can lead to an equally excessive legalism that distorts or even blinds us to a clear perception of political reality. The dynamics of political reality—which are affected by economic, social, class, and gender considerations—come to be ignored, and there develops a singular concentration on institutional frameworks and legal rules. When this occurs, political reality is not viewed as an activity designed to ameliorate unsolvable problems. The single question 'Is it legal or legitimate or procedurally correct?' replaces other more valuable questions such as 'Is it good for humans?' and "Is it appropriate for this society, this culture, and this time?' It is as if politics were independent of most of the forces actually shaping political attitudes and behaviour.[213]

It would be ridiculous to lay all of these charges at the door of Locke and ignore the economic, political, and philosophic developments of the intervening centuries. But, a Lockean political philosophy is different from an Aristotelian one, and, as a guide for evaluation, there are questions that can be asked of Locke. Can we illuminate much about political society through the hypothesis of free individuals uniting and consenting to a contract? As an historical explanation, it is simply false, and as an explanation of the ties binding actual societies together, it fails. Has Locke, then, given us a very useful moral standard for judging political systems? Societies are constituted by language, history, and common deeds; yet, these features of human life have little role in Locke. Thus, even if there is a concern for the public good in Locke, many would argue that an excessive individualism causes this concept to atrophy into an aggregation of mutual interests. Can the continued existence of a society be based upon Lockean categories?

The second area where Locke's legacy is clear is his theory of property. There are those who view it as an unmitigated good for civilization and others who view it as a key source in the development of bourgeois capitalism and its many ills.[214]

---

[213] Stephen L. Newman has an excellent survey article: "Locke's *Two Treatises* and Contemporary Thought: Freedom, Community, and the Liberal Tradition," in Edward J. Harpham, *John Locke's 'Two Treatises of Government': New Interpretations* (Lawrence: University Press of Kansas, 1994), pp. 173–208.

[214] Nozick, *Anarchy, State and Utopia*, has strongly defended Locke. The contrary view is argued by: C. B. Macpherson, *The Political Theory of Possessive Individualism* (Oxford: Oxford University Press, 1962); Sheldon Wolin, *Politics and Vision* (Boston: Little, Brown, & Co., 1961), pp. 299–305; Neal Wood, *The Politics of Locke's Philosophy: A Social Study of 'An Essay Concerning Human Understanding'* (Berkeley: University of California Press, 1983) and *John Locke and Agrarian Capitalism* (Berkeley: University of California Press, 1984).

Most recognize that Lockean property rights have been instrumental in the economic growth of the West.[215] Some have gone further and argue that welfare rights can also be built upon Lockean foundations.[216]

The third area of Locke's legacy is the model of a legitimate political structure. We have already noted that it needs to be limited in power and based upon the consent of the majority. More specifically, Locke's arguments support the separation of the legislative and the executive, the necessity of a fair and equal electoral system, and, most importantly, the dominance of the legislative branch in creating public policy. Locke himself seemed generally satisfied with the traditional Whig conception of a constitutional monarchy. Moreover, he did not explain how the principle of consent could actually be operationalized. He certainly never advocated one person, one vote, or even universal male suffrage, and he was not a social egalitarian. Yet, his ideas by themselves were more radical and influential than he could himself realize.

The fourth area is the legacy of the right of revolution. Without this right, the primacy of "the people shall be judge" would be meaningless. This is a right grounded on the protestant confidence in the capacity of individuals to reason and act, and in a confidence in human ability to act jointly as a political society, independent of a government.

The wide variety of evaluations of Locke flow from two main sources. One source is the vagueness, inconsistencies, and tensions in the *Two Treatises*. There are many examples. The distinctions between express and tacit consent and their applications are vague, if not confused. The natural law tradition utilized in the *Two Treatises* seems to be inconsistent with the epistemology of the *Essay*. Then, there are the difficulties of relating the concept of property, understood as material possessions, with the rights of life, liberty, and health. There are also tensions implict in a political philosophy that insists upon containing, as examples, both equality and liberty, the individual and the majority, or limited government and the prerogative power. It is true that these tensions can be viewed as inescapable in a democratic system. Locke, however, does not acknowledge them nor does he ever imply that they are permanent unsolvable features.

---

[215] Albert O. Hirschman has written a perceptive and balanced study examining the philosophic roots of property rights: *The Passions and the Interests* (Princeton: Princeton University Press, 1977).

[216] In addition to James Tully, see: Martin Seliger, *The Liberal Politics of John Locke* (London: George Allen and Unwin, 1968); Karen Iversen Vaughn, *John Locke: Economist and Social Scientist* (Chicago: University of Chicago Press, 1980).

A second source of the many different interpretations of his work is that Locke's arguments can be interpreted as flowing from either secular foundations or from religious ones. Locke's philosophy was composed during the transition into modernity, and he coupled the expected theological approach of the age with rational and secular arguments. Even the *Essay* utilizes theological as well as modern rational and empirical arguments. One consequence of the dual foundations that he utilized has been the great fecundity of Locke's political thought. The contract approach within political philosophy is still producing a wealth of works.[217]

Given the contemporary plurality of plausible interpretations of Locke, it is to be expected that Locke's supposedly indisputable claim to being the philosophic founder of the United States has been questioned. The traditional view has been eloquently expressed by Nathan Tarcov:

> The document by virtue of which we Americans are an independent people, occupying our special station among the powers of the earth, derives its principles and even some of its language from the political philosophy of John Locke. Practically speaking, we can recognize in his work something like our separation of powers, our belief in representative government, our hostility to all forms of tyranny, our insistence on the rule of law, our faith in toleration, our demand for limited government, and our confidence that the common good is ultimately served by the regulated private acquisition and control of property as well as by the free development and application of science.[218]

Other contemporary scholars have argued that the republican tradition developing from the Renaissance with Machiavelli and others was a more powerful influence than the Lockean liberal tradition with its stress on natural law and rights. In contrast, the republican tradition focused on questions of citizenship, virtue, corruption, and

---

[217] Nozick, *Anarchy, State, and Society*; John Rawls, *A Theory of Justice* (Cambridge: Harvard University Press, 1971) and *Political Liberalism* (New York: Columbia University Press, 1993); David P. Gauthier, *Morals by Agreement* (Oxford: Clarendon Press, 1986).

[218] Nathan Tarcov, *Locke's Education for Liberty* (Chicago: University of Chicago Press, 1984), p. 1.

change.[219] The Founding Fathers in the United States certainly were not aware of two separate and distinct traditions. John Adams was the most knowledgeable and theoretical of the Founding Fathers, and he happily coupled together people in the republican tradition with the natural law tradition of Grotius, Locke, and Sydney. His contemporaries, too, would view all of these thinkers as complementary. The predominance of Locke's influence on American political culture and institutions, for good or ill, is very difficult to dispute.[220]

Modern liberal political philosophy is the legacy of both Hobbes and Locke. There are four great themes that characterize their thought and continue to permeate Western liberal thought. First, there is a new understanding of science, emanating from the Renaissance and characterized by the reductive model for explanations, new scientific methods, and a claim of real knowledge and certainty. Second, there develops an extraordinary confidence in humanity's capacity to know and even to master nature, society and the self. Third, the problems of politics are not simply to be mitigated, but they are to be permanently solved. Fourth, the autonomous individual, rather than society, is assumed to be the starting point for constructing a political system that would provide the grounds for legitimating and justifying a political system. Each of these themes pervade the thought of Hobbes and Locke, although, as we have seen, they come to quite different conclusions about many questions within political philosophy.

First, the new science, as was noted in the previous chapter, provides an essential break with the medieval world. How Descartes and Hobbes came to be founders of liberal rationalism has already been explained. Locke joins them as a founder.

---

[219] The republican tradition is explained in the following works: J. G. A. Pocock, *The Ancient Consitution and the Feudal Law* (Cambridge: Cambridge University Press, 1967); Gordon Wood, *The Creation of the American Republic, 1776–1787* (New York: W. W. Norton, 1969); Bernard Bailyn, *The Ideological Origins of the American Revolution* (Cambridge: Belknap Press, 1967). For criticisms of this interpretation: Joyce D. Appleby, *Capitalism and a New Social Order: The Republican Vision of the 1790s* (New York: New York University Press, 1984) and Thomas Pangle, *The Spirit of Modern Republicanism: The Moral Vision of the American Founders and the Philosophy of Locke* (Chicago: University of Chicago Press, 1988).

[220] Jerome Huyler, *Locke in American: The Moral Philosophy of the Founding Era* (Lawrence: University Press of Kansas, 1995); Michael P. Zuckert, *Natural Rights and the New Republicanism* (Princeton: Princeton University Press, 1994); Catherine H. Zuckert, *Natural Right and the American Imagination: Political Philosophy in Novel Form* (Savage, Md.: Rowman, Littlefield, 1990).

They were all well aware that a revolutionary break had occurred. Two features were particularly significant: the reductive model and the search for certainty. Knowledge was achieved by reducing complex matters to their constituting parts. The reductive model is central to the new natural and social sciences, to use modern terminology. The new methods, whether they emphasized the rational approach of Descartes and Hobbes or the observation and experiment approach of Locke, were designed to provide "real" knowledge, and this new science with its knowledge was gleefully contrasted with the "science" of Aristotle and the schoolmen.[221]

Second, through the new science, its methods, and the resulting knowledge, our reason frees us from the bands of the past and of custom so that we can exercise a far greater control and even mastery over nature, society, and ourselves. An extraordinary mood of confidence and power permeates the works of Descartes, Hobbes, and Locke. We can shape and control the future. Recall the famous boast of Descartes that we can "make ourselves, as it were, the lords and masters of nature."[222] Hobbes's introduction to the *Leviathan* reflects this mood: human knowledge and power are parallel with God's. Locke, less dramatically perhaps, also has the same extraordinarily confident attitude toward the future, once we apply the new epistemology and its methods: "We are born with faculties and powers capable almost of any thing, such at least as would carry us farther than can easily be imagined: but it is only the exercise of those powers, which gives us ability and skill in any thing, and leads us towards perfection."[223] With these faculties and power, claims Locke in the *Essay*, we can advance "Man's Progress" and attain a "profitable Knowledge."[224]

Descartes's, Hobbes's, and Locke's confident claims about attaining "real" knowledge through the new science—whether the stress is on geometry, logic, or experiment and observation—applies to human nature as well as to society and physical reality. Both Hobbes and Locke, we should remember, advocate a true

---

[221] For the relation between Descartes and Locke, see Schouls, *Reasoned Freedom: John Locke and Enlightenment*, pp. 27–37 and *The Imposition of Method: A Study of Descartes and Locke* (Oxford: Oxford University Press, 1980).

[222] *Discourse on Method*, Part 6, in *The Philosophical Writings of Descartes*, 3 Vols., trans. John Cottingham, Robert Stoothoff, and Dugald Murdoch (Cambridge: Cambridge University Press, 1985), Vol. I, p. 143.

[223] *The Conduct of the Understanding*, section 4 in *The Locke Reader*, ed. John W. Yolton (Cambridge: Cambridge University Press, 1977), pp. 173–74.

[224] Bk. IV, xii, 12.

science of morality. Locke concludes his recommendation on educating the young with these words: "Teach him to get a Mastery over his Inclinations, and submit his Appetite to Reason."[225] There is a possible control and mastery over ourselves far greater than that sought by the early Calvinist and Puritan theologians with their schemes of self-imposed rules and regulations for a righteous life.

Third, Hobbes and Locke both address political reality as a set of problems to be solved. With their philosophic stance, it is first necessary to be clear about the fundamental nature of political reality. What are the key constituting ingredients of political life? Hobbes finds the great drive for self-preservation and the passions plus a calculating self-interest as chief factors. Locke finds natural equality and liberty plus the great rights. In both cases, the method is to go behind culture and civilization and to discover the original, natural, and basic parts that will form the whole. Both thinkers provide solutions to politics. The urbane pessimism of the ancients has not survived. There is a solution, supported by science and knowledge, and confidently asserted. The problem of achieving order with legitimacy and other traditional problems are solvable.

Fourth, the autonomous individual becomes the focus for creating a political system and for evaluating its claim to legitimacy. The epistemologies of Hobbes and Locke support the model of the autonomous and free individual. It is the individual's own capacities that provide knowledge. One, in fact, must not rely upon the authority of the Church, state, or tradition. There is an epistemic autonomy supporting political autonomy for the individual. Hobbes's *Leviathan*, as described earlier, is replete with witty and snide comments aimed at debunking the authorities of his time. Each person can rely on his or her own capacity to reason. Locke, more judicious with his comments, does the same. In the *Essay*, Locke calls on humans to think for themselves and employ their own reason.[226] With revolutionary fervour he calls for an individual to "dare Shake the foundation of all his past Thoughts and Actions."[227] The individual's capacity to reason, guided by the epistemology of the *Essay*, and the power of freedom to decide and act make it possible for humans to create a political system regardless of custom and tradition. The prerequisite for an individual to enter a political compact is to become a

---

[225] John W. Yolton and Jean S. Yolton, eds., *John Locke: Some Thoughts Concerning Education* (Oxford: Clarendon Press, 1989), paragraph 200.

[226] Bk. I, iii, 23.

[227] Bk. I, iii, 25.

"Master of himself, and his own Life."[228] As one scholar of Locke writes, "men begin to feel that the whole world is new for everyone and we are all absolutely free of what has gone before."[229] The autonomous individual as a knower and maker is primary; a society is derivative. Rights thus take precedence over duties, just as the individual is prior to society. Some have called this model of political reality, political atomism: individuals have become the base particles that compose society and government.[230]

Political liberalism in later centuries develops into two streams, both of which can cite originating passages from Hobbes and Locke. In the main, however, Hobbes and Locke belong to the *rights* stream of political philosophy. For this stream, individual rights are the source of legitimacy and the referee for all political discourse and disagreements. A government is illegitimate where rights are consistently violated; political decisions are justified according to the consequences for human rights. Such attitudes permeate our political culture.[231]

Another stream is *utilitarian* and is associated with Jeremy Bentham (1748–1832) and John Stuart Mill (1806–1873). For thinkers in this stream rights are philosophically unsupportable. Rights are not truly basic. For utilitarians, humans are viewed as creatures moved by pain and pleasure who seek happiness. Thoughts and actions are evaluated from the standpoint of their utility in mitigating pain and enhancing pleasure, for such constitutes the happiness all seek. Such ideas can also be found in Hobbes and Locke, as we have seen, but for Hobbes and Locke these ideas are inscribed within a larger philosophical context.

Regardless of the stream, liberalism retained its stress on the four great themes. At the height of the Age of the Enlightenment, when liberal rationalism was predominate in political thought, an original thinker appeared who attacked many of the essential tenets of liberalism and started another branch of political philosophy through focusing on the community, Jean-Jacques Rousseau.

---

[228] IIT.172.

[229] Laslett, *Two Treatises of Government*, "Introduction," p. 97.

[230] Charles Taylor has written an influential article explaining and criticizing this perspective: "Atomism," in *Philosophy and the Human Sciences*, Vol. II (Cambridge: Cambridge University Press, 1985), pp. 187–210.

[231] There are scores of books that study the long-term effects of rights-liberalism on contemporary political culture. Two of the best are Ronald Beiner, *What's the Matter with Liberalism?"* (Berkeley: University of California Press, 1992), and Mary Ann Glendon, *Rights Talk: The Impoverishment of Political Discourse* (New York: Free Press, 1993).

SUGGESTIONS FOR FURTHER READING

For the only two book-length biographies see Cranston (1950) (the most reliable) and Fox-Bourne (1876). Laslett's edition of *Two Treatises* and Wootton's edition of *John Locke: Political Writings* are valuable recent studies on the complicated and often secretive details that have obscured Locke's political activities and writings. Ashcraft's *Revolutionary Politics and Locke's 'Two Treatises of Government'* (1986) is a fascinating study on Locke's thought and life.

Yolton, *John Locke: Problems and Perspectives*, Ashcraft, *John Locke: Critical Assessments*, 4 volumes, and Harpham, *John Locke's 'Two Treatises of Government': New Interpretations* are collections of articles on interpretations of Locke.

For secondary literature on Locke's epistemology and moral theory see Yolton's various works that attempt to understand and explain Locke. Woolhouse and Jenkins are more critical short studies. Ayers works are encyclopedic in coverage. Colman provides a definitive study of Locke's moral theory, and Schouls is also useful.

For serious study of Locke's political philosophy three recent works are necessary. Grant, Simmons, and Ashcraft have extensive bibliographies, discuss the massive secondary literature, and are careful treatments of Locke's writings. Yolton, *John Locke: An Introduction*, and Dunn, *Locke* are two short works providing excellent introductions to Locke. Parry and Lloyd-Thomas are analytical treatments of Locke's political thought.

Dunn, Mitchell, and Marshall defend the theological foundation to Locke's thought.

Strauss, *Natural Right and History* is an interpretation linking Locke to Hobbes and Cox and Pangle also develop this position, whereas Grant, Yolton, Simmons, and Ashcraft provide criticisms.

Macpherson and Wood are highly critical approaches to Locke's theory of property and Nozick provides a highly laudatory approach. Tully, Vaughn, Seliger and Ryan are particularly helpful in sorting out the arguments.

Jones, Trevelyan, and Hill are useful for social and intellectual background, as are the articles in *The Cambridge History of Political Thought*, edited by Burns. The works listed in the chapter on Hobbes are also applicable.

Works

Abrams, Philip, ed. *Two Tracts on Government*. Cambridge: Cambridge University Press, 1967.

De Beer, Esmond S., ed. *The Correspondence of John Locke*. 8 Vols. Oxford: Clarendon Press, 1976–85.

411

Laslett, Peter, ed. *Two Treatises of Government.* 2nd ed. Cambridge: Cambridge University Press, 1967.

Nidditch, Peter H., ed. *An Essay Concerning Human Understanding.* Oxford: Clarendon Press, 1975.

Tully, James H., ed. *A Letter Concerning Toleration.* Indianapolis: Hackett, 1983.

von Leyden, W., ed. *Essays on the Law of Nature.* Oxford: Clarendon Press, 1954.

Wootton, David, ed. *John Locke: Political Writings.* London: Penguin, 1993.

The Works of John Locke. 12th ed. 9 Vols. 1824.

Yolton, John W., and Jean S. Yolton, eds. *John Locke: Some Thoughts Concerning Education.* Oxford: Clarendon Press, 1989.

Commentaries

Aaron, Richard I. *John Locke.* 3rd ed. Oxford: Oxford University Press, 1971.

Andrew, Edward. *Shylock's Rights: A Grammar of Lockian Claims.* Toronto: University of Toronto Press, 1988.

Appleby, Joyce D. *Capitalism and a New Social Order: The Republican Vision of the 1790s.* New York: New York University Press, 1984.

Ashcraft, Richard. *Locke's Two Treatises of Government.* London: Allen & Unwin, 1987.

———. *Revolutionary Politics and Locke's Two Treatises of Government.* Princeton: Princeton University Press, 1986.

———. ed. *John Locke: Critical Assessments.* 4 Vols. New York: Routledge, 1991.

Ayers, Michael. *Locke.* 2 Vols. London: Routledge, 1991.

Bailyn, Bernard. *The Ideological Origins of the American Revolution.* Cambridge: Belknap Press, 1967.

Beiner, Ronald. *What's the Matter with Liberalism?* Berkeley: University of California Press, 1992.

Bennett, John F. *Locke, Berkeley, Hume.* Oxford: Oxford University Press, 1971.

Colman, John. *John Locke's Moral Philosophy.* Edinburgh: Edinburgh University Press, 1983.

Cox, Richard H. *Locke on War and Peace.* Oxford: Clarendon Press, 1960.

Cranston, Maurice. *John Locke: A Biography.* London: Longmans, 1966.

Dunn, John. *Locke*. New York: Oxford University Press, 1984.

———. *The Political Thought of John Locke: An Historical Account of the Arguments of the 'Two Treatises of Government.'* Cambridge: Cambridge University Press, 1969.

Fox-Bourne, H. R. *The Life of John Locke*. 2 Vols. London: King, 1876.

Franklin, Julian H. *John Locke and the Theory of Sovereignty: Mixed Monarchy and the Right of Resistance in the Political Thought of the English Revolution.* Cambridge: Cambridge University Press, 1978.

Glendon, Mary Ann. *Rights Talk: The Impoverishment of Political Discourse*. New York: Free Press, 1993.

Gough, J. W. *John Locke's Political Philosophy: Eight Studies*. Oxford: Oxford University Press, 1950.

Grant, Ruth W. *John Locke's Liberalism*. Chicago: University of Chicago Press, 1987.

Harpham, Edward J., ed. *John Locke's 'Two Treatises of Government': New Interpretations.* Lawrence: University Press of Kansas, 1992.

Hirschman, Albert O. *The Passions and the Interests*. Princeton: Princeton University Press, 1977.

Huyler, Jerome. *Locke in American: The Moral Philosophy of the Founding Era.* Lawrence: University Press of Kansas, 1955.

Jenkins, John L. *Understanding Locke*. Edinburgh: Edinburgh University Press, 1983.

Lamprecht, S. P. *The Moral and Political Philosophy of John Locke*. New York: Columbia University Press, 1918.

Lloyd Thomas, D. A. *Locke on Government*. London: Routledge, 1995.

Lowe, F. J. *Locke on Human Understanding*. New York: Routledge, 1995.

Macpherson, C. B. *The Political Theory of Possessive Individualism*. Oxford: Oxford University Press, 1962.

Marshall, John. *John Locke: Resistance, Religion and Responsibility*. Cambridge: Cambridge University Press, 1994.

Minogue, Kenneth. *The Liberal Mind*. New York: Random House, 1968.

Mitchell, Joshua. *Not by Reason Alone*. Chicago: University of Chicago Press, 1993.

Morgan, Edmund. *Inventing the People: The Rise of Popular Sovereignty in England and America*. New York: Norton, 1988.

Nozick, Robert. *Anarchy, State, and Utopia.* New York: Basic Books, 1974.

Pangle, Thomas. *The Spirit of Modern Republicanism: The Moral Vision of the American Founders and the Philosophy of Locke.* Chicago: University of Chicago Press, 1988.

Parry, Geraint. *John Locke.* London: Allen & Unwin, 1978.

Rapaczynski, Andrzej. *Nature and Politics: Liberalism in the Philosophies of Hobbes, Locke, and Rousseau.* Ithaca: Cornell University Press, 1987.

Ryan, Alan. *Property and Political Theory.* Oxford: Basil Blackwell, 1984.

Schouls, Peter A. *The Imposition of Method: A Study of Descartes and Locke.* Oxford: Oxford University Press, 1980.

———. *Reasoned Freedom: John Locke and Enlightenment.* Ithaca: Cornell University Press, 1992.

Seliger, Martin. *The Liberal Politics of John Locke.* London: George Allen and Unwin, 1968.

Simmons, A. John. *The Lockean Theory of Rights.* Princeton: Princeton University Press, 1992.

Strauss, Leo. *Natural Rights and History.* Chicago: University of Chicago Press, 1953.

Tarcov, Nathan. *Locke's Education for Liberty.* Chicago: University of Chicago Press, 1984.

Tully, James. *A Discourse on Property.* Cambridge: Cambridge University Press, 1980.

Vaughn, Karen Iversen. *John Locke: Economist and Social Scientist.* Chicago: University of Chicago Press, 1980.

Wolin, Sheldon. *Politics and Vision.* Boston: Little, Brown & Co., 1961.

Wood, Gordon. *The Creation of the American Republic, 1776–1787.* New York: W. W. Norton, 1969.

Wood, Neal. *John Locke and Agrarian Capitalism.* Berkeley: University of California Press, 1984.

———. *The Politics of Locke's Philosophy: A Social Study of 'An Essay Concerning Human Understanding.'* Berkeley: University of California Press, 1983.

Woolhouse, R. S. *Locke.* Brighton: Harvester Press, 1983.

Yolton, John W. *John Locke: An Introduction.* New York: Basic Blackwell, 1985.

————. *John Locke and the Way of Ideas*. Oxford: Oxford University Press, 1956.

————. *Locke and the Compass of Human Understanding*. Cambridge: Cambridge University Press, 1970.

————, ed. *John Locke: Problems and Perspectives*. London: Cambridge University Press, 1969.

Zuckert, Catherine H. *Natural Right and the American Imagination: Political Philosophy in Novel Form*. Savage, Md.: Rowman, Littlefield, 1990.

Zuckert, Michael P. *Natural Rights and the New Republicanism*. Princeton: Princeton University Press, 1994.

Intellectual Background

Burgess, Glen. *The Politics of the Ancient Constitution: An Introduction to English Political Thought, 1603-1642*. University Park: Pennsylvania State University Press, 1992.

Burns, J. H., ed. *The Cambridge History of Political Thought: 1450-1700*. Cambridge: Cambridge University Press, 1991.

Daly, James. *Sir Robert Filmer and English Political Thought*. Toronto: University of Toronto Press, 1979.

Greenleaf, W. H. *Order, Empiricism and Politics: Two Traditions of English Political Thought*. Oxford: Oxford University Press, 1964.

Hill, Christopher. *The World Turned Upside Down: Radical Ideas During the English Revolution*. London: Temple Smith, 1972.

Jones, J. R. *Country and Court: England, 1658–1714*. Cambridge: Harvard University Press, 1978.

Laslett, Peter, ed. *Patriarcha and other Political Works of Sir Robert Filmer*. Oxford: Blackwell, 1949.

Plumb, J. H. *The Growth of Political Stability in England, 1675–1725*. London: Macmillan, 1967.

Pocock, J. G. A. *The Ancient Constitution and the Feudal Law*. Cambridge: Cambridge University Press, 1967.

Rabb, T. K. *The Struggle for Stability in Early Modern Europe*. Oxford: Oxford University Press, 1975.

Schochet, Gordon J. *Patriarchalism in Political Thought*. Oxford: Blackwell, 1975.

Skinner, Quentin. *The Foundations of Modern Political Thought.* Vol. 2. *The Age of Reformation.* Cambridge: Cambridge University Press, 1978.

Trevelyan, G. M. *England under the Stuarts.* London: Methuen, 1965.

Tuck, Richard. *Natural Rights Theories: Their Origins and Development.* New York: Cambridge University Press, 1979.

Western, J. R. *Monarchy and Revolution: The English State in 1680s.* London: Blandford Press, 1972.

JEAN-JACQUES ROUSSEAU

Between 1712 and 1778 Jean-Jacques Rousseau rose to great fame and notoriety as the author of the most popular novel of the century, the *New Héloise*, and one of the few classics in political philosophy, the *Social Contract*. After his death, the leaders of the new French Revolution paid homage to their philosophic patron by disinterring his body, placing it on a magnificent funeral carriage, and bringing it to Paris to be buried along side Voltaire in the Panthéon. It has always been a source of controversy that Robespierre, a fervent believer in Rousseau and the leader of the Terror in the final stages of the Revolution, claimed to be realizing Rousseau's political vision. To this day the dispute continues: Was Rousseau a totalitarian or a liberal?[1] That Rousseau could still elicit such a controversy is befitting a person who lived a life of passion, contradiction, daring, and originality.

There was a great personal contrast between Rousseau and John Locke. Indeed, Rousseau's writings were a critique of, and an alternative to, the great liberal concepts of Hobbes and Locke. The liberal conception of a limited government based upon a political society of freely-consenting individuals was, for Rousseau, fundamentally harmful to humanity. Although Rousseau would use the categories of consent, contract, and liberty, his meanings were dramatically different from Hobbes and Locke. In general, Rousseau found modern liberal thought atomistic, egocentric, and excessively individualistic. In his eyes, a wrong turn had been taken because of a misunderstanding of human nature. Humans should not be

---

[1] John Chapman, *Rousseau—Totalitarian or Liberal?* (New York: Columbia University Press, 1956). For an examination of Rousseau's influence on the French Revolution, see: Carol Blum, *Rousseau and the Republic of Virtue: The Language of Politics in the French Revolution* (Ithaca, N.Y.: Cornell University Press, 1986), and Joan McDonald, *Rousseau and the French Revolution: 1762–1791* (London: University of London Press, 1965).

viewed as egocentric calculators who were, in principle at least, independent of society. Rather, humans were creatures of will, capable of perfection, and in need of a communal home. He once said of his fellow Genevans that they were bourgeois and not citizens. Their self-identity, in short, came from being in an economic middle class rather than from being in a community of equal citizens.

Perhaps the most striking difference from liberal thought was Rousseau's goal for politics. A liberal political system is primarily designed to provide liberty by protecting individual rights. Liberty enables individuals to be relatively untrammeled and to pursue their lives according to their individual abilities and purposes. Rousseau's political goal, in contrast, is *liberté*, translated as freedom, or more precisely, moral liberty.[2] Freedom and virtue are not separate for Rousseau; the goal of freedom is the highest state humans can achieve. His aim, thus, is the full realization of our individual natures. In contrast, the concept of liberty does not mean or entail that the individual will be either virtuous and fully realized or lacking in virtue and incompletely realized. The full meaning of Rousseau's use of freedom will await the description of his writings, but the difference from liberty can be seen in many phrases of Rousseau's, not found in Locke, such as the "transformation of human nature" or "perfection" or "realization of the self." However one assesses Rousseau and his influence, no one questions his originality in creating for modernity an alternative vision of political life to the liberal individualism of Hobbes and Locke.

Rousseau's personal life is an integral part of his political philosophy. This is not because he was particularly involved in political activity, as was Locke, but because he insisted that the personal and psychological dimensions were not to be distinguished from the political. The dynamics of the psyche were integrated with the dynamics of the political society. Rousseau wrote three biographical works, published after his death, *Confessions, Rousseau Judge of Jean-Jacques* or *The Dialogues,* and *The Reveries of a Solitary Walker.* The *Confessions,* his largest work, contains no confessions and is a testament to personal authenticity rather than to traditional virtues. All three works are justifications and even flauntings of his life, mistakes and all. These biographical writings are fascinating in themselves, but, more importantly, they indicate his insistence

---

[2] The English language has the words "liberty" and "freedom"; the French language has only the word "*liberté.*" The concept of freedom has traditionally been associated with religion and liberty with politics. See chapter 4 on Saint Augustine.

that his own extreme psychological pains and strivings uniquely equipped him to probe human nature. He begins the *Confessions* as follows:

> I have resolved on an enterprise which has no precedent, and which, once complete, will have no imitator. My purpose is to display to my kind a portrait in every way true to nature, and the man I shall portray will be myself.
>
> Simply myself, I know my own heart and understand my fellow man. But I am made unlike any one in the whole world. I may be no better, but at least I am different. Whether Nature did well or ill in breaking the mould in which she formed me, is a question which can only be resolved after the reading of my book.[3]

His has been, he claims, a unique life and, at the same time, the source of all his understanding of human nature and politics.[4]

A description of Rousseau's youth up to the age of 16 (1712–1728) has understandably tempted scholars to resort to psychological explanations for his later behaviour and for his political philosophy. Regardless of the pertinence of such personality factors, Rousseau's analysis of modernity and his attempts to present an alternative vision are of lasting philosophic importance.

ROUSSEAU: His Life and Works

Jean-Jacques Rousseau was born, in 1712, in Geneva, Switzerland. His mother died a few days after his birth. His father was a watchmaker and sometimes a dance master, though not a very good provider in either profession. He was affectionate, highly emotional, and a bit of a romantic. He often read popular stories to the young, highly imaginative Jean-Jacques. One work was a French translation of Plutarch's *Lives*, which gave Rousseau a permanent and romantic attachment to the ancient Roman Republic. Rousseau was actually raised in his early years by an aunt. His father's sporadic attachment was broken when Rousseau was ten years old. In 1722, on some question of honour, his father was involved in a duel and had to flee Geneva to escape arrest. Rousseau was then raised by a Protestant pastor, Pastor Lambercier, for a time. In the *Confessions* he recounts

---

[3] Rousseau, *The Confessions*, trans. J. M. Cohen (New York: Penguin Books, 1953), p. 17.

[4] The best work that examines Rousseau's political philosophy through the *Confessions* is by Christopher Kelly, *Rousseau's Exemplary Life: The 'Confessions' as Political Philosophy* (Ithaca, N.Y.: Cornell University Press, 1987).

being spanked by the Pastor's sister and, as he tells the story, he developed a lasting taste for maschochism as a consequence. He remembered this time with the Pastor's family, however, as he did the early years with his father, in idyllic terms: "The manner of life... suited me so well that if only it had lasted longer it could not have failed to fix my character for ever. It was founded on the affectionate, tender, and peaceable emotions."[5] A malleable nature being formed by a society is a recurring theme in Rousseau. He was apprenticed into several trades, none of which he liked. He craved affection but also prized his independence. One day, March 14, 1728, he found himself outside the gates of the city just as they closed shut. Rather than face the punishment of his master, he simply left Geneva.

For the next 14 years (1728–1742) Rousseau traveled throughout Europe. He lived with peasants and attended royal courts. But, his greatest experience was his introduction to Mme. de Warens who was a beautiful, recent convert to Catholicism. She took him into the Church and, after a time, introduced him to sex. He became part of a *ménage à trois* and a devoted member of her "family." He called her *Maman* and she called him *petit*, a matter of some significance in psychiatry. He traveled, sporadically, throughout Europe and had myriad jobs, from secretary to music instructor to interpreter. He also educated himself by reading widely. But, his attachment to Mme. de Warens, who was only 12 years his senior, remained the most intense attachment of his life. He wrote of it, too, in idyllic terms just a few weeks before his death: "There is not a day when I do not remember with joy and tenderness this unique and brief time of my life, when I was fully myself, without mixture and without obstacle, and when I can truly say I lived."[6] In 1742, his need for independence lead him to Paris where he hoped to make his name through a musical career and by introducing his new system of musical notation.

In Paris he was alone again and, initially, unsuccessful. He was dismissed as the secretary to the French ambassador to Venice, was unsuccessful with his musical career, and had to become a copier of musical scores. He did meet an attractive, uneducated laundress, Thérèse Levasseur. They lived in a common-law

---

[5] *Confessions*, Bk. I, pp. 24–25.

[6] Jean-Jacques Rousseau, *The Reveries of a Solitary*, trans. John Gould Fletcher (New York: Franklin, 1971), Tenth Promenade, p. 194. This work is also translated as *The Reveries of a Solitary Walker*.

relationship for most of their lives, relatively faithful to each other, and at the close of his life in 1768 they married. They had five children; at birth, all of them were placed in an orphanage. He defends the nobility of his actions in the *Confessions*, but his sense of shame is easy to detect.[7] In addition to a new mistress, Rousseau became acquainted with some of the great figures of the time. Two of these *philosophes*, Diderot and d'Alembert, created the *Encyclopédie*, which would reflect the new science and knowledge of the Enlightenment, and Rousseau was asked to write for it. Although still unknown, he had become a member of an influential and famous group of intellectuals or *philosophes*.

Rousseau's greatest achievements were produced during the period 1749–1762. During these incredibly productive years, he wrote his most famous works, *New Héloise* (1760), *Social Contract* (1762), and another novel *Emile* (1762). He also had a minor success with an opera, *Devin du Village*, and was even offered a pension from the King, which he refused. But it was his new political and philosophic writings that changed his life and gained him lasting fame.

Rousseau's explanation of the catalyst for this new outburst of writing is extraordinary. He describes a conversion experience that occurred while he was traveling on the road to Vincennes where he would see his friend Diderot who was imprisoned there. Rousseau had taken along a publication to read. In it he discovered that the Academy of Dijon had advertised for a prize essay on the question: "Has the revival of the arts and sciences done more to corrupt or to purify morals?" Upon reading these words, Rousseau "beheld another world and became another man," as he writes in the *Confessions*.

> If ever an experience resembled sudden inspiration, it was the emotion which gripped me as I read these words: suddenly I felt my mind dazzled by a thousand lights: a host of exciting ideas occurred to me at one and the same time and so forcefully and incoherently that I was thrown into a state of indescribable confusion. My head began to swim as if I were drunk. A violent palpitation made it difficult for me to breathe, and caused my chest to heave; being unable to get my breath or to walk, I sank down under one of the trees in the avenue and remained there for half an hour in such a state of agitation that when I finally rose to my feet, I perceived that the front of my jacket was damp with my tears, although I had no recollection

---

[7] *Confessions*, Bk. VIII, pp. 366–69.

of having shed any. Ah, sir, had I been able to write down one quarter of what I saw and felt beneath that tree, with what clarity I would have exposed all the contradictions inherent in our social system.[8]

This description was written some 15 years after the event, and its literary and stylized phrasing seem meant to remind the reader of Paul traveling on the road to Damascus. Nevertheless, Rousseau claimed that this level of energy and imagination lasted for four or five years, and the ideas certainly lasted a lifetime.

His prize essay, *Discourse on the Sciences and Arts* (1750), was original in that he did not give the expected answer. Instead of arguing that the expansion of knowledge, the new science, and progress separated the modern age from the superstitious and religious ages of the past, Rousseau argued that progress in science and in civilization was actually corrupting humanity. The optimistic belief that the human mind and morals would be properly formed through reason, experience, and science was not shared by Rousseau. He saw victims and oppression resulting from this progress. It was as if he were intentionally attacking the very faith of the *philosophes*.[9] The originality, dash, and style of the essay won the prize for Rousseau and made him famous. It also introduced themes he would expand and defend for the rest of his life: that the simple life close to nature was morally superior to sophisticated urban life, and that the pursuit of material possessions entraps and warps human nature. Rousseau even altered his form of dress, and from this time on wore simple and unaffected clothes, regardless of the style of the age.[10]

A few years later, in 1754, the Academy of Dijon advertised a new contest on the origin of inequality. Rousseau responded unsuccessfully. The *Second Discourse*, as it is often called, or the *Discourse on Inequality* did not win the prize, but it expands the nascent philosophy of history found in the *First Discourse*. Both *Discourses* created a storm of pamphlets and replies that only increased

---

[8] *Confessions*, Bk. VII, as quoted in Jean Guéhenno, *Jean-Jacques Rousseau, Vol. I: 1712–1758* (London: Routledge and Kegan Paul, 1967), pp. 208–09.

[9] The following books, in order of difficulty, will provide useful background on the Enlightenment: Carl L. Becker, *The Heavenly City of the Eighteenth-Century Philosophers* (New Haven: Yale University Press, 1932); Peter Gay, *The Enlightenment: An Interpretation* (New York: Knopf, 1966); Ernst Cassirer, *The Philosophy of the Enlightenment*, trans. F. C. A. Koelln and J. P. Pettegrove (Boston: Beacon Press, 1955); Eric Voegelin, *From Enlightenment to Revolution*, ed. John H. Hallowell (Durham: Duke University Press, 1975).

[10] *Confessions*, Bk. VIII, pp. 374–75.

Rousseau's growing notoriety and his readership.[11] Of more significance, these two essays are preparatory for understanding his classic work, the *Social Contract*.

Almost at the same time that he achieved his fame, his final years (1762–1778) became filled with persecution, estrangement from his friends, and paranoia. When the novel *Emile* (1762) was published, it was immediately condemned in Paris, and an arrest order was issued for Rousseau. His religious views were suspect. He had abandoned the Catholicism of Mme. de Warens some years earlier. Although he signed both discourses and the *Social Contract* "Citizen of Geneva" and even dedicated his *Second Discourse* to the Republic of Geneva, his Calvinism was hardly orthodox. There were deist sentiments found in *Emile*, and these were, apparently, unacceptable to both Catholic Paris and Calvinist Geneva. In Geneva both the *Social Contract* and *Emile* were condemned. Oddly, Rousseau had recently lived for a brief time in Geneva and had several commendatory remarks about Geneva in the *Social Contract*. But, the city fathers could read, and they understood the import of his writing to have some relevance to controversies within the Republic. They, too, issued a warrant for his arrest. Several cities throughout Europe did likewise. Rousseau's response was to travel quietly to various isolated places where he would live for a time. Once, the Scottish philosopher David Hume took pity on him and brought him to England where the King even offered Rousseau a pension, but Rousseau refused, just as he had the French King. Rousseau's paranoia soon re-emerged. Suspecting a conspiracy against him, he returned to Paris and its environs, where he remained from 1770 until his death in 1778. He agreed not to publish and lived relatively quietly, constantly suspicious, isolated from former friends, and suffering from permanent bladder complications.[12]

Rousseau is the one political philosopher who should be studied in part through his self-explorations. He himself would insist upon it. Rousseau considered his thought to be fundamentally coherent and guided by permanent themes that

---

[11] Victor Gourevitch has edited Rousseau's major replies to the two discourses: *Jean-Jacques Rousseau: The First and Second Discourses Together with the Replies to the Critics, and Essay on the Origin of Languages* (New York: Harper and Row, 1986).

[12] There are two large biographies: Maurice Cranston's is detailed, thorough, and devoid of any psychoanalysis, *Jean-Jacques: The Early Life and Work of Jean-Jacques Rousseau, 1712–1754* (New York: Norton, 1982) and *The Noble Savage: Jean-Jacques Rousseau, 1754–1762* (Chicago: University of Chicago Press, 1991). The works by Jean Guéhenno are personal, psychoanalytical, readable, and without any footnotes for the extensive citations, *Jean-Jacques Rousseau, Vol. I: 1712–1758*, and *Jean-Jacques Rousseau, Vol. II: 1758–1778*, trans. John and Doreen Weightman (London: Routledge and Kegan Paul, 1967).

unite his original experience on the road to Vincennes and the *First Discourse* with his final writing, *The Reveries of a Solitary Walker*. One of the themes permeating his personal and philosophical writings is the need to unite his desire for independence or autonomy with an intimate, supporting, nurturing relationship. Rousseau's fervent and deepest belief was that it was possible to be both autonomous and united with others. Indeed, it was only in such a union that one could be complete and free. The pattern of his own relationship invariably oscillated from a close and eventually suffocating intimacy to a life of independence, autonomy, and eventual estrangement and loneliness. Can one have an intimate relationship without experiencing the loss of self-identity? Can one be autonomous without the experience of being alone? Are intimacy and autonomy jointly attainable? His most powerful and eloquent writings address these problems, for he believes that they are the key to both personal happiness and political legitimacy.

He wrote three works devoted to possible resolutions. *The Reveries of a Solitary Walker* has a rhapsodic description of his communion with nature while living briefly on an island. As an amateur botanist, he would roam the fields and feel enveloped by the beauty of nature. He felt at peace, happy, and complete:

> …there is a state where the soul finds a position sufficiently solid to repose thereon, and to gather together all its being, without having need for recalling the past, nor to climb on into the future; where time counts for nothing, where the present lasts forever, without marking its duration in any way, and without any trace of succession, without any other sentiment of privation, neither of enjoyment, of pleasure nor pain of desire nor of fear, than this alone of our existence, and which this feeling alone can fill entirely: so long as this state lasts, he who finds it may be called happy… a sufficing happiness, perfect and full, which does not leave in the soul any void which it feels the need of filling.…
>
> What is the nature of one's enjoyment in such a situation? Nothing external to oneself, nothing except oneself and one's own existence; so long as this state lasts, one suffices to oneself, like God.[13]

A second possible resolution between intimacy and autonomy is provided by a properly formed family. This is the central topic of both *New Héloise* and of *Emile*. *Emile* was also designed to show how a properly raised child, an eventual

---

[13] *The Reveries of a Solitary*, Fifth Promenade, pp. 113–14.

marriage, and the resulting family could form a person capable of living in society and attaining that union of independence and intimacy which would produce freedom and happiness.[14]

The third attempt at a resolution is at the political level and is developed in his great classic work, *Social Contract*. Rousseau states the task as follows:

"Find a form of association which defends and protects with all common forces the person and goods of each associate, and by means of which each one, while uniting with all, nevertheless obeys only himself and remains as free as before?" This is the fundamental problem for which the social contract provides the solution.[15]

This political formulation of the problem is, in principle, the same problem Rousseau faced throughout his personal life and for which he provided resolutions in his writings: within nature for the person, within the family, and within the political society.

DISCOURSE ON THE SCIENCES AND ARTS (The First Discourse)

In writing this short discourse, Rousseau was building upon some rather traditional republican themes. Machiavelli, it will be recalled, had attacked luxury for enervating a people; he had also lauded ancient Sparta rather than Athens, and the Roman Republic rather than the Roman Empire. The Baron Montesquieu (1689–1755) also wrote in this republican tradition and clearly influenced Rousseau. Montesquieu had linked economic growth with luxury, which was followed by moral decay and the loss of liberty.[16]

---

[14] Judith N. Shklar, "Rousseau's Images of Authority," in *American Political Science Review* 58 (December, 1964), pp. 919–32; Allan Bloom, trans. *Emile or On Education* (New York: Basic Books, 1979), Introduction, pp. 3–28.

[15] Donald A. Cress, trans. and ed., *Jean-Jacques Rousseau: Basic Political Writings* (Indianapolis: Hackett, 1987), The Social Contract, ch. VI, p. 148. The citations for the *Discourse on the Sciences and the Arts* and the *Discourse on Inequality* will also be from this collection.

[16] Kingsley Martin, *The Rise of French Liberal Thought*, 2nd ed. (New York: New York University Press, 1954), pp. 137–62; J. G. A. Pocock, "Virtue, rights and manners, a model for historians of political thought," in his *Virtue, Commerce, and History: Essays on Political Thought and History, Chiefly in the Eighteenth Century* (Cambridge: Cambridge University Press, 1985); Nannerl O. Keohane, *Philosophy and the State in France* (Princeton: Princeton University Press, 1980).

Rousseau's argument was a unique variant. The arts and sciences themselves, learning and culture, had enervating effects on morals and society. His argument was not entirely consistent. But, in the main, he saw that while the recovery of Western Civilization from the Dark Ages through the introduction of the learning of the ancient Greek world precipitated the progress of the Western world, the problem was that the evolution of the arts and sciences made life pleasant at the price of deforming and stifling human nature. The resulting oppression of *liberté* (moral liberty) by the government and laws is actually hidden by the sciences, letters, and arts. These seduce us into obedience and conformity by making possible the luxuries, comforts, and pleasantries of civilization. In reality, the sciences and arts are "garlands of flowers" spread over the iron chains of rule; they "stifle in [humans] the sense of that original liberty for which they seem to have been born, make them love their slavery, and turn them into what is called civilized people."[17] Originally, "our mores were rustic but natural" but now civilized manners hide who we are: "One no longer dares to seem what one really is." Our very civilization has meant that there is "no more sincere friendship, no more real esteem, no more well founded confidence." All of this has been replaced by a "veil of politeness" and "vaunted urbanity." Beyond doubt, he concludes, "our souls have become corrupted in proportion as our sciences and our arts have advanced toward perfection."[18]

Rousseau then turns to history to vindicate this judgment. He provides a litany of peoples who were successful before the enervating effects of luxury and the arts. The first Persians conquered Asia; the early German tribes conquered the effete Roman Empire; the early Roman Republic in her "poverty and ignorance" rose to greatness. Echoing Machiavelli, Rousseau praises virtuous Sparta in contrast to the cultivated and corrupt Athens. History shows, he then finishes, that "luxury, dissolution and slavery have at all times been the punishment for the arrogant efforts that we have made to leave the happy ignorance where eternal wisdom had placed us."[19]

These horrific effects of the sciences and arts are a consequence of their origins in human pride and vanity:

---

[17] *The First Discourse*, p. 3.

[18] *Ibid.*, pp. 4–5.

[19] *Ibid.*, p. 10.

426

Astronomy was born of superstition, eloquence of ambition, hatred flattery, lying; geometry of avarice; physics of vain curiosity; all of them even moral philosophy, of human pride. Thus the sciences and the arts owe their birth to our vices; we would be less in doubt about their advantages, if they owed it to our virtues.[20]

The very practice of the arts harms our nature: "While the conveniences of life increase, the arts are perfected and luxury spreads, true courage is enervated, military virtues disappear, and this too is the work of the sciences and of all those arts which are practised in the darkness of the study."[21] The very practice of these disciplines becomes an alternative to practical action and to the duties of citizenship.

Rousseau has introduced topics that he will then develop with greater care in his subsequent works. First, modern society has somehow deprived humans of their true selves; authenticity has been lost. Second, ignorance, innocence, and virtue are tied. Third, the history of peoples has moved from rustic simplicity, allied with a common public identity, to sophisticated luxury allied with selfishness, and decay of the public identity. Fourth, there is a spirit of pessimism about the inexorable march of history. The harm from advancing civilization to human nature seems irreversible.[22]

DISCOURSE ON INEQUALITY
(The Second Discourse)

The *Second Discourse* builds upon the philosophy of history developed in the *First Discourse* and ranges from a biological theory of evolution beginning with orangutans to the origin of language, property, and government.[23] It is divided into

---

[20] *Ibid.*, p. 11.

[21] *Ibid.*, p. 15.

[22] For a full analysis of this short discourse, see: Robert Wokler, "The *Discours sur les arts* and its offspring," in *Reappraisals of Rousseau: Studies in Honour of R. A. Leigh*, eds. S. Harvey et al. (Manchester: University of Manchester, 1980); John Hope Mason, "Reading Rousseau's *First Discourse*," in *Studies on Voltaire and the Eighteenth Century*, 249 (1987), pp. 251–66. The notes to the *First Discourse*, edited by Victor Gourevitch, are very helpful.

[23] For interpretations that stress the biological dimension of the *Second Discourse*, see Roger D. Masters, *The Political Philosophy of Rousseau* (Princeton: Princeton University Press, 1968); Jean Starobinski, *Jean-Jacques Rousseau: Transparency and Obstruction*, trans. Arthur Goldhammer (Chicago: University of Chicago Press, 1988).

two parts. Part One provides the primitive stage, and Part Two explains the process of evolution culminating in inequality. The *Second Discourse* did not achieve the immediate fame of the *First Discourse*, but it has had a more long-lasting influence on European politics and philosophy. It has been an inspiration for socialist and Marxist thought; Rousseau's views on language, morality, and culture were major influences on the German philosophers Immanuel Kant (1724–1804) and Johann Herder (1744–1803); his use of the scanty knowledge then available about Aboriginals in Africa and the Americas has qualified him as a founder of modern anthropology. It is a remarkable essay.[24]

Rousseau begins by promising to probe into what humans actually were like in nature. "Nature," he says, "never lies. Everything that comes from nature will be true." Other philosophers have read back into nature human traits that could only have existed in society; the issue is to determine clearly what are human characteristics prior to socialization and civilization. Rousseau quickly notes that he cannot claim actually to have found the historical origin and that his is an exercise in "hypothetical and conditional reasonings."[25] But, as his argument develops, it becomes obvious that Rousseau is not proceeding in the manner of Hobbes or Locke. He is attempting to discern what humanity was like before the forming influence of society, culture, civilization, and even language.

Physically, Rousseau pictures the savage man by piecing together what knowledge was then available on primates and Aboriginal peoples. The primitive or savage man he characterizes as hardy, fearless, adapted to nature: "I see him satisfying his hunger under an oak tree, quenching his thirst at the first stream, finding his bed at the foot of the same tree that supplied his meal; and thus all his needs are satisfied."[26]

---

[24] For Rousseau's influence on the German philosophers, Kant, Hegel, and Marx, see: John Plamenatz and Nathan Rotenstreich, *Basic Problems of Marx's Philosophy* (New York: Bobbs-Merrill, 1965); Andrew Levine, *The Politics of Autonomy* (Amherst: University of Massachusetts Press, 1976); Louis Althusser, *Politics and History: Montesquieu, Rousseau, and Marx*, trans. Ben Brewster (London: Routledge, 1982); G. D. H. Cole, "Introduction," in *Jean-Jacques Rousseau: The Social Contract and Discourses* (London: Everyman's Library, 1950); Ernst Cassirer, *Rousseau, Kant, Goethe* (Princeton: Princeton University Press, 1944). There is an excellent work on Rousseau and Herder by F. M. Barnard, *Self-Direction and Political Legitimacy: Rousseau and Herder* (Oxford: Clarendon Press, 1988).

[25] *The Second Discourse*, pp. 38–39.

[26] *Ibid.*, p. 40. Rousseau's endnotes contain his anthropological speculations on primates and on Aboriginal peoples. Notes, 3–6.

Rousseau then turns to an examination of the state of nature from "a metaphysical and moral point of view." Human rational capacity, he discovers, differs from animals "only in degree."[27] Reasoning to any extent is developed only after society has developed. In one of his many dramatic phrases, Rousseau writes that "the state of reflection is a state contrary to nature and that the man who meditates is a depraved animal."[28] Rousseau, however, admits two features that do distinguish humans from animals:

> Therefore it is not so much understanding which causes the specific distinction of man from all other animals as it is his being a free agent. Nature commands every animal, and beasts obey. Man feels the same impetus, but he knows he is freed to go along or to resist; and it is above all in the awareness of this freedom that the spirituality of his soul is made manifest. For physics explains in some way the mechanism of the senses and the formation of ideas; but in the power of willing, or rather of choosing, and in the feeling of this power, we find only purely spiritual acts, about which the laws of mechanics explain nothing.[29]

Being a free agent is possible because humans are so constructed—"the spirituality of his soul." We will, choose, and feel, and are aware of this power. The will and the consciousness of this will are not found in animals governed by instincts.

"Another very specific quality," in Rousseau's words, that distinguishes us from animals is the "faculty of self-perfection, a faculty which, with the aid of circumstances, successively develops all the others, and resides among us as much in the species as in the individual. On the other hand, an animal, at the end of a few months, is what it will be all its life; and its species, at the end of a thousand years, is what it was in the first of those thousand years."[30] It is this capacity of learning, changing, and adapting that enables the malleable savage to outdistance the animals.

In the primitive state, however, there is little use of this capacity because desires and fears are still benign and simple:

---

[27] *Ibid.*, pp. 44–45.

[28] *Ibid.*, p. 42.

[29] *Ibid.*, p. 45.

[30] *Ibid.*

For one can desire or fear things only by virtue of the ideas one can have of them, or from the simple impulse of nature; and savage man, deprived of every sort of enlightenment, feels only the passion of this latter sort. His desires do not go beyond his physical needs. The only good he knows in the universe are nourishment, a woman and rest; the only evils he fears are pain and hunger. I say pain and not death because an animal will never know what it is to die; and knowledge of death and its terrors is one of the first acquisitions that man has made in withdrawing from the animal condition.[31]

This is a static state where desires and needs are balanced. The primitive man has little to fear, no curiosity, and no sense of beauty or wonder: "His soul, agitated by nothing, is given over to the single feeling of his own existence, without any idea of the future, however, near it may be, and his projects, as limited as his views, hardly extend to the end of the day."[32] His days are "tranquil and innocent," and Rousseau likens them to the Orinoco Indians who use boards to bind their children's temples, thereby assuring them a life of imbecility and happiness.[33]

Humans behave in a generally constant way. Passions triggered by some need of nature or of circumstance will lead to some "progress of the mind." At this stage, though, there is very little of it. Language would be necessary for there to be sustained development, and language requires society. The nature of language, Rousseau argues, is very complex and is certainly more than labelling. In fact, language and society appear to be coeval and neither exists in this savage state.[34]

Rousseau detects in this savage state two natural principles that operate within human nature and govern human conduct. First is self-preservation. This passion is not egocentric, as claimed by Hobbes, nor does it inevitably cause violence. There would be no need for violence, as Rousseau explains later in the essay, for self-preservation leads naturally to peace. Another principle that operates

---

[31] *Ibid.*, p. 46.

[32] *Ibid.*

[33] *Ibid.*, p. 45.

[34] The nature of language is a serious topic for Rousseau, and it is one area where the difference from Hobbes and Locke is the clearest. His thought is developed at length in his *Essay on the Origin of Languages*, in Gourevitch. Richard Noble has written a careful treatment of the topic in *Language, Subjectivity, and Freedom in Rousseau's Moral Philosophy* (New York: Garland Publishing, 1991).

within humans is pity or compassion, "a disposition that is fitting for beings that are as weak and subject to ills as we are; a virtue all the more universal and all the more useful to man in that it precedes in him any kind of reflection, and so natural that even animals sometimes show noticeable signs of it."[35] These two principles, as he calls them, are quite sufficient for guiding humans within the state of nature: "In instinct alone, man had everything he needed in order to live in the state of nature."[36] Humans have neither virtue nor vices, moral relationships or duties. How can this state be one of misery, Rousseau asks? The savage is a "free being whose heart is at peace and whose body is in good health."[37]

Conflict will come about only after reason enters and warps each of the two natural principles. Self-preservation becomes sheer egocentricism, hardening the individual to pity. With eloquence and obvious bitterness, Rousseau describes what happens:

> Reason is what engenders egocentrism, and reflection strengthens it. Reason is what turns man in upon himself. Reason is what separates him from all that troubles him and afflicts him. Philosophy is what isolates him and what moves him to say in secret, at the sign of a suffering man, "Perish if you will; I am safe and sound".... Savage man does not have this admirable talent, and for lack of wisdom and reason he is always seen thoughtlessly giving in to the first sentiment of humanity....[38]

In this primitive stage of nature conflict is virtually non-existent. There are no grounds for it. There is no private property and not "the slightest notion of mine and thine." There is no vanity or contempt, which are the causes of such great conflicts within society. Competitiveness just does not exist. Pity serves to moderate the love of oneself or the instinct to self-preservation:

> It is... quite certain that pity is a natural sentiment, which, by moderating in each individual the activity of the love of oneself, contributes to the mutual preservation of the entire species. Pity is what carries us without

---

[35] *The Second Discourse*, p. 53.

[36] *Ibid.*, p. 52.

[37] *Ibid.*

[38] *Ibid.*, pp. 54–55.

reflection to the aid of those we see suffering. Pity is what, in the state of nature, takes the place of laws, mores, and virtue, with the advantage that no one is tempted to disobey its sweet voice.[39]

Even the sex drive will not lead to a conflict. The savage man has neither ideas of beauty nor moral views on monogamy. Love is only physical and "any woman suits his purpose."[40] There are no relationships so permanent and intense that a conflict could occur. Rousseau notes that "savage man, subject to few passions and self-sufficient, had only the sentiments and enlightenment appropriate to that state; he felt only his true needs;... and that his intelligence made no more progress than his vanity."[41]

In retrospect, the original state of nature has a balance between needs and desires that keeps us innocent, ignorant, and happy. Humanity is in a general, common condition. All face the same needs, and all are remarkably self-sufficient. Even the experience of mothering, Rousseau asserts, is quickly forgotten, and the female proceeds on her self-sufficient path. There is a striking equality, too, among humans; no one is dependent upon any other. (Rousseau's personal abhorrence of dependence led him to refuse pensions from both the King of France and King of England.) Here in nature, there is only an impersonal dependence on things and not on other persons. Savages experience their lives as free. The *Social Contract*, Rousseau promises, will restore our natural state with a difference; it will provide a political structure of such a nature that civilized humans can once again experience their lives as being free.

---

[39] *Ibid.*, p. 55.

[40] *Ibid.*, p. 56. This understanding of sex also applied to women within the state of nature: "With hunger and other appetites making him experience by turns various ways of existing, there was one appetite that invited him to perpetuate his species; and this blind inclination, devoid of any sentiment of the heart, produced a purely animal act. Once this need had been satisfied, the two sexes no longer took cognizance of one another, and even the child no longer meant anything to the mother once it could do without her." *Ibid.*, p. 60. The passion of sex and the role of women were personal issues for Rousseau and, as usual, philosophic ones. His personal inability to utilize the drive successfully was viewed as a paradigmatic social problem too. Joel Schwarz has a full study that relates Rousseau's personal difficulties with his philosophic position, *The Sexual Politics of Jean-Jacques Rousseau* (Chicago: University of Chicago Press, 1984); Allan Bloom has a perceptive treatment in *Love and Friendship* (New York: Simon and Schuster, 1993); Jean Bethke Elshtain has a balanced treatment of Rousseau's view of women, politics, and human relations, *Meditations on Modern Political Thought* (Westport: Praeger, 1986), pp. 37–54.

[41] *The Second Discourse*, p. 57.

In the primitive stage of human development inequality is "hardly observable." There would be no reason for superiority and subordination ever developing among humans. And, as Rousseau makes clear, the picture provided by Hobbes and Locke is plainly wrong. The egocentricism of Hobbes does not exist. In nature a healthy self-preservation is twinned with pity or compassion, and there would be no conflict among humans that would require government. Contrary to Locke, Rousseau finds no property right inherent in the state of nature, and no conflict could derive from this source that would lead to the need for government. Locke is further criticized for his depiction of a family life in the original state.[42] The true state of nature has only individuals existing in nature and has no such social institutions as property or family.

The import of Part One of the *Second Discourse* is that Hobbes, Locke, and others have been wrong on the state of nature and on human nature. Rousseau is aware that the original question about the origin of inequality is still not answered: "it remains for me to consider and to bring together the various chance happenings that were able to perfect human reason while deteriorating the species, make a being evil while rendering it habituated to the ways of society, and, from so distant a beginning, finally bring man and the world to the point where we see them now."[43]

The "chance happenings" may have been any event that lead to the recognition of common interests and the value of the "assistance of his fellowmen."[44] Living together will foster the establishment of families and all the concomitant sentiments as well as the need for language. At the same time, the psyche undergoes a critical change. The original and natural love of self, ***amour de soi***, which was twinned with compassion or pity, mutates into an understanding of oneself as presented by others. It turns into vanity, ***amour propre***. Rousseau explains the process:

> Each one began to look at the others and to want to be looked at himself, and public esteem had a value. The one who sang or danced the best, the handsomest, the strongest, the most adroit or the most eloquent became the most highly regarded. And this was the first step toward inequality and, at the same time, toward vice. From these first references were born vanity

---

[42] *Ibid.*, notes 12–13.

[43] *Ibid.*, p. 59.

[44] *Ibid.*, p. 61.

and contempt on the one hand, and shame and envy on the other. And the fermentation caused by these new leavens eventually produced compounds fatal to happiness and innocence.[45]

This new situation will lead to competitiveness, success, and progress but with a loss of innocence, happiness, and one's natural self. Humans will become artificial creations of society.

The oft quoted first sentence of Part Two eloquently places the chief blame of inequality at the door of private property:

> The first person who, having enclosed a plot of land, took it into his head to say *this is mine* and found people simple enough to believe him, was the true founder of civil society. What crimes, wars, murders, what miseries and horrors would the human race have been spared, had someone pulled up the stakes or filled in the ditch and cried out to his fellow men: "Do not listen to this impostor. You are lost if you forget that the fruits of the earth belong to all and the earth to no one!"[46]

By this time people have started to live together, and the primitive stage of individual self-sufficiency has been left. The advantages of joint activities has blinded humans to the disadvantages, as Rousseau recounts the story:

> But as soon as one man needed the help of another, as soon as one man realized that it was useful for a single individual to have provisions for two, equality disappeared, property came into existence, labour became necessary. Vast forests were transformed into smiling fields which had to be watered with men's sweat, and in which slavery and misery were soon seen to germinate and grow with the crops.[47]

Rousseau proceeds to delineate more precisely three stages, or "revolutions" as he calls them, that culminate in the great inequalities found in modern societies. First, he cites the development of metallurgy and agriculture. With iron and agricultural cultivation the creation of wealth became inevitable. The original minor inequalities resulting from differences in skills or more favourable locations were now accentuated and translated into inequalities of wealth, rank, and power.

---

[45] *Ibid.*, p. 64.

[46] *Ibid.*, p. 60.

[47] *Ibid.*, p. 65.

Then major competitions and rivalries start to occur, leading to disorder and war. It did not take much reflection for both the rich and the poor to see the need for some order. Some clever rich person convinces both sides that all should choose to enter into a new political arrangement. This second stage or "revolution" leads directly to a government:

> They all ran to chain themselves, in the belief that they secured their liberty, for although they had enough sense to realize the advantages of a political establishment, they did not have enough experience to foresee its dangers....
>
> Such was, or should have been, the origin of society and laws, which gave new fetters to the weak and new forces to the rich, irretrievably destroyed natural liberty, established forever the law of property and of inequality, changed adroit usurpation into an irrevocable right, and for the profit of a few ambitious men henceforth subjected the entire human race to labour, servitude and misery.[48]

The rich have cleverly solidified their dominance with government and laws. Inequality has now become a permanent feature of human existence.

The final stage or revolution occurs when legitimate governmental power is transformed into plain, arbitrary power. Human political history has evolved from the rich and the poor to the strong and the weak, and, finally, in this last stage to the master and the slave. In this final stage, despotism concentrates power in one person, and humanity returns, in Rousseau's language, to a new and worse state of nature. Force dominates, and the human psyche has been unalterably changed. It is the destruction of the original psyche that is the most terrifying:

> ...the savage lives in himself; the man accustomed to the ways of society is always outside himself and knows how to live only in the opinion of others. And it is, as it were, from their judgment alone that he draws the sentiment of his own existence.... [We] have merely a deceitful and frivolous exterior: honour without virtue, reason without wisdom, and pleasure without happiness. It is enough for me to have proved that this is not the original state of man, and that this is only the spirit of society, and the inequality that society engenders, which thus change and alter all our natural inclinations.[49]

---

[48] *Ibid.*, p. 70.

[49] *Ibid.*, p. 81.

Our very capacity for perfectibility has allowed our nature to be moulded, unwittingly, by accidents, circumstances, and economic historical forces. Our nature has, thus, been corrupted. The happy and innocent savage has become civilized, and, to use a contemporary term, alienated. Nature was better for human happiness and freedom than society and civilization. Progress, as Rousseau argued in the *First Discourse* and has now more fully explained in the *Second Discourse*, has not lead to our true betterment.[50]

ON THE SOCIAL CONTRACT

The *Discourse on Inequality* proclaimed civilized humanity to be hopelessly corrupt and politically enslaved. The once happy, self-sufficient, free, and ignorant savage has become vain (*amour propre*), intelligent, and competitive. Our potential for perfectibility has engendered progress and civilization, but this same potential has also caused our original human nature to become warped. In *The Social Contract* Rousseau relies upon this same assumption of human perfectibility to construct a civilized political system that would undo the warping and develop free and happy citizens.

The work is divided into four books. The first two books justify Rousseau's subtitle, *Principles of Political Right*. He demonstrates how a society can legitimately be formed on the principles of right, through a radically new understanding of a social contract. The last two books, equally original, deal primarily with maintaining a government and popular sovereignty.

In three brief introductory paragraphs Rousseau promises the reader that he will present a legitimate political system by "taking men as they are and laws as they might be" and that he will unite "justice and utility."[51] Given the title, one would assume that all of this will be accomplished by working within the social contract tradition of Hobbes, Locke, and Hugo Grotius (1583–1645), an influential Dutch legal thinker. Yet, as becomes quickly evident, there is no two-way contract in Rousseau's theory between a society and a government,

---

[50] For full treatments of the *Second Discourse*, see: Victor Gourevitch, "Rousseau's Pure State of Nature," *Interpretation* 16 (1988); Arthur M. Melzer, *The Natural Goodness of Man: On the System of Rousseau's Thought* (Chicago: University of Chicago Press, 1990); Asher Horowitz, *Rousseau, Nature, and History* (Toronto: University of Toronto Press, 1987).

[51] The text used is found in Donald A. Cress, trans. and ed., *Jean-Jacques Rousseau: The Basic Political Writings*. The citations are to book and chapter.

with defined duties and rights for each side. Moreover, there is no transfer of any rights and powers to a government, whether it is the full transfer of Hobbes or the modified transfer of Locke. By the end of the work, it is clear that Rousseau has fundamentally indicted the contract tradition itself and has developed a radical alternative.

The originality of Rousseau's approach is foretold in the dramatic opening of his first chapter.

> Man is born free, and everywhere he is in chains. He who believes himself the master of others does not escape being more of a slave than they. How did this change take place? I have no idea. What can render it legitimate? I believe I can answer this question.[52]

The claim in the first sentence that we are born free but as civilized humans are in chains is the conclusion of the *Discourse on Inequality*. All political systems are indicted. The second sentence points to the self-delusion created by progress, civilization, and modernity. Those who are masters are actually more slaves than an actual slave, who at least recognizes to some degree the pain in the condition. There is no delusion of happiness for a slave, but the master is hopelessly caught and deluded. In the third sentence, Rousseau, of course, does know how the change occurred, his denial to the contrary, because this is the topic of the *Second Discourse*. But, his task here is to explain how we can get legitimacy out of this enormous political tragedy. He promises to do so.

He begins by noting that the social order, which is prior to government, is created by human choice. Wisely or unwisely, human choices did propel the long evolution from the state of nature into a social order. A social order, accordingly, is a human convention and does not flow from nature. Using Locke's arguments, Rousseau dismisses the Filmer contention that political rule evolves from the family. Once a child reaches the age of reason, "he thereby becomes his own master."[53] He also quickly dismisses the Hobbesian view that the necessity of force will induce obligation and order. Rousseau asks, "What kind of right is it that perishes when the force on which it is based ceases?"[54]

---

[52] Bk. I, ch. 1.

[53] Bk. I, ch. 2.

[54] Bk. I, ch. 3.

Not only must there be a convention to establish a social order, it has to be one consistent with humans as original free agents. In chapter 4, Rousseau particularly criticizes the idea, associated with Grotius, that a people can totally transfer or, in a legal sense, alienate its power to a king. This cannot be the origin of a legitimate and sovereign political system, says Rousseau. It is contrary to what humans are: "They are born men and free."[55] Rousseau proceeds to expand his argument:

> Renouncing one's liberty is renouncing one's dignity as a man, the rights of humanity and even its duties. There is no possible compensation for any-one who renounces everything. Such a renunciation is incompatible with the nature of man. Removing all morality from his actions is tantamount to taking away all liberty from his will.[56]

Governments founded upon conquest or war are, therefore, not legitimate. "These words, *slavery* and *right*, are contradictory," he declares.[57] Right must be based upon human **free will**.

The use of force creates only a multitude or aggregation not a society or as-sociation. For the latter, in which there is a true uniting bond, there will have to be unanimous agreement at some point in order even to agree to majority deci-sion making. Only in this fashion, where there has been a "public deliberation," can free will create a true society.[58] The important question, quoted earlier, was whether it is possible to find a "form of association which will defend the person and goods of each member with the collective force of all, and under which each individual, while uniting himself with the others, obeys no one but himself, and remains as free as before."[59] The task appears formidable.

The contract that purportedly will create this kind of association requires the "total alienation of each associate, together with all of his rights, to the entire community."[60] This total alienation, or transferral, has three key features that

---

[55] Bk. I, ch. 4.

[56] *Ibid.*

[57] *Ibid.*

[58] Bk. I, ch. 5.

[59] Bk. I, ch. 6.

[60] During Rousseau's time the word "alienation" had the legal meaning of transferring an item from one person to another. The word in English has the psychological meaning of a loss of iden-tity. In this sense, Rousseau was instrumental in introducing the idea, though he relied upon dif-ferent words to express the modern meaning.

protect the individual from experiencing any kind of subservience or psychological dependence. These features replicate in civil society the conditions that envelop the solitary human in nature. First, "since each person gives himself whole and entire, the condition is equal for everyone; and since the condition is equal for everyone, no one has an interest in making it burdensome for the other."[61] There is, in short, a general condition all share, as there was in nature. Second, there is no privileged position for some vis-à-vis others. No member or associate "has anything further to demand." If members tried to keep some rights, each would become wary of losing some of those rights to others. With respect to one another, the associates are all equal, just as humans were equal in nature. Third, Rousseau asserts that this contract will replicate the impersonal order found in nature: "in giving himself to all, each person gives himself to no one. And since there is no associate over whom he does not acquire the same right that he would grant others over himself, he gains the equivalent of everything he loses, along with a greater amount of force to preserve what he has."[62] There is no dependence or sense of subservience because each transfers all power to *all*, not to one person or a group.

How can a contract with these three features actually be created? With Hobbes, the critical moment in establishing his contract, described in chapter 17 of the *Leviathan*, is an imaginary act of reasoning: it is *as if* each person looks at the other and agrees to give up the right of governing him- or herself to the ruler or rulers if the other will do so as well. With Locke, the terms of the contract among the members forming the society and the terms of the contract between the society and the government are carefully delineated, and consent is given. With Rousseau, the act of contracting is actually an act of full, personal commitment that will alter one's nature:

If ... one eliminates from the social compact whatever is not essential to it, one will find that it is reducible to the following terms. *Each of us places his person and all his power in common under the supreme direction of the **general will**; and as one we receive each member as an indivisible part of the whole.*

At once, in place of the individual person of each contracting party, this act of association produces a moral and collective body composed of as many members as there are voices in the assembly, which receives from this same act its unity, its common *self*, its life and its will.[63]

---

[61] Bk. I, ch. 6.

[62] *Ibid.*

[63] *Ibid.*

The social tie that has been formed by entering the **general will** is not between individuals but between each individual and the whole community. Rousseau emphasizes many times that there is no personal dependence since "in giving himself to all, each person gives himself to no one." A new corporate body and a new identity have been simultaneously formed. The transformation creates new citizens as well as a new moral entity with its own common ego, life, and will. The nature of the general will is key to this transformation, but Rousseau waits until Book II to explain its meaning.

Politically, this social contract has established a sovereign body. In fact, there can be no prior fundamental law that limits the sovereign. The sovereign itself is the source of all law, and there is no outside appeal to judge its actions. Within its domain each individual, as Rousseau explains, is under a two-fold commitment. First, each person is a citizen and member of the sovereign; second, each person is a subject obliged by the laws of the state. Since the sovereign is composed of the private individuals, it could have "no interest contrary to theirs." Thus, there is no need for individual rights to protect the citizens, since "it is impossible for a body to want to harm all of its members.... The sovereign, by the mere fact that it exists, is always all that it should be."[64] (One can imagine Locke's response to this assurance.)

A difficulty immediately arises in that "each individual can, as a man, have a private will contrary to or different from the general will that he has as a citizen."[65] In this circumstance, a person could well refuse to do the "duties of a subject" while enjoying "the rights of a citizen." In a phrase quoted frequently by Rousseau's critics, he provides a solution:

> Thus, in order for the social compact to avoid being an empty formula, it tacitly entails the commitment—which alone can give force to the others—that whoever refuses to obey the general will will be forced to do so by the entire body. This means merely that he will be forced to be free.[66]

The new identity will be lost if the person returns to the life of *amour propre*. The individual will need the power of the community to sustain the new identity

---

[64] Bk. I, ch. 7.

[65] *Ibid.*

[66] *Ibid.*

and freedom gained by the social contract. In the state of nature, it will be re-called, individuals are "forced" by necessity and circumstances to make choices and to develop their will and other faculties. The institutional structures of all present societies "force" individuals into a life that is morally corrupting. The *Social Contract* is designed to create an institutional structure for civil society that will also "force" individuals to develop properly, but this time individuals can be free. In this sense, Rousseau's notorious phrase becomes, perhaps, less terrifying. In any case, the justification for forcing people to be free is derived from the general will, which is the only political source of right.

In the next chapter Rousseau amplifies his claim that entering the social contract does create a new moral being. He first distinguishes between three kinds of liberty: natural, civil, and moral. Natural liberty is derived from an in-dividual's physical power and is found in the state of nature: "The right to everything that tempts him and that he can acquire." Civil liberty is found in so-ciety and is derived from the laws of the state and, as Rousseau says, "is lim-ited by the general will." Moral liberty is unique to a society based upon the social contract, and it "makes man the master of himself; for to be governed by appetite alone is slavery, while obedience to a law one prescribes to oneself is free-dom."[67] Moral liberty provides one with a sense of self-sufficiency ("master of oneself") through combining will ("prescribe to oneself") with law.[68] The "en-tire soul is elevated," and the individual is "transformed...from a stupid, limited animal into an intelligent being and a man." In the state of nature, humans were free and happy, but in this new civil society another dimension is added—moral liberty—which elevates the entire soul.

---

[67] Bk. I, ch. 8.

[68] John Plamenatz warns: "It is worth noticing that Rousseau, who was among the first to try to show in any detail how men develop the capacities peculiar to their species through activities which make social and moral beings of them, who recognized that society (at least in its earlier stages) must be the largely unforeseen and intended product of forms of behaviour which may be voluntary and purposeful but are not consciously directed to social aims, and who urged men to control and transform society to achieve a kind of freedom which he called *moral* and defined as obedience to a law prescribed to oneself, never used such expressions as 'self-realization,' 'self-fulfillment,' and 'self-improvement.'" *Karl Marx's Philosophy of Man* (Oxford: Oxford University Press, 1975), p. 233. "Self-sufficiency" or a derivative was perhaps his most common phrasing. See the thorough study by Ronald Grimsley, "Rousseau and the Ideal of Self-Sufficiency," *Studies in Romanticism* 10 (Autumn, 1971), pp. 283–99.

These three kinds of liberty can be distinguished by the place or context in which each can be found: the state of nature, a civil society, and a society formed by the social contract. In other words, each occurs within certain boundaries: natural liberty within the boundaries of the power of the individual and nature; civil liberty within the boundaries of the laws one prescribes for oneself. The last is of the greatest significance since the realization of moral liberty constitutes the transformation from individual to citizen.

Moral liberty, or autonomy, requires the conjoining of will and law. Rousseau's use of law is unremarkable, but his use of will is strikingly original. There are three discernible meanings to liberty of the will. One can be called procedural, that is, there is liberty of the will when one voluntarily prescribes. A person is dependent— lacks free will—when obeying even a "good" law if the person has not voluntarily prescribed it. A second meaning to liberty of the will can be called rational and formal and this is created when individuals enter society. The will in the state of nature was under the influence of particulars and appetites; however, its potentiality can be seen even in that state. Within the civil society established by the social contract one can escape the appetites and particulars that determine choice, and one can will, instead, the general and universal. The individual substitutes a "rule of conduct in the place of instinct," "duty replaces physical impulse," and man "consults his reason before listening to his inclinations."[69] Here, there is a rational and formal element to willing because reason is the guide, not instincts or appetites, and the object is to will what is general and universal, not particular and contingent.

The final meaning of liberty of the will could be called experiential or substantive and is contained in the idea of self-mastery. Liberty of will in this experiential or substantive sense is found in the state of nature ("Everyone is there his own master") as well as in the civil society formed by the contract where moral liberty makes "man the master of himself." This explains why Rousseau believes that he has provided a solution to his central problem: find a form of association in which "each one, uniting with all, nevertheless obeys only himself and remains as free as before."[70] We can be free as *before* only in the procedural and the substantial or experiential senses, but we have also gained, through the rational and formal element, moral liberty, which we did not have as primitive humans

---

[69] Bk. I, ch. 8.

[70] Bk. I, ch. 6.

in the state of nature. The rational and formal element becomes the means for retaining in society the core experience of being a free actor—control and mastery. Precisely how this occurs is left for Book II.

Rousseau completes Book I by briefly discussing the place of property in the social contract. When the act of union takes place, the individuals place their property as well as their selves "under the supreme direction of the general will." This does not deprive a person of private property but gives private possessions the protection of the whole community. Rousseau concludes by reiterating the non-Lockean principle that "each private individual's right to his very own store is always subordinate to the community's right to all."[71]

In Book II Rousseau provides a fuller explanation of the general will and of sovereignty. Through the commitment to the general will, a new social bond has been created as well as new moral personalities for the citizens. For Hobbes and Locke, there is always some loss of liberty in entering a social contract, but, for Rousseau, the new commitment actually increases our sense of moral liberty. We are liberated from the destructive social bonds of modern life. This promise must also be consistent with Rousseau's claim that the individual retains a sense of mastery. Thus, in what appears to be paradoxical, Rousseau reiterates that the general will and sovereignty are essential for the new self and its sense of mastery: "The very moment there is a master [other than of oneself], there no longer is a sovereign, and thenceforward the body politic is destroyed."[72]

The core to the idea of the general will is that each individual will learn to think in terms of what would be generally applicable rather than what would be in his or her private interest. It is this act that also creates the sovereign. He notes in chapters 2 and 3 that the sovereign is indivisible and inalienable, by which he means that we either think and will in terms of what is generally applicable or we do not. If we separate our particular group or place from the whole community in our thinking, willing, and decision making, then there is no general will and no sovereignty.

The concept of a general will had a long history in French intellectual circles, which Rousseau is subtly using for his own purpose. Theologians for a century or more had argued that God rules by general laws rather than by particular ones.

---

[71] Bk. I, ch. 9.

[72] Bk. II, ch. 1.

To rule in particular cases would be simply arbitrary, but to rule through general laws provides universal justice and right. Rousseau is relying upon these well-known themes.[73]

Rousseau has reversed the normal liberal view of authority that tries to curb and limit authority in the name of liberty. For Rousseau, moral liberty requires the authority of the general will. Rousseau is convinced that there is an objective common good for every political controversy. Politics is not a matter of probable solutions to unsolvable problems. Rather, the problem in politics is making an institutional framework so that the general will can be expressed. As Rousseau says, "the general will is always right and always tends toward the public utility."[74] It is not enough simply to ask people to express their wills or views on a matter. As he wryly notes, "it does not follow that the deliberations of the people always have the same rectitude."[75] Even the will of all is not the general will. It is not a matter of aggregating a majority of private interests or even the interests of everyone. If everyone can learn to think about what would be generally applicable or good for the whole, then the general will would be expressed. "The populace," he notes, "is never corrupted, but it is often tricked, and only then does it appear to want what is bad."[76] The point of this seeming paradox is that it is only the individuals who have learned to think in terms of the whole and to will what would fit the whole ("general") who constitute the sovereign and the general will. It is not the number of people willing but the nature of the willing that instantiates the general will.

Once the identification with the whole is lost, then the general will cannot operate. It is always right, but it may not be expressed. Accordingly, Rousseau constantly warns against practices and institutions that would tend to diminish the commitment to the general will. He is adamantly opposed to special interests or, to use a modern term, political parties:

---

[73] The precise paternity of Rousseau's concept of the will is too complicated a task to pursue here. Patrick Riley argues that "Rousseau is not conceivable without Augustine and various seventeenth-century transformations of Augustinianism," *Will and Political Legitimacy* (Cambridge: Harvard University Press, 1982), p. 5. See also, Keohane, *Philosophy and the State in France*, pp. 420–29. Riley further shows how the "general will" was a notion used by many of Rousseau's immediate predecessors and some of his contemporaries: Pascal, Montesquieu, Malebranche, Leibniz, and Diderot: *The General Will Before Rousseau: The Transformation of the Divine into the Civic* (Princeton: Princeton University Press, 1986).

[74] Bk. II, ch. 3.

[75] *Ibid.*

[76] *Ibid.*

If, when a sufficiently informed populace deliberates, the citizens were to have no communication among themselves, the general will would always result from the large number of small differences, and the deliberation would always be good. But when intrigues and partial associations come into being at the expense of the large association, the will of each of these associations becomes general in relation to its members and particular in relation to the state....

For the general will to be well articulated, it is therefore important that there should be no partial society in the state and that each citizen make up his own mind.[77]

Each individual deliberating and directing his or her thoughts toward the task of discovering what would be generally applicable to all will create the general will. But there must be that critical commitment to others, "each to all and all to each."[78] It must be remembered that there is to be "no communication among themselves." Thus, there can be no forming of alliances or amalgamating of views. The proper commitment is done by each person, in solitude, thinking of and willing for the whole, not thinking of and willing for any actual person or group. The commitment to the whole forms an identity. When that stance is taken by each member, the general will exists and is always right.

Why is the general will always right, and why do all constantly want the happiness of each of them, if not because everyone applies the word *each* to himself and thinks of himself as he votes for all? This proves that the quality of right and the notion of justice it produces are derived from the preference each person gives himself, and thus from the nature of man; that the general will, to be really such, must be general in its object as well as in its essence; that it must derive from all in order to be applied to all; and that it loses its natural rectitude when it tends toward any individual, determinate object.[79]

Rousseau enforces the themes of identity and commitment by arguing that even the individual's life is owed to the sovereign. The citizen's life "is not only a kindness of nature, but a conditional gift of the state. If the state says to a citizen,

---

[77] *Ibid.*

[78] Bk. II, ch. 4.

[79] *Ibid.*

'it is expedient for the state that you should die', he should die."[80] A person who breaks the social contract ceases to be "a moral person" and becomes "but a man, and in this situation the right of war is to kill the vanquished."[81] The sovereign is sacred, in Rousseau's eyes, and is to be respected as such.

Part of the definition of moral liberty is "obedience to the law one has prescribed for oneself."[82] In order to obtain this moral liberty, the law must be prescribed by the citizen, and in order to obtain consistency with the general will, the law must in form be both general and abstract:

> When I say that the object of the laws is always general, I have in mind that the law considers subjects as a body and actions in the abstract, never a man as an individual or a particular action…. On this view, it is immediately obvious that it is no longer necessary to ask who is to make the laws, since they are the acts of the general will; nor whether the prince is above the laws, since he is a member of the state; nor whether the law can be unjust, since no one is unjust to himself; nor how one is both free and subject to the laws, since they are merely the record of our own wills.[83]

In addition to formal attributes, true law must be derived from the general will, that is, the will created in the formation of the civil society. The general will as the source of law contains the objective, general interests of the whole community. So, both the source and the form of law make it objective, rational and universal.

Law and will, so defined, coalesce. Within the social contract the will is guided by reason rather than by appetite and is directed at the general rather than at the particular; the law instantiates through its rational form and source the objective and general interest. This internal coherence among the structural features of law and will provides moral liberty.[84]

---

[80] Bk. II, ch. 5.

[81] *Ibid.*

[82] Bk. I, ch. 8.

[83] Bk. II, ch. 6.

[84] In the *Geneva Manuscript*, a first draft of the *Social Contract*, Rousseau notes this connection between the form of law and will: "when the entire people enacts something concerning the entire people, it considers only itself…without any division of the whole. Then the object of the enactment is general like the will that enacts, and it is this act that I call a law." Roger D. Masters, ed., *On the Social Contract with Geneva Manuscript and Political Economy*, trans. Judith R. Masters (New York: St. Martin's Press, 1978), p. 190.

At several points, Rousseau warns that the populace "is often tricked" or the judgment "is not always enlightened."[85] He now introduces a most curious institution—the great legislator. There needs to be a great charismatic leader who can form an aggregate into a people. He explains the task:

> He who dares to undertake the establishment of a people should feel that he is, so to speak, in a position to change human nature, to transform each individual (who by himself is a perfect and solitary whole), into a part of a larger whole from which this individual receives, in a sense, his life and his being; to alter man's constitution in order to strengthen it…. Thus if each citizen is nothing and can do nothing except in concert with all the others, and if the force acquired by the whole is equal or superior to the sum of the natural forces of all the individuals, one can say that the legislation has achieved the highest possible point of perfection.[86]

This extraordinary person will have the tasks of moulding a people sufficiently, so that these people can create the social contract, and of framing the laws. But, the legislator is not part of the government nor would this charismatic figure exercise any power. The legislator would use religion "to compel by divine authority those whom human prudence could not move."[87] Rousseau escapes the accusation of hyperbole for once when he calls this legislator a "true miracle."

Rousseau actually does give some practical advice for implementing a government and laws. First of all, the laws are to be framed by the legislator and "submitted to the free vote of the people."[88] In practice, these laws must be appropriate to a particular people. Moreover, the people must first be prepared by some great acts of patriotism and revival. If the people are too debased, the task is impossible. "Liberty can be acquired, but it can never be recovered."[89] If a great leader can reach a people at the proper moment, then he can work with a people's peculiar history, culture, and aptitudes. Rousseau cites Peter the Great of Russia as a negative example. He had both tried "too early" in Russian history to enact his reforms

---

[85] Bk. II, chs. 3, 6.

[86] Bk. II, ch. 7.

[87] *Ibid.*

[88] *Ibid.*

[89] Bk. II, ch. 8.

and tried to turn Russians into "Germans and Englishmen, when he should have made Russians." The result is that "the Russians will never be truly civilized."[90]

Although it is necessary to work with the peculiar features of a people, it is also the case that the chief purpose of the legislator and the institutions is to form potential citizens so that they can live under the "supreme direction of the general will." This idea that human nature must be changed to fit the legitimate government also occurs in Rousseau's practical works. Rousseau believed himself to be a legislator of sorts, and, upon the request of some friends, he wrote a tract on Corsica (1765) and one on Poland (1771), both published after his death. In the *Constitutional Project for Corsica*, Rousseau advises "form the nation to fit the government," and in *The Government of Poland*, Rousseau praises great legislators of the past—Moses who founded the Jewish nation, Lycurgus who founded Sparta, and Numa who founded the Roman Republic—for creating patriotic peoples through rigorous institutions, "peculiar rites and ceremonies."[91]

Rousseau mentions other conditions that are important in implementing a government and laws founded on the general will. The state must be small so that the people can know each other and the social bond can remain strong: "a small state is proportionately stronger than a large one."[92] He prefers a hardy, liberty-loving people for the creation of a general will, and he gives the island of Corsica as a prime example.[93] There also needs to be equality among the people: "no citizen should be so rich as to be capable of buying another citizen, and none so poor that he is forced to sell himself."[94] At the end of Book II he lists the condition "on which depends the success of all the others; a part with which the great legislator secretly occupies himself."[95] The condition is that every political society has constitutional, civic, and criminal laws, but the most important is that the "law" be composed of the mores, customs, and beliefs of the people. These touch the "hearts of citizens" and are the great bond of a society.

---

[90] *Ibid.*

[91] Frederick M. Watkins, ed., *Rousseau: Political Writings* (New York: Nelson, 1953), pp. 277 and 165.

[92] Bk. II, ch. 9.

[93] Bk. II, ch. 10.

[94] Bk. II, ch. 11.

[95] Bk. II, ch. 12.

The state that has been developed up to this point in the first two books of the *Social Contract* is more than just a political system. It is a moral order: law and order are tied; the general will is always right by its very nature; and the great charismatic legislator teaches and nurtures the laws of the heart. Above all, this is an order that replicates features in nature so that we become free of any sense of dependence or subservience, and as we regain our natural sense of mastery we gain the new experience of moral liberty.

The last two books discuss the operation of government and the preserving of popular sovereignty. Book III focuses on the structure and administration of the government, and Book IV discusses various means for preserving the general will and legitimate government.

Rousseau begins Book III by making a distinction between the sovereign and the government. The latter is the administration in charge of the execution of the laws. The legislative power belongs only to the people who, united by the general will, are sovereign. Although the government has "only a borrowed and subordinate life" to the sovereign people, it is still a potential danger to a legitimate state. The government, or administration, will have "assemblies, councils, a power to deliberate and decide, rights, titles and privileges," all of which could well give it a "sensibility" distinct from the sovereign. In a rather fanciful couple of paragraphs, Rousseau uses geometry to illustrate the balance required among the government, people, and the sovereign. The size of the administration needs to be in inverse proportion to the size of the population. The idea is that an administration increases in power in order to have "more repressive force." So, Rousseau says, "in order to be good, the government must be relatively stronger in proportion as the populace is more numerous." The concomitant problem is that, inevitably, the administrators are presented with "more temptations and the means of abusing their power." The major point is that a balance needs to be kept so that the government interest is always sacrificed to the people "and not the people to the government."[96]

Rousseau gives an original twist to the traditional classification of governments into monarchy, aristocracy, and democracy. When the government or administration is operated by all of the people, it is a democracy; when it is run by a few, it is an aristocracy; and when it is run by one, it is a monarchy. These

---

[96] Bk. III, ch. 1.

forms can also be mixed. In general, the small states fit democracy; the intermediate ones fit an aristocracy; and large ones fit a monarchy.[97]

It may seem odd, but Rousseau does not advocate a democratic government or administration. As a general rule, he says, "it is not good for one who makes the law to execute them." The danger will be that the private interests of the many will take precedence over the general will. There will be the temptation to make laws that aid the one class. It would, thus, simply be too difficult to operate such a democratic administration: "a true democracy has never existed and never will."[98] Rousseau actually argues for an elective aristocracy to run the administration, because this will bring experience and enlightenment into the government. An hereditary aristocracy reflects grave inequalities and decay in a society; and a natural aristocracy is for "simple people." The monarchical form is the most dangerous, in part, because of its very effectiveness. Too easily, the king's interest engulfs the common good of the general will.

Rousseau does not hide his contempt for monarchical governments and administrations. They are composed of "petty burglars, petty swindlers, petty intriguers, whose petty talents, which cause them to attain high positions at court, serve only to display their incompetence to the public as soon as they reach these positions."[99] One can easily suspect that, here, Rousseau is targeting several fellow *philosophes* who believed in the role of an enlightened despot and even worked for the king.

Rousseau relates each governmental form to economic and social conditions. The democratic form, for example, needs an "equality in rank and fortune."[100] An aristocracy is based upon an inequality of wealth and, if the offices are elected, of merit.[101] The monarchical form is appropriate for large states where great inequalities will occur, but even there it is much worse than a republic. As evidence, he cites with approval the arguments found in Machiavelli's *The Prince*, "the book of republicans."[102]

---

[97] Bk. III, chs. 2–3.

[98] Bk. III, ch. 4.

[99] Bk. III, ch. 6.

[100] Bk. III, ch. 4.

[101] Bk. III, ch. 15.

[102] Bk. III, ch. 6.

Rousseau follows a tradition from Aristotle to Montesquieu that correlates climate and geography with types of political regimes. If the climate is too cold, there is not enough economic surplus to support a civilized state; if the climate is too warm, the surplus is too great, the population is too large, and empires and monarchies are the rule. He begins chapter 8 with the announcement: "Since liberty is not a fruit of every climate, it is not within the reach of all people."[103] It is necessary to see precisely how much surplus different climates and soils produce. This, in turn, will determine the population and affect the type of government:

> Places where men's labour yields only what is necessary ought to be inhabited by barbarous peoples; in places such as these all polity would be impossible. Places where the surplus of products over labour is moderate are suited to free peoples. Those where an abundant and fertile soil produces a great deal in return for a small amount of labour require a monarchical form of government, in order that the subject's excess of surplus may be consumed by the prince's luxurious living.[104]

The best government, he notes in the next chapter, is one where "the citizens become populous and multiply the most."[105] This is an infallible sign of good government.

All governments will eventually degenerate. Just as a private will "acts constantly against the general will" so, too, does the government act against the sovereign. Thus, what happens is that gradually "the government usurps sovereignty, the social compact is broken, and all ordinary citizens, on recovering by right their natural liberty, are forced but not obliged to obey."[106] Such a change is "a natural and inevitable tendency." It is like the human body, he declares, in that the body politic "begins to die from the very moment of its birth, and carries within itself the causes of its destruction."[107]

A major difficulty faced by a regime founded upon the social contract is that the "sovereign can act only when the populace is assembled."[108] It is most difficult to keep the commitment and moral virtue required for such a state: "It is

---

[103] Bk. III, ch. 8.

[104] *Ibid.*

[105] Bk. III, ch. 9.

[106] Bk. III, ch. 10.

[107] Bk. III, ch. 11.

[108] Bk. III, ch. 12.

our weakness, our vices and our prejudices that shrink them. Base souls do not believe in great men; vile slaves smile with an air of mockery at the word liberty."[109] Nevertheless, the only steps that can be taken to preserve the regime are ones that stress the assemblies of the people. The sovereignty of the assembled people protects the body politic and also puts a "curb on the government."[110]

Because it is only the sovereign people in assembly that can legitimately direct and protect the body politic, Rousseau is adamantly opposed to representation of the people's legislative power. Also, he argues that the use of money to relieve individuals of civic obligations will only enhance the decline of the state. He warns that "the cooling off of patriotism, the activity of private interest, the largeness of states, conquests, the abuse of government: these have suggested the route of using deputies or representatives of the people in the nation's assemblies."[111] The only antidote is to have the body politic remain small and to keep the public active in its operation. The English, in contrast, believe themselves to be free because of their representatives. This is false because their only free act is to elect the representatives. "Once they are elected, the population is enslaved; it is nothing."[112]

Only the people meeting in assembly can be the sovereign, exercise the legislative power, and control the administration. Rousseau proposes two questions that should always be placed upon the agenda:

> The first: *Does it please the sovereign to preserve the present form of government?*
> The second: *Does it please the people to leave its administration to those who are now in charge of it?*[113]

Such questions will demonstrate the source of authority for the government and will confirm that sovereignty resides in the assembly. Rousseau does not advocate a legislative chamber with standing committees and the customary compromises between interests and opinions. The function of the assembly of all citizens is not to represent, but to instantiate the general will through responding to questions put by the government.[114]

---

[109] *Ibid.*

[110] Bk. III, ch. 14.

[111] Bk. III, ch. 15.

[112] *Ibid.*

[113] Bk. III, ch. 18.

[114] Richard Fralin, *Rousseau and Representation* (New York: Columbia University Press, 1978), p. 156.

In Book IV Rousseau turns to historical examples to find some means for preserving a legitimate government. The key remains a common, uniting general will, and this appears to be possible only in small states. In one of his many paeans for simpler and smaller states, Rousseau asks: "When, among the happiest people in the world, bands of peasants are seen regulating their affairs of state under an oak tree, and always acting wisely, can one help scorning the refinements of other nations, which make themselves illustrious and miserable with so much art and mystery?"[115] The general will itself is "always constant, unalterable, and pure," but the task is to keep it from being made subordinate to other wills. One way of accomplishing this task is to ensure that the public assembly is asked proper questions—questions that engender a general will response. We have already seen at the end of Book III that the questions are plebiscitary in nature, requiring a yes or no answer. The questions do not call for a judgment on the merit of some policy; the questions require an act of will to agree or not. Rousseau continues this approach. The assembly of citizens should be asked what is advantageous to the state rather than what is advantageous to this person or group. Then, the response will create the general will; the "social bond of unity" will not be "broken in all hearts."[116]

Rousseau devotes chapter 2 to the mechanism of voting that would be appropriate for his regime. The creation of the social compact itself requires unanimous consent; otherwise it would not be voluntary. Those who do not join, in effect, have the legal status of foreigners, who, by staying, in fact give tacit consent and are thereby obliged to obey the government. The sovereignty of the populace refers only to those citizens who have entered the compact. There is no idea of universal suffrage.[117] Once the regime is established, a simple majority among the citizens is sufficient when dealing with minor matters and

---

[115] Bk. IV, ch. 1.

[116] *Ibid.*

[117] There has been a long controversy about who is included within Rousseau's idea of popular sovereignty and about how consistent his practical works on Corsica and Poland are with the *Social Contract*. He refers in some writings to classes within a population and with only a select few as voting members. The reason for the small group voting rather than the entire population, which would be only males in any case, is that citizens alone make up the sovereign, and citizens are only those who have unanimously consented to the social compact. See the definitive article by David Rosenfeld, "Rousseau's Unanimous Contract and the Doctrine of Popular Sovereignty," *History of Political Thought* VIII (Spring, 1987), pp. 83–110. See also, the full study by Fralin, *Rousseau and Representation.*

when some speed is required. But, as Rousseau says, the "more important and serious the resolutions are, the closer the prevailing opinion should be to unanimity."[118] Votes are not designed to be a method for settling disputes and balancing interests, a civilized substitute for conflict and war. Voting is perceived by Rousseau as a means of enhancing harmony and unity. At the conclusion of a vote, assuming that the citizens have been asked a proper question and that the citizens are actually focusing on what would be generally applicable, the general will is known. Rousseau explains the consequence for the minority voter after such a vote:

> Each man, in giving his vote, states his opinion on this matter, and the declaration of the general will is drawn from the counting of votes. When, therefore, the opinion contrary to mine prevails, this proves merely that I was in error, and that what I took to be the general will was not so. If my private opinion had prevailed, I would have done something other than what I had wanted. In that case I would not have been free.
>
> This presupposes, it is true, that all the characteristics of the general will are still in the majority.[119]

After the vote we know, indisputably, the general will and can accept it. Unity and harmony can now easily be achieved because the citizens know that the general will never errs. A majority vote composed of the right kind of voter will show the general will, but the ideal remains to get as close to actual unanimity in voting as possible: "The more harmony reigns in the assemblies, that is to say, the closer opinions come to unanimity, the more dominant too is the general will."[120]

In the rest of the book Rousseau describes practical institutions used by ancient republics to preserve their regimes and vigour. Chapter 4, the largest chapter in the book, examines how the Roman council, "made of two hundred thousand men," was actually able to make decisions while being a popular assembly. The next chapter looks at the Tribunate. This institution, as described by Rousseau, was a

---

[118] Bk. IV, ch. 2.

[119] *Ibid.*

[120] Bk. IV, ch. 1.

very small number of men whose task was to "protect the sovereign against the government, as the tribunes of the people did in Rome; sometimes to sustain the government against the people, as the Council of Ten now does in Venice."[121] Given Rousseau's explanation, the institution is strikingly similar to the legislator because none of the examples of a Tribunate was a part of either the legislative or the executive power. Rousseau writes approvingly in chapter 6 of the dictatorship techniques used by the Roman Republic to address certain emergencies. Chapter 7 describes the ancient institution of the public censor. This particular institution uses example and even ridicule to shape public opinion and, in that way, forestall the corruption of morals. These various institutions illustrate that Rousseau envisages a circular interplay among the laws that "give rise to morals" and beliefs and the morals and beliefs that support laws. There apparently needs to be some trans-governmental institutions, such as the great charismatic legislator, the tribunate, or the public censor to keep the interplay in motion. The fundamental purpose of all these institutional devices is to preserve and nurture the commitment to the general will.

The final chapter presents the most important means for sustaining the general will, the civil religion. The use of religion by the legislator[122] was a calculated subterfuge to add transcendental authority to his pronouncements. The civil religion, in contrast, is meant to be taken in deadly earnest.

Rousseau first gives the reader a thumbnail sketch of the history of religions prior to Christianity. He finds that the first states were all theocratic; that is, religious and political rule were not distinguished. The boundaries of the state were the boundaries of a people's gods, and, if a people were conquered, they accepted the new gods of the conquerors. A great change in history came with Judaism and, particularly, Christianity. The Jewish people refused to accept the gods of Babylon and Syria, which "brought them the persecutions we read of in their history." Later, Christianity entered the world by establishing a spiritual kingdom on earth. The effect was disastrous: "since there has always been a prince and civil laws, this double power has given rise to a perpetual jurisdictional conflict that has made all good polity impossible

---

[121] Bk. IV, ch. 5.

[122] Bk. IV, ch. 8.

in Christian states, and no one has ever been able to know whether it is the priest or the master whom one is obliged to obey."[123] The only philosopher who has seen this conflict clearly is Hobbes. Rousseau lauds the solution of the *Leviathan* of combining the two realms with the ruler as supreme. Since "no state has ever been founded without religion serving as its base" and since the distinct secular and religious realms declared by Christianity hopelessly divide a society, the place of religion in the political system has to be addressed, regardless of one's opinion of Hobbes.[124]

Rousseau lists three types of religion that might be utilized. First is the "pure and simple religion of the Gospel," or as he sometimes names it, the religion of man. Second is the religion of the pagans, where civil and religious laws are one and identify a single state. Third is the religion of the priests, found in Roman Christianity, the Lamas, and Japan. Each of these religions has its faults. Because the third type leads to disunity, Rousseau says, it "is so bad that it is a waste of time to amuse oneself by proving it." The second type does unite "the divine cult with love of the laws." Yet, these are religions of superstitions and deceits, and too easily they can make people "bloodthirsty and intolerant." The religion of man, which he distinguishes from the Christianity of the day, is "holy, sublime, and true," but, he adds, "I know nothing more contrary to the social spirit."[125] It is so otherworldly that, if practised, a political society—let alone an army— would be an impossibility. Indeed, he says, the very terms "a Christian Republic... are mutually exclusive."[126]

The solution is a civic religion. The subjects may have any other religion they want "as long as they are good citizens in this life." Whatever theological dogmas are believed, they must not interfere with the morality and duty of citizens. Civil and theological intolerance are inseparable, and Rousseau warns that "whoever dares to say *outside the church there is no salvation* ought to be expelled from the state."[127] Harmony is always the goal, and the dogmas of the civil religion are designed precisely for this purpose:

---

[123] *Ibid.*

[124] *Ibid.*

[125] *Ibid.*

[126] *Ibid.*

[127] *Ibid.*

The existence of a powerful, intelligent, beneficent divinity that foresees and provides; the life to come; the happiness of the just; the punishment of the wicked; the sanctity of the social contract and of the laws. These are the positive dogmas. As for the negative dogmas, I limit them to just one, namely intolerance. It is part of the cults we have excluded.[128]

Rousseau calls these "sentiments of sociality," but they are not lightly to be believed, for "without [them] it is impossible to be a good citizen or a faithful subject." The person who does not believe them will be banished. Furthermore, "if, after having publicly acknowledged these same dogmas, a person acts as if he does not believe them, he should be put to death; he has committed the greatest of crimes: he has lied before the laws."[129] The civil profession is a matter of life and death; the commitment to the whole is not a matter of mere utility but is of one's whole being.

In the *Discourse on Political Economy* (1755) Rousseau provides an eloquent statement of the mission of education in instilling the civic religion:

If…they are trained early enough never to consider their persons except in terms of being related to the body of the state, and not to perceive their own existence except as part of the state's existence, they will eventually come to identify themselves in some way with this larger whole; to feel themselves to be members of the country, to love it with that exquisite sentiment that every isolated man feels only for himself, to elevate their soul perpetually toward this great object, and thereby to transform into a sublime virtue [love for all] this dangerous disposition [*amour propre*] from which arises all our vices.[130]

Consequently, Rousseau's phrase "sanctity of the social contract and of the laws" is meant quite literally. To mock, ridicule, disobey, or show disbelief, in

---

[128] Bk. IV, ch. 8. The precise nature of Rousseau's religious beliefs are much disputed. The traditional interpretation is to endorse the views expressed by the Savoyard Vicar, a character in *Emile*, as those of Rousseau. The views are of a romantic natural religion and a repudiation of such doctrines as revelation, original sin, divine interventions, and the authority of the Church. See Ronald Grimsley, *Rousseau and the Religious Quest* (Oxford: Clarendon Press, 1968); *The Philosophy of Rousseau* (Oxford: Oxford University Press, 1973). In a carefully reasoned and well-documented article Peter Emberley has criticized this understanding of Rousseau, "Rousseau versus the Savoyard Vicar: The Profession of Faith Considered," *Interpretation*, Vol. 14 (Nos. 2 and 3), pp. 299–329. Joshua Mitchell is also insightful: *Not by Reason Alone* (Chicago: University of Chicago Press, 1993), pp. 98–124.

[129] Bk. IV, ch. 8.

[130] *Discourse on Political Economy* as contained in Cress, *The Basic Political Writings*, p. 125.

effect, deprives the social contract and the laws of their sacred power. The requisite personal commitment of citizenship would be dissolved.[131]

CONCLUSIONS

There is an understandable tendency for students of Rousseau to view him through the eyes of those who were influenced by him, directly or indirectly, and, in this manner, to provide a coherent and intelligible explication of Rousseau's original and heady but rather mysteriously concocted political philosophy. This method of analysis could be called the successor explanation: through the eyes of the German philosophers Immanuel Kant (1724–1804), G. W. F. Hegel (1770–1831), and Karl Marx (1818–1883) one can see more clearly and, thus, unravel the essential themes compressed by Rousseau. Certainly, Kant and Hegel explicitly found in Rousseau themes which they used. Of especial importance to them, for example, was the idea of the rational development of the free will as the road to human freedom and happiness.[132] With Marx, the influence of Rousseau was not clearly acknowledged, but Marxian categories are used by commentators: "What Rousseau is... describing in the *Social Contract* is the best possible polity that might be formed within the state of alienation characteristic of market society."[133]

Another approach is to see how Rousseau uses the ancient societies of Sparta and Rome, plus the teachings of Plato, to criticize modern societies and to construct a

---

[131] This view of civil religion constitutes another striking difference from Locke who was insistent, in his words, on a "wall of separation" and on keeping the civil society limited to "outward things, such as Money, Lands, Houses, Furniture, and the like." Locke would have been horrified at the scope of the civil religion in Rousseau. See, John Locke, *A Letter Concerning Toleration*, ed. James Tully (Indianapolis: Hackett, 1983), p. 26.

[132] An excellent assessment of the mass of literature that stresses the Kantian themes in Rousseau is provided by Stephen Ellenburg, "Rousseau and Kant: Principles of Political Right," in *Rousseau After Two Hundred Years*, ed. R. A. Leigh (Cambridge: Cambridge University Press, 1982), pp. 3–22. Andrew Levine's study is a perfect example of a Kantian interpretation: *The Politics of Autonomy* (Amherst: University of Massachusetts Press, 1976).

[133] Asher Horowitz, "Will, Community and Alienation in Rousseau's *Social Contract*," *Canadian Journal of Political and Social Theory* (Fall, 1986), p. 79. Andrew Levine also argues for a strong influence: *The General Will: Rousseau, Marx, and Communism* (Cambridge: Cambridge University Press, 1993). Robert Wokler provides a careful analysis of the influence of Rousseau on Marx and of the secondary literature on this topic: "Rousseau and Marx," in *The Nature of Political Theory*, eds. David Miller and Larry Siedentop (Oxford: Clarendon Press, 1983), pp. 219–46.

legitimate political system. This method of analysis could be called a predecessor explanation. It seems obviously helpful in understanding Rousseau's social institutions, which have the strikingly non-modern but classical trait of combining the moral with the political. Rousseau's many laudatory references to the Roman Republic and to Sparta are well known.[134] There have been many interpreters, particularly of Rousseau's political system, who have also found it illuminating to read Rousseau in conversation with Plato.[135]

Nevertheless, particularly with a thinker as genuinely original as Rousseau, one must be wary of assuming that his political philosophy is undistorted by a successor or predecessor explanation. If there were any one overwhelming factor that would cast doubt on the view that Rousseau is working fundamentally within the Greek and Roman philosophic and political traditions, it surely would be the clear primacy Rousseau places on the will over reason. Because the concept of will supports his model of a legitimate political system, starting with this concept should more clearly demonstrate the coherence and originality of Rousseau's thought and should make possible a more adequate assessment of the consequences of his political system. Even here, the differences in interpretations are quite wide. Some see a totalitarian democracy;[136] others see a modern sensitivity toward alienation and the need for authenticity and community.[137] Certainly, literature has been greatly influenced by

---

[134] Judith N. Shklar, *Men and Citizens: A Study of Rousseau's Social Theory* (London: Cambridge University Press, 1969) is one of the best interpretations stressing the republican theme in Rousseau.

[135] No one has written an essay critically examining the claim of Plato's influence on Rousseau. M. J. Silverthorne cites the various interpreters since 1918 who do see significant Platonic influence on Rousseau's thought. Silverthorne himself documents Rousseau's use of the *Laws*: "Rousseau's Plato," *Studies on Voltaire and the Eighteenth Century* 116 (1973), pp. 235–49. In addition to these, there are others who argue that Rousseau was often responding to Plato: Allan Bloom, ed., *Emile* (New York: Basic Books, 1979) and Hilail Gilden, *Rousseau's Social Contract: The Design of the Argument* (Chicago: University of Chicago Press, 1983); Masters, "Introduction," in *On the Social Contract*.

[136] J. L. Talmon, *The Origins of Totalitarian Democracy* (London: Sphere Books, 1970); David Gathier, "The Politics of Redemption," in *Trent Rousseau Papers*, ed. J. MacAdam, M. Neumann, and G. LaFrance (Ottawa: University of Ottawa Press, 1980), pp. 71-98; Michael Walzer, *The Revolution of the Saints* (New York: Atheneum, 1969).

[137] Carole Pateman's *Participation and Democratic Theory* (Cambridge: Cambridge University Press, 1970) is a classic Rousseauistic explanation. See also, Benjamin Barber, *Strong Democracy: Participatory Politics for a New Age* (Berkeley: University of California Press, 1984); Marshall Berman, *The Politics of Authenticity* (New York: Atheneum, 1970).

Rousseau. His works are one of the sources of romanticism with its stress on the natural and its critique of the debilitating effect of modernity on the psyche.[138]

An examination of three broad topics, as perceived by Rousseau—the general will with moral liberty; popular sovereignty and participation; the institutional structure within the political system—will quickly establish that his thought continues to have an enormous influence.

The General Will with Moral Liberty

The general will alone makes possible moral liberty, which is the greatest of human goals, and the general will is central to almost all that Rousseau thought. As one of the best commentators has written: "The general will expresses so much for Rousseau—divinity, voluntariness, generality, Sparta, citizenship, equality, lawfulness, the common good, antiquity, modernity, Plato, Locke, Machiavellian civic *virtù*—that it is too resonant not to be heard."[139]

Because Rousseau begins a major alternative to the dominant liberal tradition, it is essential to understand the philosophic break he made. His originality is particularly evident in the transformation he makes in the key ideas of will and freedom. Although Rousseau's concept of the will differs in several respects from Augustine's, it is, nonetheless, closer to the Judeo-Christian theological tradition than it is to that of classical Greece. With the latter there was no clear idea of will or free agency independent of the functioning of the mind. Albrecht Dihle draws the contrast:

> Our term "will" denotes only the resulting intention, leaving out any special references to thought, instinct, or emotion as possible sources of that intention. Greek, on the other hand, is able to express intention only together with one of its cause, but never in its own right.[140]

---

[138] Paul M. Spurlin, *Rousseau in America* (Tuscaloosa: University of Alabama Press, 1969); Catherine Zuckert shows the influence on James Fenimore Cooper's novel in *Natural Right and the American Imagination: Political Philosophy in Novel Form* (Savage, Md.: Rowan and Littlefield, 1990); Hannah Arendt has a brilliant analysis of Herman Melville's *Billy Budd* in which she demonstrates Rousseau's presence: *On Revolution* (New York: Viking Press, 1963), pp. 74–83. Arthur Miller's play, *Death of a Salesman*, is, in effect, a Rousseauian analysis: the father has no identity other than his economic role; he views himself only through the eyes of others; he is motivated solely by *amour propre*; he is both incapable of union with his family and with others, and he is alone; his death is that of a salesman, not of a person.

[139] Riley, *The General Will Before Rousseau*, p. 260.

[140] Albrecht Dihle, *The Theory of Will in Classical Antiquity* (Berkeley: University of California Press, 1982), pp. 25–26.

Thus, the intention behind a human action is always conflated with the originating reason or emotion.[141] For the Greeks, the equivalent to the ideal of moral freedom, which is for Rousseau the mark of a full and uncorrupted self, would be a certain kind of intellectual activity: "freedom is brought about when the human intellect has chosen the aim of action according to the true order of being, and has not been hindered in its efforts by error, emotion, or compulsion."[142] The opposite also holds; that is, when human intellectual activity is restricted and the "rational order of being" has been inadequately perceived, then to that degree human freedom of action has been diminished.[143]

Perhaps the key difference between the philosophical anthropology of the Judeo-Christian tradition and that of classical antiquity is that willing or free agency was conceived of as independent of, though related to, human intellectual activity. The concept of the will remains notoriously problematic, but with the Judeo-Christian formulation the activity of the will has been clearly differentiated from the functioning of the mind.[144] In examining the will by itself, usually two dimensions are articulated. One dimension is free choosing or deciding. Willing, in this sense, is viewed as undetermined or uncaused. It is often argued that a condition for moral autonomy is just such a free or uncaused will. Patrick Riley captures this position:

> One must assume the possibility of a free action that is binding for the reason that morality depends in part on undetermined choice: not undetermined in the sense that there is no reason for such willing but in the sense that we are free to accept or reject the reason, thereby earning justifiable praise or blame, and that the will is not determined, in the strictly causal sense in which a stone is necessitated to fall, by anything whatsoever.[145]

---

[141] "Intention itself, whether originating from reasoning or from emotion, can never be named, in the language of Homer, without reference to one or the other of these origins." *Ibid.*, p. 26.

[142] *Ibid.*, p. 71.

[143] *Ibid.*, p. 47.

[144] As was discussed in chapter 4, Augustine is usually held to be the "discoverer" of the will as a distinct concept.

[145] Riley, *Will and Political Legitimacy*, p. 12.

This autonomous or voluntaristic feature of the will, of course, is evident in Rousseau and is particularly stressed in Kantian interpretations.[146]

The second dimension of the will is experiential. The will is described as an organ or faculty with experiential content and structure. It is common in the Judeo-Christian tradition, beginning with Augustine, for thinkers to discuss the constituting experiences of the will. It is this second dimension that needs to be explored in order to see Rousseau's originality. The experiential content provides the point of reference for defining the self or human nature. With this dimension of the will one can understand the intentions behind his model of a legitimate political system.

Rousseau's analysis of the will is briefly discussed in the *Second Discourse*, as we have already seen, but his major analysis is found in the novel *Emile*. In this work he states that materialism cannot explain the existence or the nature of a self that has self-consciousness and a sense of free will. Rousseau asks through the Savoyard Vicar, one of the characters in the novel, "if it is true that all matter senses, where shall I conceive the sensitive unity or the individual *I* to be? Will it be in each molecule of matter or in the aggregate bodies?"[147] Neither can the self be reduced to instincts. In the famous quotation from the *Second Discourse*, Rousseau claims that humans are "free to acquiesce, or to resist, and it is above all in the consciousness of this freedom that the spirituality of his soul shows itself."[148]

The will, then, cannot be understood by looking for some deeper level from which it can be derived. Rather, Rousseau provides a map of the experiential domain of the will. There are three essential parts to his map. It is grounded in nature and passion; it is self-sufficient; and it emanates a sense of mastery.[149]

[146.] F. M. Barnard has perceptively probed the relationship in Rousseau among self-choosing, right acting, and political rationality, "Will and Political Rationality in Rousseau," *Political Studies* 32 (1984), pp. 369–84.

[147] Bloom, *Emile*, p. 279. After his criticism of materialism, the Vicar concludes that man is "animated by an immaterial substance" (p. 281).

[148] *Second Discourse*, p. 114.

[149] I am accepting Rousseau's oft repeated claim to being consistent in his writings. Although there is a discussion of the will in the *Second Discourse*, it is quite brief. *Emile* is clearly his masterpiece on the will. It should be added that it would have made little sense for Rousseau to have provided his summary of the *Social Contract* in the *Emile* if he did not view the *Social Contract* as constructed for Emile (Bloom, *Emile*, p. 462). For a discussion of Rousseau's consistency, see: John Charvet, "Rousseau and the Ideal of Community," and Robert Wokler, "A Reply to Charvet: Rousseau and the Perfectibility of Man," *History of Political Thought* 1 (Spring, 1980), pp. 69–90.

Rousseau's genealogy of human moral character, as described in *Emile*, differs slightly from the story in the *Second Discourse*. He begins again with the natural primitive and with the one original passion: "The source of our passions, the origin and the principle of all the others, the only one born with man and which never leaves him so long as he lives is self-love—a primitive, innate passion, which is anterior to every other, and of which all others are in a sense only modifications."[150] Rousseau posits two principles in human nature in the *Second Discourse*, but here self-love is the original natural passion and pity or compassion is derivative. This natural origin guarantees that humans begin good and potentially perfectible.

> Let us set now as an incontestable maxim that the first movements of nature are always right. There is no original perversity in the human heart. There is not a single vice to be found in it of which it cannot be said how and whence it entered. The sole passion natural to man is *amour de soi* or *amour-propre* taken in an extended sense. This *amour-propre* in itself or relative to us is good and useful; and since it has no necessary relation to others, it is in this respect naturally neutral. It becomes good or bad only by the application made of it and the relations given to it.[151]

As Rousseau reconstructs the story of human progress, also recounted in the *Second Discourse*, the initial unity of the will becomes fragmented in society when humans abandon their "true needs" and when the insatiable *amour propre* expands through comparisons with others: "What makes man essentially good is to have few needs and to compare himself little to others; what makes him essentially wicked is to have many needs and to depend very much on opinion."[152]

The skeleton description of a united and good self applies only to the natural primitive. In society imagination increases human needs and dependence on others, the will becomes corrupted and the individual becomes unhappy. It is essential to note that human unhappiness cannot be explained by a division or flaw within the will, as is depicted by the doctrine of original sin. Also, human unhappiness cannot be traced to a failure of reason or a lack of knowledge. In fact,

---

[150] Bloom, *Emile*, pp. 212–13.

[151] *Ibid.*, p. 92.

[152] *Ibid.*, p. 214.

as Rousseau says in the *Second Discourse*, "Reason engenders *amour propre* and reflection fortifies it."[153] In the first explanation of unhappiness (division or flaw within the will), one would need God's help to unite the will and to provide happiness, and in the second explanation (a failure of reason), better reasoning or information would be necessary. Since Rousseau does not accept either the Christian doctrine of original sin or the Greek view of the potential primacy of the rational faculty over passion, he finds the causes and solutions of human unhappiness elsewhere.

In brief, alien causes corrupt human natural passions, including *amour propre*, and these occur with the very development of civilization.[154] In place of a Christian catechism Emile is given a more appropriate one: "Let him know that man is naturally good; let him feel it; let him judge his neighbour by himself. But let him see that society depraves and perverts men."[155] Why does humanity's "fatal progress" lead to suffering and evil? The answer, which repeats with more detail the answer already given in the *Second Discourse*, is found in the peculiar nature of the will. The malleable and perfectible will needs boundaries or an order, and in nature there are provided just such boundaries through non-personal necessity. No self in this state experiences a debilitating loss of power or worth. There is a natural order for the will. In society there is only conventional order, and the self is constantly experiencing unrealized desires and a debilitating loss of power and worth. Rousseau's explanation is: "Dependence on things, since it has no morality, is in no way detrimental to freedom and engenders no vices. Dependence on man, since it is without order, engenders all the vices, and by it, master and slave are mutually corrupted...."[156] Without boundaries and order the will, initially united and good, succumbs to the temptations of society. Why does it succumb? Augustine, in his own exploration of the will, had noted that to will and to be able are not the same, and Rousseau comes to a similar conclusion:

> I always have the power to will, I do not always have the force to execute. When I abandon myself to temptations, I act according to the impulsion of external objects. When I reproach myself for this weakness, I listen

---

[153] *Second Discourse*, p. 132.

[154] Bloom, *Emile*, pp. 212–13.

[155] *Ibid.*, p. 237.

[156] *Ibid.*, p. 85.

only to my will. I am enslaved because of my vices and free because of my remorse. The sentiment of my freedom is effaced in me only when I become depraved and finally prevent the voice of the soul from being raised against the law of the body.[157]

If the cause of evil and suffering is not in human will but in external causes, there also must lie the solution. The external order must be so constructed that a will (of this nature) can regain its strength (the force to execute), its unity, and its happiness.

In what then, consists human wisdom or the road of true happiness? [It] is in diminishing the excess of the desires over the faculties and putting power and will in perfect equality. It is only then that, with all the powers in action, the soul will nevertheless remain peaceful and that man will be well ordered.[158]

The grounding of the will in nature and passion is the first part of Rousseau's map of the will. He is able to demonstrate both what humans are and how humans came to be civilized and, in our terms, alienated. Thus, the very functioning of the will, its nature and passion, entails the political system of the *Social Contract*. Humans need a structure providing an external order that does not debilitate but that nurtures our nature. It is easy to recognize the intention that permeates the *Social Contract*.

The second part of Rousseau's map of the experiential domain of the will is self-sufficiency. We have already seen that this ideal permeated the *Second Discourse*. But, it is a premise necessary for Rousseau's notions of happiness, perfectibility, goodness, immortality, and freedom. The reverse also holds true in that the lack of self-sufficiency explains the unhappiness in human existence. There are, in Rousseau's account, no structural flaws in nature or in the human will, and, as a consequence, the existence of evil and corruption is laid at the door of the fall from self-sufficiency into dependence on others. Personal wickedness is traced to weakness of the will relative to the temptations of the imagination engendered by society. In short, one is unable to be self-sufficient. The causes of unhappiness are

---

[157] *Ibid.*, p. 280. With Augustine there is a counter will, as it were, but with Rousseau the will is simply weak relative to the temptation. See the analysis by Walter B. Mead, "Will and Moral Faculty," in *The Ethical Dimension of Political Life*, ed. Francis Canavan (Durham: Duke University Press, 1983), pp. 61–77.

[158] *Ibid.*, p. 80.

outside the will; in principle, the will is self-sufficient. Humans need only the proper context—the *Social Contract* or the educational program for the young Emile—in which to develop. Indeed, the faculty of perfectibility, which caused humanity's facade of progress but real moral decline, logically requires a premise of self-sufficiency; otherwise, self-perfectibility would be impossible.

Even Rousseau's uses of freedom in the senses of self-choosing and of right-choosing depend upon this attribute of self-sufficiency. He clearly thinks that the greater the self-sufficiency, the greater the freedom. Thus, he constantly advises the individual person to perfect the balance between desires and strength, needs and wants. When the balance is achieved, as it was in the state of nature, humans are self-sufficient and free. When the balance is lost, the choosing self is propelled by alien causes that destroy the capacity for free-choosing. Only the self-sufficient will can freely choose. Freedom, in the sense of autonomous self-choosing, presumes the self-sufficiency of the will.

The notion of freedom as right-choosing also builds upon the critical attribute of self-sufficiency. With its grounding in nature and passion, a free will would, by its very nature, want only the good, according to Rousseau. Undetermined self-choosing and substantive right-choosing are but two dimensions of the will: "Doubtless, I am not free not to want my own good; I am not free to want what is bad for me. But it is in precisely this that my freedom consists—my being able to will only what is suitable to me, or what I deem to be such, without anything external to me determining."[159] Rousseau's reasoning seems like double-think to many people. But, he is making a powerful psychological point. A person who feels engaged and purposeful will experience the condition as freedom. A person who feels confused and uncertain experiences the condition as being trapped or alienated.[160]

In addition to self-choosing and right-choosing, freedom has another dimension, and this comprises the third key part of Rousseau's experiential map

---

[159] *Ibid.*, p. 280.

[160] For a modern example of the continual debate between Lockean understanding of liberty and the Rousseauian conception of freedom, see the debate on the merits of psychosurgery between Peter McL. Black, who is moved, unknowingly, by the ideal of freedom, and Thomas S. Szasz, who insists on the individual's absolute right to decide. Dr. Black argues that certain kinds of obsessive behaviour prohibit free decision making or a free life in any sense, all of which could be corrected by surgery. Then, such people would feel and, in fact, be free. Dr. Szasz views all of this as a violation of rights and a frightening use of arrogant power, *Humanist* (July-August, 1977), pp. 6–11.

of the will: the experience of mastery. Without this experience no self can be complete, free and happy. In short, no other experience is as essential to being a full person. This is not mastery in some vulgar and possessive sense. Attempts to overreach oneself—to extend desires over needs—negate the development of the sense of mastery. Rousseau asks, "Does it follow that I am not my own master, because I am not the master of being somebody else than me?"[161] In actuality, the sense of mastery serves to restrain human desires and action: "I have never believed that man's freedom consisted in doing what he wants, but rather in not doing what he did not wish…."[162] This negative formulation accentuates purposeful mastery as creating the essential sentiment of freedom, in contrast to the simple absence of impediments.

The ultimate goal of the educational regimen for Emile is to create this very sense of mastery. Only a will developed to attain this sentiment can be called truly free. Emile is repeatedly "forced" by dramas and schemes engineered by the tutor to develop his various faculties, including the will. The culmination of his education occurs at the end of the novel when Emile is taught to control his desires for his fiancé Sophie by obeying the tutor's command not to see Sophie for two years. The tutor tells Emile: "Up to now you were only apparently free. You had only the precarious freedom of a slave to whom nothing had been commanded. Now be really free. Learn to become your own master."[163] Emile is told to exert his will over man's most powerful drive: "try your strength" and "exercise for battle." The tutor explains to Emile that it is not "within our control to have or not to have passions. But it is within our control to reign over them."[164]

The experience of mastery is coeval with recognizing and accrediting this exercise of the will. Such an exercise, though, is not merely subjective. It must have an objective component. In humanity's primitive state, boundaries or limits are objective, and grounded in necessity and nature. In society, as we have seen, the institutions of the *Social Contract*, grounded in the general will, address this need

---

[161] Bloom, *Emile*, p. 280.

[162] *The Reveries of a Solitary*, Sixth Promenade, p. 132.

[163] Bloom, *Emile*, p. 445.

[164] *Ibid.*

for an objective component. In *Emile*, the tutor both shows Emile the boundaries and, as tutor, is one of those boundaries.[165] Emile is told that true freedom comes through the mastery of his desire, and, further, that this final exercise is applicable to all of his potentialities and faculties.

> All passions are good when one remains their master.... What is forbidden to us by nature is to extend our attachments further than our strength; what is forbidden to us by reason is to want what we cannot obtain; what is forbidden to us by conscience is not temptations but rather letting ourselves be conquered by temptations.[166]

Rousseau's lesson for Emile and for humanity, then, is that the minimally-conscious self found in nature can, in principle, still endure in society. By understanding the three parts of the experiential domain of the will, we now have the guides needed to diagnose the ills of political society and to construct a healthy regime.

Up to this point, Rousseau's use of autonomy and mastery may sound vaguely similar to the goals of Plato, Aristotle, and the Stoics. But, Rousseau's differences from both the Greek and Christian traditions can be displayed by examining the kinds of human associations and relationships, possible with his new understanding of the will. The nature of the Rousseauian virtues show these differences. There are virtues that primarily depict relationships *with* others and those that are responses *to* others. Pity and love, for example, are two modes of establishing bonds with others; repentance and gratitude are types of responses to others. Rousseau's analysis of these four virtues is derived from his map of the will, and they illuminate the kind of human relationships Rousseau wishes to nourish.

The most striking feature of these four virtues, as defined by Rousseau, is that they are peculiarly non-personal; that is, the practice of these virtues does not sensitize one to acknowledge a distinctive other person. The psychic operation of pity, as reported by Rousseau, will serve to illustrate. Pity is the emotion engendered through imaginatively comparing one's own superior position with one who suffers, and it is the reverse of envy.

---

[165] A full explanation of the political philosophy in *Emile* and its relationship with the *Social Contract* is provided by Judith Shklar, "Rousseau's Images of Authority," *American Political Science Review* 58 (December, 1964), pp. 919–32.

[166] Bloom, *Emile*, p. 445.

Pity is sweet because, in putting ourselves in the place of the one who suffers, we nevertheless feel the pleasure of not suffering as he does. Envy is bitter because the sight of a happy man, far from putting the envious man in his place, makes the envious man regret not being there.[167]

Emile quickly learns to get an "inner enjoyment" through the practice of pity.[168] This sweet emotion is not about or for the person suffering, but it is a particular emotion derived from the relative state of the person who has it. The emotion makes one aware of oneself; it does not "focus" on another person. Further, this natural emotion can be safely utilized only when it is "generalized and extended to the whole of mankind."[169] Thus, pity is non-personal in two ways. First, it is not a concern for the other person but is derived from not being the other person. Second, in order to keep this natural impulse from being destroyed through excessive selfishness, or, as Rousseau says, "to prevent pity from degenerating into weakness," it is the species, not the neighbour, toward whom pity must be directed.[170] Again, the virtue is non-personal. The self-sufficient will has been maintained: the virtue of pity does not sensitize one to a person, nor does one become obligated through pity to a person, which would create a sense of dependence and a potential loss of the sense of mastery. Yet, one still has the natural sweet emotion without threat to one's self while joined with mankind: one is independent but united.

Love is another virtue depicting a type of bond with others, and it is traditionally held to be the strongest and most personal bond among humans. Nevertheless, as Rousseau plots this most complex of natural impulses, one is again struck by how curiously non-personal it becomes. After Sophie and Emile have come to know each other well and they have fallen in love, the query is made: What has Emile gained by his love and how has he changed? The answer must rank as one of the oddest in the history of human love: "He has new reasons to be himself. This is the single point where he differs from what he was."[171] In accounts of love—romantic or religious—love is invariably described as a desire directed at something other

---

[167] *Ibid.*, p. 221.

[168] *Ibid.*, p. 253.

[169] *Ibid.*

[170] *Ibid.*

[171] *Ibid.*, p. 433.

than oneself. The person who loves is said to be drawn out by the beloved and made more worthy. Thus, in Shakespeare's *The Merchant of Venice*, Portia tells of the effect of her love for Bassanio: "To wish myself much better, yet for you... I might in virtues, beauties, livings, friends, exceed account."[172] Emile, in contrast, has a self-sufficient will. But, as with pity, a psychic operation is performed through extending a natural impulse (sexual desire) to the idealized love of Sophie. By such sublimation the self does not lose its control. Allan Bloom correctly avers of Emile:

> He has an overwhelming need for another, but that other must be the embodiment of the ideal of beauty, and his interest in her partakes of the disinterestedness of the love of the beautiful. Moreover it is not quite precise to say that he loves an "other," for he will not be making himself hostage to an alien will and thus engaging in a struggle for mastery. This woman will, to use Platonic language, participate in the *idea* he has of her. He will recognize in her his own highest aspirations. She will complete him without alienating him.[173]

Gratitude and repentance are virtues designed to bridge two properties of the human condition: the individual's sense of isolation and the need of others. The two virtues have a common feature respecting the self in that both depend upon an uncaused offering of one's self to another. Gratitude occurs, for example, when a person recognizes that he or she is not self-sufficient but limited and, thus, can receive from another. This customary understanding of gratitude, though, is not taught to Emile; rather, gratitude is redefined to be consistent with the Rousseauian will: "If you grant him what he asks of you, he will not thank you, but he will feel that he has contracted a debt."[174] When the idea of gratitude is transformed to the metaphor of a cash debt, the person becomes objectified. Then, the self is not in question for either party. Repentance, a harder virtue, is also clearly anathema to the Rousseauian will, since it requires the sacrifice, however momentary, of one's sense of self-sufficiency and mastery.

---

[172] *Merchant of Venice*, III, ii. I am grateful to Susan Porter for this citation.

[173] Bloom, "Introduction," in *Emile*, p. 22. See also, Schwartz, *The Sexual Politics of Jean-Jacques Rousseau*, pp. 74–202; Penny A. Weiss, *Gendered Community: Rousseau, Sex, and Politics* (New York: New York University Press, 1993).

[174] *Emile*, p. 161.

Nor surprisingly, Emile experiences only a "sentiment of wrong." The wrong comes from his adolescent "ardour," but he has no sense of knowingly committing a wrong for which he is responsible.[175] Weakness is the source of any wrongdoing, not the will itself, as Rousseau constantly reiterates. His own *Confessions* are noteworthy for not providing one example of a real confession or repentance. Each famous episode is excused by a concatenation of alien causes and temptations. In contrast, the traditional view has been that by admitting self-deficiency, the practice of gratitude and repentance enabled humans to establish a personal dependence and, thus, temper their sense of isolation and mutual injustice. Virtues so understood would be incompatible with Rousseau's map of the will.[176]

Rousseau's understanding of pity, love, gratitude, and repentance is dependent upon what he calls extension. This psychic operation of extension is crucial to Rousseau's project for taking a natural primitive human and forming a free, moral and happy person. The extension enables a natural impulse, distorted by *amour propre* in society, to be general, rational, equitable and just.

> Let us extend *amour propre* to other beings. We shall transform it into a virtue, and there is no man's heart in which this virtue does not have its root. The less the object of our care is immediately involved with us, the less the illusion of particular interest is to be feared. The more one generalizes this interest, the more it becomes equitable....[177]

The individual psychic operation of moving from the person to the species in order to achieve virtue is structurally identical to the act of association where the individuals together move from the particular to the general and form the social contract. It would be tedious to cite all of the obvious parallels, but two points should be mentioned: both individually and collectively, the particular and selfish will is transformed through attachment to a non-personal, abstract or

---

[175] *Ibid.*, pp. 220–21.

[176] John Charvet argues that Rousseau cannot logically move from a self-consistent ego to altruism. If Rousseau were interested in altruism, then his position would be contrary. But, the extension of the self-contained ego is not to other persons. The "identification" with others repeatedly mentioned by Rousseau (*Emile*, pp. 222–23) has no more to do with persons than does the identification found between baby identical twins: there is neither self nor an other. If this is altruism, it is not a moral virtue. John Charvet, "Rousseau and the Ideal Community," *History of Political Thought*, 1, pp. 69–80.

[177] Bloom, *Emile*, p. 252.

general whole; the inducement for this critical act is the goal of freedom and a sense of mastery. That there could be an asymmetry between private and collective willing, responsibility and accountability does not appear to trouble Rousseau. He does not hold that the type of association significantly changes the operation of will. He literally holds, as he said in rebuke of Plato, that the good son, husband, father, makes a good citizen.[178] The idea that different roles and human contexts require different faculties and virtues, or that different types of human associations may have different goals and be in tension, if not conflict, is not seriously entertained. Indeed, his conception of the will serves to undermine such concerns. It is precisely because of the key attributes of the will that *amour propre* can be extended into virtue, that Emile can safely love Sophie, and that a social contract is possible.

Just as the nature of the virtues has been transformed from those in Augustine, so has the goal of freedom. For Rousseau, external causes have corrupted us; we must then change society in order to transform our nature. This is within our power to do. For Augustine, human freedom is an inner experiential state requiring the benevolence of friends, repentance for mutual injustices, and God's grace. Critics of Rousseau argue that individuals, by their own power, cannot make themselves free any more than they can, by power, master love of another.

The topic of general will and moral liberty is the core to Rousseau's political philosophy. His originality can be seen in the transformation that he has made in the concept of the will. His experiential domain of the will—grounded in nature and passion, needing self-sufficiency and mastery—presents a unique and, in large measure as a consequence of his writings, a modern view of human nature. Critics have long questioned his portrayal of the will and its concomitant virtues. Others have lauded a view of human nature that accentuates humanity's ability to radically change a corrupting political order and to attain the goals of self-sufficiency, mastery, and moral liberty.

---

[178] Rousseau criticizes Plato as follows: "… as though there were no need for a natural base on which to form conventional ties; as though the love of one's nearest were not the principle of the love one owes the state; as though it were not by means of the small fatherland which is the family that the heart attaches itself to the large one; as though it were not the good son, the good husband, and the good father who make the good citizen!" (*Emile*, p. 363).

Popular Sovereignty and Participation

The general will, along with moral freedom, clearly forms the pivotal topic for Rousseau's political philosophy. The second topic of immense importance is that of popular sovereignty and participation. Again, Rousseau is original. No political philosopher had ever before made such a mixture of claims. When citizens, instilled with the general will to guide their decision making, meet in solemn assembly, they are sovereign. There is no outside appeal either to another institution, such as the Church, or to some transpolitical source, such as conscience or the natural law or natural rights. The duly constituted sovereign never errs and is always right, which is to say that the decision will be objectively true and not simply an aggregate of private interests. Moreover, participation in the sovereign general assembly and in many other political events and ceremonies instills in the citizens an ennobling, liberating, and nurturing sense of community. The result is a new being with a transformed self. These are all unique claims in the history of political philosophy.

In the ancient world, Socrates had introduced the philosophic life as superior to the political life and often in tension with it. Even Machiavelli, who stressed the importance of political virtues and of the state, never claimed moral certitude for the decisions of the sovereign. Participation, for him, was not done to increase a sense of community so that a person could achieve a new identity with a new self. Hobbes simply wanted a final arbitrator to make a decision where controversy could cause disorder. Rousseau has given a new level of meaning to sovereignty and participation.

In case Rousseau's claims seem impossible, one needs only to recall that for well over a century there were organizations of humans who actually acted on the belief that participation in the proper manner would guarantee a right decision and personal freedom. After the Reformation, and following Calvin, in particular, there were many sects who advocated an institutional structure in which each member voluntarily committed him- or herself to a general good applicable to all. Each church member, properly guided by the commitment, was both a subject and a part of the whole, which provided a new sense of identity and freedom. Freedom was experienced as the result of taking on a law and making it one's own.

> As long as we submit ourselves to this Law, we are not the less free for it: On the contrary, it is that Law itself which renders us free, because it liberates

us from the tyranny of our Passions. In obeying this Law, we are elevated above all worldly things, above all goods & evils, above prosperity & adversity, above grandeur, riches, pleasures of the senses, above promises & threats, above corrupt maxims and the bad examples of men. There is not one of these things, which can harness us; we are free, we are independent in all these respects.[179]

Autonomy and freedom were united. Finally, the decision made by a group so constituted was held to be always right. This is a sketch of a Calvinist congregation and their beliefs. The phrase, used above, of a "commitment to a general good" in theological language signs God. The phrase about being "subject and part of the whole" refers in theological language to a church congregation composed of members who are both subject-sinners and part of the body of Christ. The above quotation on law comes from a Calvinist theologian writing in 1734. Instead of stating that the general will never errs and is always right, the theological language is that the voice of the people is the voice of God (*vox populi, vox dei*). There is also a striking similarity between Calvin's analysis of the will and Rousseau's. In general, Rousseau has transformed elements of Calvinism into a secular political theory of the state and of the self. Calvinism itself was extraordinarily influential as a political force. The secular transformation by Rousseau has added new force.[180]

Rousseau is neither confused nor impractical with his views on sovereignty and participation. Whether these concepts adequately depict the nature of politics and enhance our political well-being would still need to be analyzed. Two scholars, W. G. Runciman and A. K. Sen, have defended Rousseau's claims that if the general will is properly put in operation the outcome is objectively right.

---

[179] Turrettin, *Sermon sur la loy de la Liberté* (1734), as quoted by Pamel A. Mason, "The Communion of Citizens: Calvinist Themes in Rousseau's Theory of the State," *Polity* (Fall, 1993), p. 46.

[180] The article by Pamel A. Mason contains an excellent summary of the influence of Calvinism on Rousseau, "The Communion of Citizens: Calvinist Themes in Rousseau's Theory of the State," pp. 26–49. The similarity in the operation of the will between Rousseau and Calvin can be seen in Michael Walzer, *The Revolution of the Saints* (New York: Atheneum, 1969); Eric Voegelin, *The New Science of Politics* (Chicago: University of Chicago Press, 1952), pp. 133–52; Norman Cohn, *The Pursuit of the Millennium*, 2nd ed. (New York: Harper, 1961); Ralph Hancock, *Calvin and the Foundations of Modern Politics* (Ithaca: Cornell University Press, 1989); William J. Bouwsma, *John Calvin: A Sixteenth Century Portrait* (New York: Oxford University Press, 1988).

In a justly famous article, they argue that the two-person, non-zero-sum, non-co-operative game known as the "prisoner's dilemma" illuminates the logical structure of the general will. The dilemma is as follows:

> Two persons are thought to be jointly guilty of a serious crime, but the evidence is not adequate to convict them at a trial. The district attorney tells the prisoners that he will take them separately and ask them whether they would like to confess, though of course they need not. If both of them confess, they will be prosecuted, but he will recommend a lighter sentence than is usual for such a crime, say 6 years of imprisonment rather than 10 years. If neither confesses, the attorney will put them up only for a minor charge of illegally possessing a weapon, of which there is conclusive evidence, and they can expect to get 2 years each. If, however, one confesses and the other does not, the one who confesses receives lenient treatment for providing evidence to the state and gets only 1 year, and the one who does not receives the full punishment of 10 years.[181]

This is a dilemma because prisoners relying strictly on a liberal, individualistic, and egocentric interest would always find it rational to confess. Consequently, the outcome would be six years. On the other hand, if each person could forego calculating his private interests and form a compact with his fellows whereby each would calculate the general interest or good of the other, then they would each will what would be to their general or common advantage, that is, neither would confess. Runciman and Sen note the parallels with Rousseau: "The general will is general not only in its origins, and is 'applicable to all as well as operated by all.' It tends always to equality, and all citizens being equal by virtue of the contract, 'none has the right to demand that another should do what he does not do himself.'"[182] The question still remains of the applicability of Rousseau's general will and popular sovereignty to the whole range of issues and contentions in political life.

---

[181] W. G., Runciman and A. K. Sen, "Games, Justice and the General Will," *Mind* 74 (1965), p. 554. Brian Barry, less successfully, examines theories of decision making to illustrate an objective element in the general will, "The Public Interest," in Anthony Quinton, *Political Philosophy* (Oxford: Oxford University Press, 1967), pp. 119–25.

[182] *Ibid.*, p. 556. Quotations are from the *Social Contract*. Bertrand de Jouvenel carefully examines the actual political advice found in Rousseau and interprets Rousseau as providing some practical guidelines for maintaining a democratic regime, "Rousseau's Theory of the Forms of Government," in Maurice Cranston and Richard S. Peters, eds., *Hobbes and Rousseau: A Collection of Critical Essays* (Garden City: Anchor Books, 1972).

The practicality of Rousseau's idea of participation is easier to recognize. In a faithful explication of Rousseau, Carole Pateman discerns three major features of participation when put into practice. First, there is an educative aspect: "As a result of participating in decision making the individual is educated to distinguish between his own impulses and desires, he learns to be a public as well as a private citizen." And, she continues, "he comes to feel little or no conflict between the demands of the public and private spheres." Second, freedom is enhanced through participation: "The individual's actual, as well as his sense of, freedom is increased through participation in decision making because it gives him a very real degree of control over the course of his life and the structure of his environment." Third, participation has an integrative function: "It increases the feeling among individual citizens that they 'belong' in their community." It is, in Pateman's phrase, these "psychological qualities and attitudes" of individuals that are enhanced by activity within Rousseau's political institutions.[183]

Rousseau accordingly develops practical institutions so that we will not be deceived or have partial interests. The legislator, laws, civil religion, educational system, and even festivals and celebrations are all means for guaranteeing the authenticity and success of participation. Authority, proper institutions, and participation are integrated, because, for Rousseau, authority and law are prerequisites for freedom.

Critics of Rousseau take issue with this description of participation because it stresses cohesiveness and unanimity, or close to it. Participation, for Rousseau, as we have seen, requires a general interest that is objective, and participation concludes in a general will that is always right. If judged by these two standards, political activity has no room for differences. Consequently, the thoughts and actions of individuals who might differ with the general will can only be explained as the result of deception, or of being simply wrong, or of a partial interest.[184] "Political actitivity" that is born from such partial, contentious interests and that concludes in compromises or the victory of one side cannot have the "psychological qualities and attitudes" sought by Rousseauian participation. There can be no grounds for recognizing merit in wrong answers in mathematics; and there are no grounds for recognizing the accompanying activity as worthwhile.

---

[183] Carole Pateman, *Participation and Democratic Theory* (Cambridge: Cambridge University Press, 1970), pp. 25–27. For a more balanced view of the complexity in political participation for Rousseau, see Barnard, "Will and Political Rationality in Rousseau, Political Studies 32 (1984), pp. 369–84."

[184] Bk. II, ch. 3; Bk. IV, ch. 2.

Politics, for Rousseau, is also supposed to conclude with a right answer, and there is also no respect for the process of getting a "wrong" answer.[185] This is a type of participation and an understanding of political reality far removed from either Aristotle or Locke.[186]

In retrospect, the topic of popular sovereignty and participation has faired better historically than the idea of the general will. This would make no sense to Rousseau because his concept of sovereignty is derivative of a general will that unites and informs the citizenry. Nevertheless, popular sovereignty when wedded to nationalism has been an extraordinarily powerful force in the last two centuries. Rousseau's thought was a significant contribution to this wedding. His unique concept of participation is clearly held by many to be superior to Aristotle's or Locke's. These people envision a community sustaining itself through Rousseauian participation and contrast it favourably with the individualistic and self-interest dominated societies of today.

The Institutional Structure within the Political System

The third great topic that demonstrates Rousseau's originality and influence is the institutional structure he creates for the political system. One of the questions that is often posed for examining Rousseau's project is, "Has Rousseau created a unitary or pluralistic system?" A traditional way of approaching this question has been to describe the powers, processes and institutions of Rousseau's political system and to draw conclusions about the consequences for political life. The unending controversies that characterize this approach result, in part, from a lack of agreement about Rousseau's philosophic premises and about their influence on the development of democracy.[187] Because Rousseau's premises themselves are often viewed as in

---

[185] Bk. II, ch. 4.

[186] It may well be viewed as unfair to defenders of Rousseau, but he does give one striking example of participation in a footnote in the *Social Contract*. The example cited by Rousseau is the religious act of communion: "It must, indeed, be remarked that it is not so much the formal assemblies, like those in France, that bind the clergy into one body, as the communion of churches. Communion and excommunication are the social pact of the clergy, a pact by means of which they will always be the masters of peoples and Kings. All priests who are of the same communion are fellow citizens, though they are as far asunder as the poles. This invention is a masterpiece of politics." (Bk. IV, ch. 8). Rousseau's solution is a secular masterpiece.

[187] James Miller provides a useful synopsis of the arguments and literature, "Epilogue: Democracy after Rousseau," in *Rousseau: Dreamer of Democracy* (New Haven: Yale University Press, 1986).

tension further compounds the difficulties in assessing his political system. For example, it is said that Rousseau attempted to combine the virtue of the ancient city with the lessons of nature.[188] Another formulation is that he tried to unite ancient cohesiveness with modern voluntarism.[189] One can plausibly stress one or the other of these paired premises. Inevitably, there are more conflicting interpretations.

For most commentators it is hard to support the view that there are significant pluralist elements within Rousseau's political system. A better question might be, "Should a state above all seek harmony and unity?" Rousseau's answer is positive. The originality of his institutional structure and its significance for modern life have been hidden to some degree by his advocacy of a small state. He was adamant in his view that only a small state would have the social and economic equality necessary for sustaining the social bond and the commitment to the general will. But, the plebiscitary and spectator qualities of his theory of political participation seem to be the same qualities that modern mass-media technology encourages in modern political life. A large modern state might conceivably have a place for Rousseauian political institutions after all.

It is true that Rousseau wanted no representation of sovereignty, but the members of the sovereign are citizens only, not the population at large, and the citizens in popular assembly vote only in a plebiscitary fashion (yes or no). The citizens are not a standard legislative chamber, either. They are even told to not consult each other, vote publicly, and have no partial interests. Given these facts, it would seem possible for a large state to accommodate Rousseau's principles. In any case, the key institutions for Rousseau's political system are not the standard legislative, executive, and judicial branches, but are the legislator, the civil religion, the laws, the educational system, and great patriotic events and celebrations. These are all concerned with the interplay of laws, beliefs, and mores that support the general will and provide the new identity for the person.[190]

---

[188] Leo Strauss, *Natural Right and History* (Chicago: University of Chicago Press, 1953).

[189] Riley, *Will and Political Legitimacy* and Keohane, *Philosophy and the State in France.*

[190] Ira Shcharansky, a former Soviet political prisoner who was ultimately freed by the Soviet Union, tried to explain to some reporters why it was so hard for the former Soviet Union to let the Soviet Jews go. In his explanation, he alludes to the type of community identity sought by Rousseau: "In the United States [and other Western states], the law is something that defends the individual against the possible arbitrariness of the state. The opposite is the case in the Soviet Union. In the Soviet Union the individual is part of the system and the people feel self-respect only through belonging to this big system." (*The New York Times,* 10 May 1988).

When these elements all work properly, so it is argued, individual autonomy and social unity will result. Curiously, the institutional structure needs the special non-institutional hand of the great legislator and a civil religion to inculcate the sacred character of the social contract and its regime. Only then do individuals get their new identity. Sometimes, the word "dyarchy" (divided rule) is used to describe Rousseau's system. On the one side are the legislator and the civil religion, and on the otherside is the government, the people, and the sovereign. Calvin's Geneva had a similar dyarchy in that the church ministers played the equivalent role of Rousseau's legislator for the Genevan government.

Rousseau believed that he had once seen an actual political system that operated as he wished. In the vicinity of Neufchatel, Switzerland, he saw hardy farmers, independent of government control and living close enough together to experience the "tranquillity of retreat and the sweetness of society." They were each self-sufficient and escaped having to take self-defining, competing, economic roles: "Never did carpenter, locksmith, glazier, or turner enter this country; each is everything for himself, no one is anything for another." Their many tasks were done as they individually pleased, rather than as required by economic necessity or *amour propre*.[191]

Marx will echo many of these themes.[192] He, too, wants a political society where a person is not required by economic necessity to take a defining role. In communist society, Marx says, "society regulates the general production and this makes it possible for me to do one thing today and another tomorrow, to hunt in the morning, fish in the afternoon, rear cattle in the evening, criticize after dinner, just as I have a mind, without ever becoming hunter, fisherman, shepherd or critic."[193] There are other structural commonalities between Rousseau and Marx. Most importantly, in a Marxist regime the communist party plays the role of Rousseau's legislator; the party is not part of the government. Joseph Stalin, strictly speaking, was only the First Secretary of the Communist Party; he held no government position. The dyarchy method of rule, ironically, fits a political regime designed to achieve harmony and unity. Nurturing and guarding

---

[191] Allan Bloom, trans., *Jean-Jacques Rousseau: Politics and the Arts: Letter to M. D'Alembert on the Theatre* (Ithaca: Cornell University Press, 1960), pp. 60–62.

[192] Wokler, "Rousseau and Marx," in *The Nature of Political Theory*, pp. 219–46.

[193] Robert C. Tucker, ed. "The German Ideology," in *The Marx-Engels Reader* (New York: Norton, 1972), p. 160.

the ideological purity of the regime, to use modern social science terminology, becomes the tasks of separate, non-governmental institutions: in Calvin's time, it was the church ministers; in Rousseau's thought, it was the great legislator; for Marx and Lenin, it was the communist party.[194]

Critics of Rousseau argue that political institutions should be designed both to express and to moderate the inevitable differences and tensions that exist in political life and, consequently, that these institutions should enhance political discussions and compromises. But, Rousseau's form of political association, which provides a non-personal unity and, thus, a prospective solution to the tensions in social existence, transforms the meaning of the political. First, this is an association in which it makes little sense to talk of a separate public space, the traditional realm of the truly political. The private and the public are united. When the voice of God inheres in the will of the people, there is no need for the give and take of public discourse. The rhetoric of persuasion inevitably turns into the litany of belief, more characteristic of religious professions of faith. A public space has been traditionally thought necessary precisely because ultimate goals, such as truth, perfect justice, perfect unity, are not attainable through political action, only improvements upon past and present injustices or approximate solutions to ongoing problems are conceived of as possible. In other words, something less than a complete solution must be sought for a discourse to remain truly political. Second, legitimacy in Rousseau's political system is dependent upon achieving a true unity, one not born from simple agreements or compromises but from an identification among all citizens. Here, collective action is not the result of joint endeavours but is more aptly characterized as arising from a community of believers. Such a collective identity is not the road to liberty or politics.[195]

---

[194] For a fascinating treatment of China during the cultural revolution, see the Rousseauian analysis by Benjamin I. Schwartz, "The Reign of Virtue: Some Broad Perspectives on Leader and Party in the Cultural Revolution," *The China Quarterly* (July-September, 1968), pp. 1–17.

[195] I have relied heavily in this conclusion on my essay, "Rousseau: Will and Politics," in *Unity, Plurality, and Politics: Essays in Honour of F. M. Barnard*, ed. J. M. Porter and Richard Vernon (London: Croom Helm, 1986), pp. 52-74. Andrzej Rapaczynski has written a superb work discussing modern liberalism by examining the major figures of Hobbes, Locke, and Rousseau: *Nature and Politics: Liberalism in the Philosophies of Hobbes, Locke, and Rousseau* (Ithaca: Cornell University Press, 1987). The debate between Lockean liberty and Rousseauian freedom is a permanent feature of modern political thought. The classic treatment is by Isaiah Berlin, *Four Essays on Liberty* (New York: Oxford University Press, 1969). See also the various essays in Graeme Duncan, ed., *Democratic Theory and Practice* (New York: Cambridge University Press, 1983).

It must also be said that Rousseau, with dramatic eloquence, shows the psychological and social damage that liberal political institutions and practices can have. Human happiness, equality, social harmony, and moral liberty, among other values, have now been raised to political consciousness. Rousseau has clearly placed on the agenda for modernity the political vision that community and freedom should be the purposes of a political regime rather than individual liberty and economic progress. He has also introduced, at least in embryo, the powerful theme that human history is driven in large part by economic activity which, in turn, is rooted in human nature. These are themes developed by many thinkers in the next two centuries; the most famous, if not best, is Karl Marx.

The nineteenth century also had a new powerful impetus provided to liberalism by the philosophers of utilitarianism—Jeremy Bentham and John Stuart Mill.

SUGGESTIONS FOR FURTHER READING

Cranston is the work providing the best biography of Rousseau, but Starobinski and Guéhenno are also valuable works. Grimsley, Kelly, and Miller weave together Rousseau's personality, thought, and history.

Cranston and Peters, Chapman, Leigh, Harvey, and *Daedalus* (Summer, 1978), Vol. 107, No. 3, contain articles helpful for the interpretations of Rousseau.

Wokler (1995) is the best short work, taking the student through the key works and providing an extensive bibliography. Masters (1968), Shklar, and Hendel are larger works, reliable and thorough. Masters is particularly good, leading the reader through the key texts.

Riley and Keohane are essential for background on Rousseau, carefully presenting major sources and setting the context for Rousseau's originality. Berlin and Crocker have edited readings from the *philosophes*, and the contrast of their philosophies with Rousseau is easily perceivable. Becker is a delightful, small classic on the Enlightenment. Gay, Berlin, and Cassirer (1955) all provide excellent treatments of the century. Horowitz, Plamenatz and Rotenstreich, Volpe, Levine (1993), and Althusser discuss the influence of Rousseau on Marx. Levine (1976) and Cassirer (1944) are the standard works relating Rousseau and Kant.

Talmon, Walzer, Yack, and Crocker (1969) provide critical assessments of Rousseau. Levine (1993), Horowitz, and Volpe are commentators who see Rousseau's influence on Marx and tend to be less critical, but also see Pateman, Strong, and Berman.

Works

Bloom, Allan, trans. *Jean-Jacques Rousseau: Politics and the Arts: Letter to M. d'Alembert on the Theater*. Notes and Introduction by Allan Bloom. Ithaca: Cornell University Press, 1960.

Butterworth, Charles, trans. *The Reveries of the Solitary Walker*. New York: Harper & Row, 1979.

Cohen, J. M., trans. *The Confessions*. New York: Penguin Books, 1953.

Cole, G. D. H. *Social Contract and the Discourses*. Revised by J. H. Bumfitt and John C. Hall. New York: E. P. Dutton, 1973.

Cranston, Maurice. *Rousseau: The Social Contract*. Middlesex: Penguin, 1968.

Cress, Donald A., trans. and ed. *Jean-Jacques Rousseau: Basic Political Writings*. Indianapolis: Hackett, 1987.

Gourevitch, Victor. *Jean Jacques Rousseau: The First and Second Discourses, Together with the Replies to the Critics, and Essay on the Origin of Languages*. New York: Harper & Row, 1986.

Mason, John Hope, ed. *The Indispensable Rousseau*. London: Quartet Books, 1979.

Masters, Roger D., ed. *The First and Second Discourses by Jean-Jacques Rousseau*. Translated by Roger D. Masters and Judith R. Masters. New York: St. Martin's, 1969.

———. *On the Social Contract with Geneva Manuscript and Political Economy*. Translated by Judith R. Masters. New York: St. Martin's, 1978.

Masters, Roger, and Christopher Kelly, eds. *Rousseau's Collected Writings*. Hanover, N.H.: University Press of New England, 1990–.

McDowell, Judith H., trans. *La Nouvelle Héloïse*. University Park: Pennsylvania State University Press, 1968.

Sherover, Charles M. *The Social Contract*. Annotated ed. New York: Meridian, 1974.

Watkins, Frederick M., ed. *Rousseau: Political Writings*. New York: Nelson, 1953.

Vaughn, C. E., ed. *The Political Writings of Jean Jacques Rousseau*. 2 Vols. New York: John Wiley, 1962.

Commentaries

Althusser, Louis. *Politics and History: Montesquieu, Rousseau, and Marx*. Translated by Ben Brester. London: Routledge, 1982.

Barnard, F. M. *Self-Direction and Political Legitimacy: Rousseau and Herder*. Oxford: Clarendon Press, 1988.

Berman, Marshall. *The Politics of Authenticity*. New York: Atheneum, 1970.

Bloom, Allan. *Love and Friendship*. New York: Simon and Schuster, 1993.

Blum, Carol. *Rousseau and the Republic of Virtue: The Language of Politics in the French Revolution*. Ithica: Cornell University Press, 1986.

Cassirer, Ernst. *The Question of Jean-Jacques Rousseau*. Translated by Peter Gay. Bloomington: Indiana University Press, 1963.

———. *Rousseau, Kant, Goethe*. Princeton: Princeton University Press, 1944.

Chapman, John H. *Rousseau—Totalitarian or Liberal?* New York: Columbia University Press, 1956.

Charvet, John. *The Social Problem in the Philosophy of Rousseau*. Cambridge: Cambridge University Press, 1974.

Cranston, Maurice. *Jean-Jacques: The Early Life and Work of Jean-Jacques Rousseau, 1712–1754*. Vol I. New York: Norton, 1982.

———. *The Noble Savage: Jean-Jacques Rousseau, 1754–1762*. Vol. II. Chicago: University of Chicago Press, 1991.

Cranston, Maurice, and Richard S. Peters, eds. *Hobbes and Rousseau: A Collection of Critical Essays*. Garden City: Anchor Books, 1972.

Crocker, Lester G. *Rousseau's Social Contract: An Interpretive Essay*. Cleveland: The Press of Case Western Reserve University, 1968.

Einaudi, Mario. *The Early Rousseau*. Ithaca: Cornell University Press, 1967.

Ellenburg, Stephen. *Rousseau's Political Philosophy: An Interpretation from Within*. Ithaca: Cornell University Press, 1976.

Fralin, Richard. *Rousseau and Representation*. New York: Columbia University Press, 1978.

Gildin, Hilail. *Rousseau's Social Contract: The Design of the Argument*. Chicago: University of Chicago Press, 1983.

Grimsley, Ronald. *The Philosophy of Rousseau*. Oxford: Oxford University Press, 1973.

———. *Jean-Jacques Rousseau: A Study in Self-Awareness*. Cardiff: University of Wales Press, 1961.

Guéhenno, Jean. *Jean-Jacques Rousseau, Vol. I: 1712—1758; Jean-Jacques Rousseau, Vol. II: 1758–1778.* Translated by John and Doreen Weightman. London: Routledge and Kegan Paul, 1967.

Hartle, Ann. *The Modern Self in Rousseau's Confession: A Reply to St. Augustine.* Notre Dame: Notre Dame University Press, 1984.

Harvey, S., et al. *Reappraisal of Rousseau: Studies in Honour of R. A. Leigh.* Manchester: University of Manchester Press, 1980.

Hendel, C. W. *Jean-Jacques Rousseau: Moralist.* 2nd ed. Indianapolis: Bobbs-Merrill, 1962.

Horowitz, Asher. *Rousseau, Nature, and History.* Toronto: University of Toronto Press, 1987.

Hulliung, Mark. *The Autocritique of Enlightenment: Rousseau and the Philosophes.* Cambridge: Harvard University Press, 1994.

Kelly, Christopher. *Rousseau's Exemplary Life: The 'Confessions' as Political Philosophy.* Ithaca: Cornell University Press, 1987.

Leigh, R. A., ed. *Rousseau after Two Hundred Years.* Cambridge: Cambridge University Press, 1982.

Levine, Andrew. *The General Will: Rousseau, Marx, and Communism.* Cambridge: Cambridge University Press, 1993.

———. *The Politics of Autonomy.* Amherst: University of Massachusetts Press, 1976.

Masters, Roger D. *The Political Philosophy of Rousseau.* Princeton: Princeton University Press, 1968.

McDonald, Joan. *Rousseau and the French Revolution: 1762–1791.* London: University of London Press, 1965.

Melzer, Arthur M. *The Natural Goodness of Man: On the System of Rousseau's Thought.* Chicago: University of Chicago Press, 1990.

Miller, James. *Rousseau: Dreamer of Democracy.* New Haven: Yale University Press, 1986.

Mitchell, Joshua. *Not by Reason Alone.* Chicago: University of Chicago Press, 1993.

Noble, Richard. *Language, Subjectivity, and Freedom in Rousseau's Moral Philosophy.* New York: Garland Publishing, 1991.

Pateman, Carole. *Participation and Democratic Theory.* Cambridge: Cambridge University Press, 1970.

Perkins, Merle L. *Jean-Jacques Rousseau on the Individual and Society.* Lexington, Ky.: University Press of Kentucky, 1974.

Rapaczynski, Andrzej. *Nature and Politics: Liberalism in the Philosophies of Hobbes, Locke, and Rousseau.* Ithaca: Cornell University Press, 1987.

Riley, Patrick. *The General Will Before Rousseau: The Transformation of the Divine into the Civic.* Princeton: Princeton University Press, 1986.

———. *Will and Political Legitimacy.* Cambridge: Harvard University Press, 1982.

Schwartz, Joel. *The Sexual Politics of Jean-Jacques Rousseau.* Chicago: University of Chicago Press, 1984.

Shklar, Judith N. *Men and Citizens: A Study of Rousseau's Social Theory.* London: Cambridge University Press, 1969.

Starobinski, Jean. *Jean-Jacques Rousseau: Transparency and Obstruction.* Translated by Arthur Goldhammer. Chicago: University of Chicago Press, 1988.

Strong, Tracy B. *Jean Jacques Rousseau: The Politics of the Ordinary.* Thousand Oaks: Sage, 1994.

Trachtenberg, Zev M. *Making Citizens: Rousseau's Political Theory of Culture.* London: Routledge, 1993.

Viroli, Maurizio. *Jean-Jacques Rousseau and the 'Well-ordered Society'.* Cambridge: Cambridge University Press, 1988.

Volpe, Galvano della. *Rousseau and Marx.* Translated by John Fraser. Atlantic Highlands: Humanities Press, 1979.

Wokler, Robert. *Rousseau.* Oxford: Oxford University Press, 1995.

———. *Social Thought of J. J. Rousseau.* New York: Garland, 1987.

Intellectual Background

Becker, Carl L. *The Heavenly City of the Eighteenth-Century Philosophers.* New Haven: Yale University Press, 1932.

Berlin, Isaiah., ed. *The Age of Enlightenment: The Eighteenth Century Philosophers.* New York: New American Library, 1956.

———. *Four Essays on Liberty.* New York: Oxford University Press, 1969.

Cassirer, Ernst. *The Philosophy of the Enlightenment.* Translated by F. C. A. Koelln and J. P. Pettegrove. Boston: Beacon Press, 1955.

Cobban, Alfred. *In Search of Humanity: The Role of the Enlightenment in Modern History.* New York: Braziller, 1960.

Crocker, Lester, ed. *The Age of Enlightenment.* New York: Walker and Co., 1969.

Duncan, Graeme, ed. *Democratic Theory and Practice.* New York: Cambridge University Press, 1983.

Gay, Peter. *The Enlightenment: An Interpretation.* New York: Knopf, 1966.

———. *The Party of Humanity: Essays in the French Enlightenment.* New York: Knopf, 1964.

Hancock, Ralph. *Calvin and the Foundations of Modern Politics.* Ithaca: Cornell University Press, 1989.

Havens, George. *The Age of Ideas: From Reaction to Revolution in Eighteenth Century France.* New York: Holt, 1965.

Keohane, Nannerl O. *Philosophy and the State in France.* Princeton: Princeton University Press, 1980.

Manuel, Frank E. *The Eighteenth Century Confronts the Gods.* Cambridge: Harvard University Press, 1959.

Martin, Kingsley. *The Rise of French Liberal Thought.* 2nd ed. New York: New York University Press, 1954.

Plamenatz, John, and Nathan Rotenstreich. *Basic Problems of Marx's Philosophy.* New York: Bobbs-Merrill, 1965.

Talmon, J. L. *The Origins of Totalitarian Democracy.* London: Sphere Books, 1970.

Vaughan, C. E. *Studies in the History of Political Philosophy Before and After Rousseau.* Manchester: Manchester University Press, 1925.

Voegelin, Eric. *From Enlightenment to Revolution.* Edited by John H. Hallowell. Durham: Duke University Press, 1975.

Walzer, Michael. *The Revolution of the Saints.* New York: Atheneum, 1969.

Wilson, Arthur M. *Diderot.* New York: Oxford University Press, 1972.

Yack, Bernard. *The Longing for Total Revolution: Philosophic Sources of Social Discontent from Rousseau to Marx and Nietzsche.* Berkeley: University of California Press, 1992.

UTILITARIANISM: JEREMY BENTHAM AND JOHN STUART MILL

The liberal tradition of Hobbes and Locke received a challenge from the utilitarianism of Jeremy Bentham (1748–1832) and John Stuart Mill (1806-1873). The challenge was not as radical as that presented by Rousseau, but there was a philosophic difference that could not be reconciled with the natural rights position, and has not been to this day. Although utilitarianism shares many fundamental tenets with the liberal tradition of Hobbes and Locke, it has developed into a distinct branch of liberalism. For example, utilitarianism also begins with the individual as the base. The individual, however, is described in utilitarianism as wholly a creature of interests. These interests, in turn, are derived from our purportedly pain-avoiding, pleasure-seeking nature. Both Hobbes and Locke, it is true, utilized to some extent the pain-pleasure mechanism for explaining human behaviour. The mechanism played a major role, particularly in Hobbes's political philosophy, much less so in Locke's but, in both of their philosophies, rights came to be the building blocks of their political theories.

Another example of a shared tenet is the claim that science, however understood, is the only accepted intellectual framework for achieving knowledge about such topics as human nature, obligation, and the causes of revolution. Science, for Hobbes and Locke, was a tool of enormous significance, but it did not encompass all of reality. They both believed in God, were authentically religious, and personally advocated human relationships characterized by a relatively traditional set of virtues and vices. For utilitarians, these attributes of Hobbes's and Locke's lives and thought were irrelevant encumbrances from a dead past. Bentham himself believed that religion should be eliminated as soon as possible because it blinded people to their own interest and led to irrationality.[1] It seemed to utilitarians that Hobbes and Locke simply lacked the courage of their philosophic premises. For philosophic utilitarians, science was not just an indispensable tool, it encompassed all of reality.

BENTHAM: His Life and Works

It would be easy when describing Bentham to slip into a parody simply by listing facts about his long life. His pets were a cat and a mouse, which some view as emblematic of the inconsistency of his thought. He took immense delight in coining words for his various ideas: "international" to cover people like himself who were not confined to the boundaries of a state; "fridigarium," which was a device for freezing vegetables to be consumed later in winter; "panopticon," which was a prison with a warden who, from the centre of the building, could see into all the cells; "codification," "epistemo-threptic," "maximize" and "minimize"; "chrestomathic" school, where children learned how to systematize and construct trees of knowledge. Perhaps the best example of Bentham's quirky genius was the "auto-icon." In a pamphlet entitled *Further Uses of the Dead to the Living* he advocated that the bodies of benefactors and malefactors be mummified; the one would serve to commend and the other to warn. He followed his own advice and, after his death, had his own body mummified and put on display at University College, London, for the edification of his followers and the public.

As one would expect, Bentham has been the subject of vituperation and jest to an extent almost equaled by that suffered by Hobbes. In the nineteenth century Bentham was labeled as: a "metaphysico-critico-politico-patriotico-phoolo—philosopher"; by the American philosopher, Ralph Waldo Emerson, "a stinking philosophy"; by Karl Marx, "the arch philistine, Jeremy Bentham, the insipid pedantic leather-tongued oracle of the common place bourgeois intelligence of the nineteenth century…a genius in the way of bourgeois stupidity." In the twentieth century, the founder of modern economic theory, Lord Maynard Keynes, said of Bentham's influence that it has been "the worm which has been gnawing at the insides of modern civilization and is responsible for its present moral decay." A contemporary historian of economic thought, Joseph A.

---

[1] James Steintrager, "Morality and Belief: The Origin and Purpose of Bentham's Writings on Religion," *The Mill News Letter* VI (Spring, 1971), pp. 3–15.

Schumpeter, concluded that Bentham's utilitarianism was "the shallowest of all conceivable philosophies of life."[2] In spite of the vituperation, Bentham was a founder of an influential movement, much as he had wished.

Bentham was extraordinarily precocious as a child. He entered Queen's College, Oxford at 12 years of age, entered Lincoln's Inn at the age of 15 for an apprenticeship to law, received his B.A. in 1764 and his M.A. in 1767. Instead of developing a successful legal career like his father and stepfather, Bentham discovered in 1769, "that wonderful year," the works of the French *philosophes*: Helvétius, and other thinkers of the Enlightenment, such as Beccaria, Voltaire, D'Alembert, and Diderot. Bentham then embarked on the task of creating a legal code that was scientific and rational, one ultimately derived from the simple principle of maximizing happiness for the greatest number. This principle (**utilitarianism**) he sometimes called the utility principle; the word "utility" was from the Scottish philosopher, David Hume. He also called it the greatest felicity or happiness principle, and sometimes just the pleasure principle. In his first work, *A Fragment of Government*, he announced the principle as a great discovery, and he never abandoned it:

> Correspondent to *discovery* and *improvement* in the natural world, is *reformation* in the moral; if that which seems a common notion be, indeed, a true one, that in the moral world there no longer remains any matter for *discovery*. Perhaps, however, this may not be the case:…with so little method and precision have the consequences of this fundamental axiom, *it is the greatest happiness of the greatest number that is the measure of right and wrong,* been as yet developed.[3]

Bentham's life work expanded from civil and penal law to constitutional law and then to all manner of reforms for the political society and government. In 1780 he actually dreamed that he would be able to accomplish an enormous reformation

---

[2] See the collation of quotations in the biography by M. P. Mack, *Jeremy Bentham: An Odyssey of Ideas: 1748–1792* (New York: Columbia University Press, 1963), pp. 1–27.

[3] J. H. Burns and H. L. A. Hart, eds. *A Fragment of Government* (Cambridge: Cambridge University Press, 1988), Preface, p. 3. Bentham's use of the famous slogan varied throughout his life. After 1776, he dropped the "greatest number" and used "greatest happiness" or "universal interest." He added "greatest number" again in 1816. He had become more radical and supportive of the democratic cause by then. See Bhikhu Parekh, ed., *Bentham's Political Thought* (London: Croom Helm, 1973), Introduction, pp. 15–17; R. Shackleton, "The Greatest Happiness of the Greatest Number: The History of Bentham's Phrase," *Studies on Voltaire and the Eighteenth Century* XC (1972).

of the world: "I dreamt the other night that I was a founder of a sect; of course, a personage of great identity and importance. It was the sect of utilitarianism."[4] He called himself the "Newton of the Moral Sciences" and wrote to his editor, Etienne Dumont: "our way will cover the whole world: Locke and Helvétius, offering incense to us every morning, both of them on their knees."[5]

Utilitarianism was successful in many ways. As the Industrial Age expanded, so did reforms to mitigate the enormous sufferings that accompanied it. Poor laws, electoral reforms, prison reforms, child labour laws, aid to the destitute, public health measures, and the Great Reform Bill of 1832 (passed two days after Bentham's death) were all topics benefiting from the political activity of utilitarians. Indeed, Bentham confidently announced toward the end of his life that only poverty and disease were yet to be conquered.[6]

Bentham's influence came from writing an immense amount of material on an enormous range of topics throughout his long life. He did not write, however, a single classic work on political philosophy. In fact, he was fortunate in having solicitous followers to edit and publish many of his publications. It was not easy to do. His handwriting was almost illegible, and his early writings were often written in French and then translated into English for publication. Yet another difficulty in bringing his voluminous writings to publication was his disconcerting habit of never quite finishing his work. The two published writings most often cited are appropriately entitled, *Fragment of Government* (1776) and *An Introduction to the Principles of Morals and Legislation* (printed in 1780, published in 1789).

Bentham was a true son of the Enlightenment and viewed himself as a part of it. He was profuse in his praise of Helvétius, D'Alembert, Voltaire, and, the father

---

[4] David Baumgardt, *Bentham and the Ethics of Today* (Princeton: Princeton University Press, 1952), Appendix I.

[5] Mack, *Jeremy Bentham: An Odyssey of Ideas*, pp. 9, 96–98, 129.

[6] How much credit can be taken by utilitarians for the reforms that occurred throughout the nineteenth century is much debated. Elie Halévy, *The Growth of Philosophic Radicalism*, trans. Mary Morris (London: Faber & Faber, 1928) gives considerable credit to Bentham, his supporters, and their influential journal, the *Westminster Review*. Bentham was, initially, far more famous outside of Britain than at home. He had written letters to many leaders throughout his life as a way of implementing his various reforms. His contacts ranged from the Czar of Russia to the future President of the United States, John Quincy Adams. Some have argued that Benthamites should be given credit for the beginnings of the welfare state. David Roberts, *Victorian Origins of the British Welfare State* (New Haven: Yale University Press, 1960) and Geoffrey Finlayson, *Decade of Reform: England in the Eighteen Thirties* (New York: W. W. Norton, 1970).

of them all, Locke, and he built upon them. Bentham's primary position, upon which he founded all of his thought, is confidently and economically expressed in the opening paragraph of the *Introduction to the Principles of Morals and Legislation*:

Nature has placed mankind under the governance of two sovereign masters, *pain* and *pleasure*. It is for them alone to point out what we ought to do, as well as to determine what we shall do. On the one hand the standard of right and wrong, on the other the chain of causes and effects, are fastened to their throne. They govern us in all we do, in all we say, in all we think: every effort we can make to throw off our subjection, will serve but to demonstrate and confirm it. In words a man may pretend to abjure their empire: but in reality he will remain subject to it all the while. The *principle of utility* recognizes this subjection, and assumes it for the foundation of that system, the object of which is to rear the fabric of felicity by the hands of reason and law. Systems which attempt to question it, deal in sounds instead of senses, in caprice instead of reason, in darkness instead of light.[7]

Bentham has welded together the descriptive and the prescriptive, science and morality. Human thought and behaviour can, in principle, be explained through a reductive analysis to the indisputable base where the sovereigns of pain and pleasure rule. Human action is always caused, and causes flow from the human motives of pursuing pleasure and avoiding pain.

Most human behaviour can be explained by the desire for pleasure. It is clear that those seeking wealth or power in business and politics are motivated by the pleasure associated with each. Even the martyr desires the pleasure that is associated with the act. What are called virtues and vices can be also be explained by their relationship to pleasure and pain. The principle of utility provides the link: if the behaviour promotes happiness, that is, there is pleasure associated with the activity, then its utility is clear, and the behaviour is viewed as virtuous. Bentham often repeats that only "by indication of the relation born to happiness, that is, to pleasure and pains, can any clear conception be attached to the words virtue and virtues, vice and vices."[8]

---

[7] Wilfrid Harrison, ed., *A Fragment on Government and An Introduction to the Principles of Morals and Legislation* (Oxford: Basil Blackwell, 1967), ch. I, para. 1. As a devoted worshipper of codification, Bentham proceeds to draw up a list of 14 simple pleasures and 12 simple pains. There are also complex perceptions of pleasures, of pains, and of pleasures and pains (ch. V).

[8] "Virtue," in Parekh, *Bentham's Political Thought*, p. 94.

Bentham identifies good with pleasure. His position is that of a hedonist: the sensation of physical pleasure is what *is* good; it is the only good. Bentham is blunt: "Now, pleasure is in *itself* a good: nay, even setting aside immunity from pain, the only good; pain is in itself an evil; and indeed without exception, the only evil; or else the words good and evil have no meaning."[9] Since good is identical with pleasure, human motives are simply neutral. A motive is good or bad dependent upon its tendency to produce pain or pleasure. It is all quite simple. For example, the pleasure of wealth engenders a neutral motive called pecuniary; when the effect causes pain, it is called avarice; when the effect causes pleasure, it is called industry or frugality.[10] Bentham's insistence on the absolute neutrality of motives includes sexual desire:

> 1. A man ravishes a virgin. In this case the motive is, without scruple, termed by the name of lust, lasciviousness, and so forth; and is universally looked upon as a bad one. 2. The same man, at another time, exercises the rights of marriage with his wife. In this case the motive is accounted, perhaps, a good one, or at least indifferent.... In both cases it may be neither more nor less than sexual desire.[11]

There is a chasm between Bentham and Aristotle or Augustine on the constitution of human nature. Even Hobbes's analysis of virtues and vices was limited to what to one could "know" in his highly restricted sense. How a person ought to behave was quite another matter and one to which science, as he understood it, could provide no answer. Such a distinction does not exist for Bentham. Ethical and rational behaviour are one and the same. Rational behaviour is operating the principle of utility in pursuing pleasure. To be precise, Bentham should actually be called a scientific hedonist for two reasons: first, the twin sovereigns of pleasure and pain cause human thought and action, and this means that a reductive explanation is possible; second, pleasure itself can be objectively quantified, at least in principle. Pleasure is not just a subjective matter of how a particular person feels at any one time.

---

[9] Harrison, *Principles of Morals and Legislation*, ch. X, para. 10.

[10] *Ibid.*, ch. X, para. 19.

[11] *Ibid.*, ch. X, para. 16.

Newton's law of gravity served to explain movements in the physical world and, thus, served to focus observations and experiments. Analogously, Bentham believed that his principle of utility explained human thoughts and actions, and directed the study of law, morals, and government toward empirical observations. The proper and fruitful question to ask of any human behaviour is, "What is the utility of it?" Bentham's definition is,

> By the principle of utility is meant that principle which approves or dis-approves of every action whatsoever, according to the tendency which it appears to have to augment or diminish the happiness of the party whose interest is in question: or, what is the same thing in other words, to promote or to oppose that happiness.[12]

The principle of utility, as he goes on to explain, is built into "the natural constitution of the human frame; on most occasions of their lives men in general embrace this principle, without thinking of it: if not for the ordering of their own actions, yet for the trying of their own actions, as well as of those of other men."[13] It makes no sense to ask for proof, he says, "for that which is used to prove every thing else, cannot itself be proved." In any case, to give such proof "is as impossible as it is needless."[14]

Bentham next provides a calculus by which one can empirically quantify utility. Whether it is a calculation required for an individual person or for a community, a numerical value should be given to six "circumstances": intensity, duration, certainty or uncertainty, propinquity or remoteness, fecundity, and purity. If one is calculating for a community, then the extent (or number of persons affected) of the pleasure or pain makes the seventh category for measuring. The empirical claim is that we can measure the pain or pleasure caused by an act or event by giving a value to each of these six or seven categories:

> Sum up all the values of all the *pleasures* on the one side, and those of all the pains on the other. The balance, if it be on the side of pleasure, will give the *good* tendency of the act upon the whole, with respect to the interests of that *individual* person; if on the side of pain, the *bad* tendency of it upon the whole.[15]

---

[12] *Ibid.*, ch. I, para. 1.

[13] *Ibid.*, ch. I, para. 12.

[14] *Ibid.*, ch. I, para. 11.

[15] *Ibid.*, ch. IV, para. 5.

Many have noted the obvious difficulty in giving a numerical value to the six "circumstances," let alone the matter of determining which should be given a higher numerical value, intensity or duration. Bentham further complicated the matter by noting in one of his writings that there should be a lexical ordering in making the calculation. A lexical ordering is one in which one first makes certain that everyone get a minimal level of "happiness" and then one makes the calculation of the greatest happiness for the greatest number. As Bentham explains: "the greatest happiness of the greatest number of them, on every occasion on which the nature of the case renders the provision of an equal quantity of happiness for everyone of them possible."[16] This complication added an element of equality. In the main, however, it was the elegant simplicity of the calculus—however impossible it would be to actually do—that delighted his followers.

Although Bentham repudiated the political philosophy of Locke, he was an admirer of the *Essay on Human Understanding,* and for Bentham, in company with other members of the Enlightenment, rationalism was held to be as essential as empiricism for a philosophy. Bentham was fond of saying that utilitarianism was built upon plain reason. He also cited with approval Locke's insistence upon clear definitions, "the grand prescription of those great physicians of the mind, Helvétius and before him Locke,"[17] These clear definitions must, of course, be in principle reducible to an empirical, pain-pleasure base.

With the scientific and analytic tools provided by utilitarianism, Bentham believed that he could construct a great moral and legal science. The outline of this project can be seen in his *A Fragment on Government.* In it he is actually addressing the work of Sir William Blackstone, who had written a famous commentary on the British legal and constitutional system, but the wide scope of Bentham's criticism also leads in the end to a refutation of the Lockean tenets that permeated Blackstone's work.

Bentham ridicules the Lockean conceptions of the state of nature, of contract, of obligations and consent, of rights and duties, and of revolution or resistance. All of them, for Bentham, become fictions and sources of confusion. It would be preposterous to think that they illuminate any significant features of political reality. The state of nature and the original contract are both judged to be

---

[16] *Parliamentary Candidate's Declaration,* p. 7, cited in Frederick Rosen, *Jeremy Bentham and Representative Democracy* (Oxford: Oxford University Press, 1983), p. 212.

[17] Burns, *A Fragment on Government,* Appendix, p. 123; ch. V, para. 6, fn. 1.

fictions, and the confusion in their use only compounds the harm they cause. The solution is to use a clear empirical definition. When people are in the habit of obeying a certain subset (government), there is a political society; when there is no government, the people are in a natural society or state of nature:

> When a number of persons (whom we may style *subjects*) are supposed to be in the *habit* of paying *obedience* to a person, or an assemblage of persons, of a known and certain description (whom we may call *governor* or *governors*) such persons altogether (*subjects* and *governors*) are said to be in a state of *political* SOCIETY.
>
> The idea of a state of *natural SOCIETY is, as we have said, a* negative one. When a number of persons are suppposed to be in the habit of *conversing* with each other, at the same time that they are not in any such habit as mentioned above, they are said to be in a state of *natural* SOCIETY.[18]

There are societies, Bentham notes, that alternate from one condition to the next. For example, during a time of war the "American Indians" will take orders from "a common chief," but afterwards they will return to a state of nature.[19]

The idea of an original contract where consent and obligation were first inaugurated is a "chimera," but one still, Bentham regrets, embraced by some. It may have been a useful fiction at one time for some political battles; but, he writes, "the season of *Fiction* is now over." There never was, nor ever could be, such a contract. He concludes that "the indestructible prerogatives of mankind have no need to be supported upon the sandy foundations of a fiction."[20] In place of the original contract, obligation, and consent, Bentham places utility as the ground for obligation and consent. It makes no sense to talk about justice, right reason, or the law of nature commanding obedience to an original contract. Going a step further than Locke, Bentham argues that such phrases have no empirical reference. They belong to Locke's category of mixed modes, but in order to analyze such abstract terms they have to be translated into whole sentences. Bentham coins, as was his wont, a new term for this exercise—paraphrasis. He takes the idea of obligation, translates it into full sentences, and derives a "clear" meaning. Thus, as Bentham argues, obligation occurs in a society because it is to the advantage of the people,

---

[18] *Ibid.*, ch. I, paras. 10–11.

[19] *Ibid.*, ch. I, paras. 19–20.

[20] *Ibid.*, ch. I, paras. 36–37.

and punishments will occur if obligations and promises are broken.[21] In Bentham's words, "every reflecting man may satisfy himself, I think, beyond a doubt, that it is the consideration of *utility*, and no other, that, secretly but unavoidably, has governed his judgment upon all these matters."[22]

The Lockean theory of rights and duties and the theory of revolution are handled with the same aplomb. The principle of utility operates to show the only meaning that can be attached to the categories of right and duty.

1. That may be said to be my *duty* to do (understand political duty) which you (or some other person or persons) have a *right* to have me made to do. I then have a DUTY *towards* you: you have a RIGHT as *against* me.

2. What you have a right to have me made to do (understand a political right) is that which I am liable, according to law, upon a requisition made on your behalf, to be *punished* for not doing.

3. I say *punished*: for without the notion of punishment (that is of *pain* annexed to an act, and accruing on a certain *account*, and from a certain *source*) no notion can we have of either *right* or *duty*.[23]

Rights, in short, occur where there is a government for enforcing them. Rights are created by law; they cannot exist without law; and they are not antecedent to law. Bentham became quite short-tempered with the Declaration of Rights promulgated during the French Revolution. In a long, crotchety critique, he calls rights "dangerous nonsense" and, in a flourish, "natural and imprescriptible rights, rhetorical nonsense, nonsense upon stilts." He concludes his critique of the Declaration of Rights by calling the use of rights "a *moral* crime, and not undeserving of being constituted a legal crime, hostile to the public peace."[24]

Revolution meets the same fate as the other Lockean concepts. Bentham makes plain that there is no abstract theory of revolution that could be derived from a violation of an original contract or derived from some fundamental rights purportedly determining when to obey and when to rebel. As Bentham says again,

---

[21] *Ibid.*, ch. V, para. 6.

[22] *Ibid.*, ch. I, para. 45.

[23] *Ibid.*, ch. V, para. 6.

[24] "A Critical Examination of the Declaration of Rights," in Parekh, *Bentham's Political Thought,* Article II, pp. 268, 269, 290.

"it is the principle of utility, accurately apprehended and steadily applied that affords the only clue to guide a man through these straits."[25] What one must do is simply calculate "*the probable mischiefs of resistance* (speaking with respect to the community in general) *appear less to him than the probable mischiefs of submission*. This then is to him, that is to each man in particular, the *juncture for resistance.*"[26] All of these cases—state of nature, contract, obligations, rights and duties, revolution—ultimately return to pain and pleasure, for as Bentham remarks with some satisfaction, these are "words which a man has no need, we may hope, to go to a Lawyer to know the meaning of."[27] The theories of revolutions or resistance presented by Aristotle and Locke, to take just two examples, were designed both to explain why revolutions occur and to provide a framework for a justification. Bentham has conflated the two purposes and claims, as a consequence, to provide a superior, scientific, and economical analysis.

In addition to criticizing the traditional arguments used to explain and justify British government, Bentham developed his own scheme for reforms and good government. The guiding principle was the greatest happiness for the greatest number. As a son of the Enlightenment, he began as a supporter of enlightened despotism as the vehicle for change. His reforms required a supreme legislator to enact and enforce them. After gradually becoming disenchanted with the British government, he became, for the day, a radical democrat in the last quarter of his life.[28] But even then, the roles of the legislator and of experts remained paramount. He was not a populist with faith in the people to run governments.

In 1823 he published the *Leading Principles of a Constitutional Code, for any State*, and he hoped that it could serve as a model for a new system of government. The whole scheme was designed so that people would do from their own interest what they ought to do for the general happiness. Governments, as he notes,

---

[25] Harrison, *Principles of Morals and Legislation*, ch. V, para. 20.

[26] *Ibid.*, ch. V, para. 21.

[27] *Ibid.*, Preface, p. 28.

[28] Bentham's frustration with getting approval for his proposal for a panopticon—the prison with cells arranged in a circle around the warden—led to considerable disillusionment with a central bureaucracy and the government. For almost a quarter of a century he was repeatedly led on by bureaucrats to the extent that he even invested money in land for a prison. In a story that sounds as if it were written by Charles Dickens, whose disdain for lawyers matched Bentham's, the government, in 1813, was finally forced by a court of law to award him compensation of £23,000.

"cannot be exercised without coercion," and this, too, is useful in obtaining the greatest happiness for the greatest number. A government can offer both rewards and punishments, and the latter, he believes, is the most effective. Habits and considerations of pain and pleasure will normally produce obedient subjects, but, as a check and balance on governments, the ultimate limitation on governmental power is that subjects, too, can calculate the utility of obedience or of resistance to their general happiness.

Bentham was keenly aware that governments operate in their own interest. His proposed reforms, he believed, would address an overweening government. He advocated annual elections, full access to information, and universal suffrage, which he hoped would, in time, include both sexes.[29] The implication of these reforms is that the government will have primarily negative functions, and he often speaks in this manner:

> Every law is an evil, because every law is a violation of liberty; so that government ... can only choose between evils. What should be the aim of the legislator when making this choice? He should satisfy himself of two things: *First*, that in all cases the events which he strives to prevent are really evils; and *secondly*, that these evils are greater than those he is about to employ as the means of prevention.[30]

Yet the four goals Bentham sets for government in his *Constitutional Code* are surprisingly broad: "Immediately specific, and jointly all-comprehensive, ends of this constitution are—subsistence, abundance, security, and equality; each maximized, in so far as is compatible with the maximization of the rest."[31] The realization of these four ends would necessarily require an active government. The first goal, subsistence, he says, refers to physical suffering and "nothing more." Nevertheless, since 1791 he had proposed houses of industry, workhouses, and poorhouses throughout Britain, which would provide work, education, and houses for the

---

[29] Terence Ball, "Utilitarianism, Feminism and the Franchise," *History of Political Thought*, I (Spring, 1980), pp. 91–115. For Bentham's general list of suggested reforms see, "Parliamentary Reform Catechism," (1817) in *A Bentham Reader*, ed. Mary Peter Mack (New York: Pegasus, 1969), pp. 306–28.

[30] C.K. Ogden, ed., *The Theory of Legislation*, trans. Richard Hildreth (London: Kegan Paul, 1931), ch. x, p. 48.

[31] "Constitutional Code," in Parekh, *Bentham's Political Thought*, para. 5.

poor. He even suggested how marriages could be encouraged among the inhabitants. The second goal, abundance, would enable subsistence to be reached, and he advocated using government policy to realize this goal.[32]

In regard to the third goal, security, Bentham lists person, property, power, reputation, and conditions of life as matters for which the government must provide protection against injury and the "appropriate services."[33] The fourth goal, equality, entails efforts to reach some rough equality of wealth and power. Bentham is quite explicit: "The more remote from equality are the shares possessed by the individuals in question, in the mass of the instruments of felicity, the less is the sum of the felicity produced by the sum of those same shares."[34] One way to reduce inequalities of power is to pay the minimum possible salaries to officials and to make all citizens eligible for office. Bentham also warns against the flaunting of intellectual and moral superiority, which can disturb the sense of equality in a society. In order to instil a sense of equality, Bentham actually created a catechism of political morality to be taught in schools and from the pulpit.[35] Bentham is well aware that he has expanded considerably the role of government from that espoused by Locke. The protection of individual rights in Locke's philosophy, says Bentham, "missed sight of so many other valuable subject matters."[36] Philosophically, Bentham's four comprehensive ends do provide the grounds for an active and positive state, in spite of his many other statements that limit governments to the negative functions of protection.

It is clear that there are tensions inherent in Bentham's political philosophy. On the one hand, there is evidence for viewing him as a major defender of liberal individualism. He begins with the calculation of pain and pleasure for each individual as the first step in forming his political philosophy. The formula of the

---

[32] "The Defence of a Maximum," in *Jeremy Bentham's Economic Writings*, 3 Vols., ed. W. Stark (London: Allen & Unwin, 1952-54), Vol. III, pp. 257–58.

[33] Parekh, *Bentham's Political Thought*, para. 8.

[34] *Ibid.*, para. 24.

[35] The political catechism—done in the religious catechism mode of questions and answers— is called "Summary of Basic Principles," (1820) and is found in Parekh, *Bentham's Political Thought*, pp. 295–308. There are dozens of hints throughout Bentham's writings, many unpublished, that suggest ways to create a condition of equality. Bhikhu Parekh, "Bentham's Theory of Equality," *Political Studies* XVIII (December, 1970), pp. 478–95.

[36] "On Locke," in Parekh, *Bentham's Political Thought*, pp. 313–14.

greatest happiness for the greatest number, which is the purportedly scientific substitute for the confused and metaphysical idea of justice, is achieved by aggregating the pain and pleasure of individuals. There appears to be no glimmer of a Rousseauian idea of community. The individual is paramount. Bentham also sometimes writes of the private property of the individual in terms that would have pleased Adam Smith, the thinker whose economic theories were essential to explaining and justifying capitalism. Bentham was highly critical of the French revolution for violating private property, and he even criticized Adam Smith himself for not letting interest rates fluctuate according to the market. Bentham's argument was that this would spur investment and productivity.[37] These clearly seem to be views of a free-market individualist.

He was also, particularly in his later years, vehement in his attack on the establishment of the day. But even in his early *A Fragment on Government* (1776), he points to the "sinister interests" of the government bureaucracy, ruling statesmen, and lawyers. The latter "tribe," as he called lawyers, was particularly to be watched. In the *Constitutional Code* (1823), he is more scathing in his remarks about government. The greatest threat to security, one of the four comprehensive ends of government, is not from "foreign and declared enemies"; rather, the greatest danger is from the "professed protectors" in government.[38] All of these views lead to a negative role for government and would appear to emanate from a professed individualism, and so it was believed throughout the nineteenth century.[39]

There are a variety of other positions found in Bentham's voluminous writings that appear to hearken in the opposite direction. The four comprehensive ends mentioned in his *Constitutional Code* lay the groundwork for a very active government. The role of the central government in welfare and education appears to be identical to that of a modern, twentieth-century, welfare state. Bentham was also quite candid about the comprehensive power of the legislator. In the scheme for education called *Chrestomathia* (1815), he developed a comprehensive encyclopedic tree of all knowledge, which could be used by the legislator in form-

---

[37] "Defense of Usury" (1787), in Stark, *Economic Writings*, Vol. I, pp. 123–207.

[38] "Constitutional Code," in Parekh, *Bentham's Political Thought*, para. 19.

[39] For a full presentation of Bentham's theory of government, see: Douglas G. Long, *Bentham on Liberty* (Toronto: University of Toronto Press, 1977) and Rosen, *Jeremy Bentham and Representative Democracy*.

ing public policy: "Exercising dominion over almost every branch of art and science...in furtherance of the interest of the whole community, the legislator, on pain of acting blindfold, has the need of an insight—the more clear, correct, and extensive the better—into the matter of every such branch of art and science."[40] Here, the expert relying upon the science of utilitarianism becomes the vital centre of the government. Bentham explicitly writes that leadership by the expert is necessary to persuade people to accept the *Constitutional Code* and all the other reforms. To be sure, persuasion is used and not the whip, but Bentham's own "job description" for the legislator is telling:

> Preach to the eye, if you would preach with efficacy. By that organ, through the medium of the imagination, the judgment of the bulk of mankind may be led and moulded almost at pleasure. As puppets in the hand of the showman, so would men be in the hand of the legislator, who, to the science proper to his function, should add a well-informed attention to stage effect.[41]

Even in his economic writings, there are places where Bentham seems decidedly modern in calling for government intervention: "I never had, nor ever shall have any horror...of the hand of government."[42] In all of these cases, the role of the government is paramount in importance over the individual.

It would be difficult to deny that there are deep tensions, if not inconsistencies, in Bentham's thought. There are three obvious difficulties. First, when Bentham thought of change and reforms in philosophical and abstract terms, he invariably resorted to rational schemes, conceived, directed, and imposed by the expert, the legislator, and the government. There was no room for the politics of pluralism, compromise, and negotiation. Pluralism, compromise, and negotiation do not characterize and are hardly compatible with the activity of science, nor should they be present in the new utilitarian science of public policy formation. This, in short, can be called the politics of rationalism where the importance of

---

[40] "Chrestomathia," in Mack, *A Bentham Reader*, p. 278.

[41] John Bowring, ed., *The Works of Jeremy Bentham* (Edinburgh: William Tait, 1838-43), Vol. VI, p. 321.

[42] "The Defense of a Maximum" (1801), in Bowring, *ibid.*, Vol. III, pp. 257–58; T. W. Hutchison, "Bentham as an Economist," *The Economic Journal* (1956), pp. 288–306.

the individual is secondary to the implementation by the expert and the government of the greatest happiness for the greatest number.[43] But, when addressing the government of his own day, Bentham was often quite fervent in defending the security of the individual. His political rationalism and theory of change were never reconciled with his defence of the individual.[44] Second, and at a deeper level, there is an inescapable shallowness to Bentham's conception of the person. Humans have no constituting centre for Bentham; they are primarily, if not wholly, mere calculators of interest. Such creatures would be easily moulded and shaped.[45] Lastly, the goal of happiness promised by the utility principle is not identical with the goal of liberty, and in many minds the two goals are incompatible. Happiness as pleasure, even assuming that it is the good for humans, is quite different from liberty, conceived as the necessary condition for the development of one's mind and character. The latter consideration is not recognized by Bentham.

It is a great irony that Bentham's "secular godson," John Stuart Mill, who was actually raised according to strict utilitarian principles, found Bentham inadequate. Mill endeavoured to redeem utilitarianism by providing more adequate conceptions of political change, of the person, and of liberty.[46]

MILL: His Life and Works

James Mill, trained as a Presbyterian minister, was a convert to utilitarianism and was chiefly responsible for bringing Bentham's philosophy to public notice. As Bentham's most famous disciple, James Mill was convinced that the education

---

[43] See the classic treatment by Michael Oakeshott, *Rationalism in Politics and Other Essays* (London: Methuen, 1962), pp. 1–36. See also, D. H. Manning, *The Mind of Jeremy Bentham* (London: Longmans, Green, 1968).

[44] For a favourable treatment of Bentham, see Warren Roberts, Jr., "Bentham's Conception of Political Change: A Liberal Approach," *Political Studies* (October, 1961), pp. 254–66; and "Behavioural Factors in Bentham's Conception of Political Change," *Political Studies* (June, 1962), pp. 163–79.

[45] See the highly critical analysis of Bentham by Sheldon S. Wolin, *Politics and Vision* (Boston: Little, Brown, 1960), pp. 343–51. Wolin cites the *Deontology* as evidence, but this essay is believed by some Bentham scholars to be the work of the overzealous editor of the *Works*, John Bowring. For a stalwart defence of Bentham, see the essay by David J. Crossley in which he argues that Bentham has a moral right to equality, "Utilitarianism, Rights and Equality," *Utilitas: A Journal of Utilitarian Studies* (May, 1990), pp. 40–54.

[46] The apt phrase "secular godson" was used by Ross Harrison in his excellent treatment of Bentham's life and philosophy, *Bentham* (London: Routledge & Kegan Paul, 1983), p. 3.

of his young son, John Stuart Mill, by utilitarian principles would demonstrate the merit of that philosophy. Bentham and Mill were fortunate in one respect; John Stuart Mill was as much a natural prodigy as Jeremy Bentham had been. John Stuart Mill started lessons in Greek at the age of three, Latin at eight, and arithmetic, history, economics, the great philosophers, and literature were quickly added. There was a prodigious amount of work required of the child. The regimen was also startling. Between five and six in the morning James Mill and his son began work. Breakfast was served at nine o'clock; then work began again until lunch at one; if a mistake was made in the studies, lunch was simply skipped until the dinner meal at nine in the evening. As John grew older, he was also responsible for the education of his younger sister and brother.

This daily regimen under the tutelage of his father and Bentham came to an end when John was 14. He was sent to France for the year to live with Jeremy Bentham's younger brother Samuel and his family. The family tried to interest the young teenager in games, dancing, and the like, but without much success.[47] When he returned to England, he read more or less on his own, and his father had him study law under John Austin, a supporter of Bentham who advocated the rational construction of a legal system deduced from the premise that law was only a command of the sovereign. John also helped his father complete a *History of British India* (1818). This worked earned James Mill an instant reputation and, happily for the Mill family, gained him a position with the East India Company and financial security.[48]

John Stuart Mill had already imbibed a great deal of utilitarianism by his midteens. The "great turning point" in his education, however, was the reading of Etienne Dumont's edition, in French, of Bentham's three-volume *Treatise on Legislation.* The work began with the *Introduction to the Principles of Morals and Legislation.* Mill was astounded: "The feeling rushed upon me, that all previous moralists were superseded, and that here indeed was the commencement of a new era in thought."[49] It served as the "keystone" linking together all that he had learned:

---

[47] Anna J. Mill, ed., *John Stuart Mill's Boyhood Visit to France: A Journal* (Toronto: University of Toronto Press, 1960).

[48] The Mill family was aided financially by Bentham while James Mill was working on the *History.* The family lived in houses either on Bentham's estate or next to it from 1814 to 1829.

[49] "Autobiography," in *John Stuart Mill: A Selection of His Works,* ed. John M. Robson (Toronto: Macmillan, 1966), p. 256.

It gave unity to my conceptions of things. I now had opinions; a creed, a doctrine, a philosophy; in one among the best senses of the word, a religion; the inculcation and diffusion of which could be made the principal outward purpose of a life. And I had a grand conception laid before me of changes to be effected in the condition of mankind through that doctrine.[50]

One of John Stuart Mill's first tasks as a young adult of 19 was to edit for publication Jeremy Bentham's 5 volumes of *The Rationale of Judicial Evidence* (1825). Given Bentham's almost illegible handwriting and the mass of material to be collated, this was an extraordinary achievement. John's diligence and capacity for hard work had become a permanent pattern. Because a university education was clearly superfluous, at the age of 17 his father attained for John a position, directly under his own supervision, with the East India Company (1823). John Stuart Mill worked at the company for the next 35 years, retiring when the British government took over from the company the direct rule of India. He was also active in his self-appointed task of being "a reformer of the world."[51] He formed a society of like-minded young utilitarians, wrote for the *Westminster Review*, and campaigned for the great causes of the day.

His career and future seemed very bright until he was struck down by a severe depression in the winter of 1826-1827. He describes in moving terms what happened to him:

> But the time came when I awakened from this as from a dream. It was in the autumn of 1826. I was in a dull state of nerves, such as everybody is occasionally liable to; unsusceptible to enjoyment or pleasurable excitement; one of those moods when what is pleasure at other times, becomes insipid or indifferent; the state, I should think, in which converts to Methodism usually are, when smitten by their first "conviction of sin." In this frame of mind it occurred to me to put the question directly to myself: "Suppose that all your objects in life were realized; that all the changes in institutions and opinions which you are looking forward to, could be completely effected at this very instant: would this be a great joy and happiness to you?" And an irrepressible self-consciousness distinctly answered, "No!" At this my heart sank within me: the whole foundation on which my life was constructed fell

---

[50] *Ibid.*

[51] *Ibid.*, p. 279.

down. All my happiness was to have been found in the continual pursuit of this end. The end had ceased to charm, and how could there ever again be any interest in the means? I seemed to have nothing left to live for.[52]

It was a devastating experience, and neither books, nor friends, nor his father ("the last person to whom in such a case as this, I looked for help") could guide him.[53]

He considered himself to be a "mere reasoning machine" with hopelessly ingrained analytic habits, no longer capable of sentiments and feeling. His education, he believed, had failed him. All the information diligently planted in him from age 3 to 14—and he had had discussions with his father and Bentham too—did not seem to have affected deeply his "will and feelings." As he notes, sympathy for others and the good of others "were the greatest and surest sources of happiness." Yet, the "dissolving influence of analysis" destroyed such sentiments and feelings in himself.[54]

During Mill's childhood, if such an inappropriate word could be used, he had never had friends or even playthings. Visitors would comment on the precocious son of James Mill and more than one would wonder how much true education was occurring. Even at the age of 14—the age at which he went to France—it seems hardly plausible that one so young and protected could understand such minds as Shakespeare or Plato to any depth. Mill echoes such views in his *Autobiography*, but in a surprisingly mild fashion. He does not explicitly attack either Bentham or his father in the published *Autobiography*, though the implications are clear enough. In the first unpublished draft of the manuscript, he is most explicit: "I thus grew up in the absence of love and in the presence of fear: and many and indelible are the effects of this bringing-up, in the stunting of my moral growth."[55] In the apt phrase of one of the best Mill scholars, James Mill and Jeremy Bentham were inculcators rather than educators.[56]

---

[52] *Ibid.*, p. 280.

[53] *Ibid.*, p. 281.

[54] *Ibid.*, pp. 281–83.

[55] Jack Stillinger, ed., *The Early Draft of John Stuart Mill's Autobiography* (Urbana: University of Illinois Press, 1961), p. 184. See the excellent article by Stillinger, "John Mill's Education: Fact, Fiction, and Myth," in *A Cultivated Mind: Essays on J. S. Mill Presented to John M. Robson*, ed. Michael Laine (Toronto: University of Toronto Press, 1991), pp. 19–43.

[56] John M. Robson, *The Improvement of Mankind: The Social and Political Thought of John Stuart Mill* (Toronto: University of Toronto Press, 1968), p. 27.

Mill continued to work and even to make speeches; but, as he says, it was all done "mechanically, by the mere force of habit," and it was a year "of which I remember next to nothing."[57] He was able eventually to climb slowly out of the depression by reading a sentimental French novel. Mill explains what happened:

> I was reading, accidentally, Marmontel's *Mémoires*, and came to the passage which relates his father's death, the distressed position of the family, and the sudden inspiration by which he, then a mere boy, felt and made them feel that he would be everything to them—would supply the place of all that they had lost. A vivid conception of the scene and its feelings came over me, and I was moved to tears. From this moment my burden grew lighter. The oppression of the thought that all feeling was dead within me, was gone. I was no longer hopeless: I was not a stock or a stone. I had still, it seemed, some of the material out of which all worth of character, and all capacity for happiness, are made.[58]

Just to read about a father dying and a son then taking over—"supply the place of"—was enough, apparently, to relieve Mill of his dark depression and to begin his recovery. It is an episode that seems designed for a case study by psychoanalysis.[59] In any case, this mental crisis provided a main theme for Mill's political and philosophic writings: the necessity of uniting the development of character and political philosophy.

The period up to this mental crisis constitutes the first major stage in Mill's philosophic journey. The second stage, lasting about a decade, begins with his slow recovery (of five years or so) from his depression. It is a period when he meets new people outside the utilitarian "religion," and he falls in love with a married woman, Harriet Taylor. He gradually reassesses his father's and Bentham's philosophic positions. Perhaps no change was as valuable to his recovery as was the realization that happiness was a proper goal, but that it was not to be sought as a direct physical gratification:

---

[57] "Autobiography," in Robson, *John Stuart Mill*, p. 284.

[58] *Ibid.*, p. 285.

[59] Peter Glassman has written a psychoanalytic study: *J. S. Mill: The Evolution of a Genius* (Gainesville: University of Florida Press, 1985). See also, A. W. Levi, "The 'Mental Crisis' of John Stuart Mill," *Psychoanalytic Review* 32 (January, 1945), pp. 86–101.

But I now thought that this end was only to be attained by not making it the direct end. Those only are happy (I thought) who have their minds fixed on some object other than their own happiness; on the happiness of others, on the improvement of mankind, even on some art or pursuit, followed not as a means, but as itself an ideal end. Aiming thus at something else, they find happiness by the way. The enjoyments of life (such was now my theory) are sufficient to make it a pleasant thing, when they are taken *en passant*, without being made a principle object. Once make them so, and they are immediately felt to be insufficient. They will not bear a scrutinizing examination. Ask yourself whether you are happy, and you cease to be so. The only chance is to treat, not happiness, but some end external to it, as the purpose of life. Let your self-consciousness, your scrutiny, your self-interrogation, exhaust themselves on that; and if otherwise fortunately circumstanced you will inhale happiness with the air you breathe, without dwelling on it or thinking about it, without either forestalling it in imagination, or putting it to flight by fatal questioning. This theory now became the basis of my philosophy of life. And I still hold to it as the best theory for all those who have but a moderate degree of sensibility and of capacity for enjoyment, that is, for the great majority of mankind.[60]

Aristotle would have approved.

Mill became acquainted with the poetry of Alfred Tennyson, Samuel Taylor Coleridge, and William Wordsworth. He credits the latter for leading him from his "habitual depression," and he writes that he "was never again subject to it." Wordsworth's treatment of rural scenery and mountains appealed to Mill's sense of beauty, but, more importantly, Wordsworth was able in his poetry to so lead the mind—at least as Mill explained it—that the reader experienced the "states of feeling." These, Mill could share with all human beings, and he felt a new connection with the "common destiny of human beings."[61] Gradually, he was shedding the view that self-interest and simple gratification were the only motivations for human actions.

---

[60] "Autobiography," in Robson, *John Stuart Mill*, p. 286.

[61] *Ibid.*, pp. 290–91.

In general, his philosophy became "more complex and many-sided."[62] He was impressed, no doubt to his father's annoyance, by Thomas Macaulay's analysis of his father's *Essay on Government*, which had near official status as the position of utilitarianism. James Mill's essay represented the standard rational and deductive Benthamite approach: self-interest and utility determined all behaviour, and a political system could be deductively constructed from such premises. Macaulay suggested that one should actually look at politics directly. As Mill approvingly writes in the *Autobiography*, Macaulay "stood up for the empirical mode of treating political phenomena."[63]

Others whose writings Mill read were the French philosopher Alexis de Tocqueville, who gave him a new understanding of history and of the rising tide of egalitarianism; Thomas Carlyle, an English essayist and historian of a romantic and conservative bent; several French philosophers—contemptuously dubbed Utopian socialists by Karl Marx—August Comte, Charles Fourier, and Saint Simon. After reading these and many more, Mill began to lose faith in Bentham's and his father's political rationalism and became more sensitive to the idea of historical growth and to the complexity of political reality. He was particularly struck by Saint Simon, who saw an ebb and flow, from an organic to a critical period and back again, throughout history. The idea, briefly, was that periods occur when the beliefs, the type of economic system, and the political and social systems are all organically tied. But these tend to break apart, and such a time of breakdown, according to Mill, was his own century. There were a host of thinkers, in Britain and on the continent, who now interested him, broadened his thought, and gave him a confident independence from strict Benthamism.[64] This did not lead to a repudiation of utilitarianism, but Mill was able to give it a new, more appealing voice.

A major, if not the chief, influence that led to Mill's new and confident voice was his friendship with Harriet Taylor, wife of John Taylor. They met in 1830 and became devoted friends. He was 24; she was 22 and had 3 children. Although Mill apparently asked her, she refused to leave her husband and children. In any case, she lived apart from her husband most of the time, and, to the consternation

---

[62] *Ibid.*, p. 298.

[63] *Ibid.*, p. 297.

[64] Particularly valuable in tracing Mill's evolution during this time are: Robson, *The Improvement of Mankind*, pp. 69–114; R. J. Halliday, *John Stuart Mill* (London: Allen & Unwin, 1976), pp. 13-68; Alan Ryan, *J. S. Mill* (London: Kegan & Paul, 1974), pp. 29–58.

of family, friends, and society, she and Mill were constant companions. Without question, the social ostracism they personally experienced helps to explain the passionate and eloquent critique of social tyranny in Mill's most famous work, *On Liberty*. John Taylor died in 1849, and Harriet and John Mill married two years later. Harriet died in 1858, in Auvignon, in southern France, where they had gone to live. Their relationship had been wholly platonic in the beginning and remained so throughout their lives. For an apparently unconsummated marriage, his hymns of praise for her are a puzzle and even an embarrassment to modern ears.[65] The epitaph on her tombstone, which he made into a shrine and visited daily, reads: "Were there even a few hearts and intellects like hers, this earth would already become the hoped for heaven."[66] The dedication to Mill's most read work, *On Liberty*, reads in part:

> Were I but capable of interpreting to the world one half the great thoughts and noble feelings which are buried in her grave, I should be the medium of a greater benefit to it, than is ever likely to arise from anything that I can write, unprompted and unassisted by her all but unrivalled wisdom.

These effusions are mild in comparison with other remarks he made. His judgment of her sterling mind and character, as one would suspect, was not shared by others. Indeed, there is a clear identity between the "states of feelings" created in his mind by romantic poetry and the "state of love" he and Harriet created and genuinely inhabited. He had only a slightly milder assessment of Harriet's daughter Helen, who, immediately upon Harriet's death, came and lived with Mill until his death in 1873. Mill said of both women: "Whoever, either now or hereafter, may think of me and of the work I have done, must never forget that it is the product not of one intellect and conscience but of three, the least considerable of whom, and above all the least original, is the one whose name is attached to it."[67]

---

[65] For an analysis of their relationship and marriage, see: Phyllis Rose, *Parallel Lives: Five Victorian Marriages* (New York: Knopf, 1982), pp. 95–140; F. A. Hayek, *John Stuart Mill and Harriet Taylor* (London: Routledge & Kegan Paul, 1951); Michael St. J. Packe, *The Life of John Stuart Mill* (London: Secker and Warburg, 1954). The friendship and marriage make a marvelous case study for those of a psychoanalytic bent: see, Glassman, *J.S. Mill*, pp. 88–105.

[66] Quoted in Robson, *The Improvement of Mankind*, p. 53.

[67] "Autobiography" in *The Collected Works of John Stuart Mill*, 35 Vols., ed. J. M. Robson (Toronto: University of Toronto Press, 1963-91), Vol. I, pp. 264–65.

His praise is not feigned; thus, the question remains of the nature of the collaboration, such as it was. There is ample evidence that both women enabled Mill to function far better than he could have by himself. His major writings and publications continued after Harriet's death, and he was even able to run successfully (once) for Parliament (1863-1865). Still, there is no significant evidence to suggest joint authorship of his works.[68] One of Harriet's accomplishments was to decrease, though it would not be possible to eliminate, Mill's infinite capacity for self-belittlement and self-denigration. Mainly, she encouraged his intellectual growth and stabilized his new-found confidence and independent philosophic stance.

With the publication, in 1843, of *A System of Logic*, Mill enters the third and final stage of his philosophic life. This work announces his independence and, in all major matters, sets the philosophic foundation for the rest of his life. He had been musing on the topic in the 1830s and had finished the manuscript by 1841. It shows Mill free of any parroting of Bentham or of his father; nevertheless, he was still convinced that utilitarianism, once revised, was the proper philosophy.

A System of Logic and *Utilitarianism* (written in the 1850s and published in 1859) publicly established the new version of utilitarianism. Mill's writings in political philosophy, government, and economics were now also distinctive. His major writing in economics was the *Principle of Political Economy* (1848), the same year of publication as Karl Marx's *Communist Manifesto*. Marx's work was obscure and unknown, but Mill's work went through many editions and revisions. His essay on *Representative Government* (1861) was a sharp contrast to the writings of both his father and Bentham. Lastly, his masterpiece, *On Liberty* (1859), written while Harriet was still alive, firmly placed him as a new, original voice for a reconstituted liberalism.

Utilitarianism Reconsidered

In the *System of Logic* Mill devotes the final book to the "logic of the Moral Sciences." His design in the *System* is to provide both a scientific framework consistent with the principle of utility and a "knowledge of duties; practical ethics, or morality." The latter does not refer to matters of fact, which is the realm of science,

---

[68] Robson, in *The Improvement of Mankind*, examines the secondary literature on this topic and reaches this sensible conclusion (pp. 50–68). See also Ann P. Robson on Helen's contribution, "Mill's Second Prize in the Lottery of Life," in Laine, *A Cultivated Mind*, pp. 215–41.

but to matters of practice or of art.[69] This use of "art" to express his point is, as he notes, an older usage, but it serves to accentuate that judgment, practice, and sensitivity to the particular are necessary in the realm of politics and ethics. In Mill's terms the "Art of Life" consists of "three departments, Morality, Prudence or Policy and Aesthetics; the Right, the Expedient, and the Beautiful or Noble in human conduct and works."[70] These topics express what are worthy and desirable in human life, and are jointly called the doctrine of ends or of teleology. Mill then draws a contrast with the concerns of a scientist:

> His part is only to show that certain consequences follow from certain causes, and that to obtain certain ends, certain means are the most effectual. Whether the ends themselves are such as ought to be pursued, and if so, in what cases and to how great a length, it is no part of his business as a cultivator of science to decide, and science alone will never qualify him for the decision.[71]

The unity expressed by Bentham in his utilitarianism has been broken. Mill has escaped the simple-minded vulgarity of Bentham's ethics, but he faces, in turn, his own philosophic difficulties.

The overarching problem facing Mill is that his central principle remains utility and his model of knowing is a scientific cause and effect model. Both of these features are ahistorical, and yet Mill wants to provide some base of knowledge (albeit not purely scientific knowledge) for the practical art of governing in any particular society. As a utilitarian of sorts, Mill maintains that the calculation of consequences is not merely subjective and that it alone can guide humans in a wise choice of actions. The calculation of utility, for Mill, cannot be the simply ahistorical, universal, mechanical operation of pain and pleasure found in Bentham and James Mill. John Mill's position is far more complicated: he has to reconcile general scientific laws of an explanation with an explanation of the behaviour of particular societies and individuals who seek to realize ends worthy of human pursuit.

---

[69] "A System of Logic," in Robson, *Collected Works*, Vol. VIII, *On the Logic of the Moral Sciences*, Bk. VI, ch. xii, 1.

[70] *Ibid.*, Bk. VI, ch. xii, 6.

[71] *Ibid.*

Mill begins his argument by denying that there is a separation between the science of physical reality and the science of humans: "It is a common notion, or at least it is implied in many common modes of speech, that the thoughts, feelings, and actions of sentient beings are not a subject of science, in the same strict sense in which this is true of the objects of outward nature."[72] Mill holds this position to be false. He sees no difference in kind between natural science and what today is called social science. Rather, social phenomena are simply extremely complex, and, as a consequence, the social scientist needs to examine the more complex of the physical sciences for a model. Hobbes's mistake, for example, was to reduce human thought and activity to one cause—the drive for self-preservation; just as Bentham's explanation of human activity was dependent upon the sole motivation of selfish interest.[73] Human activities are actually too complicated for such single-causation theories. To be sure, the predictive certainty of astronomy cannot be duplicated by social science for the history of human society "for thousands of years to come." We simply cannot obtain all of the data necessary about human society to achieve such predictive certainty, but we can get knowledge about social affairs that would be "most valuable for guidance."[74] In principle, Mill argues, there is sufficient knowledge available now.

> The science of society would have attained a very high point of perfection if it enabled us, in any given condition of social affairs, in the condition, for instance, of…any European country at the present time, to understand by what causes it had, in any and every particular, been made what it was; whether it was tending to any, and to what, changes; what effects each feature of its existing state was likely to produce in the future; and by what means any of those effects might be prevented, modified, or accelerated, or a different class of effects superinduced. There is nothing chimerical in the hope that general laws, sufficient to enable us to answer these various questions for any country or time with the individual circumstances of which we are well acquainted, do really admit of being ascertained.... Such is the object of Social Science.[75]

---

[72] *Ibid.*, Bk. VI, ch. iii, 1.

[73] *Ibid.*, Bk. VI, ch. viii, 2–3.

[74] *Ibid.*, Bk. VI, ch. vi, 2.

[75] *Ibid.*

The comparison with the current situation of social science, as Mill sees it, however, should not be with the science of astronomy but with the science of tidology, or the study of ocean tides. We already know what causes the changes in tides: the changing gravitational effects of the moon as it rotates around the earth. But we cannot predict with precision the exact height of a tide because there are so many intervening factors that we are not in practice able to know: the wind, temperature, storms far out at sea, and so on. The general scientific law we know, gravity; it is the complexity of the intervening causes and the lack of sufficient data that keeps us from precision.

The kind of exactness that tidology can currently attain is parallel to that attainable by the science of human nature. According to Mill: "the agencies which determine human character are so numerous and diversified…that in the aggregate they are never in any two cases exactly similar."[76] Just as tidology is not an exact science yet, neither is the science of human nature. But it is critical to note that there is no "inherent capacity" that keeps tidology or the science of human nature from being an exact science. Furthermore, what is not an exact predictive generalization in individual cases may become more nearly so for a large group:

> …an approximate generalization is, in social inquiries, for most practical purposes equivalent to an exact one: that which is only probable when asserted of individual human beings indiscriminately selected, being certain when affirmed of the character and collective conduct of masses.[77]

Differences in human behaviour in similar situations—like irregularities in tides—can be explained by looking for other unsuspected intervening causes. Mill's full science of human nature has three connected levels. First, there are empirical generalizations about social behaviour. Second, one deduces from these generalizations "laws of the mind" or a psychology of how the mind works. (This process, he believes, is parallel to the practices of the physical sciences in that, first, empirical generalizations are drawn and, second, the laws, such as the law of gravity, are deduced from them.) Third, and finally, from the laws of the mind are deduced explanations of individual thoughts, feelings, and actions.

Mill was quite confident that from these three levels a true claim of knowledge about individual behaviour, at least in mass, could be made. We have the knowledge in principle to explain scientifically the formation of human character.

---

[76] *Ibid.*, Bk. VI, ch. iii, 2.

[77] *Ibid.*

Excepting the degrees of uncertainty which still exist as to the extent of the natural differences of individual minds, and the physical circumstances on which these may be dependent (considerations which are of secondary importance when we are considering mankind in the average, or *en masse*) I believe most competent judges will agree that the general laws of the different constituent elements of human nature are even now sufficiently understood to render it possible for a competent thinker to deduce from these laws, with a considerable approach to certainty, the particular type of character which would be formed in mankind generally by any assumed set of circumstances.[78]

One slight qualification was in order. Mill was not sure if the laws of mind or psychology had a physiological base or not.[79] Nevertheless, one could deduce from them a science of the formation of character. He called this "ethology" or the exact science of human nature. Its task was not to discover general laws but to show us "what makes one person, in a given position feel or act in one way, another in another." These individual acts are also all explained causally.

The actions and feelings of human beings in the social state, are no doubt, entirely governed by psychological and ethological laws: whatever influence any cause exercises upon the social phenomena, it exercises through these laws. Supposing therefore the laws of human actions and feelings to be sufficiently known, there is no extraordinary difficulty in determining from those laws, the nature of the social effects which any given cause tends to produce.[80]

Education would be the application of the laws of ethology to individuals.[81] We would then have progress in morals and in society at large.

By building our knowledge upon empirical generalization of social behaviour, upon the laws of mind that are deduced from these generalizations, and upon ethology or the science of the development of character, we can have a full science of human nature for explaining the social order and human progress. One theorem that

---

[78] *Ibid.*, Bk. VI, ch. v, 6.

[79] *Ibid.*, Bk. VI, ch. iv, 2.

[80] *Ibid.*, Bk. VI, ch. ix, 1.

[81] *Ibid.*, Bk. VI, ch. v, 6.

can be drawn from our present knowledge is the general "tendency toward a better and happier state." This is a fundamental fact that must be recognized in social science: "The progressiveness of the human race is the foundation on which a method of philosophizing in the social science has been of late years erected...."[82] Mill was especially impressed by Auguste Comte's claim that humanity has progressed from the early and primitive theological stage of development, to the metaphysical or philosophic stage, and, finally, to the positive or scientific stage of the present. He was confident, too, that the science of human nature enabled humans to understand human development in history and, thus, to guide it.

> But whatever decision competent judges may pronounce on the results arrived at by any individual inquirer, the method now characterized is that by which the derivative laws of social order and of social progress must be sought. By its aid we may hereafter succeed not only in looking far forward into the future history of the human race, but in determining what artificial means may be used, and to what extent, to accelerate the natural progress in so far as it is beneficial...and to guard against the dangers or accidents to which our species is exposed from the necessary incidents of its progression. Such practical instructions, founded on the highest branch of speculative sociology, will form the noblest and most beneficial portion of the Political Art.[83]

Mill's use of the phrase political art helps to clarify the earlier distinction he made between science and art or practice. It now appears that his distinction is not at all similar to Aristotle's distinction between the theoretical and practical sciences; rather, Mill's distinction, and the relationship between science and art, is more like that between a physicist and a mechanic.

The three levels constituting the science of human nature are, as we have seen, related through deduction: ethology is deduced from laws of the mind, which, in turn, are deduced from empirical generalizations about social behaviour. In this case one is trying to explain individual character development, which is at the top of the three tiers. Mill also holds that there should be a science of political ethology as well, which would be a study of national character and how it is formed.[84]

---

[82] *Ibid.*, Bk. VI, ch. x, 3.

[83] *Ibid.*, Bk. VI, ch. x, 8.

[84] *Ibid.*, Bk. VI, ch. ix, 4.

Mills argues that a reverse model of an explanation is required to understand large historical developments. Again, there are three levels, but he calls the relationship inverse deduction. First, one draws the empirical generalizations from observing a society and its history; second, these generalizations are related to (inverse deduction) our knowledge of the laws of the mind, ethology; third, these laws of the mind are related to (inverse deduction) individual psychology. The two approaches of deduction and inverse deduction can be combined:

> Either of these processes, apart from the other, diminishes in value as the subject increases in complication…but the reliance to be placed in the concurrence of the two sorts of evidence, not only does not diminish in anything like the same proportion, but is not necessarily diminished at all…. [I]nstead of deducing our conclusions by reasoning, and verifying them by observation, we in some cases begin by obtaining them provisionally from specific experience, and afterwards connect them with the principles of human nature by *à priori* reasonings, which reasonings are thus a real Verification.[85]

Here, Mill has developed, however adequately, a conception of political change and of historical development far more complex and sophisticated than that of Bentham. Yet, there is still the fundamental confidence in moral progress and in the expanding human knowledge that guides it.

The essay on *Utilitarianism* completes the break with Bentham. It was written for a wide audience and served to demark the full changes that Mill was making in the philosophy of utilitarianism. He begins his defence of utilitarianism by restating the Greatest Happiness Principle:

> The creed which accepts as the foundation of morals, Utility, or the Greatest Happiness Principle, holds that actions are right in proportion as they tend to promote happiness, wrong as they tend to produce the reverse of happiness. By happiness is intended pleasure, and the absence of pain; by unhappiness, pain, and the privation of pleasure. To give a clear view of the moral standard set up by the theory, much more requires to be said; in particular what things it includes in the ideas of pain and pleasure; and to what extent this is left an open question. But these supplementary explanations do not affect the theory of life on which this theory of morality is grounded—

---

[85] *Ibid.*, Bk. VI, ch. ix, 1.

namely, that pleasure, and freedom from pain, are the only things desirable as ends; and that all desirable things (which are as numerous in the utilitarian as in any other scheme) are desirable either for the pleasure inherent in themselves, or as means to the promotion of pleasure and the prevention of pain.[86]

Although this statement appears consistent with Bentham's formulation, Mill proceeds to make several significant qualifications. The most significant is his re-definition of pleasure. There are differences in quality and kinds of pleasure. He is less than forthright in acknowledging the change: "there is no known Epicurean theory of life which does not assign to the pleasures of the intellect, of the feelings and imagination, and of the moral sentiments, a much higher value as pleasures than to those of mere sensation."[87] But, of course, this is pre-cisely not what Bentham had argued. Mill is clear that some pleasures are "in-trinsically" better and different in "kind." Quality must be considered, he asserts, as well as quantity.[88]

Apparently, it is surprisingly easy to distinguish between these kinds of plea-sure. Fortunately, humans are so constructed that recognition is quite natural:

> Few human creatures would consent to be changed into any of the lower an-imals, for a promise of the fullest allowance of a beast's pleasures; no intel-ligent human being would consent to be a fool, no instructed person would be an ignoramus, no person of feeling and conscience would be selfish and base, even though they should be persuaded that the fool, the dunce, or the rascal is better satisfied with his lot than they are with theirs.[89]

If there should be some difference of opinion about the quality of some pleasure, the solution is to consult the "superior person." Happiness is not equated with the "beast's pleasure" of mere ignorant contentment: "It is better to be a human being dissatisfied than a pig satisfied; better to be Socrates dissatisfied than a fool satisfied."[90]

---

[86] *John Stuart Mill: On Liberty and Other Essays*, ed. John Gray (Oxford: Oxford University Press, 1991), "Utilitarianism," p. 137.

[87] *Ibid.*, p. 138.

[88] *Ibid.*, pp. 138–39.

[89] *Ibid.*, p. 139.

[90] *Ibid.*, p. 140.

Those who have experienced both kinds of pleasures are the only "competent judges" in any controversy, and if they should differ, a "majority among them, must be admitted as final."[91]

Just as the meaning of pleasure shifts from that held by Bentham; morality and its relation to happiness undergo a change in meaning. Mill begins with a standard utilitarian formulation, which would have been acceptable both to James Mill and to Bentham: "happiness is the sole end of human action, and the promotion of it the test by which to judge of all human conduct; from whence it necessarily follows that it must be the criterion of morality since a part is included in the whole."[92] Mill proceeds to amplify the definition and in so doing makes two emendations. First, he makes clear that the happiness, which is the consequence of human conduct, must be broadened to include all concerned and not just the single person. "As between his own happiness and that of others, utilitarianism requires him to be as strictly impartial as a disinterested and benevolent spectator." It is not "the agent's own happiness" that is to be consulted "but that of all concerned."[93] Indeed, Mill insists, utilitarian morality recognizes that the highest virtue can be to make a sacrifice for the good of others.

The second emendation, and even more startling, is an introduction of the idea of justice. He gives this concept a distinct and higher status over other virtues:

> Justice remains the appropriate name for certain social utilities which are vastly more important, and therefore more absolute and imperative, than any others are as a class (though not more so that others may be in particular cases); and which, therefore, ought to be, as well as naturally are, guarded by a sentiment not only different in degree, but also in kind; distinguished from the milder feeling which attaches to the mere idea of promoting human pleasure or convenience, at once by the more definite nature of its commands, and by the sterner character of its sanctions.[94]

---

[91] *Ibid.*, p. 141.

[92] *Ibid.*, p. 172.

[93] *Ibid.*, p. 148.

[94] *Ibid.*, p. 201.

Justice is based, ultimately, upon utility but in a indirect way. He states, as a short definition, that "justice implies something which it is not only right to do, and wrong not to do, but which some individual person can claim from us as his moral right."[95] A society is obligated to defend individual rights. One can hardly square Mill's language with Bentham's gibe about rights as "nonsense upon stilts."

Mill also defines justice as a name for certain classes of moral rules:

> Justice is a name for certain classes of moral rules, which concern the essentials of human well-being more nearly, and are therefore of more absolute obligation, than any other rules for the guidance of life; and the notion which we have found to be of the essence of the idea of justice, that of a right residing in an individual, implies and testifies to this more binding obligation.[96]

The examples he gives of rights include the rights to property and to protection from harm by others; examples of moral rules are the keeping of friendships and promises.[97]

In all cases the reason Mill gives for recognizing and supporting these rights and moral rules is "general utility."[98] Somewhat disingenuously, he refers to both moral rules and rights as social utilities. The difficulty is in the application of the principle of utility in explaining and justifying rights and moral rules. If one considers, for instance, whether or not to break a particular promise in terms of utility, it may be in the interest of one's own or even a majority's happiness to do so. This formulation of the principle is called, by modern philosophers, "act utilitarianism." Mill would formulate the decision-making process differently. First, in making the calculation, as has already been noted, each individual would have to be "as strictly impartial as a disinterested and benevolent spectator."[99] Second, moral rules and rights would have to be a class of social utilities and, as such, the calculation must be made in terms of having or not having the class as a whole.

---

[95] *Ibid.*, p. 185.

[96] *Ibid.*, p. 195.

[97] *Ibid.*, pp. 196–97.

[98] *Ibid.*, p. 189.

[99] *Ibid.*, p. 148.

The question would then become one of determining whether the particular class of moral rules (here having to do with keeping promises) enhances the general happiness. This formulation of the principle of utility is now called "rule utilitarianism." One, in short, does not simply calculate the utility of breaking a promise, but it is necessary to calculate the utility of having the moral rule of promise-keeping in a society. Bentham's position is allied with the act utilitarianism approach and Mill's position with rule utilitarianism.[100]

With the publication of *Utilitarianism* the shift from Bentham's egotistic individual as the base for utilitarianism to a conception of a person constituted, to use Mill's phrases, by the intellect, feelings and imagination, and moral sentiments is completed. The concomitant pleasures that fit this conception of a person are different in kinds from those of a "beast's pleasures." Such a person has rights, duties and obligations to the whole, and moral rules. The appropriate standard of conduct for a person so constituted is justice, and Bentham's conception of the person ruled by self-interest has been fundamentally transformed.

On Liberty

Along with his altered version of utilitarianism—a version that recognizes the complexity of political change in history and views the person as far more than a calculator of interests—Mill also develops a political philosophy with an emphasis that is different from Bentham's political rationalism.

The work in which one can best see Mill's philosophy is the essay *On Liberty.* It is a short work of only five chapters, but it remains one of the most eloquent defences of individual liberty ever to be written. In the first chapter, Mill states the question to be addressed. He wants to examine civil or social liberty: "the nature and limits of the power which can be legitimately exercised by society over the individual." Human history has consistently featured a clash between liberty and authority, with subjects on one side facing the government on the other side. The resolution of this old quarrel between liberty and authority, as Mills says, has traversed through three stages. First, governments were forced to recognize the rights of the individual, and if the individual's rights were violated, governments could justifiably be resisted. Second, the very structure of government was altered to

---

[100] Michael D. Bayles has selected some contemporary articles defending the idea of rule utilitarianism as found in Mill: *Contemporary Utilitarianism* (Garden City: Anchor, 1968).

provide further protection for the liberty of the subject. In particular, says Mill, the evolution of representative institutions enabled the people to exercise control over the government so that the interests of the people would become identical with the interests of the government. This seemed to be a solution: "The nation did not need to be protected against its own will. There was no fear of its tyrannising over itself."[101]

Although these two stages have clearly increased protection for the subjects, Mill discerns a third stage in the old quarrel between liberty and authority. The danger now comes from the power of the people themselves, which boils down to the most active part of the people, the majority. A real threat has developed from the "tyranny of the majority." It is a threat not exercised so much by traditional political oppression as by a form of social tyranny, and this new form of tyranny requires a new kind of defence of liberty:

> there needs protection also against the tyranny of the prevailing opinion and feeling; against the tendency of society to impose, by other means than civil penalties, its own ideas and practices as rules of conduct on those who dissent from them; to fetter the development, and, if possible, prevent the formation, of any individuality not in harmony with its ways, and compel all characters to fashion themselves upon the model of its own.[102]

Social tyranny shows itself in innumerable ways throughout society, and public opinion, rather than government, becomes the instrument for oppression. Public opinion, accordingly, must be reformed and in a manner consistent with individual liberty. The bulk of the essay is directed to this task. Mill's first step is to announce a "simple principle," which, if properly explained and justified, would convert public opinion into an opponent of social tyranny:

> The object of this Essay is to assert one very simple principle, as entitled to govern absolutely the dealings of society with the individual in the way of compulsion and control, whether the means used be physical force in the

---

[101] *J. S. Mill: On Liberty and Other Writings*, ed. Stefan Collini (Cambridge: Cambridge University Press, 1989), pp. 5–7.

[102] *Ibid.*, p. 8. The phrase "tyranny of the majority" was taken from Alexis de Tocqueville's classic study, *Democracy in America*. Mill had written two long reviews of the work in 1840 and had been impressed by de Tocqueville's argument about the ties between egalitarianism and social conformity. De Tocqueville apparently got the phrase "tyranny of the majority" from John Adams.

form of legal penalties, or the moral coercion of public opinion. That principle is, that the sole end for which mankind are warranted, individually or collectively, in interfering with the liberty of action of any of their number, is self-protection. That the only purpose for which power can be rightfully exercised over any member of a civilised community, against his will, is to prevent harm to others. His own good, either physical or moral, is not a sufficient warrant. He cannot rightfully be compelled to do or forbear because it will be better for him to do so, because it will make him happier, because, in the opinions of others, to do so would be wise, or even right.[103]

This principle limits both the government and public opinion to self-protection as the only justification for interference. The phrase in the third sentence, "harm to others," would seem to be a less stringent limitation. Mill further explains that both action and inaction might cause harm, but it is only when harm has been committed that legal punishment, where appropriate, or "general disapprobation" would be justified. The "simple principle" is an extraordinary limitation on any government, but it would have been a particularly shocking limitation to suggest for nineteenth-century Britain. All societies expect, and governments enact, legislation that is designed to help individuals. Food and tobacco regulations are the most obvious examples. Many such regulations would be forbidden by Mill's reasoning: "His own good, either physical or moral, is not a sufficient warrant." This "very simple principle" gives the autonomous individual a very wide circle of non-interference.

Mill immediately presents some qualifications. The principle applies only to people in "the maturity of their faculties." The young and those incapable of taking care of themselves are exempt. He also notes that the principle does not apply to "those backward states of society in which the race itself may be considered as in its nonage." In this situation, despotism is appropriate, provided, he adds, that the goal is truly the improvement of the people, and the goal is being realized. The "simple principle" of liberty is applicable only "when mankind have become capable of being improved by free and equal discussion."[104] A final qualification

---

[103] *Ibid.*, p. 13.

[104] *Ibid.*, pp. 13–14. Mill worked at the East Indian Company for 35 years, and he was of the firm opinion throughout his tenure that the people of India could not "be trusted to govern themselves" but that they would be in time. Mill himself never went to India, never mentioned wanting to go there during his long retirement, and probably never met anyone from India. Trevor Lloyd, "John Stuart Mill and the East India Company," in Laine, *A Cultivated Mind*, pp. 44–79.

Mill makes is that only arguments from utility will be used as a defence of the "simple principle" of liberty. This appeal to utility, however, "must be utility in the largest sense, grounded on the permanent interests of man as a progressive being."[105] This curious phrase, as has been often noted, seems to be little more than an echo of the idea of a structured human nature, one with built-in capacities and excellences or virtues.

The goal is to defend a "region of human liberty," and Mill lists three facets of this region that will be defended. First is the "inward domain of consciousness; demanding liberty of conscience, in the most comprehensive sense; liberty of thought and feeling; absolute freedom of opinion and sentiments on all subjects, practical or speculative, scientific, moral, or theological." Second is the liberty "of tastes and pursuits; of framing the plan of our life to suit our own character." Third is the liberty to make friends and alliances with whomever one wants.[106] The value of these three parts of the region of liberty is supported by utility. Thus, Mill, in the rest of the essay, provides arguments designed to convince each person of the personal and social utility in supporting these three areas of liberty. Once each person sees the personal advantages to each of the three areas, public opinion will have been metamorphosed into a protection for, rather than a threat to, liberty.

Chapter 2, "Of the liberty of thought or discussion," is the heart of the essay. Mill restates the issue: suppression of opinion is wrong even if the government "is entirely at one with the people." Coercion of opinion, assuming that opinion involves no harm to others, is not justified: "If all mankind minus one, were of one opinion, and only one person were of the contrary opinion, mankind would be no more justified in silencing that one person, than he, if he had the power, would be justified in silencing mankind." The reason that it is unjustified is utilitarian:

> that it is robbing the human race; posterity as well as the existing generation; those who dissent from the opinion, still more than those who hold it. If the opinion is right, they are deprived of the opportunity of exchanging error for truth: if wrong, they lose, what is almost as great a benefit, the clearer perception and livelier impression of truth, produced by its collision with error.[107]

---

[105] *Ibid.*, p. 14.

[106] *Ibid.*, pp. 15–16.

[107] *Ibid.*, p. 20.

As evidence, Mill tests three hypothetical cases to demonstrate the consequences of suppression: first, he examines the consequences of suppressing an opinion that might be true; second, he tests the utility of suppressing an opinion that actually is true; third, he shows the consequences of suppressing an opinion that shares truth with other opinions.

To silence an opinion that might be true, Mill's first hypothesis, assumes infallibility. The blunt truth of the matter, he argues, is that every age has confidently suppressed what later ages discovered to be true; moreover, the oddity of time and place mainly determines most people's beliefs in any case. The same person, except for birth, would be a "Churchman in London…a Buddhist or a Confucian in Peking."[108] People do indeed have to make decisions and take actions, but the grounds for so doing are justified only if the particular opinion has been subject to the liberty of cross-examination and disputation. This is the only condition that "justifies us in assuming truth for purposes of action; and on no other terms can a being with human faculties have any rational assurance of being right."[109]

The history of persecution further discredits any assumption that infallibility could support the silencing of opinion. Socrates and Jesus were both subject to persecution, Mill reminds the reader. The greatest and most enlightened of all Roman emperors and a stoic philosopher in his own right, Marcus Aurelius, persecuted Christianity. It is true, Mill continues, that we no longer put heretics to death. But he cites as contemporary examples of the assumption of infallibility the revival of religious bigotry in certain "narrow and uncultivated minds" and the attempt to limit religious toleration in India only to Christian sects.[110] It is necessary to allow freedom to think so that truth can gain from errors. Moreover, it is not the great person who needs the freedom as much as the average person. Freedom of thought enables "average human beings to attain the mental stature which they are capable of."[111]

The second hypothetical case is that the opinion is actually true, but the "truth is not freely and openly canvassed."[112] In this case, the consequence is that the truth gradually ossifies and becomes dead dogma. In the beginning, ethical doctrines and

---

[108] *Ibid.*, p. 21.

[109] *Ibid.*, p. 23.

[110] *Ibid.*, p. 33.

[111] *Ibid.*, p. 36.

[112] *Ibid.*, p. 37.

religious creeds "are full of meaning and vitality to those who originate them, and to the direct disciples of the originators."[113] But, once the creed becomes hereditary, and the mind does not "exercise its vital powers" in questioning, "a dull and torpid assent" characterizes the believers, and the "inner life of the human being" ceases to be touched. Mill eloquently describes the consequences:

> Then are seen the cases, so frequent in this age of the world as almost to form the majority, in which the creed remains as it were outside the mind, in-crusting and petrifying it against all other influences addressed to the higher parts of our nature; manifesting its power by not suffering any fresh and liv-ing conviction to get in, but itself doing nothing for the mind or heart, except standing sentinel over them to keep them vacant.[114]

Mill does believe that "as mankind improves" the number of undisputed truths will rightly increase. Even here, there needs to be "some contrivance" for remaking a question contentious so that the answer can be rethought, and Mill recommends the Socratic dialogue for this role.[115]

The third hypothetical case is that truth is shared with other opinions. This is the situation most often found in a society, and it particularly characterizes the realm of politics: "a party of order or stability, and a party of progress or reform, are both necessary elements of a healthy state of political life."[116] It is virtually impossible for both elements, each having some truth, to be reconciled and combined in one mind: "very few have minds [being] sufficiently capacious and impartial to make the adjustment with an approach to correctness."[117] It is only in the rough process of a struggle, he argues, that both sides can be given their just due. He gives some examples of contentious differences where both sides must be presented to have a healthy political society: democracy and aristocracy, luxury and abstinence, prop-erty and equality, co-operation and competition, sociality and individuality, liberty and discipline. Without the open discussion of these and many other contentious issues, the "tendency to all opinions to become sectarian" would not be checked.[118]

---

[113] *Ibid.*, p. 41.

[114] *Ibid.*, p. 42.

[115] *Ibid.*, p. 45.

[116] *Ibid.*, p. 48.

[117] *Ibid.*, p. 49.

[118] *Ibid.*, pp. 48–53.

He concludes the second chapter with four solid reasons for freedom of opinion. These reasons are drawn from the examination he has just provided of practical consequences in the history of suppressing opinions. First, to silence an opinion is to assume infallibility. One can look at history to see how untenable this position is. Second, a silenced opinion, which is in error, may still contain "a portion of truth." This portion of truth would then be lost. Third, a wholly true opinion will become a prejudice, and the rational grounds will be lost, unless it, too, is subject to challenge. Fourth, "the vital effect on the character and conduct" of individuals is lost when opinions, even when true, become mere dogma. In this case, beliefs become "a mere formal profession, inefficacious for good, but cumbering the ground, and preventing the growth of any real and heartfelt conviction, from reason or personal experience."[119]

Mill listed in the first chapter "liberty of tastes and pursuits" and the liberty of uniting with whomever one wants as essential parts of the "region of human liberty." Chapter 3, "Of individuality, as one of the elements of well-being," is written to convince the public that these two particular liberties are valuable to all. There is one difference, according to Mill, between liberty of thought and liberty of action. The latter cannot be as free as opinions, but the key limitation governing freedom remains the same: harm to others. If the action "concerns himself, the same reasons which show that opinion should be free, prove also that he should be allowed, without molestations, to carry his opinions into practice at his own cost."[120] Just as there is a need for a variety of opinions to be expressed there should be,

> different opinions, so is it that there should be different experiments of living; that free scope should be given to varieties of character, short of injury to others; and that the worth of different modes of life should be proved practically, when any one thinks fit to try them. It is desirable, in short, that in things which do not primarily concern others, individuality should assert itself. Where, not the person's own character, but the traditions or customs of other people are the rule of conduct, there is wanting one of the principal ingredients of human happiness, and quite the chief ingredient of individual and social progress.[121]

---

[119] *Ibid.*, pp. 54–55.

[120] *Ibid.*, pp. 56–57.

[121] *Ibid.*, p. 57.

Mill wishes to show that both individual and social progress depend upon the appreciation of individuality, that without individuality both are stunted. Thus, he advocates the acceptance of spontaneity and eccentricity among individuals, and the acceptance of different experiments of living. Both have valuable, which is to say utilitarian, consequences. The problem with contemporary society is that the "intrinsic worth" of individual spontaneity is not accredited by the majority. The use of the word "intrinsic" seems, on the surface, incompatible with a utilitarian argument "Intrinsic value" means that it is not valued just for the consequences; spontaneity itself is valuable. But, Mill, apparently untroubled by such an argument, proceeds to argue that mental and moral development, "like the muscular powers," needs exercise. Unless an action flows from a person's own choices and reasons, there will be no growth as a human being:

> He who lets the world, or his own portion of it, choose his plan of life for him, has no need of any other faculty than the ape-like one of imitation. He who chooses his plan for himself, employs all his faculties. He must use observation to see, reasoning and judgment to foresee, activity to gather materials for decision, discrimination to decide, and when he has decided, firmness and self-control to hold to his deliberate decision. And these qualities he requires and exercises exactly in proportion as the part of his conduct which he determines according to his own judgment and feelings is a large one. It is possible that he might be guided in some good path, and kept out of harm's way, without any of these things. But what will be his comparative worth as a human being?[122]

Regrettably, present society keeps individuals from developing: "society has now fairly got the better of individuality." Differences in tastes and eccentricity of conduct are treated as if they were crimes, Mill laments. Human capacities are "withered and starved" by the lack of use imposed through social conformity.[123] It is only by the cultivation of individuality that one can become a well-developed human.

Even if a person is not swayed by these arguments for his or her own development, there are still good grounds for allowing individuality in others. First, originality makes a variety of contributions to society. New truth, new practices, and more enlightened conduct are the by-products of those few persons of genius.

---

[122] *Ibid.*, p. 59.

[123] *Ibid.*, pp. 61–62.

The contributions of geniuses require "the atmosphere of freedom." Eccentricity, genius, "the amount of mental vigour, and moral courage" actually go together, Mill contends, and there is a great danger to society in that so few now dare to be eccentric. It is in our interest as a society, he argues, to see the value of such individuals. With an uncharacteristically patriotic argument, he warns that it was great individuals "that made England what it has been," and such men are needed again "to prevent its decline."[124]

The second argument he makes to those who are not interested in the practice of individuality is that the "despotism of custom" will stop human advancement. Where there is no individuality and diversity, progress stops. The example is China. Europe has made extraordinary progress precisely because of its "remarkable diversity of character and culture."[125] To continue progress, there must be a "variety of situations," but such variety has now diminished:

> Formerly, different ranks, different neighbourhoods, different trades and professions, lived in what might be called different worlds; at present, to a great degree in the same. Comparatively speaking, they now read the same things, listen to the same things, see the same things, go to the same places, have their hopes and fears directed to the same objects, have the same rights and liberties, and the same means of asserting them.[126]

The recognition and the nourishment of individuality are necessary for individual and social progress. It is only then that the human being becomes "a noble and beautiful object of contemplation" and "by the same process human life also becomes rich, diversified, and animating, furnishing more abundant ailment to high thoughts and elevating feelings, and strengthening the tie which binds every individual to the race, by making the race infinitely better worth belonging to."[127] In sum, there will be benefits for all by the encouragement of individuality.

After explaining and justifying the liberty of the individual, Mill turns, in chapter 4, to what the individual owes to the society. He describes three duties or obligations. First, individuals should not harm "the interests of one another."

---

124 *Ibid.*, pp. 65–70.

125 *Ibid.*, pp. 70–72.

126 *Ibid.*, p. 73.

127 *Ibid.*, p. 63.

He then adds that he means interests of such importance that they "ought to be considered as rights." Given the definition of rights in the essay on *Utilitarianism*, Mill does not mean just any legal rights but key rights, such as liberty, property, and contract, and he also wants to cover moral rules. Second, each individual should bear a fair share of the burden of supporting the society. Taxes are an obvious example. Such burdens are duties the individual owes to society, and a breach of them would justify punishment by law. The third duty is to refrain from any actions that are harmful to others, "without going the length of violating any of their constituted rights." In this case, the punishment is not by law but by opinion.[128]

Mill's arguments about how to draw the line between individual liberty and the authority of society and of government turn on his distinctions between self-regarding and other-regarding actions. (Curiously, Mill uses the word "self-regarding," but he does not use "other-regarding.") If the conduct "affects the interest of no other persons beside himself," there should be "perfect freedom, legal and social, to do the action and stand the consequences." Because it is quite easy to imagine how self-regarding actions can ease over into affecting others, at least in the minds of those affected, Mill has added the word "interests" to provide an objective criterion for the distinction. He also uses the more precise phrase "a distinct and assignable obligation to any other person or persons," to clarify what he means by the interest of another.[129] He sometimes assigns his own conception of rights to capture the objective and permanent interests he has in mind.[130]

Self-regarding faults (such as "rashness, obstinacy, and conceit") and self-regarding immoralities (such as malice, envy, greed, and dissimulation) are subject to "loss of consideration of others," to pity, and to dislike. However odious these faults and immoralities are, they do not enter the other-regarding area, since

---

[128] *Ibid.*, p. 75.

[129] *Ibid.*, p. 81.

[130] Even in Mill's own day, the distinction between self-regarding and other-regarding was often viewed as hopelessly slippery and vague. The most astute critic was James Fitzjames Stevens, *Liberty, Equality and Fraternity*, originally published in 1873 (Chicago: University of Chicago Press, 1991). See the survey of early critics by John C. Rees, *John Stuart Mill's 'On Liberty'* (Oxford: Oxford University Press, 1985), pp. 78–105. Rees is also recognized for his interpretation of the distinction, which strengthens Mill's argument. See "A Re-Reading of Mill On Liberty," in *Limits of Liberty: Studies of Mill's 'On Liberty'*, ed. Peter Radcliff (Belmont, Calif.: Wadsworth, 1966), pp. 87–107. Also, C. T. Ten is excellent: *Mill On Liberty* (Oxford: Clarendon Press, 1980), pp. 10–41.

no rights or permanent interests of others are involved. When conduct does affect other's interests, "a distinct and assignable obligation to any other person," then society has jurisdiction and may punish by law or public disapprobation. If a father spends all his money—an immoral extravagance—the punishment can only be for the "breach of duty to his family or creditors, not for the extravagance."[131] Likewise, a drunk should not be punished for just being drunk but for dereliction of duties.

The final chapter provides examples of how the major arguments of the essay are to be applied to social issues. Mill summarizes his arguments into two maxims:

> The maxims are, first, that the individual is not accountable to society for his actions, in so far as these concern the interests of no person but himself. Advice, instruction, persuasion, and avoidance by other people if thought necessary by them for their own good, are the only measures by which society can justifiably express its dislike or disapprobation of his conduct. Secondly, that for such actions as are prejudicial to the interests of others, the individual is accountable, and may be subjected either to social or to legal punishments, if society is of opinion that the one or the other is requisite for its protection.[132]

The second maxim makes clear that in protecting a society the punishment may be either social disapprobation or legal punishment by the government.

In sorting out how to apply these two maxims, there are six major examples he uses. First, he notes that there are areas where competition unavoidably means that the winner will affect the interests of someone else. This does not place such activity into the other-regarding category, since this is an inescapable consequence of an activity that generally helps humanity. Competition for a position in an overcrowded profession and economic trade are illustrations. When fraud or treachery interfere with the process, then society can enter. One can certainly regulate economic activity to protect others from unsafe working conditions or food adulteration. But, the choices of people, wise or unwise, are in the realm of liberty protected by the first maxim.

---

[131] *J. S. Mill: On Liberty and Other Writings*, p. 81.

[132] *Ibid.*, p. 94.

Second, Mill has a category called the "preventive function of government." This role of government is "liable to be abused to the prejudice of liberty." There needs to be a "certainty" of some harm before the state can interfere. The two maxims, when applied, allow for the self-regarding misconduct of a drunk, but if such a person has caused violence to others, then preventive punishment can be applied for drunkenness. Indecent exposure, Mill remarks, is another example where the conduct injures the public and should be prohibited. Mill refuses to take a position on pimps and on the owners of public gambling houses. Both activities are self-regarding and, thus, in the realm of liberty, but the solicitations by the pimp and gambling proprietor are in a different category, because they stimulate interest in activities that the "State believes to be wrong." He admits, too, the anomaly "of fining or imprisoning the procurer, but not the fornicator, the gambling-house keeper, but not the gambler." Maybe, he suggests, the best policy would be to let such places exist in "secrecy and mystery, so that nobody knows anything about them but those who seek them."[133] He is certain about the application of the two maxims to liquor laws. Prohibition is an infringement on liberty, but taxing can be allowed because it enables the state to gain revenue from substances of little real value to the consumers.

The third issue, slavery, is easily handled. Slavery that is non-voluntary would obviously be prohibited, and so is voluntary slavery. The reason for the latter is: "The principle of freedom cannot require that he should be free not to be free. It is not freedom, to be allowed to alienate his freedom."[134] A contemporary philosopher, Ronald Dworkin, calls this "constitutive liberty." Liberty in itself is the value; the value is not in its utility. But, if liberty is a higher value than utility, Mill's defence of liberty does not rest, contrary to his promise, on purely utilitarian arguments.[135]

The fourth issue is marriage and the family. The contract of marriage should not be enforced "at the costs to the happiness of the reluctant party." In short, divorce must be possible or the principle of liberty would be violated. The great problem is that the present despotic power of husbands, by law and custom, violates liberty: "wives should have the same rights, and should receive the protection

---

[133] *Ibid.*, pp. 99–100.

[134] *Ibid.*, pp. 102–03.

[135] Ronald Dworkin, *Taking Rights Seriously* (Cambridge: Harvard University Press, 1977).

of law in the same manner, as all other persons."[136] Moreover, the parents have the duty ("or, as law and usage now stand, the father") to care for and to educate children, enforced by law.

> It still remains unrecognised, that to bring a child into existence without a fair prospect of being able, not only to provide food for its body, but instruction and training for its mind, is a moral crime, both against the unfortunate offspring, and against society; and that if the parent does not fulfill this obligation, the State ought to see it fulfilled, at the charge, as far as possible, of the parent.[137]

Fifth, in what may seem an anomaly, Mill adamantly opposes public education: "it establishes a despotism over the mind, leading by natural tendency to one over the body."[138] What the state can do in this area is to require that an education is provided.

The sixth issue is birth control. Mill was influenced by Thomas Malthus, the demographer and economist who argued that population increases were outstripping food production. Mill has no patience for those who, as a "consequence of their indulgence," produce children who suffer lives of "wretchedness and depravity" and believes both social disapprobation and the law should be applied.

> The laws which, in many countries on the Continent, forbid marriage unless the parties can show that they have the means of supporting a family, do not exceed the legitimate powers of the State: and whether such laws be expedient or not (a question mainly dependent on local circumstances and feelings), they are not objectionable as violations of liberty. Such laws are interferences of the State to prohibit a mischievous act—an act injurious to others, which ought to be a subject of reprobation, and social stigma, even when it is not deemed expedient to superadd legal punishment.[139]

Procreation is truly an other-regarding activity. Mill notes the oddity of a society that delights in interfering with solely self-regarding actions and opinions but abhors regulating the procreation of children.

---

[136] *J. S. Mill: On Liberty and Other Writings,* pp. 104–05.

[137] *Ibid.,* p. 105.

[138] *Ibid.,* p. 106.

[139] *Ibid.,* p. 108.

Mill concludes the essay with three objections to government interference, which, if adopted by citizens, would instill a healthy attitude useful to individual self-development. The first objection to government is that many things are "better done by individuals than by government." Those who should conduct any business should be the very people personally interested in it. Second, there are some activities that a government may even do better than individuals, but "it is nevertheless desirable that it should be done by them, rather than by the government, as a means to their own mental education."[140] Individuals and voluntary associations provide the diversity and experiments required for a public-spirited citizenry. Lastly, government interference always increases governmental power, a "great evil."[141]

A political culture must be created where the free individuals and their associations hold themselves to be capable and responsible for the conduct of a nation's business:

> What the French are in military affairs, the Americans are in every kind of civil business; let them be left without a government, every body of Americans is able to improvise one, and to carry on that or any other public business with sufficient amount of intelligence, order, and decision. This is what every free people ought to be: and a people capable of this is certain to be free; it will never let itself be enslaved by any man or body of men because these are able to seize and pull the reins of the central administration.[142]

The worth of a state, Mill concludes, is in the "worth of the individuals composing it." Thus, the emphasis must be on having governmental institutions that nourish free mental and moral development.

The essay *On Liberty* can be read as a hymn to political participation, but this is the theory of participation of Aristotle and not of Rousseau. Participation, for Mill, is necessary for the development of human mental and moral capacities; participation is necessary or else the dead hand of custom and tradition will destroy civilization; participation is necessary because there is no other way to reconcile the diversity and plurality among humans. The political rationalism of James Mill and Jeremy Bentham has been repudiated.

---

[140] *Ibid.*, p. 109.

[141] *Ibid.*, p. 110.

[142] *Ibid.*, p. 112.

The essay *On Liberty* has been the subject of the most praise and the most intensive criticism of all Mill's writings. One area on which criticism has focused is the coupling Mill makes between a vibrant, original, individualism and liberty. For Mill, individualism is associated with genius, original thinkers, and heartfelt convictions; and liberty, in turn, requires a society free of any dominant religion, philosophy, or ideology. Historically, Mill's coupling is suspect: such original thinkers such as Shakespeare, Newton, Galileo, and Milton all lived in societies that would not meet Mill's criteria in *On Liberty*. Sir Isaiah Berlin has made the historically sound observation that "integrity, love of truth and firey individualism grow at least as often in severely disciplined communities among, for example, the puritan Calvinists of Scotland or New England, or under military discipline, as in more tolerant or indifferent societies."[143] Mill's own attack on "official" belief systems is itself carried by two indisputable, dominant beliefs: the unsurpassed superiority of modern science to encompass all questions about human existence, and the necessity and inevitability of progress. Moreover, when these two beliefs are expanded in his ethology, an educational system supposedly can be created to mould and form human character, a position quite at odds with the clear intention of the essay *On Liberty*.

A second area of criticism focused on the coherence of Mill's key categories. The self-regarding and other-regarding distinction requires amendments in order to work, because many self-regarding activities clearly slide into the other-regarding camp. Mill's application of the distinction to drinking, procreation, gambling, and prostitution would appear to reflect the prejudices of the Victorian age, which casts further doubts on the validity of the distinction. The categories of "the human race" and "posterity" are also problematic, and they carry great rhetorical weight for Mill. To limit freedom of speech, for example, would be to the detriment of both categories. The implication is that awareness of such a detrimental effect would automatically affect judgments about questions whether or not to limit free speech, as if there were a recognized and accepted meaning to both categories. Mill's faith in posterity or progress was common enough in the nineteenth century, but the precise meaning of the term is not explored. The human race is also a self-evident concept for Mill; its meaning, too, is little explored. Both of these major categories, however, do a great deal of the philosophic work for Mill's argument.

---

[143] "The Notion of 'Negative' Liberty," in Radcliff, *Limits of Liberty*.

Lastly, friends as well as foes have argued that *On Liberty* depends upon a concept of a person that is incompatible with utilitarianism. It is empirically possible, to take one obvious example, that the greatest happiness ascertained by utility may require less liberty for some individuals than for others, which is a position that act utilitarians readily accept. Such may be the price, they would say, for the greatest happiness. If one takes literally the claim that the greatest happiness is a summation, the individual as an individual is not recognizable in the total. If one argues that there should be a lexical ordering whereby each person must attain some minimal threshold of happiness before the final summation, new problems surface for a utilitarian. First, the standard of the greatest happiness would no longer apply, since the sum may not be the greatest happiness possible. Second, the question has to be faced, Why have an equality threshold anyway? What is there about each individual as an individual that merits this protection? The response that each individual is a pain-pleasure mechanism begs the question. If the response refers to "mental and moral faculties" or "the permanent interests of a man as a progress being," the meaning of these phrases will need to be explicated, or they will simply be banalities. What, in short, is there about these alleged faculties that entail an equal respect for each person as a person? If some substantive meaning is supplied, which Mill does not do, the concept of a person would have priority over the twin sovereigns of pain and pleasure, and utilitarianism would have been shunted aside. Mill never expands on the few phrases he does use to characterize the individual. As one philosopher recently noted, Mill has "no coherent conception of a human personality at all."[144] Still, it is Mill's clear intention to argue that there is a region of liberty required for each person, which cannot be abridged. Not surprisingly, some commentators have made Mill's essay coherent by jettisoning the utilitarian arguments and supplying instead a rights framework or even an Aristotelian one.[145]

---

[144] John Dunn, *Western Political Theory in the Face of the Future* (Cambridge: Cambridge University Press, 1979), p. 52.

[145] Albert William Levi has argued that there is implicitly an Aristotelian conception of human nature lurking in Mill's thought: "The Value of Freedom: Mill's Liberty (1859-1959)," in Radcliff, *Limits of Liberty*, pp. 6–18. Major critics of Mill are: Maurice Cowling, *Mill and Liberalism* (Cambridge: Cambridge University Press, 1963); Shirley R. Letwin, *The Pursuit of Certainty* (Cambridge: Cambridge University Press, 1965); Isaiah Berlin, *Two Concepts of Liberty* (London: Oxford University Press, 1958). Ten, *Mill on Liberty*, looks at the various criticisms and gives a judicious defence. John Gray gives a qualified support: *Mill on Liberty: A Defence* (London: Routledge & Kegan Paul, 1983).

There is also a political aspect to the utilitarian failure to have a conception of a person. The utilitarians equate the weighing of desires, pains, and pleasures in the individual to the weighing of alternative courses of actions in the political process. When an individual makes a decision, the weighing of desires is that single person's decision over his or her own set of desires. But, when a political society must decide between alternative courses of actions, it is separate and distinct people who are winners and losers. There is no analogy. Utilitarianism misses this dimension of political life; indeed, utilitarianism desensitizes public discourse to the separate integrity of individuals and the tragic dimension in political existence. Our words or discourse provide the means for recognizing and accrediting significant features of political reality, such as the existence of authentically different and separate persons. Utilitarianism dulls our ability to do so.

Government and Society

Much like Bentham, Mill wrote on a wide variety of contemporary issues. Two are particularly informative of his political thought: the proper structure of government and the role of women.

The structure of government advocated by Mill in his work *Considerations on Representative Government* (1861) reflects a mix of often paradoxical influences and beliefs. As the essay *On Liberty* indicates, Mill was less than sanguine about English society. He saw, through Tocquevillian eyes, the tendency toward conformity and mediocrity that accompanied the rising tide of democratic egalitarianism. He viewed the middle class as particularly selfish and narrow in its view; the aristocracy had long been lazy and corrupt; and the lower class was not much better than the others.[146] He, nevertheless, was a democrat, but one who insisted on the need for expertise. For 35 years he had been a professional bureaucrat, and it is impossible not to detect in his writing the bureaucrat's fastidious disdain for politicians and representative chambers. Also, he, too, was an heir of the *philosophes*, as were James Mill and Jeremy Bentham. The general political stance for many of the Enlightenment figures was that leadership by the enlightened was necessary for any change. There was a faith in the role of the intellectual to guide reforms. Democracy was to be practised with reluctance and under the mantel of the expert.

---

[146] "On the Condition of England," in Robson, *Collected Works*, pp. 443–44.

Another feature of Mill's political thinking was his utilitarian conviction that self-interest did drive politics. It would be irrational to construct a government on the premise that individuals will be governed by a "disinterested regard for others, and especially for what comes after them, for the idea of posterity, of their country, or of mankind, whether grounded on sympathy or on a conscientious feeling."[147] It is ridiculous not to realize that the majority will follow "their own selfish inclinations and short-sighted notions of their own good, in opposition to justice, at the expense of all other classes and of posterity."[148] The despotism of the majority and of its class interest is a major worry in the democratic form of government. Monarchies and aristocracies are worst, to be sure, but the task in constructing a political system is to have the necessary democratic representation of all, however prone to selfishness and class interests, combined with a minority who would subordinate such interests to "reason, justice, and the good of the whole." Mill concludes, rather weakly, that the latter qualities tend to "carry the point" because the "selfish interests of mankind are almost always divided."[149]

The key parts to Mill's political system are the representative assembly, an administration to perform executive functions, and a Commission on Legislation. The assumption is that these would be reforms for improving a standard parliamentary system. The best form of government is one where sovereignty is "vested in the entire aggregate of the community." He adds that the public should, "at least occasionally," actually perform some governmental function.[150] Sovereignty of the people is then exercised through deputies "periodically elected by themselves, the ultimate controlling power."[151]

Mill sees many difficulties associated with representative assemblies, and he immediately begins to fence in the power of the legislature. The existence of selfish interests, the potential tyranny of the majority, and the generally low level of competence, just to mention a few of the inadequacies Mill perceives, all point to the conclusion that representative assemblies are "radically unfit" to govern. Their proper function is different:

---

[147] "Considerations on Representative Government," in Gray, *John Stuart Mill: On Liberty and Other Essays*, Ch. VI, p. 298.

[148] *Ibid.*, Ch. VI, p. 299.

[149] *Ibid.*, Ch. VI, pp. 300–01.

[150] *Ibid.*, Ch. III, p. 244.

[151] *Ibid.*, Ch. V, p. 269.

> Instead of the function of governing, for which it is radically unfit, the proper office of a representative assembly is to watch and control the government: to throw the light of publicity on its acts: to compel a full exposition and justification of all of them which any one considers questionable; to censure them if found condemnable, and, if the men who compose the government abuse their trust, or fulfil it in a manner which conflicts with the deliberate sense of the nation, to expel them from office, and either expressly or virtually appoint their successors.[152]

Mill adds that he knows "not how a representative assembly can more usefully employ itself than in talk."[153]

The actual running of the government belongs to those who are trained for it. A clear distinction exists between "controlling the business of government, and actually doing it."[154] When a legislature crosses the line, the consequences are "almost always injurious." Mill's contempt for a legislature's interference in government is not hidden: "At its best, it is inexperience sitting in judgement on experience, ignorance on knowledge: ignorance which never suspecting the existence of what it does not know, is equally careless and supercilious, making light of, if not resenting, all pretensions to have a judgement better worth attending to than its own."[155] A bureaucracy composed of skilled persons, chosen by contests and through examinations, and "bred to it as an intellectual profession" is essential.[156]

Both representative government and bureaucracy are necessary. But, just as the bureaucracy adds to the political system the experience and intelligence of the professional, which are qualities lacking in the democratic legislature, the bureaucracy has potential dangers that need to be balanced by the legislature. There is the tendency of bureaucracy to "pedantocracy," which develops when the same routine and pattern of decisions come to dominate. Mill's solution for this problem seems decidedly odd, given his previous disdain, and even contempt, for the

---

[152] *Ibid.*, Ch. V, p. 282.

[153] *Ibid.*, Ch. V, p. 283.

[154] *Ibid.*, Ch. V, p. 271.

[155] *Ibid.*, Ch. V, p. 274.

[156] *Ibid.*, Ch. V, p. 291.

judgment of the many and of the legislature. But he says that a democratic government can add the "conceptions of the man of original genius among them, to prevail over the obstructive spirit of trained mediocrity."[157]

He completes his political system with a Commission on Legislation. As he says, "any government fit for a high state of civilization" needs one. A small number of members would be appointed for set terms and would have the function of writing legislation—a function the legislature is incapable of performing. Mill defends this proposed institution by arguing that it adds a balancing element to the whole structure:

> the Commission would only embody the element of intelligence in their construction; Parliament would represent that of will. No measure would become a law until expressly sanctioned by Parliament; and Parliament, or either House, would have the power not only of rejecting but of sending back a Bill to the Commission for reconsideration or improvement. Either House might also exercise its initiative, by referring any subject to the Commission, with directions to prepare a law.... Once framed, however, Parliament should have no power to alter the measure, but solely to pass or reject it; or, if partially disapproved of, remit it to the Commission for reconsideration.[158]

By adding a skilled administration and a Commission on Legislation to the legislative body, Mill believes that his system provides the qualities required for good government and for the popular sovereignty required in a democracy. The system has the "benefits of popular control to be enjoyed in conjunction with the no less important requisites (growing ever more important as human affairs increase in scale and in complexity) of skilled legislation and administration." In an Aristotelian allusion, he says that the few and the many are respected in his scheme.[159]

The danger to representative government caused by class legislation imposed through the despotism of the many and the danger caused by the "low grade of intelligence in the representative body" lead Mill to offer some reforms to voting, which he believes would mitigate these problems. He sets the task as follows:

---

[157] *Ibid.*, Ch. V, p. 290.

[158] *Ibid.*, Ch. V, pp. 279–80.

[159] *Ibid.*, Ch. V, p. 284.

Democracy is not the ideally best form of government unless this weak side of it can be strengthened; unless it can be so organized that no class, not even the most numerous, shall be able to reduce all but itself to political insignificance, and direct the course of legislation and administration by its exclusive class interest. The problem is, to find the means of preventing this abuse, without sacrificing the characteristic advantages of popular government.[160]

Mill consistently argued that universal suffrage, including women, is a prerequisite for any democratic government, but since the majority can become despotic, it is necessary to provide a protection for the minority. The voting system of his contemporary Thomas Hare addressed this problem best, according to Mill. The voting system is a variation of proportional representation with the candidates ranked by voter preference. The minority would have a voice in the representative chamber, and there would be direct representation for each voter, though it may not be the voter's first preferred candidate who is elected. This method of voting would, therefore, help check the potential chance of a tyranny of the majority.[161]

Mill also advocated plural voting. As Mill directly explains, "I do not look upon equal voting as among the things which are good in themselves," or, equally frank, "It is not useful, but hurtful, that the constitution of the country should declare ignorance entitled to as much political power as knowledge."[162] Plural voting, in short, should be allowed for those who are qualified. His suggestions, he admits, would be difficult to implement, but, in principle at least, those who are educated or who belong to certain professions should have more votes. Those who pay taxes should "exclusively" elect those who impose the taxes. Those on relief should not vote. Again, the principle is to combine the democratic element of all voting with the aristocratic element of knowledge.

---

[160] *Ibid.*, Ch. VIII, pp. 326–27.

[161] *Ibid.*, Ch. VII. See the excellent article by Duff Spafford, "Mill's Majority Principle," *Canadian Journal of Political Science* (September, 1985), pp. 599-608. See also, P. B. Kern, "Universal Suffrage without Democracy: Thomas Hare and J. S. Mill," *Review of Politics* (July, 1972), pp. 306–23.

[162] "Representative Government," in Gray, *John Stuart Mill: On Liberty and Other Essays*, Ch. VIII, p. 340.

Mill's political system has elements that are reminiscent of Bentham's. The administration and the Commission on Legislation smack of a guided democracy by the educated bureaucrat. Mill was disdainful of the selfish interests of the majority voters and of the tendency toward class legislation. Yet, the views expressed in *On Liberty* keep breaking through: democracy is the best form of government for all people; the mental and moral development of each requires a system open to all; participation of all in the conduct of the government is the path to good government and a "high civilization."[163]

The *Subjection of Women* (written in 1861 and published in 1869) addressed one of the great social issues of the day. Mill wrote to convince a public of the advantages of recognizing the equality of women, and, as such, it remains a classic presentation of liberal feminism. His rhetoric is not subtle; he associates arguments for the subjugation of women with thoughtless custom and with the practice of slavery.

Mill presents the advantages of equality in five major areas. First, the injustice of the present condition is harmful to males and makes them worse:

> All the selfish propensities, the self-worship, the unjust self-preference, which exist among mankind, have their source and root in, and derive their principal nourishment from, the present constitution of the relation between men and women. Think what it is to a boy, to grow up to manhood in the belief that without any merit or any exertion of his own, though he may be the most frivolous and empty or the most ignorant and stolid of mankind, by the mere fact of being born a male he is by right the superior of all and every one of an entire half of the human race.... What must be the effect on his character, of this lesson?[164]

The subtle self-worship engendered by this pervasive sense of superiority is identical to the neurotic self-worship found in feudal monarchs.

Perhaps more persuasive to his reader was the second advantage equality would bring. By free choice for employment, equal access to occupations, and

---

[163] Letwin, *The Pursuit of Certainty,* is critical of Mill; Ryan, *J. S. Mill,* is very good on Mill and government; Bruce L. Kinzer shows that in political practice Mill was more radical than his writings would suggest, "John Stuart Mill and the Experience of Political Engagement," in Laine, *A Cultivated Mind,* pp. 182–214.

[164] "The Subjection of Women," in Collini, *J. S. Mill: On Liberty and Other Writings,* pp. 196–97.

equal encouragement for women, the society would be "doubling the mass of mental faculties available for the higher service of humanity."[165] The third advantage of equality would be an improvement in the quality of public opinion. As Mill states, "the wife is the auxiliary of the common public opinion." He illustrates his claim by noting that women have an aversion to war and an "addiction to philanthropy." His contention is that there would be a marked improvement in public opinion with the social and political emancipation of women.[166]

As he argued in *On Liberty*, the institution of marriage would be vastly improved with equality.

> What marriage may be in the case of two persons of cultivated faculties, identical in opinions and purposes, between whom there exists that best kind of equality, similarity of powers and capacities with reciprocal superiority in them—so that each can enjoy the luxury of looking up to the other, and can have alternatively the pleasure of leading and of being led in the path of development—I will not attempt to describe. To those who can conceive it, there is no need; to those who cannot, it would appear the dream of an enthusiast. But I maintain, with the profoundest conviction, that this, and this only, is the ideal of marriage; and that all opinions, customs, and institutions which favour any other notion of it, or turn the conceptions and aspirations connected with it into any other direction, by whatever pretences they may be coloured, are relics of primitive barbarism.[167]

With equality and independence, such marriages would be the norm. Only with these changes in marriages, he repeatedly warns, will there be a "moral regeneration of mankind."[168]

Lastly, the advantage of equality is simply an increase in individual happiness. Personal dignity requires equality: "the free direction and disposal of their own faculties is a source of individual happiness, and to be fettered and restricted in it [is] a source of unhappiness, to human beings, and not least to women."[169]

---

[165] *Ibid.*, p. 199.

[166] *Ibid.*, pp. 203–05.

[167] *Ibid.*, p. 211.

[168] *Ibid.*

[169] *Ibid.*, p. 214.

Mill consistently advocated changes in property and marriage laws as he did in voting laws. The patriarchal marriage he viewed as a peculiarly pernicious force in society. The harm was to women and men, and to the moral life of the society.

Many critics have noted that there is still a considerable remnant of the traditional woman's role in Mill's analysis. There does appear to be the standard gender division of labour within the family, and it is assumed that "in most cases" the male will be older and will make the "preponderance" of decisions. At best, this is an equality for two relatively exceptional, economically privileged, and, perhaps, sexless individuals. In parts of his portrayal of the role of women, the woman often appears paradoxically sexless but an equal as an intellectual friend, and in other parts she appears unequal, in the traditional roles of mother and household manager. However inadequate Mill's view may be from a contemporary perspective, it is hard to deny the power of his arguments to provide individual independence and dignity for half of humanity and to reconstitute marriage as a locus of friendship and moral development.[170]

CONCLUSIONS

At first glance, Bentham's utilitarianism seemed to provide the framework for democratic politics and a new philosophically-sounder liberalism. The following Benthamite principles appeared particularly plausible: the basic purpose of the body politic is to maximize the satisfaction of the individual's self-interest; individuals are the best judges of their own interest; legitimacy depends upon an identity between public policy and the totality of individual interests.

Mill's metamorphosis of utilitarianism undermines each of these Benthamite principles. The individual's self-interest, within Mill's analysis, is no longer conceived of as simply selfish and constituted by physical pleasures. Happiness in Mill's utilitarianism has been expanded to include pleasures of varying quality, different in kind, and intrinsic to the constitution of human nature. An individual

---

[170] Most commentators have been critical in various degrees of Mill's essay: Jean Bethke Elshtain, *Public Man and Private Woman: Women in Social and Political Thought* (Princeton: Princeton University Press, 1981), pp. 134–46; Julia Annas, "Mill and the Subjection of Women, *Philosophy* 52 (1977), pp. 179–94; Diana H. Coole, *Women in Political Theory* (Boulder: Lynne Rienner, 1988), pp. 133–53; Jennifer Ring, *Modern Political Theory and Contemporary Feminism* (Albany: State University of New York Press, 1991), pp. 59-84. For a more sympathetic approach see Mary Lyndon Shanley, "Marital Slavery and Friendship: John Stuart Mill's *The Subjection of Women*," *Political Theory* (May 1981), Vol. 9, No. 2, pp. 229–47.

is not always the best judge, Mill believes. The superior person is to be consulted at the individual level, and the professional bureaucrat and the Commission on Legislation at the public level. For Mill, what is "best" is not determined simply by finding out what people want or desire. It is true that in a well-structured political system and with a proper education, individuals are the final arbiters. Yet legitimacy, for Mill, cannot be a simple identity of interest between government and people. This would easily lead to the tyranny of the majority. Legitimacy, furthermore, is dependent upon several new ideas, such as moral rules, rights, and justice.

Even if Mill's version of utilitarianism is accepted as a decided improvement over James Mill's and Jeremy Bentham's, his version of utilitarianism needs to be further assessed, particularly from the standpoint of how adequately it supports his political philosophy. The *Logic of the Moral Sciences* particularly has received harsh treatment. The major point of contention is that the relationship between the three levels of his model of human development is causal. Mill insists that the difference between physical and social sciences is only that the latter is more complicated, as tidology is more complicated than astronomy. Two major criticisms are often made of Mill's framework. One is that he has simply made a conceptual blunder in thinking that the behaviour of a physical phenomena is of the same nature as the behaviour of an animate creature or a human. The appropriate description varies with the type of being described. As one critic explains:

> The reaction of a cat which is seriously hurt is very much more complex than that of a tree which is being chopped down. But is it really intelligible to say it is only a difference in degree? We say the cat 'writhes' about. Suppose I describe his very complex movements in purely mechanical terms, using a set of space-time co-ordinates. This is, in a sense, a description of what is going on as much as is the statement that the cat is writhing in pain. But the one statement could not be substituted for the other. The statement which includes the concept of writhing says something which no statement of the other sort, however detailed, could approximate to.... Anyone who thought that a study of the mechanics of the movement of animate creatures would throw light on the concept of animate life would be the victim of a conceptual misunderstanding.[171]

---

[171] Peter Winch, *The Idea of a Social Science* (London: Routledge & Kegan Paul, 1958), pp. 73–74.

Similarly, it is contended that a proper description of the behaviour of tides would not be applicable to a behaviour where a human makes a choice.

Another criticism is that the so-called laws of social development, discovered by Mill's inverse deduction method, are not laws but trends. Human intentions and decisions can change social behaviour. The laws of history must, accordingly, be different in kind from the physical laws of gravity or the various laws affecting tides. In sum, Mill has tried to explain human thoughts and actions as if they were just effects of complicated causes.[172]

One consequence of these criticisms of Mill's theory of knowledge is that his model of an explanation of human behaviour does not fit his own conception of a person, at least that conception implicit in *On Liberty*. His explanatory model is causal, but the person in *On Liberty* is a moral actor, responsible for the reasons and decisions made. This is a language hardly appropriate to tides. Furthermore, modern philosophers in the right's stream of liberalism are quick to point out that Mill's whole conception of the person is hopelessly mired in his utilitarian framework. The result is that the uniqueness of the individual eventually gets lost. Since the greatest happiness shown by utility is the ultimate sanction, whether this is rule or act utilitarianism, the individual will inevitably dissolve into the collective happiness.[173] Mill faces two choices. If he sticks with his strict utilitarianism and the theory of knowledge found in *The Logic of the Moral Sciences*, the individual as a unique person fades into a causal creature molded by ethology. If Mill drops strict utilitarianism and quietly forgets the promise of ethology to form human character, then the concept of a person that supports the essay *On Liberty* comes to life.

It is true that Mill was eclectic in his reliance on a variety of other thinkers, and he was also sensitive to the practical complexities of political reality, which led him to take more than one perspective and to try to reconcile opposites. His political structure, for example, is a blend of a variety of positions and his arguments seem to shift. Yet, the development of the individual's mental and moral faculties remains

---

[172] Stefan Collini provides an excellent defence of Mill. "The Tendencies of Things: John Stuart Mill and the Philosophic Method," in Stefan Collini, Donald Winch, John Burrow, *That Noble Science of Politics: A Study in Nineteenth-Century History* (Cambridge: Cambridge University Press, 1983), pp. 129–59.

[173] The most famous modern defence of the right's tradition is by John Rawls, *A Theory of Justice* (Cambridge: Harvard University Press, 1971). See the collection of essays edited by Alan Ryan, *The Idea of Freedom: Essays in Honour of Isaiah Berlin* (Oxford: Oxford University Press, 1979).

the core to his thought throughout. For this reason, it does seem plausible to argue for a rough coherence in Mill's philosophy. The self-development of the person is the source for human progress and for the health of a society. The essay *On Liberty* is a testament to this faith in the person.

The political structure is carefully designed to provide the conditions for individual development and social progress. There is a balance between democratic sovereignty and bureaucratic competence that would mitigate the evils to which each is prone. Even when he is most rigid in stressing the need for the trained intellectuals to staff the bureaucracy and when he is most critical of the legislative branch, the idea of participation will suddenly appear. He was well aware of the selfish interest of individuals and of classes, but he was also aware that real participation in government would enhance each person's mental and moral capacity, would lead to self-development, and would provide moral progress.[174]

SUGGESTIONS FOR FURTHER READING

Harrison (1983) has the best biography of Bentham and is reliable for his philosophy. Dinwiddy is a shorter work but an excellent survey. Mack is an enthusiastic work but not quite reliable; Everett is a reliable text. Parekh's edited work of Bentham's writings (1973) has a generally sympathetic summary. Steintrager and Manning are good short works on Bentham's political philosophy; the latter is more critical. Baumgardt, Lyons and Smart examine ethics as well as Bentham's general philosophy. Long and Rosenblum are well worth reading for Bentham's theory of government; Rosen and Hume are also worth consulting.

Robson's work on Mill (1968) is magesterial and the best place to start a study. Hayek, Borchard, and Packe are sound studies on Mill's life. Ryan is the best large work covering all of Mill's work; Halliday and Thomas are short but very good introductions, primarily to Mill's political philosophy. Rees, Ten, and Gray are the best analyses devoted to *On Liberty*. Schneewind, Radcliff, Ryan, and Laine are edited works containing articles representing a variety of different interpretations of Mill. Anschutz and Britton are particularly supportive of Mill; Cowling, Himmelfarb, and Letwin are particularly critical.

---

[174] Mill is ably defended by Ryan, *J. S. Mill;* R. J. Halliday, *John Stuart Mill* (London: Allen & Unwin, 1976); John Gray, *Mill on Liberty: A Defence* (London: Routledge & Kegan Paul, 1983).

Bentham's Works

Bowring, John, ed. *The Works of Jeremy Bentham.* 11 Vols. Edinburgh: William Tait, 1838-43.

Burns, J. H., and H. L. A. Hart, eds. *A Fragment of Government.* Cambridge: Cambridge University Press, 1988.

Burns, J. H., J. R. Dinwiddy, and F. Rosen. *The Collected Works of Jeremy Bentham.* Athlone Press and Oxford University Press, 1968–.

Harrison, Wilfrid, ed. *A Fragment on Government and An Introduction to the Principles of Morals and Legislation.* Oxford: Basil Blackwell, 1967.

Mack, Mary Peter, ed. *A Bentham Reader.* New York: Pegasus, 1969.

Parekh, Bhikhu, ed. *Bentham's Political Thought.* London: Croom Helm, 1973.

Stark. W., ed. *Jeremy Bentham's Economic Writings.* 3 Vols. London: Allen & Unwin, 1952-54.

Mill's Works

Collini, Stefan, ed. *J. S. Mill: On Liberty and Other Writings.* Cambridge: Cambridge University Press, 1989.

Gray, John, ed. *John Stuart Mill: On Liberty and Other Essays.* Oxford: Oxford University Press, 1991.

Mill, Anna J., ed. *John Mill's Boyhood Visit to France: Being a Journal and Notebook written by John Stuart Mill in France, 1820–21.* Toronto: University of Toronto Press, 1960.

Robson, John M., ed. *The Collected Works of John Stuart Mill.* 35 Vols. Toronto: University of Toronto Press, 1963-91.

———. *John Stuart Mill: A Selection of His Works.* Toronto: Macmillan, 1966.

Stillinger, Jack, ed. *The Early Draft of John Stuart Mill's Autobiography.* Urbana: University of Illinois Press, 1961.

Commentaries

Anschutz, R. P. *The Philosophy of J. S. Mill.* New York: Oxford University Press, 1953.

Baumgardt, David. *Bentham and the Ethics of Today.* Princeton: Princeton University Press, 1952.

Borchard, Ruth. *John Stuart Mill: the Man.* London: Watts, 1957.

Britton, Karl. *John Stuart Mill.* London: Penguin, 1953.

Collini, Stefan, Donald Winch, and John Burrow. *That Noble Science of Politics: A Study in Nineteenth-Century History.* Cambridge: Cambridge University Press, 1983.

Cowling, Maurice. *Mill and Liberalism.* New York: Cambridge University Press, 1963.

Dinwiddy, John. *Bentham.* Oxford: Oxford University Press, 1989.

Duncan, Graham. *Marx and Mill: Two Views of Social Conflict and Social Harmony.* Cambridge: Cambridge University Press, 1973.

Everett, C. W. *The Education of Jeremy Bentham.* New York: Columbia University Press, 1931.

Glassman, Peter. *J. S. Mill: The Evolution of a Genius.* Gainesville: University of Florida Press, 1985.

Gray, John. *Mill on Liberty: A Defense.* London: Routledge & Kegan Paul, 1983.

Halliday, R. J. *John Stuart Mill.* London: Allen & Unwin, 1976.

Harrison, Ross. *Bentham.* London: Routledge & Kegan Paul, 1983.

Hayek, F. A. *John Stuart Mill and Harriet Taylor.* (London: Routledge & Kegan Paul, 1951.

Himmelfarb, Gertrude. *On Liberty and Liberalism: The Case of John Stuart Mill.* New York: Knopf, 1974.

Hume, L. J. *Bentham and Bureaucracy.* Cambridge: Cambridge University Press, 1981.

Laine, Michael, ed. *A Cultivated Mind: Essays on J. S. Mill Presented to John M. Robson.* Toronto: University of Toronto Press, 1991.

Letwin, Shirley R. *The Pursuit of Certainty.* Cambridge: Cambridge University Press, 1965.

Long, Douglas G. *Bentham on Liberty.* Toronto: University of Toronto Press, 1977.

Lyons, David. *In the Interest of the Governed.* Oxford: Oxford University Press, 1973.

Mack, M. P. *Jeremy Bentham: An Odyssey of Ideas, 1748-1792.* New York: Columbia University Press, 1963.

Manning, D. H. *The Mind of Jeremy Bentham.* London: Longmans, Green, 1968.

Mazlish, Bruce. *James and John Stuart Mill.* New York: Basic Books, 1975.

McCloskey, Henry J. *John Stuart Mill: A Critical Study.* London: Macmillan, 1971.

Packe, Michael St. J. *The Life of John Stuart Mill.* London: Secker and Warburg, 1954.

Parekh, Bhikhu, ed. *Jeremy Bentham: Ten Critical Essays.* London: Frank Cass, 1973.

Plamenatz, John. *The English Utilitarians.* Oxford: Blackwell, 1949.

Radcliff, Peter, ed. *Limits of Liberty: Studies of Mill's 'On Liberty.'* Belmont, Calif.: Wadsworth, 1966.

Rees, John C. *John Stuart Mill's 'On Liberty.'* Oxford: Oxford University Press, 1985.

Robson, John M. *The Improvement of Mankind: The Social and Political Thought of John Stuart Mill.* Toronto: University of Toronto Press, 1968.

Rosen, Frederick. *Jeremy Bentham and Representative Democracy.* Oxford: Oxford University Press, 1983.

Rosenblum, Nancy. *Bentham's Theory of the State.* Cambridge: Harvard University Press, 1978.

Ryan, Alan. *J. S. Mill.* London: Kegan & Paul, 1974.

———, ed. *The Idea of Freedom: Essays in Honour of Isaiah Berlin.* Oxford: Oxford University Press, 1979.

Schneewind, J. B., ed. *Mill: A Collection of Critical Essays.* Garden City: Anchor, 1968.

Semmel, Bernard. *John Stuart Mill and the Pursuit of Virtue.* New Haven: Yale University Press, 1984.

Steintrager, James. *Bentham.* London: Allen and Unwin, 1977.

Stephen, Leslie. *The English Utilitarians.* 3 Vols. London: Duckworth, 1900.

Stevens, James Fitzjames. *Liberty, Equality and Fraternity.* Chicago: University of Chicago Press, 1991.

Ten, C. T. *Mill on Liberty.* Oxford: Clarendon Press, 1980.

Thomas, William. *Mill.* Oxford: Oxford University Press, 1985.

Thompson, Dennis F. *John Stuart Mill and Representative Government.* Princeton: Princeton University Press, 1976.

Intellectual Background

Bayles, Michael D., ed. *Contemporary Utilitarianism.* Garden City: Anchor, 1968.

Berlin, Isaiah. *Four Essays on Liberty.* Oxford: Oxford University Press, 1969.

Dworkin, Ronald. *Taking Rights Seriously.* Cambridge: Harvard University Press, 1977.

Finlayson, Geoffrey. *Decade of Reform: England in the Eighteen Thirties.* New York: W. W. Norton, 1970.

Halévy, Elie. *The Growth of Philosophic Radicalism.* Translated by Mary Morris. London: Faber & Faber, 1928.

Oakeshott, Michael. *Rationalism in Politics and Other Essays.* London: Methuen, 1962.

Rawls, John. *A Theory of Justice.* Cambridge: Harvard University Press, 1971.

Robbins, Lionel. *The Theory of Economic Policy in English Classical Political Economy.* London: Macmillan, 1961.

Roberts, David. *Victorian Origins of the British Welfare State.* New Haven: Yale University Press, 1960.

Smart, J. C. C. *An Outline of a System of Utilitarian Ethics.* Melbourne: Melbourne University Press, 1961.

Willey, Basil. *Nineteenth Century Studies.* London: Chaltto & Windsor, 1949.

KARL MARX

For most of the last half of the twentieth century, about half of the world's population has lived under regimes that, purportedly, were Marxist in their governing philosophy or ideology. Since the Soviet Union's collapse in the mid 1990s and with the client states on its perimeter following suit, the number of people living under the banner of Marxism has declined dramatically. Moreover, if the introduction of market principles is continued in China, it would be difficult to refer to it as Marxist in any real sense, and the number of people under the banner of Marxism would further decline. Nevertheless, the extent of Marx's influence over this century cannot be exaggerated. He has influenced academics in the major universities of the Western world and illiterate peasants in the rice fields of Southeast Asia. The extent alone of this man's influence merits a careful scrutiny of his philosophy.

MARX: His Life and Works

In 1818, Karl Marx was born in the small town of Trier, province of the Rhineland, Prussia. He was the oldest son, the second child, in a family of eight. On both sides of his family there had been generations of rabbis. His father, however, had received a secular education, had broken the connection with Judaism, and had become a successful, middle-class lawyer. Until the Napoleonic wars, discrimination against Jews had existed throughout Germany. Napoleon's victories, however, resulted in the imposition of liberal and enlightened laws on the various German states. (Germany had not yet been united into one nation.) After Napoleon was defeated, these laws were replaced by traditional discriminatory legislation (1816), and, as a consequence, Marx's father was barred from practising law. He responded by getting baptised in 1817. He had long considered himself as secular, in any case, and had only vague deist views on religion. Many years before he had changed his name from Levi to Marx, and because he did not belong to any synagogue, the baptism was a small matter. He then resumed his law practice. There is no evidence that Karl Marx himself experienced any significant anti-semitism in his life. In fact, as a boy Karl Marx was befriended by a neighbour, Ludwig von Westphalen a prominent Prussian official. In due course, Marx fell in love with the daughter, Jenny von Westphalen, whom he eventually married.

During Marx's childhood a dramatic political event occurred. When Karl Marx was 16, his father gave a mild speech for social reform; this brought the Prussian police to the door, and he immediately recanted. His son remembered this as a great humiliation. Marx's father apparently did not, and he always thought of himself as a loyal Prussian citizen and patriot.[1] Generally, Marx's youth was spent quite comfortably. He was, by all accounts, an excellent student whose interests in school seemed to be primarily in literature and art. Westphalen, to Marx's lifelong gratitude, had loaned books to the young man, had long conversations with him, and treated him as an intellectual equal. Marx was naturally precocious, and he quickly developed an extraordinary self-confidence, if not arrogance, which was his hallmark for the rest of his life. His father, understandably, had high hopes that his unusual son would have a successful career in law. It was not to be. The first year at the University of Bonn (1835) was spent in a fashion that delighted a 17-year-old boy but was less than pleasing to a father. Marx's achievements for the year included an arrest for drunkenness and a small scar from duelling. The next year his father sent him to the University of Berlin, one of the great universities of the day, for some serious academic work. Marx's father died in 1838, and this served to focus Karl's studies on earning a living.

His father's profession of law never interested Marx, and he turned, instead, to philosophy and history. George Wilhelm Friedrich Hegel (1730-1831) was the most famous philosopher at the time, and Marx became associated with one particular branch of Hegelianism, called the Young Hegelians or, sometimes, the Hegelians of the Left. Marx took his doctorate formally from the University of Jena (1841), though he did not study there. He originally planned on getting a position at a university, but the Prussian ministry of education officially condemned the Left Hegelians with whom Marx had close ties.

---

[1] Isaiah Berlin, *Karl Marx: His Life and Environment*, 4th ed. (Oxford: Oxford University Press, 1978), pp. 19–21.

Moreover, a close associate of Marx, Bruno Bauer, was dismissed from his university position. The option of the university for a livelihood was thus closed.

Both Right and Left Hegelians accepted the master's central thesis that the sweep of human history was intelligible if viewed as the subtle and often hidden workings of mind or reason or *geist* (also translated as spirit). Hegel, they thought, provided a method for studying history and showed history's direction. The method was the dialectic, which is to say that within any historical movement the conflicting forces and ideas reach a rough synthesis over time. Within the synthesis are further divisions that continue the dialectical process of change. The direction is the actualization of reason or *geist* in time and in history. One of Hegel's more famous aphorisms was that the rational is real and the real is rational. Thus, the actual or real historical situation contains the rational to some degree, since it incarnates at least a stage of the dialectical process and is also, for that reason, the best and morally justified situation.

Another of Hegel's aphorisms was that world history is world justice. The question that agitated Hegel's followers was the degree of the actual or real embodied in any particular stage. As an illustration, German culture was a superior synthesis, according to Hegel, of the preceding Oriental and Greco-Roman cultures. Since the last stage is necessarily the best, it would be morally wrong to try to subvert it. The Hegelians of the Right stressed this interpretation of Hegel. The Prussian ministry of education approved of the Right Hegelians, not surprisingly, since it meant that Prussia, the largest and most powerful of all the German states, must represent the pinnacle of civilization. The response of the Hegelians of the Left was that Hegel truly had made intelligible the course of civilization, but that it was their duty to be active in supporting the continuing movement or dialectic in history. Consequently, they became revolutionaries. Isaiah Berlin captures their mood:

> The plain duty of the philosopher who bears the burdens of civilization on his shoulders is, therefore, to promote revolution by the special technical skills which he alone commands, that is by intellectual warfare. It is his task to stir men from their indolence and torpor, to sweep away obstructive and useless institutions with the aid of his critical weapons much as the French philosophers had undermined the *ancient régime* by the power of ideas alone.[2]

---

[2] *Ibid.*, pp. 49–50.

The Prussian ministry of education was less than pleased with the Left Hegelians.

Because the university as a profession was closed to him, Marx took a job as a journalist for a newspaper in Cologne, *Rheinische Zeitung* (Rhenish Gazette). He was eminently successful and was the editor within a year (1842). In the main, the paper was of a liberal cast, and, in Prussia, this would entail calling for political and social reforms. The authorities closed the paper in 1843, and Marx began a series of moves through different cities and nations, ending in London. In conjunction with his moves, Marx also began a philosophic journey that culminated in communism, a revolutionary idea that could be advocated from the safety of London.

After a seven-year engagement, Jenny von Westphalen and Karl Marx were married (1843). This was one of Marx's most intelligent decisions. Jenny, against the wishes of most of her family, married Marx because she loved him, and she devoted her life to carrying for the great man that she was certain he was. They had six children; three died in childhood. Jenny's devotion sustained him and the family through poverty, several moves, and various other crises. One such crisis was the birth of their housekeeper's illegitimate child, fathered by Marx. The baby was sent to foster parents, but the housekeeper stayed with the family. Jenny, it is quite clear, was convinced of her husband's greatness, which was most fortunate for him. His own family, however, was not convinced, and he did not keep in contact with them.

The newly-married couple moved to Paris where Marx had been offered the co-editorship of a new publication, *Deutsch-Französische Jahrbücher* (German-French Annals). The first issue appeared in February 1844. The Prussian authorities again were less than pleased and they seized the entire shipment sent to Germany. They also issued a warrant for Marx's arrest, and the paper was forced to close. Marx, again, was working on his own.

He put his time to good use. The years 1834-1835 were the crucible that forged Marx's life. He changed from an idealist who viewed history as the field of contesting ideas (*geist*), moulding the course of humanity and civilization, to a materialist who saw history as propelled by economic forces. He read the French socialists; became acquainted with Pierre Proudhon (1809-65), a famous leader of French socialism and, later, subject to one of Marx's notorious and savage attacks, *The Poverty of Philosophy* (1847); and met Frederick Engels, who would become a lifelong friend and financial supporter. Engels came from a wealthy German family and owned a cotton factory in Manchester. This period came to an end when the Prussian government, in 1845, pressured the French government to expel Marx.

The Marx family was able to move to Brussels because Marx had given an understanding to the government that he would not take part in any political activity. Instead, he organized a group of Communists, continued to write a variety of works, and, in conjunction with Engels, produced the *Communist Manifesto* in 1848. This caused him to be expelled.

Prior to the publishing of the *Communist Manifesto*, Europe was convulsed with a series of rebellions, and many thought that a great working class revolution was beginning. Marx believed that the economic conditions were not propitious and that the revolutions would be crushed. He was right. But, the turmoil did present him with an opportunity to return to Germany.

Late in 1848 he was successful in getting some financial backing in Cologne for a *Neue Rheinische Zeitung* (New Rheinish Gazette). Marx was a true revolutionary by this time. In an article, he called for the people in Paris to resist the dissolution of their new revolutionary assembly by refusing to pay their taxes. Such a suggestion tends to make governments irritable. It most certainly irritated the Prussian government, and he was arrested for sedition. At his trial he rose to the occasion by giving a powerful and lengthy oration on contemporary economics, history, and politics. The jury was impressed, thanked him, and freed him of all charges. The Prussian government was not so impressed, and he was expelled from Prussia.

Britain agreed to let him immigrate, and he moved to London where he lived for the rest of his life. Financially, Marx depended upon handouts from Engels and, for eight years (1853–1861), upon a small journalist's income from the *New York Tribune*. Most of his time was spent in the library of the British Museum, where he read and wrote. In Britain, he was not well known. John Stuart Mill was his contemporary, but there is no evidence that Mill had ever heard of Marx. Mill was knowledgeable about French communist writings and wrote against them, but Marx was never mentioned.[3] Marx was aware of both Bentham and Mill and, as was his wont, expressed great contempt for them.

---

[3] "Chapters on Socialism" (1879) in Stefan Collini, ed., *John Stuart Mill: On Liberty and Other Writings* (Cambridge: Cambridge University Press, 1989).

In 1859 Marx published a part of his great work, *Capital* (*Das Kapital*), using the title *Critique of Political Economy*. The whole first volume of *Capital* was not published until 1867; the final two volumes were not published until after his death. He did receive some attention in Europe for *The Civil War in France* (1871). This little work was about the Paris Commune, a short-lived revolutionary government in Paris at the end of the Franco-Prussian war of 1870. It was crushed mercilessly and over 20,000 people lost their lives. Marx described it as the first proletarian class revolt. In fact, the Commune was led by a variety of people and had supporters from various segments of the population. Still, his writing convinced the European public that Marxists were of critical importance in forming the Commune. Marx praised the communes as the means for decentralizing government into the hands of the people, uniting the workers, and, in some vague way, still combining all with a central government. The upshot was that the atrocities of the commune were also associated with Marx as well as its abolition of private property and its commune governmental structure. He relished the publicity, bad or not.

In one sense, it is amazing how much Marx did accomplish during the 1850s and 1860s. He was extremely poor; his three surviving daughters, the housemaid, Jenny, and Marx all lived in two dirty rooms in the worst slums of London. He suffered seriously from various ailments, particularly boils and liver disease. His illegitimate child was an added stress. Marx had tried to get his friend and benefactor, Engels, to accept paternity so that Marx himself might thereby escape any scandal. It was a suggestion that reflected Marx's arrogance, and it sorely tested Engels's friendship. In spite of all these troubles, Marx worked extremely hard at his research and writing.

He also became active politically. He helped organize the first International meeting in London (1864), which was a blend of labour organizations and various socialist movements throughout Europe. He came to be the most dominant personality in this movement and a master of organizational intrigue. It was his constant purpose to have his brand of communism accepted as the official and guiding ideology. Two other congresses of the International were held in 1867 and 1868, but by the third, in 1872, he had lost his influence. He had maneuvered to get the International headquarters, such as it was, moved to New York, and this served to end the organization.

In 1869, Jenny had inherited some money from her parents, and the Marx family finally were able to leave the slums of London. Marx's fame and influence was increasing in Europe, but he now did not have any organizational outlet for his ideas. The German socialist movement pointedly ignored him, to his considerable anger. As one instance, a meeting was held at Gotha, Germany, of various workers' organizations with the purpose of preparing a platform of agreed policies. Marx was irate when he heard of it, and he wrote a vitriolic treatise against the program, *The Critique of the Gotha Program*. It never got to Gotha, however, and was not published until after his death.

His last decade was not very happy in spite of his comfortable situation. He did not wholly approve of his daughters' marriages, and his own health continued to deteriorate even though he now could afford medical care and vacations to health spas. He watched international affairs very closely and became convinced, repeatedly, that the great proletariat revolution would start in Russia or, perhaps, Turkey. He apparently even learned enough of these languages to follow events. Jenny died in 1881, and Marx never recovered from her death. A daughter, also named Jenny, died in January, 1882, and on March 14, 1883, Marx died of a lung infection.[4]

PHILOSOPHIC BACKGROUND

At Marx's funeral, Engels gave a moving speech that serves as an introduction to the powerful set of ideas that made Marxism the single most powerful ideology of the twentieth century. In the speech he first associates Marx with the great scientists of the age. Marx's achievement has been the discovery of two great laws of human history, one for all of human history and the other the particular law for this time period or epoch. Engel elaborates:

> Just as Darwin discovered the law of development of organic nature, so Marx discovered the law of development of human history: the simple fact, hitherto concealed by an overgrowth of ideology, that mankind must first of all eat, drink, have shelter and clothing, before it can pursue politics, science, art, religion, etc.; that therefore the production of the immediate material means of subsistence and consequently the degree of economic development attained by a given people or during a given epoch form the

---

[4] For information about Marx's life see: Isaiah Berlin, *Karl Marx: His Life and Environment*, 4th ed. (New York: Oxford University Press, 1963); David McLellan, *Karl Marx: His Life and Thought* (New York: Harper & Row, 1973); Franz Mehring, *Karl Marx* (London: Allen & Unwin, 1936); Heinz F. Peters, *Red Jenny: A Life with Karl Marx* (London: Allen & Unwin, 1986).

foundation upon which the state institutions, legal conceptions, art, and even the ideas on religion, of the people concerned have been evolved, and in the light of which they must, therefore, be explained, instead of vice versa, as had hitherto been the case.

But that is not all. Marx also discovered the special law of motion governing the present-day capitalist mode of production and the bourgeois society that this mode of production has created. The discovery of surplus value suddenly threw light on the problem, in trying to solve which all previous investigation of both bourgeois economists and socialist critics, had been groping in the dark.[5]

Darwin's theory of evolution provided a causal explanation of the evolution of the species, and Marx's two laws provide a causal explanation for the evolution of human thoughts and actions. The economic forces of production are the "foundation," and politics, literature, art, and religion are to be explained by recourse to the economic forces, not the other way around. The economic theory of surplus value supposedly explains the rise of capitalism. This, too, is an economic explanation.

Marx's second achievement was a moral and political revolution. He showed how it was possible to liberate humanity by liberating the proletariat. This liberation was political, economic, cultural, and moral. A new humanity would be born. In Engels's words:

> For Marx was before all else a revolutionist. His real mission in life was to contribute, in one way or another, to the overthrow of capitalist society and of the state institutions which it had brought into being, to contribute to the liberation of the modern proletariat, which he was the first to make conscious of its own position and its needs, conscious of the conditions of its emancipation. Fighting was his element. And he fought with a passion, a tenacity and a success such as few could rival....
>
> And he died beloved, revered and mourned by millions of revolutionary fellow workers—from the mines of Siberia to California, in all parts

---

[5] "Speech at the Graveside, 17 March 1883," in *The Marx-Engels Reader*, 2nd ed., ed. Robert C. Tucker (New York: W. W. Norton, 1972), pp. 681–82. Hereafter cited as the *Marx-Engels Reader*.

of Europe and America—and I make bold to say that though he may have had many opponents he had hardly one personal enemy.

His name will endure through the ages, and so also will his work![6]

A moral impulse, the liberation of humanity, was united by Marx with the power of science.

Engels has correctly expressed Marx's philosophic achievements, a moral vision expressed through science, but this is not a traditional conception of science. For Marx there was a human science that encompassed the evolution of humanity; it is an all-inclusive framework that explains the rise and fall of civilizations, law, governments, arts and literature, and even philosophy itself. Hegel, who Marx considered the finest philosopher of all time, had a similar scheme in his works. Marx, as we shall see, altered Hegel's scheme, but even prior to Hegel there was a tradition of thought, as perceived by Marx and his fellow Young Hegelians (also called Left Hegelians), which they held themselves to be completing. They believed German philosophy to be the glory of the German nation and, indeed, of Western civilization. Marx would look back many years later and argue that he had built upon past German philosophers, and communism was the final and inevitable outcome. Such a claim horrified Hegel scholars then, as it does now.

Specifically, there was a continuity in the minds of Marx and the Young Hegelians that certainly began at least with Immanuel Kant (1724-1804). The sequence was that Hegel improved Kant; Ludwig Feuerbach (1804-1872) transformed Hegel; and Marx completed the philosophic movement. Although Hegel was recognized as the most important figure, his contribution is more obvious when we know his own reflections on his predecessor, Immanuel Kant.

Kant was a philosopher and theologian who attempted to respect both the new empirical science and the truths of Christianity. This led him to make a sharp distinction between the moral or mental and the physical realms. A connection was still possible because the mind had the capacity of synthesizing sense data. He argued that the mind has certain built-in principles, which it relies upon for this task. For example, the idea of causality is in the mind; it is not in the world but comes from the way the mind synthesizes data. When explaining human nature, Kant stressed this same sharp distinction between the physical and the mental. In his

---

[6] *Ibid.*, p. 682.

view, human nature is divided into two parts. One part is the physical realm, which explains our physical being, and this he calls *homo phenomenon*. The second part is the mind dimension, which he calls *homo noumenon* (spirit).

Not only are humans fundamentally dual in nature, according to Kant, these two parts are in tension with each other. Humans, as Kant develops his philosophy, experience themselves as part of two realms: we know that we are physical beings and finite (*homo phenomenon*); we also know we are spiritual creatures in that we perceive the ideal of perfection and are aware of moral truths (*homo noumenon*). The difficulty is for finite beings to achieve the realm of *homo noumenon*. Moral-like perfection is beyond our ability to realize, but we nevertheless feel its pull and, indeed, we have a duty to try and be perfect. Our human unhappiness, or more precisely alienation, is born from the tensions and conflict we experience at being finite, material creatures with the capacity for permanent, transcendent moral perfection. We experience ourselves as caught in a physical world but actually more at home in the spirit world (*noumenon*). In the physical world we are unsatisfied, and we feel like strangers and aliens. This world does not fit what we are; it is the other world we desire. All human strivings are finally traceable to this deep psychological drive for perfection and completion; and it is our inability to realize this drive, Kant concludes that is the real source of human alienation or unhappiness.

Kant had a solution of sorts to this human dilemma of conflict within ourselves. The divided personality, at war with itself, could realize the drive to be perfect through following various moral imperatives such as the Golden Rule: "Do unto others as you would have others do unto you." Kant's own unique philosophical formulation of the Golden Rule was: "Act only on that maxim through which you can at the same time will that it should become a universal law."[7] When guided by such moral imperatives, and Kant had several, humans could realize the drive to be perfect; we would also be autonomous because we would have willed the imperatives and applied them to ourselves; we would also experience ourselves, as a consequence, as masters. Kant, obviously, was influenced by Rousseau's conception of a free, autonomous person. Mastery or autonomy is attained, in Rousseau, through obeying a law one has prescribed for oneself, and, by so doing, moral liberty is realized.

---

[7] *Grounding for the Metaphysics of Morals*, second section, "Transition from Popular Moral Philosophy to a Metaphysics of Morals," in *Classics of Moral and Political Theory*, ed. Michael L. Morgan (Indianapolis: Hackett, 1992), p. 1013.

The striking feature of Kant's speculation about human unhappiness or alienation was that it resulted from the inability to realize the drive to be perfect. The drive to be perfect is traditionally called pride, the failure to accept human limitations. The desire to be God-like and to have certainty, control, and power is, in theological terms, a sin; yet, in Kant's analysis it is precisely this failure to accept human limitations that results in human unhappiness. According to Kant, we cannot attain perfection in this life, but with the various moral imperatives we can, by our own mind and will, continually try to reach perfection: "For a rational but finite being, the only thing possible is an endless progress from the lower to the higher degree of moral perfection."[8] The very drive that instigated human unhappiness could also provide the solution. Escaping from the phenomenal world and entering, by our own power, the world of the *noumenon* could be accomplished to some degree by the categorical imperatives. The drive was not the problem; the inability to realize it was.

As a young seminary student, Hegel was aware of Kant but became disenchanted with his solution. Hegel accepted the dualism of the human personality, though his conception of dualism was different. Simply, humans experience themselves as finite creatures, but they also can participate in what is infinite. We can know incontestable truths of logic, for instance, which are not finite, and we can perceive the movement of the stars in the infinity of space. There is, indeed, a tension, and it results from a drive to participate in the infinite and to escape our finite existence.

By adding the dimension of history to his philosophy, Hegel was able to widen considerably the explanatory power of his philosophy. He held that human nature did not contain a "God-like" capacity for perfection, as Kant had argued. Rather, "Mind," "Reason" or "Spirit" (*geist*)—Hegel used these terms synonymously—actually *was* God. There have always been differences of opinion as to the precise meaning of Hegel's concept of *geist*, and the fact that it can be translated in these different ways has not helped the matter. Roughly, the idea is that individual minds, through their capacity to participate in the infinite, are part of God or Mind as a whole. Further, the evolution of Mind or Reason is an historical and dialectical process, which can be seen by looking back at all of human history. The gradual emergence of Reason of Mind, can be seen slowly unfolding through the turbulence of human history.

---

[8] *Kant's Critique of Practical Reason*, as quoted in Robert C. Tucker, *Philosophy and Myth in Karl Marx* (Cambridge: Cambridge University Press, 1961), p. 35.

In the *Phenomenology of Mind* Hegel illustrates how the dialectic works by using the relationship between a master and slave, or, as he says, "Lordship and Bondage." There is, initially, an antithesis or true conflict between the two, and neither would see the other as participating in Mind or Reason. Yet, over time, the very work of the slave alters the world around him and, simultaneously, alters the slave himself. The slave becomes conscious of his own power and develops a new identity, an "independent being as its self."[9] Over time, the master becomes dependent upon the slave, and the self-awareness that develops will lead to the liberation of the slave and to the defeat of the master-slave conflict. A new synthesis is established. Thus, in a hidden, unconscious, and unrecognized fashion, Mind or Reason or Spirit, embodied in the various actors, does work toward freedom and show itself in retrospect. In a rare, pithy remark, Hegel speaks of the "cunning of Reason" as it unfolds in history. For Hegel, this is the very pattern of all of human history.

The dialectical pattern of human history, however, can be seen only on the large scale and when looking backward. In any actual historical situation, there will be warring sides, neither side recognizing the inherent existence of Mind or Reason in the process. It is as if Mind has been splintered into small parts and has become alienated from itself in history, Hegel says. Mind is, by definition, infinite and all-encompassing; therefore, the inability to recognize itself in history serves to block and to frustrate Mind's ability to exercise its power. Within the confines of any one historical time period, all we experience are the contentious ideas, beliefs, and movements that are pulling and pushing human organizations and civilizations. It is only through looking over history, with the philosophic glasses of Hegel, that one can see a bumpy, but gradual unfolding toward more knowledge, more rational governmental structures, and more freedom. As the alien competing forces in any one situation are gradually overcome, the working of Reason or Mind is more clearly seen; the power of Reason or Mind to organize reality according to its dictates increases; and the freedom of Mind increases with its mastery over nature. It is as if Reason or Mind comes to its own self-realization and completion in history.

Hegel's solution is also different from Kant's. Mind or Reason or God, Hegel argues, manifests itself in two ways.[10] First, God or Mind can be seen in nature; in the rational, infinite structure of reality. This manifestation of Mind stands over

---

[9] J. B. Baille, trans., *The Phenomenology of Mind* (New York: Harper, 1967), p. 238.

[10] *Ibid.*, pp. 789–808.

against us; its perfectibility and immortality taunts us, in that nature constantly reminds us of our own finitude. The separateness, independence, and otherness of reality serve to accentuate our impotence. We, accordingly, feel ourselves to be aliens or strangers in reality. Second, Mind or God also is manifested in human history, as we have seen. But, in any particular time period, humans are caught in a flow of history, which they did not make nor can they control. We again experience our condition as one of powerlessness and of alienation. The very separateness of history from our individual lives, its otherness, its mysterious and unfolding power, is alienating. There is an apparent unresolvable conflict between the sense of mastery and freedom we want to experience and the alienation we, in fact, do experience.

Hegel has a solution: both forms of alienation, in nature or in human history, can be escaped through the act of knowing. First, the otherness of the external world is overcome through appropriating with our own mental activity the rational structure of reality. As Hegel says, Mind, then, recognizes Mind; Spirit recognizes Spirit. Finiteness is lost and infinity gained. The same mental operation takes place in overcoming the otherness of history. By seeing the unfolding of Reason or Mind or Spirit in the rise and fall of civilizations, our minds again participate in the working of Mind or Reason through our knowledge. Hegel uses rather colourful language to explain this mental operation. It is likened to the same act of will by which an animal devours things.

> All things may become man's property, because man is free will and consequently is absolute, while what stands over against him lacks this quality.... Thus, 'to appropriate' means at bottom only to manifest the pre-eminence of my will over the things and to prove that it is not absolute, is not an end in itself.... The free will, therefore, is the idealism which does not take things as they are to be absolute, while realism pronounces them to be absolute, even if they only exist in the form of finitude. Even an animal has gone beyond this realist philosophy since it devours things and so proves that they are not absolutely self-subsistent.[11]

Spirit recognizes itself as Spirit, but it is an act of will and power that provides a sense of mastery. The experience of alienation thus dissolves.

To reiterate, Kant had an inner dialect between the two sides of the self. Hegel follows this lead, but, for him, the self has been transposed onto an historical

---

[11] T. M. Knox, trans., *Hegel's Philosophy of Right* (Oxford: Clarendon Press, 1953), p. 236.

stage, and the inner conflict has become conflicts within history. Humans within history experience their differences of positions and ideas as antithetical, but, as a whole, humanity's strivings and conflicts in history are all manifestations—hidden and unknown to the actors—of the slow unfolding of Mind, gradually coming to its full realization. Hegel's illustration was the master-slave antithesis where the slave, through work and labour, gradually comes to consciousness and self-realization; Mind or Reason within humanity is making this same journey of self-realization. Humans have been striving by their own power to become divine or absolute, that is, to complete the full process of self-realization. Although humans have not known of this operation of *geist* or Spirit or Mind, it has worked through them to the final goal of completion. As Hegel makes the point in his own inimitable fashion:

> Itself is its own object of attainment, and the sole aim of Spirit. This result it is, at which the process of the World's History has been continually aiming; and to which the sacrifices that have ever and anon been laid on the vast altar of the earth, through the long lapse of ages, have been offered. This is the only aim that sees itself realized and fulfilled; the only pole of repose amid the ceaseless change of events and conditions, and the sole efficient principle that pervades them.[12]

The clear implication of Hegel's philosophy is politely suggested by one commentator:

> Hegel's philosophy has an odd consequence which would have been embarrassing to a more modest author. If all history is the story of Mind working towards the goal of understanding its own nature, this goal is actually reached with the completion of the *Phenomenology* itself. When Mind, manifested in the mind of Hegel, grasps its own nature, the last stage of history has been reached.[13]

---

[12] G. W. F. Hegel, *The Philosophy of History*, trans. J. Sibree (New York: Dover, 1956), pp. 18–20.

[13] Peter Singer, *Karl Marx* (Oxford: Oxford University Press, 1980), p. 13. Other commentators are not so polite. See Eric Voegelin's interpretation: *The Collected Works of Eric Voegelin*, Vol. 12, *Published Essays, 1966–1985*, ed. Ellis Sandoz (Baton Rouge: Louisiana State University Press, 1990), pp. 213–55.

There is no doubt that the Young Hegelians did believe that history had reached a defining moment.[14]

Hegel's solution is similar to Kant's in one respect: the very drive that manifests itself in alienation and conflict in history is the source of the solution. The drive for full self-realization culminates in power and freedom for humanity. In Hegel's phrase, "The hand that inflicts the wounds is also the hand that heals it."[15]

Marx and the Young Hegelians accepted most of Hegel's philosophy in the beginning. They were not willing to accept the implicit idolatry of the Prussian state as the final stage in the self-realization of Mind or God. Also, they took Hegel to task for his views on religion. There still was in Hegel, they contended, the view that God or Mind or *geist* was above and separate from humans and that the task, for humans, was to overcome this alienation by joining or participating in Mind or Spirit. Marx's friend, Bruno Bauer, and the other Young Hegelians simply abolished the pretense that God or Spirit realizes itself in history. Humans are the divine, not just a little part of the divine in a hidden, mysterious way. Marx makes the point in the preface to his doctoral dissertation:

> Philosophy makes no secret of it. The proclamation of Prometheus—in a word, I detest all the Gods—is her own profession, her own slogan against all the gods of heaven and earth who do not recognize man's self-consciousness as the highest divinity. There shall be none other beside it.[16]

Ludwig Feuerbach was an even stronger critic of Hegel, which proved to be key in changing Marx to his final philosophical position of historical materialism. Feuerbach argued that religion actually alienated humans, but not because it was an outside force shaping and oppressing humanity. Religion is the consequence of human self-alienation in that humans project onto this God-illusion,

---

[14] For more charitable interpretations of Hegel, see Raymond Plant, *Hegel* (New York: Basil Blackwell, 1984); Charles Taylor, *Hegel and Modern Society* (Cambridge: Cambridge University Press, 1979); Peter Singer, *Hegel* (Oxford: Oxford University Press, 1983). For the Young Hegelians' interpretation of Hegel, see Sidney Hook, *From Hegel to Marx: Studies in the Intellectual Development of Karl Marx* (Ann Arbor: University of Michigan, 1962); David McLellan, *The Young Hegelians and Karl Marx* (London: Macmillan, 1969).

[15] *The Logic of Hegel*, quoted in Tucker, *Philosophy and Myth in Karl Marx*, p. 44.

[16] "Doctoral Thesis," in *Karl Marx: Selected Writings*, ed. David McLellan (Oxford: Oxford University Press, 1977), pp. 12–13. Hereafter cited as *Selected Writings*.

as Feuerbach called it, a compendium of perfect qualities and then use this illusion as a judge of themselves. God is described as all-powerful, all-knowing, immortal, holy and the like; humans are described, in contrast, as weak, limited, mortal, sinful and so on. But, the compendium of God-like qualities are only generic human qualities, and by recognizing this God-illusion as only a projection we can begin to liberate ourselves from alienation. We would no longer experience ourselves as the opposite to God, because there is only a God-illusion. The full solution is to focus on the divine qualities within ourselves and within our fellows. We could then become whole and authentic selves who would not treat each other competitively or instrumentally; we could truly know one another in a personal "I-thou" relationship based on love and friendship. Indeed, Feuerbach spoke of the goal as becoming philosophical communal humans or communists, because human relations would be personal and communal, not individualistic and egocentric. There is a self-realization and completion in history, as Hegel said, but it is not of Mind or *geist* coming to its completion; rather, there is human self-realization in history.

It is Feuerbach's contention, in brief, that human alienation does not result from individual minds or spirits trying to express and grasp the Mind or God in history, the so-called World Spirit of Hegel. This is all unnecessary metaphysical jargon. The root of alienation is within the human. Hegel covertly saw, according to Feuerbach, that alienation shows itself in history, but he got the explanation upside down. Feuerbach provides a "transformative criticism" of Hegel so that one can see what actually is occurring in history. History is indeed, as Hegel showed, the stage of human alienation, and there is an unfolding of sorts leading to greater clarity. But, Mind or *geist* is not guiding humans and history in subtle and hidden ways; humans themselves are the engines of history and of their own alienation.

At the end of 1843 Marx wrote an article for the soon-to-be defunct *Deutsch-Französische Jahrbücher* in which he marks his agreement with Feuerbach.

> The abolition of religion as the *illusory* happiness of men, is a demand for their *real* happiness. The call to abandon their illusions about their condition is a *call to abandon a condition which requires illusions*. The criticism of religion is, therefore, *the embryonic criticism of this vale of tears* of which religion is the *halo*....
>
> The immediate *task of philosophy*, which is in the service of history, is to unmask human self-alienation in its *secular form* now that it has been

unmasked in its *sacred form.* Thus the criticism of heaven is transformed into the criticism of earth, the *criticism of religion* into the *criticism of law,* and the *criticism of theology* into the *criticism of politics.*[17]

Marx's message is that Feuerbach has shown how the reification of religion has created the institution of religion and a set of ideas that actually have served to judge, condemn, and, in short, alienate humanity. By exposing the religion-illusion, we become free of its oppression. Marx then adds that the same kind of analysis needs to be done of other institutions such as the legal and political systems.

Marx, it should be noted, always disagreed with Feuerbach's "love your neighbour" solution. Marx wants a revolution, and philosophy, he believes, will lead the struggle. "It is clear that the arm of criticism cannot replace the criticism of arms. Material force can only be overcome by material force; but theory itself becomes a material force when it has seized the masses."[18]

One more element was attached to Feuerbach's revision of Hegel, and it came from a friend of Marx's, Moses Hess. Hess made the case that Feuerbach's God-illusion argument was itself only a reflection of a deeper cause, the drive for money, or, more broadly, the drive for material acquisitions. Prior to Hess others had certainly argued that the source of alienation was in economic life.[19] Hess placed the argument into a philosophic frame. Feuerbach had argued that humans became estranged by positing a God they worshipped and pursued. Human ego and pride to be God-like was the driving force, but by creating the God-illusion (the institutions and practices of religion) the desire to be God-like had been frustrated, and humans had become used, judged, and generally alienated. Hess said that the pursuit of money works in exactly the same way. The desire for money or the acquisitive urge leads to the creation of all sorts of institutions and practices which, in turn, judge, condemn, and alienate humanity. Humans, as in reiigion, experience themselves as powerless instruments of a ruling force, and the force is real and is the economic system.

---

[17] "Contribution to the Critique of Hegel's Philosophy of Right: Introduction," in *The Marx-Engels Reader,* p. 54.

[18] *Ibid.,* p. 60.

[19] Pierre Proudhon was the most famous contemporary to make this case. For an excellent survey of other contemporaries, see Leszek Kolakowski, *Main Currents of Marxism: Its Rise, Growth, and Dissolution,* Vol. I, *The Founders,* trans. P. S. Falla (Oxford: Clarendon Press, 1978), pp. 182–233.

There was indeed, concluded Hess, a material base for alienation, whether alienation was contributed to by religion, law, state, family, or economics. All of these institutions and their supporting beliefs were alienating, and all of them need to be analyzed to show their root in the drive for money, or, to put it more philosophically, in the labouring process, which is Marx's term. In the labouring process, humans provide for their food, clothing, shelter, and other needs, and through that process create economic systems. Marx, during the years 1843-1844, wrote and published "On the Jewish Question" in the *Deutsch-Französische Jahrbücher*, which expands on Hess's position. This essay was written as a response to his friend Bruno Bauer who had written that the difficult position of Jews in society was a consequence of their religion. Marx argues, using anti-semitic allusions, that the true, basic cause is not religion but is the economic system.

> Let us not seek the secret of the Jew in his religion, but let us seek the secret of the religion in the real Jew.
>
> What is the profane basis of Judaism? *Practical* need, *self-interest*. What is the worldly cult of the Jew? *Huckstering*. What is his worldly god? *Money....*
>
> Money is the jealous god of Israel, beside which no other god may exist. Money abases all the gods of mankind and changes them into commodities. Money is the universal and self-sufficient *value* of all things. It has, therefore, deprived the whole world, both the human world and nature, of their own proper value. Money is the alienated essence of man's work and existence; this essence dominates him and he worships it.
>
> The god of the Jews has been secularized and has become the god of this world. The bill of exchange is the real god of the Jew. His god is only an illusory bill of exchange.[20]

Marx further expanded the economic perspective to include the proletariat, which, he argued, was the perfect embodiment of human alienation. As it struggled to free itself, it was actually freeing humanity, or so Marx explains:

> A class must be formed which has *radical chains*, a class in civil society which is not a class of civil society, a class which is the dissolution of all classes, a sphere of society which has a universal character because

---

[20] "On the Jewish Question," in *The Marx-Engels Reader*, pp. 48, 50.

its sufferings are universal, and which does not claim a *particular redress* because the wrong which is done to it is not a *particular wrong* but *wrong in general.* There must be formed a sphere of society which claims no *traditional* status but only a human status...a sphere, finally, which cannot emancipate itself without emancipating itself from all the other spheres of society, without, therefore, emancipating all these other spheres, which is, in short, a *total loss* of humanity and which can only redeem itself by a *total redemption of humanity.* This dissolution of society, as a particular class, is the *proletariat.*[21]

The conception of the proletariat completes Marx's philosophic journey to his final position, which he did not alter. As is now clear, Marx's philosophic position stresses the primary role of economics, but this position was reached through Hegel, not through reading economists or through empirical economic studies.

In sum, Marx accepted Hegel's view that history was intelligible and had a direction.[22] With the help of Feuerbach and his so-called transformative criticism, Marx saw that Hegel needed to be turned right side up. When Hegel saw all of history as the reflection of Mind or God or Spirit gradually, through the rise and fall of civilizations, coming to self-realization and completion in history, he had unknowingly inverted the story. Hegel did not realize that he was actually describing, symbolically and confusedly, material forces of alienation. In particular, the labouring process creates a succession of economic stages in history, which have been necessary but have also served to alienate humanity. In speaking of Hegel's *Phenomenology of Mind,* Marx wrote, in 1843, of his discovery of how to read Hegel:

The *Phenomenology* is, therefore, an occult critique—still to itself obscure and mystifying criticism; but inasmuch as it keeps steadily in view man's *estrangement,* even though man appears only in the shape of mind, there

---

[21] "Contribution to the Critique of Hegel's Philosophy of Right: Introduction" (1844), in *The Marx-Engels Reader,* p. 65.

[22] Both Hegel and Kant deserve to be read through eyes other than that of Marx and the Young Hegelians. For Kant, see Patrick Riley, *Kant's Political Philosophy* (Totowa, N.J.: Rowman & Littlefield, 1983). For Hegel see the following works. The book by Melzer and others discusses another way of interpreting Hegel's view that history has a direction and a closing: Arthur M. Melzer, Jerry Weinberger and M. Richard Zinman, eds., *History and the Idea of Progress* (Ithaca: Cornell University Press, 1995); Walter Kaufman, ed., *Hegel's Political Philosophy* (New York: Atherton, 1970).

lie concealed in it *all* the elements of criticism, already *prepared* and *elaborated* in a manner often rising far above the Hegelian standpoint.[23]

To reiterate, the history of humanity is not God or Spirit or Mind working and weaving its troubled path toward self-realization, but it is humans, through their labouring activity, creating an external, economic world, which, in turn, captures humans in its powerful grip. This is the real cause of alienation. Marx repeats his debt to Hegel in the preface to the second edition of *Capital*, published in 1873:

> My dialectic method is not only different from the Hegelian, but is its direct opposite. To Hegel, the life-process of the human brain, i.e., the process of thinking, which, under the name of 'the Idea', he even transforms into an independent subject, is the demiurgos of the real world, and the real world is only the external, phenomenal form of 'the Idea'. With me, on the contrary, the ideal is nothing else than the material world reflected by the human mind, and translated into forms of thought.
>
> The mystifying side of Hegelian dialectic I criticized nearly thirty years ago, at a time when it was still the fashion.... With him it is standing on its Head. It must be turned right side up again, if you should discover the rational kernel within the mystical shell.[24]

HISTORICAL MATERIALISM

Marx has reached the stage where he believes that he can now answer all the questions previously probed by German philosophers, and that all his answers are better than those of his predecessors. Marx is confident, first, that his view of history is philosophically and scientifically the best; second, that his conceptions of the dialectic in history and the dualized self are the only ones that are coherent and philosophically sound; third, and above all, that his solution to alienation is the only true and practical solution.

First, Hegel held that history is Mind or *geist* unfolding in history in a manner unknown to the actors themselves, but, as Feuerbach showed, this was only

---

[23] "Critique of the Hegelian Dialectic and Philosophy as a Whole," in *The Marx-Engels Reader*, p. 111. As an antidote to Marx's interpretation of the *Phenomenology*, see Judith N. Shklar, *Freedom and Independence: A Study of the Political Ideas of Hegel's 'Phenomenology of Mind'* (Cambridge: Cambridge University Press, 1976).

[24] "Preface" to *Capital*, in *Selected Writings*, p. 420.

so much metaphysical jargon. All the talk about Mind or Reason or God was simply, as Feuerbach diagnosed, a projection of human qualities that were then worshipped and used to judge humanity. There is a true movement in history, but it is not one of "ideas" or "ideals," which are splinters of Mind unconsciously trying to reach completion and self-realization. Nor is history driven, as Feuerbach suggested, by succeeding desires to be God-like. History is not driven by either ideas or illusions; it is, says Marx, driven by the actual labouring activity whereby humans produce goods for their needs. This drive, rather vulgarly described by Moses Hess as money worship, results in a succession of economic systems that manifests man's desire to create a world satisfying humanity's wants. History is the productive power of humanity unfolding in history.

Second, it is true, as Hegel perceived, that history is a dialectical movement. For Hegel, this movement was the consequence of the portions of Mind in humans seeking, blindly, to achieve some completion and self-realization in Mind. The antithesis created by Mind in the striving but minute manifestations in humans produces a dynamic progress that, ultimately, leads to self-realization and absolute knowledge. Thus, self-realization in history is the self-realization of Mind or God. Feuerbach's conflict is in history and is propelled, as has already been noted, by the drive to be God-like, which is a projection of actual human qualities onto a God-illusion. Marx's dialectic in history is economic in character. He wrote the "Theses on Feuerbach" in early 1845 to summarize in epigrammatic style the differences between himself and Feuerbach.

> Feuerbach starts out from the fact of religious self-alienation, of the duplication of the world into a religious, imaginary world and a real one. His work consists in resolving the religious world into its secular basis. He overlooks the fact that after completing this work, the chief thing still remains to be done. For the fact that the secular basis detaches itself from itself and establishes itself in the clouds as an independent realm can only be explained by the cleavage and self-contradictions within this secular basis.[25]

The Feuerbachian dialectic between a real world of actual humans and an imaginary one of the God-illusions is itself, says Marx, only a reflection of a deeper cause in the secular world itself. In the 1844 *The Holy Family: A Critique of Critical Criticism* he spells out his shift from Feuerbach to his own explanation of the cause

---

[25] "Theses on Feuerbach," IV, in *The Marx-Engels Reader*, p. 144.

of the dialectic in history. The dialectic, Marx states, is the antithesis between the capitalist or "possessing class" and the proletarian class. The dialectic between the two is parallel to the analysis Hegel provides of the master-slave, but, as Marx will now repeatedly write, his own dialectic of history is in the real, actual world in contrast to the ideal, abstract, mental worlds of Feuerbach and of Hegel. The dualized self of both Hegel and Feuerbach are actually just expressions of two real classes. Marx has perceived, hidden under the Hegelian mystical claim of Mind or *geist* unfolding in history, that human labouring, productive power is unfolding in history. The dialectic movement is not from the splinterings of Mind trying to realize Mind, but from the expression of the love of money or the acquisitive urge into two actual, real forces and classes.

> Private property as private property, as wealth, is compelled to preserve *its own existence* and thereby the existence of its opposite, the proletariat....
>
> The proletariat, on the other hand, is compelled to abolish itself and thereby its conditioning opposite—private property—which makes it a proletariat....
>
> The possessing class and the proletarian class represent one and the same human self-alienation. But the former feels satisfied and affirmed in this self-alienation, experiences the alienation as a sign *of its own power*, and possesses in it the *appearance* of a human existence. The latter, however, feels destroyed in this alienation, seeing in it its own impotence and the reality of an inhuman existence. To use Hegel's expression, this class is, within depravity, an *indignation* against this depravity, an indignation necessarily aroused in this class by the contradiction between its human *nature* and its life-situation, which is a blatant, outright and all-embracing denial of that very nature.[26]

The antithesis between labour and capital, the proletarian and capitalist classes, produces real alienation in humans and in history. It is not a religious or psychological phenomena; there is a real dialectic in history, and, as Marx will soon announce in the 1848 *Communist Manifesto*, it is the class struggle.

Third, Marx asserts that his solution to the "riddle of history" is indisputably the best. Hegel has the Mind realizing itself in history and, thus, attaining absolute

---

[26] *The Holy Family,* in *The Marx-Engels Reader,* pp. 133–34.

knowledge, mastery, and freedom. Feuerbach has the dissolution of the judgmental and alienating God-illusion and the birth of the authentic, communal selves. Marx follows Feuerbach in that the goal is human self-realization in history, and that self-realization contains the experiences of freedom and mastery. Marx's solution is communism because it completes the natural forces shaping the human condition (naturalism) and, in so doing, releases the authentic whole self (humanism) hidden and abused by the economic process:

> *Communism* as the *positive* transcendence of *private property*, or *human self-estrangement*, and therefore as the real *appropriation of the human* essence by and for man; communism therefore as the complete return of man to himself as a social (i.e., human) being—a return becomes conscious, and accomplished within the entire wealth of previous development. This communism, as fully-developed naturalism, equals humanism, and as fully-developed humanism equals naturalism; it is the *genuine* resolution of the conflict between man and man—the true resolution of the strife between existence and essence, between objectification and self-confirmation, between freedom and necessity, between the individual and the species. Communism is the riddle of history solved, and it knows itself to be this solution.[27]

Feuerbach may have solved religious alienation, but this was only of "man's inner life," whereas Marx claims his solution is in "real life" and, thus, "embraces both aspects."[28] Since the alienation is in the real world, the solution, too, is realized by action in the real world—a revolution. Hegel's "appropriation" was through a mental operation whereby the individual's mind recognizes Mind; Marx has real "appropriation" by the practical activity of the proletariat, who will eventually destroy the capitalist class ruling over them and establish a classless society. One of Marx's more widely quoted epigrams expresses the point: "The philosophers have only *interpreted* the world, in various ways; the point, however, is to *change* it."[29]

---

[27] "Private Property and Communism," *The Economic and Philosophic Manuscript of 1844*, in *The Marx-Engels Reader*, p. 84.

[28] *Ibid.*, p. 85.

[29] "Theses on Feuerbach," XI, in *The Marx-Engels Reader*, p. 145.

Given Marx's own analysis of history, of the dialectic, and of the solution to alienation, his claim that his philosophy completed the German philosophic tradition is, perhaps, understandable. At this point in his writing, Marx is an historical materialist; he will now demonstrate how it is that economics is the locus of human alienation and of the dialectic in history.

In the *Economic and Philosophic Manuscripts of 1844* Marx begins his lifelong study on economics, to be completed in the three-volume *Capital*, and of these volumes only the first was actually completed and published in his lifetime (1873).[30] The early manuscripts of 1844 present Marx's full analysis of alienation using his new-found tool of economics. Alienation is an inevitable consequence of the natural labouring process whereby humans attain their means of subsistence: food, clothing, and shelter. In an argument that echoes Rousseau, Marx describes how the necessary act of labouring produces alienation. Specifically, he shows how humans become alienated from their products, from their own labouring activity, from their own nature or "species being," and from other people.

Humans become alienated from their products when they work to create objects for an economic system. The cheap and efficient production of objects commands the attention and labour of the worker. In this sense, the object confronts the worker as "*something alien, as a power independent* of the producer." Furthermore, the more efficient and productive the worker is and the more sophisticated the economic system becomes, the less significant is the individual worker. The efficiency gained by narrowing the division of labour to ever more minute functions increases productivity, but the worker becomes an even less significant part of a large economic machine. Marx draws an analogy with Feuerbach's analysis of religion. The economic system now replaces the role of God: "The more man puts into God, the less he retains in himself. The worker puts his life into the object; but now his life no longer belongs to him but to the object."[31]

Even more debilitating, as Marx describes the process, is the effect of the economic system on human labouring activity. Labour, too, has become an object—a commodity purchased by a wage. Labouring does not express one's own personality, and, again, Marx alludes to Feuerbach's analysis of religion to explain:

---

[30] Engels was instrumental in publishing the last two, in 1885 and 1894, respectively.

[31] "Estranged Labour," *The Economic and Philosophic Manuscript of 1844*, in *The Marx-Engels Reader*, p. 72.

the external character of labour for the worker appears in the fact that it is not his own, but someone else's, that it does not belong to him, that in it he belongs, not to himself, but to another. Just as in religion the spontaneous activity of the human imagination, of the human brain and the human heart, operates independently of the individual—that is, operates on him as an alien, divine or diabolical activity—in the same way the worker's activity is not his spontaneous activity. It belongs to another; it is the loss of his self.[32]

Marx uses the phrase "**species being**" to refer to the free ability of humans to create a world to manifest their full nature. This creative capacity separates humans from animals. Animals produce only from physical need, but, says Marx, "man produces even when he is free from physical need and only truly produces in freedom therefrom." The capacity to make or create is the defining feature of human nature:

It is just in the working-up of the objective world, therefore, that man first really proves himself to be a *species being*. This production is his active species life. Through and because of this production, nature appears as *his* work and his reality. The object of labour is, therefore, the *objectification of man's species life*: for he duplicates himself not only, as in consciousness, intellectually, but also actively, in reality, and therefore he contemplates himself in a world that he has created.[33]

But, in the economic system we are no longer spontaneous, free, and creating creatures; we are defined and tied to the economic system.

Lastly, alienation shows itself in the "estrangement of man from man." In the real practical world, alienation or estrangement is "manifest through the real practical relationship to other men."[34] It is other men who incarnate the alienating power over the worker:

[If] the product of his labour, his labour *objectified*, is for him an *alien*, hostile, powerful object independent of him, then his position towards it is such that someone else is master of this object, someone who is alien, hostile,

---

[32] *Ibid.*, p. 74.

[33] *Ibid.*, p. 76.

[34] *Ibid.*, p. 78.

powerful, and independent of him. If his own activity is to him an un-free activity, then he is treating it as activity performed in the service, under the dominion, the coercion and the yoke of another man.[35]

It is not only the relationship between owners and workers that shows alienation but also alienation occurs throughout since all are defined by their position in the economic system.

In all the forms of alienation—products, labour activity, species being, and other people—the individual is unable to be fully a person. The human qualities of self-expression, spontaneity, creativity, and self-determination are engulfed by the economic system. The ability and experience of being able to create for one-self and to attain a sense of mastery are critical for human freedom. Yet, as Marx's analysis of economic systems demonstrates, it is precisely this ability and experience that is destroyed. Humans experience themselves as separate from, and ob-jectified by, the economic process. Humans are separate in the sense that it is only the labouring activity that is wanted, and that activity is objectified and paid for by a wage. The full human is kept separate and objectified as a mere in-strument or cog to be fitted into the larger economic machine. As a consequence, the individual experiences the alienating sense of surrender to another and of domination by another. Marx captures the experience in the following passage:

> A *being* only considers himself independent when he stands on his own feet; and he only stands on his own feet when he owes his *existence* to him-self. A man who lives by the grace of another regards himself as a dependent being. But if I live completely by the grace of another if I owe him not only the sustenance of my life, but if he has, moreover, *created* my *life*—if he is the *source* of my life; and if it is not of my own creation, my life has nec-essarily a source of this kind outside it.[36]

It is an alienation with this psychological depth and one located in the real eco-nomic world that the revolution to communism must remove. Because it is the economic force that causes alienation, it is the working class that ultimately resolves

---

[35] *Ibid.*

[36] "Private Property and Communism," in *The Marx-Engels Reader*, p. 91. The best full-length study of the doctrine of alienation in Marx is by Bertell Ollman, *Alienation: Marx's Conception of Man in Capitalist Society* (Cambridge: Cambridge University Press, 1971).

the situation. The revolution can occur only after the full historical development of the economy. The revolution is not an act of power by a small or a large number of people; it is the inevitable culmination of historical forces. A political revolution can solidify only what has become potential in history, and, in the case of capitalism, it is the proletarian who will eventually reach the final stage in history. In a speech given in 1855, Marx makes this point:

> To revenge the misdeeds of the ruling class, there existed in the middle ages in Germany a secret tribunal, called the 'Vehmgericht'. If a red cross was seen marked on a house, people knew that its owner was doomed by the 'Vehm'. All the houses of Europe are now marked with the mysterious red cross. History is the judge—its executioner, the proletarian.[37]

There are three stages to the revolution, according to Marx. First, there is the stage of raw communism. This is the stage where vast numbers of workers are fully alienated, are driven by the same desire as the capitalists, and simply want to take what the rich few have. Marx is explicit about their desire and uses a brutal sexual analogy for their method of expropriation. Raw communism

> is really nothing but the logical expression of private property, which is this negation. General *envy* constituting itself as power is the disguise in which *avarice* re-establishes itself and satisfies itself, only in *another* way....
>
> In the approach to *woman* as the spoil and handmaid of communal lust is expressed the infinite degradation in which man exists for himself, for the secret of his approach has its *unambiguous*, decisive, *plain* and undisguised expression in the relation of *man* to *woman* and in the manner in which the *direct* and *natural* procreative relationship is conceived.[38]

The very drive—the acquisitive urge for material goods or "private property"— that created an external economic world that, in turn, alienated humanity is finally satisfied. When the bulk of humanity satisfies their acquisitive urge by taking the wealth and power of the controlling few, they not only have satisfied the drive but also have liberated all humanity from its yoke. The Hegelian phrase, "the hand that inflicts the wound, is the hand that heals," has been given a concrete, practical meaning.

---

[37] "Speech on the Anniversary of the People's Paper, 14 April 1856," in *Selected Writings*, p. 339.

[38] "Private Property and Communism," in *The Marx-Engels Reader*, pp. 82–83.

The second stage features a governmental structure, though there are little more than implications about its nature. The third stage is also only vaguely described as the "administration of things." It is in this final stage, though, that one can see clearly the fruits of the revolution. Where there is abundance, where there no longer is a government or ruling-class oppression, and where the lust for "appropriating" the wealth of the few has been satisfied, then the full and free development of all human potentialities will occur. In a commentary on the utilitarian philosophy of James Mill, Marx gives his contrasting vision:

> Supposing that we had produced in a human manner; each of us would in his production have doubly affirmed himself and his fellow men. I would have: (1) objectified in my production my individuality and its peculiarity and thus both in my activity enjoyed an individual expression of my life and also in looking at the object have had the individual pleasure of realizing that my personality was objective, visible to the senses and thus a power raised beyond all doubt. (2) In your enjoyment or use of my product I would have had the direct enjoyment of realizing that I had both satisfied a human need by my work and also objectified the human essence and therefore fashioned for another human being the object that met his need. (3) I would have been for you the mediator between you and the species and thus been acknowledged and felt by you as a completion of your own essence and a necessary part of yourself and have thus realized that I am confirmed both in your thought and in your love. (4) In my expression of my life I would have fashioned your expression of your life, and thus in my own activity have realized my own essence, my human, my communal essence.[39]

The four manifestations of alienation—products, labouring activity, species being, and other people—have all been overcome.

As to the final stage, Marx notes that communism itself is about ownership of property, only it is an ownership by one large class that eventually will include all. Still, the real goal is not to have the acquisitive urge or the drive for possessions at all. It is the drive that produces economic systems and that objectifies and alienates us; we want a world where we labour and produce as artists would—

---

[39] "On James Mill," in *Selected Writings*, pp. 121–22.

to express our own perceptions, personalities, and creative power. Then, we would be truly free. As Marx says, communism trumps (or "negates") all property getting, but we want more:

> Communism is the position as the negation of the negation, and is hence the *actual* phase necessary for the next stage of historical development in the process of human emancipation and recovery. *Communism* is the necessary pattern and the dynamic principle of the immediate future, but communism as such is not the goal of human development—the structure of human society.[40]

By explaining alienation and its solution in economic terms, Marx believes that he has achieved a better understanding than any of his philosophic forebears. He also argues that the course of history can be more clearly perceived through economic categories. In 1845 to 1846, Marx, with the help of Engels, wrote the first clear statement of his new materialistic conception of history, *The German Ideology*. Regrettably, the work was not published until 1932, but it has become a classic statement of Marx's mature philosophy and one that links his early philosophic period with the later economic analyses. Marx spends some time clarifying his break with Feuerbach and the Young Hegelians, whom he now ridicules for their "innocent and childlike fancies."[41] In the process, however, he presents historical materialism.

The first "premise," as he calls it, of this new philosophy of history is that history begins not with thought or consciousness but with practical human activity: "[Humans] themselves begin to distinguish themselves from animals as soon as they begin to produce their means of subsistence, a step which is conditioned by their physical organization. By producing their means of subsistence men are indirectly producing their actual material life."[42] A "definite mode of life" follows from whatever means of production is used to get food, clothing, and shelter. The type of production followed depends primarily upon the extent of the division of labour. For example, there is a clear division of "industrial and commercial from agricultural labour, an hence to the separation of *town* and *country* and

---

[40] "Private Property and Communism," in *The Marx-Engels Reader*, p. 93.

[41] "The German Ideology," in *Selected Writings*, p. 160.

[42] *Ibid.*

to the conflict of their interests."[43] Within agriculture and industry, there are further divisions of labour, which are made as people learn to be more efficient. The lesson Marx draws is that the "existing stage in the division of labour determines also the relations of individuals to one another."[44]

Historically, Marx sees four major forms of ownership that invariably result from changes in the divisions of labour. The first form of ownership is tribal, and people live by "hunting and fishing, by the rearing of beasts or, in the highest stage, agriculture." A definite mode of life follows, one that is little more than the simple division of labour found in a family: "The social structure is limited to an extension of the family; patriarchal family chieftains, below them the members of the tribe, finally slaves."[45] The second form of ownership "is the ancient communal and State ownership which proceeds especially from the union of several tribes into a city by agreement or by conquest, and which is still accompanied by slavery."[46] The mode of life begins to change too. In particular, a fully developed class system emerges, and the conflicts between town and country intensify. The third form of ownership is feudal or estate property. The chief change is that the antagonism is no longer between slaves and the tribal or communal ownership but is between the peasantry and the aristocracy. A distinctive feudal mode of life develops with "the differentiation of princes, nobility, clergy and peasants in the country, and masters, journeymen apprentices and soon also the rabble of casual labourers in the towns."[47] The conflicts between town and country increase as the towns gradually develop into centres of trade with their own social hierarchy. The political structure that was appropriate for this economic system, according to Marx, was a monarchy.

The fourth form of ownership is private property, which has already come into existence, but its major impact on historical developments comes after the rise of the middle class and the decline of feudalism.

---

[43] *Ibid.*, p. 161.

[44] *Ibid.*

[45] *Ibid.*, p. 162.

[46] *Ibid.*

[47] *Ibid.*, p. 163.

It is because individuals are producing in a certain way that they develop certain social relations or modes of life. The conclusion is that law Engels summarizes in his "Speech at the Graveside": material production precedes and explains all other aspects of human existence. Marx states unequivocably the primacy of human material activity:

> The production of ideas, of conceptions, of consciousness, is at first directly interwoven with the material activity and the material intercourse of men, the language of real life. Conceiving, thinking, the mental intercourse of men, appear at this stage as the direct efflux of their material behaviour. The same applies to mental production as expressed in the language of politics, laws, morality, religion, metaphysics, etc. of a people. Men are the producers of their conceptions, ideas, etc.—real, active, men, as they are conditioned by a definite development of their productive forces and of the intercourse corresponding to these, up to its furthest forms. Consciousness can never be anything else than conscious existence, and the existence of men is their actual life-process....
>
> Morality, religion, metaphysics, all the rest of ideology and their corresponding forms of consciousness, thus no longer retain the semblance of independence. They have no history, no development; but men developing their material production and their material intercourse, alter, along with this their real existence, their thinking and the products of their thinking. Life is not determined by consciousness, but consciousness by life.[48]

Marx now claims that his new philosophy is "real, positive science: the representation of the practical activity, of the practical process of development of men."[49]

The study of history cannot rely upon philosophy, and as is befitting a positive science, it must examine the actual mode of production used by a people. The mode of production is more than one factor affecting human life; it is the determining factor:

> It follows...that a certain mode of production, or industrial stage, is always combined with a certain mode of co-operation, or social stage, and this

---

[48] *Ibid.,* p. 164.

[49] *Ibid.,* p. 165.

mode of co-operation is itself a 'productive force'. Further, that the multitude of productive forces accessible to men determines the nature of society, hence, that the 'history of humanity' must always be studied and treated in relation to the history of industry and exchange.[50]

Because the mode of production is the determining factor, it must be examined to find the root of changes in history. With every change in the division of labour and in the productive force, a new element is added, changing the mode of life of the individuals. The dictates of the economic system assign individuals an "exclusive sphere of activity" and a corresponding identity: "He is a hunter, a fisherman, a shepherd, or a critical critic, and must remain so if he does not want to lose his means of livelihood."[51] Marx immediately counters this picture of the alienated individual with a Rousseauistic picture of individuals in a communist society: the whole "society regulates the general production" and one can "hunt in the morning, fish in the afternoon, rear cattle in the evening, criticize after dinner, just as I have a mind, without ever becoming hunter, fisherman, cowherd, or critic."[52] Until the advent of the communist society, individuals are trapped and the experience of alienation is inescapable:

> The social power, i.e. the multiplied productive force, which arises through the co-operation of different individuals as it is determined by the division of labour, appears to these individuals, since their co-operation is not voluntary but has come about naturally, not as their own united power, but as an alien force existing outside them, of the origin and goal of which they are ignorant, which they thus cannot control, which on the contrary passes through a peculiar series of phases and stages independent of the will and the action of man, nay even being the prime governor of these.[53]

The phases and stages of production operate "independent of the will and action" of humans. The history of productive forces, therefore, is a history of alienation, and the only solution will also have to be an outcome of history itself.

---

[50] *Ibid.*, p. 166.

[51] *Ibid.*, p. 169.

[52] *Ibid.*

[53] *Ibid.*, p. 170.

The goal is to have an economic system that does not assign roles as required by the division of labour and the mode of production. There will have to be the abolition of private property and humans will have to "get exchange, production, the mode of their mutual relations, under their own control again."[54] For this to occur, Marx states that two "practical premises" must also exist (the large figure of Hegel can be seen looming over Marx's "practical premises"). First, the economic situation must become truly intolerable, "a power against which men make a revolution." Also, the large mass of humans would have to be propertyless so that the contrast or, as he says, contradiction with wealth and culture is as sharp as possible. Second, there has to be a "universal development of productive forces" that will then create "world-historical" humanity. This would make it possible to have a "propertyless mass" in "all nations simultaneously." If communism occurred in only one isolated nation, it would not last. As Marx concludes: "Empirically, communism is only possible as the act of the dominant peoples 'all at once' and simultaneously, which presupposes the universal development of productive forces and the world intercourse bound up with communism."[55] Marx's philosophical agenda was set by Hegel; Marx just claims to have given better answers. World history is not an unfolding of Mind through the strivings of partial individual manifestations of Mind; world history is the unfolding of human productive power. In both cases, the unfolding occurs independently of the will and the consciousness of the individuals; and the culmination will occur only in history's good time.

The German Ideology contains the general framework for Marx's historical materialism. His economic studies and writings are designed to demonstrate empirically the validity of his philosophy. There are three features that are particularly distinctive to Marx's position and that need to be explored. First, Marx constantly refers to the forces of production as determining, at least in some general sense, the type of economic system and the attached modes of life. The great Darwinian-like "law of development" mentioned by Engels entails that there is some kind of causal structure; otherwise, it could hardly claim the status of a scientific law. Second, Marx emphasizes that the forces of production operate independently of the will and consciousness of the individual. Consciousness is,

---

[54] *Ibid.*

[55] *Ibid.*, p. 171.

as he says, an efflux of the economic forces. The religious beliefs, legal systems, political structures, artistic styles and so on, are the different forms of consciousness that correspond, in some unspecified fashion, to the locus of production. The nature of the relationship between the "superstructure," which is the term for all of these different forms of consciousness, and the forces of production has to be made more precise. What, in short, is the status of the superstructure? Third, because Marx's philosophy is now a "positive science," his theory of history supposedly captures empirically the true unfolding of history. In other words, the process of change in history needs to be delineated. The causal structure, the status of the superstructure, and the process of change in history have been central topics for Marxian scholarship, with defenders and detractors on each topic. Marx's precise position on the status of the superstructure has been the most difficult to discern, whereas the causal structure and the process of change were discussed at length directly by Marx.

The classic statement of Marx's historical materialism is found in the *Contribution to the Critique of Political Economy* (1859). He provides a three-layered model of his economic framework, which can be used to diagnose any system. At the base are the productive forces that determine the relations of production and, ultimately, the superstructure. By productive forces, Marx is referring to two factors: the labour power used by humans and the "means of production" utilized by the labour power. Labour power itself varies with the different ways humans attain their subsistence. For instance, the type of labour power used by a hunter and gatherer would be quite different from that used by an agricultural worker or a computer operator. The means of production (the instruments and the raw material needed) likewise vary. A hunter needs a good piece of wood for a bow and sharp rocks for arrows. The instruments of production and raw material in a manufacturing industry, obviously, would be different. The relations of production refers to who owns and who hires and fires, but they also include the social relations and classes that are formed. Finally, the forms of social consciousness (the superstructure) are the last to be determined. Marx summarizes his position as follows:

> In the social production of their life, men enter into definite relations that are indispensable and independent of their will, relations of production which correspond to a definite stage of development of their material productive forces. The sum total of these relations of production constitutes the

economic structure of society, the real foundation, on which rises a legal and political superstructure and to which correspond definite forms of social consciousness. The mode of production of material life conditions the social, political and intellectual life process in general. It is not the consciousness of men that determines their being, but, on the contrary, their social being that determines their consciousness.[56]

Figure 11–1 diagrams the three-fold causal structure. The combination of the forces of production and the relations of production Marx sometimes calls the economic foundation and, at other times, the economic structure. The relation between the productive forces and the relations of production is held to be determinative in a precise sense, and he uses the phrase "with the precision of natural science" to accentuate his claim. But, the relation of the economic foundation or the economic structure to the superstructure is considerably looser. Marx explains:

At a certain stage of their development, the material productive forces of society come in conflict with the existing relations of production, or—what is but a legal expression for the same thing—with the property relations within which they have been at work hitherto. From forms of development of the productive forces these relations turn into their fetters. Then begins an epoch of social revolution. With the change of the economic foundation the entire immense superstructure is more or less rapidly transformed. In considering such transformations a distinction should always be made between the material transformation of the economic conditions of production, which can be determined with the precision of natural science, and the legal, political, religious, aesthetic or philosophic—in short, ideological forms in which men become conscious of this conflict and fight it out.[57]

The process of change is driven by changes in the productive forces. Once an improvement of some sort takes place, this is immediately reflected in a tension or a "contradiction" with the relations of production. A simple example would be the development of agriculture in an hunter-gatherer society. Early in this society, the relations of production would have the hunter as the dominant or ruling

---

[56] "Contribution to the Critique of Political Economy," in *The Marx-Engels Reader*, p. 4.

[57] *Ibid.*, pp. 4–5.

FIGURE 11-1   MARX'S ECONOMIC FRAMEWORK

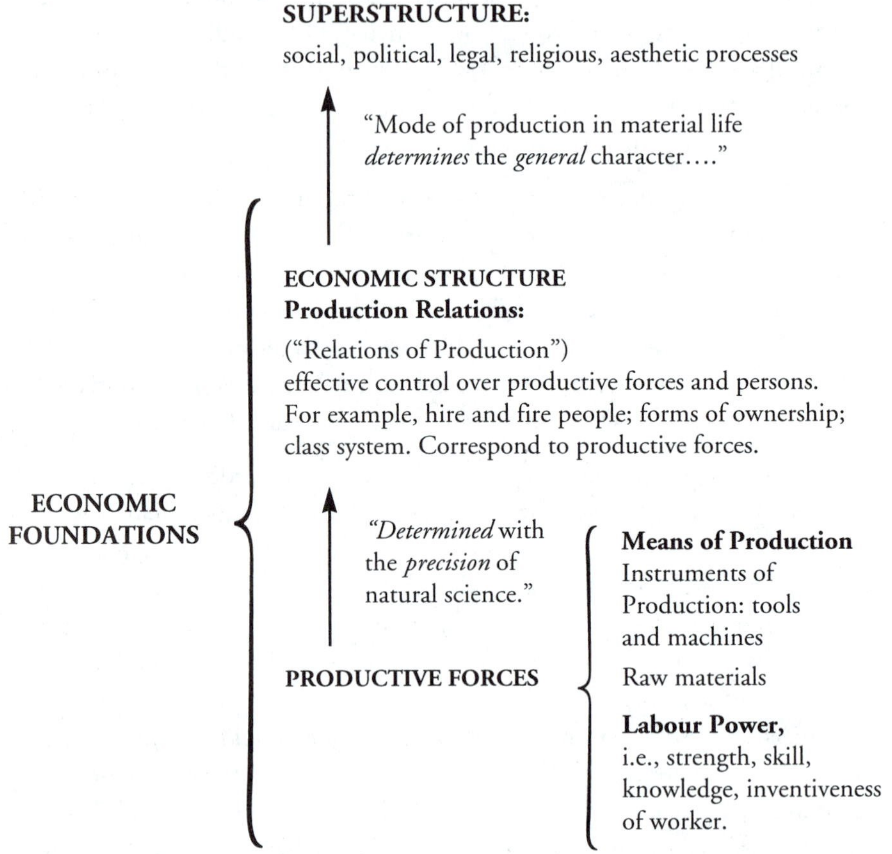

SUPERSTRUCTURE:

social, political, legal, religious, aesthetic processes

"Mode of production in material life
determines the general character...."

ECONOMIC STRUCTURE
Production Relations:

("Relations of Production")
effective control over productive forces and persons.
For example, hire and fire people; forms of ownership;
class system. Correspond to productive forces.

ECONOMIC
FOUNDATIONS

"Determined with
the *precision* of
natural science."

Means of Production
Instruments of
Production: tools
and machines

PRODUCTIVE FORCES   Raw materials

Labour Power,
i.e., strength, skill,
knowledge, inventiveness
of worker.

---

class. As agriculture develops, those who produce in this fashion would be in tension with the old ruling system; there would be a contradiction between the new productive forces and the old relations of production. The agricultural producers will eventually insist on control, and the old order vanishes. There are corresponding changes in the superstructure: a legal system with defined ownership accompanies a stable agricultural society but not a hunter-gatherer society; the gods in the hunter-gatherer society reflect the fear and awe of animals, but in the agricultural societies the gods are more apt to reflect the weather and the seasons. The same type of change occurs throughout the superstructure because consciousness has been altered by the change in the forces of production.

The changes that occur in history are not sporadic but follow a path of economic development where production and efficiency generally improve over time. Any major social and political change that does occur can only be successful and be a true revolution if it follows from the real change in the economic foundation. There have been communist revolutions for centuries, but, says Marx, they are always premature and fail. The path of history is like boiling water: boiling requires going through all of the degrees to reach 212 Fahrenheit or 100 centigrade; one cannot decide to skip 10 degrees and jump ahead. Marx argues this point and also presents the economic system of capitalism as the last stage:

> No social order ever perishes before all the productive forces for which there is room in it have developed; and new, higher relations of production never appear before the material conditions of their existence have matured in the womb of the old society itself. Therefore mankind always sets itself only such tasks as it can solve; since, looking at the matter more closely, it will always be found that the task itself arises only when the material conditions for its solution already exist or are at least in the process of formation. In broad outlines Asiatic, ancient, feudal, and modern bourgeois modes of production can be designated as progressive epochs in the economic formation of society. The bourgeois relations of productions are the last antagonistic form of the social process of production—antagonistic not in the sense of individual antagonism, but of one arising from the social conditions of life of the individuals, at the same time the productive forces developing in the womb of bourgeois society create the material conditions for the solution of that antagonism. This social formation brings, therefore, the prehistory of human society to a close.[58]

In one long paragraph, Marx has succinctly stated his position. The major difficulty with the statement is that the dynamics of change, of which Marx is acutely aware, are not as clear as they could be. It is true that any period of time can be directed and placed into the three-layered model. In that sense, his statement illuminates the real structure of any society, from the forces of production, to the relations of production, to the superstructure. Figure 11–2, "Marx's Economic Interpretation of History," illustrates the true unfolding of history as

---

[58] *Ibid.*, p. 5.

FIGURE 11-2 MARX'S ECONOMIC INTERPRETATION OF HISTORY

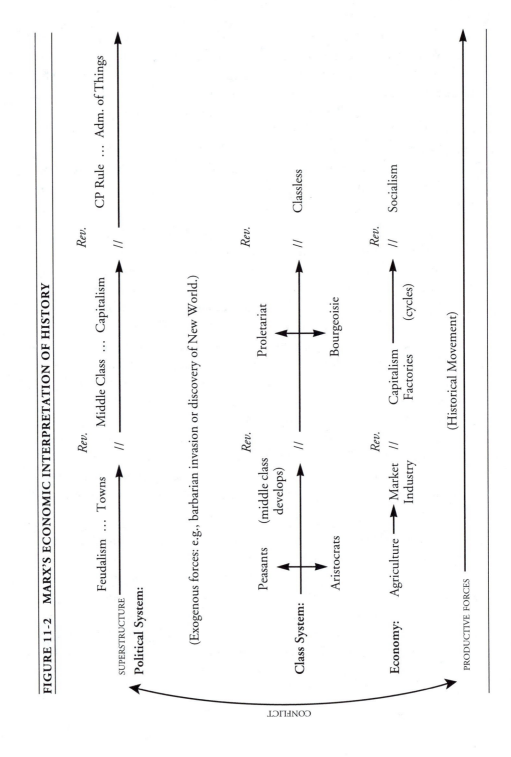

perceived by historical materialism. As the productive forces inevitably evolve, the relations of production, the class system, the political system, and the entire superstructure also change. At the beginning of any period, all of these elements are synchronized, but, as change occurs in the productive forces, these various elements cease to be synchronized and come into tension or contradiction. If it is a major change, a revolution will eventually occur. This creates a new synchronization and the process begins again. The final change is the move from the capitalist system to communism.

The transition from a feudal society to a bourgeois society illustrates the dynamic process of change portrayed in Figure 11–2. Initially, the feudal estates strove to be self-sufficient in order to provide protection and stability. In time, it was clear that there were advantages to trade. The effectiveness of protection and stability enabled more goods to be produced. Small villages became centres for trade and for services such as the blacksmith for iron work and the mill for the grinding of grain. Gradually, a new force of production grew in these middling groups. Yet, the old relations of production and superstructure still applied. There was the feudal system itself with its legal privileges for a certain class; the government was run according to the aristocracy's interests; and the superstructure—religion and arts for example—accentuated the "ordained" nature of the system. From the perspective of the new middle class and their economic interests, the whole system was oppressive and backwards. Inevitably, middle-class revolutions occurred throughout Europe. A new legal system is created that abolishes the privileges of the aristocracy. All types of professions and businesses are now opened to everyone. The government changes to one that reflects the power of the middle class and protects its rights. The class system ceases to be as important or as rigid. It even becomes common for literature to refer to the corrupt, lazy, and effete aristocracy; these adjectives, needless to say, do not characterize the literature at the height of feudalism. Religion now stresses individual responsibility and choice, and an ethic that propels the middle class and the proletariat to work. The honour ethic of the aristocracy comes to be viewed as quaint and is replaced by an ethic of individual work and responsibility. Thus, the superstructure or forms of consciousness change as did the forces of production and the relations of production. The whole, three-layered framework, as in Figure 11–1, is synchronized again. As we will see after examining Marx's economic thought, the bourgeois world has built into its very nature its own demise. The unfolding of history through the evolution of productive forces continues.

For a fair assessment of Marx's mature philosophy of history, the new positive science, it is necessary to combine both Figure 11–1 and Figure 11–2 in order to accredit the complexity Marx actually saw in history. There are odd changes that occur, such as the exogenous factors noted in Figure 11–2. The discovery of gold in the New World made Spain a power of note, quite independent of its real economic foundation. Figure 11–2 also illustrates that a dialectical conflict will occur between the superstructure and the productive forces. It is not simply the one-directional effect that the economic foundation has on the superstructure. The major difficulty scholars have always had in deciphering Marx's various statements about the three elements in his model is to arrive at a coherent and precise interpretation of their interrelationship.

There are three possible models of interpretations for explaining this interrelationship. First is the base-superstructure model, which seems to be the plain meaning of the classic statement found in the *Contribution to the Critique of Political Economy*. There is no doubt that Marxisms as a political ideology traded on this model. It enabled Marxists to debunk their opponents by treating them as a mere efflux of some economic causes.[59] But, Marx and Engels would also, from time to time, note the effect that the superstructure could have on the foundation. After all, the *Communist Manifesto* and Marx's political activity make no sense if conscious and human activity are wholly determined by the economic foundation. Marx and Engels worked assiduously to change the consciousness and political activity of their fellows.

A second, less simple-minded model is the dialectical version of the base-superstructure relationship. There are passages in Marx's and Engel's writings that speak in general of the dominance of the economic foundation, but, at the same time, they noticeably refrain from a single-causation explanation. Marx was always quick to attack any hint of quietism or of waiting until history took its course. He would call for political action that would affect changes.[60] In the *Grundrisse* (1857–1858) Marx purposely softens the tone of determinism and uses the phrase "in the last analysis."[61] Engels, in letters written after Marx's death, also insists that

---

[59] Eugene Kamenka, *Marxism and Ethics* (New York: St. Martin's Press, 1969).

[60] "Circular Letter to Bebel, Liebknecht, Brock, and Others," in *The Marx-Engels Reader*, p. 552.

[61] Karl Marx, *Grundrisse*, trans. Martin Nicolaus (New York: Vintage, 1973), p. 495.

neither Marx nor he himself had a single-causation theory. They meant only that the economic foundation was the "*ultimately* determining element in history."[62]

A third mode for interpreting Marx is that of an organic totality. This model captures Marx's insistence on the interlocking features of the entire economic and social order, and on the dynamic movement of the system as a whole. There is a well-known instance in Marx's *Grundrisse* where he does use the organic metaphor:

> For example if the market, i.e. the sphere of exchange, expands, then production grows in quantity and the divisions between its different branches become deeper. A change in distribution changes production, e.g. concentration of capital, different distribution of the population between town and country, etc. Finally, the needs of consumption determine production. Mutual interaction takes place between the different movements. This the case with every organic whole.[63]

Little can be done to resolve the precise meaning of Marx's various utterances.[64] What does seem clear is that he did not waver from the view that Hegel was ultimately correct about the dialectic movement toward completion in history. Hegel just mistook what was the operating force. It was not Mind but human productive power. He never changed in referring to these forces as real and actual; conversely, he never gave such a status to the realm of the superstructure but characterized it by such words as "efflux," "echo," and "phantasmagoria." The progress of the forces of production are just as necessary and inevitable in their unfolding as the equivalent Mind or Reason category was in Hegel. Humans can be useful tools for advancing the process of history and, thus, be conscious of their role. This lucky position is only for those who have looked back over history with Marx's philosophic

---

[62] "Letter to Joseph Block (1890)," in *The Marx-Engels Reader*, p. 767.

[63] *Grundrisse*, pp. 99–100.

[64] The best survey of the different interpretations is by Melvin Rader, *Marx's Interpretation of History* (New York: Oxford University Press, 1979). For a defence of Marx's view of history, see G. A. Cohen, *Karl Marx's Theory of History: A Defense* (Princeton: Princeton University Press, 1978). He modifies his defence considerably in his later, *History, Labour, and Freedom: Themes from Marx* (Oxford: Clarendon Press, 1988). John McMurtry writes a defence, *The Structure of Marx's World-View* (Princeton: Princeton University Press, 1978), pp. 157–239. Jon Elster defends Marx but concludes that Marx was ultimately wrong about the culmination of history in the final revolution: *Making Sense of Marx* (Cambridge: Cambridge University Press, 1985), pp. 513–31.

glasses and have discerned the evolution. For all others, and those prior to Hegel and Marx, history would operate "independent of [their] will and consciousness."

The *Communist Manifesto of 1848* was a direct attempt to have an effect on history. It has come to be the single most influential document for the history of socialism and communism. The ten specific policies advocated by Marx now seem relatively tame. They range from a graduated income tax, a central bank, abolition of the right of inheritance, to free public education.[65] The *Communist Manifesto* also has several themes that capitalized on a century or more of political and social thought. These themes not only enhanced the appeal of the *Manifesto* but they became associated in the public mind with Marxian communism.

Marx begins with the bold announcement that the "history of all hitherto existing society is the history of class struggles."[66] This is a position at odds with his philosophical position, because the class system itself is only a reflection of the productive forces. Still, there is a powerful, political rhetoric in naming the opponents and associating the conflict with the forces of history at the same time. Also, Marx makes the working class the moral centre of the entire social system by referring to the misery of their lives in the bourgeois society and by referring to the exploitation by the bourgeoisie of the proletariat. The idea that the situation of the labouring class would deteriorate catastrophically over time and the idea that the coming of socialism was a result of the inexorable law of capitalism were also central to the appeal of the *Manifesto*. The proletariat and the communists were the force of the future. The *Manifesto* several times alludes to the creative role of violence in inaugurating the new age. All in all, these themes were a summation of other socialist thinkers, primarily French, and not original with Marx, but he attached them to the force of history and delivered them with a powerful moral rhetoric that condemned opponents and confidently called for unity with all other workers.

ECONOMICS

Engels mentioned during the "Graveside Speech" that Marx had discovered a second great law, the theory of surplus value, and this theory was the clue to explaining the economic developments of the capitalist epoch. Prior to the mid 1840s, Marx had read primarily German philosophy and the French socialist

---

[65] *The Communist Manifesto of 1848*, in *The Marx-Engels Reader*, p. 490.

[66] *Ibid.*, p. 473.

thinkers. He was to contemptuously dismiss the latter as Utopian socialists while he was a scientific socialist, but the very phrase "scientific socialism" he got from Proudhon.[67] Engels wrote in 1880 that there were three great Utopian writers, Henri de Saint-Simon, Charles Fourier, and Robert Owen.[68] If Engels had been more generous, he would have in fairness also cited Proudhon. After German philosophy, these writers became the second major influence on Marx's thought. They introduced several themes Marx was to use: there was an historical sequence of stages, concluding in socialism; a society needed central planning and administration; social harmony would be regained once the economy was properly managed; humans can be transformed in a new economic order, and co-operation will replace competition, and equality will replace inequality. Such themes are also in Marx, but his genius was to ground them on his economic theory and to give them a far greater plausibility—or scientific stature, in the eyes of Marx's followers—than they had before. In addition to German philosophy and the Utopian thinkers, there was a third influence on Marx's thought: the classical economists Adam Smith (1723-1790) and David Ricardo (1772-1823). Marx's own economic theory begins with them.

The labour theory of value has a long history before Marx, but Marx takes this original Lockean idea as it was expanded by the later classical economists and develops from it his own economic theory, which he believes demonstrates the inescapable contradictions in the capitalist system. The value of a commodity, it is held, depends upon the quantity of labour, understood to be the socially necessary labour time required to produce the commodity. The phrase "socially necessary" reflects the point that it is the average amount of time and skill in normal circumstances. Marx further distinguishes between the use value and exchange value: use value means that it satisfies some human want; exchange value refers to what one can get in exchange, which is to say, in money.

---

[67] Marx's insistence upon being a scientific socialist is best illustrated in *The Gotha Program*. This was a platform put together by various union leaders and socialist thinkers. It was full of talk about fair distributions, equality, and rights. Marx vehemently attacks these as "obsolete verbal rubbish," and as mere slogans derived from the bourgeoisie. Such slogans are only the efflux of a dying economic system. A proper analysis of the economic system requires his historical materialism; the slogans are simply rhetorical band-aids and not drawn from science. "Any distribution whatever of the means of consumption is only a consequence of the distribution of the conditions of production themselves." He does quote the phrase "from each according to his ability, to each according to his needs." This phrase is not repeated in any of his major works and comes from the Bible: Acts 4: 35.

[68] "Socialism: Utopian and Scientific," in *The Marx-Engels Reader*, p. 685.

The theory of surplus value, to take a simple example, explains the behaviour of the market, of workers, and of owners in the capitalist system. Assume that a commodity takes 12 hours of labour to produce and that 4 hours of the labour value of the product is required to pay the wages of the workers, for the exchange value of the labour, the worker, in effect, receives the equivalent of 4 hours worth of the total 12 hours used to produce the commodity. The labour power of the worker for the extra 8 hours now is surplus value for the owner. In other words, the difference between the value of what the worker actually produces and the value of the wage actually paid for the labourer—the exchange value—is surplus value.

The process is one in which the labour power of the worker comes under the control of the capitalist. The latter pays only for the exchange value of the worker (a subsistence wage), but gets the use value of the worker's labour power. Thus, there is the real alienation of being controlled by an outside alien force, as was described philosophically in the *Economic and Philosophic Manuscripts of 1844*. Marx now repeats this point as expressed through his economic analysis:

> The worker receives means of subsistence in exchange for his labour power, but the capitalist receives in exchange for his means of subsistence labour, the productive activity of the worker, the creative power whereby the worker not only replaces what he consumes but *gives to the accumulated labour a greater value than it previously possessed*. The worker receives a part of the available means of subsistence from the capitalist. For what purpose do these means of subsistence serve them? For immediate consumption. As soon, however, as I consume the means of subsistence, they are irretrievably lost to me unless I use the time during which I am kept alive by them in order to produce new means of subsistence, in order during consumption to create by my labour new values in place of the values which perish in being consumed. But it is just this noble reproductive power that the worker surrenders to the capitalist in exchange for means of subsistence received. He has, therefore, lost it for himself.[69]

The system is driven by the need of the capitalists to increase surplus value because only in that way is there sufficient capital for profits and investments. A successful capitalist competes through a better product and lower prices. In both cases, capital is required, and it can come only from surplus value. There are three

---

[69] "Wage, Labour and Capital (1849)," in *The Marx-Engels Reader*, p. 209.

main methods for sustaining and increasing surplus value: lower wages and longer hours, better technology and equipment, and larger scale production. There is a biological limit on the number of hours one can require someone to work, and there is a similar type of limit on the subsistent wage or what Marx calls the "cost of existence and reproduction of the worker."[70] The best the worker can hope for is a rapidly growing economy where there is more need for workers and where there is also more need for surplus value to enhance the capacity to compete. The positions of the worker and the capitalist are inseparably entangled. By increasing the surplus value for the capitalist, the workers lose even more of their labour power, and the social gap between the wealth of the few and the poverty of the many relatively increases. Even in the most favourable economic situation for the capitalist and the workers—growth— the real situation gets worse:

> The indispensable condition for a tolerable situation of the worker is, *therefore, the fastest possible growth of productive capital.*
>
> But what is the growth of productive capital? Growth of the power of accumulated labour over living labour. Growth of the domination of the bourgeoisie over the working class....
>
> Even the *most favourable situation* for the working class, the *most rapid possible growth of capital,* however much it may improve the material existence of the worker, does not remove the antagonism between his interests and the interests of the bourgeoisie, the interests of the capitalists. *Profit and wages* remain as before in *inverse proportion.*
>
> If capital is growing rapidly, wages may rise; the profit of capital rises incomparably more rapidly. The material position of the worker has improved, but at the costs of his social position. The social gulf that divides him from the capitalist has widened.[71]

The nature of the system is such that neither the capitalist nor the workers have control over it. The system is the most efficient of all economic systems, and it will make abundance possible. But, in the process it unfolds with such a dynamic force that the mass of humanity is dehumanized. Figure 11–3 illustrates the key features of the competitive business cycle. At the beginning of any expansion,

---

[70] *Ibid.*, p. 206.

[71] *Ibid.*, pp. 210–11.

FIGURE 11–3   MARX: BUSINESS CYCLE: COMPETITION

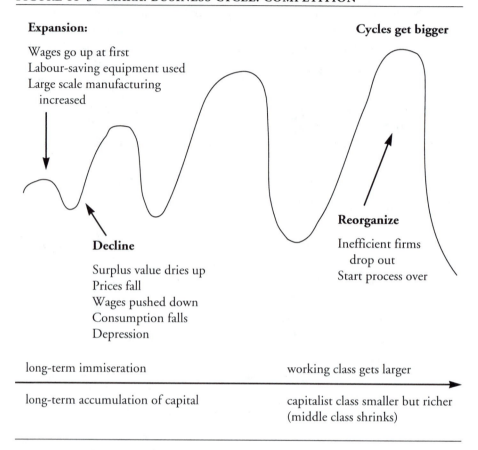

Expansion:

Wages go up at first
Labour-saving equipment used
Large scale manufacturing
   increased

Cycles get bigger

Decline

Surplus value dries up
Prices fall
Wages pushed down
Consumption falls
Depression

Reorganize

Inefficient firms
   drop out
Start process over

long-term immiseration   working class gets larger

long-term accumulation of capital   capitalist class smaller but richer
                                          (middle class shrinks)

there is a bump in wages, and productivity increases with new methods and technology. But, competition lowers wages, consumption, prices and profits; the result is decline. After a period of reorganization, the inefficient firms are consolidated, and the process begins again. This two-fold dynamic is inescapable in the capitalist system. The long-term trends are for the position of the worker to gradually get worse. There will be, as he says, an immiseration of their condition. Most of the middle class will fall into the proletariat, and only a few wealthy will survive. He predicts the inevitable forming of an "industrial reserve army" of the unemployed. The long-term consequence for the capitalist class will be the gradual creation of oligopolies in industry after industry. For example, in North

America the auto industry evolved from 50 manufacturers at the beginning of the century into 3. Also, the accumulation of capital will be centred in fewer hands. Marx describes in the first volume of *Capital* the final scene and history's judgment:

> Along with the constantly diminishing number of the magnates of capital, who usurp and monopolise all advantages of this process of transformation, grows the mass of misery, oppression, slavery, degradation, exploitation; but with this too grows the revolt of the working-class, a class always increasing in number, and disciplined, united, organised by the very mechanism of the process of capitalist production itself. The monopoly of capital becomes a fetter upon the mode of production, which has sprung up and flourished along with, and under it. Centralisation of the means of production and socialisation of labour at last reach a point where they become incompatible with their capitalist integument. This integument is burst asunder. The knell of capitalist private property sounds. The expropriators are expropriated.
>
> The capitalist mode of appropriation, the result of the capitalist mode of production, produces capitalist private property. This is the first negation of individual private property, as founded on the labour of the proprietor. But capitalist production begets, with the inexorability of a law of Nature, its own negation. It is the negation of negation.[72]

Real human history can now begin. We will no longer make a fetish out of commodities by falsely and neurotically objectifying their importance to us, just as we have learned from Feuerbach not to make a fetish of, and to objectify, the God-illusion. We will no longer be driven by the acquisitive urge for material things, by which we have identified and judged ourselves. Now, we will produce for the joy of it and to serve our wants. In economic language, products will have only a use value, rather than an exchange value.

CONCLUSIONS

An assessment of Marx's philosophy has become more daunting as the century closes. There are many who profess to be Marxists, but they want to make several fundamental revisions in past interpretations, if not to Marx directly. There are two examples: first, there has long been a quarrel whether Marx can be

---

[72] *Capital*, in *The Marx-Engels Reader*, p. 438.

viewed as a revolutionist or as an evolutionist on the topic of changing the capitalist system. His major philosophic writings clearly support the revolutionary
interpretation, but there are some who argue that in later years Marx became
more flexible and did allow for evolution where the political system was open to
the proletariat's influence. In an oft-quoted speech, in Amsterdam (1872) Marx
mentioned America, England, and Holland as places "where the workers can
attain their goals by peaceful means."[73] The problem is that this "amendment"
to Marx's thought was never reconciled to his other writings. It would seem impossible to reconcile the evolutionary interpretation with Marx's views on the status of the superstructure or with his peculiar Hegelian framework, which was
always praised and never recanted.[74]

The second example is that there are many modern scholars who wish to save
various "insights" of Marx by treating his work as heuristic: "It is a work of art, of
philosophical reflection and of social polemic, all in one, and it has the merits
and the defects of all three of these forms of writing. It is a painting of capitalism,
not a photograph."[75] There is no doubt that Marx would be livid at such an assessment; yet, that may be the best that can be done.

Defence of his economic predictions requires considerable effort. Some obvious
failed predictions are: the proletariat revolutions have not occurred in the most advanced countries; polarization of classes has not taken place; immiseration of the
workers has not happened; capitalism has not collapsed because of the various
internal contradictions. The prediction that business cycles would become increasingly extreme was the pride of the communist party during the 1930s, but
it, too, has fallen on hard times. The prediction about oligopolies does seem true,
but it is a prediction that does not require the economic theory of *Capital*. More
generally, it is hard to imagine a contemporary social scientist who would not
be sensitive to the economic factor when examining social and political behaviour.
The class struggle motif has also entered political consciousness as a feature of
political life. Neither of these is wholly the consequence of Marx's writings, but
it would be ridiculous to pretend that his writings were not a major influence.

---

[73] "The Possibility of Non-Violent Revolution," in *The Marx-Engels Reader*, p. 523.

[74] Michael Evans provides a good survey of the issues, *Karl Marx* (London: Allan & Unwin,
1975), pp. 136–63. George Lichtheim argues for the evolutionary interpretation, *Marxism: An
Historical and Critical Study* (New York: Praeger, 1965), pp. 122–29.

[75] Peter Singer, *Karl Marx* (Oxford: Oxford University Press, 1980), p. 58.

There are two areas where criticisms have been strongest. Politically, Marx did claim that governments are the reflection of a class system and that with the destruction of the class system governments would turn into an administration of things. This promise, most political philosophers would argue, is ill-founded. Governments are born from the need for a society to make, justify, and enforce decisions. Unless one works from the assumption that there can be a self-regulating order—an assumption that would need to be proved—the necessity of government is a necessity of the human condition, not of a class system. Thus, even if one did abolish a class system, the need for a government would remain. A more serious charge is that his philosophical framework makes political life impossible. Marx has claimed to know with scientific certainty the course of human history, and he has coupled this knowledge with a moral condemnation, in the name of history, of one group. As an illustration, he wrote the following in late 1843:

> This state of affairs is *beneath the level of history, beneath all criticism*; nevertheless it remains an object of criticism just as the criminal who is beneath humanity remains an object of the *executioner*. In its struggle against this state of affairs criticism is not a passion of the head, but the head of passion. It is not a lancet but a weapon. Its object is an *enemy* which it aims not to refute but to *destroy*. For the spirit of this state of affairs has already been refuted. It is not, in itself, an object worthy of our thought; it is an *existence* as contemptible as it is despised. Criticism itself has no need of any further elucidation of this object, for it has already understood it. Criticism is no longer an end in itself, but simply a means; *indignation* is its essential mode of feeling, and *denunciation* its principal task.[76]

Even allowing for the fact that this was written in exile, there is no framework here for discourse. Some 30 years later, in 1874, the same attitude can be seen in the marginal notes Marx made to a work by the Russian revolutionary, Michael Bakunin. The latter ruminates on the danger of having only the radical, "privileged minority" rule the majority. He is prescient. Marx is contemptuous, and he

---

[76] "Contribution to the Critique of Hegel's Philosophy of Right: Introduction," in *The Marx-Engels Reader*, pp. 55–56.

responds that the "so-called will of the people disappears in order to make way for the real will of the cooperative."[77] Bakunin's fears were realized in the Soviet Union; Marx was wrong. John Stuart Mill provides an edifying contrast. He states that in a discussion one should have the "calmness to see and honesty to state what his opponents and their opinion really are, exaggerating nothing to their discredit, keeping nothing back which tells, or can be supposed to tell, in their favour. This is the real morality of public discussion."[78] There is no such political morality in Marx. One might add that both Locke and Aristotle faced greater difficulties, personally and politically, than Marx, and neither one conceived of political discourse or political activity as did Marx.

The second area of criticism is also one where Marx often receives high praise: alienation and freedom. Defenders note that his analyses of how the economic system alienates and deprives humans of freedom are a lasting contribution to political philosophy. Critics believe that he misunderstood the nature of both alienation and freedom. Alienation was the result of being unable to realize one's full, productive power as a person. Instead of making a world that reflects our own personality, we have made an economic world that has captured us. The solution is the full realization or satisfaction of the very drive that enslaved us. Raw communism requires the expression of powers Marx identifies with rape and lust, and once these forces are satisfied (the negation of the negation) freedom begins. This is psychologically unpersuasive: the alienating drive will be destroyed by envy, greed, hate, and lust, but these are themselves debilitating and alienating passions.[79] Freedom is described by Marx as a state without a sense of subjection and one with a sense of control and mastery. It is instructive to compare Mill or Aristotle or Augustine with Marx. When Marx stated that it was servility that he hated most, he was being quite consistent. Servility is a vice, but it could only be the worst condition if the opposite would be the best, a sense of mastery. For Augustine or Mill or Aristotle, freedom would be tied to a purpose that enabled humans to flourish and to live well.

---

[77] Singer, *Karl Marx*, p. 76.

[78] "On Liberty," in Collini, *John Stuart Mill: On Liberty*, p. 55. Graeme Duncan has written an excellent study: *Marx and Mill: Two Views of Social Conflict and Social Harmony* (Cambridge: Cambridge University Press, 1973).

[79] This argument is pursued by Tucker, *Philosophy and Myth in Karl Marx*.

SUGGESTIONS FOR FURTHER READING

Berlin and McLellan (1973) provide the best biographies. Tucker (1969 and 1972) and Avineri are the best for the connection between the early works and the later works, but Ollman and McLellan on the Young Hegelians are also worthwhile. Cohen (1980), Elster, McMurtry, and Rader are very good sophisticated defences that are not apologetic. Singer (1983), Freedman, and Evans are good short works. Bottomore, Roemer, Carver (1991), and Cohen, Nagel and Scanlon are four useful collections of articles. Kolakowski's three volumes are encyclopedic in their coverage.

Works

Bottomore, T. B., trans. and ed. *Karl Marx: Early Writings*. New York: McGraw-Hill, 1963.

Elster, Jon. *Karl Marx: A Reader*. Cambridge: Cambridge University Press, 1986.

Marx, Karl. *Collected Works*. New York: International Publishers, 1975–.

———. *Grundrisse*. Translated by Martin Nicolaus. New York: Vintage, 1973.

McLellan, David, ed. *Karl Marx: Selected Writings*. Oxford: Oxford University Press, 1977.

———. *Karl Marx: Early Texts*. Oxford: Oxford University Press, 1971.

Tucker, Robert C., ed. *The Marx-Engels Reader*. New York: W. W. Norton, 1972.

Commentaries

Althusser, Louis. *For Marx*. Translated by Ben Brewster. New York: Random House, 1970.

Avineri, Shlomo. *The Social and Political Thought of Karl Marx*. New York: Cambridge University Press, 1968.

Berlin, Isaiah. *Karl Marx: His Life and Environment*. 4th ed. Oxford: Oxford University Press, 1978.

Bober, M. M. *Karl Marx's Interpretation of History*. 2nd ed. New York: Norton, 1948.

Bottomore, Tom. *Modern Interpretation of Marx*. Oxford: Blackwell, 1981.

Carver, Terrell, ed. *The Cambridge Companion to Marx*. Cambridge: Cambridge University Press, 1991.

———. *Marx and Engels: The Intellectual Relationship.* Bloomington: Indiana University Press, 1983.

Cohen, G. A. *History, Labour, and Freedom: Themes From Marx.* Oxford: Clarendon Press, 1988.

———. *Karl Marx's Theory of History: A Defense.* Princeton: Princeton University Press, 1978.

Cohen, Marshall, Thomas Nagel, and Thomas Scanlon, eds. *Marx, Justice and History.* Princeton: Princeton University Press, 1980.

Duncan, Graeme. *Marx and Mill: Two Views of Social Conflict and Social Harmony.* Cambridge: Cambridge University Press, 1973.

Dupré, Louis. *The Philosophical Foundations of Marxism.* New York: Harcourt, 1966.

Elster, Jon. *Making Sense of Marx.* Cambridge: Cambridge University Press, 1985.

Evans, Michael. *Karl Marx.* London: Allen & Unwin, 1975.

Freedman, Robert. *The Marxist System: Economic, Political, and Social Perspectives.* Chatham: Chatham House, 1990.

Fromm, Erich. *Marx's Concept of Man.* New York: Ungar, 1961.

Giddens, Anthony. *Capitalism and Modern Social Theory: An Analysis of the Writings of Marx, Durkheim, and Max Weber.* Cambridge: Cambridge University Press, 1971.

Gilbert, Alan. *Marx's Politics: Communists and Citizens.* Boulder: Lynne Rienner, 1981.

Gould, Carol C. *Marx's Social Ontology: Individuality and Community in Marx's Theory of Social Reality.* Cambridge: MIT Press, 1980.

Heilbroner, Robert. *Marxism: For and Against.* New York: Norton, 1980.

Hook, Sidney. *From Hegel to Marx: Studies in the Intellectual Development of Karl Marx.* Ann Arbor: University of Michigan Press, 1962.

Kamenka, Eugene. *Marxism and Ethics.* New York: St. Martin's Press, 1969.

Kolakowski, Leszek. *Main Currents of Marxism: Its Rise, Growth, and Dissolution.* 3 Vols. Translated by P. S. Falla. Oxford: Clarendon Press, 1978.

Lichtheim, George. *Marxism: An Historical and Critical Study.* New York: Praeger, 1965.

Lobkowicz, Nicholas, ed. *Marx and the Western World.* Notre Dame: University of Notre Dame Press, 1967.

MacIntyre, Alasdair. *Marxism and Christianity.* Revised edition. New York: Shocken Books, 1968.

Mandel, Ernest. *Marxist Economic Theory.* 2 Vols. Translated by Brian Pearce. New York: Monthly Review Press, 1970.

Mazlish, Bruce. *The Meaning of Karl Marx.* Oxford: Oxford University Press, 1987.

McLellan, David. *Karl Marx: His Life and Thought.* New York: Harper & Row, 1973.

———. *Marx before Marxism.* New York: Harper & Row, 1970.

———. *The Young Hegelians and Karl Marx.* London: Macmillan, 1969.

McMurtry, John. *The Structure of Marx's World-View.* Princeton: Princeton University Press, 1978.

Meszaros, Istvan. *Marx's Theory of Alienation.* New York: Harper & Row, 1972.

Meyer, Alfred. *Marxism: The Unity of Theory and Practice.* Cambridge: Harvard University Press, 1954.

Miliband, Ralph. *Marxism and Politics.* Oxford: Oxford University Press, 1977.

Ollman, Bertell. *Alienation: Marx's Conception of Man in Capitalist Society.* Cambridge: Cambridge University Press, 1971.

Padover, Saul K. *The Man Marx.* New York: McGraw-Hill, 1978.

Rader, Melvin. *Marx's Interpretation of History.* New York: Oxford University Press, 1979.

Roemer, John., ed. *Analytical Marxism.* Cambridge: Cambridge University Press, 1986.

Singer, Peter. *Karl Marx.* Oxford: Oxford University Press, 1980.

Sowell, Thomas. *Marxism, Philosophy and Economics.* London: Allen and Unwin, 1985.

Tucker, Robert C. *The Marxian Revolutionary Idea.* New York: Norton, 1969.

———. *Philosophy and Myth in Karl Marx.* 2nd ed. Cambridge: Cambridge University Press, 1972.

Zeitlin, Irving M. *Marxism: A Re-Examination.* Princeton: Van Nostrand, 1967.

Intellectual Background

Avineri, Shlomo. *Hegel's Theory of the Modern State.* Cambridge: Cambridge University Press, 1972.

Cole, G. D. H. *The Life of Robert Owen.* London: Macmillan, 1930.

Findlay, John N. *Hegel: A Reexamination.* London: George Allen, 1958.

Gray, Alexander. *The Socialist Tradition: Moses to Lenin.* New York: Longmans, Green & Co., 1946.

Hook, Sidney. *From Hegel to Marx.* New York: Humanities Press, 1950.

Kaufmann, Walter, ed. *Hegel's Political Philosophy.* New York: Atherton, 1970.

Kelly, George A. *Idealism, Politics and History: Sources of Hegelian Thought.* Cambridge: Cambridge University Press, 1969.

Lichtheim, George. *The Origins of Socialism.* New York: Praeger, 1969.

Loewith, Karl. *From Hegel to Nietzsche.* New York: Holt, Rinehart and Winston, 1964.

MacIntyre, Alasdair, ed. *Hegel: A Collection of Critical Essays.* Notre Dame: University of Notre Dame Press, 1976.

Manuel, Frank. *The Prophets of Paris.* New York: Harper & Row, 1965.

Marcuse, Herbert. *Reason and Revolution.* London: Routledge & Kegan Paul, 1974.

Morton, A. L. *The Life and Ideas of Robert Owen.* New York: International Publishing, 1969.

Pelczynski, Z., ed. *The State and Civil Society: Studies in Hegel's Political Philosophy.* Cambridge: Cambridge University Press, 1984.

Plant, Raymond. *Hegel.* New York: Basil Blackwell, 1984.

Riedel, Manfred. *Between Tradition and Revolution: The Hegelian Transformation of Political Philosophy.* Cambridge: Cambridge University Press, 1984.

Singer, Peter. *Hegel.* Oxford: Oxford University Press, 1983.

Taylor, Charles. *Hegel.* Cambridge: Cambridge University Press, 1975.

———. *Hegel and Modern Society.* Cambridge: Cambridge University Press, 1979.

THE END OF HISTORY AND FRIEDRICH NIETZSCHE

Writing a conclusion to the history of political philosophy is as impossible as it would be to put a conclusion to political history itself, for our political-social existence remains an historical one in which decisions continuously have to be made, enforced, and justified. Furthermore, any absolute claim to know what the end of history would be is logically impossible because one would have to be both at the end of history and external to it before one could make such a claim. Finally, history and the history of political thought tell us that there could no more be a conclusion to reflections upon politics than there could be conclusions to reflections upon those two other modes of human relationship, love and friendship; for politics, love, and friendship are indispensable and constitutive activities of human life and, as such, could not conclude in some sort of static end-state that at the same time allowed for the continuation of human life.

MEANING IN HISTORY

It seems that human history is a story without a conclusion, and it is the course and meaning of this endless story that have occupied political philosophers. Individuals clearly have historical existences in that we are all involved in a journey from birth to death. Moreover, we strive to find meaning in our individual historical existences, and humans truly unable to perceive any purpose or meaning to their historical existence become unhappy, dysfunctional, and, indeed, mentally ill. Few would dispute that individuals need some sense of purpose or goal to

provide meaning to their historical existence. It is also empirically the case that societies and civilizations do not define themselves as simply efficient organizations
for providing food, clothing, and shelter. They all claim to represent some meaning and purpose other than that of providing for the necessities of mere physical
survival. History is full of these representations, noble and ignoble: the Aryan
race, the proletariat, various gods, humanity, the "last great hope of mankind," and
many more.[1] Does it follow that humanity as a whole also needs some purpose or
goal to provide meaning to its historical existence? What would such a purpose be
like? Can it be represented by political organizations or a civilization? These questions have led philosophers to quite different conceptions of history.

A humbling, cyclical view of history was common in Greek and Roman cultures. Augustine had countered in the fourth century A.D. with a bifurcated theory of history: empirical, political history was held to have no detectible meaning
or goal, but providential history revealed a spiritual meaning and goal for humanity independent of the rise and fall of empires and civilizations. Over the
centuries there were challenges to Augustine's sharp distinction between meaningless
secular history and meaningful providential history. Certainly, by the nineteenth
century the dominant view was the reverse of Augustine: secular history did have
a meaningful linear pattern, and providential history was relegated to the museum of ancient and irrelevant ideas. The important question became What is
the precise nature of the meaning and goal of secular history?

Various answers were given to this question throughout the nineteenth and twentieth centuries. Some were darkly pessimistic and others quite optimistic, but in the
nineteenth century optimism characterized most philosophies of history. There was
an unshakeable, if vague, faith in the evolution of scientific knowledge, and it permeated the thought of thinkers as different as Mill and Marx. For example, in spite
of their major differences, both worked on the assumption that it was possible to understand the course of history and even to provide some degree of guidance to history; such was the widespread faith in empirical science and in progress.

The belief that empirical science can solve all problems does seem to entail
a conclusion of some sort to history. The history in which humans are buf-
feted by fate and chance and about which we have only limited knowledge and

---

[1] "The last great hope of mankind" was a phrase used by Abraham Lincoln in *The Gettysburg Address.*

over which we have little control does seem to become more manageable with scientific knowledge. At least, Mill and, especially, Marx were so convinced. It was as if scientific knowledge could provide the power to free humanity from the clutches of history. Yet, the twentieth century has produced such horrors that this nineteenth-century faith in the social and political benefits that would flow from the inevitable evolution of scientific knowledge now seems hopelessly naive and even dangerous.

There have been, consequently, considerably fewer philosophies of history in the twentieth century, and these few do not exude a sense of optimism and of inevitable progress.[2] The nineteenth century did bequeath to the twentieth the strong suspicion that at least some turning point, if not conclusion, was being reached in history. Immanuel Kant had argued that there were laws in history that progressively inclined humanity toward republican constitutions. He, nevertheless, found it morally repugnant that prior generations were instruments for the happiness of future generations. This was a clear violation of the moral autonomy and worth of each individual, and Kant ultimately gave up on having a philosophy of history.[3] G. W. F. Hegel was less modest and did claim to know of the end of history. His contemporary interpreters argue that the rational process in history described by Hegel has led to liberal democracy with its ideals of equality and freedom. Only in this political system, the argument goes, can individuals finally recognize and respect each other's self-worth.[4] During the last half of the twentieth century many scholars have written about the end of great ideological conflicts just because the political system of liberal democracy appears unassailable as the accepted form of political organization

[2] Oswald Spengler, *The Decline of the West*, 2 Vols., originally published in 1918 (New York: Alfred A. Knopf, 1926–1928); Arnold J. Toynbee, *A Study of History*, 12 Vols. (Oxford: Oxford University Press, 1948-1961); Eric Voegelin, *Order and History*, 5 Vols. (Baton Rouge: Louisiana State University Press, 1956-1987). See the comparison of Voegelin and Toynbee by Ellis Sandoz, *The Voegelinian Revolution: A Biographical Introduction* (Baton Rouge: Louisana State University Press, 1981), pp. 127–45.

[3] For a succinct and fair treatment of Kant, see Susan Shell, "Kant's Idea of History," in *History and the Idea of Progress*, eds. Arthur M. Melzer, Jerry Weinberger, and M. Richard Zinman (Ithaca: Cornell University Press, 1955), pp. 75–96.

[4] Francis Fukuyama has most famously argued this case in *The End of History and the Last Man* (New York: Free Press, 1992). See the article by Fukuyama and the responses by other scholars analyzing his thesis in Melzer et al., *History and the Idea of Progress*.

for humanity. The violent turmoil instigated by Nazism and Communism have finally passed, and, so they argue, there is little reason to expect that equivalent ideologies will reappear to challenge the ideals of liberal democracy.[5]

There was one philosopher at the very end of the nineteenth century who forecast quite a different future for the twentieth century and for human history as a whole, Friedrich Nietzsche (1844–1900). From the standpoint of the political and military turmoil of the twentieth century, his judgments, given at the end of the nineteenth century, appear prescient to many people, and some argue that it is critical for understanding the future history of humanity—its meaning and purpose—to take cognizance of Nietzsche's philosophy. Accordingly, a brief examination of his thought is in order.

NIETZSCHE: His Life and Works

The most radical bequest of the nineteenth to the twentieth century clearly came from Nietzsche. In his famous aphorism "God is dead" Nietzsche was announcing that to rely upon the metaphysical support of a rational universe and a sovereign deity to provide meaning and purpose to humanity was no longer possible; in the modern scientific age such metaphysical support was no longer believable. Moreover, Nietzsche saw that there was no belief system to take the place of the traditional belief in a rational universe created by God. Humanity was entering an age of nihilism, empty of meaning, that could be overcome only by a new and radical understanding of the human predicament. Humans were now absolutely alone in a silent universe, and only their own will to power would garner the meaning necessary for their existence.

There seems to be nothing in Nietzsche's background that could be said to have led to this radical and dark conception of the human condition. His family were traditional Lutherans; both grandfathers were Lutheran pastors, and his father was pastor of the church in Röchen, Prussia, where Friedrich was born. His father died when Friedrich was five, and the family left the parsonage and moved to Naumburg where he was raised in a comfortable household consisting of his

---

[5] For a sampling of these arguments, see Edward Shils, "Ideology and Civility: On the Politics of the Intellectual," originally published in 1958 and reprinted in Richard Cox, ed. *Ideology, Politics, and Political Theory* (Belmont, Calif.: Wadsworth, 1969); Daniel Bell, *The End of Ideology* (Glencoe, Ill.: Free Press, 1960); Chaim Isaac Waxman, ed., *The End of Ideology Debate* (New York: Funk and Wagnalls, 1969).

mother, sister, grandmother, and two maiden aunts. His childhood was happy and normal by any standard. At the age of 14 he was sent to a famous private boarding school, Pforta, where he showed himself to be a precocious student, but not overly so. In fact, he failed the mathematic examination required for graduation from Pforta and was passed only because of his outstanding work in Greek and Latin.[6]

In 1864 he went to the University of Bonn to study theology and to follow in the footsteps of his grandfathers and father. By the time the year was over he had given up theology. He had also visited a brothel during this year and apparently contracted syphyilis, from which he was eventually to die. In August, 1865, he transferred to the University of Leipzig where his professor of philology, Friedrich Ritschl, had moved. Nietzsche's university career now became outstanding, and even before he completed his studies for his Ph.D., he was recommended for a position at the University of Basel in Switzerland. He received the appointment, somewhat to his surprise, and was awarded his Ph.D. from Leipzig without having to take the usual examination. He seemed poised to have an outstanding career as a philologist, specializing in the classical Greek world.

It was not to be. The years spent at the University of Basel, 1869-1879, were not particularly happy. His interests were changing even at Leipzig from philology to philosophy, and by the end of the decade he clearly conceived of himself as a philosopher and one with an original vision. Two people were instrumental in this shift: one was the philosopher Arthur Schopenhauer (1788-1860), and the other was the opera composer Richard Wagner (1813-1883). While a student at Leipzig, Nietzsche had discovered *The World as Will and Idea* by Schopenhauer. According to Schopenhauer, the will was the primary force of life and the intellect merely its instrument. The goal for human life was to deny the will and achieve a Buddhist-like serenity. Nietzsche became a disciple, though it seems that he was drawn to Schopenhauer as much by emotions as by philosophical arguments. Schopenhauer was darkly pessimistic about the evils of the age; he was alienated by the philistinism of bourgeois society, and he perceived himself as an original genius standing alone against the age. All of these features appealed to Nietzsche as well. Of more importance to Nietzsche's early career, however, was Richard Wagner's charismatic and dominating personality, which captivated

---

[6] Curiously, Nietzsche did not show a penchant for languages in general. A good deal of his life was spent in Italy, yet, he never learned Italian, nor French for that matter.

Nietzsche for several years. Wagner also professed to be a disciple of Schopenhauer, and he, too, conceived of himself as an original genius fighting against bourgeois society. Nietzsche did break free of both influences, but the intense relationship with the Wagner entourage made it very difficult for him. Finally (after what now appears to be psychosomatic illnesses), Nietzsche broke with Wagner in the fall of 1877. Nietzsche's health actually deteriorated over the years, and in 1879 he permanently resigned from the University of Basel.

From 1879 to 1889 Nietzsche wrote and lived in boarding houses mainly in Switzerland and Italy. His writings were not successful with the public; nevertheless, he had firmly established his own clear vision. Also, it could be said that Nietzsche had now become successful in "becoming a genius."[7] The lessons from Schopenhauer and Wagner had been learned well. He was publishing steadily and working extremely hard through these years, but in January 1889, he physically collapsed. Upon regaining consciousness, it was clear that he had become insane. The syphilitic disease was incurable, and he died 11 years later.[8]

After his death, the Nazis brought Nietzsche his first great fame. They supported him in spite of his many vehement attacks against nationalism and anti-semitism.[9] In the 1930s Hitler bestowed the honour of his patronage on the Nietzsche museum established by Nietzsche's worshipful sister. During World War II, the German army had a mass edition printed of Nietzsche's *Thus Spake Zarathustra*, which was distributed to the troops. Unfortunately, such notoriety can tend to make an interpreter either too defensive or too critical in an analysis of Nietzsche's works; his notoriety has, consequently, hindered a full assessment of his writings.

---

[7] The phrase is used by Carl Pletsch, *Young Nietzsche: Becoming a Genius* (New York: Free Press, 1991).

[8] When he returned to consciousness after the collapse, he suddenly sent off a spate of letters to a variety of leaders asking them to assemble in Rome. He signed his name "the Crucified One." The best biography is by R. J. Hollingdale, *Nietzsche: The Man and His Philosophy* (Baton Rouge: Louisiana State University Press, 1965). Walter Kaufmann's encyclopedic work is also useful: *Nietzsche: Philosopher, Psychologist, Antichrist*, 4th ed. (Princeton: Princeton University Press, 1974). Pletsch, *Young Nietzsche*, is insightful on the forming of young Nietzsche's personality.

[9] Even during World War I Nietzsche was attacked for his purported philosophy of power and for contributing to German nationalism, regardless of his diatribes against nationalism. See Ernest Barker, *Nietzsche and Treitschke: The Worship of Power in Modern Germany*, Oxford Pamphlet No. 20 (London: Oxford University Press, 1914). For Nietzsche's words against German nationalism and explicitly against "Herr von Treitschke," as Nietzsche contemptuously refers to him, see *Ecce Homo*, "The Case of Wagner," in *The Philosophy of Nietzsche* (New York: Modern Library, 1954), pp. 916–20. *Ecce Homo* is an autobiography and a retrospective on Nietzsche's writings.

Nietzsche's influence has been greater in Germany and France than in the English world, but since World War II his works have gradually been given new translations and new assessments in both philosophy and literary theory. Nietzsche's early writings are essays, but his later ones are often full of aphorisms and are sometimes written as literary works with songs, poems, stories and myths used to persuade the reader. He did not write any work strictly in political philosophy, though many works have portions that are pertinent to the study of political life. Particularly useful are the following: *On Truth and Lies in an Extra-Moral Sense* (written in 1873 and published posthumously); *Untimely Meditations* (1873–1876); *Human, All Too Human* (1878–1879); *The Gay Science* (1882, the fifth part done in 1887); *Thus Spake Zarathustra* (1883–1885); *Beyond Good and Evil* (1886); *A Genealogy of Morals* (1887); and *The Will to Power* (1883–1888 and left unfinished).

Philosophy

It is a scholarly commonplace to point to the contradictions, some apparent and some real, that abound throughout Nietzsche's writings; thus, there is value in remembering that a unifying thread does bind his writings. He begins with the death of God, and it is this realization, explored in depth by Nietzsche, that leads to nihilism for humanity. The overcoming of nihilism requires the *übermensch* (translated as overman or superman) and the concept of the eternal return or recurrence.[10] All of these unusual categories—death of God, nihilism, superman, and eternal return—are linked, and they are critical for understanding the unity of Nietzsche's thought.

The pronouncement that "God is dead" is actually central to his whole philosophy. There are two dimensions to the claim that God is dead, which Nietzsche develops at length: first, humanity, he argues, must now unflinchingly face its position in reality; second, it is necessary to have a new conception of the activity of philosophizing or of the search for truth.

With Nietzsche's customary dramatic flare, he opens *On Truth and Lies in an Extra-Moral Sense* with the following description of the human condition:

In some remote corner of the universe, poured out and glittering in innumerable solar systems, there once was a star on which clever animals invented

---

[10] Karl Löwith, *From Hegel to Nietzsche: The Revolution in Nineteenth-Century Thought*, trans. David E. Green (New York: Holt, Rinehart and Winston, 1964), pp. 193–94.

knowledge. That was the haughtiest and most mendacious minute of "world history"—yet only a minute. After nature had drawn a few breaths the star grew cold, and the clever animals had to die.[11]

There is, for Nietzsche, no built-in reason for human existence within reality. The universe is cold, uncaring, and silent. We owe to science and its unrelenting search for truth this new realization of the human predicament.

In his work *The Gay Science*, Nietzsche uses the literary device of having a madman announce the death of God as a murder, for indeed, in contrast to humanity's traditional beliefs, it is as if the world has gone mad. In this fashion, he attempts to force the reader to experience in depth humanity's stark position.

> "Whither is God" he cried. "I shall tell you. *We have killed him*—you and I. All of us are his murderers. But how have we done this? How were we able to drink up the sea? Who gave us the sponge to wipe away the entire horizon? What did we do when we unchained this earth from its sun? Whither is it moving now? Whither are we moving now? … Is there any up or down left? Are we not straying as through an infinite nothing? Do we not feel the breath of empty space? Has it not become colder? Is not night and more night coming on all the while? Must not lanterns be lit in the morning? Do we not hear anything yet of the noise of the gravediggers who are burying God? Do we not smell anything yet of God's decomposition? Gods too decompose. God is dead. God remains dead. And we have killed him.[12]

In yet another of his powerful images, Nietzsche has Zarathustra describe the human condition through the metaphor of a rope: "Man is a rope, tied between beast and overman—a rope over an abyss. A dangerous across, a dangerous on-the-way, a dangerous looking-back, a dangerous shuddering and stopping."[13] We are of nature and, in that sense, belong to the animal world, but it is still true that the vast majority of humanity has not yet experienced to the depth its real predicament and needs to see the new stance of the overman or superman. As Nietzsche explains in other passages, only the few can attain the

---

[11] *On Truth and Lies in an Extra-Moral Sense*, written in 1873, in Walter Kaufmann, ed., *The Portable Nietzsche* (New York: Viking Press, 1954), p. 42.

[12] *The Gay Science*, section 125, in Kaufmann, *The Portable Nietzsche*, p. 95.

[13] *Thus Spake Zarathustra*, Prologue, section 4, in Kaufmann, *The Portable Nietzsche*, p. 126.

overman or superman stance. In any case, humanity is without the support of God or of the *logos*, and in this sense it is as if each person is a rope over an abyss.

Nihilism, argues Nietzsche, results from the fatal belief that no meaning is possible without the metaphysical support of a God or of a rational nature. Although only the weak and cowardly become nihilist, they are the vast majority of humanity. Without the belief in so-called eternal truths, such people succumb, and this becomes a great danger to a civilization. The futility engendered by nihilism saps humanity of its power. Nihilism enervates and perverts our most powerful and creative instincts, in particular the will to power. But, according to Nietzsche, meaning in human life is possible. Thus, he himself is not a nihilist since he believes that there is a sense in which philosophizing or the search for truth, as he understands it, and the stance of the overman or superman can provide a creative and noble life.

Nietzsche's particular conception of philosophy, the search for truth as he repeatedly calls it, is usually named perspectivism. Simply, perspectivism is the view that there can be no single truth to be discovered on any question and then impartially and objectively seen by all. Truth is not independent of one's position but results from one's perspective. In this sense, truth is always an interpretation, a reflection of someone's perspective. In a direct contrast with Plato's form or *eidos*, Nietzsche describes how the use of language distorts knowing:

> Every concept originates through our equating what is unequal. No leaf ever wholly equals another, and the concept "leaf" is formed through an arbitrary abstraction from these individual differences, through forgetting the distinctions: and now it gives rise to the idea that in nature there might be something besides the leaves which would be "leaf"—some kind of original form after which all leaves have been woven, marked, copied....[14]

It is the refusal to see the differences that confuses us and leads to the illusory assertion of some objective knowledge about reality.

The conclusion he reaches is that truth is perspectival and no one, accordingly, can claim to have absolute and impartial knowledge:

> What then is truth? A mobile army of metaphors, metonyms, and anthropomorphisms—in short, a sum of human relations, which have been

---

[14] Kaufmann, *On Truth and Lies in an Extra-Moral Sense*, p. 46.

enhanced, transposed, and embellished poetically and rhetorically, and which after long use seem firm, canonical, and obligatory to a people: truths are illusions about which one has forgotten that this is what they are; metaphors which are worn out and without sensuous power; coins which have lost their pictures and now matter only as metal, no longer as coins.[15]

In one of his many, apparent contradictions, Nietzsche also constantly asserts the primacy of honesty and of the search for truth. The figure Zarathustra, who sees the meaninglessness of reality and yet has the will to overcome it, is used by Nietzsche to speak this harsh truth of the loss of meaning, which has been exposed by the death of God: Zarathustra's "teaching and his alone defines truthfulness as the highest virtue—that is to say, as the reverse of the cowardice of the 'idealist' who flees at the sight of the reality."[16]

Given the true nature of the human condition framed by the death of God, Nietzsche provides a new understanding of morality and of what the true source of "morality" must now be. Nietzsche calls himself an immoralist.[17] In the *Genealogy of Morals* he presents his diagnosis of morality and his solution.

As the very word genealogy implies, Nietzsche argues that our moral values are not inscribed in our nature, to be discovered and developed; rather, they result from a concatenation of interpretations and interests in human history. He sees in history a distinction, now lost, between good and bad, and good and evil. The good and bad distinction is the original and natural distinction. The origin was from

---

[15] *Ibid.*, pp. 46–47. Nietzsche has helped to spur, along with many others, an examination in philosophy and literary theory of the relationship among language, reality, and truth. Erich Heller has written an eloquent essay relating Nietzsche to Ludwig Wittgenstein, in the eyes of many the greatest philosopher of the twentieth century: *The Importance of Nietzsche: Ten Essays* (Chicago: University of Chicago Press, 1988), pp. 141–57. Also of value are the articles by Jacques Derrida, Giles Deleuze, and Jean Granier in David B. Allison, ed., *The New Nietzsche: Contemporary Styles of Interpretation* (Cambridge: MIT Press, 1985). Also useful is Arthur C. Danto, *Nietzsche as Philosopher: An Original Study* (New York: Columbia University Press, 1965), pp. 68-99. For a discussion of deconstruction in literary theory, see: Daniel R. Ahern, *Nietzsche as Cultural Physician* (University Park: Pennsylvania State University Press, 1995), pp. 2-6, 187–93; Alan D. Schrift, *Nietzsche and the Question of Interpretation: Between Hermeneutics and Deconstruction* (New York: Routledge, 1990).

[16] *Ecce Homo*, "Why I am a fatality," section 3, in *The Philosophy of Nietzsche*, p. 925. The word "fatality" should be translated "destiny."

[17] *Ibid.*, section 6, p. 929.

the "aristocratic, the powerful, the high-stationed, the high-minded, who have felt that they themselves were good, and that their actions were good, that is to say of the first order, in contradistinction to all the low, the low-minded, the vulgar, and the plebian."[18] The bad arises from the contrast with the "meaner race, an under race," and "this is the origin of the antithesis of good and bad."[19]

Good originally had nothing to do with altruism or some particular set of excellences within human nature. As Nietzsche states in one of his aphorisms: "There is no such thing as moral phenomena, but only a moral interpretation of phenomena."[20] The natural good of the aristocrats flowed from their physical nature itself:

> The knightly-aristocratic "values" are based on a careful cult of the physical, on a flowering, rich, and even effervescing healthiness, that goes considerably beyond what is necessary for maintaining life, on war, adventure, the chase, the dance, the tourney—on everything, in fact, which is contained in strong, free, and joyous action.[21]

Although there are still fleeting remnants of the good-bad valuation in contemporary culture, Nietzsche believes that for all practical purposes it has been superseded by the good-evil valuation. There has, he says, been a "revolt of the slaves":

> It was the Jews who, in opposition to the aristocratic equation (good=aristocratic=beautiful=happy=loved by the gods), dared with a terrifying logic to suggest the contrary equation, and indeed to maintain with the teeth of the most profound hatred (the hatred of weakness) this contrary equation, namely, "the wretched are alone the good; the poor, the weak, the lowly, are alone the good; the suffering, the needy, the sick, the loathsome, are the only ones who are pious, the only ones who are blessed, for them alone is salvation....[22]

---

[18] *The Genealogy of Morals*, First Essay, section 2, in *The Philosophy of Nietzsche*, p. 634.

[19] *Ibid.*, p. 635.

[20] *Beyond Good and Evil*, section 108, in *The Philosophy of Nietzsche*, p. 459.

[21] *On the Genealogy of Morals*, First Essay, section 7, in *The Philosophy of Nietzsche*, p. 642.

[22] *Ibid.*, p. 643.

The aristocratic had given a "yes" to life, but the "herd morality" has given a "no." The slave's revolt is a revenge upon the strong, and it has succeeded.

The race of the weak with their "squinty souls" are, nevertheless, very clever and even creative, and it is they who have developed the morality of society to fit their interests and capacities. Thus, slave morality now predominates everywhere.[23] It is from this origin that there are such ideas as bad conscience and guilt. These were brutally pressed upon our collective memory in order to shape and mould humanity.[24]

Nietzsche explains the psychological steps followed in developing the phenomenon of a bad conscience as the consequence of sublimating and, thus, perverting natural and instinctual drives:

> All instincts which do not find a vent without, *turn inwards*—this is what I mean by the growing "internalisation" of man: consequently we have the first growth in man, of what subsequently was called his soul. The whole inner world, originally as thin as if it had been stretched between two layers of skin, burst apart and expanded proportionately, and obtained depth, breadth, and height, when man's external outlet became *obstructed*. These terrible bulwarks, with which the social organization protected itself against the old instincts of freedom (punishments belong pre-eminently to these bulwarks), brought it about that all those instincts of wild, free, prowling man became turned backwards *against man himself*. Enmity, cruelty, the delight in persecution, in surprises, change, destruction—the turning of these instincts against their own possessors: this is the origin of the "bad conscience."[25]

There is an ascetic ideal, Nietzsche notes, that is asserted by philosophers and theologians to provide meaning and happiness to humanity. But, this ideal with its so-called virtues of poverty, humility, and chastity are merely manifestations of the irrepressible will to power.[26] Humans saw no meaning to their existence: "a tremendous *void* encircled man—he did not know how to justify himself, to explain himself, to affirm himself, he *suffered* from the problem of his

---

[23] *Ibid.*, First Essay, sections 10, 13.

[24] *Ibid.*, Second Essay, sections 3–4, 6.

[25] *Ibid.*, Second Essay, section 16, p. 702.

[26] *Ibid.*, Second Essay, section 12 and Third Essay, section 8.

own meaning."[27] The ascetic ideal provided our answer: "suffering *found an explanation*; the tremendous gap seemed filled; the door to all suicidal Nihilism was closed."[28] What is essential for humans is that they will something even if it is, as provided by the ascetic ideal, a hatred of beauty and happiness.

In addition to unmasking Christianity by diagnosing the origins and illness of modern slave morality, Nietzsche provides an alternative to the dominant theological conception of the relationship between God and humanity. In the place of a God who provides meaning and purpose to existence, he puts the overman or superman; in the place of a divine grace that provides guidance and nurture, he puts the will to power; and in place of eternal life that would provide the escape from meaningless death, he puts eternal return or recurrence.

Throughout his writings Nietzsche stresses that the will to power is behind all great founders of religions and philosophies. They have hidden behind "eternal truths" or "God's revelation" as justifications for their actions. Indeed, all human actions, virtues, and vices can be traced to the instinctual and overwhelming **will to power** without which no human can live. He customarily speaks of the drive in physiological terms to underscore that it is an inescapable, material, and natural part of human nature. The will to power is not conceived of as merely an ideal or simply a psychic need.[29]

The superman or overman is designed to incarnate the will to power. After the murder of God, the proper response is self-deification: "Must not we ourselves become gods simply to seem worthy of it?"[30] Such a step is only a completion of the drive inherent in humans, whether saints, caesars, scientists, artists, philosophers, or members of the herd. All show in various confused or often sublimated ways the desire and need to express the will to power. The need to live, control, and master is the source of human meaning and happiness.

Only the overman has fully realized the death of God and has the unstinting integrity to face the consequences without falling into the deadening morass of nihilism. The overman, represented by the figure of Zarathustra, is constituted less by a set of

---

[27] *Ibid.*, Third Essay, section 28, p. 792.

[28] *Ibid.*, pp. 792–93.

[29] The excellent work, Ahern, *Nietzsche as Cultural Physician*, provides the best treatment of the physical, physiological, and biological themes.

[30] *The Gay Science*, section 125, in Kaufmann, *The Portable Nietzsche*, p. 96.

virtues and attributes than by a stance toward life. The overman affirms life and its value against the death of God. Such an affirmation requires forgetting the bonds of both history and the slave morality so that a new postmodern culture can be willed—one that is consistent with the reality of God's death. Zarathustra is an immoralist in the particular sense that the unsparing search for truth entails the conclusion that traditional morality has no warrant and that all humanity's deeds reflect the will to power. Thus, Nietzsche calls Zarathustra the first immoralist: "The defeat of morality by itself, through truthfulness, the moralist's defeat of himself in his opposite—in me—that is what the name Zarathustra means in my mouth."[31] The overman redeems what has been destroyed. As one interpreter of Nietzsche properly concludes of the overman: "he is the man of the future who will redeem humanity from nihilism by teaching the liberation of the will; he is the victor over God and nothingness."[32]

The victory of the overman is completed by the doctrine of eternal return or recurrence. This curious doctrine is explained by Nietzsche in *The Gay Science*:

> *The greatest stress.* How, if some day or night a demon were to sneak after you into your loneliest loneliness and say to you, "This life as you now live it and have lived it, you will have to live once more and innumerable times more; and there will be nothing new in it, but every pain and every joy and every thought and sign and everything immeasurably small or great in your life must return to you—all in the same succession and sequence—even this spider and this moonlight between the trees, and even this moment and I myself. The eternal hourglass of existence is turned over and over, and you with it, a dust grain of dust."[33]

As Nietzsche proceeds to say, the response to this new understanding of eternity might be one of feeling crushed by utter futility or it might be the reverse: "You are a god, and never have I heard anything more godly."[34] Presumably,

---

[31] *Ecce Homo*, "Why I am a fatality," section 3, in *The Philosophy of Nietzsche*, p. 925.

[32] Keith Ansell-Pearson, *Nietzsche Contra Rousseau: A Study of Nietzsche's Moral and Political Philosophy* (Cambridge: Cambridge University Press, 1991), p. 152. For a full analysis of the will to power and of the overman or superman, see Kaufmann, *Nietzsche: Philosopher, Psychologist, Antichrist*, pp. 178–207; Bernard Yack, *The Longing for Total Revolution* (Princeton: Princeton University Press, 1986), pp. 356–64; Peter Berkowitz, *Nietzsche: The Ethics of an Immoralist* (Cambridge: Harvard University Press, 1995), pp 176–227.

[33] *The Gay Science*, section 341, in Kaufmann, *The Portable Nietzsche*, p. 101.

[34] *Ibid.*, p. 102.

this enthusiastic response is possible because the doctrine of eternal recurrence gives humans the same relationship to reality and time as God has. By definition, God as God is outside of time and does not have to abide by some existing rational structure of reality into which he must fit and which would serve as a limitation on his freedom and power to create the world. With the doctrine of eternal recurrence the overman also is not bound by time and some existing rational structure in which he must fit and which provides a boundary to his freedom and power to create a world of meaning. God pronounced in *Genesis* that his creations were good and, thus, established his dominion and mastery over reality. The overman, too, can create and enjoy. He, too, has freedom and mastery in the eternal return.

Thus Spake Zarathustra is the major work wherein Nietzsche explores the psychology of overcoming. In brief, Zarathustra teaches that by a continual testing of the will one can consciously experience overcoming, and, thus, this very act of willing affirms one's own life. It is necessary to will to forget the valuelessness of the world or else we will return to an animal nature. Yet, the overman does realize that the world is valueless—carries no inherent meaning—while willing its value. The doctrine of the eternal recurrence instantiates the continual act of willing against the world's valuelessness. The eternal return unites the contradiction in the overman between willing value over a valueless reality.

Both the meaning and plausibility of the doctrine of eternal return are often questioned, even by those sympathetic to Nietzsche. Some interpret the doctrine to be about physical nature and the cosmos. Others interpret the doctrine in existential terms; i.e., it is a way of creating meaning in a meaningless world by one's own willful bestowing of value on human actions and the world. In Nietzsche's words, "to impose upon becoming the character of being—that is the supreme will to power."[35] The eternal return, however interpreted, still contains the inescapable contradiction that the valueless world infinitely recurs and is valued for that. We must will to believe this contradiction or be doomed to nihilism and dehumanization.

In another of his striking metaphors, Nietzsche illustrates the position of the overman with an eagle and a snake. The eagle represents willful pride and the snake represents wisdom: "the proudest animal under the sun and the wisest animal under the sun." "An eagle soared through the sky in wide circles,

---

[35] *The Will to Power*, cited in Yack, *The Longing for Total Revolution*, p. 353.

and on him hung a serpent, not like prey but like a friend: for she kept herself wound around his neck."[36] Pride and wisdom soaring without any support, such is the stance of the overman.[37]

Great Politics

Nietzsche called for a time of "great politics." His harsh indictment of political life and his harsh predictions and prescriptions have troubled even his defenders. He held modern rulers to be hypocrites who rule in the name "of the constitution, of justice, of the law, or of God himself." The human herd stupidly follows.[38] The rulers are helped by religion, which keeps the majority of people in some degree of contentedness:

> . . . to ordinary men, to the majority of the people, who exist for service and general utility, and are only so far entitled to exist, religion gives invaluable contentedness with their lot and condition, peace of heart, ennoblement of obedience, additional social happiness and sympathy, with something of transfiguration and embellishment, something of justification of all the commonplaceness, all the meanness, all the semi-animal poverty of their souls.[39]

It is Nietzsche's fear that European civilization is entering a stage dominated by what he calls "the last man." The last man is the polar opposite of the overman and is the subject of some of Nietzsche's most virulent rhetoric. The possibility of human greatness is suffocated by the self-satisfied mediocrity of the last man and his search for self-preservation and for dull and secure comforts. These are the human creatures who have been debased by the slave morality, by democracy, and by technology. They want security and comfort, little more. Zarathustra

---

[36] *Thus Spake Zarathustra*, Prologue, section 10, in Kaufmann, *The Portable Nietzsche*, p. 137.

[37] For interpretations of the eternal return, see Hollingdale, *Nietzsche: the Man and His Philosophy*, pp. 197–202, 311–12; Yack, *The Longing for Total Revolution*, pp. 352–56; Berkowitz, *Nietzsche: The Ethics of an Immoralist*, pp. 195–210; Kaufmann, *Nietzsche: Philosopher, Psychologist, Antichrist*, pp. 316–27.

[38] *Beyond Good and Evil*, section 199, in *The Philosophy of Nietzsche*, pp. 488–99. In Nietzsche's early writing, *Human, All Too Human* (1878), his views were more moderate, but by the time he wrote *Beyond Good and Evil* (1886) and *Thus Spake Zarathustra* (1883-1885) he had clearly established his position of "great politics." Yet, even in *Human, All Too Human* he talks about the need to breed a new mixed European race (section 475, in Kaufmann, *The Portable Nietzsche*, pp. 61–63).

[39] *Ibid.*, section 61, p. 447. See also, *Ecce Homo*, "Morality as Prejudice," section 2.

forecasts their coming: "Alas, the time is coming when man will no longer give birth to a star. Alas, the time of the most despicable man is coming, he that is no longer able to despise himself. Behold, I show you the *last man.*"[40]

It is into this political environment that Nietzsche throws his teachings about great politics. As he modestly describes the effect of his thought, "I am not man, I am dynamite."

> For when Truth engages in struggle with the falsehood of ages, we must expect shocks and a series of earthquakes, with a rearrangement of hills and valleys, such as has never yet been dreamed of. The concept "politics" is thus raised bodily into the realm of spiritual warfare. All the mighty forms of the old society are blown into space—for they all rest on falsehood: there will be wars, whose like have never been seen on earth before. Politics on a grand scale will date from me.[41]

The great politics has features horrifying to most ears, though Nietzsche is sometimes defended as simply perceiving the new, harsh reality of the twentieth century. As an instance, he foresees the development of Russia as a threat to Europe, but this threat, however deplorable, may finally force Europe to unite:

> I do not say this as one who desires it; in my heart I should rather prefer the contrary—I mean such an increase in the threatening attitude of Russia, that Europe would have to make up its mind to become equally threatening— namely, *to acquire one will,* by means of a new caste to rule over the Continent, a persistent, dreadful will of its own, that can set its aims thousands of years ahead; so that the long spun-out comedy of its petty-statism, and its dynastic as well as its democratic many-willedness, might finally be brought to a close. The time for petty politics is past; the next century will bring the struggle for the dominion of the world—the *compulsion* to great politics.[42]

---

[40] *Thus Spake Zarathustra*, Prologue, section 5, in Kaufmann, *The Portable Nietzsche*, p. 129. Lawrence Lampert, with justification, associates the last man to the liberal political philosophies of Hobbes and Locke. *Nietzsche's Teaching: An Interpretation of 'Thus Spake Zarathustra'* (New Haven: Yale University Press, 1986), pp. 22-29. Barry Cooper shows how modern technology enforces Nietzsche's picture of the last man: "Nihilism and Technology," in *Nietzsche and the Rhetoric of Nihilism*, eds. Tom Darby, Béla Egyed, and Ben Jones (Ottawa: Carleton University Press, 1989), 165–81.

[41] *Ecce Homo*, "Why I am a fatality," section 2, in *The Philosophy of Nietzsche*, pp. 923, 924.

[42] *Beyond Good and Evil*, section 208, in *The Philosophy of Nietzsche*, pp. 509–10.

A new age of aristocratic rulers will, thus, transform politics. The consequence will be a nobler and higher kind of men who can create a new, great culture.

> The essential thing... in a good and healthy aristocracy is that it should *not* regard itself as a function either of the kingship or the common-wealth, but as the *significance* and highest justification thereof—that it should therefore accept with a good conscience the sacrifice of a legion of individuals, who, *for its sake*, must be suppressed and reduced to imperfect men, to slaves and instruments. Its fundamental belief must be precisely that society is *not* allowed to exist for its own sake, but only as a foundation and scaffolding, by means of which a select class of beings may be able to elevate themselves to their higher duties, and in general to a higher *existence*: like those sun-seeking climbing plants in Java...which encircle an oak so long and so often with their arms, until at last, high above it, but supported by it, they can unfold their tops in the open light, and exhibit their happiness.[43]

It is clear that, like Machiavelli and Marx, Nietzsche advocates a creative role for violence. He wants rulers who will have the qualities of the overman: "In order that there may be institutions, there must be a kind of will, instinct, or imperative, which is anti-liberal to the point of malice: the will to tradition, to authority, to responsibility for centuries to come, to the solidarity of chains of generations....[44] Rulers of this type are necessary for a state in which politics is always a contest and war a necessity. For Nietzsche it is obvious that humans are not political-social animals with a common life directed toward developing human potentialities. Such a view of politics, in Nietzsche's judgment, is based on a slave morality and is incompatible with a creative culture and the overman.[45]

---

[43] *Ibid.*, section 258, pp. 576–77.

[44] *Twilight of the Idols*, section 39, in Kaufmann, *The Portable Nietzsche*, p. 543.

[45] Nietzsche's great politics is discussed and criticized by B. Detwiler, *Nietzsche and the Politics of Aristocratic Radicalism* (Chicago: University of Chicago Press, 1990); Tracy B. Strong, *Friedrich Nietzsche and the Politics of Transfiguration* (Berkeley: University of California Press, 1975), pp. 192-202; Ansell-Pearson, *Nietzsche Contra Rousseau*, pp. 200–24; Yack, *The Longing for Total Revolution*, pp. 356–64. Walter Kaufmann gives his usual spirited defence of Nietzsche, *Nietzsche: Philosopher, Psychologist, Antichrist*, pp. 284–306.

Evaluation

Nietzsche's influence has increased throughout the twentieth century. In political philosophy there are those who accept, at least to a degree, Nietzsche's assessment of the stark human predicament and the stance one should then take toward it. One interpreter of Nietzsche writes: "We want to matter, and on the deepest level we do not matter and nothing we do matters." Since this is the case, we must courageously take the stance left for an honest person: "We must try to live an honourable life and die an honourable death."[46] Sometimes the defence of Nietzsche also includes supporting his assessment of democracy and of politics.[47] Seldom, however, will there be an explicit defence of his great politics or of the qualities he demanded for the ruling aristocracy. There is the odd exception. Michael Haar has written that Nietzsche's theory of rule is a "nonviolent Caesarism": "The 'Masters of the Earth' will, as artists do, mould and fashion the masses of humanity to the extent to which, unknown to these masses, they can serve the 'masters' as an instrument."[48] Nietzsche's diagnosis might be acceptable, but most interpreters get squeamish at his remedy.[49]

Perhaps, his greatest influence has been his conception of philosophy as perspectivism. It is a refinement of historicism—the view that an historical period does inscribe thought—which is a powerful school of thought.[50] Perspectivism has been particularly influential in literary theory. Nietzsche argued that language does not mirror reality, that language expresses meaning by closing off

---

[46] Werner Dannhauser, "Nietzsche and Spengler on Progress and Decline," in Melzer et al., *History and the Idea of Progress*, p. 133. Leo Strauss also respects much in Nietzsche. He sees an unsolvable tension in Nietzsche's implicit reliance on nature and reason and his express attempt to repudiate them. "Notes on the Plan of Nietzsche's *Beyond Good and Evil*," in *Studies in Platonic Political Philosophy* (Chicago: University of Chicago Press, 1983).

[47] See Allan Bloom for one kind of defence in *The Closing of the American Mind* (New York: Simon and Schuster, 1987), pp. 200–08, 307–12.

[48] "Nietzsche and Metaphysical Language," in Allison, *The New Nietzsche*, pp. 26–27.

[49] In spite of his support for Nazism, the most influential exponent of Nietzsche's thought has been the German philosopher Martin Heidegger: *Nietzsche*, 4 Vols., ed. David F. Krell (New York: Harper and Row, 1979–1982). Heidegger's article, "The Will to Power," in Allison, *The New Nietzsche*, pp. 37–63, is a good introduction to his thought.

[50] A famous contemporary advocate is Richard Rorty. One of his many books is, *Contingency, Irony, Solidarity* (Cambridge: Cambridge University Press, 1989).

other possible interpretations, and that the multiplicity of different interpretations must be rediscovered. The literary theory of deconstruction owes its origin to these themes in Nietzsche.[51]

Criticism of Nietzsche's thought has been voluminous. Perspectivism, and historicism in general, has been criticized for its claim that truth is perspectival, except for the privileged truth-claim that all other truth is perspectival. Also, as many philosophers have argued, it is impossible to escape a metaphysical framework, in the sense that any philosophic framework implicitly is an assertion of what is real and lasting, and, as such, provides a "moral horizon" or "orientation" for humanity.[52]

The death of God pronouncement, which served as the axis for Nietzsche's thought, can also be questioned. The persuasive power of the announcement—namely, that within the physical universe humanity appears to be a mere blink in time and a speck of dust—depends in large measure upon the backdrop of the extraordinary claim for knowledge and mastery begun with Descartes, Bacon, Hobbes, and many others. Had not Descartes promised that we would be "masters of the universe"? But, given the new and expanded understanding of the vastness of the universe in the late nineteenth century, the consequent realization of human finiteness and powerlessness would be dramatic and shocking. Would this realization be equally shocking to the writers of the books of *Ecclesiastes* and *Job* in the Old Testament, or to Socrates, Plato, Aristotle, and Augustine? The answer is a clear no. It is true that the various cosmologies in the ancient world did not have expanding galaxies in which the earth and sun are minute particles. Yet, for these thinkers, it was not the cosmology that carried the meaning for human existence in any case. For these ancient writers, regardless of their cosmologies, consciousness and death were the inescapable poles of human existence, and meaning was tenuously placed between these poles. Further, they believed that a sign of wisdom was the recognition of the limitations on human knowledge and power. In sum,

---

[51] Jacques Derrida has many works explaining deconstruction. See, for example, *Dissemination*, trans. Barbara Johnson (Chicago: University of Chicago Press, 1988).

[52] The phrases are from Charles Taylor. For arguments in support of this general position see Taylor, *Sources of the Self: The Making of the Modern Identity* (Cambridge: Harvard University Press, 1989), pp. 98–103, 516–21; Alasdair MacIntyre, *Three Rival Versions of Moral Enquiry* (Notre Dame: University of Notre Dame Press, 1990), pp. 45–46. Berkowitz, *Nietzsche: The Ethics of an Immoralist,* is an excellent book primarily devoted to exploring how and why Nietzsche failed in his attempt to break free of the history of philosophy.

Nietzsche has created a particularly modern, but still false, dichotomy through linking meaning to the freedom and mastery of a god and linking meaninglessness to the limitations on humanity's knowledge and power.

Nietzsche's great politics has received the most criticism, even from those who are sympathetic with his historicism. It is difficult to sympathize with these views: politics should be characterized as struggle, contest, and war; a new aristocratic breed with a will hardened to conscience and pity is necessary; the mass of people are merely instruments so that the powerful and noble few may thrive and create a great culture. Moreover, it is ludicrous to argue, as Nietzsche does, that the two classes of overman and the many will not be in conflict and that the overman will not rule:

> *One* movement is unconditional: the leveling of humanity, the great anthills....
>
> The *other* movement: my movement: is, on the contrary, the enhancement of all antitheses and chasms, abolition of equality, the creation of men of superior power.
>
> The former produces the last man. My movement the overman.
>
> The goal is *absolutely not* to conceive the latter as masters of the former. But: two types and species are to exist side by side—separated as far as possible; *like the gods of Epicurus the one paying no heed to the other.*[53]

Nietzsche recognizes in other passages that, inescapably, there would be coercion over the weak by the overman caste of aristocrats. Nietzsche's protests that Zarathustra goes down among the people but does not impose on them is hardly credible.[54] Great politics is a remaking of humanity by the few who have achieved mastery of the human will. Such a politics unleashes enormous hatreds, resentments, and destruction on a society. It would hardly provide the conditions for a great culture or for humans worthy of the name.

The potentially horrific consequences of Nietzsche's great politics follow from the flaws in his doctrines of the will to power and of the eternal return. The will to power does not adequately express, and indeed distorts, human capacities. The doctrine reflects the modern position that mastery and freedom are linked. Such an idea is found in theology where the two are linked in God, who created

---

[53] *The Will to Power* as cited in Ansell-Pearson, *Nietzsche Contra Rousseau*, p. 211.

[54] Nietzsche makes this claim in the Prologue to *Thus Spake Zarathustra*, section 9, in Kaufmann, *The Portable Nietzsche*, pp. 135–37.

reality *ex nihilo* (out of nothing). Here, there is a creative, willful action that was not constrained or limited; thus, mastery and freedom are shown. The eternal recurrence doctrine supposedly shows that humans, too, can do the same by continually asserting their wills each returning moment over a meaningless reality, which by definition means that there are no limits (the equivalent of *ex nihilo*) on our assertion of meaning. The belief that we, too, are free and can express our willful mastery is a true self-deification.

Ignoring the question of what scientific sense eternal recurrence could conceivably have, there is still the problem of whether the assertion of the will, the consequent sense of mastery and freedom, and the necessary escape from the boundary of time can actually occur even in a psychological or spiritual sense, for the taunt of time, the great boundary of morality, is inescapable. As one perceptive critic of Nietzsche analyzes the doctrine of eternal recurrence,

> In the Eternal Recurrence the problem [of time] disappears; every moment is significant by virtue of its eternal return. The Eternal Recurrence is the extreme *epic* philosophy—epic to the point of grandiose absurdity, a cosmic therapy against the terror of the passing of every moment, a vanishing into nothingness, into absolute oblivion. A mathematical magic is at work in this philosophy. The endless repetition of a senseless life is assumed to yield an immensity of spiritual significance, as if one could arrive at an overwhelmingly positive sum by frantically multiplying zero.[55]

It will not work.

The doctrine of the will to power can also be disputed. All human purposes and actions cannot be plausibly reduced to the will to power any more than they can be reduced to the alleged economic drive or the self-preservation drive in humans. More importantly, the will to power in practice distorts and demeans humans. Human capacities become warped by the drive to dominate; experiences that actually constitute human well-being and joy are eviscerated. The capacity to reason, for example, cannot be relegated to an instrument of the will to power. Reason is not passive or impotent. After all, it enables Nietzsche to conceive and to present his philosophy, just as it enables science to develop theories of cosmology. In neither case does reason function in any plausible sense, only as an instrument of a supposedly more fundamental desire for power. Also,

---

[55] Heller, *The Importance of Nietzsche*, p. 185.

human experiences such as love, friendship, compassion, and generosity are discredited and perverted by the will to power. Although the remark may seem flippant, Daniel Ahern correctly comments of Nietzsche: "I think he underestimated the tenacity of human beings, their capacity for generosity and courage. He believed that these would eventually be undermined, so he 'jumped ship', went AWOL on humanity."[56]

Such criticism of Nietzsche does not imply that the will to power does not exist. In fact, the will to power is not a new experience articulated by Nietzsche but is one well known and examined by many. The plays of Shakespeare and the novels of Dostoyevsky and Melville illuminate the disastrous effects of this drive on a psyche and the consequent effect on other people. For writers such as Shakespeare, Dostoyevsky, and Melville, it would come as no surprise that Nietzsche's great politics would lead to the destruction of much that is human and worthy of respect.

The final remarks on Nietzsche should belong to another German philosopher. A century prior to Nietzsche, J. G. Herder wrote that "Humanity is the treasure and prize of all human effort, the art of our race. Education to it is a labour which must be continued without cease, or we sink back…into brutality." He concludes with a statement whose truth he assumed to be self-evident: "no honourable man would willingly have written letters for the promotion of brutality."[57] Even if it was not the intention of Nietzsche, the great politics born from the will to power and the eternal recurrence could be read as "letters for the promotion of brutality" and, some would argue, they were.

Retrospective

It is as foolhardy to predict the future of political philosophy as it is to place a conclusion upon it.[58] The best type of political order, one in which humanity can flourish, is not a problem to be solved but an inescapable and continual responsibility placed upon us as social animals. The particular set of issues and problems

---

[56] Ahern, *Nietzsche as Cultural Physician*, p. 195.

[57] *Letters for the Advancement of Humanity* (1793-77), cited in Löwith, *From Hegel to Nietzsche*, p. 325.

[58] There are exceptions. John Dunn has bravely and usefully reflected upon the future: *Western Political Theory in the Face of the Future* (Cambridge: Cambridge University Press, 1993).

that humanity must face varies with the age. At one time in history, the great issue to be addressed might be one of probing the human psyche and its constituting experiences. At another time, the issues might focus on the institutional means of limiting power. At still other times, the great political questions might evolve around protecting the individual against governments.

The three most striking features of political life in the twentieth century are still commanding reflection. These are: the extraordinary growth of the executive or administrative branch everywhere in the world, whether the form of government is democratic or authoritarian; the development and power of mass ideological movements with their authoritarian or totalitarian governments; the collapse of the Soviet Union from within. The first feature has led to continual reflection by contemporary political philosophers in the liberal utilitarian and rights traditions, as well as by those in the communitarian tradition, and by all those who reflect on the nature of democracy.[59] The second feature has led to reflections on the history and nature of Western civilization and on the meaning of history itself.[60] The third feature has yet to be fully digested, though the view that politics is fundamentally about force has become much harder to sustain. These three features of twentieth-century political life hardly exhaust the philosophic issues to be probed. There has, for example, been continuing attention devoted to questions about equality and gender.[61]

---

[59] See the helpful study by James Wiser on the minimal and extended state. *Political Theory: A Thematic Inquiry* (Chicago: Nelson-Hall, 1986), pp. 191–226. General evaluations of the democratic form of government are provided by Jean Bethke Elshtain, *Democracy on Trial* (Concord, Ont.: Irwin Publishing, 1993) and Roland Axtmann, *Liberal Democracy into the Twenty-First Century* (Manchester: Manchester University Press, 1996). The debate continues between the liberal and communitarian thinkers. See the reader edited by Stephen Mulhall and Adam Swift, *Liberals and Communitarians* (Oxford: Basil Blackwell, 1992).

[60] The four political philosophers most cited are: Hannah Arendt, Michael Oakeshott, Leo Strauss, and Eric Voegelin. John Rawls and Charles Taylor should also be added to this list.

[61] The following works are only illustrations of the many contemporary examinations of the place of gender in political philosophy, past and present: Diana H. Coole, *Women in Political Theory: From Ancient Misogyny to Contemporary Feminism* (Boulder: Lynne Rienner, 1988); Arlene W. Saxonhouse, *Women in the History of Political Thought: Ancient Greece to Machiavelli* (New York: Praeger, 1985); Jean Bethke Elshtain, *Public Man, Private Woman: Women in Social and Political Thought* (Princeton: Princeton University Press, 1981); Susan Maller Okin, *Women in Western Political Thought* (Princeton: Princeton University Press, 1979); Ellen Kennedy and Susan Mendus, eds., *Women in Western Political Philosophy: Kant to Nietzsche* (New York: St. Martin's Press, 1987); Nancy Tuana, *Woman and the History of Philosophy* (New York: Paragon, 1992); Mary Lyndon Shanley and Carole Pateman, eds., *Feminist Interpretations and Political Theory* (Cambridge: Polity Press, 1991).

Providing a political order so that humans can develop their capacities and flourish remains a permanent task of all citizens. This task depends upon an understanding of human nature, its capacities and purposes. If a society is permeated by the belief that human nature is governed by self-interest and the satisfaction of appetites, the political order and culture will come to reflect and nourish this belief, which authorizes and justifies the society's existence. If a society is permeated by the belief that the glory of a military *esprit de corps* and of conquest provides for human flourishing, yet another political order and culture results. If a society is permeated with the belief that the life of the mind—the search for the true, good, and beautiful—provides the best nourishment for developing human capacities, the political order and culture will come to reflect and nourish this belief, which will, in turn, authorize and justify this society's existence.

The poet George Faludy eloquently expresses how the life of the mind sustained him and his compatriots through his time (1950-1953) in an Hungarian concentration camp:

> For those who steep themselves in it, it provides both a guide and a goal far surpassing all the half-baked ideologies that have blown up at our feet in this century like landmines. Sitting comfortably in the present and looking forward to longevity in an unknown future does nothing to ensure our survival nor even to make it desirable. In any case we do not live in the future: we live in the present, and all we have to guide us in this present is the accumulated thought and experience of those who have lived before us.[62]

There is no doubt in which political order the politics of discussion and persuasion will best flourish. The doubts are about the sustainability of such a political order once the belief in the life of the mind becomes ridiculed, ossified, and repudiated.

SUGGESTIONS FOR FURTHER READING

Hollingdale provides the best biography of Nietzsche. Pletsch's work is a psychoanalytic study of the development of the young Nietzsche and is quite good. Kaufmann, *Nietzsche: Philosopher, Psychologist, Antichrist*, is encyclopedic in its coverage, but also unrelentingly defensive and apologetic. Stern and Tanner

---

[62] Convocation Address to the University of Toronto, 29 November 1978, reprinted in and Gillien Thomas, Richard J. H. Perkyns, Kenneth A MacKinnon, Wendy R. Katz, eds., *Introduction to Literature*, 3rd ed. (Toronto: Harcourt, Brace, 1995), p. 36.

have useful short works on Nietzsche's philosophy. Berkowitz is a particularly excellent treatment of Nietzsche's philosophy and political thought as well as an introduction to secondary literature. See Yack, Ansell-Pearson, Strong, Detwiler, and Ahern for a general critical approach to Nietzsche's political thought. Defence of Nietzsche varies: Dannhauser, Bloom, and Strauss (1983) respect his steely-eyed view of the human condition; Heidegger and Kaufmann (1974) appreciate the substance of his political thought. Koelb, Sedgwick, Solomon, Solomon and Higgins, Allison, and Pasley are readers providing a good sampling of the various interpretations of Nietzsche's thought. Given the excessive claims about Nietzsche's originality, it is important to put his thought into a context. Blackham, Löwith, Megill, and Heller are very useful for this purpose.

Works

Hollingdale, R. J., trans. Human, All Too Human. London: Cambridge University Press, 1986.

———. *Thus Spake Zarathustra.* Harmondsworth: Penguin, 1975.

———. *Twilight of the Idols.* Harmondsworth: Penguin, 1972.

———. *Untimely Meditations.* Cambridge: Cambridge University Press, 1983.

Kaufmann, Walter, ed. *The Portable Nietzsche.* New York: Viking Press, 1963.

———. trans. *Beyond Good and Evil.* New York: Vintage, 1966.

———. *The Birth of Tragedy and The Case of Wagner.* New York: Vintage, 1967.

———. *The Gay Science.* New York: Vintage, 1974.

Kaufmann, Walter, and R. J. Hollingdale, trans. *On the Genealogy of Morals and Ecce Homo.* New York: Vintage: 1966.

———. *The Will to Power.* New York: Vintage, 1968.

The Philosophy of Nietzsche: Thus Spake Zarathustra, Beyond Good and Evil, The Genealogy of Morals, Ecce Homo, The Birth of Tragedy. New York: Modern Library, 1954.

Commentaries

Ahern, Daniel R. *Nietzsche as Cultural Physician.* University Park: Pennsylvania State University Press, 1995.

Allison, David B., ed. *The New Nietzsche: Contemporary Styles of Interpretation.* Cambridge: MIT Press, 1985.

Ansell-Pearson, Keith. *Nietzsche Contra Rousseau: A Study of Nietzsche's Moral and Political Philosophy*. Cambridge: Cambridge University Press, 1991.

Berkowitz, Peter. *Nietzsche: The Ethics of an Immoralist*. Cambridge: Harvard University Press, 1995.

Blackham, H. J. *Six Existentialist Thinkers*. London: Routledge & Kegan Paul, 1961.

Blondel, Eric. *Nietzsche: The Body and Culture*. Translated by Séan Hand. Stanford: Stanford University Press, 1991.

Brinton, Crane. *Nietzsche*. Cambridge: Harvard University Press, 1941.

Dannhauser, Werner. *Nietzsche's View of Socrates*. Ithaca: Cornell University Press, 1974.

Danto, Arthur C. *Nietzsche as Philosopher: An Original Study*. New York: Columbia Press, 1965.

Deleuze, Gilles. *Nietzsche and Philosophy*. Translated by Hugh Tomlinson. New York: Columbia University Press, 1983.

Detwiler, B. *Nietzsche and the Politics of Aristocratic Radicalism*. Chicago: University of Chicago Press, 1990.

Eden, Robert. *Political Leadership and Nihilism: A Study of Weber and Nietzsche*. Gainesville: University Press of Florida, 1983.

Gillespie, M. A., and Tracy B. Strong, eds. *Nietzsche's New Seas*. Chicago: University of Chicago Press, 1988.

Hayman, Ronald. *Nietzsche: A Critical Life*. New York: Penguin, 1984.

Heidegger, Martin. *Nietzsche*. 4 Vols. Edited by David F. Krell. New York: Harper and Row, 1979-1982.

Heller, Erich. *The Importance of Nietzsche: Ten Essays*. Chicago: University of Chicago Press, 1988.

Higgins, Kathleen Marie. *Nietzsche's 'Zarathustra'*. Philadelphia: Temple University Press, 1987.

Hollingdale, R. J. *Nietzsche: The Man and His Philosophy*. Baton Rouge: Louisiana State University Press, 1965.

Jaspers, Karl. *Nietzsche: An Introduction to the Understanding of His Philosophical Activity*. Translated by Charles F. Wallraff and Frederick J. Schmitz. South Bend: Gateway, 1979.

Kaufmann, Walter. *Nietzsche: Philosopher, Psychologist, Antichrist*. 4th ed. Princeton: Princeton University Press, 1974.

Koelb, Clayton, ed. *Nietzsche as Postmodernist: Essays Pro and Contra*. Albany: State University of New York Press, 1990.

Lampert, Laurence. *Nietzsche's Teaching: An Interpretation of 'Thus Spake Zarathustra'.* New Haven: Yale University Press, 1986.

Löwith, Karl. *From Hegel to Nietzsche: The Revolution in Nineteenth-Century Thought.* Translated by David E. Green. New York: Holt, Rinehart and Winston, 1964.

Magnus, Bernd. *Nietzsche's Existential Imperative.* Bloomington: Indiana University Press, 1978.

Magnus, Bernd, and Kathleen M. Higgins, eds. *The Cambridge Companion to Nietzsche.* Cambridge: Cambridge University Press, 1996.

Megil, Allan. *Prophets of Extremity: Nietzsche, Heidegger, Foucault, Derrida.* Berkeley: University of California Press, 1985.

Nehamas, Alexander. *Nietzsche: Life as Literature.* Cambridge: Harvard University Press, 1985.

Pasley, Malcolm, ed. *Nietzsche: Imagery and Thought.* London: Methuen, 1978.

Pletsch, Carl. *Young Nietzsche: Becoming a Genius.* New York: Free Press, 1991.

Rosen, Stanley. *Nihilism: A Philosophical Essay.* New Haven: Yale University Press, 1969.

Schacht, Richard. *Nietzsche.* London: Routledge and Kegan Paul, 1983.

Schrift, Alan D. *Nietzsche and the Question of Interpretation: Between Hermeneutics and Deconstruction.* New York: Routledge, 1990.

Sedgwick, Peter R., ed. *Nietzsche: A Critical Reader.* Oxford: Blackwell, 1995.

Solomon, Robert C., ed. *Nietzsche: A Collection of Critical Essays.* New York: Anchor, 1973.

Solomon, Robert C., and Kathleen M. Higgins. *Reading Nietzsche.* New York: Oxford University Press, 1988.

Stambaugh, Joan. *Nietzsche's Thought of Eternal Return.* Baltimore: Johns Hopkins University Press, 1972.

Stern, J. P. *Nietzsche.* Hassocks, Sussex: Harvester Press, 1978.

Strong, Tracy B. *Friedrich Nietzsche and the Politics of Transfiguration.* Berkeley: University of California Press, 1975.

Tanner, Michael. *Nietzsche.* Oxford: Oxford University Press, 1994.

Thomas, R. Hinton. *Nietzsche in German Politics and Society 1890-1918.* Manchester: Manchester University Press, 1983.

Warren, Mark. *Nietzsche and Political Thought.* Cambridge: MIT Press, 1987.

Yack, Bernard. *The Longing for Total Revolution.* Berkeley: University of California Press, 1992.

Political Background

Arendt, Hannah. *The Human Condition.* Chicago: University of Chicago Press, 1958.

———. *The Life of the Mind.* 2 Vols. New York: Viking, 1978.

Axtmann, Roland. *Liberal Democracy into the Twenty-First Century.* Manchester: Manchester University Press, 1996.

Bloom, Allan. *The Closing of the American Mind.* New York: Simon Schuster, 1987.

Camus, Albert. *The Rebel: An Essay on Man in Revolt.* New York: Vintage, 1956.

Coole, Diana H. *Women in Political Theory: From Ancient Misogyny to Contemporary Feminism.* Boulder: Lynne Rienner, 1988.

Derrida, Jacques. *Dissemination.* Translated by Barbara Johnson. Chicago: University of Chicago Press, 1988.

Dunn, John. *Western Political Theory in the Face of the Future.* Cambridge: Cambridge University Press, 1993.

Elshtain, Jean Bethke. *Democracy on Trial.* Concord, Ont.: Irwin Publishing, 1993.

Fukuyama, Francis. *The End of History and the Last Man.* New York: Free Press, 1992.

Kennedy, Ellen, and Susan Mendus, eds. *Women in Western Political Philosophy: Kant to Nietzsche.* New York: St. Martin's Press, 1987.

MacIntyre, Alasdair. *After Virtue: A Study of Moral Theory.* Notre Dame: Notre Dame University Press, 1981.

———. *Three Rival Versions of Moral Enquiry.* Notre Dame: University of Notre Dame Press, 1990.

McKnight, Stephen A., ed. *Eric Voegelin's Search for Order in History.* Baton Rouge: Louisana State University Press, 1978.

Melzer, Arthur M., Jerry Weinberger and M. Richard Zinman, eds. *History and the Idea of Progress.* Ithaca: Cornell University Press, 1995.

Oakeshott, Michael. *On Human Conduct.* Oxford: Clarendon Press, 1975.

———. *Rationalism in Politics.* London: Methuen, 1962.

Okin, Susan Maller. *Women in Western Political Thought.* Princeton: Princeton University Press, 1979.

Rorty, Richard. *Contingency, Irony, Solidarity.* Cambridge: Cambridge University Press, 1989.

Saxonhouse, Arlene W. *Women in the History of Political Thought: Ancient Greece to Machiavelli.* New York: Praeger, 1985.

Shanley, Mary Lyndon, and Carole Pateman, eds. *Feminist Interpretations and Political Theory.* Cambridge: Polity Press, 1991.

Strauss, Leo. *Natural Right and History.* Chicago: University of Chicago Press, 1958.

————. *Studies in Platonic Political Philosophy.* Chicago: University of Chicago Press, 1983.

————. *What is Political Philosophy? and Other Studies.* Glencoe, Ill.: Free Press, 1959.

Taylor, Charles. *Sources of the Self: The Making of the Modern Identity.* Cambridge: Harvard University Press, 1989.

Toynbee, Arnold J. *A Study of History.* 12 Vols. Oxford: Oxford University Press, 1948–1961.

Tuana, Nancy. *Woman and the History of Philosophy.* New York: Paragon, 1992.

Voegelin, Eric. *Order and History.* 5 Vols. Baton Rouge: Louisiana State University Press, 1956-1987.

Wiser, James. *Political Theory: A Thematic Inquiry.* Chicago: Nelson-Hall, 1986.

CREDIT LIST

CHAPTER 1

Cushman, Robert E., *Therapeia: Plato's Conception of Philosophy.* Copyright ©1958 The University of North Carolina Press. Reprinted by permission.

Hackforth, R., trans., *Phaedrus,* in *The Collected Dialogues of Plato,* eds. Edith Hamilton and Huntington Cairns. Cambridge: Cambridge University Press, 1961. Reprinted by permission.

Lippmann, Walter, *The Public Philosophy: On the Decline and Revival of the Western Society.* Copyright 1955 by Walter Lippmann; © renewed 1983 by Bank of New York. By permission of Little, Brown and Company.

Pangle, Thomas, trans., *The Laws of Plato.,* Basic Books, 1956. Reprinted by permission.

Plato, *Apology.* R. E. Allen, trans., *The Dialogues of Plato,* Vol. I. Yale University Press, 1984. Reprinted by permission.

Plato's *Republic.* Hackett Publishing Company: Indianapolis and Cambridge, 1974. Reprinted by permission.

Voegelin, Eric, *Order and History: The World of the Polis,* Vol. II. Louisiana State University Press, 1957. Reprinted by permission.

Voegelin, Eric, *Plato and Aristotle.* Louisiana State University Press, 1957. Reprinted by permission of the publisher.

CHAPTER 2

Everson, Stephen, ed., Benjamin Jowett, trans., revised by Jonathan Barnes, *Aristotle: The Politics.* Cambridge: Cambridge University Press. Reprinted by permission.

McKeon, Richard, ed., *Introduction to Aristotle, Metaphysics,* trans. W. D. Ross. Oxford: Oxford University Press. Reprinted by permission.

Ross, W.D., *Aristotle.* Methuen & Co., 1930. Reprinted by permission.

CHAPTER 3

Bevan, Edwyn, "Hellenistic Popular Philosophy," J. B. Bury and others, *The Hellenistic Age.* Cambridge University Press, 1925. Reprinted by permission.

Chilton, C.W., *Diogenes of Oenoanda: The Fragments.* Oxford: Oxford University Press, 1971. Reprinted by permission.

Lapidge, Michael, "The Stoic Inheritance," *A History of Twelfth-Century Western Philosophy,* ed. Peter Dronke. Cambridge: Cambridge University Press, 1988. Reprinted by permission.

Long, A.A., and D.N. Sedley, translations with commentary, *The Hellenistic Philosophers,* Vol. I. Cambridge University Press, 1987. Reprinted by permission.

Nichols, James H., Jr., *Epicurean Political Philosophy: The 'De rerum natura' of Lucretius.* Copyright © 1972, 1976 by Cornell University. Reprinted by permission.

Reprinted by permission of the publishers and the Loeb Classical Library from Volume XVI, translated by Clinton W. Keyes, Harvard University Press, 1928; Volume XVII translated by H. Rackham, Harvard University Press, 1914; Volume XXI translated by Walter Miller, Harvard University Press, 1913.

Shuckburgh, Evelyn S., trans., *Polybius on Roman Imperialism: The Histories of Polybius.* Copyright © 1980 by Alvin H. Bernstein. All rights reserved. Reprinted by special permission from Regnery Gateway, Inc. Washington, D.C.

CHAPTER 4

Augustine, Saint, *A Select Library of the Nicene and Post-Nicene Fathers of the Christian Church,* Vol. VIII, *Saint Augustine: Expositions on the Book of Psalms.* William B. Eerdmans Publishing Co., 1956.

Bettenson, Henry, ed., *Stromateis* in *Documents of the Christian Church.* Oxford University Press, 1947.

Deane, Herbert A., *The Political and Social Ideas of St. Augustine.* Copyright © 1963. Columbia University Press. Reprinted by permission.

Dvornik, Francis, *Early Christian and Byzantine Political Philosophy: Origins and Background.* The Dumbarton Oaks Center for Byzantine Studies, 1966.

Falls, Thomas B., trans., *Writings of Saint Justin Martyr,* in *The Fathers of the Church,* Vol. VI, ed. Ludwig Schopp. The Catholic University of America Press, 1965.

Gilson, Étienne, *The Christian Philosophy of St. Augustine,* trans. L.E.M. Lynch. Random House, 1960. Reprinted by permission.

Greenslade, S.L., trans., *Early Latin Theology,* in *The Library of Christian Classics,* Vol. V, SCM Press, 1956.

Leff, Gordon, *Medieval Thought* (Penguin Books, 1958), coypyright © Gordon Leff, 1958. Reprinted by permssion.

McIlwain, Charles, H., *The Growth of Political Thought in the West.* Copyright 1932 by The Macmillan Company; copyright renewed © 1960 by Charles H. McIlwain. Reprinted by permission.

Niebuhr, Reinhold, *Christian Realism and Political Problems.* Yale University Press, 1953. Reprinted by permission.

Ogg., F.A., ed., *A Source Book of Mediavel History.* Rowman & Littlefield, 1972. Reprinted by permission.

Revised Standard Version Bible, copyright 1946, 1952, 1971 by the Division of Christian Education of the National Council of Churches of Christ in the USA. Reprinted by permission.

Ullmann, Walter, *Medieval Political Thought* (Penguin Books, 1975), copyright © Walter Ullmann, 1965. Reprinted by permission.

Voegelin, Eric, *Order and History, Volume 1: Israel and Revelation.* Copyright © 1956 by Louisiana State University Press. Reprinted by permission.

CHAPTER 5

Aquinas, St. Thomas, *Summa Theologiae* translation of the *Fathers of the English Dominican Province,* 3 volumes. Benziger Publishing, 1948.

Canning, J.B., "Introduction: politics, institutions and ideas," *The Cambridge History of Medieval Political Thought, 350–c. 1450,* ed. J.H. Burns. Cambridge University Press, 1988.

Niebuhr, Richard H., *Christ and Culture.* Copyright 1951 by Harper & Row, Publishers, Inc. Reprinted by permission of HarperCollins Publishers.

Voegelin, Eric, *Science, Politics, and Gnosticism.* Regnery, 1968. Reprinted by permission.

CHAPTER 6

Bondanella, Peter, and Mark Musa, "The Art of War," "The Discourses," "The Prince," from *Portable Machiavelli.* Copyright © 1979 by Viking Penguin, Inc. Reprinted by permission of Viking Penguin, a division of Penguin Books USA Inc.

Butterfield, Herbert, *The Statecraft of Machiavelli.* George Allen & Unwin, now Unwin Hyman, an imprint of HarperCollins Publishers Limited.

Gilbert, Allan, ed. and trans., *The Letters of Machiavelli: A Selection of His Letters.* The Putnam Publishing Group. Reprinted by permission.

Hulling, Mark, *Citizen Machiavelli.* Copyright © 1983 by Princeton University Press. Reprinted by permission.

CHAPTER 7

Burtt, E.A., *The Metaphysical Foundations of Modern Physical Science.* Humanities Press International, Inc. Atlantic Highlands, NJ, 1955.

Crew, Henry, and Alfonso de Saliro, trans., *Galileo Galilei, Dialogues Concerning Two New Sciences.* Dover, 1954. Reprinted by permission.

Descartes, Rene, *The Philosophical Writings of Descartes,* Vols. I & II, trans. John Cottingham, Robert Stoothoff and Dugald Murdoch. Cambridge University Press, 1985. Reprinted by permission.

Hobbes, Thomas, *Leviathan,* ed. Michael Oakeshott. Macmillan Publishing, 1962.

Keeling, S.V., *Descartes.* Oxford University Press, 1934. Reprinted by permission.

Sedgwick, W.T. and H. W. Tyler. *A Short History of Science.* Copyright © 1917 by Macmillan Publishing Company, renewed 1939 by Macmillan Publishing Company. Reprinted by permission.

Spragens, Tom, *The Irony of Liberal Reason.* The University of Chicago Press.

Temple, William, *Nature, Man and God.* Macmillan Publishing Company, 1935.

Whitehead, Alfred North, *Science and the Modern World.* Macmillan Publishing, 1960.

Willey, Basil, *The Seventeenth Century Background.* Doubleday Anchor Books, 1953.

CHAPTER 8

Andrew, Edward, *Shylock's Rights: A Grammar of Lockian Claims.* Toronto: University of Toronto Press, 1988. Reprinted by permission.

Barker, Ernest, "Reflections on English Political Theory," *Political Studies,* Vol. I (1953-54). Oxford: Blackwell Publishers. Reprinted by permssion.

von Leyden, W., ed., *Essays on the Law of Nature,* VII. Oxford: Clarendon Press, 1958. Reprinted by permission.

Locke, John, *Locke: Two Treatises of Government,* ed. Peter Laslett. New York: Cambridge Univeristy Press, 1967. Reprinted by permission.

Tarcov, Nathan, *Locke's Education for Liberty.* Chicago: Univeristy of Chicago Press, 1984. Reprinted by permssion.

CHAPTER 9

Barry, Brian, "Games, Justice and the General Will," *Mind* 74 (1965). Reprinted by permission of Oxford University Press.

Turrettin, *Sermon sur la loy de la Liberté* (1734), as quoted by Pamela A. Mason, "The Communion of Citizens: Calvinist Themes in Rousseau's Theory of the State," Originally printed in *Polity,* Fall 1993 (Vol. 26, #1). Reprinted by permission.

CHAPTER 10

Bentham, Jeremy, *A Fragment on Government* and *An Introduction to the Principles of Morals and Legislation,* ed. Wildred Harrison. Oxford: Blackwell Publishers. Reprinted by permission.

Burns, J.H. and H.L.A. Hart, eds., *A Fragment of Government.* Cambridge: Cambridge University Press, 1988. Reprinted by permission.

Collini, Stefan, ed., "The Subjection of Women" in *J.S. Mill:On Liberty and Other Writings.* Cambridge: Cambridge University Press, 1989. Reprinted by permission.

Mill, John Stuart, *On Liberty and Other Essays,* ed. John Gray. Oxford: Oxford University Press, 1991. Reprinted by permission

Nidditch, Peter H., ed., *An Essay Concerning Human Understanding.* "The Epistle Reader." Oxford: Clarendon Press, 1975. Reprinted by permission.

Robson, John, M., ed., *Autobiography* in *John Stuart Mill: A Selection of His Works.* Toronto: University of Toronto Press, 1963-91. Reprinted by permission.

Winch, Peter, *The Idea of a Social Science.* Routledge, 1958. Reprinted by permission.

CHAPTER 11

Berlin, Isaiah, *Karl Marx: His Life and Environment,* 4/e. Oxford: Oxford University Press, 1978. Reprinted by permssion.

Hegel, G.W.F., *The Philosophy of History,* trans. J. Sibree. New York: Dover, 1956. Reprinted by permssion.

Knox, T.M., trans., *Hegel's Philosophy of Right.* Oxford: Clarendon Press, 1953. Reprinted by permssion.

Singer, Peter, *Marx.* Oxford: Oxford University Press, 1980. Reprinted by permssion.

Tucker, Robert C., *The Marx-Engels Reader,* 2/e. Copyright © 1978, 1972 by W.W. Norton & Company, Inc. Reprinted by permission.

GLOSSARY

Agathon: the Good. In Plato, the term is used for the final goal of knowing in the stages of cognition. It is best understood as the orientation point for all knowing. It is synonymous with the greatest good.

Aitia: The translation from Greek is usually "cause," but level of explanation is better. Aristotle has four levels: material, formal, efficient, and final. The efficient level of explanation refers to what, in modern language, causes something to come into existence.

Amour de soi: the love of self. This term is used in Rousseau to refer to the natural self-love found in nature before society has warped it into vanity and envy.

Amour propre: self-love or vanity. Rousseau uses this category to express what happens when humans in society compare themselves to each other. Ultimately, this produces an alienated individual whose self-understanding is determined by social position and status.

Arete: The word refers to the proper function or operation of something and can be translated as excellence, goodness, or virtue. The *arete* of the eye is to see. With a human, for example, the full and proper development of a person's faculties is the life of virtue.

Aristocracy: Strictly speaking, the term means the rule of the best and is used by Plato to designate the guardian rulers of the Republic. It is a just form of government in contrast with the timocracy, oligarchy, tyranny, or democracy—all of which rule in their own interests and without law.

Caritas: This term is the Latin version of the Greek *agape*. It is the love of God for humans and of humans for God.

Cause: See *Aitia*.

Democracy: In Plato and Aristotle, the term refers to the rule by the many poor in their own class interest. The term does not become associated with law, limited government, and individual rights until modernity.

Dialectic: In Greek, the term used is often *dianoetic*. The process whereby thought moves from hypothetical starting points to a conclusion. More generally, it may mean the critical reflectiveness characteristic of genuine, open philosophizing. The term is often associated, somewhat unfairly, with Hegel's purported triad of thesis, antithesis, and synthesis.

Diffidence: In Hobbes, this is one of the three causes of quarrels within society, along with competition and glory, and it too will lead to a state of war unless a government imposes order.

638

Dike: This can be defined variously as right, justice, and order.

Doxa: opinion or judgment. This is a lesser degree of knowledge and is contrasted with *episteme* in Greek philosophy.

Dualism: Any view that posits two irreducible principles or forces for explaining reality, such as good and evil, mind and body, spirit and matter.

Eikasia: imagining. This is the lowest stage in Plato's stages of cognition. Here the senses simply record the impressions received from reality.

Empiricism: This is the philosophy that holds that sense perception is the sole source of knowledge about reality.

End: For Aristotle, the completion of a thing, or its full development, is its *telos* or end. See *Teleology*.

Episteme: theoretical knowledge in Greek philosophy. It is contrasted with opinion or *doxa*, and is sometimes translated as science.

Epistemology: the science of knowing. It is that part of philosophy that examines how humans know and the methods for knowing.

Essence: the intrinsic or ultimate nature of something. It is a term often used in Greek philosophy to denote the inherent substance of something. The essence or nature of an acorn is to be an oak tree; the essence or nature of a particular fetus is to be the fully grown creature of that species. Essence is contrasted with accidental properties that do not constitute the nature of a thing. Essence is also contrasted with existence, i.e., whether something exists is a question independent of its essence.

Eudaimonia: happiness. In Aristotle, it refers to well-being of a fully functioning human, with all the faculties operating according to their potentials. Euphoria refers only to the happiness associated with the appetites.

Form: The Greek term is *eidos*, which is translated as idea or form. In earlier translations "ideal" was improperly used. The idea of something is permanent, in contrast with the actual material thing itself, which can die, decay, burn, or be destroyed in some way.

Fortune (fortuna):   For Machiavelli, *fortune* is what chance and fate continually present to each person as a challenge. Sometimes one can successfully conquer *fortune*; at other times, one may fail.

Free will: This doctrine holds that human behaviour is not completely determined. The human, as agent, can decide and act; as a consequence, human actions are free, and humans can be viewed as accountable and responsible moral agents.

General will: The term is used by Rousseau to refer to the case in which each individual in a community simultaneously and voluntarily will what would be applicable to the whole community. This would be an instantiation of the general will, and it is always right.

639

Gnosticism: (1) The term was used by Eric Voegelin to represent the type of ideological thinking where cognitive mastery is claimed. It can be seen in both religious and secular movements when a claim for certainty is put forward. The claim may take intellectual, emotional, or volitional forms. (2) There were early Christian gnostics in the first century A. D. who argued that with the proper discipline they could make themselves immortal.

Hedonism: This is the doctrine that holds that pleasure is the sole good of humans. The good may be simple physical pleasure (Bentham) or a more complicated psychological and mental pleasure (Mill).

Humanism: The term is used in various ways. One use is to contrast religious ethics and secular ethics with one derived from a transcendental source and the other derived from human nature. Another use is to label the cultural movement in the fourteenth century that emphasized the study of the re-discovered Greek texts and classical literature in general.

Immanent: dwelling in. What is within empirical, mundane reality is called immanent. The contrast is with transcendent.

Innate Ideas: These are ideas antecedent to all experience and are built-in to the mind. Plato, Descartes, and Leibnitz are usually associated with this view. Locke is viewed as an opponent.

Jus gentium: law of the tribes or people. This was judge-made law in ancient Rome and was based upon practice and common sense.

Justice: The term has two standard meanings. (1) It is synonymous with right or order and is a translation of the Greek *dike*. (2) The term is used to refer to the state of a well-balanced soul, as described by Plato, where reason guides the two other faculties, appetite and spirit.

Kallipolis: the just or beautiful city. The city in speech, described by Socrates in his conversation with Glaucon and Adeimantus.

Labour theory of value: The first intimation of the idea is found in Locke's argument that value comes by humans mixing their labour with nature. More precisely, it refers to the theory that a commodity's value—the exchange value or its worth in money—results from the average amount of labour time required to make the commodity.

Law: In Greek, the term is *nomos*. It can be written or unwritten and is sometimes translated as convention. The contrast is often with *physis* or nature. The former can be other than the way it is, but the latter cannot.

Logos: The word literally means speech, but its meaning and use are far broader. It can refer to reason, the rational capacity, and, more generally, the rational structure of reality.

Materialism: This is the doctrine that all reality is wholly matter and is contrasted with idealism. Strict materialists hold that mind, consciousness, spirit, and other such categories are either nonsensical or reducible to material components.

Metaphysics: In Aristotle, the word refers to the search for the ultimate cause and nature of reality.

Metaxy: in-between. The term is used by Plato to represent the tension between the divine and human, imperfection and perfection, ignorance and knowledge and other poles.

Millenarian: A variety of movements, beginning in the Middle Ages, contended that history was coming to an end and that the actual Kingdom of God would be established on earth. History would be over. There are secular equivalences.

Monism: the doctrine that everything is reducible to one kind of thing whether it is material or ideational. Hobbes is viewed by some as a monist materialist, and Hegel is held to be an ideational monist.

Mysticism: This is the view that reality is inexpressible in standard concepts or rational categories; therefore, one must use nonrational categories, such as images and metaphors, to refer to the transcendent.

Myth: In Plato, myth is a story or fable with a philosophic point, such as the myth of Er at the end of the *Republic*. The story may be fictional, but it is used to illuminate and evoke a new perception and understanding.

Naturalism: Sometimes this term is used synonymously with humanism and secularism, and the contrast is with dualism or some religious position. It is also used to mean that there is only a difference in degrees between animals and humans—all are natural creatures. In this use, the contrast is with humanism.

Natural Law: (1) The term can be used to refer to scientific and empirical laws, such as gravity. (2) Philosophically, the term has been associated with the view that humans have a rational structure and purpose that has been ordained or at least built into the structure of reality. One is thus bound, as in a law, by the structure of one's nature and of reality. Reason can be used to detect its applicability. The idea is intimated in Plato and developed in Aquinas and others. (3) Aquinas limits the term to what can be discovered by reason without revelation; it is that part of the eternal law that humans can naturally detect through reason.

Natural right: The term is used more generally to mean roughly the same as the second meaning for natural law. But, with modernity, the term has been associated with the position that there is a source, or sources, that are indisputable and provide authority. In Hobbes, self-preservation is the indisputable source of right; in Locke, there are four great rights that can be used to determine the legitimacy of a state.

Nature: The Greek word is *physis* and is used to denote origins or growth. In Aristotle, the nature of a thing is its full development. Also, nature implies a standard for evaluating that is independent of human wishes or convention.

Nominalism: This is the view that reality can be attributed only to particular empirical things, not to universals or general ideas. Hobbes is often called a nominalist because he argues in Part One of *Leviathan* that humans can know only empirical things.

641

Oligarchy: This is rule by the rich few in their own interest.

Ontology: the theory or account of being. It refers to what is real or being, rather than what is illusory or derivative.

Periagoge: turning around or conversion. The term is used in Plato's cave allegory to refer to the mysterious turning around that leads to the breaking of the chains of ignorance and the long ascent to the sun or the Good. It designates a new and fundamental orientation point.

Phronesis: The usual translation is practical wisdom or prudence. In Aristotle, this is the practical reason that guides virtuous human conduct. It is a mixture of both principles and experience.

Physis: See *Nature*.

Pistis: belief. This is the second stage of cognition in which there is no real knowledge, but the empirical reality of things is recognized. Common sense is a synonym.

Polis: This is the Greek word for city, or more generally, political society. It means more than the institutional structure and includes the common cultures and goals of the society.

Politeia: The closest translation from the Greek is regime. But, it includes the constitutional order as well as the way of life.

Politeuma: Aristotle uses the phrase to refer to the ruling civic body.

Polity: This form of rule has control exercised by the middling group, which would be the largest group in society. There is rule by law and for the common good; thus, the rich and the poor would be protected and have a degree of participation in the political system. This is the best practical regime for Aristotle.

Prudence or practical wisdom: See *Phronesis*.

Rationalism: This is usually contrasted with empiricism. It is held that the operation of reason can discern the essential features of reality.

Realism: (1) This is the position that universals are more real than particulars or sense experience. Plato would be a realist and Hobbes would be a nominalist. (2) The view that stresses how humans actually behave when motivated by self-interest is often called realist. In this sense, Machiavelli and Hobbes are realists, and Plato and Aristotle are not.

Regime: See *Politeia*.

Relativism: This is the position that human judgments and beliefs are relative to one's culture, class, gender, or any other determinative factors.

Revolution: In Aristotle's categories, a full revolution—or social revolution—occurs when the ruling group (*politeuma*) and the way of life (*politeia*) are changed.

Science: see, *Episteme*. In modernity, the word is associated with the mathematical and empirical methods of the natural sciences. In general, it means a body of organized and formal knowledge and is contrasted with arts or skills (*techné*).

Scientism: This term refers to the belief that all of reality can be knowable by the empirical and quantifiable methods of the physical sciences. It stresses the control that humans can have over reality. Hobbes represents this position.

Skepticism: This is the position that denies the possibility of true knowledge. Hobbes, for example, is skeptical about the possibility of knowledge about any transcendental subject but claims certainty about other areas.

Sophia: wisdom. Aristotle defines *sophia* as "intuitive reason combined with scientific knowledge—of the highest objects which has received as it were its proper completion."

Soul: In Aristotle, this is the vital principle or formal cause constituting living things; so, there are vegetative and animal souls as well as human souls. In Christian theology, the word refers to the spiritual dimension of human nature and is not dependent upon the material for its existence; it is, thus, immortal.

Sovereignty: This is the doctrine that final and ultimate power rests with some centre, which is sovereign. Hobbes is a representative thinker advocating the creation of a sovereign political centre without limitation.

Species being: This term is used by Marx to designate human potential as free, self-conscious labour. Our species being is warped by economic systems, particularly capitalism, and this causes alienation.

Spirit: in Greek, *thymos*. Plato uses the word to label one of the three faculties of human nature—reason, spirit, and appetite. It refers to human self-consciousness of its own identity, particularly with respect to other humans, and it shows itself in courage or anger, ambition or humility, etc.

Spoudaioi: serious or mature persons. The phrase is used by Aristotle to refer to mature, rational, and ethical persons. These would be fully developed persons.

State of nature: This is a hypothetical or imaginative device utilized by Hobbes so that one could allegedly conceive of human nature free of past cultural and philosophic influences. It was a state prior to government and even society.

State of war: The state of nature is a state of war for Hobbes. Locke and others distinguish between the two on the grounds that in the state of nature humans are not automatically in competition or without peaceful means of resolving whatever conflicts that may occur.

Summum bonum: the highest good. It is the Latin equivalent for Plato's *agathon*.

Synderesis: In Aquinas, the term is used to refer to the innate human capacity, deeper than conscience, which can, in principle, enable humans to recognize the Good or God's will.

Teleology: The term is derived from the Greek word *telos*, which means end or goal. A teleological explanation is one of a goal or purpose. Bentham explains human behaviour in regard to the goal of pleasure; Plato explains human behaviour in in regard to the Good. Both explanations are teleological.

Timocracy: This is rule by the military. It is directed to the goal of honour.

Transcendent: This refers to what is beyond some limits of some kind, and it need not be religious. The contrast is with immanent.

Tyranny: This is the rule by one in his own interest and by decree; it is, accordingly, an unjust rule.

Universal: A universal is a feature that is common to all examples of a thing. A standard example is that "male" is common to all individual men. Realists argue that universals are constitutive of reality in some sense; others would argue that they are merely concepts or names of likeness with no ontological status.

Utilitarianism: This is the position associated with Jeremy Bentham and John Stuart Mill, in which good is measured in terms of the pleasure produced, and the greatest happiness for the greatest number becomes the criterion for a just government. John Stuart Mill tried to deepen and broaden the philosophy.

Virtue: See *Arete*. (1) In Greek thought, the four great virtues or excellences are wisdom, courage, moderation, and justice. The first three are the full or excellent uses of, respectively, the rational, spirited, and appetitive faculties. Justice is the state that results. (2) St. Thomas also added the theological virtues of faith, hope, and charity. (3) Aristotle developed a catalogue of other moral virtues in the *Nichomachean Ethics*.

Virtù: Machiavelli used this Latin equivalent of *arete* to mean those qualities that make for a successful political life. Such *virtù*, for example, could include cruelty or clemency, depending whether or not the behaviour was required to get or to keep power. If it was necessary, the behaviour or personality trait would be an example of *virtù*.

Will to power: The term is used by Nietzsche to express the elemental force in humans to assert themselves over nature and others.

SUBJECT INDEX

A

Absolutism
  Filmer, 366–377
  Hobbes, 316–318
  Locke, 381, 399–402
Academy, Plato, 8, 55, 97
Agathon, 29–31, 62, 157, 635
Aitia, 60–61, 635
Alienation
  Hegel, 561–569
  Marx, 571–576
  Rousseau, 433–436, 460, 466
American Revolution, xii, 108, 323–324, 406
Amour de soi, 433, 635
Amour propre, 433, 635
Anti-Semitism, 212–213, 568, 615–616
Aquinas, St. Thomas, Ch. 5, 283, 285, 287, 333, 367
  Aristotle, 176, 181–183, 190–195, 206–209
  Augustine, 183, 194–195
  Church-State, 212–213
  Conscience, 196
  Faith, 190
  Grace, 189
  Justice, 191, 195, 214
  Kingly Rule, 206–209, 215
  Law, human, divine, and natural, 195–206
  Property, 210–211
  Reason and Revelation, 186–194, 219
  Tyrannicide, 208
  Virtue, 191–192, 196, 204
  War, 210
  Women, 211, 213–215
Arete, 18, 22, 62–63, 635. *See also* Plato.
Aristocracy, 20–21, 34, 84, 635
Aristotle, Ch. 2, 109–110, 155, 157, 181–183, 286, 334, 341–342, 367, 404, 477, 492, 507, 535, 600
  Aitia or cause, 60–61

Compared with Plato, 90–92
  Criticism of Plato, 58–59, 62, 77–79
  Democracy, 82–83, 85–86
  Education, 74, 89
  Ethics, 62–72
  Family, 72–73, 75, 77–79
  Friendship, x–xi, 71–72
  Happiness, 61, 63, 190
  Human Nature, 73, 92
  Justice, 66–67
  Law, 66–67, 73, 74–75, 82–89
  Mean, 63–65. *See also* Virtue.
  Metaphysics, 57–62
  Oligarchy, 82–83, 85–86
  Phronesis or Practical Wisdom, 68
  Pleasure, 70–71
  Polis, 72–73, 79–80
  Polity, 82–83, 86–87
  Property, 77, 78–79
  Reason, Theoretical and Practical, 63, 67–70
  Revolution, 87–88
  Sciences, Theoretical and Practical, 67–70
  Slavery, 75–77
  Statesmanship, 69, 84–85, 91
  Teleology, 60
  Typology of States, 82
  Tyranny, 82, 88–89
  Virtue, 63–65
  Virtues, Theoretical and Practical, 67
  Wisdom, 68–69
  Women, 75
Art of War, The, 231, 246
Astrology, 228, 255
Atheism, 45–47, 332, 335
Athens, 3–4, 7–8, 52, 55–56, 72
Augustine, Ch. 4, 140–160, 180, 261, 272, 312, 333, 444, 460, 461, 492, 600, 606, 624

Church and State, 148–152
Comparison of Greek and Christian Thought, 155–160
  Evil, 143–146
  Freedom, 144–145
  Grace, 145, 158
  History, Theory of, 159–160
  Human Nature, 142–146
  Justice, 148–150
  Manichean, 140
  Peace, 151–152
  Platonism, 141
  Property, 152–155
  Sin, 144–145
  Slavery, 152–154
  State, 148–152
  Two Cities, Two Loves, 146–148
  Will, 143, 159
  Women, 159–160
Autobiography (Mill), 505–508

B

Behavioralism, 334
Behemoth, The (Hobbes), 297
Bentham, Jeremy, Ch. 10, 555
  Blackstone, 494–495
  Calculus, 493–494
  Ethics, 491–493
  Government, 497–499
  Justice, 498–500
  Law, 500
  Legislation, 500–501
  Liberalism, 489–490
  Mill, James, 502–503, 505
  Pleasure and Pain, 491
  Revolution, 496–497
  Rights, 496
  Social Contract, 495
  Society, 495
  Utility, 493–494
Beyond Good and Evil, 611
Bible, 306, 372
  Old Testament, 126, 128–132, 134, 167, 179, 200, 299, 325

New Testament, 126, 133–136, 200, 325

C

Calvinism
  Hobbes, 316, 333
  Locke, 370
  Rousseau, 423, 473–474
Capital (Marx), 556, 570
Capitalism, 323, 336, 381–385, 404–405, 407, 458, 587–589, 594–597, 598
Caritas, 143, 635. *See also* Love.
Cause, 60, 195. *See also Aitia.*
Christian Creeds, 136–139
Christianity, 33, 47
  Feuerbach, 565–567
  Hegel, 561–565
  Hobbes, 308–309, 322, 324–333
  Kant, 559–561
  Locke, 342, 346, 366
  Machiavelli, 245, 260–262
  Origins, 133–139
Church Fathers, 136–142, 159
Church and State
  Aquinas, 212–213
  Augustine, 148–152
  Hobbes, 309, 332
  Locke, 342, 366
  Middle Ages, 160–168
  Rousseau, 456, 458
Cicero, 107, 110–117, 141, 148, 226, 257, 259, 263, 271–272
  Commonwealth, 115–117
  Equality, 114–115
  Justice, 112–113
  Law, 116
  Natural Law, 113–114
City of God, 141, 159
Common Good, 19, 49, 83–84, 116, 148, 197, 202–204, 207–211, 253, 255, 257, 259, 265, 334, 380, 403
Communism, 573, 577–579, 583
Communist Manifesto, 555, 592
Confessions (Rousseau), 418–422
Confessions of St. Augustine, 142–144

Conquest
  Aristotle, 81–82
  Hobbes, 319, 399
  Locke, 381–382, 397–399
  Machiavelli, 234–235, 251–255, 262–266
  Rousseau, 437–438
Consent, see Hobbes, Locke, and Rousseau
Contract, Social. *See also* Bentham, Epicurus, Hobbes, Locke, Rousseau
Constitutional Code, 497–500
Constitutionalism, 215, 322
Covenant, 128–132
Critique of the Gotha Program, 557, 593
Critique of Political Economy, 556, 584–590
Cynics, 97–99

D

De Cive (Hobbes), 296–297, 329
Declaration of Independence, 406
Declaration of Rights of Man, 496
Deconstruction, 614, 623–624
Democracy, 36, 635
  Aristotle, 82–83, 85–86
  Bentham, 489–490, 497–499
  Locke, 368–369, 377, 393
  Mill, 536–541
  Plato, 35–37
  Rousseau, 459, 477, 480
Descartes, René, 287–295, 301, 304, 342, 354, 361, 402, 408
Dialectic, 636
  Hegel, 553, 561–565
  Marx, 570–574, 590–592
  Plato, 29
Diffidence, 310–311, 636
Dike, 17, 66, 636. *See also* Justice.
Discourses on the First Ten Books of Titus Livius, 231, 247–267
Discourse on Inequality (Second Discourse), 422–436
Discourse on Method (Descartes), 288–291
Discourse on the Sciences and Arts (First Discourse), 422, 425–427

Divine Law, 167, 197, 201–202
Divine Right, 372–377, 391. *See also First Treatise.*
Division of Labour
  Marx, 580, 583
  Plato, 19–20
  Rousseau, 479
Dominicans, 178, 184
Doxa, 28, 636
Dualism, 145, 636

E

Early Christianity, 133–136
Economic and Philosophic Manuscripts, 573–579, 594
Economics, *see* Property
  Aristotle, 77–79
  Locke, 382–386, 404
  Marx, 569, 592–597
  Rousseau, 434–436, 479
Education
  Aristotle, 74, 89
  Hobbes, 300–301, 324
  Locke, 346, 364, 409
  Mill, 514–515, 532
  Plato, 11, 26–28
  Rousseau, 457, 464, 467
  Sophists, *See Gorgias.*
Eikasia, 28, 636
Elements of Philosophy (Hobbes), 295–296
Emile, 423, 462–469
Empiricism, 103, 195, 294, 302–304, 342, 360–361, 365, 636
End, 60, 304, 636. *See also* Teleology.
England
  Civil War (1640s), 296–297
  Revolution (1688), 347, 398
Enlightenment, 410, 490–491, 497, 536
Epicureanism, 91–102
  Human nature, 100–101
  Pleasure, 100
  Social Contract, 101
Episteme, 67–70, 636
Epistemology, 111, 300–306, 348–366, 636
Equality
  Aquinas, 211, 214–215
  Aristotle, 62–63, 75–76, 80, 87

Augustine, 144, 153, 159–160
Hobbes, 310, 319
Locke, 379, 388–389
Marx, 583, 593
Mill, 541–543
Plato, 24, 45
Rousseau, 433, 439–440
Erastrianism, 309, 332
*Essay Concerning Human
    Understanding* (Locke),
    344, 346, 348–366
Essays on the Law of Nature
    (Locke), 342
Essay on Toleration (Locke),
    344, 346
Essence, 59, 194, 304, 360,
    573, 636
Eudaimonia, 636. *See also*
    Happiness.
Exclusion Controversy, 345
Exodus, 128–132
Exploitation
    Marx, 571–576, 594–597
    Rousseau, 434–435

F

Family
    Aristotle, 72–73, 75–79
    Hobbes, 319
    Locke, 386–389
    Marx, 568, 580
    Mill, 531–532, 541–543
    Plato, 24–27, 45
    Rousseau, 424–425, 472
Feudalism, 169–171
First Treatise (Locke), 366–377
Forms, 28–29, 58, 103, 304, 637
Fortune, 110, 242–244, 637
Fragment of Government,
    489–490, 494–496
Franciscans, 184
Freedom
    Augustine, 143–145
    Hegel, 562–563
    Hobbes, 320–321
    Locke, 378–381
    Marx, 573–575, 600
    Mill, *See On Liberty*
    Rousseau, 437, 440–441
    Stoics, 98, 100–106, 109
Free Will, 142–146, 207, 303,
    387, 438, 458, 637
French Revolution, 417, 500
Friendship, x–xi, 71–72

G

Gelasian Doctrine, 161–164
Genealogy of Morals, 614–615
General Will, 439–440,
    443–446, 452–453,
    460–473, 474–475,
    637
German Ideology, The, 583–584
Glorious Revolution (1688),
    347, 398
Gnosticism, 136, 227, 637
Gorgias, 3, 10–16, 56, 97
Government, *see*
    Republicanism
    Bentham, 497–499
    Locke, 393–397
    Machiavelli, 248, 250,
        254–259
    Mill, 536–541
    Rousseau, 449, 479–480

H

Happiness
    Aquinas, 190, 192
    Aristotle, 61, 63
    Augustine, 147
    Bentham, 489, 494–495
    Hobbes, 307
    Locke, 350, 357, 364, 410
    Mill, 517–518, 543–544
    Nietzsche, 616
    Plato, 14–17, 18, 22
    Rousseau, 433–436, 441,
        458, 465–467
Hebraic Tradition, 127–132
Hedonism, 70, 492, 637
Hegel, 130, 268, 552–553,
    559, 561–565,
    569–570, 577, 594, 598
Historicism, xi, 623–624. *See*
    Nietzsche and
    Perspectivism.
History of Florence, 231, 250
Hobbes, Thomas, Ch. 7.
    232, 417–418, 428, 430,
    433, 436–437, 439, 456,
    487, 492
    Aristotle, 301, 304,
        306–307, 318, 331,
        333–334
    Conscience, 286, 322, 326,
        328
    Consent, 316–317, 319

Contract or Covenant,
    315–319
Family, 319
Free Will, 303
Good and Evil, 304–305
Human Nature, 300–305,
    310
Influence, 333–335
Law, 311–312, 322
Liberty, 320–321
Motion and Matter,
    304–305, 334
Natural Law, 312–315
Natural Right, 312
Obligation, 316
Religion, 308–309,
    324–333
Science, 303, 334
Self-preservation, 312–314
Sense, 300–303
State of Nature, 311–313
State of War, 311–313
Holy Family, The, 571–572
Human Nature, *see listing
    under each philosopher*
Humanism, 226–229, 242,
    637

I

Idea, 28, 351.
    See also Forms.
Idealism, 40, 89
Ideology, 581, 590, 607–608,
    628
Immanent, 145, 637
Incarnation, 134, 186–188
Individualism, 286
    Hobbes, 286, 334
    Locke, 403–404, 407,
        409–410
    Mill, 526–528, 535
    Rousseau, 417, 477–479
Industrial Revolution
Inequality
    Locke, 381–384, 386–388
    Marx, 583, 593
    Rousseau, 434
Innate Ideas, 103, 349–351,
    637. See Locke, *Essay on
    Human Understanding.*
*Introduction to the Principles of
    Morals and Legislation*,
    490
Israel, 128–131, 134

J

Jesus of Nazareth, 126,
133–135
Jus Civile, 117, 202
Just Gentium, 118, 202, 638
Just Naturale, *see* Natural law
Justice, 5, 149, 168, 311–314,
317, 334, 360, 379–380,
392–393, 638. *See also*
Plato, Aristotle, Cicero,
Augustine, Aquinas.
Justinian Code, 176

K

Kallipolis, 22, 40–41, 638
Kant, Immanuel, 559–561, 563
Kingdom of Darkness, 298,
330–333
Kingdom of God, 133–135,
147, 153, 158, 328, 330
Kingship
Aquinas, 206–209
Aristotle, 82, 88–89
Filmer, 367–370
Hobbes, 318
Plato, 20–22, 25, 41–42,
47–48

L

Labour Theory of Value, 638
Locke, 383–386
Marx, 593–594
Laissez-faire, 385, 587–589,
594–597
Law, *see each thinker*, 18,
166–172, 638
Laws (Plato), 41–48, 90
Legislator, 447–448, 479–481
Leviathan, 296–335
Liberalism
Bentham, 489–490
Hobbes, 292–295,
334–335, 407
Locke, 403–410, 477–481
Mill, 510, 545–546
Rousseau, 460
Liberty, *see* Freedom
Locke, John, 292, 294,
417–418, 428, 433,
436–437, 458, 477, 480,
487, 491, 494–496, 600
American Founding Fathers,
xii

Comparison with Hobbes,
354, 363, 379–380, 392,
399, 407–409
Conquest, 381–382, 397–399
Consent, Express and Tacit,
381, 391–392, 399
Divine Right, 372–377, 391
Education, 346, 409
Family, 374–375, 380,
386–389
First Treatise, 366–377
Human nature, 343, 380
Human Understanding,
Epistemology, 348–366
Influence, 402
Innatism, 103, 349–352
Law, 393–396
Liberalism, 403–410
Money, 384–385
Natural Law, 342–343,
378–381
Natural Rights, 356–357,
378
Political Society, 389–390
Property, 356–357,
362–363, 373, 382–386,
393, 404
Religious Toleration, 342,
366
Revolution, 399–402, 405
Second Treatise, 377–402
Separation of Powers,
396–397, 405
State of Nature, 378–381
Structure of Government,
393–397
Tyranny, 399
War, 345, 379–380, 405
Whig Party, 397
Logos, 3, 10, 46, 73, 121, 134,
171, 334, 613, 638
Love, xi, 143, 191, 216–217,
469–470, 627
Lyceum, 55, 97

M

Machiavelli, Niccolo, Ch. 6,
286, 297, 299, 318, 406,
450, 473, 622
Compared with Aristotle,
232, 236, 239, 245, 252,
270–272
Education, 237–238
Forms of States, 254–255
Fortuna, 242–248, 259, 266

Founding of a State, 242,
245, 251–255
Great Men, 236–238
Human Nature, 237–238,
249, 256
Law, 252–253, 262–263
Militia, 257
Necessity, 238–239, 241,
244, 259
Religion, 258, 260–262
Republicanism, 248, 250,
254–259
Significance, 268–273
Statecraft, 236–238,
249–250, 253–254,
262–266
Violence, 243, 246–247, 250,
253, 259, 262, 265–266
Virtù, 234–242 *passim*,
244–248, 252, 259, 270
Woman, 243, 270
Majority
Hobbes, 316
Locke, 390–393, 395
Mill, 521, 537–538
Rousseau, 453–454
Mandragola, 231, 243
Manicheans, 140
Marx, Karl, Ch. 11, 488, 508,
510, 606, 607, 622
Accumulation, 595–597
Alienation, 571–576
Capitalism, 587–589,
594–597, 598
Class, 580, 588–589, 592
Communism, 573, 577–579
Critics, 597–600
Engels, Frederick, 554–556,
590–592
Exchange value, 593–594
Exploitation, 571–576,
594–597
Feuerbach, 565–567,
571–573, 597
Forces of Production,
581–586
Foundation, Economic,
585–586
Freedom, 569, 573, 575,
578, 600
Hegel, 552–553, 559,
561–565, 569–570, 577,
591, 598
Historical Materialism,
557–558, 570–574,
579–80, 584–592

Immiseration, 595–597
Kant, 559–561, 563
Labour Theory of Value, 593–594
Liberation
Ownership, 580
Predictions, 598–599
Proletariat, 568–569
Religion, 565–567
Revolution, 577–579, 583, 588, 598
Surplus Value, 594
Mastery
Bentham, 493, 497–498, 501–502
Descartes, 294
Hegel, 562–563
Hobbes, 299–334
Locke, 408–409
Marx, 5765, 600
Mill, 511–515
Nietzsche, 618–619, 622–623, 625–626
Rousseau, 467–470
Materialism, 45, 59, 103–104, 638
Metaphysics (Aristotle), 56–62, 638
Metaxy, 9, 638
Methodology, xi–xiii
Middle Ages, Early
Church and State, 160–166
Law, 166–169
Mill, John Stuart, Ch. 10, 555, 600, 606, 607
Bureaucracy, 536, 538
Coercion, 521–422
Conscience, 517, 523
Equality, 541–543
Ethics, 511
Ethology, 514–515
Family, 531–532, 541–543
Happiness, 517–518, 543–544
Human Nature, 513–515, 523
Individuality, 526–528, 535
Justice, 518–519
Laws of Mind, 513
Liberty, 520–536
Morality, 518, 527
Pleasures, 516–518
Progress, 512, 525, 534
Public Opinion, 521–522
Representation, 536–541

Rights, 519, 529–530
Self-Protection Principle, 521–522
Self-Regarding, Other-Regarding, 529–530
Tidology, 512–513
Tyranny of Majority, 521, 537–538
Utility, 516–517, 519–520, 522–523
Women, 531–532, 541–543
Millenarian Movements, 132, 178–180, 194, 638
Mixed Government, *see* Republicanism
Aquinas, 209
Aristotle, 82–83, 86–87
Hobbes, 321–322
Locke, 393–397, 406–407
Machiavelli, 254–256
Mill, 536–541
Plato, 43
Polybius, 109–110
Rousseau, 449–450, 459, 477–480
Monism, 143, 638
Mysticism, 639
Myths, 10, 639
Myth of Er, 16, 39–40
Myth of the Metals, 21–22

N

Natural Law, 639
Aquinas, 196–206, 217–218
Aristotle, 66–67, 73
Hobbes, 312–313
Locke, 342–343, 378–381
Middle Ages, 167–168
Plato, 40–41
Rousseau, 438–439, 473
Stoics, 106–107, 113–114
Natural Right, 639
Bentham, 496
Hobbes, 312–314
Locke, 356–357
Mill, 519, 529–530
Rousseau, 418, 437–440, 473
Naturalism, 639
Nature, 59, 71, 73–74, 121, 277–281, 284–285, 294, 334, 350, 639. *See also* Descartes.
Neo-Platonism, 121, 141, 145
Nichomachean Ethics, 62–72,

91, 187
Nietzsche, Friedrich, Ch. 12, 130, 133
Aristocratic ruler, 615–616, 622, 625
Death of God, 611–612, 624–625
Eternal recurrence or eternal return, 619–620, 626
Great Politics, 620–622
Last man, 620–621
Nihilism, 613
Overman or Superman, 617–618, 622, 625
Perspectivism, 613–614, 623–624
Slave morality, 615–616
Zarathustra, 612, 614, 617–618, 620–621, 625
Nihilism, 613
Nominalism, 304, 360, 639
Nous, 3, 67, 71–72, 92

O

Oligarchy, 34–35, 85–86, 639
Old Testament. *See* Hebraic Tradition and Bible.
On Kingship, 185, 206–209, 234
On Liberty, 509, 520–536
On Truth and Lie in an Extra-Moral Sense, 611–612
On the Truth of the Catholic Faith, 186, 194
Ontology, 639
Original Sin, 144–146, 463

P

Patriarcha. (Filmer), 366–377
Periagoge, 33, 640
Phenomenology of Mind, 569–570
Philosophical Anthropology, 23–24, 40, 461
Phronesis, 68, 191, 198, 239, 640
Physics (Aristotle), 56, 639
Pistis, 28, 640
Plato, Ch. 1, 109–110, 116, 155–160, 282, 299, 304, 318, 458–459, 472, 473, 624
Agathon, the Good, 29–31, 48, 49–50

Arete, 18, 22
Auxilaries, 20
Cave, Allegory of, 31–33
Censorship, 26
Decline of States, 34–40
Despotism, 37–38
Education, 8, 11, 20–21,
    26–28, 45
Excellence or Virtue, 22–25.
    See also Arete.
Family, 24–27, 45
Gorgias, 10–16
Guardians, 20–22, 42
Human Nature, 23–24, 40
Idea of *Eidos*, 28. *See* Forms.
Justice, 17, 19, 22–25, 38–40
Laws, 18, 41–48
Nocturnal Council, 47–48
Philosopher-Kings, 20–22,
    25, 41–42, 47–48
Poetry, 26–27
Property, 22, 44
Rhetoric, 10–16
Socrates, 7
Sophists, 10, 46. *See also*
    Gorgias, Callicles,
    Thrasymachus.
Soul, 15, 23
Stages of Cognition, 28–31
Statesmanship, 40, 42–43
Sun, 29–30
Utopianism, 40–41
Virtue, 18, 22
Waves, Three, 24–25
Wisdom, 22–23, 28–31
Pleasure. *See also* Happiness.
    Aristotle, 70
    Bentham, 491–494
    Epicurus, 99–102
    Hobbes, 305, 307
    Locke, 351
    Mill, 516–518
    Plato, 15, 22
Polis, 72, 79–80, 640
Politics (Aristotle), 62, 72–89
Politeuma, 81, 640
Politieia, 81, 640
Polity, 82, 86–87, 640. *See also*
    Mixed Government.
Popular Sovereignty, 117, 440,
    443, 449, 451–454,
    473–478
Power, 231–232, 238, 279, 302,
    308, 356–357, 377–378
Pre-Socratics, 1–3
Prince, The, 231, 233–247

Progress, 293, 408, 422, 623
Property
    Aquinas, 210–211
    Aristotle, 77, 78–79
    Hobbes, 321–322
    Locke, 356–357, 362–363,
        373, 382–386, 393, 404
    Marx, 571–577, 592–597
    Rousseau, 431, 433–434,
        443
Prophets, 130–131
Proportional Representation,
    540
Protestants, 136, 139, 216
Providence, 139, 160, 207,
    215, 242
Providential history, 160, 606
    See Augustine
Prudence or practical wisdom,
    68, 191, 239, 249, 268,
    640. *See also Phronesis.*
Puritans, 325, 330–331, 386

R

Rationalism, 103, 287–295
    passim, 365, 500, 502,
    640
Realism, 159, 183, 210, 248,
    269, 270, 287, 304, 640
Reason of State, 253
Reductionism, 289, 299–300,
    408, 491, 510, 516
Reformation, 216, 219, 327,
    333
Regime, 81, 640. *See also*
    Politeia.
Relativism, 640
Religion, See each thinker.
Renaissance, 225–229,
    286–287, 406
Representation, 314–315, 395,
    452
Representative Government
    (Mill)
Republic (Cicero), 111
Republic (Plato), 16–41,
    72–79, 83, 101, 116
Republican Government
    Locke, 406–407
    Machiavelli, 248, 254–259,
        273
    Rousseau, 425, 459
Resurrection, 133–135
Revelation, 128–131, 134,
    285, 287, 327, 366, 617

Reveries of a Solitary Walker,
    418, 424
Revolution, 691
    Aristotle, 87–88
    Locke, 309–402, 405
    Machiavelli, 251–255
    Marx, 577–579, 583, 588,
        598
    Rousseau, 417–418,
        424–425, 447–448
Rights
    Bentham, 496
    Hobbes, 312–314, 316–317
    Locke, 356–357
    Mill, 519, 529–530
    Rousseau, 418, 437–440,
        473
Ring of Gyges, 18
Roman Law, 117–120,
    175–177
Romanticism, 460
Rome, 108–117 *passim*,
    161–165, 171–172,
    176–177, 247–267, 425,
    459
Rousseau, Jean-Jacques, Ch. 9,
    215, 268
    Alienation, 433–436, 460,
        466
    Amour de soi, 433
    Amour propre, 433–434,
        440, 463–464
    Autonomy, 438–441, 462,
        468–472, 474
    Civil Religion, 447,
        456–457
    Coercion, 440
    Compared with Augustine,
        444, 460–461, 465, 472
    Compared with Marx, 458,
        479–481
    Conquest, 437–438
    Contract, 438–441
    Death Penalty, 457
    Dyarchy, 479–480
    Equality, 433, 439–440
    Evolution, 428
    Family, 424–425, 472
    Freedom, 418, 437,
        440–441
    General Will, 439–440,
        443–446, 452–453,
        460–473, 474–475
    Inequality, 434–436
    Influence, 428, 460
    Law, 446–448, 473

Legislator, 447–448
Moral Liberty, 418, 441–443
Perfectibility, 429, 436
Progress, 422, 437, 463
Property, 431, 433, 434, 443
Self-Preservation, 430–431
Sovereignty, 440, 443, 449, 451–452, 454, 473–478
State of Nature, 429–433
Toleration, 456, 458, 476–477
Virtues, 430–431, 468–472
Voting, 452–454, 478
Will, 418, 438–443
Women, 432, 469–470

S

Salvation, 135, 188, 328–329
Scholastsicism, 216–219, 283, 285–286, 290, 331, 341, 360, 408
Science, 31, 641
   Aristotle, 67–70, 90
   Hobbes, 302–303, 304
   Locke, 348–365
   Marx, 558–559, 581, 590
   Mill, 510–516, 544–545
   Modern History, 227–228, 277–286
   See, Episteme.
Scientism, 641
Second Treatise (Locke), 377–402
Self-Creation, 576
Self-Preservation, 312–314, 409, 430–431
Separation of Powers, 322, 396–397, 405
Skepticism, 4, 50, 141, 641
Slavery, 21, 42, 75–77, 153, 211, 381–382, 531
Social Contract (Rousseau), 417, 436–458
Socialism, 555, 593
Socrates, 5–7, 138, 624
Sophia, 67, 641. *See also* Wisdom.
Sophists, 10, 46, 74. *See also* Plato.
Soul, 3, 12–15, 18, 23–27 *passim*, 34–46 *passim*, 56, 92, 105, 157, 430–431, 441, 616, 641

Sovereignty, 245, 316–318, 321–322, 398, 641
Sparta, 7, 41, 52, 72, 257, 425, 458–459
Species-being, 575, 641
Spirit (thymos), 23–24, 641
Spoudaios, 80, 641
State of Nature, 311, 642. *See also* Hobbes, Locke, and Rousseau.
State of War, 311, 379, 642
Stoicism, 102–117
   Citizens, 106–107
   Law, 106–107
   Materialism, 103–104
   Regimes and Polybius, 109–110
   Virtue, 105, 107
Summa contra Gentiles, 185–186
Summa Theologiae, 185–194, 196–206
Summum Bonum, 89, 334, 642. *See also* Agathon and Common Good.
Synderesis, 196, 199–201, 642
System of Logic (Mill), 510–516

T

Tacit Consent, 316, 391–392
Taxation, 395
Teleology, 60, 195, 642
Terror, 265, 318
Theses on Feuerbach, 571, 573
Third International, 556
Thus Spake Zarathustra, 611, 619–620
Timocracy, 34, 642
Toleration
   Locke, 342, 366, 458
   Mill, See *On Liberty*.
   Rousseau, 456, 458, 476–477
Totalitarianism, 50, 335, 417, 459, 628
Transcendence, 4, 50, 642
Two-Sword Doctrine, See Selasian Doctrine.
Two Treatises of Government (Locke), 346–347, 366–402
Tyrannicide, 208, 322
Tyranny, 36–38, 88–89, 319, 399, 642

U

Unam Sanctum, 165–166
Universal, 5, 59, 67, 106, 113, 115–116, 158, 196, 217, 304, 642
University, 8, 175–178, 180, 184, 219
Utilitarianism (Mill), 516–520
Utilitarianism, 297, 642. *See also* Bentham and Mill.
Utopia, 40–41, 593
Utopian Socialists, 593

V

Violence, 7, 167, 247–248, 253, 265, 269, 310–312, 390, 430, 622
Virtú, 234–242 *passim*, 244–247, 643
Virtue, *See Arete* and Plato, Aristotle, Stoics, Augustine, Aquinas, Machiavelli, and Hobbes.

W

War, 34–35, 42, 108, 113, 151, 171, 210, 238, 248, 257, 311, 379–380
Welfare State, 216, 490
Whig, 345, 397, 405
Will
   Augustine, 142–146, 159
   Hobbes, 307
   Rousseau, 438–443, 460–473
Will to Power, 617, 626–627, 643
Wisdom, 22–23, 67
Woman, 24–27, 45, 74, 115, 319, 389, 432, 469–470, 498, 531–532, 541–542, 628

Y

Yahweh, 128–132
York Tracts, 165
Young Hegelians, 552, 559, 565

INDEX OF PERSONS

Certain philosophers are listed in the Subject Index: Socrates, Plato, Aristotle, Cicero, Stoicism, Aquinas, Machiavelli, Hobbes, Locke, Bentham, Mill, Marx, and Nietzsche.

A

Aaron, Richard, 349
Ackrill, J. L., 93
Adams, John, 255, 407, 521
Adams, Robert M., 273
Adeimantus, 16, 18–20
Agathocles, 246–247
Ahern, Daniel R., 614, 617, 627, 630
Albert the Great, 184, 236
Alexander the Great, 55–56, 96, 258
Alexander VII, Pope
Alfieri, Vittorio
Allison, David, 630
Althusser, Louis, 481
Ambrose, St., 140
Amyntas II, King, 55
Anaximenes, 1
Andrew, Edward, 403
Anglo, Sydney, 273
Annas, Julia, 51
Anschutz, R. P., 546
Ansell-Pearson, Keith, 618, 629
Antiochus IV, 127
Antisthenes, 97
Aquinas, St. Thomas, 3
Arendt, Hannah, 120, 143, 460, 628
Aristophanes, 5
Armstrong, A. H., 155, 172
Armstrong, R. A., 220
Ashcraft, Richard, xi, 346, 411
Ashley, Lord, see Earl of Shaftesbury
Athenian Stranger, 41–44
Aubrey, 297, 333
Augustine, St., 3
Austin, Jane, xi

Austin, John, 297, 503
Averröes or Ibn Roschd, 180–184, 190, 193
Avineri, Shlomo, 601
Ayers, Michael, 350
Ayton, Robert, 295
Azo, 177

B

Bacon, Francis, 268, 277, 286, 294, 295
Bacon, Roger, 286
Bailey, D. R., 122
Baldry, H. C., 122
Barker, Sir Ernest, 51, 93, 347, 610
Barnard, Frederick M., 428, 476
Barnes, Jonathan, 93
Baron, Hans, 229, 248, 273
Baumgardt, David, 490, 546
Baumgold, Deborah, 336
Baumrin, Bernard, 335
Beccaria, 489
Becker, Carl L., 422, 481
Beiner, Ronald, 92, 217
Berkowitz, Peter, 618, 620, 630
Berlin, Sir Isaiah, 240, 269, 321, 480, 481, 535, 552, 553, 557, 601, 624
Berman, Harold J., 220
Berman, Marshall, 481
Bevan, Edwyn, 122
Black, Antony, 220
Blackham, H. J., 630
Blackstone, Sir William, 494
Bloom, Allan, xii, 41, 51, 425, 432, 459, 470, 623, 630
Bock, Gisela, 273
Bodin, Jean, 232
Bondanella, Peter, 250, 273
Boniface VIII, Pope, 165–166
Boonin-Vail, David, 333, 335
Borchard, Ruth, 546
Borgia, Cesare, 230, 233, 236, 246
Botticelli, 229

Bottomore, Tom, 601
Boyle, Robert, 277, 342, 348–349, 354–355
Braden, Gordon, 229, 244, 273
Bradshaw, Leah, 75
Brandt, Frithiof, 336
Brauer, Bruno, 565, 568
Bréhier, Émile, 103, 122, 287
Britton, Karl, 546
Brown, Keith, 332, 335
Brown, Peter, 136, 160, 172
Brutus, Marcus, 263
Burckhardt, Jacob, 229
Burns, J. H., 172, 220, 335, 411
Burnyeat, M., 122
Burtt, E. A., 281
Bury, J. B., 122
Butterfield, Herbert, 236, 250–251, 273, 282

C

Caesar, 302
Caesar Augustus, 302
Callicles, 13–16, 38
Calvin, Jean, 296, 480
Canning, J. G., 176
Carmichael, D. J. C., 323
Carver, Terrell, 601
Cassirer, Ernst, 229, 272, 422, 428, 481
Cephalus, 16
Chabod, Frederico, 232, 273
Chadwick, Henry, 172
Chapman, John H., 481
Charles I, 341, 382
Charles II, 296, 344–345, 396, 399–400
Chenu, Marie Dominique, 220
Chroust, Anton-Hermann, 93
Chrysippus, 102
Cistercians, 178
Clark, Stephen R. L., 93
Cleanthes, 102, 106
Cleinias, 41–42
Clement of Alexandria, 139, 154

Cohen, G. A., 591, 601
Cohn, Norman, 132
Coleridge, Samuel Taylor, 507
Colish, M., 121, 122, 142, 271
Colman, John, 363, 364, 411
Columbus, 225
Comte, August, 508
Connolly, William E., 336
Constantine, Emperor, 136
Cooper, Barry, 621
Cooper, John M., 93
Copernicus, 277, 278–283
Copleston, Frederick, 122, 220
Cornford, Francis M., 51
Cowling, Maurice, 535, 546
Cox, Richard, 363, 411, 608
Craig, Leon, 19, 25, 51
Cranston, Maurice, 335, 385, 411, 423, 481
Crates of Thebes, 99, 102
Crocker, Lester G., 481
Cromwell, Oliver, 296, 321, 341
Crossley, David, 502
Crowe, Michael Bertram, 218, 220
Cushman, Robert E., 51
Cynics, 97–99

D

D'Alembert, Jean Le Rond, 421, 489, 490
Danielou, Jean, 172
Dannhauser, Werner, 623, 630
Dante, Alighieri, 190
Darwin, Charles, 281, 557
Deane, Herbert, 148
D'Entréves, Passerin Alexandra, 122, 220
De Grazia, Sebastian, 231, 242, 262, 270, 273
De Lange, Nicholas, 172
Democritus, 100–102
Derrida, Jacques, 614, 624
Descartes, René, 277, 287–295
Des Pres, Terrence, 72
Detwiler, B., 630
Diaz, Rodrigo, 225
Diderot, Denis, 421, 444
Dietz, Mary G., 335
Dihle, Albrecht, 460
Dinwiddy, John, 546
Diocletian, 120
Diogenes of Oenoanda, 102
Diogenes of Sinope, 98

Dion, 8
Dionysius II, 8
Dobbs, Betty Jo Teeter, 228
Donatello, 228
Dostoevsky, Fyodor, 143, 627
Duncan, Graeme, 600
Dunn, John, xii, 363, 402, 403, 411, 535, 627
Duns Scotus, John, 219, 285

E

Ehrenberg, Victor, 122
Einstein, Albert, 282
Elshtain, Jean Bethke, 75, 159–160, 214, 270, 432, 543, 628
Elster, Jon, 591, 601
Emberley, Peter, 457
Emerson, Ralph Waldo, 488
Engels, Frederick, *see* Marx
Epictetus, 103
Epicureans, 99–102, 517, 625
Epicurus, 99–102
Er, 16, 39–40
Euclid, 295
Evans, G. R., 145–146
Evans, Michael, 598, 601
Everett, C. W., 546
Everson, Steven, 56
Ewin, R. E., 336

F

Fackenheim, Emil, 126, 172, 218
Faludy, George, 629
Ferdinand, King, 230
Ferguson, John, 93
Feuerbach, Ludwig, 559, 565–567
Figgis, John N., 148
Filmer, Sir Robert, 366–377 *passim*
Finnis, John, 122, 220
Flanagan, Thomas, 242, 399
Flathman, Richard, 333, 336
Fleisher, Martin, 273
Fourier, Charles, 508, 593
Fox-Bourne, H. R., 411
Francis of Assisi, St., 179
Frankl, Viktor, 72
Frederick II, Emperor, 183–184
Freedman, Robert, 601
Friedlander, Paul, 51
Frischer, Bernard, 122

Fukuyama, Francis, 607
Furley, David, J., 122

G

Gaius, 118–119
Galileo, 272, 277–285, 295
Garver, Eugene, 236, 273
Gauthier, David, 336, 406
Gay, Peter, 422, 481
Geach, Peter, 220
Gelasius, Pope, 161–162
Germino, Dante, 115
Gilbert, Allan, 273
Gilbert, Felix, 232, 240, 273
Gilbert, William, 277
Gilby, Thomas, 220
Gilson, Étienne, 141–142, 172, 220
Glaucon, 16, 18–20, 101
Goldsmith, M. M., 307, 336
Gorgias, 3, 10–16, 56, 97
Gourevitch, Victor, 427, 430, 436
Grant, Ruth, 136, 364, 366, 411
Gray, John, 535, 546
Greenleaf, W. H., 335
Gregory, Pope, 164
Grene, Marjorie, 93
Grimsley, Ronald, 481
Griswold, Jr., Charles L., 51
Grotius, Hugo, 407, 436
Grube, G. M. A., 51
Guéhenno, Jean, 423, 481
Guthrie, W. K. C., 51, 93
Gyges, 18

H

Hale, J. R., 232, 234, 273
Hall, Robert W., 51
Halliday, R. J., 333, 508, 546
Hampton, Jean, 336
Hannibal, 236, 246
Hardie, W. F. R., 93
Harding, Arthur L., 122
Haren, Michael, 220
Harpham, Edward J., 411
Harrison, Ross, 546
Harvey, S., 481
Harvey, William, 277
Hayek, F. A., 546
Hegel, G. W. F., 458, 552–553, 559, 561–565, 569–570, 577, 591, 598, 607

Heidegger, Martin, 623, 630
Heller, Erich, 614, 626, 630
Hendel, C. W., 481
Henry IV, King, 164
Heraclitus, 1, 62, 103
Herbert, Gary B., 336
Herder, Johann G., 627
Hermias, 55
Hermes Trismegistus, 228
Herod, 128
Hesiod, 26, 91
Hess, Moses, 567–568
Hexter, J. H., 126, 172, 240, 254
Hicks, R. D., 122
Higgins, Kathleen M., 630
Hildebrand, 164
Hill, Christopher, 336, 346, 411
Hillel, 133
Himmelfarb, Gertrude, 546
Hinnant, Charles H., 297, 335
Hollingdale, R. J., 610, 620, 629
Homer, 26, 296
Hood, F. C., 336
Horace, 142
Horowitz, Asher, 436, 458, 481
Hulliung, Mark, 250, 262, 272, 273
Hume, David, 294, 423
Hume, L. J., 546
Hunt, H. A. K., 122
Hutter, Horst, 271
Huyghens, Christian, 277

I

Ionian, 1, 45, 282
Irwin, Terence, 93
Isidore, Bishop of Seville, 204–205

J

Jaeger, Werner, 57, 155
James II, King, 345–346, 396, 400
Jenkins, John L., 350, 411
Jenks, Edward, 168
Jensen, De Lamar, 273
Jesus of Nazareth, 126, 133–135
Joachim of Fiore, 179–180
Jonas, Hans, 96, 132
Jones, J. R., 345, 411
Jonson, Ben, 268, 295

Jordan, Constance, 227, 388
Jordan, Mark D., 220
Julius II, Pope, 230, 233
Justinian, Emperor, 176

K

Kant, Immanuel, xiii, 294, 458, 462, 481, 559–561, 563, 607, 618, 620
Kaufmann, Walter, 610, 629, 630
Kavka, Gregory, 336
Keeling, S. V.
Kelly, Christopher, 481
Kenny, Anthony, 218, 220
Keohane, Nannerl O., 425, 444, 481
Kepler, Johannes, 277–278, 282
Kerrigan, William, 229, 244, 273
Keynes, Lord Maynard, 488
Keyt, David, 93
King, Preston, 335
Kirwan, Christopher, 172
Klosko, George, 51
Knowles, David, 182, 219, 220
Koelb, Clayton, 630
Kolakowski, Leszek, 601
Kraut, Richard, 51
Kraynak, Robert P., 336
Kristeller, Paul Oscar, 229
Kuhn, Thomas, 283

L

Laine, Michael, 522, 546
Laird, John, 336
Laslett, Peter, 411
Laurence, Margaret, 143
Leff, Gordon, 178, 219
Leibniz, Gottfried Wilhelm von, 294, 444
Leigh, R. A., 481
Leo X, Pope, 230–231
Letwin, Shirley R., 323, 535, 546
Levasseur, Thérèse, 420–421
Levine, Andrew, 428, 458, 481
Levinson, R., 51
Lichtheim, Georg, 598
Lincoln, Abraham, 606
Lippmann, Walter, 50
Livy, 226, 247–267 *passim*, 263
Lloyd, G. E. R., 93

Lloyd, S. A., 333, 336
Lloyd-Thomas, D. A., 411
Lonergan, Bernard, 220
Long, A. A., 122
Long, Doug, 500, 546
Lord, Carnes, 89, 93
Lorenzo the Magnificent, 227, 233
Louis XII, King, 233
Louis XIV, King, 344
Löwith, Karl, 132, 630
Lucian, 98–99
Lucretius, 99
Luther, Martin, 219, 232, 333
Lycurgus, 448
Lyons, David, 546

M

Macaulay, Thomas, 508
Maccabeus, Judas, 127
MacIntyre, Alasdair, 92, 93, 220, 624
Mack, M. P., 439, 546
Macpherson, C. B., 323, 336, 404, 411
Magellan, Ferdinand, 225
Maimonides, 181
Malthus, Thomas, 532
Manning, D. H., 546
Mansfield, Jr., Harvey C., 273, 315
Marcus Aurelius, 102, 524
Markus, R. A., 143, 155, 160
Marshall, John, 385, 411
Marsilius of Padua, 219
Marsilio Ficino, 227
Martinich, A. P., 332, 333, 335
Mason, Pamela A., 474
Masham, Lady, 347
Masters, Roger D., 427, 481
Maximilian I, 230, 233
McIlwain, C. H., 118, 148, 171, 215
McInerny, Ralph, 220
McLellan, David, 557, 601
McMurtry, John, 591, 601
McNeilly, F. S., 336
Mead, Waldo, 465
Medici, 229–233
Medici, Giovanni, 230–231
Megil, Allan, 630
Megillus, 41–42
Melling, David J., 51

Melville, Herman, 460, 627
Miles, Margaret R., 146, 160, 215, 220
Mill, James, 502–503, 505, 536, 578
Miller, Jr., Fred D., 93
Miller, James, 477, 481
Mitchell, Joshua, 333, 363, 385, 411
Mitchell, T. N., 122
Mitteis, H., 220
Montesquieu, 108, 425, 444
Morrall, John B., 93
Morrow, Glenn R., 51
Moses, 129, 236, 244–245, 319
Mulgan, R. G., 76, 93
Murdoch, Iris, 27
Murray, Alexander, 220

N

Nero, Emperor, 136
Nettleship, Richard Lewis, 51
Newton, Isaac, 228, 277–282, 285, 347–349, 352, 493
Nichols, Jr., James H., 21, 122
Nichols, Mary P., 75, 93
Nichomacus, 55
Niebuhr, H. Richard, 216
Niebuhr, Reinhold, 148, 216–217
Noah, 367–368
Noble, Richard, 430
Nozick, Robert, 403, 404, 406, 411
Numa, 253, 260–261
Nussbaum, Martha C., 51, 78, 93

O

Oakeshott, Michael, 323, 502, 628
Oakley, Francis, xii, 316, 333
O'Connor, Daniel J., 218, 220
O'Connor, David K., 93
Ollman, Bertell, 601
Owen, Robert, 593

P

Packe, Michael St. J., 546
Pagel, Elaine, 136
Panaetius of Rhodes, 107
Pangle, Thomas, 51, 407, 411
Parekh, Bhikhu, 479, 489, 546

Parel, Anthony, 218, 220, 255, 262, 273
Parmenides, 2–3, 62
Parry, Geraint, 411
Pasley, Malcolm, 630
Pateman, Carol, 459, 476, 481
Paul of Tarsus, 135, 332, 422
Pelikan, Jaraoslav, 220
Peter of Ireland, 184
Peters, Richard, 332, 335, 481
Petrarch, 225, 227
Philip of Macedon, 55
Philip the Fair, 165
Pico della Mirandola, 227
Pieper, Joseph, 182, 220
Pilate, Pontius, 128
Pitken, Hannah Fenichel, 242, 270, 315
Plamenatz, John, 428, 441, 481
Pletsch, Carl, 610, 629
Plotinus, 141
Plutarch, 263, 419
Pocock, J. G. A., xi, 244, 270, 273, 333, 407, 425
Polanyi, Michael, 31, 282, 293, 359
Polemarchus, 16–17
Polus, 11–12
Polybius, 107, 108–110, 254–255
Pompey, 128
Popper, Karl, 51
Porphery, 141
Protagoras, 3–5, 227
Proudhon, Pierre, 554, 593
Ptolemy, 278
Pythagoras, 282
Pythagorean, 2
Pythias, 55

Q

Quinton, Anthony, 286

R

Rabil, Jr., Albert, 273
Radcliff, Peter, 546
Rader, Melvin, 591, 601
Ramus, Peter, 286
Randall, John Herman, 93, 155
Rapaczynski, Andrzej, 336, 480
Raphael, D. D., 335

Rawls, John, 406, 545, 628
Rawson, Elizabeth, 122
Rebhorn, Wayne, 231, 236, 262, 273
Rees, John C., 529, 546
Regan, Richard J., 211, 215, 220
Ricardo, David, 593
Ridolfi, Roberto, 232, 273
Riley, Patrick, 444, 460, 461, 478, 481
Rist, J. M., 122
Ritschl, Friedrich, 609
Robertson, George Cromm, 297, 333
Robespierre, 417
Robson, John M., 505, 508, 510, 546
Roemer, John, 601
Rogers, G. A. J., 335
Rogow, Arnold A., 297, 333
Romulus, 236, 253, 262
Rorty, Richard, xi, 293, 623
Rosen, Frederick, 546
Rosenblum, Nancy, 546
Ross, Sir W. D., 65, 93
Rotenstreich, Nathan, 428, 481
Ruffo-Fiore, Silvia, 273
Runciman, W. G., 474
Russell, Bertrand, 78
Ryan, Alan, 335, 411, 508, 546
Ryle, Gilbert, 51

S

Saint Simon, Henri de, 508, 593
Salkever, Stephen G., 75, 92
Sallis, John, 51
Sambursky, S., 122
Sandbach, F. H., 121
Savonarola, 229–230, 245
Schneewind, J. B., 546
Schofied, M., 122
Schopenhauer, Arthur, 609–610
Schouls, Peter A., 364, 408, 411
Schumpeter, Joseph A., 489
Scipio Aemilianus, 107, 110
Sedgwick, Peter R., 630
Seliger, Martin, 411
Sen, A. K., 474
Seneca, 115

Shaftesbury, Earl of (Lord Ashley), 341, 343–345, 371
Shakespeare, William, xi, 143, 268, 271, 468, 627
Sherman, Nancy, 65, 93
Shklar, Judith N., 425, 459, 468, 481, 570
Shumaker, Wayne, 228
Siger of Brabant, 184, 190
Sigmund, Paul E., 122, 220
Simmons, A. John, 403, 411
Simon, Yves, 215, 220
Singer, Peter, 564, 598, 601
Skinner, Quentin, xi, 177, 273, 316, 333, 400
Smart, J. C. C., 546
Smith, Adam, 500, 593
Smith, Bruce James, 250, 273
Smith, Warren Thomas, 172
Snell, Bruno, 51
Soderini, Piero, 230, 262
Solomon, Robert C., 630
Solon, 52
Somers, Lord, 341, 347
Sommerville, Johann P., 333
Sophists, 3–5
Sorel, Tom, 307, 335
Spafford, D. S., 540
Spengler, Oswald, 607, 623
Speusippus, 55
Spinoza, Baruch, 294
Spragens, Jr., Thomas, 292–293, 307, 336
Stalley, R. F., 51
Starobinski, Jean, 427, 481
Steintrager, James, 546
Stern, J. P., 629
Stewart, Larry, 286
St. Justin Martyr, 138
Stockton, David, 122
Stokes, Michael C., 51
Strauss, Leo, xi–xii, 51, 217, 236, 273, 307, 336, 363, 411, 478, 623, 628, 630
Striker, G., 122
Strayer, Joseph R., 200
Strong, Tracy B., 481, 630
Sydney, Algernon, 345, 405

T

Talmon, J. L., 132, 481
Tanner, Michael, 629
Tarcov, Nathan, 403, 406
Tarlton, Charles R., 231, 273, 359
Taylor, A. E., 307, 332, 335
Taylor, Charles, 293, 321, 624, 628
Taylor, Harriet, 506, 508–510
Temple, William, 286
Ten, C. T., 529, 535, 546
Tertullian, 138
Thales, 1, 287
Thomas, William, 546
Thrasymachus, 16–18, 38
Thucydides, 226
Tierney, Brian, 176–177, 220
Tocqueville, Alexis de, 508, 521
Toynbee, Arnold, 607
Trevelyan, G. M., 345, 411
Trevor-Roper, Hugh, 126, 172
Tuck, Richard, xi, 298, 335
Tucker, Robert C., 601
Tully, James, 134, 403, 411

U

Ullmann, Walter, 161, 166, 170, 220
Ulpian, 118–119
Urban, Linwood, 172

V

Varro, 142
Vasco da Gama, 225
Vaughn, Karen I., 411
Veatch, Henry B., 93
Vettori, Francesco, 233
Vinci, Leonardo da, 277, 278
Virgil, 142, 226
Viroli, Maurizio, 254, 273
Vlastos, Gregory, 51
Voegelin, Eric, 33, 40, 51, 57, 62, 78, 91, 93, 115, 122, 130–131, 132, 172, 179, 231, 422, 474, 564, 607, 628
Volpe, Galvona della, 481
Voltaire, 268, 417, 490

W

Wagner, Richard, 609–610
Walzer, Michael, 132, 269, 459, 474, 481
Warens, Mme de, 420, 423
Warrender, Howard, 307, 332, 335
Watkins, J. W. N., 307, 333
Weinreb, Lloyd L., 122
Weisheipl, James, 220
White, Nicholas P., 51
Whitehead, Alfred North, 277, 284
Willey, Basil, 284, 335
William and Mary, 345–346
William of Occam, 219, 285, 287
Williams, Bernard
Winch, Peter, 349, 359, 544
Wiser, James L., 628
Wittgenstein, Ludwig, 359, 614
Wokler, Robert, 427, 458, 462, 481
Wolin, Sheldon S., 269, 404
Wood, Neal, 122, 240, 269, 404, 411
Woolhouse, R. S., 411
Wooten, David, 345
Wordsworth, William, 507

X

Xenocrates, 55
Xenophon, 5

Y

Yack, Bernard, 93, 481, 618, 620, 629
Yates, Francis, 228
Yolton, John, 349, 366, 411

Z

Zeller, E., 122
Zeno, 99, 102, 121
Zuckert, Catherine, 407, 460
Zuckert, Michael, 407